28th Ibero-American Conference on Software Engineering (CIbSE 2025)

Ciudad Real, Spain
12-16 May 2025

ISBN: 979-8-3313-2229-8

Printed from e-media with permission by:

Curran Associates, Inc.
57 Morehouse Lane
Red Hook, NY 12571

Some format issues inherent in the e-media version may also appear in this print version.

CIbSE - IberoAmerican Conference on Software Engineering
c/o Luca Cernuzzi
Universidad Católica "Nuestra Seóra de la Asunción",
Campus Universitario, Asunción
Barrio Santa Ana, C.C.1683, C.P. 1364
Asunción - Paraguay

Phone: +595 21 334650
Fax: +595 21 310587

lcernuzz@uca.edu.py

Additional copies of this publication are available from:

Curran Associates, Inc.
57 Morehouse Lane
Red Hook, NY 12571 USA
Phone: 845-758-0400
Fax: 845-758-2633
Email: curran@proceedings.com
Web: www.proceedings.com

TABLE OF CONTENTS

RESEARCH PAPERS

DOCTORAL SYMPOSIUM

EMERGING IDEAS

ARTICLES ON APPLIED R&D PROJECTS OR CONTRACTS

POSTERS

CIbSE2025

XXVIII Congreso Iberoamericano en Ingeniería de Software
XXVIII Congresso Ibero-Americano de Engenharia de Software
XXVIII Ibero-American Conference on Software Engineering
Ciudad Real, Spain, May 12 - 16, 2025

GENERAL CHAIRS

Marcela Genero Bocco (University of Castilla-La Mancha, Spain)

Jose Antonio Cruz-Lemus (University of Castilla-La Mancha, Spain)

PROGRAM COMMITTEE CHAIRS

Silvia Abrahão (Universitat Politècnica de València, Spain)

Andrea Delgado (Universidad de la República, Uruguay)

DOCTORAL SYMPOSIUM CHAIRS

Kelly Garces Pernett (Universidad de los Andes, Bogotá, Colombia)

Sergio Segura (University of Seville, Spain)

JOURNAL FIRST CHAIRS

Renata Guizzardi (University of Twente, The Netherlands)

Sérgio Soares (Universidade Federal de Pernambuco, Brazil)

EIbAIS CHAIRS

Ignacio García (University of Castilla-La Mancha, Spain)

Sheila Reinehr (Pontifícia Universidade Católica do Paraná (PUCPR), Brazil)

INDUSTRY TALKS CHAIRS

María José Escalona (University of Seville, Spain)

Moises Rodríguez (University of Castilla-La Mancha, Spain)

OPEN SCIENCE & PROCEEDINGS CHAIRS

Beatriz Bernárdez (University of Seville, Spain)

Breno Bernard Nicolau de França (Universidade Estadual de Campinas, Brazil)

PUBLICITY & SOCIAL NETWORKS CHAIRS

Johnny Marques (Instituto Tecnológico de Aeronáutica, Brazil)

Marisa Panizzi (Universidad Nacional de Hurlingham, Argentina)

Pedro Valderas (Universitat Politècnica de València, Spain)

SUSTAINABILITY CHAIRS

Elisa Jiménez (University of Castilla-La Mancha, Spain)

Mª Ángeles Moraga (University of Castilla-La Mancha, Spain)

WEB CHAIRS

Aurelio José Horneros Cano (University of Castilla-La Mancha, Spain)

Manuel Serrano (University of Castilla-La Mancha, Spain)

Preface

On behalf of the CIbSE 2025 Organizing Committee, we are pleased to present the proceedings of the 28th Ibero-American Conference on Software Engineering (CIbSE 2025). Since its inception in 1998, CIbSE has served as a premier forum for showcasing recent advancements in both research and best practices for engineering software-intensive systems. This year, the conference was hosted by the University of Castilla-La Mancha in Spain, marking its first edition in Europe, and providing an ideal setting for this prestigious and high-quality event.

Software Engineering research and practice play a critical role in the reliable and efficient development of increasingly complex software systems. Grounded in well-established methods, processes, and tool support, Software Engineering enables the creation of robust, maintainable, and scalable solutions. Over the past decades, software has become deeply embedded in every aspect of society—ranging from enterprise systems that support core organizational processes, to real-time embedded systems and personal mobile applications. Today, this expansion continues alongside the emergence of transformative technologies such as quantum computing, green computing, the Internet of Things (IoT), and, most notably, the integration of Artificial Intelligence (AI) and Generative AI. These advancements underscore the growing importance of Software Engineering as a discipline capable of addressing the challenges posed by innovation, scale, and societal impact.

CIbSE has established itself as the leading forum for Software Engineering research in Ibero-America, promoting high-quality scientific inquiry while fostering collaboration between academia, industry, and other organizations. The conference plays a key role in supporting its research community by providing opportunities to publish, present, and discuss their work among academic peers, while also engaging students and practitioners participation.

For this edition of CibSE, a total of 70 submissions were received (57 full papers and 13 emerging ideas papers). After six desk rejections, 64 submissions (52 full papers and 12 emerging ideas) underwent the full review process. After careful peer-reviewing by the members of the Program Committee, 12 full papers and 2 emerging ideas papers were accepted (16 were initially accepted, but four were later withdrawn by the authors), resulting in an acceptance rate of 23% for full papers and 16% for emerging ideas papers. Five distinguished papers were invited to submit extended versions to the Science of Computer Programming journal, and the best paper received an award certificate. In addition to the 17 research papers, 11 posters were accepted, providing a forum to share and discuss early-stage research and enriching the CIbSE technical program. Also, seven papers were accepted in the Applied R&D projects and contracts category, presenting ongoing research, collaboration experiences, and technology transfer with industry and organizations. Finally, seven papers were accepted in the Journal First category, providing authors the opportunity to discuss their previously published work with the CIbSE community and further broaden the scope of the technical program.

CIbSE 2025 hosted a new edition of the Doctoral Symposium, aimed at disseminating ongoing research conducted by early-career researchers. In this forum, a panel of experts engaged in discussions with twenty doctoral students, offering valuable feedback, new perspectives, and suggestions to enhance their doctoral work. The research presented by the students covered several topics aligned with CIbSE 2025's scope, including foundations, techniques, tools, and applications. The symposium was further enriched by a keynote presentation delivered by Prof. Óscar Díaz (University of the Basque Country, Spain), titled *"PhD walker, there is no research question; the question arises from literature searches"*.

This year's edition also hosted the 8th edition of the Ibero-American School on Software Engineering (EIbAIS), which aims to provide a forum for discussing both foundational and emerging technology topics in Software Engineering. EIbAIS welcomes participation from practitioners, undergraduate and graduate students, and researchers alike. For ClbSE 2025, three tutorials were offered, addressing timely and relevant topics in Software Engineering:

- *Agility on Steroids of Artificial Intelligence* (Javier Garzás, Universidad Rey Juan Carlos, Spain).
- *Fundamentals of Software Sustainability* (Félix García, María de los Ángeles Moraga, University of Castilla-La Mancha, Spain).
- *Software Engineering for ML Systems* (Silverio Martínez-Fernández, Santiago del Rey, Universitat Politècnica de Catalunya, Spain).

Another highlight of CibSE 2025 was the Industry Talks Track, presented in the form of a roundtable discussion titled *"The University-Industry Relationship: A Debate That Remains Necessary."* This session brought together professionals from both private companies and the Spanish public administration to address key topics, including: benefits and challenges of university-industry collaboration, potential alternatives or solutions for bridging gaps, the role of the artificial intelligence revolution in research and knowledge transfer between academia and industry, positive and negative aspects of using artificial intelligence in research, and successful case studies that may serve as inspiration for future collaborations.

The conference also featured three distinguished keynote presentations, each addressing prominent and timely topics in Software Engineering:

- *Are we Getting Reliable Evidence? Methodology is Critical in Empirical Studies.* Natalia Juristo (Technical University of Madrid, Spain). The keynote addresses the importance of following proper and rigorous methodology when running an empirical study, as a critical element for advancing the generation of evidence in software engineering built on reliable findings. The talk discusses the methodological status of two types of empirical studies: experiments and observational studies, empirical activities such as data analysis and aggregation, and several empirical "domains" (as laboratory, MSR, or Deep neural networks).
- *AI and the Future of Software Development: Learning from Industry, Research, and Human-Centered Theories.* Margaret-Anne Storey (University of Victoria, Canada). The keynote addresses the impact of Artificial Intelligence (AI) innovations on the developer experience, how they write code, comprehend complex systems, create innovative solutions, collaborate with peers, and in communities of practice. The talk explores what can be learned from AI's adoption in industry and early research, taking insights from cognitive science, human-computer interaction, and social learning theories to understand AI's broader implications.
- *The Cloud-IoT Continuum: Software Engineering for a Connected Ecosystem.* Ernesto Pimentel (University of Málaga, Spain). The keynote presents the challenges of systems development for the Cloud-IoT continuum ecosystem, where cloud computing services and Internet of Things (IoT) devices are seamlessly and continuously integrated. The talk addresses key elements such as interoperability between heterogeneous devices, components at different levels, security and privacy and energy efficiency, highlighting architectures to support this type of system, emerging trends and opportunities offered by the Cloud-IoT continuum.

Finally, we would like to express our sincere gratitude to all those who contributed to making this event possible. The high quality of the technical program is the result of the commitment and hard work of the Program Committee members and additional reviewers. We are also deeply thankful to the Organizing Committee, authors, keynote speakers, panelists, tutorial instructors, session chairs, sponsors, and all participants for their valuable contributions to the success of CIbSE 2025. A special word of appreciation goes to Breno de França and Beatriz Bernárdez, who, as Open Science and Proceedings Chairs, played a key role in the preparation and publication of these proceedings.

We are also grateful to the CIbSE Steering Committee for their continued support, with special thanks to Guilherme Horta Travassos and Beatriz Marín for their guidance throughout the process. Last but not least, we extend our deepest gratitude to Marcela Genero and José Antonio Cruz-Lemus, our exceptional General Chairs. Their leadership, tireless dedication, and outstanding coordination were instrumental in bringing all aspects of the conference together and ensuring that everything ran smoothly. CIbSE 2025 would not have been possible without their vision and unwavering commitment.

It has been a privilege and a pleasure to serve as Program Chairs for CIbSE 2025, and we are deeply thankful for the opportunity.

Silvia Abrahão and Andrea Delgado
CIbSE 2025 Program Chairs

Main Conference

PC Chairs

Silvia Abrahão (Universitat Politècnica de València, Spain)

Andrea Delgado (Universidad de la República, Uruguay)

Program Committee

Leandro Antonelli (LIFIA, Facultad de Informática, UNLP, Argentina)
João Araújo (Universidade NOVA de Lisboa, Portugal)
Hernán Astudillo (Universidad Andrés Bello, Chile)
Claudia Ayala (Universitat Politècnica de Catalunya, Spain)
Clara Ayora (Universidad de Castilla-La Mancha, Spain)
Monalessa Barcellos UFES, Brazil)
Pablo Becker (GIDIS_Web, Engineering School, UNLPam, Argentina)
Beatriz Bernárdez (University of Seville, Spain)
Regina Braga (UFJF, Brazil)
Isabel Sofia Brito (Instituto Politécnico de Beja, Portugal)
Antonio Brogi (Università di Pisa, Italy)
Daniel Calegari (Universidad de la República, Uruguay)
Carlos Cano Genoves (Universitat Politècnica de València, Spain)
Juan Pablo Carvallo (Universidad del Azuay, Ecuador)
Alejandra Cechich (Universidad del Comahue, Argentina)
Priscila Cedillo (Universidad de Cuenca, Ecuador)
Luca Cernuzzi (DEI - Universidad Católica, Paraguay)
Nelly Condori Fernández (Universidad de Santiago de Compostela, Spain)
Heitor Costa (Federal University of Lavras, Brazil)
Abraham Davila (Pontificia Universidad Católica del Perú, Perú)
José Luis de la Vara (University of Castilla-La Mancha, Spain)
Juan de Lara (Universidad Autónoma de Madrid, Spain)
Rafael de Mello (UFRJ, Brazil)
Ronnie de Souza Santos (University of Calgary, Canada)
J. Andrés Díaz-Pace (ISISTAN Research Institute, UNICEN University, Argentina)
Cláudio Farias (Universidade Federal do Rio de Janeiro, Brazil)
Eduardo Figueiredo (Federal University of Minas Gerais, Brazil)
Efraín R. Fonseca C. (Universidad de las Fuerzas Armadas ESPE, Ecuador)
Félix García (University of Castilla-La Mancha, Spain)
Jesús García-Molina (Universidad de Murcia, Spain)
Ignacio García Rodríguez de Guzmán (University of Castilla-La Mancha, Spain)
Alejandra Garrido (LIFIA, Facultad de Informática, UNLP, Argentina)
Giovanni Giachetti (Universitat Politècnica de València, Spain)

Magalí González (DEI - Universidad Católica, Paraguay)
María Paula González (CONICET and UNS, Argentina)
Javier González-Huerta (Blekinge Institute of Technology, Sweden)
Laura González (Universidad de la República, Uruguay)
Miguel Goulão (NOVA LINCS, Universidade Nova de Lisboa, Portugal)
César Guerra-García (Autonomous University of San Luis Potosí, México)
Renata Guizzardi (University of Twente, Netherlands)
Abel Gómez (Universitat Oberta de Catalunya, Spain)
Graciela Dora Susana Hadad (Universidad Nacional del Oeste, Argentina)
Luis Iribarne (University of Almería, Spain)
Emanuel Irrazábal (Universidad Nacional del Nordeste, Argentina)
Marcelo Jenkins (University of Costa Rica, Costa Rica)
Miguel Katrib (Universidad de La Habana, Cuba)
Uirá Kulesza (UFRN, Brazil)
Danilo Leal (Universidad Andrés Bello, Chile)
Lidia López (Universitat Politècnica de Catalunya, Spain)
Iván Machado (UFBA - Federal University of Bahia, Brazil)
Bell Manrique Losada (Universidad de Medellín, Colombia)
Johnny Marques (Instituto Tecnológico de Aeronáutica (ITA), Brazil)
Silverio Martínez-Fernández (Universitat Politècnica de Catalunya, Spain)
Beatriz Marín (Universitat Politècnica de València, Spain)
Denisse Muñante (ENSIIE & SAMOVAR, France)
Elisa Yumi Nakagawa (University of São Paulo, Brazil)
Adolfo Neto (Federal University of Technology - Paraná, UTFPR, Brazil)
Sergio Ochoa (University of Chile, Chile)
Kathia Oliveira (Université Polytechnique Hauts-de-France, France)
Toacy Oliveira (COPPE/UFRJ, Brazil)
Luis Olsina (Universidad Nacional de La Pampa, UNLPam, Argentina)
José Ignacio Panach Navarrete (Universitat de València, Spain)
Marisa Daniela Panizzi (Universidad Nacional de Hurlingham, Argentina)
Oscar Pastor (Universitat Politècnica de Valencia, Spain)
Diego Pedro Pinto Roa (Universidad Nacional de Asunción - Facultad Politécnica, Paraguay)
Sebastián Pizard (Universidad de la República, Uruguay)
Claudia Pons (LIFIA, Facultad de Informática, UNLP, Argentina)
Talita Ribeiro (UERJ, Brazil)
Sergio Rico (Mid Sweden University, Sweden)
Marcela Ridao (INTIA UNICEN, Argentina)
Andrés Rodríguez (UNLP LIFIA, Argentina)
Eric Rojas (Universidad Católica de Chile, Chile)
Julio Sandobalín (Escuela Politécnica Nacional, Ecuador)
Víctor Santander (Universidad Estadual do Oeste do Paraná, Brazil)
Gleison Santos ((Universidade Federal do Estado do Rio de Janeiro, UNIRIO, Brazil)

Elvys Soares (Federal Institute of Alagoas, Brazil)
Martin Solari (Universidad ORT Uruguay, Uruguay)
Simone R. S. Souza (ICMC/USP, Brazil)
Vitor E. Silva Souza (Federal University of Espírito Santo, Brazil)
Leopoldo Teixeira (Federal University of Pernambuco, Brazil)
Pedro Valderas (Universitat Politècnica de València, Spain)
Diego Vallespir (Universidad de la República, Uruguay)
Davi Viana (Federal University of Maranhão, Brazil)
Jéssyka Vilela (Universidade Federal de Pernambuco, Brazil)

Doctoral Symposium

DS Chairs

Kelly Garces Pernett (Universidad de los Andes, Bogotá, Colombia)
Sergio Segura (University of Seville, Spain)

DS Committee

Claudia Ayala (Universitat Politècnica de Catalunya, Spain)
Beatriz Bernárdez (University of Seville, Spain)
Jose Bocanegra (Universidad de los Andes, Colombia)
José Campos (Faculty of Engineering of the University of Porto, Portugal)
Francisco Chicano (University of Malaga, Spain)
Javier Luis Cánovas Izquierdo (Universitat Oberta de Catalunya, Spain)
Xavier Franch (Universitat Politècnica de Catalunya, Spain)
Felix García (University of Castilla-La Mancha, Spain)
Giovanni Giachetti (Universidad Andrés Bello, Chile)
María Clara Gómez (Universidad de Medellín, Colombia)
Inmaculada Medina-Bulo (Universidad de Cádiz, Spain)
Ana Moreira (NOVA University of Lisbon and NOVA LINCS, Portugal)
Elena Navarro (University of Castilla-La Mancha, Spain)
Ramón René Palacio Cinco (ITSON, México)
José Antonio Parejo Maestre (Universidad de Sevilla, Spain)
Ricardo Pérez-Castillo (University of Castilla-La Mancha, Spain)
Gleison Santos (Universidade Federal do Estado do Rio de Janeiro,UNIRIO, Brazil)
Martín Solari (Universidad ORT Uruguay, Uruguay)
Pedro Valderas (Universitat Politècnica de València, Spain)
Sira Vegas (Universidad Politécnica de Madrid, Spain)
Aurora Vizcaíno (Universidad de Castilla - La Mancha, Spain)
Jose Luis de la Vara (Universidad de Castilla - La Mancha, Spain)

Panel Experts

Claudia Ayala (Universitat Politècnica de Catalunya, Spain)
Beatriz Bernárdez (University of Seville, Spain)
Isabel Sofia Brito (Instituto Politécnico de Beja, Portugal)
Luca Cernuzzi (UC Nuestra Señora de la Asunción, Paraguay)
Óscar Díaz (University of the Basque Country, Spain)
Félix García (University of Castilla-La Mancha, Spain)
Marisa Panizzi (Universidad Nacional de Hurlingham, Argentina)
Ricardo Pérez-Castillo (University of Castilla-La Mancha, Spain)
Sebastian Pizard (Universidad de la República, Uruguay)
Martín Solari (Universidad ORT Uruguay, Uruguay)
Pedro Valderas (Universitat Politècnica de València, Spain)
Sira Vegas (Universidad Politécnica de Madrid, Spain)
Aurora Vizcaíno (Universidad de Castilla-La Mancha, Spain)

Using Real-world Scenarios to Bridge Training and Practice in Evidence-Based Software Engineering

Sebastián Pizard[1], **Leticia Marenco**[1]

[1]Instituto de Computación – Universidad de la República
Av. Julio Herrera y Reissig 565 – 11300 Montevideo – Uruguay

spizard@fing.edu.uy, letims@gmail.com

Abstract. *Context: Training is crucial for the adoption of Evidence-Based Software Engineering (EBSE), but there is a gap in its integration with professional practice. Objective: To investigate the creation and use of scenarios that enhance EBSE training by simulating the application of evidence in real-world situations. Method: A mixed methods study was conducted, starting with consultations with three Uruguayan industry and government practitioners to create a practical scenario, followed by its use to improve an EBSE course. Results: Scenario development is challenging, primarily due to limitations of evidence, but their use enhances students' ability to apply evidence. Conclusions: Using scenarios to align EBSE training with practice seems to be feasible & effective.*

1. Introduction

Evidence-Based Software Engineering (EBSE) seeks to enhance decision-making in software development by combining the best research evidence with practical experience and human values [Kitchenham et al. 2004]. EBSE is widely accepted by researchers, as shown by Kamei et al.'s identification of 446 Systematic Reviews (SRs) published in leading software engineering (SE) journals and conferences before 2019 [Kamei et al. 2021]. However, its adoption in non-academic settings remains limited [Kitchenham et al. 2015, Hassler et al. 2014, Da Silva et al. 2011].

In other fields where Evidence-Based Practice (EBP)—the broader framework from which EBSE is derived—is being studied, adequate training has been recognized as crucial. SRs highlight that a lack of knowledge and skills is one of the most common barriers to EBP adoption [Upton et al. 2014, Scurlock-Evans and Upton 2015, Zwolsman et al. 2012, Sadeghi-Bazargani et al. 2014].

Motivated by this, we launched a research program to improve EBSE adoption through the development and evaluation of a university-level training initiative. The previous stages of our research involved:

- Conducting an SR on previous EBSE training initiatives, designing an EBSE course based on learning outcomes that encapsulate the knowledge and skills required for future EBSE practitioners, and delivering and evaluating the course based on student performance and their initial feedback after the course [Pizard et al. 2021].
- Conducting a longitudinal case study to analyze the EBSE course and its impact. This included collecting data at the end of each EBSE course (delivered in 2017, 2018, and 2019) and through two follow-up surveys conducted seven months and twenty-one months after the final course, respectively [Pizard et al. 2022].

Our recent studies provide evidence that gaining an understanding of EBSE enables participants to improve their information literacy skills [Pizard et al. 2022, Pizard et al. 2023]. This can be attributed to several factors, but it is likely that, after becoming familiar with EBSE, participants develop an awareness of the quality of the information underpinning decision-making in SE, as well as the level of rigor applied in its generation. Other studies also confirm that Rapid Reviews—a lightweight form of SR designed for resource-constrained environments—and their results can be successfully used by researchers to collaborate with practitioners [Cartaxo et al. 2018, Pizard et al. 2025], or by practitioners with strong research skills [Milewicz et al. 2023], to address real-world problems using evidence.

We aim to explore another way to take advantage of the benefits of EBSE: supporting practitioners in using SR evidence to address problems in their professional practice. In particular, in this paper, we report our research aimed at better integrating EBSE training with practice by evaluating using scenarios that simulate the application of evidence in real-world professional situations.

This paper is structured as follows. In Section 2 we introduce the integration of professional practice into EBP training, the concept of scenarios, and summarize EBSE training initiatives and their relationship with practice. Section 3 outlines the EBSE & SRs course in which this study was conducted, along with the context in which it was delivered. In Section 4, we specify our research objectives and describe the research strategy used to address them. The results are presented and discussed in Section 5. Finally, we present our conclusions in Section 6.

2. Related Work

EBP training in medicine has been shown to be more effective when it is integrated or supported with clinical practice [Ilic and Maloney 2014, Larsen et al. 2019, Coomarasamy and Khan 2004], as a result of bringing practitioners even closer to scientific evidence. A commonly used method to achieve this is to apply evidence to clinical cases, clinical scenarios, or case studies [Swanberg et al. 2016].

In particular, Manns and Darrah use the term *scenario* to refer to a specific clinical situation or case that is constructed to assess the use of EBP in clinical decision-making [Manns and Darrah 2012]. These scenarios are carefully designed and developed to represent real-world clinical situations. They serve as a tool to evaluate whether individuals can recognize and apply the various components of EBP in their decision-making process.

Before creating our EBSE course, we conducted an SR on EBSE and SR training, which was last updated in December 2019 [Pizard et al. 2021]. In that review, we identified 14 initiatives for teaching EBSE to undergraduate and graduate students [Pizard et al. 2021]. The studies reported EBSE training courses with postgraduate and undergraduate students conducted by universities in seven countries (Brazil, Canada, Italy, Norway, Turkey, the UK, and the USA) prior to 2014. Each study included a practical assignment, typically involving participation in a secondary study, such as a SR, a limited SLR, or a mapping study.

Only three studies have specifically focused on teaching EBSE, as opposed to the SR process, all published by 2008 [Jørgensen et al. 2005, Rainer et al. 2006,

Rainer and Beecham 2008]. Notably, two of these studies describe teaching experiences based on the same modules of empirical evaluation for SE in the UK [Rainer et al. 2006, Rainer and Beecham 2008]. The key details of these studies are as follows:

- Jørgensen et al. report on the experience of teaching a mandatory undergraduate EBSE course in Norway from 2003 to 2005 . Students carried out individual projects that required them to formulate a research question, search for evidence (including scientific sources, expert consultations, and outreach to two companies), and draw conclusions based on the evidence they gathered. The authors observed that *"the best project reports would, according to our assessment, provide good input to real-world SE decisions."* The main challenge was the lack of relevant scientific studies for many of the topics chosen by students.
- In Rainer et al.'s study, students applied EBSE to evaluate a technology of their choice that could potentially solve a specific problem in SE, often related to their final-year projects [Rainer et al. 2006]. Few students employed SRs; instead, many evaluated the technologies themselves rather than seeking supporting evidence. Furthermore, only a small number of students effectively integrated their practical experience with the evidence they reviewed.
- Rainer and Beecham tasked students with using EBSE to evaluate one or more of four specific Requirements Management Tools [Rainer and Beecham 2008]. The tools were based on an evaluation conducted by a commercial organization in collaboration with the authors' university. While students were able to complete the evaluation, they faced significant challenges. Many selected tools based on the availability of online information about the vendor or tool rather than their relevance or suitability. Additionally, many students recommended the tool they initially chose, with some indicating that their recommendation was driven by adherence to guidelines rather than the actual evidence they analyzed.

In summary, the integration of EBSE training with professional practice has been explored only to a limited extent, and in all cases, it required students to engage in activities covering all five steps of EBSE. Moreover, previous initiatives suggest that incorporating practical elements into EBSE training presents significant challenges, often due to limitations in the availability and quality of SE evidence.

3. EBSE Training Module for University Students

In 2017, we introduced an elective course on EBSE & SRs into the five-year Computer Science degree program at Universidad de la República. Students, who typically take it in their fourth or fifth year, must first complete the mandatory SE course. The course aimed to teach practical EBSE concepts and techniques. By the end, students were expected to understand the basics of EBSE, identify SE issues that could be addressed by evidence, assess published secondary studies, and participate in SRs.

Learning outcomes (LOs) guided the course design and assessment, specifying what students should achieve [Kennedy et al. 2007]. The course grounded over fifty LOs to promote practical EBSE application [Pizard et al. 2021], covering topics such as: (i) Basics of scientific publications and SE research methods; (ii) Introduction to the EBP and SR characteristics, based on key chapters of the EBSE reference book [Kitchenham et al. 2015]: (iii) The SR process and its stages.

The course alternated between theory and practice, with weekly meeting to monitor students' progress on their team assignments (conducting a secondary study). Based on prior EBSE training challenges [Pizard et al. 2021], the teachers focused on: Limiting team assignment workload in certain EBSE stages, assisting students in selecting review topics, and supporting iterations in the team assignment.

The 14-week course included one optional in-person class per week. Table 1 shows the topics and team assignments for each week, with weeks 11-13 dedicated to completing the team assignments.

Table 1. Course timetable, including class topics and student assignments.

Week	Topics	Team assignments
1	Basic aspects of scientific publications, Introduction to SE research, Evidence-based paradigm, SRs in SE	Classify the sections of a scientific paper.
2	Planning an SR	Establish the purpose and the need for the SR to be performed by each team. Propose and validate the research questions.
3	Searching for primary studies	Define the search strategy for the SR. Create and validate the search string.
4	Study selection	Define inclusion and exclusion criteria for the SR. Define and conduct the selection process, obtaining 20-30 primary studies per student.
5	Study quality assessment	Define and conduct the quality assessment procedure for the selected primary studies.
6	Data extraction from the studies	Define an extraction form and use it to extract data from the primary studies.
7	Mapping study analysis	Classify primary studies according to commonly used schemes and schemes relevant to the research questions.
8	Introduction to data synthesis, Qualitative synthesis	Use qualitative synthesis to answer the research questions, considering the limitations of the review process.
9	Reporting a systematic review	Report the results and the whole process.
10	Knowledge translation and diffusion	-
14	Deadline for team assignment submission	

Students worked in teams of two or three to conduct a SR as a course assignment. They selected their SR topic and research questions with teacher guidance to keep the scope manageable. Weekly classes included a brief lecture on an SR stage, followed by team work time. Students applied the concepts from the lecture to their SR, with the final report due in week 14. Pre-reading from the EBSE book (i.e., [Kitchenham et al. 2015]) was required, and weekly tasks focused on completing the SR stage discussed in class.

Following EMSE journal reviewers' suggestions [Pizard et al. 2021], we made changes to the 2021 course to reduce the emphasis on the SR process and better balance it with EBSE concepts. The changes included adding [Kasoju et al. 2013] to the reading list as an example of EBSE in practice, assessing students' understanding of EBSE steps through a written test, and incorporating the final EBSE steps with a focus on contextual information and practical application. In addition, there was an interest in including an activity aimed at preparing students to use evidence to address problems they might encounter in their future professional practice. This interest prompted this study's conduction.

4. Research Goals and Method

We aimed to study the challenges involved in creating scenario-based exercises and their usefulness in improving the teaching of EBSE. Specifically, our research questions were:

RQ1: What challenges should be expected when creating scenario-based exercises to teach the use of evidence in professional SE practice?

RQ2: What are the benefits and challenges of using scenario-based exercises for teaching EBSE?

To address both RQs, we examined (1) how to create a practical scenario for applying evidence and (2) how to use it to improve EBSE teaching in 2021 & 2023 courses.

Our research consisted of a mixed-methods study [Venkatesh et al. 2013]. For the development of the scenario, we employed the participant-observer method [Atkinson and Hammersley 1994], while for the restructuring and delivery of the course, as well as the assessment of the scenario-based exercise within the course, we applied action research [Davison et al. 2004]. Both parts of this study are exploratory.

	Stage 1 **Collaboration with practitioners to create a scenario of use of evidence** **Aug 2021 – Oct 2021**	**Stage 2** **Using a scenario based on practice to improve EBSE teaching** **Nov 2021 & Nov 2023**
Inputs	Previous paper reviewers' comments Structured process to develop scenarios	Scenario created in Stage 1 Modifications to course materials
Participants	2 practitioners from government 1 practitioner from software industry	8 undergraduate students in 2021 10 undergraduate students in 2023
Data collection	Communications with practitioners Questionnaire for assess draft scenario Meeting to evaluate final scenario	Individual use of the scenario by students Class discussion on the use of the scenario Teacher scores of scenario-based excercise Questionnaire for collect feedback from students

Figure 1. Summary of research stages.

As shown in Figure 1, data was collected in both stages (details will be presented in the next section). The only researcher involved in these stages was Pizard, who was also the course instructor. Several months after the 2021 course concluded, the second author—a former student from the 2021 course—undertook her capstone project, which involved receiving training in qualitative analysis and conducting the analysis of the 2021 data. Pizard then validated and complemented this analysis by including his own analysis of the 2023 data.

Regarding ethical considerations, during the first meeting with both practitioners and students (hereafter referred to as participants), the first author informed them about the EBSE training research, including its goals and data collection procedures. He assured the participants that all information would be kept confidential, participation was voluntary, and for the students, withdrawing from the study would not affect their learning or evaluation. All participants voluntarily and explicitly agreed to participate, and in the case of the students, they also signed informed consent forms.

Qualitative data analysis was strongly based on thematic analysis [Braun and Clarke 2006], including inductive coding, the identification of themes, and the selection of illustrative quotes. OTranscribe[1] and TurboScribe[2] were used to transcribe audio.

[1]https://otranscribe.com/

[2]https://turboscribe.ai/

5. Results

First, we describe the process we followed to develop our scenario-based exercise in the next section, highlighting the challenges we encountered (RQ1). Second, we report how the scenario-based exercise was integrated into the EBSE course and present the results of the evaluations with students from the 2021 and 2023 cohorts (RQ2).

5.1. RQ1 Development of the Scenario

We adapted the process proposed by Manns and Darrah [Manns and Darrah 2012] to create a practice scenario to improve the teaching of EBSE (see Figure 2). Practitioners participated in specific activities based on their availability, rather than throughout the entire process. The activities involved in creating the scenario are summarized below.

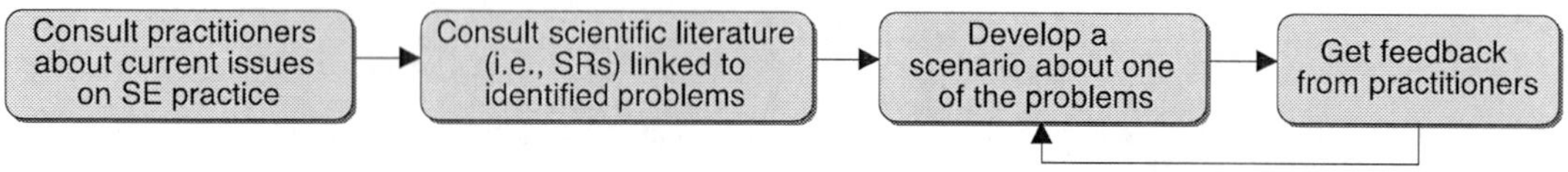

Figure 2. Scenario development process.

Consult practitioners about real problems. The three practitioners who collaborated with Pizard are acquaintances of his. They are all between 40 and 45 years old, with over 15 years of experience, consisting of two women and one man. One works in the private sector, while the other two are in the public sector –one at the government telecommunications company and the other at the Central Bank of Uruguay. Pizard explained the research purpose to them and asked about current open problems in their practice. They responded with a list of 11 issues related to process management, agile development practices, estimation, knowledge management, code quality, requirements analysis, and training (see appendix 7).

Consult scientific literature linked to identified problems. Based on the list of identified problems, Pizard conducted searches in SCOPUS and Google Scholar using terms representative of each problem. No secondary studies with research questions that addressed the identified (or similar) issues were found. Given this, Pizard referred to the study by Budgen et al. [Budgen et al. 2020], which he was already familiar with, and which presents a tertiary review in SE up to 2015. This study identifies and categorizes secondary studies with findings considered relevant for teaching industrial practice in SE. After reviewing the list, two SRs were found that relate to one of the problems identified by the practitioners [Bano and Zowghi 2015, Pacheco and Garcia 2012]. This problem, as expressed by one of the practitioners, is: *"How to prioritize equally among different stakeholder groups so that the client receives what they need as quickly as possible? How to prioritize requirements when dealing with different user groups?"*

Develop a scenario about one of the problems. Based on the identified problem and both SRs, Pizard drafts a scenario for using evidence. The following objectives, aligned with the principles used by Manns and Darrah [Manns and Darrah 2012], were pursued:

- Focus exclusively on interventions, excluding diagnostic aspects to simplify participant involvement.
- Preselect interventions for each scenario to streamline scoring and preparation.
- Avoid differentiating based on the strength of the evidence[3], given the immaturity of SE evidence.
- Given the limited time students have to use the scenario, minimize effort by providing two SRs as the sole sources for completing the assignment.

Gather feedback from practitioners. The draft scenario was shared with the practitioners, who were asked to evaluate whether it resembled real industry problems and if the proposed solutions (based on the SRs found) were appropriate for addressing these issues.

After two iterations to refine the scenario, it received an average rating of 7 out of 10 from the practitioners for its similarity to industry problems, with no major issues identified (scores between 1=Completely unrelated to industry problems; 10=Very similar to industry problems). Regarding the proposed solutions (derived from the SRs) included in the exercise, the practitioners found them somewhat adequate but felt there were other alternatives they would have preferred. When reminded that these proposals were grounded in scientific evidence and could be clarified but not replaced, two practitioners noted that this, along with the fact that SRs were found for only one of their proposed problems, aligned with their views on the gap between academia and industry. They added that academia should take a more proactive role in engaging with industry.

As detailed in the following subsection, the scenario was used in the EBSE courses of 2021 and 2023. At the end of the 2021 course, it was revised to improve its wording. Due to size constraints, we present only its latest version here (refer to Table 2).

5.2. RQ2 Use of Scenario

The scenario-based exercise, along with other improvements, was incorporated into the EBSE & SRs course. Specifically, an extra class was added after week 10 of the course to help students achieve the following these new learning outcomes:

- LO59 – Describe factors that affect the use of evidence: its nature, the context of application, and the facilitation process.
- LO60 – Participate in the analysis of scenarios involving the use of evidence.
- LO61 – Analyze the EBSE process and its improvement.

The dynamics of how students engage with the scenario are as follows. Before the new class, as part of a team practical assignment, students are required to read the scenario and reflect on whether the proposed solutions are appropriate, considering the evidence provided in the recommended SRs. During the first minutes of the class, student teams have the opportunity to ask questions and make any final adjustments to their assignment before submitting their responses.

Next, and after submission, the class engages in a group discussion centered on the scenario exercise. This is followed by a lecture from the instructor addressing the

[3]In this context, the strength of evidence refers to the robustness and reliability of the information collected, including the rigor of the methods used by researchers in each primary study.

Table 2. Exercise for applying evidence based on a real-world scenario.

Below, a professional practice scenario is outlined. The scenario describes a specific context, a problem, and two proposals for addressing it. You are asked to evaluate whether the proposals seem appropriate, using what you have learned in the course (scientific evidence, systematic reviews, etc.). To do this, it may be necessary to assess whether the proposals are supported by scientific evidence; if so, you may use the two reviews mentioned. If you use other materials, please indicate which ones. Recommendations:

- Remember the definition and steps of EBSE.
- It is likely unnecessary to start with a complete reading of both SRs.
- Consider the factors that affect the use of evidence [Kitson et al. 1998]: the nature of the evidence, the context of use, and the method or way in which the process of use is facilitated.
- During the next class, each group will have few minutes to ask questions, after which they will submit their response with a maximum of 200 words.

You are part of a project team that will develop a system for requesting and delivering per diems to be used in various ministries and government agencies.

A per diem is the money provided to employees for travel, food, and lodging expenses incurred while performing their duties away from their usual place of residence.

Your team is responsible for requirements gathering and software development. To this end, you plan to use an agile methodology due to your considerable experience. For the project's success, identifying stakeholders and their involvement is deemed crucial. This is quite challenging because there are many stakeholders from different organizations and agencies, with varying needs that are currently unclear.

Your team has proposed:

- Identifying all stakeholders and conducting personality tests to those who will participate in the requirements gathering to assign them the most suitable roles, and
- Promoting constructive interaction among all stakeholders during the requirements gathering, e.g., by determining each stakeholder's actual interests and establishing appropriate communication channels.

Materials that can be used: [Bano and Zowghi 2015, Pacheco and Garcia 2012]

complexity of using evidence in practice and the factors that influence it (LO59, see [Kitson et al. 1998]). The session concludes with a discussion on the objective of step 5 of the EBSE process (i.e., analyzing and improving the EBSE process) and how students believe this goal can be effectively achieved (LO61).

To evaluate the use of the scenario (i.e., evaluate LO60), questions were distributed that students had to answer individually and in teams during the final class of the course. In addition, we analyzed the teachers' assessments of the practical work on the evidence scenario, along with the video recordings of the open-class discussions. Figure 3 summarizes all these activities.

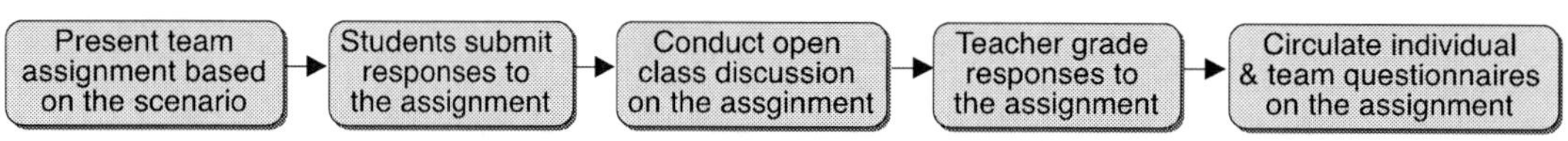

Figure 3. Activities conducted to assess the scenario in the EBSE & SRs course.

The evaluation was conducted during 2021 and 2023, in courses attended by 8 and 10 undergraduate students, respectively. Figure 4 presents their demographic data, gathered at the end-of-course individual questionnaire. All students have industry experience, with the majority having held technical roles. Most students work part-time or full-time during their final two years, as our university is public and tuition-free and there is high demand for IT professionals.

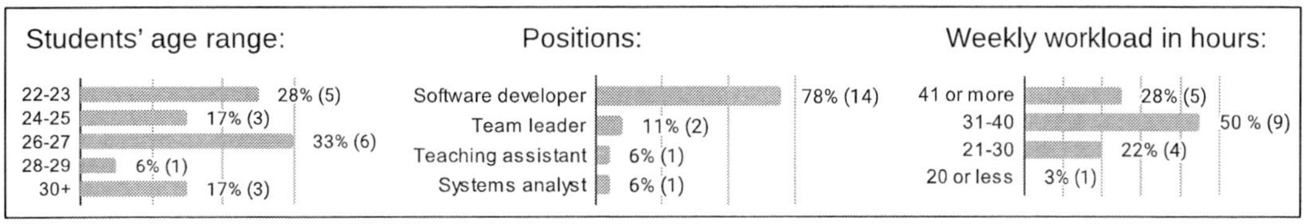

Figure 4. Students demographics.

Achievement of Learning Outcomes. Figure 5 summarizes the assessment of the LO related to the use of evidence in a practical scenario by the students. This includes both the students' opinions and the scores assigned by the teacher on the practical assignments.

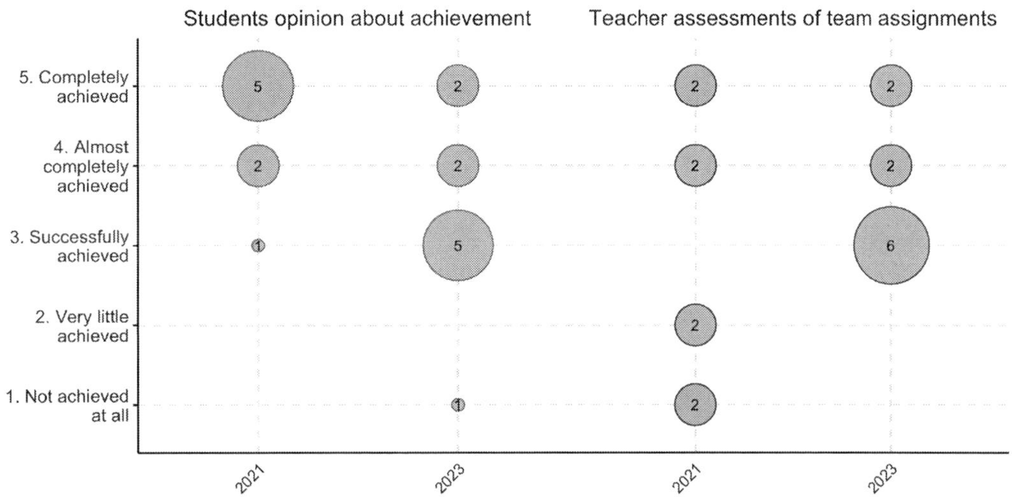

Figure 5. Students' Achievement of LO60.

In 2021, half of the students (4 out of 8) struggled to complete the exercise satisfactorily, as they reported not fully understanding what was required. However, through class discussions and reviewing their submitted responses, they improved their understanding of how to use evidence. This progress was reflected in their feedback on the achievement of LO60 at the end of the course. By 2023, the exercise instructions were revised to make the requirements clearer, which appears to have contributed to better student performance.

Benefits of Using the Scenario. More than half of the students (10 out of 18) reported that the exercise helped them gain a better understanding of the entire EBSE process, particularly the use of evidence in practice. One student remarked: *"It is an exercise that reflects the entire process we progressively followed throughout the course. It helps to understand the importance of synthesizing information and applying it to a concrete case."* Another student highlighted that using evidence to address the practical scenario helped them better recognize the value of aggregating evidence.

It is also worth noting that incorporating this scenario-based exercise did not significantly impact the students' performance or their perceptions of achieving the other learning outcomes of the course.

Challenges of Using the Scenario. Using a practical scenario to enhance the teaching of evidence-based practice presented three major challenges.

Almost half of the students (8 out of 18) highlighted the difficulty in evaluating and applying evidence. For instance, they noted that the challenge stemmed from the SRs referencing one of the recommendations proposed in the exercise and citing support from several primary studies, yet they found this evidence insufficient. One student remarked, *"There is evidence, but I'm not sure if it can be considered enough."* Another student mentioned being unsure how to compare the contexts of the SRs with the scenario, while other found the problem overly complex and the proposed solutions too simplistic.

Issues with using SE SRs. Nearly one-third of the students (5 out of 18) reported difficulties in understanding the SRs. Additionally, 3 students mentioned that the SRs did not provide actionable recommendations. We believe that both challenges also contributed to the previously mentioned difficulty in applying evidence.

Finally, 6 out of 8 students in the 2021 course indicated that they struggled to understand the exercise instructions. Similarly, 5 out of 10 students in the 2023 course also reported initial difficulties with the instructions.

5.3. Discussion of Findings

Several aspects of our results deserve reflection and analysis.

Creating scenario-based exercises for applying scientific evidence. Creating scenario-based exercises for applying scientific evidence can follow Manns and Darrah's process [Manns and Darrah 2012], but it needs adaptation to fit the nuances of SE. We recommend:

- Exploring ways to collaborate with practitioners while accommodating their skills and limited availability. In our case, this approach meant that practitioners, for example, did not engage in reading, searching for, or selecting scientific papers.
- Considering the limitations of SE evidence. We found SR evidence only for one of the eleven topics raised by practitioners. Although our searches were not exhaustive, this appears to align with other studies that discuss the limitations of SE evidence (e.g., [Jørgensen et al. 2005, Budgen et al. 2020]). This could be mitigated by consulting SR catalogs, but none exist formally in our field. We used the list of SRs reported by [Budgen et al. 2020]. Currently, the SR list published by [Kamei et al. 2021, Kamei et al. 2022] is also available.

After evaluating students' practice of the learning outcomes, we concluded that LO60 should use the verb *evaluate* instead of *analyze* to better reflect its complexity according to Bloom's taxonomy [Bloom 1956]. This adjustment is justified because students are required to focus on evaluating both the evidence and the context in which it is to be applied.

Usefulness of scenarios for teaching the use of evidence in practice. Students reported that the exercise helped them better understand how to apply scientific evidence in practice. Additionally, we believe it introduces them to the complexity of using evidence and encourages critical thinking on this subject.

Scenarios help clarify what is expected from students when applying evidence in practice, reducing issues noted in previous studies, such as selecting overly familiar or overly documented topics [Rainer et al. 2006, Rainer and Beecham 2008]. That said, instructions must be clear, and guidance should be carefully crafted to be as unambiguous as possible. An open discussion session on the use of evidence in the proposed scenario, held after students submit their responses, appears very useful for promoting reflection and consolidating learning.

In a recent paper, Wilson et al. reflect on a fundamental challenge in SE: *"how to get researchers to focus on problems that practitioners care about and practitioners to pay attention to what researchers discover"* [Wilson et al. 2024]. They suggest that the best opportunity to bridge this gap is during undergraduate education, when future researchers and practitioners are still fully engaged. They argue that if students graduate without exposure to research methods and relevant research insights, they are unlikely to seek out researchers or academic literature for support or solutions later in their careers.

We agree with Wilson et al.'s argument and believe that teaching EBSE effectively exposes future practitioners to scientific evidence. In a study on the effects of EBSE training among our former students, it was found that although no student had conducted an SR, over half of the respondents reported improvements in their work practices, particularly in their information literacy skills and confidence in using scientific evidence [Pizard et al. 2022].

Our proposal, including scenario-based practice to solve real-world problems, brings students closer to both research methods and scientific findings. This approach prepares them to incorporate evidence into their practice, a complex but essential skill.

5.4. Limitations of this study

Many of the limitations related to our EBSE training also apply here [Pizard et al. 2021]. (1) Volunteer participants may be motivated to support the study's objectives. (2) The course was optional, so it might have only attracted students interested in SE and EBSE. (3) The practical work focused on SR process possibly leading to better preparation for aggregating studies than for identifying issues that EBSE could address. (4) Learning assessments might have included teacher bias, which was minimized by using predefined grading criteria. (5) Activities and resources, like slides and an introductory EBSE report, were included in Spanish to reduce comprehension issues because some course materials were not in the students' native language.

Additional limitations of this particular study are: (6) The context of the scenario was a company that provides software for government agencies, which might be unfamiliar to students. To minimize this, the context was explained to students and some specific comments were made about general characteristics of SE in government agencies. (7) As a field study, results may be context-dependent, not generalizable, with potential low control over events and measurement precision [Stol and Fitzgerald 2018]. (8) Practitioners involved in scenario development were acquainted with Pizard possibly influencing their responses. To mitigate this, they were repeatedly reminded that honesty was paramount when providing feedback, and that both positive and negative comments were equally important. (9) The 2021 and 2023 courses had the first author as the sole instructor.

6. Concluding remarks

Using a scenario-based exercise to teach the application of scientific evidence in practice appears effective in helping students grasp the EBSE process at a more abstract level and its use to improve SE practice. For example, it allows them to better understand how evidence is aggregated and to apply what they have learned throughout the course to tackle a practical problem. Developing scenarios highlights the gap between industry and academia and shows how difficult it is to find SRs that address real-world problems, partly due to their scarcity and the lack of catalogs to easily locate them.

For future work, we plan to bring EBSE teaching even closer to practice. Specifically, our goal is to develop and offer EBSE training for industry practitioners and government agency members. Additionally, it also seems interesting to continue developing different scenarios to teach the use of evidence, in order to have more teaching material.

Artifact Availability

Data from the first stage are unavailable due to non-disclosure agreements, while second-stage data are accessible at [Pizard and Marenco 2025] (In Spanish).

Acknowledgments

We thank Prof. Barbara Kitchenham for reviewing an earlier draft of this paper. We thank the practitioners and students who participated in this study.

References

Atkinson, P. and Hammersley, M. (1994). Ethnography and participant observation. In Denzin, N. and Lincoln, Y., editors, *Handbook of Qualitative Research*. Thousand Oaks, CA.

Bano, M. and Zowghi, D. (2015). A systematic review on the relationship between user involvement and system success. *Information and Software Technology*, 58.

Bloom, B. (1956). *Taxonomy of educational objectives, the classification of educational Goals, handbook I: Cognitive domain*. D. McKay.

Braun, V. and Clarke, V. (2006). Using thematic analysis in psychology. *Qualitative Research in Psychology*, 3(2).

Budgen, D., Brereton, P., Williams, N., and Drummond, S. (2020). What support do systematic reviews provide for evidence-informed teaching about software engineering practice? *E-Informatica Software Engineering Journal*, 14(1).

Cartaxo, B., Pinto, G., and Soares, S. (2018). The role of rapid reviews in supporting decision-making in software engineering practice. In *International Conference on Evaluation and Assessment in Software Engineering*.

Coomarasamy, A. and Khan, K. (2004). What is the evidence that postgraduate teaching in evidence based medicine changes anything? a systematic review. *BMJ (Clinical research ed.)*, 329.

Da Silva, F., Santos, A., Soares, S., Frana, A., Monteiro, C., and Maciel, F. (2011). Six years of systematic literature reviews in software engineering: An updated tertiary study. *Information and Software Technology*, 53(9).

Davison, R., Martinsons, M. G., and Kock, N. (2004). Principles of canonical action research. *Information Systems Journal*, 14(1).

Hassler, E., Carver, J., Kraft, N., and Hale, D. (2014). Outcomes of a community workshop to identify and rank barriers to the systematic literature review process. In *International Conference on Evaluation and Assessment in Software Engineering*.

Ilic, D. and Maloney, S. (2014). Methods of teaching medical trainees evidence-based medicine: A systematic review. *Medical Education*, 48(2).

Jørgensen, M., Dybå, T., and Kitchenham, B. (2005). Teaching evidence-based software engineering to university students. In *International Software Metrics Symposium*.

Kamei, F., Wiese, I., Lima, C., Polato, I., Nepomuceno, V., Ferreira, W., Ribeiro, M., Pena, C., Cartaxo, B., Pinto, G., and Soares, S. (2021). Grey Literature in Software Engineering: A critical review. *Information and Software Technology*, 138.

Kamei, F., Wiese, I., Neto, C., Polato, I., Nepomuceno, V., Ferreira, W., Ribeiro, M., Pena, C., Cartaxo, B., Pinto, G., and Soares, S. (2022). Grey Literature in Software Engineering: A Critical Review.

Kasoju, A., Petersen, K., and Mäntylä, M. (2013). Analyzing an automotive testing process with evidence-based software engineering. *Information and Software Technology*, 55(7).

Kennedy, D., Hyl, Á., Ryan, N., Hyland, Á., and Ryan, N. (2007). *Writing and using learning outcomes: A practical guide*, chapter C 3.4-1.

Kitchenham, B., Budgen, D., and Brereton, P. (2015). *Evidence-based software engineering and systematic reviews*. Chapman & Hall/CRC Innovations in Software Engineering and Software Development Series. CRC Press, London.

Kitchenham, B., Dybå, T., and Jørgensen, M. (2004). Evidence-based software engineering. In *International Conference on Software Engineering*.

Kitson, A., Harvey, G., and Mccormack, B. (1998). Enabling the implementation of evidence based practice: a conceptual framework. *Quality in Health Care*, 7.

Larsen, C. M., Terkelsen, A. S., Carlsen, A. M. F., and Kristensen, H. K. (2019). Methods for teaching evidence-based practice: A scoping review. *BMC Medical Education*, 19(1).

Manns, P. and Darrah, J. (2012). A structured process to develop scenarios for use in evaluation of an evidence-based approach in clinical decision making. *Advances in Medical Education and Practice*, 3.

Milewicz, R. M., Bisila, J. D., Mundt, M. R., and Teves, J. B. (2023). Seeking enlightenment: Incorporating evidence-based practice techniques in a research software engineering team. In *Conference of the United States Research Software Engineer Association*.

Pacheco, C. and Garcia, I. (2012). A systematic literature review of stakeholder identification methods in requirements elicitation. *Journal of Systems and Software*, 85(9).

Pizard, S., Acerenza, F., Otegui, X., Moreno, S., Vallespir, D., and Kitchenham, B. (2021). Training students in evidence-based software engineering and systematic reviews: a systematic review and empirical study. *Empirical Software Engineering*, 26(3).

Pizard, S., Acerenza, F., Vallespir, D., and Kitchenham, B. (2023). Assessing attitudes towards evidence-based software engineering in a government agency. *Information and Software Technology*, 154.

Pizard, S., Lezama, J., García, R., Vallespir, D., and Kitchenham, B. (2025). Using rapid reviews to support software engineering practice: a systematic review and a replication study. *Empirical Software Engineering*, 30(1).

Pizard, S. and Marenco, L. (2025). Data & Codification from Stage 2 of the study "Using Real-world Scenarios to Bridge Training and Practice in Evidence-Based Software Engineering".

Pizard, S., Vallespir, D., and Kitchenham, B. (2022). A longitudinal case study on the effects of an evidence-based software engineering training. In *IEEE/ACM International Conference on Software Engineering: Software Engineering Education and Training (ICSE-SEET)*.

Rainer, A. and Beecham, S. (2008). A follow-up empirical evaluation of evidence based software engineering by undergraduate students. In *International Conference on Evaluation and Assessment in Software Engineering*.

Rainer, A., Hall, T., and Baddoo, N. (2006). A preliminary empirical investigation of the use of evidence based software engineering by undergraduate students. In *International Conference on Evaluation and Assessment in Software Engineering*.

Sadeghi-Bazargani, H., Tabrizi, J. S., and Azami-Aghdash, S. (2014). Barriers to evidence-based medicine: A systematic review. *Journal of Evaluation in Clinical Practice*, 20(6).

Scurlock-Evans, L. and Upton, D. (2015). The role and nature of evidence: A systematic review of social workers' evidence-based practice orientation, attitudes, and implementation. *Journal of Evidence-Informed Social Work*, 12(4).

Stol, K.-J. and Fitzgerald, B. (2018). The ABC of Software Engineering Research. *ACM Transactions on Software Engineering and Methodology*, 27(3).

Swanberg, S. M., Dennison, C. C., Farrell, A., Machel, V., Marton, C., O'Brien, K. K., Pannabecker, V., Thuna, M., and Holyoke, A. N. (2016). Instructional methods used by health sciences librarians to teach evidence-based practice (EBP): a systematic review. *J. Med. Libr. Assoc.*, 104(3).

Upton, D., Stephens, D., Williams, B., and Scurlock-Evans, L. (2014). Occupational therapists' attitudes, knowledge, and implementation of evidence-based practice: A systematic review of published research. *British Journal of Occupational Therapy*, 77(1).

Venkatesh, V., Brown, S. A., and Bala, H. (2013). Bridging the qualitative-quantitative divide: guidelines for conducting mixed methods research in information systems. *MIS Q.*, 37(1).

Wilson, G., Aranda, J., Hoye, M., and Johnson, B. (2024). Experience Report: It Will Never Work in Theory . *IEEE Software*, 41(03).

Zwolsman, S., Te Pas, E., Hooft, L., Wieringa-De Waard, M., and Van Dijk, N. (2012). Barriers to gps' use of evidence-based medicine: A systematic review. *British Journal of General Practice*, 62(600).

7. Appendix: problems identified by the practitioners (refer to section 5.1).

The following is the complete list of current practice problems identified by practitioners in Stage 2 of this study. This is an English translation of the original Spanish concerns expressed by the practitioners, although every effort was made to preserve their exact words and intentions.

1. How to ensure that the client understands how agile methodologies work? Generally, clients want fixed deadlines, fixed scope, everything delivered as quickly as possible, and often apply pressure.
2. Estimations are challenging; we use expert judgment, but clients increasingly want everything faster. They send a brief description and expect a quick and accurate estimate. How to improve estimation?
3. Managing a very large system over many years is difficult. Design ideas or specific functionalities might be used occasionally, but over time, it's easy to lose track of how they work or the correct way to implement and integrate them. How can we preserve the knowledge of processes, especially in massive applications with high team turnover? Documentation exists, but even remembering where things are documented can be a challenge.
4. Control code quality. Is very difficult to... the code reviews. At some point, you have to trust that developers are doing things correctly because reviewing every line is complex. Even though automatic analysis tools are used, they don't catch everything... and some issues slip through. How to control code quality?
5. How to balance quality with deadlines? Stress, and the pressure of arbitrary timelines can be tough. The theory is great, but in practice, it becomes very complicated.
6. How to identify the Minimum Viable Product (MVP) that adds value to the customer?
7. How to estimate when you depend on other development groups?
8. How to prioritize equally among different stakeholder groups so that the client receives what they need as quickly as possible. How to prioritize requirements when dealing with different user groups?
9. Having a fixed team with a high workload is challenging. It's hard to balance daily (urgent) tasks with research (important) tasks to make progress and incorporate, for example, new technology. How would you create a process that allows these two aspects to work together? Hiring more people isn't always an option, and when new hires finally gain the necessary expertise, they might leave (high turnover). How can we balance innovation management with development and maintenance?
10. We have many legacy systems. When considering a rebuild, the business usually asks for the new system to *"do the same as the previous one"*. It's tough to get the business to generate new requirements during the migration of legacy systems. If the initiative doesn't come from IT, business involvement isn't as strong. It's hard to get the client to see this as a new opportunity to rethink things. How to involve the business in the rebuilding of legacy systems?
11. How to introduce agile for the first time in an overstructured organization?

Integración de herramienta para el seguimiento ágil mediante el uso de Machine Learning

Yadira Jazmín Pérez Castillo[1], Sandra Dinora Orantes Jiménez[1], Patricio Orlando Letelier Torres[2], María Elena Acevedo Mosqueda[3]

[1]Centro de Investigación en Computación, Instituto Politécnico Nacional, Av. Juan de Dios Bátiz, esq. Miguel Othón de Mendizábal, Col. Nueva Industrial Vallejo, Alcaldía Gustavo A. Madero, C.P. 07738, CDMX, México.

[2]Departamento de Sistemas Informáticos y Computación, Escuela Técnica Superior de Ingeniería Informática, Universitat Politècnica de València Camino de Vera, s/n, C.P. 46022, Valencia, España.

[3]Instituto Politécnico Nacional, Escuela Superior de Ingeniería Mecánica y Eléctrica (ESIME-IPN), CDMX, 07738, México.

yperezc2022@cic.ipn.mx, dinora@cic.ipn.mx, letelier@dsic.upv.es, eacevedo@ipn.mx

Resumen. *El enfoque ágil ha impulsado la necesidad de herramientas avanzadas para la gestión de proyectos, especialmente en entornos multiproyecto. Este trabajo presenta la integración de un modelo de Machine Learning (ML) en Worki, una plataforma de seguimiento ágil, para analizar datos históricos de Sprints y evaluar el rendimiento. El modelo clasifica y evalúa el progreso y ritmo de trabajo, mostrando los resultados directamente en la plataforma. Esto permite una visión basada en datos, facilitando la detección temprana de anomalías y mejorando la eficiencia en la gestión de proyectos.*

Abstract. *The agile approach has driven the need for advanced tools in project management, especially in multi-project environments. This work presents the integration of a Machine Learning (ML) model into Worki, an agile tracking platform, to analyze historical Sprint data and evaluate performance. The model classifies and assesses progress and work pace, displaying the results directly within the platform. This enables a data-driven perspective, facilitating early anomaly detection and improving project management efficiency.*

1. Introducción

En la actualidad, el enfoque ágil ha adquirido una relevancia significativa en el desarrollo de software y la gestión de proyectos, desde sus inicios, consolidándose como un elemento clave para adaptarse a las necesidades dinámicas del mercado y de los equipos de trabajo. El Manifiesto Ágil (Sutherland, 2001), estableció los principios fundamentales que guían la práctica de desarrollo ágil, enfocándose en la colaboración, la flexibilidad y la entrega continua de valor. Este marco ha evolucionado para abordar los desafíos contemporáneos en proyectos ágiles.

Según el informe *The 17th State of Agile Report de Digital.ai (2024)* (Digital.ai, 2024), el 71% de las organizaciones encuestadas utilizan prácticas ágiles en su ciclo de vida de desarrollo de software (SDLC). Sin embargo, solo el 11% de los encuestados se sienten "muy satisfechos" con los resultados obtenidos, lo que indica que, a pesar de su amplia adopción, persisten desafíos en la implementación efectiva de estas metodologías (Digital.ai, 2024).

En este contexto, la integración de técnicas de “Machine Learning” (ML) en entornos ágiles se presenta como una oportunidad innovadora para optimizar procesos, mejorar la precisión en la planificación y facilitar la toma de decisiones en entornos ágiles, contribuyendo así a una gestión de proyectos eficiente y adaptativa.

Según (Dam, Tran, Grundy, Ghose, & Kamei, 2019), la inteligencia artificial (IA) tiene el potencial de transformar significativamente la práctica de la gestión de proyectos, ayudando a acelerar la productividad y aumentar las tasas de éxito de los proyectos. En este trabajo también proponen un marco donde las tecnologías de IA pueden ofrecer soporte para gestionar proyectos ágiles, automatizando tareas repetitivas y de alto volumen, habilitando análisis de proyectos para estimaciones y predicciones de riesgos, proporcionando recomendaciones accionables e incluso tomando decisiones. Esta perspectiva resalta la relevancia y los avances en la incorporación de técnicas avanzadas que integran ML para optimizar la Gestión Ágil de Proyectos (GAP), permitiendo a los gestores no solo supervisar el avance, sino también tomar decisiones oportunas.

Por lo anterior, en este trabajo se describe la integración de un modelo de ML en la herramienta Worki, perteneciente al enfoque TUNE-UP Process (TUNE-UP Process, 2017), que fue desarrollado para facilitar la transformación ágil de equipos de trabajo. En un contexto ágil, el término "Sprint" se refiere a un bloque de tiempo definido, generalmente de dos a cuatro semanas, en el que un equipo de desarrollo se enfoca en completar un conjunto específico de tareas previamente planificadas. Según la Guía Scrum de Schwaber y Sutherland, los “Sprint” son la base del desarrollo incremental, proporcionando una estructura iterativa para alcanzar objetivos claros dentro de ciclos breves (Schwaber & Sutherland, 2020).

La integración de algoritmos de ML en Worki busca potenciar este enfoque iterativo al analizar datos históricos de “Sprint” para evaluar el progreso y la velocidad del trabajo; permitiendo detectar anomalías en el progreso y tomar acciones correctivas oportunamente. Este trabajo analiza cómo la integración de técnicas de ML, sobre la herramienta Worki, contribuye a optimizar el seguimiento de proyectos. Se examinan los resultados derivados de la evaluación de los "Sprints" y se destacan las ventajas de emplear enfoques adaptativos para potenciar la supervisión del avance del Sprint. Estas funcionalidades subrayan el impacto transformador del ML en la GAP, especialmente en contextos multiproyecto.

El presente trabajo se organiza de la siguiente manera: en la sección 2, se presenta un panorama general sobre el uso de ML como apoyo a la GAP. La sección 3 ofrece una descripción detallada de la herramienta de seguimiento utilizada, Worki, además se describe como fue la generación del modelo a integrar. En la sección 4, se aborda el desarrollo de la integración del ML dentro de la herramienta Worki. La sección 5 se centra en la visualización de los resultados obtenidos.

En la sección 6 presenta una breve discusión sobre los hallazgos. Finalmente, las secciones 7 y 8 concluyen con las principales aportaciones del estudio y se proponen direcciones futuras de investigación.

2. Contexto

Hoy día, la GAP, especialmente en entornos multiproyecto, requiere herramientas que no solo permitan supervisar el progreso del trabajo, para así tomar decisiones oportunas.

Las herramientas de seguimiento tradicionales suelen limitarse a ofrecer una visión estática del estado actual del proyecto, sin proporcionar una capacidad integral para discernir entre los diversos proyectos en curso. Por esta razón, la integración de tecnologías avanzadas como ML se ha vuelto clave para abordar estos desafíos como la supervisión del progreso del trabajo, debido a que estas técnicas permiten analizar grandes volúmenes de datos y ofrecer predicciones y análisis más profundos.

Según (Mamatha & Suma, 2021) la aplicación de técnicas de ML en la gestión de proyectos de software ha demostrado ser efectiva para mejorar la toma de decisiones, mejorar la precisión en las estimaciones y facilitar una gestión más adaptativa. Estos avances tecnológicos permiten una visión más precisa y dinámica de los proyectos, lo que ayuda a tomar decisiones más informadas y ajustadas a las realidades cambiantes del entorno ágil (Mahdi, y otros, 2021).

De manera similar, (Mamatha & Suma, 2021) destacan el papel de ML en la mejora de la precisión de las estimaciones, la optimización de la planificación y la identificación temprana de riesgos, lo que a su vez facilita una gestión de proyectos más ágil y eficiente.

Además, en (Prasetyo, Peranginangin, Martinovic, Ichsan, & Wicaksono, 2025) destacan cómo la inteligencia artificial (IA) está ganando terreno en la gestión de proyectos de innovación abierta, subrayando la importancia de integrar tecnologías avanzadas para una gestión más eficiente y flexible.

Varios estudios han explorado la integración de ML en el contexto ágil, aunque cada uno se ha centrado en diferentes áreas de aplicación. Por ejemplo, en (Baharom, Rahman, Sabudin, & Nor, 2023) aplicaron ML en el desarrollo de herramientas de apoyo a la toma de decisiones, específicamente en un planificador inteligente, para apoyar en la planificación en proyectos ágiles, mejorando la asignación de recursos y la programación de tareas. En el área de estimación de esfuerzo y costos, en (Rodríguez Sánchez, Vázquez Santacruz, & Cervantes Maceda, 2023) utilizaron técnicas de árboles de decisión y punto de historia de usuario para predecir el esfuerzo y los costos asociados a proyectos ágiles de desarrollo de software. De manera similar, Meiliana et al. (2023) implementaron un enfoque basado en ML para estimar el esfuerzo en el desarrollo ágil, enfocándose en los elementos del backlog del producto. También, en (Tiwari, Phonsa, & Malik, 2024) la estimación en proyectos Scrum utilizando diversas técnicas de ML para mejorar la precisión de las predicciones en la planificación del esfuerzo y el tiempo.

Por otro lado, en (Gaona-Cuevas, Guerrero, & Vera-Rivera, 2024) aplicaron técnicas de ML para desarrollar un modelo de clasificación inteligente del Product Backlog, lo que permite una gestión más eficiente de las historias de usuario y una mejor priorización de tareas.

En el área de la determinación del tamaño ideal del equipo en prácticas ágiles, en (Olivares, Noel, Guzmán, Miranda, & Munoz, 2024) implementaron métodos basados en ML para optimizar la asignación de recursos y mejorar la productividad del equipo dentro del marco ágil.

Además, en (Shameem, Nadeem, & Zamani, 2023) propusieron un modelo probabilístico basado en algoritmos genéticos para predecir el éxito de los proyectos ágiles en el contexto del desarrollo global de software, mejorando la capacidad de planificación y anticipación de riesgos.

Estos trabajos destacan cómo el uso de ML se ha extendido a diversas áreas clave dentro de la GAP, como la estimación de esfuerzo, costos, riesgos y la optimización de equipos, mostrando su versatilidad y su potencial para transformar la toma de decisiones.

En el ámbito de la estimación de esfuerzo y costos, técnicas como los árboles de decisión y modelos probabilísticos se ha demostrado su capacidad para predecir con mayor precisión el esfuerzo requerido y los costos asociados, permitiendo una planificación más realista y ajustada a las necesidades del proyecto. En términos de gestión de riesgos, los algoritmos de ML permiten identificar y anticipar posibles problemas antes de que ocurran, mejorando la capacidad de respuesta ante cambios inesperados o problemas durante el desarrollo del proyecto. Además, en el área de la gestión de equipos, métodos de ML, como el análisis de datos históricos y la determinación del tamaño ideal del equipo han permitido mejorar la asignación de recursos, optimizando la productividad y asegurando que el equipo esté equilibrado para abordar las demandas del proyecto de manera más eficiente. Estos avances muestran cómo ML no solo apoya las decisiones, sino que también facilita una planificación más adaptativa, mejora las predicciones y permite un enfoque proactivo en, asegurando una mayor alineación con los objetivos estratégicos del proyecto.

Sin embargo, a pesar de los avances logrados en la integración de ML con el enfoque ágil, no se encontró trabajo en la línea de investigación enfocada al progreso del trabajo. Algunas herramientas de seguimiento como Jira (Atlassian, 2024) y Worki (Tuneupprocess, 2017), recopilan una amplia gama de datos durante el ciclo de vida de un proyecto, incluyendo tiempos de respuesta, asignación de tareas y rendimiento del equipo.

No obstante, la explotación de estos datos mediante técnicas de ML para proporcionar análisis predictivos y recomendaciones personalizadas aún está en sus etapas iniciales. Esta falta de integración, lejos de limitar la capacidad para tomar decisiones, representa una oportunidad para mejorar la calidad de las decisiones informadas y oportunas basadas en datos analíticos, especialmente en entornos multiproyecto

En este contexto, el presente trabajo tiene como objetivo explorar cómo la integración de modelos de ML en la herramienta Worki puede mejorar el seguimiento de los Sprints, en los proyectos. Mediante el análisis de los datos proporcionados por Worki, este trabajo muestra cómo la integración de ML puede contribuir al seguimiento del progreso del trabajo.

3. Desarrollo previo

Worki es una herramienta desarrollada en Valencia, España, se nutre de tres vertientes: la docencia, la investigación y la aplicación industrial. A través de su metodología "TUNE-UP Process" (TUNE-UP Process, 2017), Worki integra prácticas de los métodos ágiles más populares, como Scrum, Kanban, y Lean Development, permitiendo la gestión ágil de proyectos mediante workflows flexibles, configurables y un enfoque centrado en la gestión de requisitos a través de pruebas de aceptación. Además, facilita el seguimiento del tiempo, la gestión del backlog y la comunicación integrada en un entorno colaborativo.

Esta herramienta es un ejemplo de cómo se puede aplicar la metodología ágil en la práctica, contribuyendo a una gestión más eficiente y adaptativa de proyectos (Agilismoatwork, 2012).

Se eligió Worki como herramienta para el desarrollo de este estudio debido a su enfoque integral y su capacidad para gestionar proyectos ágiles y eficiente y particularmente por ofrecernos datos reales de 200 proyectos, considerando aproximadamente 551 Sprints para análisis. Estos datos fueron extraídos de Worki y empleados para generar el conjunto de datos destinado al entrenamiento de algoritmos de ML. Estos datos corresponden a equipos de trabajo de asignaturas de ingeniería de software, de la escuela de informática de la Universidad Politécnica de Valencia, España.

Dentro de Worki, específicamente en la sección de "dashboard", se encuentran diversos gráficos diseñados para facilitar el seguimiento de los "Sprint". Entre ellos, destacan la gráfica de Burndown y la gráfica de trabajo terminado y no terminado, tal como se ilustra en la Figura 1.

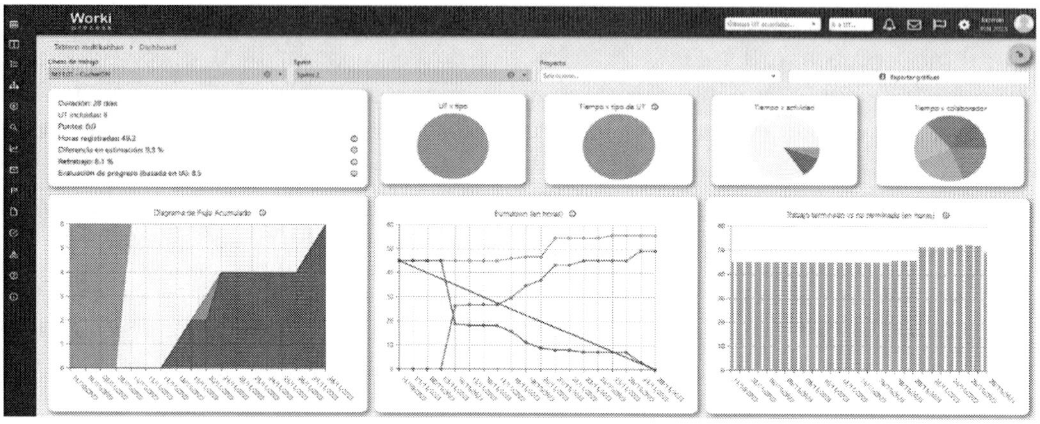

Figura 1 Dashboard de seguimiento de Sprints de Worki (Tuneupprocess, 2017)

En un trabajo previo realizado en (Pérez Castillo, Orantes Jiménez, & Letelier, 2024), se proporcionó un análisis detallado sobre el uso de estas gráficas y su importancia para evaluar el progreso y la velocidad de los Sprints. Además, se describió el proceso de extracción de datos llevado a cabo para la construcción del conjunto de datos y las consideraciones, para la generación de los rasgos y etiquetas, así como los experimentos realizados con algoritmos de ML seleccionados.

Dentro del trabajo previo realizado, se implementaron diversos experimentos utilizando algoritmos de ML. Entre los algoritmos probados en la experimentación, SVM (Support Vector Machine) destacó como el más apropiado debido a su capacidad para manejar datos complejos y ofrecer predicciones precisas. Los resultados experimentales demostraron que SVM proporciona un equilibrio óptimo entre precisión y eficiencia, lo que lo convierte en una elección sólida para evaluar el progresos y ritmo de "Sprint".

La Tabla 1 resume las métricas clave obtenidas en los experimentos realizados con diferentes algoritmos de ML, evaluando su desempeño en términos de *Recall, F1-Score, Accuracy* y *Precision*. El algoritmo SVM sobresale en varias métricas, alcanzando un *Recall* de 0.88, un *Accuracy* de 0.88 y un *Precision* de 0.88, posicionándose como el más adecuado para el análisis de los Sprints.

Otros algoritmos como *KNN*, *MLP*, *RF* y *LR* también mostraron desempeños competitivos, con métricas similares, aunque ligeramente inferiores. En contraste, NB y AB presentaron resultados menos robustos, especialmente en *F1-Score* y *Recall*.

El proceso detallado de preprocesamiento de datos y experimentación con estos algoritmos se documenta en el trabajo previo. Este trabajo fundamenta la elección de SVM como el modelo óptimo entre precisión y eficiencia.

Tabla 1 Resultados experimentación

	Recall	**F1**	**Accuracy**	**Precision**
KNN	0.86	0.86	0.86	0.87
SVM	0.88	0.87	0.88	0.88
MLP	0.86	0.86	0.86	0.87
RF	0.87	0.86	0.87	0.87
NB	0.69	0.66	0.69	0.78
LR	0.87	0.87	0.87	0.88
AB	0.77	0.75	0.77	0.75

Por otro lado, las categorías de desempeño del "Sprint" también fueron definidas como: Malo, Regular, Bueno, Excelente. Estas categorías fueron determinadas en colaboración con un experto en enfoque ágil, quien, valido los criterios utilizados para su clasificación, además de que, se basan en métricas clave como el porcentaje de tareas completadas, la consistencia en el ritmo de trabajo diario y la cantidad de días sin progreso. A través de este proceso, se definieron umbrales específicos que permiten evaluar objetivamente hasta qué punto un sprint puede considerarse exitoso o necesita mejoras, garantizando una retroalimentación precisa.

4. Proceso de Integración

Con el objetivo de facilitar la integración del modelo de ML previamente desarrollado en Worki se diseñó y desarrolló una API (Interfaz de Programación de Aplicaciones), que permite interactuar con el modelo de forma eficiente y automatizada.

Esta API fue desarrollada en Python, utilizando el framework Flask[1], que permite gestionar las solicitudes HTTP. Además de Flask, se integraron diversas bibliotecas que permiten la manipulación, validación y análisis de los datos. También se incluyó Marshmallow [2]para la validación y serialización de los datos entrantes y salientes.

[1] https://pypi.org/project/Flask
[2] https://pypi.org/project/marshmallow

Para el procesamiento y análisis de grandes volúmenes de datos, como los gráficos generados por Worki, se utilizaron Pandas [3]y NumPy[4], que permiten manipular tablas y realizar cálculos numéricos eficientes. Además, se empleó Joblib [5]para cargar y ejecutar el modelo de ML.

El principal propósito de la API es realizar la comunicación entre el modelo de ML, tomando los datos provenientes de Worki para pasarlos al modelo y asi obtener la evaluación el desempeño de un Sprint.

A través de esta comunicación, los datos de las gráficas de BurnDown y otros indicadores de progreso se analizan y clasifican en cuatro categorías: Malo, Regular, Bueno, y Excelente, basadas en el rendimiento general del "Sprint". Cada categoría incluye una retroalimentación detallada y recomendaciones prácticas para mejorar el desempeño de los equipos en futuros Sprints.

Una vez que la API fue desarrollada y probada localmente, se procedió con su integración con la plataforma de Worki (Tuneupprocess, 2017). Esta integración permite que Worki y la API trabajen de forma conjunta, agilizando el flujo de trabajo entre ambas plataformas y el modelo de ML. El flujo de interacción completo entre Worki, la API y el modelo de ML se representa de la siguiente manera: la API recibe datos directamente desde Worki, procesa la información utilizando el modelo de aprendizaje automático (ML) y devuelve los resultados junto con las recomendaciones, completando así un ciclo de retroalimentación eficiente. Este proceso de integración asegura que los datos se procesen y se devuelvan a Worki de forma inmediata, proporcionando información actualizada sobre el desempeño de los Sprints.

La interacción entre Worki, la API y el modelo de ML sigue un flujo estructurado, que se desglosa en tres fases principales:

1. **Consulta**: En esta etapa, la API valida los datos de entrada y realiza una solicitud a Worki para obtener la información necesaria sobre el estado del sprint solicitado. La validación de los datos es esencial para garantizar que la información recibida esté correctamente estructurada y sea útil, para el análisis.
2. **Análisis y Cálculo**: Tras obtener los datos, la API procede a analizar la información mediante el modelo de ML. Durante esta fase, se procesan datos de gráficas como las de Burndown y se calculan métricas clave que permiten evaluar aspectos como el ritmo de trabajo, los días sin progreso, la velocidad de entrega y la efectividad del equipo durante el "Sprint".
3. **Retroalimentación**: Finalmente, la API clasifica el desempeño del sprint en las categorías predefinidas y genera un detalle de retroalimentación. Además, con el fin de proporcionar orientación sobre el estatus del "Sprint".

La integración del modelo de ML con la plataforma Worki requirió el diseño y desarrollo de una arquitectura robusta que actúa como intermediaria entre Worki y el modelo de ML.

---

[3] https://pypi.org/project/pandas/
[4] https://numpy.org/
[5] https://joblib.readthedocs.io/en/stable/

Este proceso presentó algunos retos técnicos para garantizar que los resultados de la API se integrasen intuitivamente en el frontend de Worki, como ejemplo, validar una comunicación sin afectar tiempos de respuesta, tanto del modelo, como de frontend de Worki.

Gracias a esta integración, es posible realizar un análisis del desempeño de los Sprints en tiempo real. Los encargados del proyecto pueden conocer el estatus de cualquier "Sprint" de manera automática, lo que les permite tomar decisiones oportunas y realizar ajustes en tiempo real. Este análisis continuo contribuye a la mejora constante en entornos ágiles y a la toma de decisiones informadas basadas en datos. La implementación de esta API también abre la puerta a futuras implementaciones. Gracias a su arquitectura flexible, es posible incorporar nuevas funcionalidades, como la inclusión de métricas adicionales, la adaptación a otros tipos de gráficos. Este enfoque modular y escalable asegura que la API no solo sea útil en el contexto actual, sino que también pueda evolucionar con las necesidades futuras.

5. Resultados

Para validar la integración de la herramienta Worki con el modelo de ML desarrollado, se llevó a cabo una evaluación preliminar con un grupo de estudiantes de la asignatura *Proceso del Software* en la Escuela Técnica Superior de Ingeniería Informática de la Universitat Politècnica de València, durante el semestre B del año 2024. El grupo estuvo compuesto por 26 equipos de 4 estudiantes cada uno y la evaluación, fue aplicada específicamente en el "Sprint 3".

Durante la evaluación preliminar realizada, se planteó una pregunta clave a los participantes con el objetivo de medir su percepción sobre la utilidad de la incorporación de la evaluación del "Sprint" con ML en la herramienta Worki. La pregunta fue:

"¿Considera que la herramienta facilita la evaluación del desempeño de los Sprints ágiles y proporciona retroalimentación útil para mejorar los futuros Sprints?".

Los resultados obtenidos se encuentran resumidos en el gráfico de la Figura 2.La interpretación de estos resultados revela que una proporción considerable de los estudiantes (55%) estuvo de acuerdo o totalmente de acuerdo con que la herramienta facilita la evaluación del desempeño de los "Sprint".

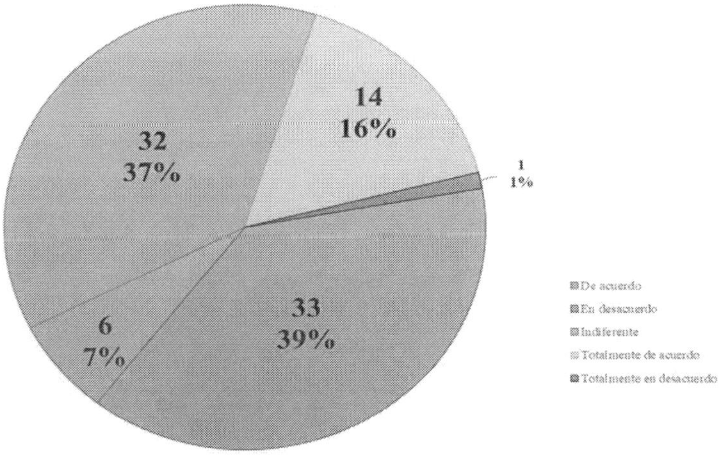

Figura 2 Respuestas al cuestionario

Lo anterior resalta la percepción positiva sobre su funcionalidad y potencial para apoyar el seguimiento ágil. Sin embargo, un 37% de los estudiantes se mostró indiferente, lo que podría estar relacionado con varios factores.

Por un lado, esta respuesta podría reflejar una falta de familiaridad con la herramienta o con los conceptos de evaluación de "Sprints" en general, lo que limitaría su capacidad para apreciar plenamente los beneficios ofrecidos.

Por otro lado, es posible que algunos estudiantes no hayan enfrentado escenarios lo suficientemente desafiantes durante los "Sprint" como para experimentar una necesidad tangible de apoyo en la evaluación.

También podría sugerir que la herramienta no logró conectar del todo con las expectativas o necesidades específicas de este grupo, ya sea por limitaciones en la interfaz, funcionalidad percibida o la relevancia de las métricas evaluadas.

En cuanto al 7% que expresó desacuerdo, este grupo podría haber encontrado dificultades específicas en el uso de la herramienta, como complejidad en la interpretación de los resultados, falta de personalización o posibles inconsistencias en los datos analizados.

Por otro lado, en la Figura 3, se puede observar un ejemplo de la interfaz de Worki, donde se muestran los detalles de la evaluación, incluyendo la categorización (calificación) del desempeño de los equipos, mostrando asi el resultado de la integración del modelo de ML y la herramienta Worki.

Cabe mencionar que, para establecer la evaluación del "Sprint" en el frontend de Worki, primeramente, se consideraron cuatro niveles, previamente establecidos con el experto: Malo, Regular, Bueno, y Excelente. Estas métricas fueron transformadas a una escala numérica, donde cada categoría corresponde a un rango específico: Malo a 4.0, Regular a 7.0, Bueno a 8.5, y Excelente a 9.5.

Este cambio permitió simplificar la interpretación de los resultados, facilitando la clasificación del desempeño de los Sprint y proporcionando retroalimentación categorizada de manera más comprensible.

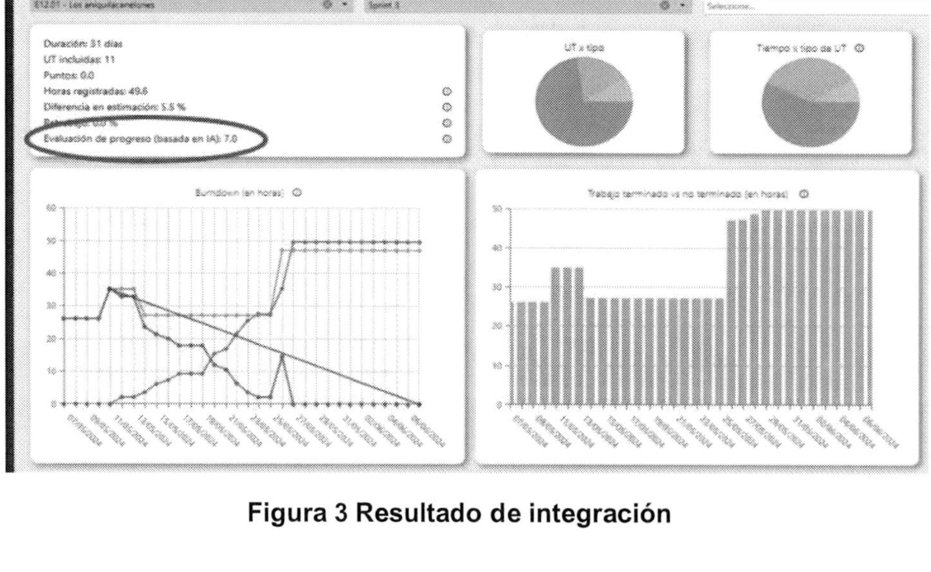

Figura 3 Resultado de integración

Finalmente, los resultados obtenidos de esta integración entre modelo y la herramienta confirman la capacidad del modelo ML para generar retroalimentación de forma precisa y eficiente, permitiendo a los equipos y el gestor identificar áreas de mejora. También se observó que, al recibir retroalimentación continua y categorizada, es posible tomar decisiones más informadas y ajustar su enfoque de trabajo para mejorar su rendimiento en los siguientes ciclos de "Sprint".

La evaluación preliminar permitió validar que la integración entre el modelo ML y Worki es una herramienta funcional y eficaz. La fluidez en el procesamiento y entrega de los resultados en tiempo real demostró efectividad para proporcionar retroalimentación inmediata.

En conclusión, los resultados obtenidos evidencian el valor de la solución implementada para la evaluación de "Sprints" ágiles. La integración de ML con Worki no solo facilita el análisis de los datos, sino que también ofrece una retroalimentación útil y personalizada, permitiendo a los equipos fortalecer uno de los valores clave del enfoque ágil que es la mejora continua.

6. Discusión

Los resultados obtenidos en la evaluación preliminar de la integración de ML con la herramienta Worki reflejan una aceptación general de esta unión como una solución viable para la evaluación del desempeño de "Sprint". Sin embargo, la diversidad en las respuestas también destaca la necesidad de analizar ciertos aspectos de la implementación y funcionalidad.

Un punto clave identificado es la percepción de utilidad expresada por el 55% de los estudiantes que estuvieron de acuerdo y totalmente de acuerdo, con que la herramienta facilita la evaluación y proporciona retroalimentación útil.

Este resultado sugiere que, el modelo de ML implementado tiene un impacto positivo en la identificación y análisis de un "Sprint". Sin embargo, el porcentaje de estudiantes indiferentes (37%) y aquellos en desacuerdo (8%) subraya posibles limitaciones, como la complejidad percibida de los resultados o la falta de familiaridad con la herramienta.

Otro aspecto importante de la integración es que, aunque se logró una comunicación eficiente entre ambas partes, el entorno académico en el que se probó la herramienta podría haber influido en las percepciones de los estudiantes. En un contexto profesional, donde los usuarios tienen experiencia en entornos ágiles y herramientas de análisis avanzadas, la aceptación y utilidad podrían variar significativamente.

Además, el diseño de las categorías de desempeño (traducidas en calificaciones numéricas: 4.0, 7.0, 8.5 y 9.5) plantea un enfoque interesante pero también subjetivo para evaluar los "Sprint". Si bien estas categorías simplifican la interpretación de los resultados, podrían requerir ajustes para reflejar de manera más precisa las complejidades del trabajo en equipo en proyectos ágiles reales.

Por otro lado, los hallazgos en los resultados invitan a una reflexión más profunda para identificar las áreas de mejora que permitan abordar las expectativas de los usuarios y potenciar la adopción de la herramienta Worki, ampliando su impacto en diferentes contextos educativos y profesionales.

Los resultados reflejan una percepción general positiva, aunque también sugiere áreas de oportunidad para mejorar la incorporación de ML en worki. El propósito de la evaluación fue medir de manera objetiva y práctica el rendimiento de los equipos en la gestión de "Sprints" ágiles.

Finalmente, la retroalimentación detallada y las recomendaciones prácticas generadas por el modelo ML ofrecen un valor añadido. No obstante, sería relevante explorar cómo los usuarios aplican esta retroalimentación y si realmente contribuye a mejorar la gestión de los "Sprint" en iteraciones posteriores. Este aspecto podría abordarse en futuras investigaciones que incluyan un análisis del impacto de la herramienta en escenarios más complejos.

En general, la evaluación preliminar resalta el potencial de la integración de Worki con ML, pero también subraya la importancia de iterar sobre su diseño e implementación para maximizar su utilidad en diversos contextos.

7. Conclusiones

Este trabajo ha explorado el potencial de integrar técnicas de ML en un entorno ágil, específicamente mediante el desarrollo de una API que se conecta con la plataforma de seguimiento de proyectos ágiles, Worki, con la finalidad de analizar el progreso de los Sprint. La implementación de esta integración ha permitido procesar datos relevantes, de gráficos como Burndown, obteniendo métricas clave, facilitando así la evaluación de un Sprint.

La evaluación preliminar realizada con estudiantes en un contexto académico ofreció información sobre la aceptación y percepción del modelo de ML en la herramienta. Los resultados mostraron que, aunque una mayoría se consideró útil la integración, persisten desafíos relacionados con la interpretación de los resultados. Esto indica la necesidad de ajustes tanto en la presentación de los resultados como en la interfaz de usuario para mejorar la experiencia de los equipos que adopten esta solución.

Una contribución importante de este trabajo es la capacidad de categorizar el desempeño de los Sprint en niveles y de generar recomendaciones prácticas para la mejora continua. Estas funcionalidades no solo simplifican la evaluación, sino que también proporcionan un enfoque basado en datos para apoyar la toma de decisiones, una característica fundamental en entornos ágiles.

Sin embargo, también se destaca la importancia de ampliar las pruebas de la herramienta en entornos reales, donde los equipos trabajan con mayor presión y complejidad. Esto permitirá evaluar con mayor precisión la efectividad del modelo ML y ajustar las métricas y recomendaciones a las necesidades específicas de proyectos del mundo profesional. Los resultados obtenidos destacan el potencial del modelo de ML para obtener la evaluación de un "Sprint" y proporcionar retroalimentación objetiva basada en datos. No obstante, se identifican diversas oportunidades para perfeccionar y expandir la solución, abordando escenarios más complejos y adaptándola a las dinámicas de equipos y proyectos más exigentes.

Este trabajo constituye un avance significativo en la integración de ML para optimizar el seguimiento ágil de proyectos en entornos multiproyecto, favoreciendo las retrospectivas del sprint curso. Worki demuestra ser una herramienta eficaz para el seguimiento ágil de proyectos, ofreciendo funcionalidades clave para evaluar el progreso y ritmo de los Sprint.

Los resultados experimentales respaldan la elección de SVM como el modelo más adecuado para la integración con Worki, gracias a su equilibrio entre Precision y Accuracy en el análisis de datos. Esto refuerza el potencial de integrar ML en herramientas ágiles para optimizar la gestión y la toma de decisiones basadas en datos, estableciendo una base prometedora para futuras mejoras y aplicaciones.

8. Trabajos Futuros

A partir de los resultados obtenidos y las limitaciones identificadas, se proponen diversas líneas de trabajo para futuras investigaciones que permitan fortalecer y ampliar el uso de ML como apoyo al seguimiento ágil:

1. **Validación de la evaluación del "Sprint" en tiempos de desarrollo específicos**: Es necesario explorar la viabilidad de evaluar sprints dentro de marcos de tiempo específicos, considerando variaciones en las duraciones de los ciclos de trabajo. Esto permitirá determinar si las métricas y clasificaciones generadas son consistentes y relevantes en diferentes contextos de planificación ágil.
2. **Incorporación de gráficas de seguimiento adicionales**: Si bien la herramienta utiliza gráficos, como la gráfica de BurnDown, para evaluar el progreso, una línea de trabajo futura podría incluir el análisis de otras métricas y gráficas relevantes, como los diagramas de flujo acumulado. Esto complementaría la evaluación del "Sprint" al proporcionar una visión más integral sobre los patrones de trabajo y la productividad del equipo.
3. **Algoritmos avanzados para la evaluación del "Sprint"**: El uso de técnicas como análisis de clustering o redes neuronales podría ser explorado para agrupar, por ejemplo, calificaciones similares y detectar puntos de discordancia o anomalías en el desempeño de los equipos de trabajo. Estas técnicas permitirían identificar dinámicas de equipo menos evidentes y ofrecer retroalimentación más específica y detallada con la finalidad de complementar la evaluación del "Sprint".
4. **Validación en entornos empresariales reales**: Ampliar las pruebas de la herramienta a entornos de desarrollo de software reales será clave para validar su aplicabilidad. La evaluación en empresas de diferentes sectores, con equipos diversos y en proyectos de alta complejidad, permitirá ajustar el modelo y los algoritmos para que respondan de manera óptima a escenarios reales.
5. **Estudio del impacto de la propuesta**: Evaluar cómo los gestores de trabajo perciben la utilidad y facilidad de uso de la herramienta, así como su impacto en la toma de decisiones, sería clave para garantizar su aceptación. Investigaciones adicionales podrían diseñarse para identificar barreras de adopción y posibles mejoras en la interfaz y la retroalimentación generada.

6. **Compatibilidad con otras herramientas de gestión**: Aunque el trabajo se centró en la integración con Worki, futuros desarrollos podrían extenderse a investigar la usabilidad de técnicas de ML con herramientas como Jira, Trello o Asana.

En conjunto, estas propuestas buscan fortalecer la herramienta desde un enfoque técnico, funcional y práctico, permitiendo una evaluación más completa de los “Sprint” y su adaptación a distintos entornos de trabajo.

Referencias

Agilismoatwork. (2012). Herramientas para gestión ágil de proyectos de desarrollo de software. Obtenido de https://agilismoatwork.blogspot.com/2012/01/herramientas-para-gestion-agil-de.html

Atlassian. (2024). Jira. Recuperado el 20 de octubre de 2024, de https://www.atlassian.com/es/software/jira

Baharom, M., Rahman, M., Sabudin, A., & Nor, M. (2023). Decision support tools: Machine learning application in smart planner. Lecture Notes in Mechanical Engineering, 753-760. https://doi.org/10.1007/978-981-19-1939-8_58

Pérez Castillo, Y. J., Orantes Jiménez, S. D., & Letelier Torres, P. O. (2024). Sprint management in agile approach: Progress and velocity evaluation applying machine learning. Information, 15(11), 726. https://doi.org/10.3390/info15110726

Dam, H., Tran, T., Grundy, J., Ghose, A., & Kamei, Y. (2019). Towards effective AI-powered agile project management. IEEE/ACM 41st International Conference on Software Engineering: New Ideas and Emerging Results (ICSE-NIER), 41-44. https://doi.org/10.1109/ICSE-NIER.2019.00019

Digital.ai. (2024). The 17th state of agile report. *Analyst Reports - Digital.ai*. Recuperado de https://digital.ai/resource-center/analyst-reports/state-of-agile-report/

Gaona-Cuevas, M., Guerrero, V., & Vera-Rivera, F. (2024). The Smart Product Backlog: A Classification Model of User Stories. IEEE Access, 12, 150008-150019. https://doi.org/10.1109/ACCESS.2024.3478833

Mahdi, M., Zabil, M., Ahmad, A., Ismail, R., Yusoff, Y., Cheng, L., Naidu, H. (2021). Software Project Management Using Machine Learning Technique—A Review. Applied Sciences, 11(11), 5183. https://doi.org/10.3390/app11115183

Mamatha, R., & Suma, K. (2021, October). Role of machine learning in software project management. Journal of Physics: Conference Series, 2040(1), 012038. https://doi.org/10.1088/1742-6596/2040/1/012038

Meiliana, Daniella, G., Wijaya, N., Putra, N., & Efata, R. (2023, January). Agile software development effort estimation based on product backlog items. Procedia Computer Science, 227, 186-193. https://doi.org/10.1016/j.procs.2023.10.516

Olivares, R., Noel, R., Guzmán, S., Miranda, D., & Munoz, R. (2024, May). Intelligent learning-based methods for determining the ideal team size in agile practices. Bioengineering, 9(5), 292. https://doi.org/10.3390/biomimetics9050292

Prasetyo, M., Peranginangin, R., Martinovic, N., Ichsan, M., & Wicaksono, H. (2025, March). Artificial intelligence in open innovation project management: A systematic literature review on technologies, applications, and integration requirements. Lecture Notes in Networks and Systems, 1005, 200-213. https://doi.org/10.1016/j.joitmc.2024.100445

Rodríguez Sánchez, E., Vázquez Santacruz, E., & Cervantes Maceda, H. (2023, March). Effort and cost estimation using decision tree techniques and story points in agile software development. Mathematics, 11(6), 1477. https://doi.org/10.3390/math11061477

Schwaber, K., & Sutherland, J. (2020). La guía definitiva de Scrum: Las reglas del juego. Recuperado de https://scrumguides.org/

Shameem, M., Nadeem, M., & Zamani, A. (2023, March). Genetic algorithm-based probabilistic model for agile project success in global software development. Journal of Software: Evolution and Process. https://doi.org/10.1002/smr.2349

Sutherland, J. (2001). Manifesto for agile software development. Recuperado el 24 de noviembre de 2024, de http://agilemanifesto.org/

Tiwari, S., Phonsa, G., & Malik, N. (2024, January). Estimation approaches of machine learning in Scrum projects. Lecture Notes in Networks and Systems, 731, 103-111. https://doi.org/10.1007/978-981-99-4071-4_9

TUNE-UP Process. (2017). Recuperado el 01 de agosto de 2023, de http://www.tuneupprocess.com/

Tuneupprocess. (2017). Worki. Recuperado el 18 de octubre de 2024, de https://cliente.tuneupprocess.com/web/#/login

Integrating Participatory Design and Dual-track Software Development Process: A Case Study From an Intelligent Mathematics Tutoring System

João Victor Assis[1], Guilherme Guerino[2], Luiz Rodrigues[3], Valmir Macario [1], Marcelo Marinho [1]

[1]Universidade Federal Rural de Pernambuco (UFRPE)
Caixa Postal 15.064 – 91.501-970 – Recife – PE – Brazil
{joao.ctassis, marcelo.marinho, valmir.macario}@ufrpe.br

[2]Universidade Estadual do Paraná
Caixa Postal 98 - 86.800-970 – Apucarana – PR – Brazil
guilherme.guerino@ies.unespar.edu.br

[3]Universidade Federal de Alagoas
Caixa Postal 57.072-970 – Maceió – AL – Brazil
luiz.rodrigues@nees.ufal.br

Abstract. *The demand for educational technology has increased research into Intelligent Tutoring Systems (ITS) for low-connectivity regions. However, misalignment between requirement discovery and software development hinders adoption. This case study examines the development of an unplugged ITS using dual-track agile development and participatory design to ensure continuous alignment with pedagogical needs. This study contributes to software engineering by demonstrating how we integrated dual-track development and participatory design to enhance agility while maintaining a user-centered approach in a project with a scalable model for ITS applications in low-resource environments.*

Resumo. *A demanda por tecnologia educacional aumentou a pesquisa em Sistemas Tutores Inteligentes (STI) para regiões de baixa conectividade. No entanto, o desalinhamento entre a descoberta de requisitos e o desenvolvimento de software dificulta a adoção. Este estudo de caso examina o desenvolvimento de um STI desplugado usando desenvolvimento com abordagem dual-track e design participativo para garantir o alinhamento contínuo com as necessidades pedagógicas. Este estudo contribui para a engenharia de software ao demonstrar como o desenvolvimento com dual-track e o design participativo auxiliam com a agilidade, mantendo uma abordagem centrada no usuário, e oferecendo um modelo escalável para aplicativos STI em ambientes de poucos recursos.*

1. Introduction

The growing demand for innovative educational methodologies has driven research into intelligent tutoring systems (ITS) and unplugged educational approaches, particularly in mathematics, a subject historically associated with learning difficulties among Brazilian students [Instituto Nacional de Estudos e Pesquisas Educacionais Anísio Teixeira (Inep) 2023].

Research suggests that ITSs and unplugged education approaches can potentially enhance students' interest and performance in regions with limited infrastructure [Hillmayr et al. 2020, Silva et al. 2023]. However, poor or nonexistent connectivity and a shortage of technological devices make it difficult for students to access online learning platforms, compromising the effectiveness of personalized learning offered by conventional ITS [Silva et al. 2023].

In this study, we present the software development process of an application for an intelligent tutoring system designed for an unplugged educational context. The project involved two synchronized workstreams: (1) a team dedicated to discovering and formalizing requirements through user interaction and participatory design techniques, and (2) a development team responsible for implementing and refining functionalities based on iterative feedback cycles. This dual-track approach was essential to ensure that pedagogical and usability aspects were effectively integrated into the Software Development Life Cycle (SDLC).

The system developed as part of this project aims to automate the correction of handwritten math problems, provide personalized feedback, and offer pedagogical materials aligned with the *Brazilian National Common Curricular Base (BNCC)*, a document that defines the essential learning topics to be worked on in Brazilian schools. To achieve the project's goals, the team employed a blend of predictive and agile approaches alongside participatory design principles, involving teachers, students, and other stakeholders in stages such as requirements gathering, prototyping, and iterative validation. In the project context, software development methodologies were adapted to accommodate distributed and remote teams while ensuring parallel and continuous user involvement.

Although the project had different teams and activities for its completion, this article focuses on the specific dynamics of the application discovery and development by the Development team. In this regard, agile methodologies, particularly dual-track development, have been proposed to balance rapid development with ongoing user research and requirement refinement [Sedano et al. 2020]. This approach enables teams to work in parallel: one team focuses on understanding user needs and defining requirements, while the other implements and tests functional components of the system. In this context, participatory design emerges as a fundamental approach to developing educational systems on teachers' behalf. It allows technological solutions to be shaped based on the real needs of users, promoting greater acceptance and impact in their final use [Spinuzzi 2005].

Despite the widespread adoption of agile methodologies and user-centered design principles in software development, their integration poses challenges in distributed and remote settings [Camara et al. 2020, Marinho et al. 2019]. In particular, the need for extensive upfront user research in User-Centered Design (UCD) contrasts with agile development's iterative, fast-paced nature [Al-Razgan et al. 2022]. Furthermore, ITS applications require careful alignment with educational objectives, making it essential to balance technical implementation with educational effectiveness [Silva et al. 2023]. The lack of structured processes for synchronizing requirement discovery with development efforts can cause misalignment between user needs and system functionalities, reducing the impact and adoption of the final product.

The **objective** of this case study is to describe the software development process of an intelligent tutoring system in an unplugged context. Specifically, we investigate applying a dual-track development approach that facilitates synchronization between user research, requirement formalization, and system implementation. In addition, we examine the role of participatory design in defining system requirements and ensuring alignment with pedagogical needs.

Thus, this work aims to answer the following research questions (RQ):

- **RQ1:** What are the key roles and team dynamics that enable the integration of dual-track development and participatory design in this distributed software development environment?
- **RQ2:** How does the dual-track development approach facilitate synchronization between requirement discovery and system implementation, and what challenges arise in maintaining this alignment?
- **RQ3:** How did the use of participatory design contribute to identifying pedagogical and technical needs?

2. Background

Intelligent tutoring systems (ITS) represent a transformative educational technology that uses artificial intelligence, machine learning, and natural language processing to provide personalized learning experiences [Nkambou et al. 2010]. These systems adapt dynamically to the needs and abilities of individual learners, significantly enhancing educational outcomes by providing personalized instruction and feedback [Silva et al. 2023].

Artificial intelligence in education (AIED) presents a trend to improve teaching and learning processes through educational systems and tools that use AI [Rodrigues et al. 2023]. However, this technology typically requires high levels of performance or connectivity [Rodrigues et al. 2024a]. To adapt to underprivileged regions, this technology must work on devices with low performance, low connectivity, and low digital literacy [Rodrigues et al. 2024c].

In this context, AIED Unplugged emerges as an approach to creating AI-based educational technologies that do not depend solely on technology [Portela et al. 2023], requiring no changes in school infrastructure, stable internet access or digital skills [Isotani et al. 2023]. This approach is especially useful for improving education in underserved regions [Rodrigues et al. 2024c].

The Software Development Life Cycle (SDLC) is a systematic process used for planning, creating, testing, and deploying software applications. It encompasses several distinct phases that provide a structured approach to software development, helping teams ensure that the software meets quality standards and fulfills business requirements. [Agarwal et al. 2023]. In this sense, agile methodologies act as a way to promote flexibility and adaptability, involve the customer, focus on delivering value, and carry out constant and iterative deliveries in software development processes [Marinho et al. 2019, Camara et al. 2020, Menezes et al. 2024].

From another perspective, [Sedano et al. 2020] describes User-Centered Design (UCD) as both a philosophy and a collection of design practices aimed at ensuring that the design of software artifacts is driven by their impact on and interaction with human users. According to [Al-Razgan et al. 2022], the integration of UCD with Agile methodologies enhances User Experience (UX) by facilitating continuous user feedback, which allows for ongoing refinement and improvement of software products. This synergy ensures that as requirements change, the software remains user-aligned, thereby promoting usability and overall satisfaction in the end product.

However, integrating Agile with UCD faces challenges as the second relies on an extensive upfront design phase, while Agile emphasizes immediate coding and iterative development [Sedano et al. 2020]. Some challenges include time constraints, prioritization of functionality over usability, communication gaps, inadequate documentation, and insufficient user involvement [Al-Razgan et al. 2022].

In this sense, according to [Sedano et al. 2020] **dual track development** emerges as an alternative to reconcile UCD with agile methods by organizing the development process into two parallel tracks: (1) One focuses on understanding user needs and product design through practices like user research and usability testing, while (2) the other emphasizes rapid programming and delivery through agile methodologies. The study emphasizes that the framework fosters continuous communication between the two tracks via mechanisms such as a product backlog, allowing teams to work simultaneously on what to build and how to build it efficiently. By integrating UCD principles with agile practices, Dual-Track Development enables a holistic approach that addresses both user-centered design and project management efficiency.

In another perspective, **participatory design** is an approach that involves end users in the creation process of products, services, and systems, allowing their perspectives, experiences, and needs to influence design decisions [Spinuzzi 2005]. This method differs from traditional approaches, treating users as data sources and active collaborators in developing solutions [Bossen et al. 2016, Bannon and Ehn 2012]. By enabling an iterative and collective process, participatory design strengthens the relationship between technology and society, ensuring that designed solutions align more with real-world contexts. Additionally, this approach contributes to the democratization of design, making it more accessible and responsive to user expectations [Spinuzzi 2005].

In developing interactive systems, this methodology has proven particularly effective in healthcare, education, and software aimed at a broad audience [Bossen et al. 2016]. Tools like co-creation workshops, exploratory testing, and collaborative prototyping help transform user contributions into concrete design elements. Beyond improving usability and acceptance, directly involving users reduces barriers to adopting new technologies and increases engagement with developed products. By giving a voice to those who will use the system, participatory design stands out as an essential strategy for creating more intuitive experiences that truly meet user needs [Spinuzzi 2005].

3. Methodology

From an interpretivist perspective, this research uses the holistic and descriptive single case study method with an inductive approach to observe the application of an adapted software development process in agile, virtual, and distributed teams for a mathematics tutoring system in an unplugged context. We highlight the strategy used to enhance collaboration, maintain agility, and ensure user-centered outcomes.

3.1. Project Context

Company A developed the project in Brazil, a group specialized in developing technological solutions for education, research, and innovation. The company has expertise in tutoring systems, teaching platforms, and technologies that promote inclusion and access to quality education. The client was Company B, a government organization responsible for coordinating educational policies and programs at the national level.

In this context, a partnership was established between companies A and B to develop an automatic correction solution for handwritten math questions. It enhances their intelligent management solution, a previous project focused on automating text correction, with a high potential for adoption by schools. The expectation is to use it in public schools across the country, with elementary school classes being the initial target audience for the Minimum Viable Product (MVP).

This project focused on automating the process of collecting, correcting, and providing pedagogical feedback on math questions to develop basic skills in elementary school students, meeting the needs of populations with limited access to technological resources. Thus, a mobile application was designed to generate open-source intelligent services, based on Artificial Intelligence and Computer Vision algorithms, to automate the correction of handwritten math questions. The project includes fieldwork to validate the parametrization of AI models, in addition to the production and provision of pedagogical materials by specialists. The project counted on nationwide distributed teams, with members from 3 regions in Brazil, as well as collaborative tools to enhance communication. It also used a hybrid project management approach with a blend of predictive (structured teams and documentation) and agile methodologies (such as dual-track development, scrum-like approaches, and kanban boards) to ensure the project's success.

The project had approximately 28 members including the project's coordinator and manager. The members were distributed across 4 teams to ensure efficiency and quality in deliveries: (1) domain experts, (2) pedagogical team, (3) development team, and (4) computer vision teams. They worked simultaneously in different activities to achieve the project goals.

The **Domain Experts Team:** Two Specialists in mathematics, the area addressed by the Intelligent Tutoring System (ITS). They were responsible for defining the competencies required for the system's pedagogical effectiveness and developing educational activities.

The **Computer Vision team**, counted with approximately 9 members including engineers and researchers, processed images of students' handwritten solutions provided by the Domain Experts. Their primary objective was to create a computer vision component capable of automatically detecting and recognizing handwritten solutions, seamlessly integrating with the tutoring system to enhance pedagogical automation.

The pedagogical team, consisting of 4 educators and ITS engineers, developed the student model integrated into the system based on artifacts provided by the Domain Experts.

Development Team: The development team, consisting of approximately 10 members, comprises developers, software testers, and user experience specialists. They were responsible for developing the app with the help of its end users, who were consulted to identify new features and points for improvement.

The project team was geographically distributed across a continental country like Brazil, therefore communication and collaboration were adapted to this scenario. As the members were in the same time zone, meeting synchronization depended on agreements based on members' availability. The tools used included:

- Weekly and biweekly synchronous meetings via the Google Meet platform.
- Asynchronous communication channels via Discord, WhatsApp, and email platforms were used respectively for official communication between teams and coordinators, quick day-to-day communication of each team, and sending documentation to be shared externally to the project.
- Task management boards on the Jira platform.
- Storage and sharing documentation via a project folder on Google Drive (general team's documents) and the Confluence platform (for UX and requirements).

Initially, the project involved other activities that culminated in the initial elaboration of the requirements. Thus, the development team began the activities by adopting a development process based on Dual-tracking while other teams followed their activities in parallel. This paper focuses on the development team's activities,

The Dual-Track Development approach was used to sustain agility in the project's complex environment, where a discovery team continuously refined requirements while the development team implemented and tested functionalities iteratively. Integrating participatory design ensured direct user involvement, aligning the system with pedagogical needs. Agile practices were reinforced through Scrum and Kanban, structured communication via Jira, Confluence, Google Meet, and Discord, and a combination of automated and manual testing to ensure quality throughout the process. Knowledge management was streamlined through lightweight documentation and synchronized workflows, allowing teams to maintain adaptability without excessive overhead. These strategies collectively enabled rapid iterations, continuous validation, and efficient coordination, ensuring that the project remained agile despite its multifaceted nature.

The SDLC analyzed is the mobile application functionalities' discovery, improvement, and development, which had already started in previous project phases. This paper focuses on the development team's activities to discover and implement improvements in the application via consulting its users, while it was being developed. In this context, to collect the data needed for the application's improvement, the UX research group carried out research activities involving information gathering and participatory design with educators from the Pedagogical team and the target users.

To discover improvements in functionalities, the research group used tools such as focus groups, observations and interviews [Guerino et al. 2024, Rodrigues et al. 2024b]. It also aimed at improve usability through usability tests, heuristic inspections, and A/B tests, and experimental application testing. Finally, to analyze the data, qualitative and quantitative analysis were made. This information was distributed in scientific publications made by the team and in the preparation of internal reports.

3.2. Threats to Validity

A challenge to **construct validity** was ensuring the study accurately measured the effectiveness of participatory design in shaping system requirements. To enhance construct validity, the researchers employed a mixed-methods approach, combining qualitative and quantitative techniques, such as thematic analysis of user feedback, usability tests, and participatory design sessions. These methods provided triangulated evidence, minimizing the risk of misrepresenting the impact of participatory design on system development.

Regarding **conclusion validity**, it may be compromised by the subjectivity in assessing the effectiveness of the dual-track development process and participatory design. Although the study uses structured reports, the lack of clear quantitative metrics to measure the effectiveness and impact of these approaches may lead to biased interpretations. Furthermore, **internal validity** is threatened by potential gaps in communication between distributed teams, which may affect the synchronization between requirements discovery and implementation. However, the paper seeks to mitigate this problem by reporting challenges faced and actions taken to improve the development process.

The study's findings may have compromised generalization due to the specific project context, team composition, and focus on an unplugged ITS application. However, to improve **external validity**, the research thoroughly documented the software development process, and methodologies facilitating replication in similar contexts. Furthermore, the involvement of diverse stakeholders, including developers, educators, and AI specialists, contributed to a wider applicability of the study's insights beyond the immediate project scope.

4. Results

4.1. RQ1: Teams and Dynamics

From the project's inception, the application development process involved the participation of 5 different functional groups from the development team, each playing complementary roles in the elicitation, prototyping, development, and evaluation of the application:

1. **UX Research:** Two members, conducting surveys with partner teachers or test users to collect feedback, organize and monitor field testing of the application, and document user feedback, helping improve the app's functionalities.
2. **Requirements:** Two members were assigned to: (1) Collect requirements from suppliers and UX researchers, (2) document requirements in Epics and User Stories, (3) keep requirements updated and prioritized, (4) communicate with other teams about changes in requirements, (5) maintain and monitor the flow of User Stories created during their development, (6) ensure understanding of project requirements with the development, and UX and Pedagogical teams.
3. **UX Design:** One member was assigned to: (1) Develop User Interface (UI) flows for Epics and User Stories described in the requirements, (2) develop and document prototypes, and (3) assist in creating the Design System used in the app.
4. **Development:** Three members were assigned to: (1) Implement project requirements, (2) document technical solutions applied in the project, (3) perform unit tests, and (4) perform integration tests.

5. **Software Testing:** Two members were assigned to: (1) Develop test flows, (2) Plan, and (3) perform manual and automated tests on the application.

These roles were clearly defined within the team to ensure the visibility of individual responsibilities, facilitating understanding of how each person contributes to the final objective. The groups maintained close and direct communication between the development team and the project manager. In this sense, an open communication channel was maintained through instant messaging platforms.

In addition, 2 weekly meetings were held between the groups to help the team align work during the week; one comprised of UX researchers, UX designers, and requirements analysts, and the other comprised developers and testers. Finally, weekly follow-up meetings were held with the project manager and the entire team to report the work done, define the activities for the following week, and resolve any challenges encountered. These meetings and reporting dynamics were essential to alignment and proper communication between discovery and development activities in a distributed software development environment.

4.2. RQ2: Dual-track Development and Project's SDLC

Initially managed in Trello, the project scaled to Jira and Confluence platforms, using Google Drive for collaboration and document sharing. The workflows were structured in Jira for different demands, such as:

- **User Stories:** Building the main features from creation to delivery, involving requirements, design, development, and testing.
- **Tasks:** Viewed in specific boards, allowing detailed control of weekly activities.
- **Bugs:** Allowing interaction between the testing and development teams to identify and correct application bugs.

Five Kanban boards were created to facilitate teams' transition to Jira, for better integration between tasks from different teams. Later, the main team boards were replaced by Scrum boards, optimizing weekly planning and generating more detailed reports.

From the beginning of the project, the development process considered the dual-track approach, to parallelize discovery and application development activities. Due to delays in validating prototyped demands, the team felt it necessary to improve the requirements discovery process. The development team was also behind on tasks, accumulating small adjustments and new requirements in the backlog. Therefore, the team studied and implemented participatory design to systematize and optimize the discovery and evaluation of the end-user experience. By going through more evaluation and correction phases before being developed, the quality and alignment of the features and fixes developed increased.

To develop the application, the teams followed a structured and continuously improved dual-track process, which evolved and stabilized as depicted in Figure 1. In this scenario, (1) the UX researchers worked on discovering new demands, functionalities, or problems, (2) the requirements engineer documented formal requirements or adjustments to them, and (3) the UX designer worked on prototyping these new requirements. Meanwhile, the previously defined requirements were going through the development phases, with (4) the development group building the front end and back end of the application, and (5) the testing group ensuring the quality of the software.

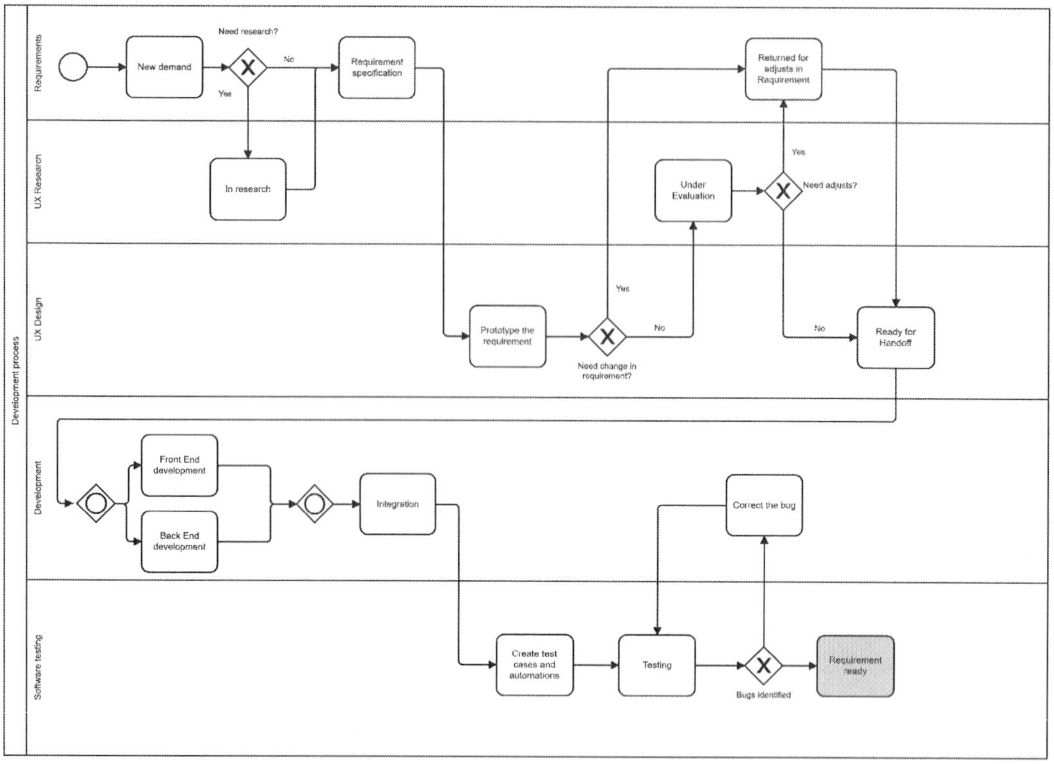

Figure 1. Development process with participatory design.

The requirements group receives, describes, and prioritizes demands. Demands may come from user testing, interviews with teachers from the team, or changes identified to improve usability. These new demands could be described in requirements directly and then prototyped or go through the 4 phases based on **participatory design**. It was applied when the need for more in-depth studies was identified to understand an educational demand and how the target audience would want it to be resolved in the application. In addition, it was also used to investigate usability improvements in a controlled scenario.

The participatory design encompassed the following phases: (1) “In research”, when interviews are conducted with teachers from the pedagogical team to understand the demand better and seek expectations for solving the problem; (2) “Requirement specification” to describe a possible solution in the system; (3) “Prototype the requirement”, when the requirement is modeled in a prototype; and (4) “Under evaluation“, when another interview is conducted to validate the designed solution with potential users and seek points for improvement.

After going through this process, a new requirement is created or an existing requirement is revised and refined through a change requirement. The developers receive some requirements created or altered after the first track of the process each week to develop the project. Two fronts take turns developing the application: one is responsible for the front end, building the user interface, ensuring a seamless and intuitive user experience, and implementing visual elements based on design prototypes [bin Uzayr 2022]. The other front handles the back end and is responsible for implementing the underlying functionality, including server-side logic, database management, and integration of

APIs to ensure the application operates efficiently and meets the specified requirements [Phaneendra et al. 2022].

After being developed, front and back end are integrated and the functionality is passed on to the test group to check the quality. Finally, after being implemented and tested, it is directly updated to the original requirement. Given the large volume of changes that emerged from user research during the project, it was difficult for developers to understand some requirements. To achieve this, some measures were taken, such as explaining in the document what was there before, how it should be using color-coded labels, and a communication channel through the Discord platform to pass on and answer developers' questions.

The development and User Experience (UX) groups maintained an open contact channel, via the requirement card itself in Jira, in case any questions arise regarding the requirements so that specific problems can be quickly resolved, avoiding delays. Close communication between these two groups led to a better understanding of the requirements' objectives, allowing the development team to give their opinion on the construction of the application, also becoming another source of feedback. In addition, it made it easier for the development team to develop feasible requirements according to the resources available for the project.

Another challenge we encountered was the alignment between development and testing groups. After reporting bugs in Jira, testers had difficulty tracking which version they were being fixed in by developers. Therefore, the team started using versioning, providing a version with release notes for each generated build. These notes comprised the changes made in each version, including bug fixes, and improvements to the application, among other changes. The testing team could base their manual tests on the sprints.

The project faced problems in assembling a team to test the software, which caused a slight delay in the start of this team's activities. Therefore, testers had a longer adaptation period to include themselves in the defined process and propose improvements.

After developers complete the integration phase, they release the stories in Jira so that testers can analyze the new requirement or change made, and create test cases and automations, and then perform the tests. The team adapted the tests to run on two simultaneous devices: one physical device and one through an emulator. This approach provided greater reliability in the results obtained. After being tested, if bugs were identified, the requirement is sent back to the developers to correct it. Finally, if there are no more bugs, the requirement is ready.

Each sprint week, all features included in the development team's build and listed in the release notes underwent manual testing. The test results were detailed in a spreadsheet that contains the scope of all the weeks (sprints) of a given month and their indicators. Changes in requirements, after being developed by the development team, were sent to the testing team to develop a new test case or adjust existing ones, in addition to reviewing the automation after the changes. Furthermore, during all pilot applications, the problems identified by the UX researchers were reported in real-time, enabling the testing team to investigate and report bugs for resolution.

There were communication problems between the testers and the project management, who were unable to visualize the number of tests being carried out, nor monitor the corrections. Therefore, the testing process was improved and included as artifacts: (1) the test plan, (2) the test execution document with some indicators, and (3) the test case execution reports generated by Testiny. For each weekly sprint, the entire test execution and the history of the activities that failed, passed, or were blocked by others, among other relevant information, were registered and presented to the other teams. In addition, test case management was essential to ensure software quality. The team used a tool to manage and execute test cases, thus optimizing their processes and improving the efficiency and reliability of the tests.

4.3. RQ3: Participatory Design

The app development process involved participatory design, involving teachers in all discovery and development cycles. This ensured that improvements and new features met their real needs and adapted to the context of use. These contributions aimed to facilitate teachers' work, improve the organization of school activities, provide more effective monitoring of students, and promote a more dynamic and interactive learning environment [Rodrigues et al. 2024a].

Different people with different roles conducted the participatory design: a UX researcher, a UX writer, a requirements analyst, a UX designer, and two teachers. The complete process for each participatory design execution lasted three weeks, including UX research, design, and evaluation. At the end of the three weeks, the goal was to obtain requirements to provide the development team with prototypes validated by the teachers participating in the research.

In the UX research stage (first week), the UX researcher and writer were responsible for preparing, conducting, and analyzing teacher interviews about a specific user pain point the team wanted to explore. To this end, virtual meetings were held to fulfill the purpose of this stage. At the end of the analysis, the requirements analyst specified the requirement(s) identified from the interview. With the requirement specified, in the second week, the objective was for the UX designer to prototype the screens and flows in high fidelity. Once prototyped, the UX researcher and writer evaluated the screens and flow to identify initial adjustments.

In the third week, the objective was to validate the prototype with the teachers. To this end, the methods and artifacts used were defined, which could vary between A/B testing, inspection, and usability testing using the System Usability Scale. In this sense, the teachers used the prototype and provided their opinions and suggestions for improvements. If the prototype was far below what the teachers expected, the demand returned to the research stage to be understood in more depth. If adequate, the requirements specified and the prototype was available for development.

The process was applied to nine pain points in the project, with two pain points often being addressed simultaneously. In the end, approximately 14 new requirements were identified, along with more than 30 modifications to previously validated requirements with the teachers. The participatory design process proved to be efficient because (i) it enabled the identification of new requirements based on users' pain points, (ii) it allowed improvements to already defined requirements, (iii) it brought the technical team closer to the users; and (iv) it provided developers with prototypes previously validated by users, reducing errors and rework.

5. Discussion

The team had the participation of early childhood education teachers, with whom interviews and usability tests were conducted with the prototype to identify problems and validate solutions. The participatory design process developed by the team predisposes research and evaluation with potential users to extract requirements and usability improvements. Through the project, 9 participatory design sessions were carried out, which generated reports from which points for improvement, bugs, recommendations for new features, and changes were extracted. In addition, pilot tests and experiments carried out with users in a real context, conducted with partner schools, contributed to the process of improving and evolving the application.

At the end of the project, an experiment was carried out with the participation of the UX team, making observations of the application's use. The use of ITS in schools in remote areas proved innovative and functional, optimizing teachers' time with diagnostic lists and clear reports that help with pedagogical understanding and motivating students with technological activities. However, there were challenges such as dependence on good quality internet, lack of school resources, and inaccuracies in the correction of activities, requiring improvements in the algorithms and lists, which in some cases were incompatible with the level of the students or confusing. The proposal to use the application during classes proved to be unfeasible due to the need for divided attention from the teacher, compromising the experience.

The application was designed to address user-centered needs through a dual-track development approach, integrating participatory design. This process ensured that teachers were consistently involved in requirement discovery, prototyping, and iterative validation, leading to a system that aligns with their real-world classroom demands. As a result, the application offers key contributions to educators, including secure access and simplified management through authentication features and tools for registering school and student information.

Teachers' feedback during participatory design sessions led to the inclusion of onboarding tutorials and help buttons, enabling them to familiarize themselves with the platform and resolve doubts efficiently. Additionally, customization and flexibility were prioritized, providing features for selecting classes, creating and managing exercise lists, and tailoring activities to the specific needs of each student.

The development process also involved tools that support teachers in monitoring student progress and optimizing classroom management. The system includes detailed performance tracking based on teacher input, allowing educators to record activity execution, generate reports, and identify areas needing intervention. The ability to export customized reports enhances documentation and facilitates efficient information sharing. The AI powered activity correction tool, refined through iterative feedback cycles, provides real-time, personalized feedback to students, enabling teachers to address learning gaps more effectively. Additionally, the centralized student profile screen consolidates performance data and teacher comments, streamlining individual student monitoring.

Instead of relying on static documents, the project maintained concise and adaptable records of requirements and design changes. Real-time communication channels, combined with regular synchronous meetings, facilitated rapid decision-making and continuous alignment between requirement discovery and implementation. Additionally, the integration of participatory design enabled direct user validation, ensuring that evolving requirements were dynamically incorporated into sprint planning without excessive documentation overhead. In other perspective, a challenge faced involved Balancing agility with clarity in requirements specifications. To address this, brief but structured documentation was maintained through the Jira platform and meeting minutes.

Overall, the project's knowledge exchange practices adhered to agile values by prioritizing collaborative decision-making, iterative learning, and continuous feedback, ensuring that knowledge flowed efficiently between teams while maintaining flexibility and responsiveness to change.

6. Conclusion

This study presented the software development process of an intelligent tutoring system (ITS) designed for an unplugged educational context, employing a hybrid approach with dual-track agile methodology and participatory design. This process enabled two parallel tracks: one dedicated to discovering and formalizing requirements through participatory design techniques and another focused on iterative development and implementation. The integration of these tracks ensured continuous synchronization between UX research, requirement engineering, and system development, effectively incorporating pedagogical and usability aspects throughout the project lifecycle.

One of the key contributions of this study is demonstrating how a structured dual-track process can bridge the gap between agile development and user-centered design. By maintaining a continuous feedback loop between requirement discovery and development, this approach minimized misalignment between user needs and system functionalities, fostering a more efficient and user-centered software development process. Additionally, the incorporation of participatory design techniques played a critical role in refining system requirements, validating features, and enhancing usability, particularly in an educational setting where teacher and student engagement is fundamental.

The approach used offers a scalable model for the development process with distributed teams, detailing the organization of roles and responsibilities across requirement elicitation, UX research, prototyping, development, and testing. This structured team organization ensures that iterative improvements align with both technical feasibility and pedagogical effectiveness.

Future work should focus on conducting longitudinal evaluations to measure the long-term impact of the application on student learning outcomes, teacher workflows, and user engagement. Another important direction is the exploration of hybrid and offline functionalities to reduce reliance on internet connectivity, thereby increasing accessibility for remote and underserved regions. Additionally, investigating how the dual-track process can be generalized to other ITS projects and educational technology solutions would contribute to a broader understanding of its applicability in various learning contexts.

By addressing these areas, future research can further optimize the integration of agile development, participatory design, and AI-driven educational systems, contributing to the advancement of software development methodologies for intelligent tutoring systems and other applications.

Acknowledgment

This work was made possible by the team's dedicated support at the Núcleo de Eficiência em Tecnologias Sociais (NEES), whose contributions were instrumental to the development of this project. Financial support for presenting this work was provided, in part, by the Coordenação de Aperfeiçoamento de Pessoal de Nível Superior – Brasil (CAPES).

Artifact Availability

Due to privacy restrictions outlined in our project's contract, we are unable to share any artifacts beyond the figures presented in this paper.

References

Agarwal, A., Agarwal, A., Verma, D. K., Tiwari, D., and Pandey, R. (2023). A review on software development life cycle. *International Journal of Scientific Research in Computer Science, Engineering and Information Technology (IJSRCSEIT)*, 9(3):384–388.

Al-Razgan, M., Aldossari, R., Albesher, L., Alshammari, M., Alotaibi, S., Alanquary, N., Alshahrani, N., and Alsaykhan, L. (2022). Challenges of integrating agile and ux/ucd: Systematic. *International Journal of Computer Applications*, 975:8887.

Bannon, L. J. and Ehn, P. (2012). Design: design matters in participatory design. In *Routledge international handbook of participatory design*, pages 37–63. Routledge.

bin Uzayr, S. (2022). *Frontend Development: The Ultimate Guide*. CRC Press.

Bossen, C., Dindler, C., and Iversen, O. S. (2016). Evaluation in participatory design: a literature survey. In *Proceedings of the 14th Participatory Design Conference: Full papers-Volume 1*, pages 151–160.

Camara, R., Alves, A., Monte, I., and Marinho, M. (2020). Agile global software development: A systematic literature review. In *Proceedings of the XXXIV Brazilian Symposium on Software Engineering*, pages 31–40.

Guerino, G., Rodrigues, L., Oliveira, L., Marinho, M., Silva, T., Amorim, L., Dermeval, D., da Penha, R., Bittencourt, I., and Isotani, S. (2024). We see you: Understanding math teachers from brazilian public schools to design equitable educational technology. *Revista Brasileira de Informática na Educação*, 32:336–358.

Hillmayr, D., Ziernwald, L., Reinhold, F., Hofer, S. I., and Reiss, K. M. (2020). The potential of digital tools to enhance mathematics and science learning in secondary schools: A context-specific meta-analysis. *Computers & Education*, 153:103897.

Instituto Nacional de Estudos e Pesquisas Educacionais Anísio Teixeira (Inep) (2023). Resultados do Índice de Desenvolvimento da Educação Básica (IDEB) 2023.

Isotani, S., Bittencourt, I. I., Challco, G. C., Dermeval, D., and Mello, R. F. (2023). Aied unplugged: Leapfrogging the digital divide to reach the underserved. In *International Conference on Artificial Intelligence in Education*, pages 772–779. Springer.

Marinho, M., Noll, J., Richardson, I., and Beecham, S. (2019). Plan-driven approaches are alive and kicking in agile global software development. In *2019 ACM/IEEE International Symposium on Empirical Software Engineering and Measurement (ESEM)*, pages 1–11. IEEE.

Menezes, R., Marinho, M., and Sampaio, S. (2024). Metrics in large-scale agile software development: A multivocal literature review. In *Anais do XXVII Congresso Ibero-Americano em Engenharia de Software*, pages 106–120, Porto Alegre, RS, Brasil. SBC.

Nkambou, R., Mizoguchi, R., and Bourdeau, J. (2010). *Advances in intelligent tutoring systems*, volume 308. Springer Science & Business Media.

Phaneendra, C., SAI PRASAD, B., Sainath, P., MUKESH REDDY, C., and Sowmya, Y. (2022). Query stand web development with user authentication. *Ymer*, 21(05):180–185.

Portela, C., Lisbôa, R., Yasojima, K., Cordeiro, T., Silva, A., Dermeval, D., Marques, L., Santos, J., Mello, R., Macário, V., Bittencourt, I. I., and Isotani, S. (2023). A case study on aied unplugged applied to public policy for learning recovery post-pandemic in brazil. In Wang, N., Rebolledo-Mendez, G., Dimitrova, V., Matsuda, N., and Santos, O. C., editors, *Artificial Intelligence in Education. Posters and Late Breaking Results, Workshops and Tutorials, Industry and Innovation Tracks, Practitioners, Doctoral Consortium and Blue Sky*, pages 788–796, Cham. Springer Nature Switzerland.

Rodrigues, L., Guerino, G., Challco, G. C., Veloso, T. E., Oliveira, L., da Penha, R. S., Melo, R. F., Vieira, T., Marinho, M., Macario, V., et al. (2023). Teacher-centered intelligent tutoring systems: Design considerations from brazilian, public school teachers. In *Anais do XXXIV Simpósio Brasileiro de Informática na Educação*, pages 1419–1430. SBC.

Rodrigues, L., Guerino, G., Silva, T. E., Challco, G. C., Oliveira, L., da Penha, R. S., Melo, R. F., Vieira, T., Marinho, M., Macario, V., et al. (2024a). Mathaide: A qualitative study of teachers' perceptions of an its unplugged for underserved regions. *International Journal of Artificial Intelligence in Education*, pages 1–29.

Rodrigues, L., Guerino, G., Veloso, T., Bianchini, L., Xavier, M., Vieira, T., Marinho, M., Macario, V., Dermeval, D., Bittencourt, I. I., and Isotani, S. (2024b). Mathaide in the classroom: A qualitative analysis of teachers' perspectives of intelligent tutoring systems unplugged. In *Anais do XXXV Simpósio Brasileiro de Informática na Educação*, pages 1515–1528, Porto Alegre, RS, Brasil. SBC.

Rodrigues, L., Pereira, F. D., Marinho, M., Macario, V., Bittencourt, I. I., Isotani, S., Dermeval, D., and Mello, R. (2024c). Mathematics intelligent tutoring systems with handwritten input: A scoping review. *Education and Information Technologies*, 29(9):11183–11209.

Sedano, T., Ralph, P., and Péraire, C. (2020). Dual-track development. *IEEE Softw.*, 37(6):58–64.

Silva, T. E. V. d., Challco, G. C., Rodrigues, L. A. L., Versuti, F. M., Penha, R. S. d., Oliveira, L. S., Guerino, G., Amorin, L. F. C. d., Marinho, M. L. M., Macario, V., et al. (2023). Its unplugged: leapfrogging the digital divide for teaching numeracy skills in underserved populations. In *Proceedings*.

Spinuzzi, C. (2005). The methodology of participatory design. *Technical communication*, 52(2):163–174.

Evaluación de la calidad de historias de usuario usando modelos de lenguaje de gran tamaño: un estudio en la industria

Erika Hernández-Agüero[1,2], Christian Quesada-López[1,2], José P. Chaves-Sánchez[2]

[1]Posgrado en Computación e Informática, Escuela de Ciencias de la Computación e Informática – Universidad de Costa Rica (UCR) –San José –Costa Rica

[2]Dirección de Tecnologías de Información y Comunicaciones – Universidad Estatal a Distancia (UNED) – San José – Costa Rica

{erika.hernandezaguero,cristian.quesadalopez}@ ucr.ac.cr,
{ehernandez,cquesadal,jpchaves}@uned.ac.cr

Abstract. *The specification and maintenance of high-quality user stories are critical and challenging activities in agile software development, due to the dynamic nature of projects, the ambiguity of natural language, and the effort required for manual evaluations. This study investigates the use of large language models (LLMs) to assess the quality of user stories in an industrial software project, using the criteria defined by the INVEST framework. The performance of three LLM tools is compared with two evaluations conducted by requirements engineering experts. The results indicate that LLMs have the potential to support the automated assessment of user stories based on INVEST.*

Keywords: software requirements, quality, NLP4RE, automation, LLM, user stories, INVEST

Resumo. *La especificación y mantenimiento de historias de usuario de alta calidad son actividades críticas y desafiantes en el desarrollo de software ágil, debido a la naturaleza dinámica de los proyectos, la ambigüedad del lenguaje natural y el esfuerzo requerido para las evaluaciones manuales. Este estudio investiga el uso de modelos de lenguaje de gran tamaño (LLM) para evaluar la calidad de historias de usuario en un proyecto de software de industria, utilizando los criterios del marco INVEST. Se compara el desempeño de tres herramientas LLM con dos evaluaciones de personas expertas en ingeniería de requisitos. Los resultados indican que los LLM tienen potencial para apoyar la evaluación automatizada de historias basado en INVEST.*

Palabras clave. requerimientos de software, calidad, NLP4RE, automatización, LLM, historias de usuario, INVEST

1. Introducción

La Ingeniería de Software Continua proporciona una perspectiva integral del flujo de trabajo que vincula la estrategia de negocio, el desarrollo de software y las operaciones, un enfoque conocido como BizDevOps [Fitzgerald and Stol 2017]. Esta disciplina abarca elementos clave como la mejora continua, la innovación, la adopción de metodologías ágiles en el desarrollo de software y la automatización de procesos [Fitzgerald and Stol 2017; Bosch 2014]. La integración fluida entre el negocio y el desarrollo de software es crucial, ya que una gestión eficaz de los requisitos permite la entrega de productos alineados con las necesidades de las partes interesadas y los objetivos estratégicos de la organización [Bourque and Fairley 2014]. Los enfoques de automatización se han enfocado en las áreas de DevOps, pero se requieren esfuerzos en la automatización de procesos que involucren el área Biz [Fitzgerald and Stol 2017]. En este contexto, el Procesamiento de Lenguaje Natural (NLP) para la Ingeniería de Requisitos (NLP4RE) ha surgido como un área de investigación que aplica sus técnicas NLP para abordar desafíos en la ingeniería de requisitos, tales como la generación, captura, análisis, validación y gestión de requisitos redactados en lenguaje natural [Marques, Silva, and Bernardino 2024; Belzner, Gabor and Wirsing 2024]. Es necesario valorar estos enfoques en proyectos reales, para determinar su potencial con el fin de apoyar este tipo de tareas en la industria.

En enfoques ágiles como Scrum, los requisitos suelen expresarse mediante historias de usuario organizadas en la pila de producto, las cuales se refinan y priorizan para facilitar eventos clave, como la planificación, la revisión y retrospectiva en cada iteración [Schwaber and Sutherland 2020]. Al redactarse en lenguaje natural, las historias de usuario incorporan una de las formas más utilizadas para representar requisitos, y capturar de forma concisa las necesidades del usuario final [Zhang et al. 2024]. Este enfoque busca responder a la evolución continua del negocio y acelerar la entrega de valor. La evaluación de la calidad de estas historias representa un desafío complejo, pues requiere adaptarse a cambios frecuentes en las especificaciones, además de analizar atributos clave como la completitud, la verificabilidad y la ambigüedad inherente al lenguaje natural, además de la variabilidad en los requisitos [Parra et al. 2015; Bosch 2014; Subedi et al. 2021]. La calidad de las historias de usuario puede evaluarse mediante marcos como INVEST, el cual define criterios específicos que deben cumplir que sean: independientes, negociables, valiosas, estimables, pequeñas y testeables [Subedi et al. 2021; Ronanki, Berger and Horkoff 2023; Zhang et al. 2024]. Se ha propuesto la adopción de técnicas de aprendizaje automático, principalmente, modelos de lenguaje de gran tamaño (LLM), como una herramienta de apoyo para las personas expertas en ingeniería de requisitos [Parra et al. 2015; Subedi et al. 2021; Ronanki et al. 2023; Krishna et al. 2024; Bosch 2014; Zhang et al. 2024] con el potencial de apoyar los procesos de evaluación y mejora de las historias de usuario, utilizando INVEST [Subedi et al. 2021; Zhang et al. 2024].

Este estudio explora el potencial uso de los LLMs en el proceso de automatización de la evaluación de la calidad de historias de usuario, integrando el marco INVEST. Se analizaron los resultados obtenidos mediante ChatGPT, Gemini y Copilot contrastándolos con la revisión de dos personas expertas en el contexto de un proyecto de desarrollo de un departamento de TI de una institución pública. El enfoque de estudio proporciona herramientas de apoyo para personas expertas, con el fin de facilitar la detección de inconsistencias, ambigüedades y deficiencias en los requisitos. Para analistas de nivel inicial, el uso de LLMs podría proporcionar una guía estructurada basada en INVEST, facilitando la adopción de buenas prácticas y la redacción de historias de usuario alineadas con principios ágiles, basado en el contexto de los proyectos de la organización. Para personas expertas en ingeniería de requisitos, estas herramientas podrían proporcionar apoyo en la revisión de especificaciones complejas y el alto volumen de requisitos. El artículo reporta la experiencia en el uso de las herramientas y los resultados obtenidos de la comparación. La unidad de desarrollo de la organización ha implementado procesos de mejora en las actividades de requisitos [Hernandez, Quesada and Chaves 2024] y busca automatizar las evaluaciones de calidad de requisitos para apoyar a las personas expertas. Se analiza la consistencia, diferencias y coincidencias entre las evaluaciones realizadas por las personas expertas y las generadas por los LLMs. Asimismo, se estudian variaciones en la evaluación de cada criterio del marco INVEST, determinando hasta qué punto los LLMs pueden complementar el juicio experto humano en la validación de historias de usuario. Además, se espera que este estudio aporte en la discusión sobre el uso de estas herramientas en dichas tareas de la ingeniería de requisitos y el alcance de los LLMs para valorar la calidad de las historias de usuario utilizando INVEST, en el contexto de un proyecto de industria.

2. Trabajo Relacionado

Distintos estudios han explorado la automatización de tareas de la ingeniería de requisitos. Los estudios recientes se centran en el uso de modelos de lenguaje de gran tamaño (LLMs) para mejorar la eficiencia y calidad en diversas fases del ciclo de vida del desarrollo de software. Estos trabajos abordan la generación y validación de documentos de especificaciones de requisitos de software, la asistencia en la elicitación de requisitos, la mejora de historias de usuario en entornos ágiles y el apoyo en diseño de sistemas, generación de código y pruebas.

[Krishna et al. 2024] analizó cómo los LLMs, específicamente GPT-4 y CodeLlama, pueden contribuir a la generación y validación de Especificaciones de Requisitos de Software (SRS). Para esto, compararon documentos generados por estos modelos con los elaborados por ingenieros de software de nivel inicial, evaluando atributos de calidad como claridad, consistencia y completitud. Los resultados mostraron que los LLMs pueden generar documentos de calidad comparable, con una reducción significativa del tiempo de elaboración. [Ronanki et al. 2023] exploró el potencial de ChatGPT para asistir en la elicitación de requisitos. Se formularon preguntas específicas para obtener requisitos tanto de ChatGPT como de expertos humanos, y se evaluaron en atributos de calidad como abstracción, atomicidad, consistencia, corrección, claridad (no ambigüedad), comprensibilidad y factibilidad. Los hallazgos indicaron que ChatGPT destaca en abstracción, atomicidad y comprensibilidad, aunque presenta deficiencias en claridad y factibilidad.

[Zhang et al. 2024] analizó el uso del sistema ALAS, que utiliza agentes basados en LLM (GPT-3.5 y GPT-4) para mejorar historias de usuario en proyectos ágiles. La metodología consistió en la implementación de agentes autónomos que colaboran para refinar historias de usuario, evaluadas posteriormente mediante el marco INVEST. Los resultados mostraron mejoras en claridad y alineación con objetivos de negocio, aunque persisten desafíos relacionados con la complejidad de las historias generadas. Por su parte, [Belzner et al. 2024] revisó los beneficios y desafíos de integrar LLMs en la ingeniería de software. Se evaluó el apoyo de modelos como ChatGPT y Bard en la ingeniería de requisitos, diseño, pruebas y generación de código. La metodología incluyó interacciones iterativas con los LLMs para desarrollar requisitos y proponer soluciones, identificando tanto el potencial para mejorar la productividad como las limitaciones en la integración con procesos existentes. Finalmente, estudios previos han aplicado técnicas de aprendizaje automático para evaluar automáticamente la calidad de requisitos, emulando el juicio de expertos con base en atributos IEEE 830, alcanzando hasta un 86,1 % de precisión [Parra et al. 2015]. En el caso de historias de usuario, se ha evaluado la calidad mediante los atributos Testeable y Valiosa del marco INVEST, destacando el clasificador de árboles de decisión y el uso de SMOTE para mejorar el recall sin comprometer la precisión [Subedi et al. 2021]. El presente estudio integra la evaluación de historias de usuario basándose en los seis atributos del marco INVEST, y busca aportar evidencia empírica sobre la capacidad de los LLMs para evaluar la calidad de los requisitos en entornos ágiles de un proyecto en la industria.

3. Metodología

El estudio investiga el uso de herramientas LLM para evaluar las historias de usuario en un proyecto de software de industria. Se evalúa su efectividad para la automatización de la evaluación en el contexto de desarrollo ágil de software. Las evaluaciones obtenidas a partir del uso de las herramientas LLMs son comparadas con las realizadas por dos personas expertas en ingeniería de requisitos del proyecto seleccionado. Para evaluar la calidad de los requisitos se utiliza el marco INVEST. El trabajo plantea la siguiente pregunta de investigación: *RQ1: ¿Cómo se comparan los resultados de la evaluación de calidad de las historias de usuario realizadas por las personas ingenieras de requisitos en un proyecto ágil con las obtenidos con el apoyo de las herramientas LLM?* En el análisis se busca identificar las diferencias y similitudes que existen entre las evaluaciones obtenidas de las herramientas LLM y de las personas expertas de acuerdo al marco INVEST.

3.1. Proyecto, Conjunto de Datos, Participantes y Herramientas

El proyecto analizado corresponde al desarrollo de una aplicación para la gestión de notas de cursos universitarios, en la cual interactúan los roles de administración, tutoría y coordinación de cátedra. El desarrollo se realiza en un entorno ágil, utilizando Azure DevOps Server para gestionar los requisitos mediante historias de usuario organizadas en la pila de producto. El equipo de trabajo sigue formalmente el marco Scrum, y la persona administradora de la aplicación cumple también el rol de persona dueña del producto. La aplicación es utilizada por un total de 1,820 personas usuarias. En este estudio, se seleccionó un conjunto de 60 historias de usuario de una pila total de 112 registros de diferentes módulos funcionales, como: mantenimiento de usuarios, mantenimiento de instrumentos de evaluación, asignación de modelos de evaluación, asignación de tutores, ingreso de notas e historial de notas, entre otras funcionalidades. Las evaluaciones de calidad se realizaron tanto por personas expertas en ingeniería de requisitos como mediante herramientas basadas en LLM. Las personas expertas cuentan con más de 15 años de experiencia en desarrollo de software, dominio de metodologías ágiles y gestión de historias de usuario bajo el marco INVEST. Las herramientas LLM utilizadas fueron ChatGPT Pro 4, Gemini Advanced 1.5 y Microsoft Copilot, todas en sus versiones de pago. La selección de estas herramientas se basa en su uso extendido en la industria y su aplicación en investigaciones previas relacionadas con la evaluación de requisitos.

Disponibilidad de artefactos: por tratarse de un estudio realizado en la industria no es posible compartir los datos.

3.2. Marco de Evaluación INVEST

La Tabla 1 muestra el marco de evaluación INVEST, basado en [Zhang et al. 2024; CertiProf 2022]. Para evaluar la calidad de las historias de usuario, se aplica este marco asignando a cada historia una puntuación en una escala de Likert del 1 al 5, donde 1 indica un fuerte desacuerdo con el cumplimiento del criterio, y 5 representa un fuerte acuerdo.

Table 1. Variables to be considered on the evaluation of interaction techniques

ID	Declaraciones y las características correspondientes al marco INVEST para las historias
I	Independiente: es autónoma, comprensible por sí sola y no depende de otras historias.
N	Negociable: tiene un nivel de detalle adecuado que permite ajustes y priorización.
V	Valiosa: proporciona un beneficio claro y medible para el sistema o usuario final.
E	Estimable: es técnicamente alcanzable y se puede estimar en términos de tiempo o esfuerzo.
S	Pequeña: presenta un alcance acotado para completarse dentro de un sprint (máximo 4 semanas).
T	Testeable: incluye criterios de aceptación que permiten validar su implementación con pruebas.

Durante el proceso de evaluación de calidad, cada persona experta evalúa la calidad de cada historia de usuario de manera independiente utilizando un instrumento estructurado, que contiene el conjunto de historias por evaluar con los espacios para la calificación de cada criterio INVEST con la escala de Likert y un espacio para sus observaciones. Cada una de las personas ingenieras de requisitos asignó la calificación de 1 a 5 siguiendo la escala por criterio. Por separado, la persona investigadora ejecuta en cada herramienta LLM el *prompt* de evaluación de calidad de las historias de usuario, obteniendo las calificaciones correspondientes para el mismo conjunto de requisitos. El conjunto de datos fue segmentado en 12 subconjuntos por las limitaciones de cantidad de tokens de las herramientas. El proceso de evaluación se basa en lo recomendado por [Zhang et al. 2024].

3.3. Implementación del Prompt

La implementación del *prompt* se basa en las recomendaciones de [Zhang et al. 2024; Ronanki et al. 2023; Krishna et al. 2024]. Se construye a partir de dos etapas de trabajo: etapa de preparación y etapa de ejecución. En la etapa de preparación se crean los *prompts* y se considera la siguiente estructura para el *prompt* inicial y de seguimiento:

$$Initial\ Prompt_i = Profile_i + Task + Context + Subtask_i,\ (1 \leq i \leq k)$$
$$Follow\text{-}up\ Prompt_i = Subtask_i + Response_{i-1},\ (i > k)$$

Donde para el *prompt* inicial:

$Profile_i$: Describe el rol, habilidades o responsabilidades específicas.

Task: Es una descripción amplia del objetivo que se busca alcanzar.

Context: Proporciona detalles sobre el entorno, limitaciones o condiciones específicas.

$Subtask_i$: Es un paso específico dentro de la tarea general.

Para el *prompt* de seguimiento:

Subtask$_i$: Es un paso específico dentro de la tarea general.
Response$_{i-1}$: La respuesta generada tras completar la subtarea anterior, permite generar las instrucciones que simulan la interacción de diferentes actividades que lleva a cabo este evaluador.

En la etapa de ejecución se realizan las actividades relacionadas con la aplicación y calibración del *prompt* generado en el diseño en cada una de las herramientas seleccionadas ChatGPT, Gemini y Copilot. Esto permite la recolección de las evaluaciones generadas por cada LLM de manera automatizada [Zhang et al. 2024].

Evaluación de los Requisitos de Software

Primero, se definió un flujo de trabajo para la evaluación de la calidad de las historias de usuario utilizando el marco INVEST, como se muestra en la Figura 1. Este proceso puede ser ejecutado tanto por una persona analista, a través del perfil de una persona ingeniera de requisitos, quien, según el contexto del proyecto, realiza la evaluación utilizando el *prompt* diseñado.

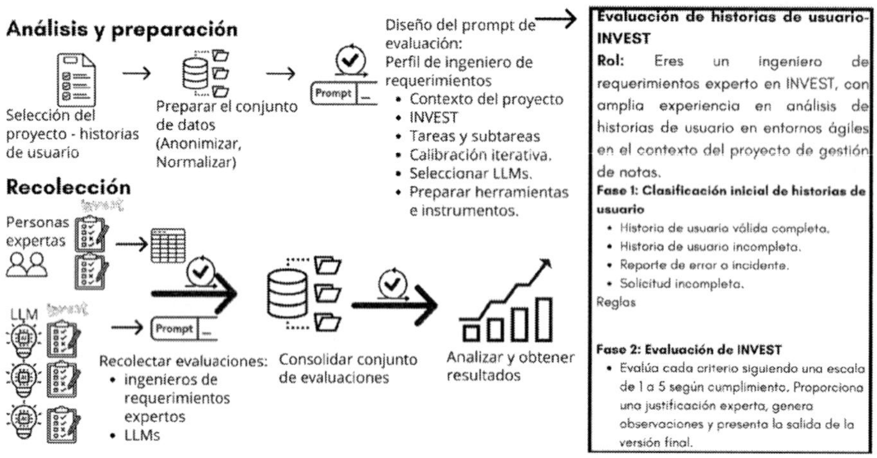

Figura 1. Evaluación de calidad de requisitos

Análisis y Preparación de los Datos

En la etapa de preparación para la recolección de datos, se llevaron a cabo actividades de preprocesamiento y normalización de las historias de usuario. Este proceso incluyó la eliminación de registros incompletos o sin información relevante, como aquellos creados en Azure DevOps que solo contenían un título sin descripción, casos generados como recordatorios de situaciones particulares que no representan funcionalidades reales, o registros correspondientes a ceremonias Scrum (planificación, refinamiento, revisión y retrospectiva). Asimismo, registros que representan funcionalidades específicas, y no cumplían con la estructura estándar de redacción de historias de usuario, fueron incluidos en el conjunto de datos con el objetivo de prever casos similares en otros proyectos y permitir que parte del proceso de validación considere la verificación de este tipo de historias. La etapa de anonimización de datos, implicó la detección y eliminación de información confidencial de la institución. Por ejemplo, se sustituyeron nombres de sistemas, identificadores personales, referencias a bases de datos y otros elementos vinculados a la infraestructura técnica del proyecto. Esto es fundamental para mitigar los riesgos asociados al uso de modelos externos o en la nube, y para garantizar el cumplimiento de los principios de seguridad y privacidad desde las fases iniciales del análisis. La estructura estándar de la historia de usuario definida por la organización es la siguiente: *Como [rol] quiero [funcionalidad/requerimiento] para [beneficio/objetivo].* Además, cada historia de usuario debe incluir criterios de aceptación, definidos bajo la estructura: Dado *[contexto inicial], cuando [acción], entonces [resultado esperado].* Los registros que no contaban con criterios de aceptación definidos fueron etiquetados con la leyenda "[No se han definido AC]", con el propósito de que los LLMs evaluaran las historias tal como fueron registradas originalmente, sin inferir ni completar la información ausente durante el proceso de evaluación. El conjunto de datos final se conformó por tres tipos de registros: (1) historias de usuario con criterios de aceptación completos; (2) historias de usuario sin criterios de aceptación explícitos; y (3) funcionalidades del sistema que no siguen la estructura estándar de redacción.

Recolección de las Evaluaciones

Previo al proceso de recolección de datos, se llevaron a cabo pruebas para calibrar el *prompt,* ajustando las instrucciones de la tarea con el fin de asegurar que los resultados fueran comparables con las evaluaciones de las personas expertas. Como parte del proceso de calibración, se implementaron mejoras para la evaluación: garantizar la lectura y calificación individual de cada historia de usuario, asegurar que cada historia de usuario reciba su propia calificación incluyendo observaciones, estandarizar la estructura de salida de las evaluaciones para que cada historia de usuario ocupe una única fila en la tabla de evaluación, evitando duplicaciones y mejorando la claridad de los resultados. Asimismo, se definen instrucciones detalladas para el procesamiento de datos, incluyendo la lectura de archivos, el formato de despliegue de los resultados y la descarga de la evaluación.

Primero se define el perfil del evaluador y su rol dentro del contexto de evaluación de la calidad de requisitos, como se ilustra en la Figura 2. Se trata de un ingeniero de requisitos que desempeña funciones específicas y realiza tareas concretas en un entorno ágil de desarrollo de software. La fase 1 del proceso abarca las actividades relacionadas con los refuerzos en la evaluación que permite establecer las reglas adicionales. Por ejemplo: si una historia de usuario no cuenta con criterios de aceptación definidos debe recibir la calificación mínima en el criterio Testeable, verificar el cumplimiento del formato estándar de la historia de usuario válidas que deben cumplir con la descripción y criterios de aceptación, historias de usuario incompletas que carecen de una descripción estructurada o criterios de aceptación definidos, registros que no corresponden a requisitos (reportes de errores o incidentes) que deben recibir la calificación más baja e incluir la observación que corresponde a otro tipo gestión para esos elementos de trabajo. Asimismo, se incorporaron ejemplos historias de usuario habilitadoras, las cuales también son relevantes en el contexto de evaluación como se ilustra en la Figura 3. La fase 2 del proceso permite realizar las evaluaciones de manera que se asigne la calificación por historia de usuario. Se realizó una segmentación en subgrupos de 5 historias de usuario por ejecución, para evitar exceder los límites de procesamiento de los modelos, facilitar la revisión y validación progresiva de las respuestas generadas y aplicar calibraciones en tiempo real para mejorar la precisión del análisis. Una vez obtenidas las evaluaciones de los LLM se integran en el consolidado junto con las evaluaciones proporcionados por los expertos para proceder con el análisis de resultados como se muestra en la Figura 3.

Prompt Ajustado para Evaluación de Historias de Usuario en SNP bajo INVEST (Versión Mejorada)

Rol del Evaluador

Eres un ingeniero de requerimientos experto en INVEST, con amplia experiencia en análisis de historias de usuario en entornos ágiles. Procedo a evaluar cada una de las historias de usuario del documento adjunto, de una en una según la solicitud en este chat y sigo las siguientes instrucciones.

Tu evaluación se basa en:

- Mejores prácticas de ingeniería de requerimientos.
- Patrones comunes de errores en historias de usuario.
- Diferenciación clara entre historias funcionales y habilitadoras.
- Clasificación automática de historias incompletas o incorrectas.
- Ajuste del tamaño de las historias según la capacidad del sprint.
- Corrección de clasificación errónea de historias que contienen "error", "fallo" o "problema", pero son mejoras o requerimientos funcionales.

Figura 2. Prompt- Rol evaluador

- Clasificación de la Entrada

Antes de evaluar INVEST, clasifica la historia en una de las siguientes categorías:

Historia de Usuario Válida

✔ Sigue la estructura: "Como [rol], quiero [funcionalidad] para [beneficio]".

✔ Tiene criterios de aceptación claros y verificables.

✔ Su propósito y alcance son comprensibles y valiosos para el negocio.

⚠ Historia de Usuario Incompleta

⚠ Es ambigua, imprecisa o carece de estructura adecuada.

⚠ Puede estar mal redactada o sin criterios de aceptación.

⚠ Se evaluará bajo INVEST con calificaciones bajas y observaciones específicas para su mejora.

- Evaluación bajo INVEST

Evalúa cada criterio en una escala de 1 a 5 y proporciona una justificación experta basada en patrones comunes de errores.

Criterio	Cómo Evaluar (Actualizado)
Independiente (I)	¿Se puede desarrollar sin depender de otras historias? 5 si es completamente independiente. 3-4 si tiene dependencias leves. 1-2 si requiere otra historia para ser útil.
Negociable (N)	¿Permite ajustes sin afectar el negocio? 4-5 si es flexible y adaptable. 1-3 si es rígida o con requisitos inmodificables.
Valiosa (V)	¿Tiene un beneficio claro para el usuario? 5 si sigue la estructura "Como [rol], quiero [funcionalidad], para [beneficio]". 3 si falta claridad. 1-2 si no tiene valor claro.
Estimable (E)	¿Se puede estimar el esfuerzo? 5 si la historia es clara y bien definida. 3-4 si tiene aspectos ambiguos. 1-2 si es muy vaga para ser estimada.
Small (S)	¿Es lo suficientemente pequeña para completarse en un sprint? 5 si puede completarse en máximo 4 semanas con 80% de capacidad del equipo. 3-4 si es grande pero reducible. 1-2 si es enorme.
Testeable (T)	¿Tiene criterios de aceptación verificables? 5 si tiene criterios de aceptación claros ("Dado, Cuando, Entonces"). 4 si son ambiguos. 3 si están incompletos. 1 si no tiene.

Figura 3. Prompt-Fases

4. Análisis de Resultados

El estudio compara las evaluaciones de historias de usuario bajo el marco INVEST, analizando las diferencias entre las evaluaciones realizadas por las personas expertas (Experto1, Experto2) y las herramientas LLM (ChatGPT, Gemini, Copilot). Se procesaron 60 historias de usuario, asignando calificaciones en seis criterios: I: Independiente, N: Negociable, V: Valioso, E: Estimable, S: Pequeña y T: Testeable.

La Figura 4 presenta las diferencias en las evaluaciones de cada una de las 60 historias de usuario, comparando los resultados de los dos expertos humanos con los obtenidos por las herramientas LLM. Se observan agrupamientos que reflejan tanto similitudes como variabilidad en las calificaciones asignadas en la escala de 1 a 5. En cada caso, se identifican concordancias y discrepancias respecto al juicio experto, lo que permite analizar la capacidad de los modelos para replicar evaluaciones humanas. Los resultados indican que los LLMs, en particular ChatGPT y Copilot, presentan un desempeño favorable bajo el marco INVEST, aunque tienden a sobrestimar atributos como Negociable y Valiosa. Estas diferencias resaltan la necesidad de calibrar y ajustar los modelos para mejorar su alineación con la perspectiva de expertos, especialmente en contextos ágiles donde la evaluación precisa de historias de usuario es clave para el éxito de los proyectos. El análisis de las 60 historias evidencia variabilidad y similitudes en los distintos criterios INVEST. La Figura 5 amplía este análisis mediante el cálculo de diferencias absolutas [Roumeliotis, Tselikas y Nasiopoulos, 2024], que permiten cuantificar la magnitud de las discrepancias en la calificación. Estas se obtienen al calcular el valor absoluto de la diferencia entre la puntuación asignada por una persona experta y la otorgada por un LLM, para cada historia y para cada criterio del marco INVEST.

Se expresa como:

$$Diferencia\ absoluta = |Evaluación_{Experto} - Evaluación_{LLM}|$$

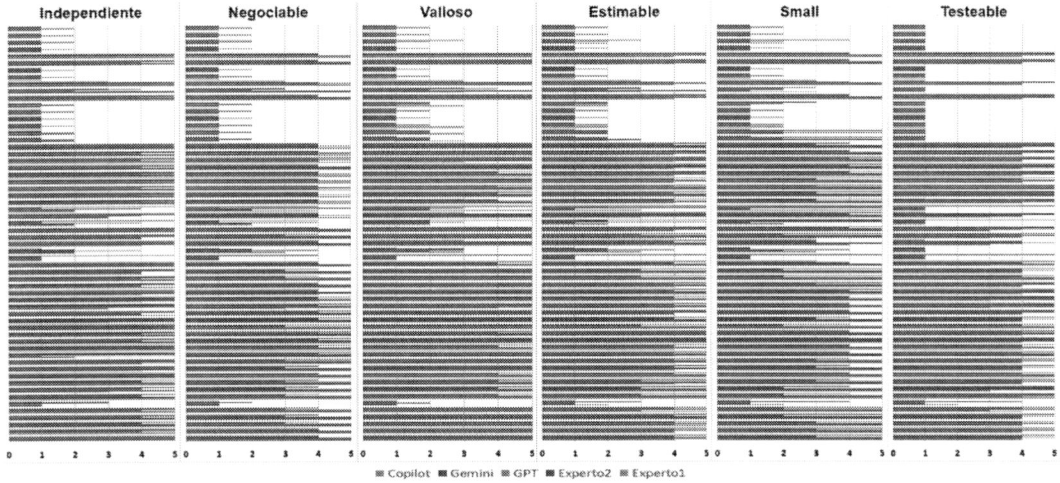

Figura 4. Evaluación de historias de usuario

El uso de diferencias absolutas ofrece una forma objetiva de medir la discrepancia, ya que elimina la influencia de la dirección del error, es decir, no importa si el LLM sobreestima o subestima en comparación con el experto, lo relevante es la magnitud de la diferencia. Esto facilita la comparación entre pares de evaluadores, permitiendo identificar tanto diferencias sistemáticas como casos atípicos que podrían reflejar inconsistencias significativas en la interpretación de los criterios INVEST.

La Figura 5 presenta la distribución de las diferencias absolutas entre las personas expertas (Experto 1 y Experto 2) y los modelos LLM (ChatGPT, Gemini y Copilot), revelando patrones relevantes en las evaluaciones de los criterios del marco INVEST. En general, la mayoría de las diferencias se concentra en el rango de 0 a 2, lo que sugiere una alta consistencia entre las evaluaciones humanas y automatizadas. Esta alineación es particularmente evidente en los criterios Independiente y Valioso, donde se observa una menor variabilidad y escasa presencia de valores atípicos. En estos casos, la objetividad de los criterios parece facilitar su interpretación por parte de los modelos. En contraste, los criterios Pequeña (S) y Testeable (T) presentan las mayores diferencias absolutas, lo que sugiere que los LLM encuentran más dificultades para evaluarlos adecuadamente. En el criterio Pequeña, la complejidad radica en estimar correctamente el tamaño o granularidad de las historias, mientras que en Testeable, los desafíos están vinculados a la ausencia o ambigüedad de los criterios de aceptación. Las comparaciones entre Experto 2 y Gemini, y entre Experto 1 y Copilot, evidencian las mayores discrepancias en estos dos atributos, reflejando limitaciones específicas en su interpretación. Al comparar el rendimiento general, ChatGPT mostró mayor consistencia con las evaluaciones humanas, mientras que Gemini y Copilot presentaron mayor dispersión, sobre todo en los criterios más complejos. Estos resultados indican que, si bien los LLM pueden aproximarse al juicio experto, es necesario fortalecer la calibración en criterios como Pequeña, Negociable y Testeable, a través de instrucciones más específicas y refuerzos dirigidos

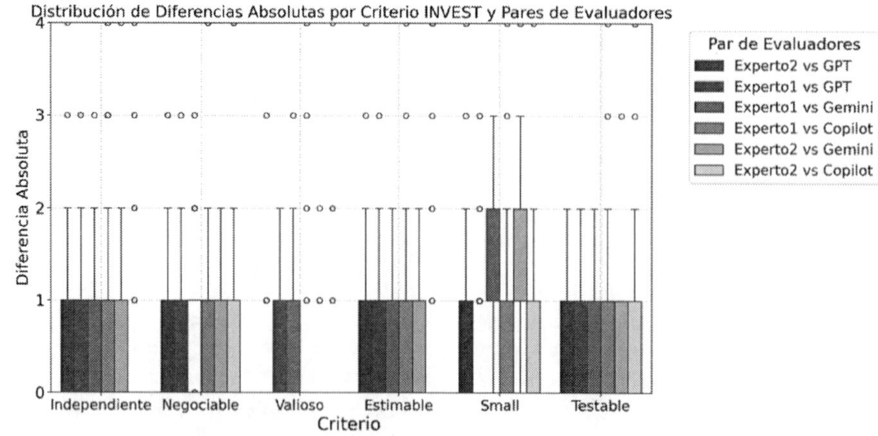

Figura 5. Distribución de diferencias absolutas

Desde la perspectiva del proyecto, los resultados indican que estas herramientas pueden apoyar los procesos de evaluación de requisitos, con supervisión de las personas expertas, aunque se requiere mejorar su precisión y consistencia, enfocándose en su capacidad para interpretar de forma más alineada con el juicio experto en algunos criterios. Se espera que, al ofrecer un contexto más amplio, junto con ejemplificaciones de evaluaciones previas realizadas por personas expertas, los LLM mejoren su rendimiento, considerando además el balance con la capacidad de procesamiento de tokens de cada herramienta. Para analizar la consistencia, la Figura 6 presenta la matriz de correlación de Spearman, que muestra asociaciones positivas entre las evaluaciones de las personas expertas y cada LLM. La correlación más alta se observa entre Experto1 y Experto2 ($\rho = 0.80$), lo que indica una fuerte correlación en sus evaluaciones. ChatGPT presenta correlaciones elevadas con ambas personas expertas ($\rho = 0.75$ con Experto1 y $\rho = 0.77$ con Experto2), lo que sugiere una mayor consistencia que permite utilizar estas medidas como base para la comparación. En contraste, Copilot y Gemini muestran correlaciones moderadas, siendo más bajas con Experto1 ($\rho = 0.56$ y $\rho = 0.59$, respectivamente) y ligeramente superiores con Experto2. Estos resultados indican que, aunque ambos LLM logran un alineamiento con los expertos, ChatGPT muestra mayor consistencia. Por otro lado, se analizó la fiabilidad de la consistencia de las escalas de medición mediante el Alfa de Cronbach [Essel et al. 2024] para cada uno de los pares evaluadores:

$$\alpha = k/(k-1)\,(1 - \Sigma/(\sigma\_t\hat{}2)\,\sigma\_i\hat{}2)$$

k = Número de elementos evaluados (criterios I N V E S T).

σ_t^2 = Varianza de cada criterio evaluado (I N V E S T).

σ_i^2 = Varianza total del conjunto de evaluaciones.

En este caso, un valor alto en la consistencia de las evaluaciones sugiere que la herramienta LLM pueden apoyar la evaluación automatizada de la calidad de los requisitos, al mostrar concordancia con las evaluaciones expertas. Los valores bajos indican diferencias en la interpretación de los criterios y la necesidad de mejorar la calibración. Se establece que un valor de $\alpha \geq 0.9$ representa una alta consistencia entre las evaluaciones expertas y las generadas por los LLM, lo que sugiere que los LLM pueden replicar el juicio humano con un alto grado de confianza. Los valores por debajo de 0.9 reflejan diferencias en la forma en que las herramientas LLM evalúan los criterios, evidenciando la necesidad de ajustes en su calibración. La Figura 7 presenta los valores de consistencia calculados mediante el Alfa de Cronbach. Los resultados muestran una consistencia aceptable en la mayoría de los criterios INVEST, aunque se identifican áreas específicas de mejora. En particular, la herramienta Gemini presenta los valores más bajos de consistencia en el criterio Pequeña (S), con $\alpha = 0.61$ y $\alpha = 0.63$ frente a las evaluaciones de los expertos, lo que indica una mayor variabilidad en sus juicios. En particular, ChatGPT y Copilot presentan la mayor consistencia con las personas expertas, lo que sugiere que sus evaluaciones son más estables y confiables. En contraste, Gemini evidencia mayores diferencias, lo que indica la necesidad de ajustes en su calibración.

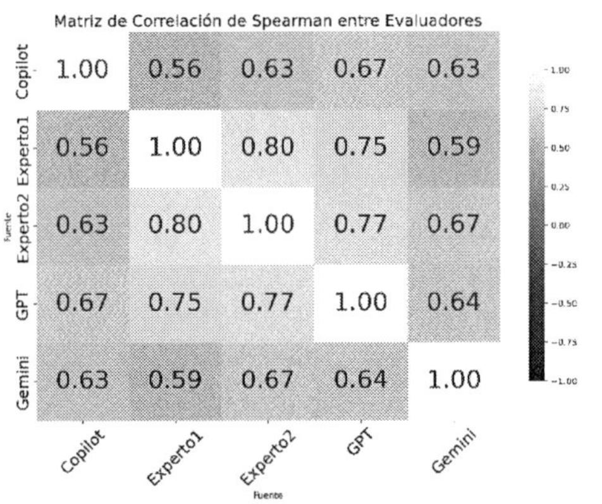

Figura 6. Correlación entre evaluadores

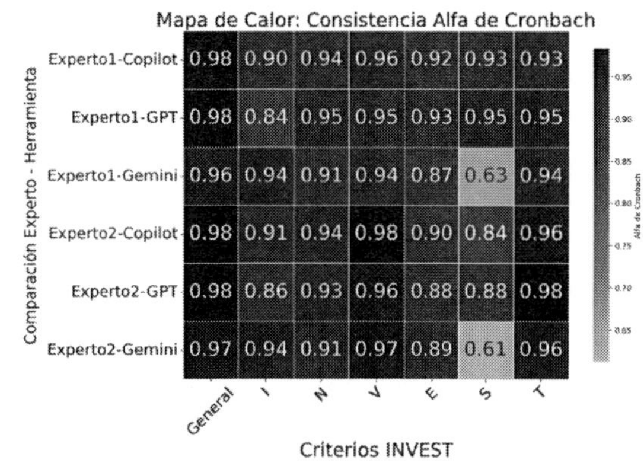

Figure 7. Consistencia de las evaluaciones

La prueba Kruskal-Wallis, permitió evaluar las diferencias globales, obteniendo un estadístico de 63.8148 y un p-valor de 0.0000, lo que confirma diferencias significativas entre los evaluadores. Previamente, se verificaron los supuestos de normalidad mediante las pruebas de Kolmogorov-Smirnov y Shapiro-Wilk, obteniendo p-valores de 0.0000 en todos los casos, lo cual indica que las distribuciones no siguen una normalidad estadística. La prueba de Homogeneidad de Levene (estadístico = 2.9207, $p = 0.0201$) mostró diferencias en la varianza entre los grupos, lo que justifica el uso de pruebas no paramétricas. Como análisis post hoc, se aplicó la prueba de Dunn con corrección de Bonferroni la cual reveló diferencias significativas entre las evaluaciones expertas y los LLM. Sin embargo, esto se debe a las diferencias que se han presentado en las evaluaciones de Gemini con todos los evaluadores ($p < 0.01$), lo que indica que su enfoque de evaluación difiere del criterio experto y de otros LLM. Copilot no presentó diferencias significativas con las personas expertas, lo que sugiere una mayor alineación con la evaluación experta. ChatGPT, mostró diferencias con una evaluación experta ($p = 0.000573$), pero no con la otra persona experta, ni con Copilot, lo que indica una alineación consistente con la evaluación humana. Los resultados sugieren que, para una automatización alineada con el juicio de las personas expertas, ChatGPT y Copilot son más consistentes. Mientras que Gemini requiere mejoras para alinearse a los criterios humanos.

Las diferencias significativas ($p < 0.0001$) en varias comparaciones refuerzan la necesidad de un análisis cualitativo para identificar los factores que influyen en la divergencia de Gemini. Estos hallazgos subrayan la importancia de calibrar los LLM para lograr evaluaciones más precisas y alineadas con los estándares utilizados en la ingeniería de requisitos. El coeficiente de concordancia de Kendall (W) obtenido fue de 0.7048, con un p-valor de 0.0000, que representa un acuerdo significativo entre los evaluadores, aunque no perfecto. Estas diferencias explican la variabilidad en la concordancia total y sugieren la necesidad de ajustes en la calibración Gemini para mejorar su alineación con el criterio experto. El análisis comparativo entre personas expertas y herramientas LLM mediante la prueba de Mann-Whitney revela que no se encontraron diferencias estadísticamente significativas en los criterios Independiente ($p = 0.4992$), Valioso ($p = 0.5693$) y Estimable ($p = 0.3365$), lo que sugiere que los LLM presentan un desempeño alineado con las personas expertas en estos criterios. Se detectaron diferencias significativas en los criterios Negociable ($p = 0.0016$), Pequeña ($p = 0.0009$) y Testeable ($p = 0.000056$), lo que indica que los LLM podrían evaluar estos criterios de manera diferente. Los hallazgos del estudio indican que los LLM pueden apoyar el criterio experto en el proceso de evaluaciones de calidad realizadas por personas expertas, para algunos de los criterios de evaluación.

Para analizar el grado de alineación entre las evaluaciones humanas y automáticas de la calidad de historias de usuario, se aplicó una clasificación semántica a las puntuaciones asignadas en cada criterio del marco INVEST. Dado que las calificaciones se otorgaron en una escala de 1 a 5, estas se agruparon en tres categorías: Positivo (4–5), Neutral (3) y Negativo (1–2). A partir de esta categorización, se definieron tres niveles de acuerdo semántico entre pares de evaluadores (persona experta y LLM): (1) Concordancia semántica, cuando ambos asignaron la misma categoría; (2) Desacuerdo leve, cuando uno evaluó como Neutral y el otro como Positivo o Negativo; y (3) Desacuerdo opuesto, cuando uno calificó como Positivo y el otro como Negativo. Esta metodología permitió cuantificar de manera cualitativa y cuantitativa la coincidencia conceptual entre evaluaciones, así como identificar discrepancias interpretativas significativas. Para garantizar la validez del análisis, se aplicó esta estrategia a las 60 historias de usuario, evaluadas por las dos personas expertas y los tres modelos LLM, de forma consistente para los seis criterios del marco INVEST.

Los resultados del análisis evidencian una alta concordancia semántica (superior al 80 %) en la mayoría de los pares de comparación, particularmente en los criterios Independiente, Pequeña y Testable, donde las definiciones más objetivas favorecen la consistencia en las evaluaciones. En contraste, se identificaron mayores niveles de desacuerdo leve y opuesto en los criterios Valioso, Estimable y Negociable, los cuales tienden a involucrar un mayor grado de subjetividad. El criterio Pequeña destaca por un desacuerdo opuesto más pronunciado en la comparación entre Experto 2 y Gemini, lo que sugiere diferencias en la interpretación del tamaño o granularidad adecuada de las historias de usuario. Estos resultados permiten identificar los criterios en los que los LLM se alejan del juicio experto, lo que constituye un insumo valioso para orientar el ajuste de los modelos y priorizar el análisis cualitativo de los casos más críticos.

Por ejemplo, al analizar los niveles de desacuerdo semántico entre las personas expertas y los LLM, el análisis detallado por historia de usuario revela que los casos con ID 4643 y 4821 presentan las mayores frecuencias de desacuerdo opuesto, con 18 y 13 casos, respectivamente. A estos les sigue el caso ID 4645, con un total de 8 desacuerdos (4 leves y 4 opuestos). Estos hallazgos sugieren que dichas historias podrían contener ambigüedades o múltiples interpretaciones asociadas a su claridad, valor o granularidad, por lo que fueron seleccionadas para un análisis cualitativo en profundidad.

La historia con ID 4643 corresponde a una solicitud de reporte de actividades evaluativas que no sigue la estructura estándar definida por la organización ni incluye criterios de aceptación. Esta falta de estructura influye a que los modelos LLM asignaran calificaciones más optimistas en varios atributos INVEST como Independiente, Negociable, Valiosa y Estimable en comparación con las personas expertas. No obstante, en el atributo Testeable, sí se observó consenso entre expertos y modelos, asignando una calificación mínima (valor 1), lo que indica el reconocimiento compartido de la ausencia de condiciones verificables. Un patrón similar se identificó en la historia ID 4821, también correspondiente a una solicitud de reporte, formulada sin estructura definida ni criterios de aceptación. Este comportamiento recurrente sugiere que los requisitos mal estructurados, especialmente aquellos relacionados con reportes sin elementos verificables, tienden a generar mayores divergencias en las evaluaciones automáticas, lo cual resalta la necesidad de establecer reglas claras de redacción para mejorar la consistencia y coherencia en los procesos de evaluación de calidad asistidos por LLM. El análisis agrupado por criterios INVEST revela que los criterios con mayor frecuencia de desacuerdo opuesto son Pequeña (11 casos), Negociable (10) y Estimable (8), lo que sugiere que los modelos LLM presentan mayores dificultades para alinearse con las valoraciones humanas en aspectos que requieren juicios más subjetivos, como la granularidad del requerimiento, su negociabilidad o estimabilidad. En contraste, el atributo Valioso registra la mayor cantidad de desacuerdos leves (17 casos), lo que indica que, aunque existen diferencias, estas tienden a ser más matizadas y posiblemente vinculadas a interpretaciones del valor percibido. En conjunto, estos hallazgos refuerzan la hipótesis de que ciertos atributos INVEST son más propensos a generar discrepancias semánticas, particularmente cuando son evaluados de manera automática, lo que subraya la importancia de complementar las técnicas automáticas con revisión cualitativa experta en contextos reales.

6. Conclusiones

Los resultados muestran el potencial de las herramientas LLM para el apoyo en la evaluación de la calidad de requisitos de software, específicamente en la valoración de historias de usuario siguiendo los criterios INVEST. Los LLMs presentan un rendimiento aceptable y que, en conjunto con las personas expertas en ingeniería de requisitos, pueden realizar evaluaciones de las historias de usuario. A pesar de la necesidad de supervisión humana, se observó que mediante procesos de calibración y mejora de *prompts* diseñados siguiendo los ejemplos prácticos indicados en otros estudios como [Krishna et al. 2024; Zhang et al. 2024; Ronanki et.al 2023], es posible ajustar el comportamiento de los modelos para que simulen de forma más precisa el criterio experto, integrando reglas específicas y ejemplos de evaluaciones previas.

Los modelos de lenguaje muestran un desempeño prometedor al alcanzar altos niveles de concordancia semántica con evaluadores humanos en la mayoría de los criterios del marco INVEST, lo que evidencia su potencial para apoyar procesos de evaluación automatizada de requisitos. Sin embargo, los resultados también revelan oportunidades de mejora, especialmente en criterios como Pequeña, Negociable y Estimable, donde los modelos presentan mayor variabilidad frente a las evaluaciones humanas. Estas diferencias son más notorias en historias de usuario sin estructura estandarizada ni criterios de aceptación, lo que resalta la importancia de seguir buenas prácticas de redacción. En este contexto, el análisis cualitativo experto resulta fundamental para complementar las evaluaciones automáticas, aportando una visión contextual y especializada que fortalece la precisión, la coherencia y la confiabilidad del proceso de validación en entornos reales de ingeniería de requisitos.

En términos de alineación con el juicio experto, Copilot y ChatGPT mostraron un desempeño más cercano al de las personas evaluadores expertas. En contraste, Gemini presentó oportunidades de ajuste. Para mejorar los resultados se requieren análisis cualitativos para identificar los aspectos que requieren calibración. Por lo que, lo anterior implica el análisis de las diferencias de interpretación de los criterios INVEST entre los LLM y expertos, ya que en algunos criterios los modelos presentan similitudes, pero en otras diferencias, y hasta qué punto pueden ser ajustados para interpretar de manera más precisa. La necesidad de calibración y validación de personas expertos en la evaluación automatizada aún parece necesaria, identificando estrategias de ajuste y calibración continua para mejorar su alineación al juicio experto.

En cuanto a generalización de los resultados, las evaluaciones se realizaron en el contexto de un proyecto real con historias de usuario, y se reconoce que su generalización puede estar limitada a el dominio y estilo de documentación o estructuras organizativas. Sin embargo, el proceso parece ser aplicable en organizaciones con procesos similares. Como trabajo futuro se recomienda investigar estrategias híbridas combinando evaluaciones de LLM con validación posterior por parte de personas ingenieras de requisitos, según criterios de calidad de la organización. Por un lado, ampliar el conjunto de datos de evaluación, incluyendo historias de usuario, con el contexto particular de cada proyecto de la organización, con el fin de reducir el sesgo en las evaluaciones y por otro lado la posibilidad de ofrecer contexto más detallado durante las evaluaciones. Desde la perspectiva práctica, se debe evaluar la posibilidad de desarrollar herramientas de apoyo integradas en plataformas de gestión de requisitos, permitiendo una automatización controlada y supervisada. Como siguientes pasos se proyecta llevar a cabo un proceso iterativo de mejora de la evaluación de las historias y de mejora de la especificación de las historias de usuario evaluadas en tres fases y utilizando dos perfiles clave: la persona ingeniera de requisitos y la dueña del producto.

7. Agradecimientos

Esta investigación fue parcialmente apoyada por el proyecto No. 0013-2024 UNED, Nodos-Investiga DTIC-UNED, No. 834-C1-011 UCR, el Posgrado en Computación e Informática y el Centro de Investigaciones en Tecnologías de la Información y Comunicación de la UCR. Se agradecen los invaluables aportes de las personas colaboradoras de los equipos de la DTIC-UNED.

8. Referencias

Belzner, L., Gabor, T. and Wirsing, M. (2023) "Large language model assisted software engineering: prospects, challenges, and a case study", In: International Conference on

Bridging the Gap between AI and Reality (pp. 355-374). Springer Nature Switzerland.

Bosch, J. (2014) "Continuous software engineering: An introduction", In: Bosch, J. (eds) Continuous Software Engineering (pp. 3-13). Springer , Cham.

Bourque, P., and Fairley, R. (2014). Guide to the Software Engineering Body of Knowledge (Swebok). 335.

CertiProf. (2022), Scrum Master Professional Certificate.

Essel, H., Vlachopoulos, D., Essuman, A. and Amankwa, J. (2024) "ChatGPT effects on cognitive skills of undergraduate students: Receiving instant responses from AI-based conversational large language models (LLMs)", In: Computers and Education: Artificial Intelligence, 6, 100198.

Fitzgerald, B. and Stol, K. (2017) "Continuous software engineering: A roadmap and agenda", In Journal of Systems and Software, 123, 176-189.

Hernandez-Agüero, E., Quesada-López, C., & Chaves-Sánchez, J. P. (in press). "Integración de enfoques ágiles para el mejoramiento continuo de procesos de software", In: Proceedings of the 13th International Conference on Software Process Improvement (CIMPS 2024), Mérida, Yucatán, México. IEEE Xplore.

Krishna, M., Gaur, B., Verma, A. and Jalote, P. (2024). "Using LLMs in software requirements specifications: an empirical evaluation", In: 2024 IEEE 32nd International Requirements Engineering Conference (RE) (pp. 475-483). IEEE.

Marques, N., Silva, R. and Bernardino, J. (2024). Using chatgpt in software requirements engineering: A comprehensive review. Future Internet, 16(6), 180.

Parra, E., Dimou, C., Llorens, J., Moreno, V. and Fraga, A. (2015) "A methodology for the classification of quality of requirements using machine learning techniques", In: Information and Software Technology, 67, 180-195.

Ronanki, K., Berger, C. and Horkoff, J. (2023) "Investigating ChatGPT's potential to assist in requirements elicitation processes", In: 2023 49th Euromicro Conference on Software Engineering and Advanced Applications (SEAA) (pp. 354-361). IEEE.

Roumeliotis, K., Tselikas, N. and Nasiopoulos, D. (2024). "LLMs in e-commerce: a comparative analysis of GPT and LLaMA models in product review evaluation", In: Natural Language Processing Journal, 6, 100056.

Schwaber, K. and Sutherland, J. (2020), La Guía de Scrum.

Subedi, I., Singh, M., Ramasamy, V. and Walia, G. (2021), "Classification of testable and valuable user stories by using supervised machine learning classifiers", In: 2021 IEEE International Symposium on Software Reliability Engineering Workshops (ISSREW) (pp. 409-414). IEEE.

Zhang, Z., Rayhan, M., Herda, T., Goisauf, M., and Abrahamsson, P. (2024). "Llm-based agents for automating the enhancement of user story quality: An early report", In: International Conference on Agile Software Development (pp. 117-126). Springer Nature Switzerland.

Modelo de Características Extendido para Sistemas Híbridos (Cuántico-Clásicos)

Samuel Sepúlveda[1], **Ricardo Pérez-Castillo**[2], **Mario Piattini**[3]

[1]Departamento de Ciencias de la Computación e Informática – Universidad de La Frontera – Av. Francisco Salazar 01145 – Temuco – 4811230 – Chile

[2]Facultad de Ciencias Sociales y Tecnologías de la Información – Universidad de Castilla-La Mancha – Av. Real Fábrica de Sedas s/n
Talavera de la Reina – 45600 – España

[3]Departamento de Tecnologías y Sistemas de Información – Universidad de Castilla-La Mancha – Paseo de la Universidad 4 – Ciudad Real – 13071 – España

samuel.sepulveda@ufrontera.cl

ricardo.pdelcastillo,mario.piattini@uclm.es

Abstract. *Quantum computing (QC) and quantum software engineering (QSE) face challenges due to the diversity of algorithms, languages, and integration strategies. This paper proposes a quantum-classical hybrid software development model following a Software Product Lines approach. Based on a previous model and a literature search, essential components were identified and structured in a hierarchy to represent the variability in these systems. The resulting model facilitates variability and configuration management of hybrid architectures, setting the basis for further evaluation and refinement and contributing to a more effective methodology for integrating QC and QSE.*

Resumen. *La computación cuántica (CQ) y la ingeniería de software cuántico (ISC), enfrentan desafíos debido a la diversidad de algoritmos, lenguajes y estrategias de integración. Este trabajo propone un modelo para el desarrollo de software híbrido cuántico-clásico, siguiendo un enfoque de Líneas de Producto de Software. A partir de un modelo previo y una búsqueda de la literatura, se identificaron componentes esenciales y se estructuraron en una jerarquía para representar la variabilidad en estos sistemas. El modelo resultante facilita la gestión de variabilidad y configuración de arquitecturas híbridas, estableciendo las bases para futuras evaluaciones y refinamientos, contribuyendo a una metodología más efectiva para la integración de CQ e ISC.*

1. Introducción

En el ámbito de la computación cuántica (CQ) y la ingeniería de software cuántico (ISC), la multiplicidad de algoritmos, lenguajes de programación, mecanismos de integración genera importantes desafíos al momento de adoptar y adaptar soluciones cuánticas [Salam and Ilyas 2024]. La falta de pautas que guíen la adopción de estas tecnologías, en continua evolución, a menudo dificulta su integración efectiva [Bisicchia et al. 2024]. Además, los sistemas software del futuro no serán puramente cuánticos, sino que estos serán sistemas híbridos (clásico-cuánticos) donde parte de la funcionalidad será soportada por software cuántico que deberá ser integrado en los sistemas software clásicos heredados [Pérez-Castillo et al. 2021].

A pesar de los avances significativos en ISC y Líneas de Productos de Software (LPS), no se han desarrollado propuestas completamente integradas que faciliten la transición de grandes sistemas clásicos hacia sistemas híbridos con alta variabilidad [Carbonelli et al. 2024]. Si bien existen propuestas que exploran el uso de LPS y modelos de características (MC) para abordar ciertos aspectos de esta transición [Sepúlveda et al. 2024, Sepúlveda et al. 2025], dichas propuestas no abordan de manera integral los desafíos asociados con la gestión de variabilidad y la escalabilidad en sistemas híbridos.

La presente investigación busca consolidar y expandir estas ideas mediante el desarrollo de un modelo más robusto, que integre ISC y LPS de manera eficiente, gestionando la variabilidad en diversos escenarios y bajo distintas restricciones. Al organizar y clasificar la compleja variedad de tecnologías cuánticas, se busca facilitar una comprensión más clara e identificar de manera sistemática las características relevantes según sus relaciones intrínsecas. En este contexto, se busca responder la siguiente pregunta: ¿Cómo la adaptación de metodologías tradicionales con artefactos cuánticos puede facilitar una integración entre sistemas clásicos y cuánticos al usar conceptos de LPS? Para abordar esta cuestión, se plantea la hipótesis de que la adaptación de metodologías tradicionales, complementadas con un artefacto diseñado para incorporar principios cuánticos, permitirá un diseño y una implementación con más calidad de los sistemas híbridos.

El resto del artículo se estructura como sigue. La sección 2 presenta los conceptos fundamentales relacionados con la propuesta. Las secciones 3 y 4 presentan el desarrollo de la propuesta y una discusión de los principales resultados, respectivamente. Finalmente, la sección 5 presenta las conclusiones del trabajo realizado.

2. Antecedentes generales

Esta sección presenta los conceptos básicos de la QC (Sección 2.1), seguido de la ISC (Sección 2.2), y finalmente los conceptos de LPS y la variabilidad (Sección 2.3).

2.1. Conceptos básicos

La CQ utiliza los principios de la superposición y el entrelazamiento para procesar información de manera más eficiente que las computadoras clásicas en ciertos tipos de problemas [Nielsen and Chuang 2001].

A diferencia de los bits clásicos (0 y 1), los qubits manejan ambos estados simultáneamente de forma probabilística, lo que permite realizar cálculos paralelos con mayor eficiencia. Este paradigma ha demostrado su potencial en áreas como la optimización, criptografía y simulación molecular. Aunque las tecnologías actuales se limitan a sistemas NISQ (Noisy Intermediate-Scale Quantum), se espera que su desarrollo impacte significativamente la industria del software según se consiguen dispositivos FTQC (Fault-tolerant Quantum Computing) tolerantes a fallos [Chen and Rengaswamy 2024].

2.2. Ingeniería de software cuántica

La ISC es una disciplina emergente que busca adaptar metodologías tradicionales de software para gestionar la complejidad del desarrollo cuántico. El concepto de

ISC [Piattini et al. 2020, Zhao 2021, Serrano et al. 2022] ha emergido en los últimos años como un conjunto de procesos, métodos y herramientas diseñados para maximizar el potencial de los sistemas de computación cuántica. El Software Engineering Institute [Carleton et al. 2021] menciona desafíos como la integración de algoritmos cuánticos en sistemas híbridos y la falta de herramientas formales para gestionar la incertidumbre en sistemas cuánticos.

Por otro lado, [Exman et al. 2024] presenta el estado actual de la ISC y el diseño de sistemas cuánticos, independientemente del hardware específico. Los autores abordan aspectos teóricos del software cuántico y aplica conceptos clásicos de ingeniería de software, como enfoques ágiles de desarrollo, validación, medición y despliegue, en entornos cuánticos o híbridos. Además, se complementa con diversas aplicaciones industriales. Un estudio secundario muestra que la mayor parte de la investigación en ISC se ha centrado en pruebas de software y en el uso de frameworks como Qiskit [De Stefano et al. 2024]. Sin embargo, todavía queda un vacío importante en áreas de gestión y diseño a nivel arquitectónico para sistemas híbridos.

Si bien ya se ha llevado a cabo un trabajo preliminar que aborda el proceso basado en principios de LPS y el uso de MC para software híbrido, la propuesta actual se centra en abarcar los diferentes aspectos involucrados en el desarrollo de software híbrido e integrar las funcionalidades necesarias para gestionar su variabilidad de manera integral.

2.3. Líneas de Productos de Software (LPS) y Modelado de Variabilidad

Las LPS se han consolidado como un enfoque eficaz para gestionar la variabilidad en sistemas complejos mediante modelos de características (MC). Estos modelos representan la diversidad de productos posibles en una línea de software, permitiendo generar múltiples configuraciones desde una base común. Benavides et al. (2010) destacan que los MC son esenciales para gestionar la complejidad en LPS, aunque aún existen retos en su aplicación a entornos colaborativos y dinámicos [Benavides et al. 2010].

Galindo et al. (2019) examinan cómo los MC han sido adoptados en la industria y sugieren que la combinación de LPS con tecnologías emergentes, como la computación cuántica, podría aumentar significativamente su aplicabilidad [Galindo et al. 2019]. Además, estudios recientes han explorado nuevas áreas de aplicación, como los sistemas ciberfísicos y los vehículos autónomos submarinos, lo que demuestra la flexibilidad de las LPS para adaptarse a dominios emergentes [Safdar et al. 2016, Cares et al. 2022].

3. Modelo de Características para Software Híbrido

La propuesta de investigación principal es un modelo de variabilidad para el desarrollo de software híbrido. Aunque un MC preliminar ya ha sido publicado por [Sepúlveda et al. 2024, Sepúlveda et al. 2025], estos trabajos exploran cómo puede usarse el MC propuesto en el contexto general de LPS en el desarrollo de software híbrido. No obstante, dicho MC no resulta ser completo ni preciso como para cubrir toda la casuística en este tipo de desarrollos de manera eficiente, gestionando la variabilidad en diversos escenarios y bajo distintas restricciones. Este es precisamente el objetivo del presente artículo. Para ello, se ha llevado a cabo una búsqueda en la literatura para descubrir y clasificar los componentes esenciales de la CQ —por ejemplo, algoritmos, lenguajes, mecanismos de integración y métodos de corrección de errores— junto con sus propiedades definitorias. Los hallazgos fueron discutidos en cuanto a su importancia y relevancia entre los autores, desarrollando un modelo cuya estructura jerárquica encapsula la diversidad de los elementos y restricciones para el software híbrido.

El modelo propuesto se define mediante formato textual con UVL (*Universal Variability Language*) [Benavides et al. 2024, Fadhlillah and Rabiser 2024]. Definir un modelo de variabilidad en UVL en lugar de un árbol gráfico facilita la escalabilidad, edición y mantenimiento en texto plano, permitiendo integración con herramientas de análisis y automatización [Rabiser 2024]. Además, UVL es más flexible para expresar restricciones como opcionalidad, alternativas y dependencias, evitando la complejidad visual de los diagramas cuando el modelo crece. Para complementar el presente estudio, se recomienda consultar el material proporcionado por [Sepúlveda et al. 2025], donde se detalla la representación gráfica del MC y se incluye su archivo de configuración en formato JSON.

La estructura del modelo se presenta en el Código 1. En las siguientes subsecciones se describen los principales grupos de características que se consideran: el tipo de funcionalidad soportada, tipo de algoritmo, los framework y lenguajes de programación, el modelo de integración, y restricciones software basadas en el hardware.

```
HQC_SPL

features:
    @Functionality:
        ...
    @Algorithm:
        ...
    @Programming:
        ...
    @Integration_model:
        ...
    @Quantum_HW_constraint:
        ...
# restricciones para todos los elmentos del modelo
constraints:
    ...
```

Código 1. Modelo de características en UVL para software híbrido

3.1. Tipo de funcionalidad soportada

Un sistema de software híbrido cuántico-clásico integra componentes cuánticos y clásicos para aprovechar las fortalezas de ambos paradigmas [Faro et al. 2023]. En la propia fase de análisis de requisitos [Pendenti et al. 2024], una de las primeras preguntas es si una determinada funcionalidad deberá ser soportada por software clásico o cuántico (véase el Código 2). Existen algunas aproximaciones para determinar si una determinada funcionalidad debe ser soportada por software clásico o cuántico. Por ejemplo, [Chancellor et al. 2020] proporcionan un marco de toma de decisiones para casos de uso de algoritmos cuánticos y cuántico-inspirados. Obviamente, esta decisión estará condicionada también por otras restricciones (entre ellas de hardware) que son modeladas en otro subárbol de características del MC propuesto. De forma similar, el propio algoritmo escogido condicionará la elección, así, por ejemplo, si se pretende resolver un problema mediante *machine learning*, también tendrá que decidirse si se hace mediante software clásico o *quantum machine learning* (QML) [Nadim et al. 2024].

Adicionalmente, es posible distinguir dos principales paradigmas de computación cuántica (véase el Código 2): la computación cuántica basada en puertas y la computación cuántica adiabática, también conocida en su implementación práctica como *Quantum Annealing* (QA) [McGeoch 2020]. Por un lado, la computación basada en puertas también se conoce como computación cuántica universal, ya que, en teoría, puede abordar todos los problemas objetivo (dado que es Turing-completa), mientras que los sistemas de QA se utilizan exclusivamente para problemas de optimización y han logrado cierta penetración en el mercado, como es el caso de D-Wave [Kahn 2020].

```
@Functionality:
    Classical
    @Quantum:
        Gate_based
        Adiabatic
```

Código 2. Características definidas en UVL para el tipo de funcionalidad software

3.2. Algoritmos Software

Los algoritmos híbridos como el Variational Quantum Eigensolver (VQE) y el Quantum Approximate Optimization Algorithm (QAOA) combinan el procesamiento cuántico y clásico. Estos algoritmos ejecutan subrutinas cuánticas, cuyas salidas son utilizadas por procesos clásicos para optimizar los resultados en tiempo real. La iteración continua entre ambas partes es clave, lo que permite que las decisiones clásicas condicionen operaciones cuánticas futuras dentro de un mismo ciclo de ejecución.

El trabajo de [Qi et al. 2024] presenta una revisión y aplicación de los algoritmos variacionales, así como sus aplicaciones y desafíos asociados su implementación dispositivos cuánticos actuales. Una revisión específica de los algoritmo VQE y QAOA, sus implementaciones prácticas y varios resultados experimentales se muestran en [Grange et al. 2023]. La variabilidad de algoritmos que se debe manejar es, en primer lugar, si estos son clásicos, cuánticos o híbridos.

En primer lugar, los algoritmos clásicos utilizan procesamiento determinista basado en bits clásicos y no aprovechan, de ninguna forma, fenómenos cuánticos como superposición o entrelazamiento. Estos son altamente maduros y aplicables a una amplia gama de problemas. Por ello, en este artículo se obvia un listado pormenorizado de estos algoritmos, aunque estos se pueden clasificar y organizar atendiendo a diferentes criterios:

- Propósito principal: Procesamiento de datos (clasificación, búsqueda, ordenación); Optimización (combinatoria, estocástica); Inteligencia artificial (aprendizaje supervisado, no supervisado, por refuerzo), Criptografía y seguridad (cifrado simétrico, cifrado asimétrico, hashing).
- Complejidad y enfoque: Deterministas (divide y vencerás, voraces, dinámicos); No deterministas (probabilísticos, heurísticos).
- Paradigma de programación: Iterativos, Recursivos, Paralelos, Distribuidos.
- Metodología de desarrollo: Exactos, Aproximados, Heurísticos.

Por otra parte, los desafíos de la gestión de la variabilidad en sistemas software híbridos residen en los algoritmos cuánticos puros o híbridos.

Los algoritmos cuánticos aprovechan fenómenos cuánticos como superposición, entrelazamiento e interferencia y están especialmente diseñados para aprovechar la aceleración cuántica en problemas específicos. A continuación se presenta una clasificación de éstos que divide en dos grandes grupos: FTQC y NISQ [Ezratty 2024]. A parte, se consideran algoritmos *quantum annealing* específicos para computación cuántica adiabática.

FTQC (Fault-Tolerant Quantum Computing): Son algoritmos diseñados para computadoras cuánticas tolerantes a fallos, que corrigen errores durante la ejecución. Se centran en aplicaciones de gran escala, como la simulación precisa de sistemas físicos y criptografía, con aceleración garantizada a largo plazo.

- Deutsch-Jozsa: Verificar si una función es constante o balanceada, consigue una ventaja exponencial (*O(1)*).
- Bernstein-Vazirani: Descubrir una clave secreta codificada en una función matemática en una sola consulta, consigue una ventaja exponencial (*O(1)*).
- Grover: Búsqueda en una base de datos no estructurada, consigue una ventaja cuadrática ($O(\sqrt{n})$).
- Simon: Encontrar un patrón oculto en una función matemática, consigue una ventaja exponencial (*O(1)*).
- Shor: Factorización de números semi-primos. Ventaja Exponencial para enteros grandes.
- QFT (Quantum Fourier Transform): Convertir un conjunto de números en una representación de frecuencias, consigue una ventaja exponencial ($O(1/\epsilon^2)$).
- QPE (Quantum Phase Estimation): Permite encontrar la fase asociada a un operador cuántico, consigue una ventaja exponencial ($O(1/\epsilon)$).
- HHL (Harrows-Hassidim-Lloyd): Resolución de sistemas lineales. Ventaja exponencial en matrices dispersas.

NISQ (Noisy Intermediate-Scale Quantum): Son algoritmos para dispositivos cuánticos actuales con ruido, sin corrección de errores completa. Son heurísticos y se usan en problemas como optimización y *machine learning*, pero su rendimiento no está garantizado de manera general.

- QAOA (Quantum Approximate Optimization Algorithm): Optimización combinatoria desde una función objetivo codificada en ansatz.
- VQE (Variational Quantum Eigensolver): Obtención de energías de estado base.
- QML (Quantum Machine Learning): Clasificación y clustering basado en QNN (Quantum Neural Networks). Potencial mejora en problemas de alta dimensionalidad.

Finalmente, los algoritmos híbridos combinan procesamiento clásico y cuántico. Usan computadoras clásicas para manejar preprocesamiento o integración con datos, delegando tareas específicas al hardware cuántico.

- Quantum-Assisted Annealing: Optimización combinatoria que mezcla simulaciones clásicas y cálculos cuánticos.
- Clustering híbrido, realiza el preprocesamiento clásico para el particionado en problemas más manejables y luego aplica un algoritmo cuántico.

- QAOA clásico-cuántico: Preprocesamiento clásico para reducir restricciones complejas y optimización cuántica del objetivo.

A modo de resumen, el Código 3 muestra el subárbol UVL que modela las características para el tipo de algoritmo considerado.

```
@Algorithm:
    {Quantum, Hybrid, Classical}:
    @Quantum:
        {0..1} {FTQC, NISQ, Quantum_Annealing}:
            FTQC:
                Deutsch_Jozsa
                Bernstein-Varizani
                Grover
                Simon
                Shor
                QFT
                QPE
                HHL
            NISQ:
                QAOA
                VQE
                QML
            Quantum_Annealing
    @Hybrid:
        Quantum_Assisted_Annealing
        Hybrid_Clustering
        Classical_Quantum_QAOA
    @Classical
```

Código 3. Características definidas en UVL para el tipo de algoritmo

3.3. Lenguajes de Programación

Los marcos de trabajo y lenguajes de programación cuánticos han evolucionado significativamente para facilitar el desarrollo de software híbrido cuántico-clásico, presentando diferencias clave en compatibilidad, sintaxis y optimización. Un análisis comparativo de plataformas como Qiskit, Cirq, Forest y Q# destaca variaciones en requisitos de instalación, sintaxis y capacidades de simulación, lo que influye en la elección de herramientas según el caso de uso específico [LaRose 2019].

La diversidad de lenguajes cuánticos permite adaptaciones para diferentes paradigmas de computación, siendo algunos más adecuados para modelos de circuitos cuánticos y otros para enfoques adiabáticos o de simulación [Heim et al. 2020]. Además, la selección del compilador cuántico adecuado es crucial, ya que impacta en la optimización de circuitos y en la eficiencia de ejecución en hardware real, lo que resalta la importancia de considerar estos factores en arquitecturas híbridas [Salm et al. 2021].

Finalmente, la portabilidad entre diferentes marcos sigue siendo un desafío, pues las diferencias en especificaciones dificultan la interoperabilidad y la reutilización de código cuántico en distintas plataformas [Schönberger et al. 2022]. Estos estudios respaldan la necesidad de estructurar de manera modular los elementos de programación en modelos como UVL, asegurando compatibilidad, flexibilidad y eficiencia en el desarrollo de software híbrido cuántico-clásico.

A modo de resumen, el Código 4 muestra el sub árbol UVL que modela las características para el tipo de framework y lenguaje de programación considerado.

```
@Programming:
    {Quantum_framework, Language}:
    @Quantum_framework:
        Qiskit
        dWave
        Cirq
        Braket SDK
    @Language:
        {quantum, classical}:
        @quantum:
            QASM
            QSharp
        @classical:
            Python
            CSharp
```

Código 4. Características definidas en UVL para el tipo de funcionalidad programación

3.4. Modelos de integración software

La integración entre computación clásica y cuántica es un desafío fundamental en la adopción de tecnologías cuánticas dentro de sistemas informáticos convencionales. Existen diversos enfoques para lograr esta interoperabilidad basada en servicios [Ahmad et al. 2024], los cuales se pueden agrupar en tres modelos principales (véase el Código 5): integración mediante APIs y computación en la nube, sistemas Quantum-SOA y orquestación mediante microservicios.

```
@Integration_model:
    {1..1} {Middleware_API, Quantum_SOA, Microservices}
```

Código 5. Características definidas en UVL para los tipos de integración software

El primer modelo, **integración mediante APIs y middleware en nube**, se basa en la interacción entre código clásico y cuántico a través de interfaces de programación de aplicaciones (APIs) y software development kits (SDKs) proporcionados por plataformas de computación cuántica en la nube. Frameworks como Qiskit, Cirq y Braket SDK permiten que lenguajes clásicos, como Python, interactúen con hardware cuántico remoto, mientras que esos servicios ofrecen infraestructura para ejecutar algoritmos cuánticos en sistemas distribuidos. Este enfoque facilita la adopción de la computación cuántica sin necesidad de poseer hardware especializado, además de permitir la integración de algoritmos cuánticos en flujos de trabajo convencionales. Sin embargo, la latencia en la comunicación y los costos asociados al uso de recursos cuánticos en la nube pueden representar limitaciones en ciertos escenarios.

El segundo modelo, **sistemas Quantum-SOA (Service-Oriented Architecture)**, aplica la arquitectura orientada a servicios para desacoplar el procesamiento cuántico y clásico en módulos independientes, permitiendo su integración flexible dentro de infraestructuras empresariales o científicas [Hevia et al. 2024]. En este enfoque, los sistemas cuánticos se exponen como servicios que pueden ser invocados bajo demanda a través de protocolos estándar como REST. Por ejemplo, un sistema de optimización en la industria logística puede delegar cálculos NP-duros a un servicio cuántico, o bien, una plataforma de banca puede integrar módulos de encriptación cuántica como parte de su infraestructura de ciberseguridad. La principal ventaja de este modelo radica en la escalabilidad y reutilización de componentes, permitiendo que distintos sistemas clásicos accedan a las capacidades cuánticas sin modificar su arquitectura base. No obstante, la orquestación eficiente entre servicios cuánticos y clásicos sigue siendo un desafío, especialmente en entornos con restricciones de tiempo real. Un estudio secundario sobre la QC como servicio (QCaaS) se presenta en [Ahmad et al. 2023].

El tercer modelo, **orquestación mediante microservicios**, extiende la idea de modularidad introducida por Quantum-SOA al ámbito de la computación distribuida, organizando los distintos componentes clásicos y cuánticos en una arquitectura de microservicios [Garcia-Alonso et al. 2021]. En este enfoque, cada unidad funcional del sistema se encapsula en un microservicio independiente que puede comunicarse con otros módulos a través de una infraestructura de mensajería asincrónica. Un caso de uso típico es la integración de modelos de aprendizaje automático donde los preprocesadores clásicos envían datos a microservicios cuánticos especializados en clustering o reducción de dimensionalidad. Tecnologías como *Kubernetes* permiten gestionar contenedores cuánticos y clásicos en la misma infraestructura, facilitando la implementación de flujos de trabajo híbridos. Aunque este modelo ofrece una gran flexibilidad y escalabilidad, la gestión de latencias y la sincronización de flujos de datos entre sistemas clásicos y cuánticos pueden representar desafíos significativos en escenarios de alta concurrencia. Una implementación de microservicios cuánticos para resolver el problema del viajante, ventajas y limitaciones se presenta en [Rojo et al. 2021].

3.5. Restricciones software basadas en hardware cuántico

Dada la naturaleza intrínseca del software cuántico y el alto impacto que tiene el hardware cuántico en él (debido a la madurez actual de la tecnología), existen numerosas restricciones derivadas del hardware que impactan fuertemente en los diferentes productos software dependiendo de la variabilidad escogida. El Código 6 resume todos estos elementos, que se explican a continuación.

Los sistemas híbridos requieren la integración de un procesador clásico y un procesador cuántico (QPU), cuya comunicación es fundamental para tareas como el control del flujo del programa y la evaluación de resultados. Los registros clásicos gestionan instrucciones y mediciones de qubits, mientras que los registros cuánticos operan los estados necesarios para las operaciones del sistema. La construcción de estas arquitecturas presenta desafíos significativos [Stirbu and Mikkonen 2023], requiriendo la adaptación del software para satisfacer las necesidades específicas de los sistemas híbridos [Ahmad et al. 2022].

La mitigación de errores y la reducción de la latencia son esenciales para el rendimiento en sistemas híbridos cuántico-clásicos. Métodos avanzados para la corrección y mitigación de errores cuánticos han demostrado reducciones significativas en experimentos recientes [Cai et al. 2023, Czarnik et al. 2021], mientras que la integración eficiente entre unidades clásicas y cuánticas contribuye a minimizar tiempos de espera. Además, las redes de comunicación cuántica han mostrado ventajas clave en términos de eficiencia y seguridad, así como en la reducción de la latencia en redes de gran escala [Ferrara et al. 2021, K.S. and Gowda 2023, Sekavčnik and Nötzel 2022].

```
@Quantum_HW_constraint:
    {Error correction,quality,optimization}:
    @Error correction:
        logic qubits
        dynamic correction
    @optimization:
        memory
        task schedule
    quality
```

Código 6. Características definidas en UVL para las restricciones basadas en hardware que impactan los diferentes productos software

3.6. Restricciones en el Modelo de Características

Además de las relaciones entre características, en el modelo de variabilidad se permiten restricciones cruzadas (*cross-tree constraints*). Estas restricciones pueden ser de dos tipos: «requires» y «excludes». La relación «requires» entre una característica *A* y una característica *B* indica que la selección de *A* obliga a seleccionar también *B*. Por otro lado, la relación «excludes» entre *A* y *B* significa que ambas características no pueden formar parte del mismo producto.

El Código 7 muestra el subárbol UVL que modela algunas de las restricciones entre características del modelo. Debido a las limitaciones de extensión del artículo, sólo se muestran cuatro de ellas.

```
constraints:
    # Restricción: Quantum require Quantum_HW_constraint
    Quantum -> Quantum_HW_constraint

    # Restricción: NISQ excluye Fault-Tolerant
    NISQ -> not Fault_Tolerant

    # Restricción: dWave require Annealing
    dWave -> Annealing

    # Restricción: Quantum_Algorithm requiere Functionality - Quantum
    Quantum_Algorithm -> Quantum
```

Código 7. Restricciones definidas en UVL entre algunas características del modelo

4. Discusión de Resultados

El modelo propuesto clarifica la interrelación entre tecnologías cuánticas, facilita comparaciones y destaca aspectos clave en sistemas híbridos cuántico-clásicos. Además, proporciona una base para futuras evaluaciones e integraciones, promoviendo una gestión más eficiente y adaptable de la variabilidad en el desarrollo de software cuántico.

4.1. Impacto esperado de las LPS y modelado de la variabilidad

La aplicación de LPS puede mejorar significativamente el diseño e implementación de sistemas híbridos cuántico-clásico en los elementos clave previamente mencionados.

En arquitecturas de procesamiento mixto, permite representar diversas configuraciones de procesadores cuánticos y clásicos, así como sus interacciones, facilitando la generación automática de arquitecturas adaptadas a distintos escenarios, como entornos locales o en la nube. Por ejemplo, se pueden definir variantes según si los QPUs están integrados localmente o accesibles a través de plataformas remotas.

Para los algoritmos híbridos, posibilita la gestión de variantes de algoritmos como VQE y QAOA, adaptando automáticamente componentes según las necesidades del sistema y las restricciones del hardware. A través de los MC, es factible modelar versiones y variantes paramétricas de los algoritmos, optimizando su configuración en tiempo real. Un ejemplo es la adaptación de VQE según la cantidad de qubits disponibles o el tiempo de coherencia del hardware cuántico.

En corrección de errores, se pueden representar múltiples estrategias y permitir la selección automática de la más adecuada según las condiciones del hardware. Una LPS facilita la integración de distintas técnicas en un sistema único, garantizando flexibilidad en su aplicación. Por ejemplo, se puede automatizar la elección entre corrección con qubits lógicos o mitigación basada en parámetros, considerando el tipo de QPU y el nivel de ruido en las mediciones.

4.2. Modelo propuesto

A continuación, se describen algunas de las diferencias clave entre el modelo propuesto y el modelo previo [Sepúlveda et al. 2025]. Se explican las modificaciones realizadas y cómo estas mejoran dicha propuesta.

Aspectos generales. Se introduce mayor granularidad, flexibilidad y precisión en la descripción de las características y restricciones. Esto facilita que el modelo sea más aplicable en escenarios reales, evitando inconsistencias y facilitando configuraciones válidas. Además, el enfoque actualizado refleja mejor las necesidades técnicas y prácticas de los sistemas híbridos, alineándose con los avances en ISC y LPS reportados en la literatura.

Uso de notación UVL. Ésta ofrece ventajas frente al modelado de la variabilidad usando MC, en particular usando modelos de texto. UVL permite una representación modular y estandarizada, facilitando la edición y mantenimiento sin depender de herramientas gráficas. Además, es compatible con herramientas de validación automática optimiza la gestión de restricciones y dependencias, asegurando configuraciones coherentes.

Interoperabilidad y algoritmos. Es posible combinar y optimizar algoritmos cuánticos y clásicos en flujos de trabajo híbridos, lo cual no estaba explícito en el modelo original. Este cambio refleja mejor la realidad actual de los sistemas híbridos cuántico-clásicos, donde algoritmos como VQE y QAOA requieren interacción continua con optimizadores clásicos. Esta nueva característica facilita el diseño de sistemas más eficientes y robustos.

Mejora en la Organización de HW-based Constraint. En este nuevo modelo, HW-based Constraint se reorganiza en subcaracterísticas como Calidad y Corrección de Errores, mejorando la granularidad del modelo. Esto permite una representación más detallada de las limitaciones y capacidades del hardware cuántico, asegurando que las restricciones se adapten mejor a las necesidades específicas de cada configuración.

Latencia y Comunicación como restricciones. Ahora estas propiedades se consideran como restricciones, lo cual simplifica el modelo al considerar que la latencia y la comunicación son propiedades del hardware y no funcionalidades seleccionables, reflejando con mayor precisión el impacto técnico de estas propiedades sin sobrecargar la descripción funcional. Además, este enfoque facilita su evaluación en configuraciones específicas sin introducir redundancia.

Posibilidad de extensión. Se considera agregar atributos a ciertas características del modelo, que permitan calcular métricas cuantitativas para evaluar restricciones como costos, tiempos de procesamiento, número de qubits requeridos, etc. Además, se considera extender el modelo para incluir nuevos algoritmos y arquitecturas emergentes. Por último, se considera incorporar características para sistemas distribuidos y auto adaptativos, incluyendo conceptos de LPS dinámicas.

5. Conclusiones

La propuesta presentada constituye un marco flexible y sólido para caracterizar soluciones en entornos híbridos cuántico-clásicos. Al incorporar conceptos y subdominios nucleares de la CQ dentro de una cuasi-taxonomía, el trabajo permite a investigadores y practicantes comprender los componentes esenciales y sus interconexiones, sentando las bases para una integración más coherente y efectiva de CQ-ISC. La inclusión de los conceptos de LPS contribuye a una gestión eficiente de la variabilidad y personalización, facilitando la selección automática de configuraciones óptimas y la integración de componentes en diferentes escenarios.

Como trabajo futuro, se plantea aplicar el modelo en distintos escenarios de integración cuántico-clásicos para validar su efectividad y flexibilidad, así como ampliar la propuesta incorporando técnicas de optimización formal que gestionen la complejidad de la computación cuántico-clásica, realizando un análisis cuantitativo de costos, recursos y otros factores, maximizando la fidelidad y garantizando el cumplimiento de restricciones.

Agradecimientos

Samuel Sepúlveda cuenta con el apoyo de ANID, Chile, FONDECYT de Iniciación en Investigación, Proyecto Nº 11240702.

Este trabajo ha sido soportado por los proyectos PID2022-137944NB-I00 (Proyecto SMOOTH) y PDC2022-133051-I00 (Proyecto QU-ASAP) financiados por MCIN/AEI/10.13039/501100011033 y por la "Unión Europea NextGenerationEU/FEDER". Adicionalmente, ha sido posible gracias a la ayuda UNION (2022-GRIN-34110) para la realización de proyectos de investigación aplicada, en el marco del Plan Propio de Investigación de la UCLM (cofinanciados con FEDER).

El trabajo cuenta con el apoyo del Programa Iberoamericano de Ciencia y Tecnología para el Desarrollo (CYTED), a través de RIPAISC - Red Iberoamericana para el avance de la Ingeniería de Software Cuántico (525RT0174).

Referencias

Ahmad, A., Altamimi, A. B., and Aqib, J. (2024). A reference architecture for quantum computing as a service. *Journal of King Saud University - Computer and Information Sciences*, 36(6):102094.

Ahmad, A., Khan, A. A., Waseem, M., Fahmideh, M., and Mikkonen, T. (2022). Towards process centered architecting for quantum software systems. In *2022 IEEE international conference on quantum software (QSW)*, pages 26–31. IEEE.

Ahmad, A., Waseem, M., Liang, P., Fehmideh, M., Khan, A. A., Reichelt, D. G., and Mikkonen, T. (2023). Engineering software systems for quantum computing as a service: A mapping study. *arXiv preprint arXiv:2303.14713*.

Benavides, D., Segura, S., and Ruiz-Cortés, A. (2010). Automated analysis of feature models 20 years later: A literature review. *Information systems*, 35(6):615–636.

Benavides, D., Sundermann, C., Feichtinger, K., Galindo, J. A., Rabiser, R., and Thüm, T. (2024). Uvl: Feature modelling with the universal variability language. *SSRN*.

Bisicchia, G., Garcia-Alonso, J., Murillo, J. M., and Brogi, A. (2024). From quantum mechanics to quantum software engineering. *arXiv preprint arXiv:2404.19428*.

Cai, Z., Babbush, R., Benjamin, S. C., Endo, S., Huggins, W. J., Li, Y., McClean, J. R., and O'Brien, T. E. (2023). Quantum error mitigation. *Rev. Mod. Phys.*, 95:045005.

Carbonelli, C., Felderer, M., Jung, M., Lobe, E., Lochau, M., Luber, S., Mauerer, W., Ramler, R., Schaefer, I., and Schroth, C. (2024). Challenges for quantum software engineering: An industrial application scenario perspective. In *Quantum Software: Aspects of Theory and System Design*, pages 311–335. Springer.

Cares, C., Lühr, D., Mora, S., Navarro, C., Olivares, L., Sepúlveda, S., and Vidal, G. (2022). Architecting autonomous underwater vehicles by adapting software product lines. In *Conference on Integrated Computer Technologies in Mechanical Engineering–Synergetic Engineering*, pages 719–730. Springer.

Carleton, A. D., Harper, E., Robert, J. E., Klein, M. H., De Niz, D., Desautels, E., Goodenough, J. B., Holland, C., Ozkaya, I., and Schmidt, D. (2021). Architecting the future of software engineering: A national agenda for software engineering research and development. Report, Software Engineering Institute, Carnegie Mellon University.

Chancellor, N., Cumming, R., and Thomas, T. (2020). Toward a standardized methodology for constructing quantum computing use cases. `https://arxiv.org/abs/2006.05846v1`. ArXiv preprint.

Chen, Z. and Rengaswamy, N. (2024). Tailoring fault-tolerance to quantum algorithms.

Czarnik, P., Arrasmith, A., Coles, P. J., and Cincio, L. (2021). Error mitigation with Clifford quantum-circuit data. *Quantum*, 5:592.

De Stefano, M., Pecorelli, F., Di Nucci, D., Palomba, F., and De Lucia, A. (2024). The quantum frontier of software engineering: A systematic mapping study. *Information and Software Technology*, page 107525.

Exman, I., Pérez-Castillo, R., Piattini, M., and Felderer, M. (2024). *Quantum Software: Aspects of Theory and System Design*. Springer Nature.

Ezratty, O. (2024). Understanding quantum technologies 2024.

Fadhlillah, H. S. and Rabiser, R. (2024). Towards a product configuration representation for the universal variability language. In *Proceedings of the 28th ACM International Systems and Software Product Line Conference*, pages 50–54.

Faro, I., Sitdikov, I., Valiñas, D. G., Fernandez, F. J. M., Codella, C., and Glick, J. (2023). Middleware for quantum: An orchestration of hybrid quantum-classical systems. In *2023 IEEE International Conference on Quantum Software (QSW)*, pages 1–8. IEEE.

Ferrara, R., Bassoli, R., Deppe, C., Fitzek, F. H., and Boche, H. (2021). The computational and latency advantage of quantum communication networks. *IEEE Communications Magazine*, 59(6):132–137.

Galindo, J. A., Benavides, D., Trinidad, P., Gutiérrez-Fernández, A.-M., and Ruiz-Cortés, A. (2019). Automated analysis of feature models: Quo vadis? *Computing*, 101:387–433.

Garcia-Alonso, J., Rojo, J., Valencia, D., Moguel, E., Berrocal, J., and Murillo, J. M. (2021). Quantum software as a service through a quantum api gateway. *IEEE Internet Computing*, 26(1):34–41.

Grange, C., Poss, M., and Bourreau, E. (2023). An introduction to variational quantum algorithms for combinatorial optimization problems. *4OR*, 21(3):363–403.

Heim, B., Soeken, M., Marshall, S., Granade, C., Roetteler, M., Geller, A., Troyer, M., and Svore, K. (2020). Quantum programming languages. *Nature Reviews Physics*, 2(12):709–722.

Hevia, J. L., Peterssen, G., and Piattini, M. (2024). qsoa®: Dynamic integration for hybrid quantum/classical software systems. *Journal of Systems and Software*, 214:112061.

Kahn, J. (2020). D-wave unveils its most powerful quantum computer to date. `https://fortune.com/2020/09/29/d-wave-5000-qubit-quantum-computer/`. Accessed on January 25, 2025.

K.S., J. and Gowda, S. (2023). Quantum network for quantum communication. In *2023 7th International Conference on Computation System and Information Technology for Sustainable Solutions (CSITSS)*, pages 1–5.

LaRose, R. (2019). Overview and Comparison of Gate Level Quantum Software Platforms. *Quantum*, 3:130.

McGeoch, C. C. (2020). Theory versus practice in annealing-based quantum computing. *Theoretical Computer Science*, 816:169–183.

Nadim, M., Hassan, M., Mandal, A. K., and Roy, C. K. (2024). Quantum vs. classical machine learning algorithms for software defect prediction: Challenges and opportunities. `https://arxiv.org/abs/2412.07698`. ArXiv preprint.

Nielsen, M. A. and Chuang, I. L. (2001). *Quantum computation and quantum information*, volume 2. Cambridge university press Cambridge.

Pendenti, H., Yepez, L. P., Castillo, R. P., Alegría, J. A. H., Antonelli, L., and Fernandez, A. (2024). ¿qué tiene de especial la ingeniería de requisitos para los sistemas cuántico-clásicos? *Memoria Investigaciones en Ingeniería*, 1(27):257–265.

Piattini, M., Peterssen, G., Pérez-Castillo, R., Hevia, J. L., Serrano, M. A., Hernández, G., De Guzmán, I. G. R., Paradela, C. A., Polo, M., Murina, E., et al. (2020). The talavera manifesto for quantum software engineering and programming. In *QANSWER*, pages 1–5.

Pérez-Castillo, R., Serrano, M. A., and Piattini, M. (2021). Software modernization to embrace quantum technology. *Advances in Engineering Software*, 151:102933.

Qi, H., Xiao, S., Liu, Z., Gong, C., and Gani, A. (2024). Variational quantum algorithms: fundamental concepts, applications and challenges. *Quantum Information Processing*, 23(6):224.

Rabiser, R. (2024). Industry adoption of uvl: What we will need. In *Proceedings of the 28th ACM International Systems and Software Product Line Conference*, pages 46–49.

Rojo, J., Valencia, D., Berrocal, J., Moguel, E., Garcia-Alonso, J., and Rodriguez, J. M. M. (2021). Trials and tribulations of developing hybrid quantum-classical microservices systems. *arXiv preprint arXiv:2105.04421*.

Safdar, S. A., Yue, T., Ali, S., and Lu, H. (2016). Evaluating variability modeling techniques for supporting cyber-physical system product line engineering. In *System Analysis and Modeling. Technology-Specific Aspects of Models: 9th International Conference, SAM 2016, Saint-Melo, France, October 3-4, 2016*, pages 1–19. Springer.

Salam, M. and Ilyas, M. (2024). Quantum computing challenges and solutions in software industry—a multivocal literature review. *IET Quantum Communication*.

Salm, M., Barzen, J., Leymann, F., Weder, B., and Wild, K. (2021). Automating the Comparison of Quantum Compilers for Quantum Circuits. In *Proceedings of the 15th Symposium and Summer School on Service-Oriented Computing (SummerSOC 2021)*, pages 64–80. Springer International Publishing.

Schönberger, M., Franz, M., Scherzinger, S., and Mauerer, W. (2022). Peel | pile? cross-framework portability of quantum software.

Sekavčnik, S. and Nötzel, J. (2022). Effects of quantum communication in large-scale networks at minimum latency. In *2022 IEEE Globecom Workshops (GC Wkshps)*, pages 802–807.

Sepúlveda, S., Pérez-Castillo, R., and Piattini, M. (2025). A software product line approach for developing hybrid software systems. *Information and Software Technology*, 178:107625.

Sepúlveda, S., Piattini, M., and Pérez Del Castillo, R. (2024). Developing hybrid quantum-classical software: a software product line approach. In *Proceedings of the 5th ACM/IEEE International Workshop on Quantum Software Engineering (Q-SE)*, page 37–40, New York, USA. ACM.

Sepúlveda, S., Perez-Castillo, R., and Piattini, M. (2025). Feature model hqc-spl cibse2025. `https://doi.org/10.5281/zenodo.15013631`. DOI: 10.5281/zenodo.15013631.

Serrano, M. A., Pérez-Castillo, R., and Piattini, M. (2022). *Quantum software engineering*. Springer.

Stirbu, V. and Mikkonen, T. (2023). Software architecture challenges in integrating hybrid classical-quantum systems. In *2023 IEEE International Conference on Quantum Computing and Engineering (QCE)*, volume 2, pages 203–204. IEEE.

Zhao, J. (2021). Quantum software engineering: Landscapes and horizons. `https://arxiv.org/abs/2007.07047`. ArXiv preprint.

Exploring the Role of Women in Hugging Face Organizations

Maria Tubella Salinas[1], Alexandra González[1], Silverio Martínez-Fernández[1]

[1]Universitat Politècnica de Catalunya

{maria.tubella@estudiantat.upc.edu,
alexandra.gonzalez.alvarez,silverio.martinez}@upc.edu

Abstract. ***Background****: Despite its impact on innovation, gender diversity remains far from fully being achieved in open-source projects.* ***Aims****: We examine gender diversity in Hugging Face (HF) organizations, investigating its impact on innovation and team dynamics in open-source development projects.* ***Method****: We conducted a repository mining study, focusing on ML model development projects on HF, to explore the involvement of women in collaborative processes.* ***Results****: Women are highly underrepresented in both organizations and commits distribution, which is also found when analyzing individual developers.* ***Conclusions****: Addressing gender disparities is essential to create more equitable, diverse, and inclusive open-source ecosystems.*

1. Introduction

Diversity is crucial in Software Engineering (SE), fostering innovation and effective problem-solving [Damian et al. 2024]. More specifically, gender diversity is being explored as, in recent decades, the software development field has been marked by a significant gender imbalance, with men overwhelmingly representing the majority of the workforce. For instance, only 26.8% of the people hired in Google's Tech area in 2023 were women [1]. This lack of gender diversity is prevalent, not only at the individual level but often across entire teams and organizations. In a survey conducted by [Kohl and Prikladnicki 2022], most respondents indicated that there is a lack of support for diversity in the SE field, with outdated patterns continuing to prevail, alongside instances of sexism and prejudice. Such gender homogeneity stands in contrast to the needs of software projects today, which rely heavily on collaboration, creativity, and diverse perspectives. Research shows that team diversity, including gender diversity, can enhance problem-solving capabilities, foster innovation, and lead to higher-quality outputs [Vasilescu et al. 2015]. Yet, many women who contribute meaningfully to the field remain underrepresented, often lacking visibility and recognition for their contributions.

Hugging Face (HF) is an advanced Machine Learning (ML) open-source platform known for its extensive library of pre-trained models, particularly in natural language processing and computer vision. Its ecosystem supports seamless model deployment, fine-tuning, and community-driven development, fostering rapid innovation. We focused our study in this platform due to its rapid growth and increasing popularity in both research and industry. Its versatility and active community make it an appealing choice for exploring modern ML workflows and tendencies.

[1]https://static.googleusercontent.com/media/about.google/ca//belonging/diversity-annual-report/2023/static/pdfs/google_2023_diversity_annual_report.pdf?cachebust=2943cac

On the HF platform, users can collaborate through entities called *Organizations* [2]. These HF Organizations serve as collaborative spaces where teams, research groups, companies, and other entities can jointly manage ML projects. By establishing an organization, members gain a shared environment for publishing, managing, and maintaining models, datasets, and other ML assets as a team. Any HF member can join one or more organizations, each of which can create and maintain an unlimited number of models. HF's openness is a foundational concept, essential for accurately interpreting the results.

Our research addresses multiple facets of gender composition and its potential influence on open-source ML projects. First, we aim to understand how HF organizations are structured in terms of gender diversity and whether this composition correlates with the popularity of the models they develop, measured by metrics such as downloads and likes. Secondly, we explore how women contribute within these organizations, particularly regarding the frequency and impact of their code commits. Analyzing commit patterns can offer insights into whether men or women tend to serve as primary contributors, potentially shaping project direction. Finally, we examine the nature of interactions between male and female members within these teams. By analyzing these dimensions, we aim to reveal how gender diversity manifests in HF organizations and explore its potential connections to organizational behavior and ML model success. This work ultimately aims to highlight the roles and contributions of women within this community, with broader implications for gender diversity in open-source software development.

2. Related Work

Extensive research has been conducted to study diversity across work groups, including both software development teams and teams from other domains. Understood broadly, diversity arises from any attribute that differentiates people [Phillips and O'Reilly 1998]. These attributes can be demographic (*e.g.*, age, gender, culture, religion, nationality), functional (*e.g.*, role, expertise), or subjective (*e.g.*, personality).

The impact of diversity on team outcomes remains a topic of debate, with conflicting findings in the literature. While some studies report a positive correlation between diversity and performance, others suggest a negative relationship. For instance, [Gomathy 2023] states that diversity can prevent grouping and lead to an inclusive workspace while also adding problems in how teammates communication.

2.1. Gender Diversity in Software Teams

Said by the World Health Organization, *gender* refers to "*the socially constructed characteristics of women and men – such as norms, roles and relationships of and between groups of women and men. It varies from society to society and can be changed*" [3]. Nevertheless, there are multiple definitions, as the American Psychology Association defines *gender identity* as a component of gender that describes a person's psychological sense of their gender. Many people describe gender identity as a deeply felt, inherent sense of being a boy, a man, or male; a girl, a woman, or female; or a nonbinary gender (*e.g.*, genderqueer, gender-nonconforming, gender-neutral, agender, gender-fluid) that may or may not correspond to a person's sex assigned at birth, presumed gender based on sex assignment [American Psychological Association 2015].

[2] https://huggingface.co/organizations

[3] https://www.who.int/health-topics/gender#tab=tab_1

Gender diversity has been increasingly recognized as a key factor in enhancing productivity and reducing turnover in software development teams. Studies show that gender-diverse teams tend to exhibit higher productivity, with partial positive effects on reducing employee turnover [Vasilescu et al. 2015]. This positive influence is linked to diverse perspectives in problem-solving and communication, which contribute to more dynamic and effective team interactions. The impact of gender diversity on employee performance is further influenced by several demographic and social factors, including the gender, age, marital status, education level, position, and work experience of employees. Research demonstrates a positive correlation between gender diversity and individual employee performance within organizations and statistical analyses reveal that gender diversity can be a predictive factor for employee performance, as diverse teams foster harmonious relationships and positive attitudes [Krishnan and Gokula 2020]. This, in turn, enhances overall team performance and adaptability to evolving market demands.

Another way to analyze the women's behaviour in teams is through studying its effect in *community smells*, which are organizational patterns associated with problematic team dynamics and communication structures [Palomba et al. 2018]. The top four more popular are: *Organizational silos*, when subgroups within a team are isolated, leading to fragmented knowledge and collaboration breakdowns; *Black clouds*, which describe persistent negative attitudes or dissatisfaction within a team, which can spread and impact morale; the *Lone wolf* phenomenon, that refers to individuals working in isolation from the rest of the team, limiting collaborative potential; and cohesion and *Radio silence*, that indicates a lack of communication, often resulting in misalignment and reduced efficiency in project execution. In terms of organizational culture, gender-diverse teams report fewer community smells compared to non-diverse teams [Catolino et al. 2019]. Specifically, gender diversity and women's participation are influential in mitigating issues such as *Black clouds* and *Radio silence*. However, the effect of gender diversity on other patterns, such as *Organizational silos* and *Lone wolves* appears to be less pronounced.

Nonetheless, women do not appear much in software teams; maybe because there are too few of them working in the field or maybe because of an inherent bias. The 2022 Stack Overflow Developer Survey [Stack-Overflow 2022] showed that only 5.17% of worldwide developers (from 180 countries) were women, while the 2023 data from Eurostat [4] revealed that just 17.4% ICT employees were women. Imtiaz *et al.*[Imtiaz et al. 2019] conducted an investigation to examine four effects on gender bias; *Tightrope*, when women behave in a restricted manner to avoid backlash, *Maternal Wall*, when women who are mothers have their competence and commitment questioned, *Prove-It-Again*, when women must provide more evidence than men to prove competence and *Tug of War*, when women are discouraging to other women. These four phenomena were first described in Williams and Dempsey's work [Williams and Dempsey 2014]. The investigation, performed with GitHub data, demonstrated that, while women are equally competent, they often limit their contributions to fewer projects and organizations compared to their male counterparts. Women also tend to demonstrate a more restrained approach in their professional interactions. Contrary to some expectations, the research has shown no significant differences between men and women in avoiding the posting of personal

[4]https://ec.europa.eu/eurostat/statistics-explained/index.php?title=ICT_education_-_a_statistical_overview

content, such as images with children, on professional platforms.

Table 1 shows a summary of the aforementioned related work. While gender diversity in software projects has been widely studied, most research is focused on larger and established platforms like GitHub [Vasilescu et al. 2015] [Imtiaz et al. 2019] or relied on survey-based approaches [Hodges and Murphy-Hill 2024] [Rastogi 2024]. This leaves a gap in understanding how gender diversity manifests itself in newer communities, such as ML engineers [Lanubile et al. 2024] in HF. This offers an opportunity to explore gender dynamics in a new area, motivating us to investigate this understudied area.

Table 1. Comparison of related work.

Study	Focus	Key Findings	Research Strategy
[Gomathy 2023]	Impact of diversity on communication in teams	Diversity can prevent grouping and create an inclusive workspace but may lead to communication challenges	Field strategy
[Vasilescu et al. 2015]	Gender diversity in software teams	Gender-diverse teams have higher productivity and lower turnover due to better problem-solving and communication	Data strategy
[Krishnan and Gokula 2020]	Gender diversity and individual performance	Gender diversity positively correlates with individual performance, fostering better relationships and attitudes	Data strategy
[Catolino et al. 2019]	Impact of gender diversity on organizational culture	Gender-diverse teams report fewer community smells, especially black clouds and radio silence	Data strategy
[Imtiaz et al. 2019]	Gender bias in software teams	Women tend to limit their contributions and restrict professional interactions due to bias	Data strategy
[Hodges and Murphy-Hill 2024]	Gender diversity in software teams	Researchers should also explore less visible challenges affecting diversity	Respondent strategy
[Rastogi 2024]	Gender diversity in software teams	Improving diversity in software development requires meaningful, sustainable solutions that balance business needs and inclusivity	Respondent strategy
This study	Gender diversity in HF	Analyzes the effects of gender diversity on HF organizations and models	Data strategy

The last column shows the research strategy based on [Storey et al. 2020].

3. Research Methodology

3.1. Goal and Research Questions

Following the Goal Question Metric (GQM) template [Basili et al. 1994], our goal is to ***analyze*** **gender diversity** ***for the purpose of*** **measuring it** ***with respect to*** **ML model commits** ***from the point of view of*** **ML engineers** ***in the context of*** **HF organizations of the HF Hub**.

To gain insights into organizational structures and ML model development processes in HF, we defined four Research Questions (RQ). **RQ1** focuses on understanding the characteristics of HF organizations in terms of gender diversity to uncover patterns that define their composition.

RQ1: How are HF organizations built in terms of gender diversity?

RQ2 and **RQ3** shift the focus to ML model commits and the contributions made by users to these projects. In this context, we aim to investigate how gender diversity within organizations relates to the number of downloads and success of the models they develop, as well as the behavioral patterns of individual contributors.

RQ2: Does the popularity of an ML model have a relation with the gender diversity in the organization developing it?

RQ3: How does gender relate to the volume and contribution of commits in HF models?

Building on the analysis of organizations and ML model contributions, **RQ4** compares gender diversity at the organizational level with that of individual contributors. We aim to see if gender patterns observed in organizations are also reflected in individual contributions.

RQ4: How does gender distribution in the top individual HF contributors compare to that in leading organizations?

3.2. Repository Mining Process

As illustrated in *Figure* 1, this repository mining study is divided into three fundamental parts: data collection from the HF API, the use of GitHub API and Large Language Models (LLMs) to augment that data, and a final analysis stage.

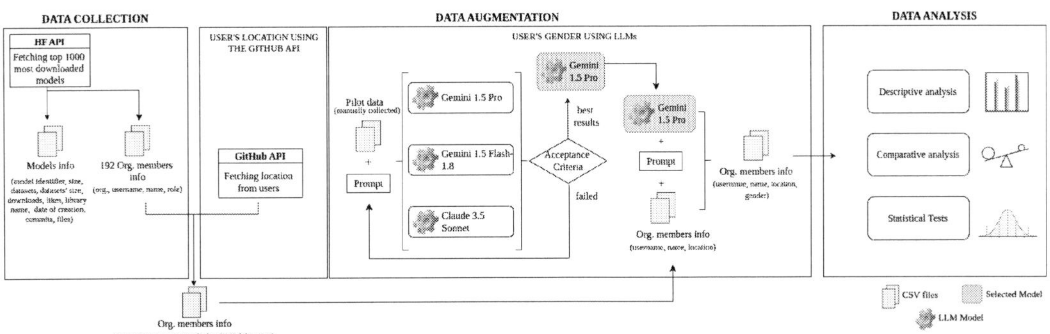

Figure 1. Repository Mining Study: Data Collection, Augmentation, and Analysis.

3.2.1. Data Collection

The data collection process began by using the HF API [5], following methods from [Castaño et al. 2024], to retrieve information about users, including their affiliations with organizations and details about the models they manage. We retrieved the **top 1,000 most downloaded models**, associated with **363 different developers**, including individual users who independently published models and organizations. Since our focus was

[5]https://huggingface.co/docs/huggingface_hub/package_reference/hf_api#huggingface_hub.HfApi

on studying organizations, we filtered the data to retain only the models associated with them, leaving us with **192 organizations** and their most downloaded models. For these organizations, we collected the necessary data. On the one hand, we obtained the data from the **models**: *model identifier, size, datasets, datasets' size, downloads, likes, library name, date of creation, commits* and *files*. However, to conduct our experiment we only used *model identifier, downloads, likes* and *commits*. Each *commits* data comprised a JSON with all ML model commits registered. Each commit is composed of these different fields: *commit identifier, authors, date of creation, title, message, formatted title* and *formatted message*. On the other hand, we saved the information about all **users** from those 192 organizations. That resulted in a total of 14,988 users from who we got *organization, username, name* and *role*.

At the same time, manually, we got the **top 100 individual contributors** from December 2024. About these users, we retrieved their *username* and *name* and obtained their *gender* by manually looking at their profile images or either of their socials.

3.2.2. Data Augmentation

User's location using the GitHub API Determining a user's gender directly from the HF API was not possible, as the platform does not include a specific field for users to disclose this information. However, the profile configuration page allows users to link external accounts, such as GitHub, X (formerly Twitter), LinkedIn, and Bluesky. While the API does not provide access to this data, it is possible to manually infer a user's gender by examining their profile photo on HF or by exploring these linked accounts.

Nevertheless, searching for the gender one by one for almost 15,000 people would mean a huge amount of time. In order to try to get the gender information we used the GitHub API. Because some users had their GitHub account linked, we used it to save their *location*. Again, obtaining gender information was not accomplished. Many are trying to but it seems like the pronouns are highly protected and, apart from doing it manually, it is not viable to know them. So, finally, the organization's members data we collected were *organization, username, name, role, has github* and *location*.

User's gender using LLMs Because the experiment's goal is the study of gender diversity, it is essential to know that about the users that compose an organization. To accomplish that, we relied on LLMs and followed the PRIMES framework [De Martino et al. 2025]. We focused on LLMs that provide an accessible API and offer some form of free credit for testing. Following a careful evaluation of available models, we selected Anthropic's *Claude 3.5 Sonnet*, which provides a $5 free credit, and Google's *Gemini 1.5 Flash* and *Gemini 1.5 Pro*, which offer $300 trial. To ensure clarity and reduce potential ambiguities arising from international naming conventions, we followed the recommendation by [Serebrenik 2024] to provide additional context beyond just names. We conducted a pilot using a manually collected **dataset of 360 randomly selected user samples** to validate the use of the LLM, and through several prompt refinements, we derived the following prompt to complete the dataset:

Final Prompt

Given the name [name] and, if not none, the location [location], tell me the gender of the username.

- The input is a name and maybe a location too.
- The output must be 'Male', 'Female', or 'Unknown'. Without any explanations or reasons. Just the predicted gender.
- Examples:
  - Christopher Pirillo: Male. Vera AxelRod: Female

We chose to introduce a third category, *unknown*, to prevent the LLM from being forced to classify individuals as either male or female. This approach was intended to mitigate the risk of the model providing correct answers purely by chance. This third category allows for more nuanced interpretations of results and reduces the potential for biased outcomes. To evaluate the accuracy, we used **Cohen's Kappa** [Cohen 1960], a statistical measure of agreement between two dependent categorical samples. An important consideration when interpreting the kappa is that the pilot data was built using additional information extracted from other platforms (such as HF, X and LinkedIn profile photos, published posts, Google Scholar pages and other socials appearances) while the models could only rely on name and location. We compared our manually collected data with the LLM gender classification to evaluate how well the model did. As shown in *Table* 2, the *Claude 3.5 Sonnet* requires more than twice the execution time of *Gemini's Flash* and nearly four times that of the *Pro*. Additionally, the free credit provided by *Anthropic* would be insufficient to process our entire dataset. Despite the comparable accuracy levels across all models, execution time and economic implications led us to select **Gemini 1.5 Pro**.

With the LLM, we augmented our dataset, which comprised each user's *organization, username, name, role, has github, location* and *gender*.

Table 2. Comparison of LLMs in the pilot test.

LLM	Execution Time	Economic Cost	Cohen's Kappa
Claude 3.5 Sonnet	12'	≈ $0.64	Moderate Agreement
Gemini 1.5 Flash	5'40"	≈ $0.50	Moderate Agreement
Gemini 1.5 Pro	3'46	≈ $0.50	Moderate Agreement

Explicit Cohen's Kappa values can be found in the Replication package 8.

3.2.3. Data Analysis

We used **descriptive analysis** to explore patterns of diversity and contributions within organizations. This method quantified important aspects such as gender distribution and commit characteristics, offering an overview of trends. Additionally, **comparative analysis** contrasted gender distributions and contributions between organizations and individual developers, providing deeper insights into diversity dynamics on the platform. Finally, we conducted **statistical tests** for each RQ, with a significance level of $\alpha = 0.05$ for all analyses. For *RQ1*, we performed a χ^2 test to determine whether there is an association between organizations and gender distribution across the dataset. To address *RQ2*, we investigated the relationship between the proportion of women in an organization and the downloads of their most popular model, applying Spearman's correlation test due to the non-normal distribution of the data. For *RQ3*, we used the Kruskal-Wallis test to examine differences in the distribution of commits between men, women, and bots, as the normality assumption was not met. Lastly, for *RQ4*, we conducted a χ^2 test to explore the relationship between gender distribution in organizations and among individual contributors. The statistical tests and the null hypotheses are summarized in *Table* 3.

Table 3. Summary of RQs, Statistical Tests, and Null Hypothesis (H_0).

RQ	Test	Null Hypothesis (H_0)
RQ1	χ^2 test	No association between organization and gender.
RQ2	Spearman's correlation	No correlation between women's proportion and ML model downloads.
RQ3	Kruskal-Wallis test	Commit distribution is equal across groups.
RQ4	χ^2 test	Organization and contributor gender distributions are the same.

4. Results

4.1. Gender diversity in HF organizations (RQ1)

As illustrated in *Table* 4, women account for 12.06% of the total users across the 192 HF organizations analyzed [6] when including those with unknown gender and 17.21% when considering only users with an assigned gender. A closer examination reveals that the proportion of women in the studied organizations ranges from 0% to 50%, with no organization having a female majority. Notably, 88 organizations have no women on their teams, and 183 have less than 30% female representation. Among the few organizations where women constitute half of the team, all consist of four members or fewer, underscoring the limited female presence across these organizations.

Table 4. Users by gender in the 192 analyzed organizations

Gender	Count	Proportion (%)	Mean Users
Men	8,696	58.02%	45.29
Women	1,808	12.06%	9.42
Unknown	4,484	29.92%	23.35
Total	14,988	100%	78.06

Finding 1. There is a significant gender imbalance within HF organizations, with the number of women remaining low, even when considering only users with known gender.

[6] https://github.com/GAISSA-UPC/HF_diversity/tree/main/HF_diversity/HF_diversity/organisations/complete_organisations

The χ^2 test yielded a p-value of 3.28×10^{-57}, which is far smaller than the significance level. Consequently, we rejected the null hypothesis, concluding that the proportions of males, females, and unknown gender differ significantly across organizations. The result is consistent with the gender imbalance observed across the different HF organizations, as well as with the diverse team sizes and highly varied gender distributions.

4.2. Relationship between ML model popularity and gender diversity in HF Organizations (RQ2)

We selected the **most downloaded model** from each organization to explore whether there is a relationship between ML model popularity and gender diversity. We then examined the behavior of the top 15 organizations - organizations that developed the 15 models with the highest download counts - including: *sentence-transformers, nesaorg, facebookAI, google-bert, Qwen, microsoft, openai, facebook, openai-community, bigscience, google, timm, distilbert, pyannote* and *M-CLIP*. *Figure* 2 shows no evident correlation between team diversity and the number of downloads. In fact, the top 3 organizations, with the highest download counts, have no women on their teams, suggesting a potential inverse relationship between gender diversity and popularity. Among the top 15 organizations, more than half are composed entirely of male members, highlighting the absence of gender representation in the most successful teams. These observations challenge the assumption that diversity is positively associated with organizational success, at least in terms of download metrics. However, it is important to note that the popularity of an ML model does not necessarily equate to the popularity of its organization, as models are often developed by contributors outside of the organization. Thus, it would not be accurate to assume that the gender distribution within a team aligns with that of the ML model authors.

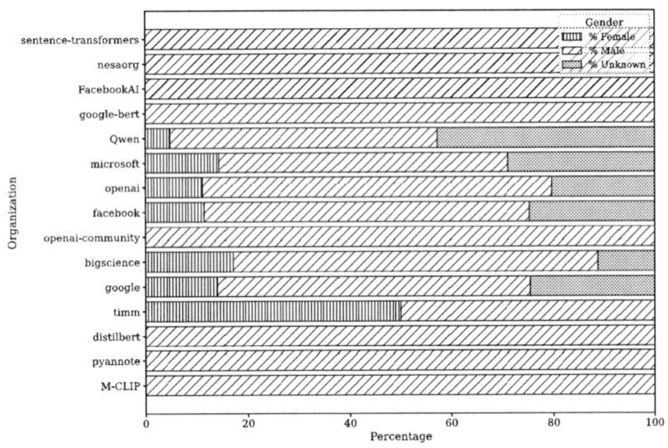

Figure 2. Normalized Gender Distribution of the Top 15 Organizations.

Finding 2.1. The most downloaded models do not exhibit a direct relationship with organizational diversity, as the top organizations often have no female team members.

Next, we analyzed **all 192 models** rather than just the top ones per organization, and obtained Spearman's correlation coefficient of -0.03 and a p-value of 0.7. The correlation value indicates a very weak negative relationship between the proportion of women and the number of downloads. Since the correlation is close to zero, it suggests that there is no clear relationship between the two variables. The negative direction implies that, on average, as one variable increases, the other decreases slightly, but this trend is negligible due to the small correlation value. Furthermore, the p-value of 0.7 is much greater than the significance threshold of 0.05, providing no evidence to reject the null hypothesis (H_0). Therefore, we conclude that there is no significant correlation between the proportion of women and the number of downloads.

Finding 2.2. No significant correlation exists between the proportion of women and ML model downloads across all models.

4.3. Commits data and gender diversity (RQ3)

We further analyzed the commit distribution of models developed by the 192 organizations selected for this study. However, before diving into the analysis, several key observations were made.

Firstly, we observed that the commit distribution does not directly correspond to the distribution of organizations. Due to the open-source nature of the platform, individuals can contribute to models without being affiliated with a particular organization or owning the model. As a result, some users make contributions to over 30 models, despite not being members of any team. Additionally, we encountered what we refer to as **Bots**, which contribute a significant number of commits. However, these commits are not critical to ML model development, as they mainly focus on file-related tasks. Two notable bots, *system* and *SFconvertbot*, rank as the top two committers. The *system* bot is responsible for managing ML model files such as *.txt, .json,* and *.bin*, as well as tasks such as updating *README.md* or making the initial commit. In contrast, the *SFconvertbot* specializes in a single type of commit: *"Adding 'safetensors' variant of this model"*.

In our analysis of commit data, we recorded 5,274 commits across 192 distinct models (one per organization). The data necessary to complete the final component of this experiment was collected manually due to the nature of authors' independent commitments to models. Consequently, when combining data from the organizations with commit data, many authors could not be identified because the LLM did not process those users.

Initially, we analyzed the gender distribution among authors who had committed the most, based on the number of models they contributed to. As observed in *Figure* 3, there were no female authors among the top committers, with only five female authors contributing to a total of two models. Further examination of the authors with the highest total number of commits revealed a similar lack of female representation. Of the 5,274 commits collected, 83.35% were done by men, 6.48% by users of unknown gender, 5.84% by bots, and the remaining 4.3% were committed by female authors.

Recovering the previous analysis - *Figure* 2 - we explored how are the commits [7] of their respective models (*Figure* 4). As stated before, both gender arrangements do differ. When comparing both perspectives - one from the organization point of view and the other from their corresponding ML model- some differences can be found. The first one and obvious, bots are not part of any organization yet they commit in majority. Furthermore, in some cases, there are women committers even though that team is male-composed. That would be the case of *google-bert*'s *bert-base-uncased*, *openai-community*'s *gpt2* or *distilbert*'s *distilbert-base-uncased.* The contrary phenomenon appears too, as the models

[7] pyannote's ML model was not authorized to download, that's why CIDAS appears

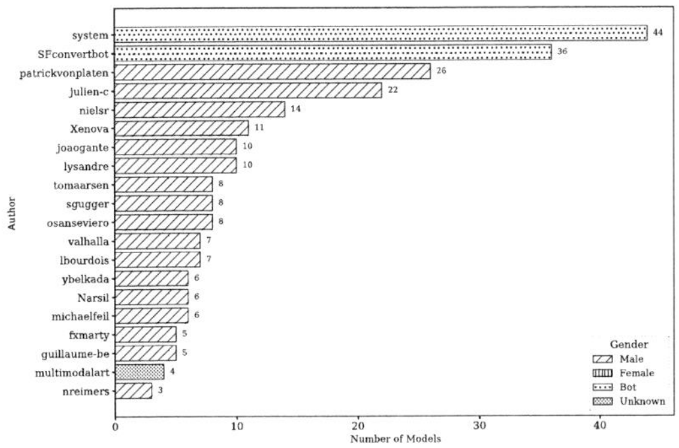

Figure 3. Top 20 Authors by Number of Models they Committed in.

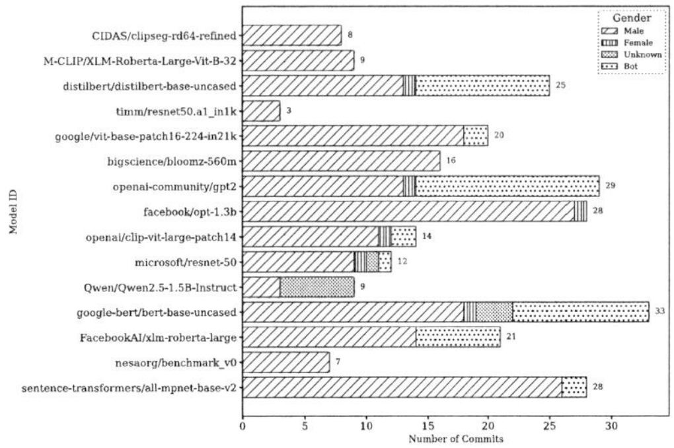

Figure 4. Number of Commits by Gender for the Top 15 Most Downloaded Models.

Qwen2.5-1.5B-Instruct, *bloomz-560m*, *vit-base-patch16-224-in21k* and *resnet50.a1-in1k* show no commits from female authors besides having women as members of the developing organization.

Finding 3.1. The gender distribution of committers does not always align with the gender composition of the developing organizations.
Finding 3.2. The most committers are men, with bots making more commits than women.

Despite the significant disparity in the quantity of contributions between men and women, we examined whether any differences could be observed in the nature of the commits rather than just their volume. By analyzing the commits' title, we categorized them into two main groups: commits related to ML model changes and those related to documentation. ML model updates such as fixing or adding variables, tokenizers, or weights were classified under the first group, while tasks such as creating and updating a README.md or a model card would be included in the second.

From a broader perspective, after conducting the Kruskal-Wallis test, we obtained a p-value of 0.008, which is smaller than the significance level of 0.05. Consequently, we rejected the null hypothesis and concluded that there are significant differences in the commit patterns across the different groups. These results are consistent with our earlier findings, where we observed that the number of commits made by men is significantly greater than those made by women or bots.

4.4. Comparison with top users outside HF organizations (RQ4)

To examine how the gender distribution in top organizations compares to that of individual contributors, we analyzed the *Top Contributors to Follow* [Valoatto]. This leaderboard, which ranks users based on metrics such as ML model downloads, dataset downloads, space likes, and profile followers, provides insight into individual developers. By focusing on ML model downloads, we applied the same approach used for organizations to study the distribution among top contributors. As shown in *Table* 5, the gender distribution among the top contributors closely resembles that of the leading organizations. While some differences exist, both groups follow a similar pattern in terms of representation across genders.

Finding 4. Gender distribution is similar across organizations and individual developers.

Table 5. Gender Distribution in Top 100 Contributors and Top 192 Organizations.

Category	Men	Women	Unknown
Top 100 Contributors	60.0%	9.0%	31.0%
Top 192 Organizations	58.0%	12.1%	29.9%

Lastly, the Chi-squared test yielded a p-value of 0.644, leading us to not reject the null hypothesis, indicating no significant differences in gender distributions. These results align with the earlier findings, as shown in *Table* 5.

5. Discussion

Our analysis shows that women are underrepresented in HF organizations. Contrary to what Vasilescu *et al*.stated in [Vasilescu et al. 2015], we found that an ML model success is not directly related to the gender diversity in it. However, we can agree with Imtiaz *et al*., whose findings in [Imtiaz et al. 2019] exhibit that "women focus their work in fewer projects". This observation does not necessarily reflect a barrier to participation in open-source coding and development. Open-source platforms inherently allow anyone to contribute regardless of organizational affiliation. Our study reveals that model popularity does not consistently correlate with organizational diversity, as many leading organizations lack female representation. Furthermore, the gender makeup of contributors often diverges from the organization's internal gender composition, indicating that external contributions may play a significant role in shaping widely adopted models. This means that while women may not be prominent in formal organizations, their contributions to the open-source ecosystem can still be significant and impactful.

However, understanding the true extent of this impact requires more than just counting commits. It is crucial to note that the quantity of commits cannot be assumed to be proportional to the quality or significance of the work performed. As we only have access to commit *titles* and *messages*, we cannot assure the actual impact of each contribution. Therefore, it would be unfair to infer that men's work is more relevant or substantial than women's based solely on commit counts. It would be valuable to develop measures that assess the relevance of a commit — such as its influence on project development, the number of dependencies affected, or the extent of community engagement it generates. Such an approach could provide deeper insights into the meaningful contributions of women in open source beyond sheer participation rates.

Interestingly, the patterns observed in HF organizations appear to mirror those seen in the broader context of software development. A similar lack of gender diversity is evident when examining the most recognized individual contributors on the platform. What is more, this is a general tendency in the SE field. Survey-method work done by Kohl and Prikladnicki in [Kohl and Prikladnicki 2024] [Damian et al. 2024] found that respondents answered "it is common to see only one woman in teams or just a few".

The nature of open-source coding has posed challenges in analyzing the relationship between team composition and ML model commits. The decentralized and collaborative nature of open-source projects has made it difficult to reliably relate contributions to specific individuals or teams. Consequently, our findings may lack the precision needed to draw definitive conclusions, and some of our results could be considered insignificant or unreliable due to these limitations.

6. Threats to Validity

In this section, we address potential threats to the study's validity, aiming to clarify the constraints and biases that could affect the interpretation of the findings.

Internal Validity: Since HF does not provide gender data, we relied on an LLM using names and locations to infer gender. To mitigate biases, we conducted a pilot and measured agreement using Cohen's Kappa. The results, however, indicate that this method cannot reliably replace human judgment, highlighting the need for human involvement to ensure accuracy in this context. Nevertheless, even though we classify some users as having an *unknown* gender due to insufficient information, if these users were indeed women, the proportions would still remain unbalanced. Additionally, analyzing contributions made by the same individual across multiple models has proven challenging. To address this, we aggregated all contributions by a user, regardless of their affiliation, ensuring a comprehensive perspective on their involvement across the platform.

External Validity: Our findings, based on HF organizations, may not fully generalize to all open-source ML communities or software ecosystems. However, by focusing on a prominent ML repository with a diverse range of organizations, our findings aim to be significant for the community. We analyzed the top 1,000 most downloaded models to assess whether model popularity is associated with gender diversity among contributors. However, the findings may not extend to less popular or niche models.

Construct Validity: Our study focuses on women's representation in HF organizations, using inferred gender data rather than self-reported identities, which may not fully capture non-binary contributors or broader diversity factors. As gender is not reported, we focus on women's roles, recognizing the existence of non-binary identities.

Conclusion Validity: Due to the absence of a gender field in HF, we inferred gender based on names and locations, considering regional variations. Despite potential variability, the study's conclusions are expected to remain reliable.

7. Conclusion and Future Work

Our study has revealed a significant gender imbalance within HF organizations, with women being notably underrepresented. However, no direct relationship was found between gender diversity in organizations and the popularity of the models they develop. Additionally, gender diversity was not present in the participation of committers, with men being the primary contributors. Despite this, no differences were observed in the quality or content of commits between men and women, indicating that women's contributions are not limited to specific tasks or roles. Their commits span a wide range of development activities, including core functionality, bug fixes, documentation, and feature enhancements. It is important to note that this analysis is based on commit titles and messages, which serve as the primary data for this study. Similar gender trends were observed among individual contributors, reflecting those in organizations. These findings highlight the need for greater gender inclusion in open-source communities, while also showing that gender does not influence the quality of contributions.

Future research could build upon this study by analyzing a broader range of models and organizations within HF. This would provide a wider and more representative view of gender diversity and contribution patterns. Moreover, integrating user feedback through surveys could shed light on the factors influencing contributors' decisions to engage in ML model development, helping to identify potential barriers or motivators for participation. Lastly, future studies could concentrate on evaluating the relevance and impact of commits by moving beyond surface-level attributes to gain deeper insights into their true contribution to ML model development and overall success. By doing so, we could be able to study different types of commits and committers, as in [Aguilera González et al. 2021].

8. Artifact availability

If wanted to reproduce the study, used codes and generated datasets can be found in this GitHub repository: https://github.com/GAISSA-UPC/HF_diversity.

Acknowledgment

This work has been funded by the Spanish research project GAISSA (TED2021-130923B-I00 by MCIN/ AEI/10.13039/501100011033).

References

Aguilera González, C., Albors Zumel, L., Antoñanzas Acero, J., Lenarduzzi, V., Martínez-Fernández, S., and Rabanaque Rodríguez, S. (2021). A preliminary investigation of developer profiles based on their activities and code quality: Who does what? In *2021 IEEE QRS*, pages 938–945.

American Psychological Association (2015). Key Terms and Concepts in Understanding Gender Diversity and Sexual Orientation Among Students.

Basili, V. R., Caldiera, G., and Rombach, H. D. (1994). The Goal Question Metric approach. *Encyclopedia of software engineering*, pages 528–532.

Castaño, J., Martínez-Fernández, S., Franch, X., and Bogner, J. (2024). Analyzing the Evolution and Maintenance of ML Models on Hugging Face. MSR '24, page 607–618.

Catolino, G., Palomba, F., Tamburri, D. A., Serebrenik, A., and Ferrucci, F. (2019). Gender Diversity and Women in Software Teams: How Do They Affect Community Smells? In *2019 IEEE/ACM ICSE-SEIS*, pages 11–20.

Cohen, J. (1960). A coefficient of agreement for nominal scales. *Educational and psychological measurement*, 20(1):37–46.

Damian, D., Blincoe, K., Ford, D., Serebrenik, A., and Masood, Z. (2024). *Equity, Diversity, and Inclusion in Software Engineering: Best Practices and Insights*. Springer.

De Martino, V., Castaño, J., Palomba, F., Franch, X., and Martínez-Fernández, S. (2025). A Framework for Using LLMs for Repository Mining Studies in Empirical Software Engineering. *WSESE@ICSE 2025*.

Gomathy, D. (2023). Workplace Diversity and its effects on team dynamics and productivity. *Intl journal of scientific research in engineering and management*, 7(06):1–8.

Hodges, M. and Murphy-Hill, E. (2024). Perceptions of Software Developer Inclusion: A Survey at Google. In Equity, Diversity, and Inclusion in Software Engineering: Best Practices and Insights (pp. 207-230).

Imtiaz, N., Middleton, J., Chakraborty, J., Robson, N., Bai, G., and Murphy-Hill, E. (2019). Investigating the Effects of Gender Bias on GitHub. In *2019 IEEE/ACM ICSE*, pages 700–711.

Kohl, K. and Prikladnicki, R. (2022). Benefits and Difficulties of Gender Diversity on Software Development Teams: A Qualitative Study. In SBES '22, 21–30.

Kohl, K. and Prikladnicki, R. (2024). Gender Diversity on Software Development Teams: A Qualitative Study. In Equity, Diversity, and Inclusion in Software Engineering: Best Practices and Insights (pp. 169-184). .

Krishnan and Gokula, D. S. (2020). Gender Diversity in the workplace and its effects on Employees' Performance. *Journal of the Social Sciences*.

Lanubile, F., Martínez-Fernández, S., and Quaranta, L. (2024). Training Future Machine Learning Engineers: A Project-Based Course on MLOps. *IEEE Software*, 41(2):60–67.

Palomba, F., Tamburri, D. A., Serebrenik, A., Zaidman, A., Fontana, F. A., and Oliveto, R. (May 2018). How do community smells influence code smells? *In ICSE 2018*, pages 240–241.

Phillips, K. and O'Reilly, C. (1998). *Demography and Diversity in Organizations: A Review of 40 Years of Research*, volume 20, pages 77–140.

Rastogi, A. (2024). Roads Ahead to Diversity and Inclusion by Software Engineering. In Equity, Diversity, and Inclusion in Software Engineering: Best Practices and Insights (pp. 3-16).

Serebrenik, A. (2024). How to Ask About Gender Identity of Software Engineers and "Guess" It from the Archival Data. In Equity, Diversity, and Inclusion in Software Engineering: Best Practices and Insights (pp. 487-505).

Stack-Overflow (2022). Stack Overflow Developer Survey. `https://survey.stackoverflow.co/2022/#developer-profile-demographics`.

Storey, M.-A., Ernst, N. A., Williams, C., and Kalliamvakou, E. (2020). The who, what, how of software engineering research: a socio-technical framework. *Empirical Software Engineering*, 25:4097–4129.

Valoatto, M. Top Contributors To Follow - a Hugging Face Space by mvaloatto — huggingface.co. `https://huggingface.co/spaces/mvaloatto/TCTF`. [Accessed 30-01-2025].

Vasilescu, B., Posnett, D., Ray, B., van den Brand, M. G., Serebrenik, A., Devanbu, P., and Filkov, V. (2015). Gender and Tenure Diversity in GitHub Teams. CHI '15, page 3789–3798.

Williams, J. C. and Dempsey, R. (2014). What works for women at work: Four patterns working women need to know. In *What Works for Women at Work*. New York University Press.

Generación de Pruebas Unitarias con LLMs en Entornos Industriales: Desafíos, Evolución y Lecciones Prácticas

Eneko Pizarro[1], Maider Azanza[2], Beatriz Pérez Lamancha[1]

[1]LKS Next
Goiru, 7
Arrasate-Mondragón, España

[2]Universidad del País Vasco (EHU/UPV)
Facultad de Informática
Donostia-San Sebastian, España

{epizarro,bperez}@lksnext.com, maider.azanza@ehu.eus

Abstract. *Large Language Models (LLMs) show potential for automatically generating unit tests, but their industrial application presents challenges. We present a longitudinal case study on the implementation and evaluation of LLMs for test generation at LKS Next, integrating standard tools such as SonarQube. Our approach reveals findings on the temporal evolution of these technologies in production environments and provides learned lessons. The results offer evidence-based industrial guidance for organizations considering adopting these solutions, highlighting practical integration and maintainability considerations often absent in theoretical studies.*

Resumen. *Los Modelos de Lenguaje de Gran Escala (LLMs) muestran potencial para generar pruebas unitarias automáticamente, pero su aplicación industrial genera desafíos. Presentamos un caso de estudio longitudinal sobre la implementación y evaluación de LLMs para generación de pruebas en la empresa LKS Next, integrando herramientas estándar como SonarQube. Nuestro enfoque revela hallazgos sobre la evolución temporal de estas tecnologías en entornos de producción y proporciona lecciones aprendidas. Los resultados ofrecen una guía industrial basada en evidencia para organizaciones que consideran adoptar estas soluciones, destacando consideraciones prácticas de integración y mantenibilidad a menudo ausentes en estudios teóricos.*

1. Introducción

Las pruebas unitarias continúan siendo un aspecto crítico y a la vez costoso en recursos dentro del desarrollo de software. Las prácticas modernas de desarrollo como DevSecOps [Prates and Pereira 2025] demandan tanto velocidad como fiabilidad en la entrega continua del software. Esto implica contar con un conjunto completo de pruebas unitarias que asegure la calidad del código. Sin embargo, estudios recientes revelan que la escritura de pruebas unitarias es una de las tareas que los desarrolladores disfrutan menos y que preferirían delegar a la inteligencia artificial [Sergeyuk et al. 2025], siendo además un proceso costoso para la organización.

Debido a esto, con la emergencia de la *Inteligencia Artificial Generativa (IAGen)* o, más concretamente *Modelos de Lenguaje de Gran Escala (LLMs por sus siglas en inglés)*, las empresas están explorando su potencial para automatizar la generación de pruebas unitarias y reducir la carga de trabajo de los desarrolladores. Si bien investigaciones recientes han estudiado extensamente las capacidades de generación de pruebas mediante LLMs [Wang et al. 2024b], su adopción industrial genera desafíos que van más allá de los abordados en estudios académicos.

Un reto clave para las empresas que adoptan estas herramientas radica en su rápida evolución: lo que era cierto sobre las capacidades de una herramienta hace seis meses puede no reflejar su rendimiento actual. Esto es particularmente desafiante para organizaciones que implementan *pipelines* de integración/entrega continua *(CI/CD)*, donde la generación de pruebas unitarias debe integrarse perfectamente con los flujos de trabajo existentes y mantener estándares de calidad consistentes, sin estar a expensas de la evolución de las capacidades de los LLM subyacentes.

Este trabajo presenta un marco práctico para la evaluación continua de generadores de pruebas unitarias basados en LLMs en entornos industriales, ilustrado mediante un estudio longitudinal de las capacidades de GitHub Copilot en LKS Next.

Las contribuciones principales de este trabajo son:

1. Un marco práctico de medición aplicado en un entorno industrial para la evaluación continua de LLMs en la generación de pruebas unitarias.
2. Un análisis longitudinal que muestra la evolución temporal de las capacidades de los LLMs en la generación de pruebas en un contexto productivo.
3. Lecciones aprendidas para otras organizaciones que estén considerando la adopción de los LLMs para la automatización de pruebas unitarias.

2. Motivación: el Caso de LKS Next

LKS Next[1], la organización donde se realiza esta investigación, es una empresa de consultoría tecnológica que ofrece soluciones personalizadas utilizando diversas tecnologías y lenguajes de programación. La empresa sigue metodologías ágiles y prácticas DevSecOps [Prates and Pereira 2025] para desarrollar software seguro y de alta calidad que sea mantenible durante todo su ciclo de vida. En este contexto, las pruebas representan un desafío crítico. La empresa debe generar suficientes pruebas para garantizar la calidad de sus proyectos, equilibrando la rigurosidad con la eficiencia en costos y tiempo, para optimizar su salida al mercado.

Las pruebas automatizadas en entornos DevSecOps proporcionan ventajas estratégicas y operativas significativas, garantizando la verificación consistente y repetible de la funcionalidad del software. Este enfoque sistemático minimiza los tiempos de ejecución, mide la cobertura de código y facilita la integración continua, proporcionando retroalimentación inmediata sobre los cambios. La infraestructura DevSecOps utiliza en los proyectos de la empresa, ejecuta automáticamente con cada *commit* una serie de pasos (*pipeline de desarrollo*) que incluyen: compilación, ejecución de pruebas unitarias y de integración, análisis de la calidad y seguridad del código y verificación de la seguridad de sus dependencias. A continuación, se despliega la nueva versión al entorno correspondiente (desarrollo, pruebas, etc.).

[1]`https://www.lksnext.com/es/`

La irrupción de herramientas de IA, particularmente los LLM, promete soluciones que parecen mejorar mucho la productividad en todas las áreas del desarrollo del software, incluyendo el testing. Las empresas sienten la presión de adoptar herramientas de IA generativa en los desarrollos, pero requieren garantías de sus resultados antes de utilizarlas en entornos productivos. Hasta ahora, el código generado por la IA requería una revisión y modificación significativas para cumplir con los estándares de la organización, pero esto ha ido cambiando a medida que aparecen nuevas herramientas o nuevas versiones de las mismas.

A esto se suma la proliferación de herramientas de IA generativa, que implica decidir qué herramienta es la más adecuada. El modelo de pago por token introduce costes variables que escalan con el uso, por lo que las organizaciones deben equilibrar productividad, los gastos en IA y la confiabilidad en la solución resultante. Es por ello que las empresas requieren mecanismos para validar y revisar el código generado por IA. En el caso del presente trabajo, el objetivo es la generación de pruebas unitarias, ya que juegan un papel crucial en los procesos DevSecOps.

Establecer un marco de referencia para poder comparar los LLMs y sus versiones en el tiempo resulta crucial para las empresas. Este marco de referencia debe tener en cuenta las técnicas de generación de casos de prueba, tanto estructurales como basadas en conocimiento de expertos, midiendo la cobertura de las pruebas generadas, el grado de parametrización y el grado de aislamiento de las pruebas unitarias mediante técnicas de dobles de pruebas (*mocks*).

Para abordar estos desafíos en un contexto industrial real, desarrollamos y aplicamos un marco sistemático de evaluación que presentamos a continuación.

3. Estructura del Marco: Métricas y Categorías de Evaluación

El acelerado desarrollo de las capacidades de los LLMs requiere un marco sólido, reproducible y longitudinal para evaluar la calidad de las pruebas generadas. Nuestro enfoque responde a los desafíos específicos de las pruebas generadas por inteligencia artificial a través de un sistema de evaluación que prioriza la reproducibilidad, la integración con herramientas industriales estándar y facilita la evaluación continua a lo largo del tiempo.

Para analizar la capacidad de los LLMs en la generación de pruebas unitarias, hemos desarrollado un conjunto de métricas organizadas en tres categorías: (1) métricas de calidad de código, (2) métricas estructurales y (3) métricas basadas en el conocimiento de expertos. Estas métricas se integran mediante un modelo de ponderación que permite calcular una valoración cuantitativa para cada LLM, facilitando la comparación objetiva entre diferentes modelos y sus versiones a lo largo del tiempo.

3.1. Métricas de Calidad de Código

Las métricas de calidad del código se centran en dos aspectos: la compilación y el análisis estático de las pruebas **IAGen**. La compilación representa el nivel más básico de evaluación y, aunque seguramente se elimine del marco de evaluación en el futuro dada la mejora en las pruebas IAGen (véase el apartado *Resultados*), resulta relevante ya que nos permite apreciar el progreso que los distintos LLM han tenido a lo largo de la toma de las mediciones. En nuestras pruebas iniciales observamos que los LLM introducían frecuen-

Tabla 1. Métricas de calidad de código

Métrica	Definición	Medición
Incidencias de compilación	Mide problemas en el uso de bibliotecas externas y declaraciones de importación, uso incorrecto de elementos específicos del proyecto (clases, métodos, constructores), problemas de corrección sintáctica y estructural básica del código de prueba generado y cantidad de errores de compilación encontrados en las pruebas IAGen.	Cantidad de errores de compilación encontrados en las pruebas IAGen
Incidencias de análisis estático de código	Mide incidencias encontradas con la herramienta Sonarqube, siguiendo el perfil SonarWay [Campbell and Papapetrou 2013]. Calcula la mantenibilidad, confiabilidad y seguridad del código de las pruebas IAGen.	Cantidad de incidencias encontradas en el análisis de código estático de las pruebas IAGen

temente fallos de compilación en las clases de las pruebas, evitando poder tomar métricas de ejecución.

Por otro lado, es importante evaluar la calidad del código generado, para lo cual utilizamos la herramienta de análisis estático de código Sonarqube[2], que proporciona reglas específicas para analizar la mantenibilidad, confiabilidad y seguridad del código generado. Herramientas como Sonarqube son especialmente importantes en entornos industriales, ya que permiten hacer un seguimiento de la calidad del código previo a la puesta en producción como parte integral de los desarrollos DevSecOps.

La Tabla 1 describe las métricas *incidencias de compilación* e *incidencias de análisis estático de código* y cómo se miden. Consideramos que esta categoría de métricas es objetiva, ya que los resultados serán los mismos, sin depender de un juicio experto que los valide. Además, consideramos que las métricas en esta categoría penalizan al resultado final del LLM siendo evaluado, ya que a mayor cantidad de errores de compilación o mayor cantidad de incidencias de calidad de código, peores son las pruebas IAGen.

3.2. Métricas Estructurales

Las métricas estructurales evalúan el grado en que las pruebas IAGen ejercitan el código bajo prueba. Estas métricas miden aspectos de cobertura del código siguiendo distintas técnicas. Además, hemos incorporado una métrica para determinar el grado de aislamiento en pruebas unitarias que alcanzan las pruebas IAGen.

La Tabla 2 muestra las cuatro métricas que utilizamos en este apartado. Las tres primeras tienen que ver con la cobertura de código, partiendo de la más simple, la *cobertura de líneas*, que indica las líneas de código que han sido ejecutadas con las pruebas IAGen. Este criterio es necesario pero no suficiente, por lo que además hemos incluido la *cobertura de condiciones*, donde se evalúa que cada condición haya sido evaluada como verdadera y falsa. Un criterio aún más restrictivo es el de *cobertura de condición/decisión*, donde se pide que todas las decisiones dentro de una condición sean probadas al ejecutar las pruebas [H. Washizaki 2024].

[2] `https://www.sonarsource.com/products/sonarqube`

Tabla 2. Métricas estructurales

Métrica	Definición	Medición
Cobertura de líneas	Porcentaje de líneas de código que se han ejecutado con las pruebas IAGen [ISO 2021]	(Cantidad de líneas ejecutadas por los test IAGen / Total de líneas ejecutables) × 100
Cobertura de condiciones	Pocentaje de condiciones que se han ejecutado con las pruebas IAGen. Prueba que cada condición del código sea ejecutada al menos una vez [ISO 2021]	(Cantidad de condiciones evaluadas por las pruebas IAGen/ Total de condiciones) × 100
Cobertura de condicion/decisión	Pocentaje de condiciones y decisiones que se han ejecutado con las pruebas IAGen. Prueba cada decisión dentro de una condición. [ISO 2021]	(Cantidad de condiciones y decisiones ejecutadas por las pruebas IAGen / Total de condiciones y decisiones) × 100
Aislamiento de las pruebas	Evalúa cuan bien las pruebas IAGen crean objetos simulados (mocks, stubs, etc.) que al ejecutarse cuenten con todo lo que necesita de su entorno. [Freeman et al. 2004]	(Cantidad de pruebas IAGen aisladas / Cantidad de pruebas aisladas que se esperaban) × 100

Para la evaluación de estas métricas de cobertura, existen herramientas que facilitan su cómputo automático. En nuestro caso, para el lenguaje Java, hemos empleado Jacoco [3], que proporciona reportes detallados sobre la cobertura alcanzada por las pruebas IAGen en cada una de estas dimensiones.

Además de la cobertura, es esencial considerar el aislamiento en las pruebas unitarias. Por definición, estas se centran en probar clases individuales y garantizar su correcto funcionamiento, controlando todos los aspectos del contexto en el cual la clase bajo prueba es ejecutada. Para lograr este aislamiento, se reemplazan los colaboradores reales por dobles de pruebas ("test doubles"), implementaciones simuladas que separan el código bajo prueba de dependencias externas como capas de servicios, sistemas y recursos [Kaczanowski 2013].

En este contexto, hemos definido la métrica *Aislamiento de las pruebas* para evaluar si las pruebas IAGen manejan apropiadamente estas dependencias, aislando el código de distracciones introducidas por servicios web, sistemas de archivos, bases de datos o software de terceros, mientras validan que el código aislado funciona según lo esperado. Esta métrica también tiene carácter objetivo, puesto que las pruebas unitarias sin un aislamiento adecuado no podrán ejecutarse correctamente en entornos de integración continua, donde frecuentemente no se dispone del entorno completo de ejecución.

3.3. Métricas Basadas en el Conocimiento de Expertos

Estas métricas se fundamentan en los requisitos y especificaciones del sistema, utilizando técnicas de caja negra. Su objetivo principal es determinar en qué medida las pruebas IAGen consideran los aspectos funcionales del código bajo prueba. A diferencia de las categorías anteriores, que se basan en criterios objetivos, la categoría de *métricas basadas en el conocimiento de expertos* incorpora elementos subjetivos que requieren validación especializada.

[3]https://github.com/jacoco/jacoco

Tabla 3. Métricas basadas en el conocimiento de expertos

Métrica	Definición	Medición
Cobertura de Partición de Equivalencia	Una clase de equivalencia es un subconjunto de los datos que se consideran iguales por el sistema bajo prueba [ISO 2021]. Evalúa qué porcentaje de la clases de equivalencia identificadas por expertos han sido cubiertas por las pruebas IAGen	(Cantidad de particiones de equivalencia identificadas por las pruebas IAGen / Total de clases de equivalencia identificadas por expertos)x100
Cobertura de Valores Límites	El análisis de valor límite se centra en los límites de las clases de equivalencia. Se prueban valores por debajo y por encima de dichos límites [ISO 2021]. Evalúa qué porcentaje de los valores límites identificados por expertos han sido cubiertos por las pruebas IAGen	(Cantidad de valores límites encontrados por las pruebas IAGen / Total de valores límites identificados por expertos) × 100
Parametrización de las pruebas	La parametrización de las pruebas unitarias y de integración permite reutilizar pruebas con distintos conjuntos de datos [Tillmann and Schulte 2005]. Evalúa que porcentaje de parametrizaciones han sido realizadas correctamente por las pruebas IAGen	(Cantidad de prueba IAGen que se han parametrizado correctamente / Cantidad de pruebas que se esperaba parametrizar) × 100
Cobertura de Pruebas de Referencia	Porcentaje de pruebas unitarias generadas por IAGen que replican pruebas manuales de expertos, las cuales cumplen con los estándares mínimos de calidad de la empresa. Evalúa la capacidad del LLM para igualar el enfoque y rigor de desarrolladores en un entorno industrial.	(Cantidad de pruebas replicadas por la IA Gen / Cantidad de pruebas manuales generadas por expertos) x 100

Para establecer una base de comparación o *ground truth*, hemos desarrollado pruebas manuales de referencia por cada caso analizado, avaladas por expertos de la empresa. Este enfoque nos permite contrastar las pruebas generadas por IAGen con aquellas que se obtendrían mediante un desarrollo manual en el mismo entorno empresarial. Si bien estas métricas incluyen juicios subjetivos utilizando técnicas de caja negra—que pueden considerar distintos valores de prueba según el criterio del tester—ofrecen una perspectiva valiosa sobre la calidad práctica de las pruebas automatizadas.

La Tabla 3 describe las métricas que utilizamos en este apartado. La técnica de *Partición de Equivalencia* divide los datos de entrada en clases que el sistema bajo prueba procesa de la misma manera. Complementariamente, la técnica de *Análisis de Valores Límites* se centra en examinar los bordes de estas clases de equivalencia, evaluando valores cercanos a los límites donde suelen ocurrir más errores [ISO 2021]. La efectividad de ambas técnicas depende fundamentalmente de la correcta identificación de las clases de equivalencia, tarea que requiere el juicio experto de profesionales en pruebas.

Particularmente importante en entornos industriales resulta la *Parametrización de las pruebas*, que permite reutilizar las pruebas con diferentes conjuntos de datos para verificar su funcionamiento bajo diversas condiciones. Las pruebas unitarias parametrizadas mejoran la reutilización, mantenibilidad y documentación del proceso de pruebas [Tillmann and Schulte 2005], aspectos cruciales para la sostenibilidad a largo plazo de los juegos de pruebas.

	Categoría	Métrica Final para valorar el LLM	Peso	Fórmula para evaluar cada ejemplo del LLM	Valoración del LLM
Métricas Objetivas	Métricas de calidad de código	Total de Incidencias de compilación (IC)*	-20%	IC para el LLM = ∑(IC para cada ejemplo del LLM)	Valoración IC para el LLM = -(IC para el LLM / MAXIMO(IC para todos los LLMs))x20%
		Total de Incidencia de Análisis de Código (IAC)*	-5%	IAC para el LLM = ∑(IAC para cada ejemplo del LLM)	Valoración IAC para el LLM = -(IAC para el LLM / MAXIMO(IAC para todos los LLMs))x5%
	Métricas Estructurales	Cobertura de Líneas (CL)	50%	CL para el LLM = ∑(CL para cada ejemplo del LLM) / Total de ejemplos	Valoración de Métricas Estructurales para el LLM = PROMEDIO(CL para el LLM, CC para el LLM, CCD para el LLM, AP para el LLM)x50%
		Cobertura de Condiciones (CC)		CC para el LLM = ∑(CC para cada ejemplo del LLM) / Total de ejemplos	
		Cobertura de Condicion/ Decisión (CCD)		CCD para el LLM = ∑(CCD para cada ejemplo del LLM) / Total de ejemplos	
		Aislamiento de las Pruebas (AP)		AP para el LLM = ∑(AP para cada ejemplo del LLM) / Total de ejemplos	
Métricas subjetivas (Juicio de expertos)	Métricas basadas en el conocimiento de expertos	Cobertura de Partición de Equivalencia (CPE)	50%	CPE para el LLM = ∑(CPE para cada ejemplo del LLM) / Total de ejemplos	Valoración de Métricas basadas en la Especificación para el LLM = PROMEDIO(CPE para el LLM, CVL para el LLM, PP para el LLM, CPR para el LLM)x50%
		Cobertura de Valores Límites (CVL)		CVL para el LLM = ∑(CVL para cada ejemplo del LLM) / Total de ejemplos	
		Prametrización de las pruebas (PP)		PP para el LLM = ∑(PP para cada ejemplo del LLM) / Total de ejemplos	
		Cobertura de Pruebas de Referencia (CPR)		CPR para el LLM = ∑(CPR para cada ejemplo del LLM) / Total de ejemplos	

Figura 1. Modelo de ponderación para valorar cada LLM

Finalmente, la *Cobertura de Pruebas de Referencia* establece una comparación directa entre las pruebas generadas automáticamente y aquellas desarrolladas manualmente por los expertos, las cuales cumplen con los estándares mínimos de calidad establecidos por la empresa. Esta métrica evalúa la capacidad del LLM para replicar patrones, escenarios y enfoques considerados fundamentales por desarrolladores experimentados en un entorno industrial. Además, permite identificar discrepancias entre los enfoques automatizados y manuales [Kracht et al. 2014], señalando posibles áreas de mejora en la generación de pruebas mediante LLM.

3.4. Modelo de Ponderación de Métricas de Prueba

Para evaluar de manera integral la calidad de las pruebas generadas por LLMs, hemos desarrollado un modelo de ponderación que combina las métricas previamente descritas en una valoración cuantitativa consolidada. Este modelo equilibra factores objetivos y subjetivos, permitiendo comparaciones sistemáticas entre diferentes modelos LLM y sus evoluciones temporales.

El modelo estructura las métricas en las tres categorías fundamentales ya presentadas:

- *Métricas de calidad de código*: Evalúan aspectos técnicos básicos como la compilabilidad y la calidad estructural del código generado.
- *Métricas estructurales*: Miden la efectividad de las pruebas para ejercitar el código bajo análisis y su capacidad de aislamiento.
- *Métricas basadas en el conocimiento de expertos*: Valoran aspectos funcionales y de diseño que requieren juicio especializado.

Para reflejar tanto criterios objetivos como subjetivos, asignamos una ponderación equitativa del 50 % a las métricas objetivas (combinando calidad de código y estructurales) y 50 % a las métricas subjetivas (basadas en conocimiento experto). Esta distribución equilibrada reconoce la importancia complementaria de ambas dimensiones en la evaluación de pruebas unitarias en entornos industriales.

Un aspecto distintivo de nuestro modelo es el tratamiento de las *Métricas de calidad de código* como factores de penalización. Dado que los errores de compilación imposibilitan la ejecución de pruebas, la métrica *incidencias de compilación* reduce un 20 % del puntaje total. Similarmente, la métrica *incidencias del análisis estático de código* penaliza un 5 % adicional, reflejando su impacto en la mantenibilidad a largo plazo.

La Figura 1 muestra el modelo completo con las ponderaciones asignadas a cada métrica y las fórmulas utilizadas para los cálculos. Para las métricas de penalización (IC e IAC), se realiza la sumatoria de incidencias detectadas en todos los ejemplos evaluados. Para las demás métricas, se calcula la puntuación promedio de los valores obtenidos en los ejemplos.

Es importante destacar que los pesos específicos reflejan las prioridades de LKS Next, y el marco está diseñado para ser adaptable. Otras empresas pueden ajustar estas ponderaciones según sus propios criterios de calidad y objetivos estratégicos, manteniendo la estructura general del modelo como base para evaluaciones comparativas coherentes.

4. Aplicación Práctica: Procedimiento y Herramientas

Para abordar los desafíos de evaluación de pruebas unitarias generadas por LLMs en un contexto industrial real, hemos definido una metodología sistemática que permite tanto la evaluación objetiva como la mejora progresiva de los resultados. Nuestro enfoque se caracteriza por su naturaleza iterativa, su integración con herramientas industriales estándar y su capacidad para adaptarse a la rápida evolución de las capacidades de los LLMs. A continuación, detallamos este proceso, comenzando por la estructura general del flujo de trabajo de evaluación.

4.1. Proceso y Entorno Iterativo de Evaluación

El proceso inicia con una fase de preparación donde configuramos el entorno de desarrollo, establecemos las dependencias y herramientas de compilación e implementamos la infraestructura de recopilación de datos para el seguimiento de métricas.

Un componente crucial de esta fase preparatoria es el desarrollo de pruebas de referencia por parte de expertos. Estas pruebas sirven como estándar de comparación (*ground truth*) y se crean siguiendo las mejores prácticas de la organización, como se ha detallado en secciones anteriores.

Una vez completada la preparación, iniciamos un ciclo iterativo estructurado que consta de cuatro pasos principales:

1. **Generación de Pruebas:** Utilizamos el LLM con el prompt actual (inicial o refinado) para generar pruebas unitarias para el código objetivo.
2. **Análisis Multidimensional:** Evaluamos las pruebas generadas mediante todas las métricas definidas en nuestro marco, contrastándolas directamente con las pruebas de referencia para las métricas basadas en conocimiento experto.
3. **Identificación de Deficiencias:** Determinamos qué aspectos específicos de las pruebas generadas difieren de las pruebas de referencia, como la falta de cobertura en ciertas condiciones, la ausencia de particiones de equivalencia relevantes, o deficiencias en el aislamiento.

4. **Refinamiento del Prompt:** Modificamos el prompt para abordar explícitamente las deficiencias identificadas. Por ejemplo, si las pruebas de referencia utilizan dobles de prueba para aislar componentes externos mientras las pruebas IAGen no lo hacen, refinamos el prompt para enfatizar esta técnica.

Este ciclo se repite hasta que: (1) las pruebas generadas se aproximan suficientemente a la calidad de las pruebas de referencia según nuestro modelo de ponderación, o (2) se alcanza un punto donde refinamientos adicionales no producen mejoras significativas.

Las pruebas de referencia cumplen así una doble función: como parámetro de evaluación contra el cual se mide el rendimiento de las pruebas generadas, y como guía para el refinamiento específico de los prompts. Esta estrategia nos permite abordar sistemáticamente las brechas de calidad y mejorar progresivamente la capacidad de los LLMs para generar pruebas que sean aplicables en entornos industriales.

4.2. Selección de Ejemplos a Probar y Pruebas de Referencia

Para garantizar una evaluación robusta y significativa, hemos aplicado criterios específicos en la selección de los ejemplos de prueba. Primero, seleccionamos código que no contara con pruebas preexistentes, ya que nuestras evaluaciones exploratorias iniciales revelaron un fenómeno de "fuga de datos"(*data leakage*) donde los LLMs, al estar entrenados con repositorios públicos, reproducían pruebas existentes en lugar de generar nuevas [López et al. 2025, Wu et al. 2024]. Esto habría distorsionado nuestra evaluación, ofreciendo una visión artificialmente optimista de sus capacidades reales.

Adicionalmente, dado que nuestro estudio se centra en la aplicación industrial práctica, priorizamos funciones y clases representativas de escenarios reales de desarrollo corporativo. Estos ejemplos debían reflejar patrones comunes y desafíos habituales encontrados en proyectos empresariales, asegurando así la relevancia de nuestros hallazgos.

Considerando estos requisitos y las limitaciones prácticas asociadas a la evaluación experta manual, seleccionamos siete funciones que representan diversos desafíos de prueba frecuentes en entornos industriales:

- **Ensamblador de Alquileres** (`assemble`): Método complejo que involucra múltiples objetos de dominio y requiere simulación (mocking) de bases de datos.
- **Comprobador de Números Primos** (`isPrime`): Función con alta complejidad ciclomática y manejo de excepciones.
- **Gestión de Usuarios** (`addUser`): Manejo de condiciones nulas (null) y simulación de acceso a bases de datos.
- **Calculadora de Bonificaciones** (`getBonus`): Lógica condicional compleja con dependencias externas.
- **Validador de IPV4** (`isIPV4Valid`): Requiere pruebas de integración mediante funciones auxiliares.
- **Número Estrobogramático** (`isStrobogrammic`): Manipulación de estructuras de datos.
- **Detector de Palíndromos** (`palindrome`): Integración de múltiples funciones.

Para cada una de estas funciones, expertos en pruebas de la empresa desarrollaron pruebas de referencia siguiendo las mejores prácticas y estándares de calidad establecidos.

Estas pruebas de referencia constituyeron nuestro *ground truth* contra el cual evaluamos las pruebas generadas por los LLMs.

4.3. Metodología de Ingeniería del Prompt

Nuestro enfoque de ingeniería de prompts se fundamenta en una estrategia de Prompt Chaining [Wu et al. 2022], diseñada para guiar a los LLMs en la generación de pruebas unitarias que cumplan con los estándares de calidad industrial. Esta técnica divide el proceso de generación en componentes secuenciales que abordan diferentes aspectos de las pruebas, permitiendo un control más preciso sobre los resultados. El desarrollo del prompt siguió un proceso iterativo alineado con nuestro marco de evaluación, refinándolo progresivamente según los hallazgos cuantitativos de cada iteración. Nuestro análisis reveló que el uso del inglés mejoraba significativamente los resultados en comparación con el español, lo que es consistente con otros estudios sobre el impacto del idioma en la generación de código mediante LLMs [Jiang et al. 2024, Wang et al. 2024a]. El prompt final optimizado, disponible en nuestro paquete de replicación, se estructura en cuatro componentes principales:

1. **Calidad de código y análisis estático:** Instrucciones específicas para evitar incidencias detectables por SonarQube, incluyendo directivas como: *"When creating the test class, do not generate any line of code that could create any Issue, nor Bug nor Code Smell."*
2. **Cobertura estructural:** Requisitos explícitos para maximizar la cobertura, por ejemplo: *"You must use the White Box method using Condition/Decision coverage, so use the truth tables to cover all the cases of the composed condition statements"* y *Ïneed a 100 % of line, condition and condition/decision coverage."*
3. **Técnicas de caja negra:** Instrucciones para implementar partición de equivalencias y análisis de valores límite: *"You must do the Black Box testing using equivalence partitioning and boundary value analysis. If you find redundancy with any of the other methods, remove the redundant tests."*
4. **Buenas prácticas de ingeniería de pruebas:** Directrices sobre estructura, nomenclatura y técnicas de refactorización: *Üse proper naming conventions for the tests and structure them correctly. If there is repeated code you must use @BeforeAll, @BeforeEach @AfterAll and @AfterEach statements."*

Este enfoque estructurado nos permitió mejorar progresivamente la calidad de las pruebas generadas, abordando sistemáticamente las debilidades identificadas en cada iteración del proceso evaluativo.

4.4. Infraestructura y Herramientas

Nuestro marco de evaluación emplea herramientas estándar de la industria para garantizar la robustez y reproducibilidad del análisis. Para la ejecución y parametrización de pruebas utilizamos JUnit, mientras que el análisis estático se realiza mediante Sonarqube Cloud y Sonarqube IDE, herramientas que proporcionan las métricas de calidad del código. La cobertura se analiza con JaCoCo, que ofrece informes detallados sobre líneas, condiciones y decisiones ejecutadas. Todo el proceso se integra en un flujo de trabajo automatizado utilizando GitHub y GitHub Actions como plataformas de control de versiones y CI/CD, respectivamente. La gestión de dependencias se centraliza mediante Maven, asegurando así la reproducibilidad de las compilaciones y la coherencia en las versiones de las herramientas a lo largo de todas las evaluaciones. Esta infraestructura, además de facilitar la evaluación sistemática, refleja el entorno real de desarrollo industrial, aumentando la validez externa de nuestros resultados.

5. Resultados

Nuestro análisis abarca la evolución de GitHub Copilot entre marzo y diciembre de 2024, ofreciendo una perspectiva longitudinal sobre cómo esta herramienta de generación automatizada ha mejorado sus capacidades para crear pruebas unitarias en entornos industriales.

	Categoria	Nombre de Métrica	Peso	ChatGPT-4-1º Vez (Marzo 2024)	ChatGPT-4 - Iterativo (Mayo 2024)	o1-Mini (Dic. 2024)	GPT-o (Dic. 2024)	o1-Preview (Dic. 2024)
Métricas Objectivas	Métricas de Calidad de Código	Total de Incidencias de Compilación (IC)*	-20%	31	3	7	2	0
		Total de Incidencia de Análisis de Código (IAC)*	-5%	45	18	10	29	15
	Métricas Estructurales	Cobertura de Líneas (CL)	50%	39,14%	65,57%	28,57%	70,14%	98,00%
		Cobertura de Condiciones (CC)		39,14%	65,57%	28,57%	71,29%	95,71%
		Cobertura de Condicion/Decisión (CCD)		36,57%	61,57%	28,57%	68,29%	95,71%
		Aislamineto de las Pruebas (AP)		85,71%	100,00%	100,00%	100,00%	100,00%
Métricas Subjetivas (Juicio de Expertos)	Métricas Basadas en el Conocimiento de Expertos	Cobertura de Partición de Equivalencia (CPE)	50%	71,19%	75,00%	85,12%	79,88%	84,52%
		Cobertura de Valores Límite (CVL)		69,39%	71,77%	83,57%	78,20%	81,53%
		Parametrización de las Pruebas (PP)		12,70%	38,89%	88,10%	83,81%	91,84%
		Cobertura de Pruebas de Referencia (CPR)		65,77%	75,36%	81,57%	66,23%	97,94%
		Evaluación del Peso Total		27,45%	65,28%	59,88%	72,72%	91,49%

*Errores de compilacion sobre el valor maximo de las iteraciones

Figura 2. Resumen de los resultados obtenidos (marzo 2024 - diciembre 2024)

La Figura 2 presenta un resumen completo de los resultados obtenidos. Es importante destacar que GitHub Copilot ha ido evolucionando en el periodo analizado, incorporando diferentes modelos LLM subyacentes. En nuestra primera evaluación (marzo 2024), Copilot utilizaba ChatGPT-4 como modelo base. En evaluaciones posteriores, Copilot incorporó nuevos modelos como GPT-4-turbo (mayo 2024), o1-Mini (octubre 2024), GPT-o y o1-Preview (diciembre 2024), lo que nos ha permitido observar cómo la herramienta ha mejorado sus capacidades a medida que integra modelos más avanzados.

Respecto a las métricas de calidad de código, observamos una mejora notable y consistente. El total de incidencias de compilación muestra una clara tendencia descendente, comenzando con 31 incidencias en la primera evaluación con ChatGPT-4 (marzo 2024) y reduciéndose a 0 con o1-Preview (diciembre 2024). De manera similar, las incidencias de análisis de código disminuyeron desde 45 hasta 15 en la configuración más reciente, evidenciando una mejora sustancial en la calidad estructural del código generado.

En el ámbito de las métricas estructurales, los avances son igualmente significativos. La cobertura de líneas aumentó desde un modesto 39,14 % inicial hasta un notable 98 % con o1-Preview. La cobertura de condiciones y la cobertura de condición/decisión siguieron una progresión similar, alcanzando ambas un 95,71 % en la configuración más reciente. Particularmente destacable es el aislamiento de las pruebas, que alcanzó y mantuvo un rendimiento óptimo del 100 % en las tres últimas evaluaciones.

Las métricas basadas en conocimiento de expertos también reflejan mejoras sustanciales. La cobertura de partición de equivalencia mejoró desde un 71,19 % hasta alcanzar un 84,52 % con o1-Preview. Especialmente notable es el progreso en la parametrización de las pruebas, que evolucionó desde un modesto 12,70 % hasta un sobresaliente 91,84 %. La cobertura de valores límite y la cobertura de pruebas de referencia también experimentaron mejoras significativas, alcanzando 81,53 % y 97,94 % respectivamente en la configuración más reciente.

La evaluación del peso total, calculada según nuestro modelo de ponderación, refleja esta tendencia positiva, evolucionando desde un 27,45 % inicial hasta un 91,49 % con o1-Preview. Esta progresión evidencia cómo GitHub Copilot ha mejorado consistentemente su capacidad para generar pruebas de calidad industrial a medida que integra modelos LLM más avanzados..

6. Lecciones Aprendidas

Este trabajo nos ha permitido extraer lecciones aprendidas que son susceptibles de ser generalizadas a otras organizaciones. En primer lugar, el marco ha tenido un impacto directo en la toma de decisiones de la organización. En marzo de 2024, cuando GitHub Copilot generaba pruebas que apenas compilaban y requerían considerable intervención manual, la inversión en esta tecnología probablemente hubiera aumentado el esfuerzo de pruebas en lugar de reducirlo. Sin embargo, las mejoras observadas en diciembre de 2024 (ver sección anterior) han llevado a la organización a revaluar su postura, ya que los últimos resultados sugieren potenciales ganancias en productividad con su uso.

Además, ha quedado de manifiesto la necesidad de realizar una evaluación longitudinal continua. La rápida evolución de las capacidades de los LLMs significa que las evaluaciones se desactualizan rápidamente. Lo que era cierto sobre hace seis meses puede no reflejar el rendimiento actual. Las organizaciones necesitan mantener procesos de evaluación continuos en lugar de basarse en evaluaciones puntuales.

En tercer lugar, se reafirma la necesidad de la supervisión por expertos. A pesar de las altas puntuaciones alcanzadas en nuestras métricas, ésta sigue siendo esencial. Las métricas basadas en conocimiento experto muestran que, si bien los LLMs han mejorado en la aplicación de técnicas de prueba, aún no igualan la experiencia humana en decisiones de diseño de pruebas. Cabe recalcar que los ejemplos utilizados son básicos, pero por la tendencia que vemos, dichos ejemplos deberán ser escalados a ejemplos más complejos.

Estos hallazgos sugieren que, aunque las herramientas de generación de pruebas basadas en LLMs son cada vez más viables para uso industrial, su adopción exitosa requiere tanto marcos de evaluación sistemáticos como expectativas realistas. Las empresas deberían ver estas herramientas como ayudas para aumentar la productividad del desarrollador, no como reemplazos del conocimiento experto.

7. Limitaciones y Amenazas a la Validez

Nuestro estudio presenta ciertas limitaciones que deben considerarse al interpretar los resultados:

Validez de Constructo: Aunque nuestro marco es exhaustivo, podría no captar todos los aspectos relevantes del valor real de las pruebas generadas por LLMs. Para mitigar esto, combinamos métricas automatizadas con evaluaciones expertas validadas por profesionales de QA experimentados.

Validez Interna: La mejora observada podría atribuirse tanto a la evolución natural de los LLMs como al refinamiento de nuestras estrategias de prompt. Hemos documentado rigurosamente los cambios metodológicos y validado mediante múltiples ejecuciones para aislar estos factores.

Validez Externa: Los resultados provienen principalmente de una organización y tipos específicos de proyectos. El marco se diseñó para ser adaptable a diferentes contextos organizacionales, centrándose en herramientas y prácticas estándar de la industria.

Fiabilidad: Para abordar la subjetividad inherente a las evaluaciones expertas, establecimos criterios de evaluación claros y documentados, manteniendo registros detallados de todos los procedimientos y criterios de decisión.

A pesar de estas limitaciones, consideramos que nuestras estrategias de mitigación proporcionan un nivel razonable de confianza en los hallazgos presentados.

8. Trabajo Relacionado

Desde la emergencia de los LLMs en el desarrollo de software, la investigación sobre su aplicación en pruebas ha avanzado rápidamente. Wang et al. [Wang et al. 2024b] analizaron 102 artículos sobre LLMs en pruebas de software, identificando su uso principal en generación de pruebas unitarias, oráculos y entradas para pruebas del sistema, señalando también limitaciones en cobertura y confiabilidad. Complementando este análisis, nuestro trabajo aporta evidencia empírica longitudinal sobre cómo estas limitaciones han evolucionado en un entorno industrial real.

En cuanto a frameworks específicos, Liu et al. [Liu et al. 2024] presentaron AutoTestGPT con prompts estructurados y refinamiento iterativo, reduciendo el tiempo de generación en más del 70 % comparado con métodos manuales. Chen et al. [Chen et al. 2024] desarrollaron ChatUniTest incorporando mecanismos de generación-validación-reparación. Mientras estos enfoques se centran en la optimización técnica del proceso de generación, nuestro marco evalúa además la integración con herramientas estándar de la industria (SonarQube, JaCoCo) y considera métricas basadas en conocimiento experto, aspectos críticos para la adopción empresarial.

En evaluaciones empíricas, Siddiq et al. [Siddiq et al. 2024] analizaron varios LLMs usando benchmarks HumanEval y EvoSuite SF110, revelando desafíos en cobertura y compilabilidad. Schäfer et al. [Schäfer et al. 2024] evaluaron sistemáticamente la generación de pruebas unitarias con LLMs en JavaScript. Estos estudios ofrecen evaluaciones puntuales valiosas, pero carecen de la perspectiva longitudinal de nuestro trabajo, que permite observar cómo las capacidades de los LLMs han evolucionado a lo largo de nueve meses en aplicaciones industriales reales.

La principal contribución de nuestro trabajo respecto a la literatura existente radica en tres aspectos diferenciadores: (1) un marco práctico para evaluación continua en entornos industriales reales con métricas ponderadas adaptables a diferentes contextos organizacionales, (2) evidencia empírica sobre la evolución temporal de las capacidades de LLM en generación de pruebas, y (3) lecciones prácticas derivadas de la implementación real en una empresa de desarrollo de software. Esta combinación ofrece orientación concreta para organizaciones que consideran adoptar estas tecnologías.

9. Conclusiones y Trabajo Futuro

Este estudio presenta un marco sistemático para la evaluación continua de las capacidades de generación de pruebas unitarias mediante LLMs en entornos industriales. Los resultados obtenidos durante el período de marzo 2024 a diciembre 2024 demuestran una mejora significativa en las capacidades de los LLMs, con modelos recientes como o1-Preview alcanzando valoraciones superiores al 90 % en nuestras métricas ponderadas.

Las principales contribuciones incluyen: (1) la validación de un marco de evaluación que integra métricas objetivas y subjetivas, permitiendo una evaluación holística de las pruebas generadas, (2) la demostración empírica de la evolución de las capacidades de generación de pruebas de los LLMs en un entorno industrial y (3) la identificación de lecciones aprendidas relevantes para organizaciones que buscan adoptar estas tecnologías. Sin embargo, nuestros hallazgos también sugieren que, si bien las herramientas basadas en LLMs han alcanzado un nivel de madurez prometedor, aún deben considerarse como complementos al conocimiento experto más que como reemplazos. Las métricas basadas en el conocimiento de expertos indican que los LLMs, aunque han mejorado significativamente en la aplicación de técnicas de prueba, todavía no igualan la experiencia humana en aspectos críticos del diseño de pruebas.

El trabajo futuro se centrará en la evaluación de casos más complejos, incluyendo pruebas combinatorias, y en la realización de una nueva replicación del estudio en seis meses para continuar monitoreando la evolución de estas tecnologías. Además, planeamos expandir el marco para incluir evaluaciones de eficiencia en términos de tiempo y recursos necesarios para la generación y mantenimiento de pruebas.

Disponibilidad de Artefactos

Tanto las funciones como los resultados están disponibles en `https://doi.org/10.5281/zenodo.15076786` para facilitar la reproducibilidad de este estudio.

Agradecimientos

Este trabajo ha sido financiado por MCIN/AEI/10.13039/501100011033, el *European Union NextGeneration EU/PRTR* con la referencia PID2021-125438OB-I00, Universidad del País Vasco dentro del programa *Universidad-Empresa-Sociedad* (US24/10).

Referencias

Campbell, A. and Papapetrou, P. (2013). *SonarQube in action*. Manning Publications Co.

Chen, Y., Hu, Z., Zhi, C., Han, J., Deng, S., and Yin, J. (2024). Chatunitest: A framework for llm-based test generation. In *Companion Proceedings of the 32nd ACM International Conference on the Foundations of Software Engineering (FSE)*. ACM.

Freeman, S., Mackinnon, T., Pryce, N., and Walnes, J. (2004). jMock: supporting responsibility-based design with mock objects. In *Companion to the 19th Annual ACM SIGPLAN Conference on Object-Oriented Programming, Systems, Languages, and Applications, OOPSLA*. ACM.

H. Washizaki, e. (2024). *Guide to the Software Engineering Body of Knowledge (SWEBOK Guide)*. IEEE Computer Society.

ISO (2021). IEEE/ISO/IEC international standard - software and systems engineering–software testing–part 4: Test techniques. *ISO/IEC/IEEE 29119-4:2021(E).*

Jiang, W., Gao, X., Zhai, J., Ma, S., Zhang, X., and Shen, C. (2024). From effectiveness to efficiency: Comparative evaluation of code generated by lcgms for bilingual programming questions.

Kaczanowski, T. (2013). *Practical Unit Testing with JUnit and Mockito*. Tomasz Kaczanowski, POL.

Kracht, J. S., Petrovic, J. Z., and Walcott-Justice, K. R. (2014). Empirically evaluating the quality of automatically generated and manually written test suites. *14th International Conference on Quality Software*, pages 256–265.

Liu, H., Liu, L., Yue, C., Wang, Y., and Deng, B. (2024). Autotestgpt: A system for the automated generation of software test cases based on chatgpt. *Journal of Software*, 19(4).

López, J. A. H., Chen, B., Saad, M., Sharma, T., and Varró, D. (2025). On inter-dataset code duplication and data leakage in large language models. *IEEE Transactions on Software Engineering*, 51(1).

Prates, L. and Pereira, R. (2025). Devsecops practices and tools. *International Journal of Information Security*, 24(1):1–25.

Schäfer, M., Nadi, S., Eghbali, A., and Tip, F. (2024). An empirical evaluation of using large language models for automated unit test generation. *IEEE Transactions on Software Engineering*, 50(1):85–105.

Sergeyuk, A., Golubev, Y., Bryksin, T., and Ahmed, I. (2025). Using ai-based coding assistants in practice: State of affairs, perceptions, and ways forward. *Information and Software Technology*, 178.

Siddiq, M., Da Silva, J., Tanvir, R., Ulfat, N., Al Rifat, F., and Carvalho, V. (2024). Using large language models to generate junit tests: An empirical study. In *Proceedings of the 28th International Conference on Evaluation and Assessment in Software Engineering (EASE)*. ACM.

Tillmann, N. and Schulte, W. (2005). Parameterized unit tests. In *Proceedings of the 10th European Software Engineering Conference*. ACM.

Wang, C., Li, Z., Gao, C., Wang, W., Peng, T., Huang, H., Deng, Y., Wang, S., and Lyu, M. (2024a). Exploring multi-lingual bias of large code models in code generation.

Wang, J., Huang, Y., Chen, C., Liu, Z., Wang, S., and Wang, Q. (2024b). Software testing with large language models: Survey, landscape, and vision. *IEEE Transactions on Software Engineering*, 50(4):911–936.

Wu, T., Terry, M., and Cai, C. (2022). Ai chains: Transparent and controllable human-ai interaction by chaining large language model prompts. In *Proceedings of the 2022 CHI Conference on Human Factors in Computing Systems*. ACM.

Wu, Y., Li, Z., Zhang, J. M., and Liu, Y. (2024). Condefects: A complementary dataset to address the data leakage concern for llm-based fault localization and program repair. In *Companion Proceedings of the 32nd ACM International Conference on the Foundations of Software Engineering (FSE)*. ACM.

Viagem à Lua - RPG aplicado ao ensino de Testes de Software com elementos do Design Socialmente Consciente

Flávia Belintani Blum Haddad[1,2], **Cléber Gimenez Corrêa**[1] **e Leticia Mara Peres**[2]

[1]Universidade Tecnológica Federal do Paraná (UTFPR)
Cornélio Procópio - PR - Brasil

[2]Universidade Federal do Paraná (UFPR)
Curitiba - PR - Brasil

{flaviahaddad, clebergimenez}@utfpr.edu.br

lmperes@inf.ufpr.br

Abstract. *This paper presents the use of a framework for creating RPGs (Role-playing Games) applied to Software Engineering (SE) teaching to stimulate active participation and increase students' protagonism in the teaching and learning process. The framework, named CreativEduc, has basic elements for creating RPGs combined with Socially Aware Design (SAwD) artifacts, which allows obtaining a systemic and social view of the problem. An RPG was created for the Software Testing discipline of an undergraduate SE course. The planning, execution and evaluation of the game and the framework are reported. Questionnaires were applied, resulting in positive indications regarding its use and application.*

Resumo. *Este artigo apresenta o uso de um framework para criação de RPG (Role-playing Game), aplicado ao ensino de Engenharia de Software (ES), para estimular a participação ativa e ampliar o protagonismo dos alunos no processo de ensino e aprendizagem. O framework, chamado CreativEduc, possui elementos básicos para criação de RPG somados aos artefatos do Design Socialmente Consciente (DSC), que possibilita a obtenção de uma visão sistêmica e social do problema. Foi criado um RPG para a disciplina Teste de Software de um curso de graduação de ES. Relata-se o planejamento, execução e avaliação do jogo e do framework. Foram aplicados questionários resultando em indícios positivos ao seu uso e aplicação.*

1. Introdução

A ACM (*Association for Computing Machinery)* em conjunto com a *IEEE Computer Society* publicaram o *Computing Curricula 2020 (CC2020)* que contém paradigmas para educação global em computação, elaborado por 50 membros de 20 países, recomenda a transição do aprendizado baseado em conhecimento por aprendizado baseado em competência nos currículos de cursos de computação [Association for Computing Machinery 2020].

O CC2020 descreve a competência como a combinação de conhecimentos, habilidades técnicas, cognitivas e metacognitivas, interpessoais, intelectuais, práticas e valores éticos dentro de um contexto computacional

[Association for Computing Machinery 2020]. A Sociedade Brasileira de Computação (SBC) disponibilizou uma nova versão do Referencial de Formação (RF), baseado no CC2020 e adaptado à realidade brasileira, considerando também as Diretrizes Curriculares Nacionais (DCNs). O RF serve como um guia para a implantação de currículos por competência nas instituições de nível superior do Brasil. cujos projetos pedagógicos estão sendo alterados de forma gradativa [Ferreira et al. 2024].

O desenvolvimento de competências técnicas, sociais e emocionais devem estar explícitas nos objetivos instrucionais e a escolha por métodos de ensino que facilitem e/ou motivem aos alunos a se tornarem protagonistas no processo de ensino e aprendizagem é recomendada [Ferreira et al. 2024].

Métodos ativos de aprendizagem propõem estratégias de ensino que inserem os alunos em cenários conectados a realidade do seu cotidiano, ao mesmo tempo em que estudam o conteúdo da disciplina, criando um ambiente propício para o desenvolvimento de competências [Ferreira et al. 2018a].

Aprendizagem baseada em problemas, ambiente integrado automatizado de processos de Engenharia de Software (ES), uso de projetos de software, aprendizagem baseada em jogos (GBL - *Game based learnig*), atividades lúdicas, *storytelling*, sala de aula invertida são exemplos de métodos ativos aplicados no ensino de ES [Ferreira et al. 2018b]; [Lemos et al. 2019]. GBL permite que os alunos desenvolvam habilidades, estratégias e competências importantes para ampliar sua capacidade cognitiva e intelectual [Brenda Alexandre 2024]. Assim, acredita-se que o uso de jogos em sala de aula pode colaborar com a proposta do desenvolvimento de competências e habilidades relacionadas ao ensino e aprendizagem de ES.

Em ES encontram-se jogos educacionais que abrangem requisitos, qualidade, processo, testes, gerenciamento de projetos de software, métodos ágeis e programação, por exemplo, mas percebe-se que esses jogos concentram-se em objetivos de ensino específicos e falham em fornecer interdisciplinaridade e exercitar habilidades interpessoais e sociais [Rodríguez et al. 2021]; [Haddad et al. 2024].

Importante enfatizar que o aprendizado por meio de jogos não acontece por si só. Devem-se considerar teorias contemporâneas de aprendizagem, como por exemplo aprendizagem situada, construtivismo ou construcionismo ao projetar jogos educacionais [Ivan et al. 2020] e ampliar o conhecimento do contexto social em que o jogo será inserido [Ferrari et al. 2019].

A construção de narrativas compartilhadas para produção de conhecimento é relatada em um estudo sobre a dimensão social do construcionismo, o qual define socioconstrucionista como um ambiente de aprendizagem que estimula o aluno a ser ativo, com liberdade para criar objetos concretos ou conceituais que sejam de seu interesse pessoal, sociossituado, favorecendo a construção conjunta do conhecimento. [Baranauskas and Posada 2017].

Para a criação de ambientes de aprendizagem que contenham uma abordagem socioconstrutivista sugere-se um processo que inclua o Design Socialmente Consciente (DSC). O DSC pode guiar a criação de jogos que abordem o modelo socioconstrucionista proposto por [Baranauskas and Posada 2017].

Por sua vez, o RPG (Role-playing Game) é um tipo de jogo que possui propriedades e atributos para a construção de narrativas compartilhadas, permite trabalhar habilidades técnicas, bem como socialização, cooperação, criatividade, interatividade e interdisciplinaridade [Grando and Tarouco 2008].

O RPG é um jogo de interpretação de papeis onde os jogadores assumem os papeis de personagens em um cenário fictício criado por meio de uma narrativa. Os jogadores assumem a responsabilidade de representar os papeis dentro da narrativa, podendo seguir um roteiro ou por meio de um processo de tomada de decisão estruturada e desenvolvimento de personagens que podem os levar a diferentes caminhos e resultados [Zuppiroli et al. 2012], e ainda utilizar o DSC para descobrir e caracterizar personagens, descobrir problemas e soluções relacionados ao tema e conhecer o contexto social envolvido.

O DSC propõe a construção de sistemas interativos mais humanizados visando descobrir dentro de um grupo social, requisitos nos níveis informal (hábitos, valores e cultura) e formal (procedimentos e regras), que se somem aos requisitos de nível técnico (tecnologias) [Baranauskas 2014]. Para produzir sistemas sustentáveis, inclusivos e com a devida atenção a possíveis impactos negativos que possa causar o DSC envolve diferentes partes interessadas no processo de *design* [Ferrari et al. 2019]; [Baranauskas 2014].

Assim, neste artigo, é relatado o uso de um *framework* conceitual, chamado CreativEduc, para criação de RPGs voltados ao ensino de ES com elementos do DSC, aplicado na disciplina Teste de Software de um curso de ES.

Na seção 2, são apresentados alguns trabalhos relacionados, na seção 3, consta os materiais e métodos utilizados, na seção 4, os resultados e discussão sobre o CreativEduc e sobre o RPG criado e na seção 5, as considerações finais.

2. Trabalhos Relacionados

Esta seção, apresenta alguns trabalhos que motivaram e colaboraram com esta pesquisa.

Um Mapeamento Sistemático da Literatura (MSL) realizado em 2017 sobre jogos educacionais destinados ao ensino de ES apontou que a GBL foi a metodologia mais utilizada seguida da aprendizagem baseada em desenvolvimento de jogos (GDBJ - *Game Development Based Learning*), que permite a experiência prática por meio do desenvolvimento de jogos e defende o uso de *frameworks* de desenvolvimento de jogos como instrumentos de aprendizagem simplificados que permitem aos alunos concentrarem esforços em objetivos específicos de aprendizagem [De Almeida Souza et al. 2017].

O trabalho de [Grando and Tarouco 2008] apresenta um estudo sobre estratégias dos diversos tipos de jogos educacionais para uma aprendizagem mais efetiva, com ênfase nos jogos de RPG, citando suas características e potencialidades. [Barreto et al. 2008] apresentam um trabalho sobre a utilização de um RPG no ensino de Gerenciamento e Processo de Desenvolvimento de Software, por meio de um jogo chamado SE•RPG (*Software Engineering • Role-playing Game*). Interessante citar também o ConES, um RPG elaborado para simular a construção de um software [Guerra et al. 2024] e o SimScrumF que utiliza elementos de RPG para ensinar Scrum [Ferreira et al. 2024].

Em *Tangible and Shared Storytelling: Searching for the Social Dimension of Constructionism*, [Baranauskas and Posada 2017] projetam um ambiente socioconstrucionista, o CPES (Ambiente Programável Colaborativo para Contação de Histórias). [Ferrari et al. 2020] realizam oficinas de design propostas pelo DSC na concepção de um jogo para apoiar crianças em exercícios fonoaudiológicos e [Haddad et al. 2022] aplicam conceitos do DSC na construção de um jogo digital para o ensino de Gerenciamento de Projeto de Software.

3. Materiais e Métodos

Esta pesquisa foi realizada em três etapas: a elaboração do RPG, seguindo as diretrizes do *framework* CreativEduc; a aplicação em sala de aula e uma avaliação realizada com o professor e com os alunos da disciplina para obtenção de *feedback* em relação ao CreativEduc e ao RPG.

3.1. Elaboração

Para a elaboração do RPG, o professor da disciplina de Teste de Software recebeu o material de apoio do CreativEduc, que contém um processo explicativo das etapas de elaboração do RPG, dividido em três etapas: objetivos de aprendizagem, *design* do jogo e materiais, bem como um manual de uso.

O CreativEduc disponibiliza fichas para facilitar o processo de elaboração,e também um formato simplificado que utiliza o *Game Design Canva* (GDC). Assim o professor pode optar pelas fichas ou pelo GDC, desde que siga as instruções do manual de uso do *framework*.

O CreativEduc enfatiza a importância de trabalhar habilidades interpessoais (*softskills*) inclusas no *framework* a partir das orientações dispostas no CC2020 [Association for Computing Machinery 2020], de uma pesquisa realizada por [Pereira et al. 2021], que aponta 17 habilidades importantes a serem trabalhadas durante os cursos de computação e do resultado de uma oficina de DSC durante a elaboração do próprio CreativEduc, além de recomendações para evitar, no contexto do RPG criado, situações que ensejem algum tipo de preconceito racial, sexual, de gênero ou outros que possam causar mal estar nos participantes.

Foi disponibilizado ainda um fluxo de execução do CreativEduc (Figura 1), que mostra o que deve ser feito e a ordem de execução, incluindo os artefatos do DSC que colaboram no *design* do jogo e no exercício de habilidades, tais como colaborativismo, visão sistêmica, questões sociais e culturais por meio de análise de contexto de forma não técnica, ética e responsabilidade, entre outras.

As atividades em laranja (Figura 1) são atividades macro para a criação do RPG educacional, seguidas das atividades em branco, que complementam as laranjas. As atividades em amarelo representam os artefatos do DSC, com a recomendação de realizá-las com os alunos. O Diagrama das Partes Interessadas (DPI) colabora na identificação dos principais envolvidos e de outras pessoas interessadas na situação-problema e na solução podendo, no RPG, serem transformadas em personagens: protagonistas, antagonistas e coadjuvantes. O Quadro de Avaliação levanta questões/problemas de acordo com a visão de cada parte interessada, com a proposta de ideias/soluções que comporão a estética do jogo. A Torta de Valores trabalha as áreas dos Blocos de Construção da Cultura elaborado por [Hall 1959] e adaptado por [Liu 2000] cuja utilização amplia a visão do

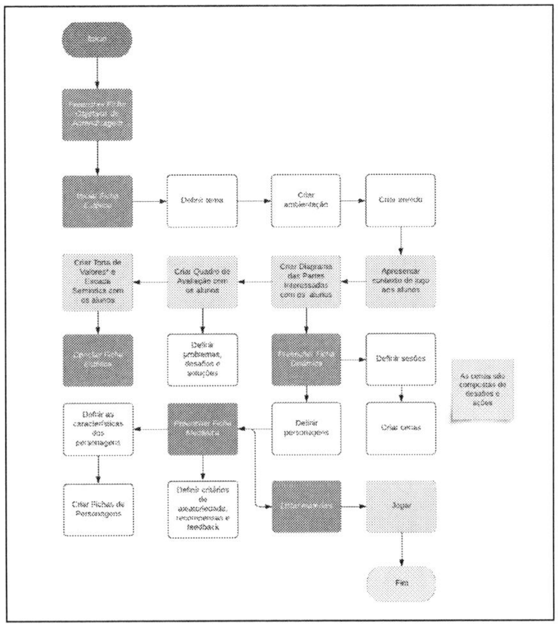

Figura 1. Fluxo de execução do CreativEduc.

contexto do ambiente do jogo e a Escada Semiótica permite a elaboração de requisitos sociotécnicos para solucionar o problema, dispostos em seis degraus (mundo social, pragmático, semântico, sintático, empírico e mundo físico).

Importante salientar que a Torta de Valores é um elemento opcional a ser trabalhado com os alunos, ficando a critério do professor o quanto ele quer que detalhe o contexto socioambiental do jogo. Neste jogo, o professor optou por não utilizar a Torta de Valores por causa do pouco tempo disponível em aula para a sessão do jogo.

Para facilitar o entendimento dos artefatos do DSC, foram disponibilizadas cartas (no formato digital) que possuem questões para ajudar aos alunos e ao professor a rechearem estes artefatos. As cartas estão disponíveis em: https://l1nk.dev/2hwV9 (ao clicar, aguardar a validação para encaminhamento automático às cartas).

3.2. Aplicação

Para a aplicação o professor deve ter em mãos as diretrizes para o jogo, tais como quantidade de sessões (aulas), quantidade de participantes por grupo, contexto do jogo, regras e estar com o material, listado na etapa anterior, disponível.

O professor deve expor as regras e objetivos, tanto objetivos de aprendizagem quanto objetivo do jogo, tirar dúvidas e iniciar a sessão.

Ao final de cada sessão, o professor deve perguntar aos alunos se gostaram da dinâmica, se visualizaram e compreenderam o conteúdo técnico e o que pode melhorar para a próxima sessão.

3.3. Avaliação

Além do *feedback* informal ao final de cada sessão e da observação do professor durante a condução do jogo, foram disponibilizados questionários, pré e pós execução, para o professor e para os alunos, bem como termo de consentimento livre e esclarecido, visando a participação voluntária e consciente. Esta pesquisa, bem como os questionários aplicados foram analisados e aprovados pelo Comitê de Ética da Universidade Tecnológica Federal do Paraná.

Para avaliar o *framework*, foi aplicado um questionário ao professor participante para identificação do perfil (duração estimada de 3 minutos) e um questionário para coleta de dados quanto ao uso do *framework* (duração estimada de 10 minutos).

Para avaliar o RPG, o professor aplicou um questionário aos alunos para identificação do perfil (duração estimada de 3 minutos) e um questionário para coleta de dados quanto às características do jogo e resultados de aprendizagem (duração estimada de 20 minutos).

Os questionários foram elaborados visando verificar a eficiência e facilidade de uso do *framework* e do RPG, além de buscar evidências de melhorias no processo de ensino e aprendizagem. Para isso, as questões de avaliação do RPG foram baseadas na ferramenta MEEGA+, um modelo de questionário elaborado para avaliação de jogos educacionais para o ensino de Computação [Giani Petri 2019], adaptado para RPG.

4. Resultados e Discussão

Esta seção apresenta a criação do jogo, o jogo, os artefatos gerados pelos participantes e a avaliação do CreativEduc pelo professor e do jogo pelos alunos.

4.1. O Jogo

O RPG criado a partir do CreativEduc foi idealizado pelo professor da disciplina de Teste de Software, do curso de graduação de Engenharia de Software da Universidade Tecnológico Federal do Paraná durante o segundo semestre de 2024.

O professor preencheu o GDC disponibilizado pelo CreativEduc (versão simplificada) para criação do jogo, conforme Figura 2. O primeiro quadrante do GDC diz respeito aos objetivos de aprendizagem, em que o professor define qual conteúdo técnico irá trabalhar com os alunos, com a possibilidade de incluir conteúdos interdisciplinares e determinar quais habilidades interpessoais podem ser estimuladas durante do jogo, o que se espera e como será possível atingir os objetivos de aprendizagem. Também são determinados quais problemas serão abordados, desafios enfrentados e possíveis soluções para os problemas.

Os quadrantes cujos títulos estão em verde, ainda na Figura 2, representam o *design* do jogo, baseado no *framework* MDA, cujo acrônimo vem de mecânica, dinâmica e estética (*Mechanics, Dynamics, Aesthetics*) [Marín et al. 2019]. A estética relaciona-se com a definição do tema, ambientação (cenário, espaço, tempo) e enredo, a dinâmica com a definição dos personagens e quantidade de sessões previstas e a mecânica envolve as regras do jogo, com as características dos personagens, aleatoriedade, recompensas e *feedback*, se houver. Finalizando, o professor descreveu quais os materiais necessários para a execução do jogo. O jogo foi relacionado ao projeto Apollo da década de 1960, para viabilizar a viagem à Lua, com a participação da NASA (National Aeronautics and Space Administration - Administração Nacional de Aeronáutica e Espaço) e as empresas desenvolvedoras de produtos para o projeto.

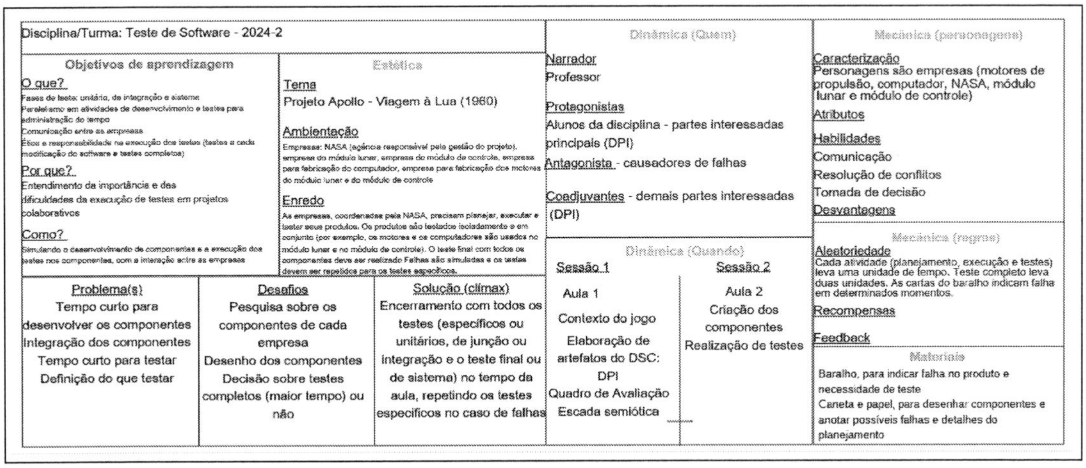

Figura 2. GDC preenchido pelo professor.

Na sequência, o professor elaborou um roteiro a ser entregue aos alunos participantes com informações iniciais: quantidade de participantes por grupo, quantidade de unidades de tempo para finalizar o jogo (até 17 unidades). As atividades, sendo que cada atividade leva uma ou duas unidades são: **planejamento geral** (NASA/Todas as empresas e 1 unidade), **planejamento específico** (cada empresa e 1 unidade), **execução** (cada empresa e 1 unidade de tempo), **teste específico** (cada empresa e 1 ou 2 unidades), **teste de junção de produtos** (NASA/2 empresas e 1 unidade), **teste de todos os produtos** (NASA e 1 unidade), **correção em caso de falha** (cada empresa e 1 unidade de tempo).

O teste específico completo utiliza 2 unidades, o teste específico incompleto 1 unidade. Cada empresa decide se fará teste completo ou não. Cada grupo representa uma empresa. A cada correção um novo teste é necessário. A falha é determinada por cartas de um baralho. Uma carta que não é figura indica que foi observada uma falha. Uma carta é retirada para cada empresa a cada teste. Uma carta pode ser utilizada para uma determinada empresa de todos os grupos. A cada um ou dois testes específicos, deve-se realizar um teste de junção de produtos, e após um ou dois testes de junção deve-se, realizar o teste de todos os produtos, dependendo da ocorrência de falhas.

Os atores (protagonistas) representados pelos alunos são: **NASA** (especifica o projeto e ajuda as empresas); **Empresa de motores de foguetes** (fabrica os motores do módulo de serviço); **Empresa para o módulo de serviço** (fabrica o módulo considerando aerodinâmica, fonte de energia e componentes eletrônicos); **Empresa de computadores** (fabrica o computador do módulo lunar); e **Empresa para o módulo lunar** (fabrica o módulo considerando aerodinâmica, fonte de energia e componentes eletrônicos).

A comunicação entre os integrantes do grupo é realizada durante toda a sessão e as atividades para chegar ao clímax do jogo são: **Planejamento geral:** NASA escreve o que cada empresa deve fazer e o prazo (uma frase para cada empresa). Todos os grupos elaboram o Diagrama de Partes Interessadas, o Quadro de Avaliação e a Escada Semiótica de forma colaborativa; **Planejamento da empresa:** pode pensar em peso, capacidade energética, volume do produto; **Execução:** cada empresa desenha seu produto, podendo consultar páginas na Internet; **Teste específico:** cada empresa escreve o que deve ser testado (1 item); **Teste de junção de produtos:** NASA e 2 empresas escrevem o que deve ser testado (1 item); **Teste de todos os produtos:** NASA e todas as empresas escrevem o que deve ser testado (1 item); e **Correção em caso de falha:** cada empresa escreve o tipo de falha (1 item).

4.2. Execução

Foram realizadas duas sessões do jogo, conforme previsto no planejamento do professor. Cada sessão equivale ao tempo de 2 aulas de 50 minutos (1 hora e 40 minutos cada sessão). Participaram 29 alunos matriculados na disciplina de Teste de Software no segundo semestre de 2024, porém apenas 14 responderam aos questionários. O motivo pode ter sido a iminência do recesso de final de ano, visto que a última sessão foi na última aula antes da prova e a solicitação de preenchimento do questionário foi após a aula.

4.2.1. Sessão 1

Na primeira sessão, inicialmente, foram divididos os grupos, entregue um roteiro para cada grupo, enfatizados os objetivos e regras e apresentado o conceito do DSC.

Na sequência, iniciou-se uma oficina de *design* participativo para levantamento das partes interessadas e elaboração do quadro de avaliação. Ainda nessa sessão, estava prevista a elaboração da escada semiótica.

Os alunos, motivados pelo enredo e pelo professor, com apoio das cartas explicativas sobre os artefatos do DSC, preencheram o DPI e o Quadro de Avaliação. O resultado está representado na Figura 3.

O DPI possui 5 camadas, sendo a camada central o produto do projeto (APOLLO), quanto mais próximo da camada central, maior o envolvimento no projeto. Assim, na camada de Contribuição estão a NASA, as empresas que irão construir os módulos, designers, testadores, engenheiro espacial, na camada Fonte estão físicos, matemáticos, universidades, governo, na camada mercado estão metalúrgicas (representando fornecedores), Rússia (representando concorrentes), investidores e na camada comunidade estão os americanos, a Organização das Nações Unidas (ONU), o planeta Terra de modo geral para refletir sobre os benefícios e impactos do projeto.

Na sequência os alunos preencheram o Quadro de Avaliação, que possui uma área para cada parte interessada de cada camada do DPI se manifestar quanto aos problemas e soluções relacionados à viagem à Lua. Ainda na Figura 3, o resultado final do quadro de avaliação após o preenchimento contém considerações importantes quanto ao material a ser utilizado na confecção da espaçonave, quanto ao risco de vida dos tripulantes, quanto aos impactos para outros países, entre outras.

Na Figura 4, está registrado o momento em que os alunos preenchem este artefato no quadro branco.

Não foi possível, durante essa sessão, elaborar a Escada Semiótica e os alunos tiveram dificuldade em executar essa tarefa sozinhos. Assim, o professor optou por dar sequência no jogo sem este artefato.

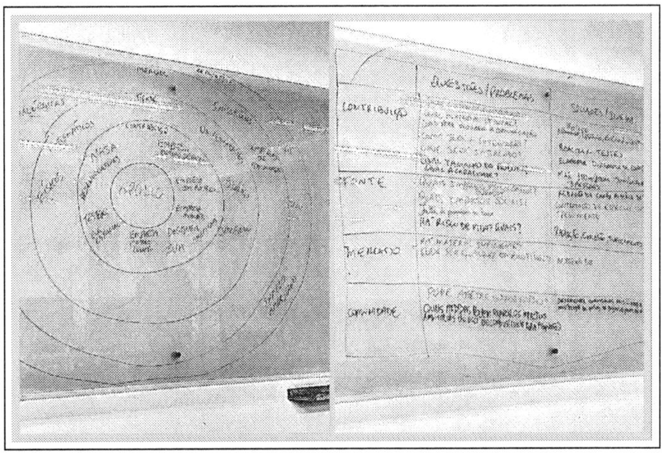

Figura 3. DPI e Quadro de avaliação preenchidos.

Figura 4. Elaboração do Quadro de Avaliação.

4.2.2. Sessão 2

Na segunda sessão, os alunos, representando as empresas e a NASA e considerando as informações obtidas no Quadro de Avaliação, construíram o protótipo do produto por meio de desenhos que podem ser visualizados na Figura 5, sendo cada desenho de um grupo distinto, e realizaram os testes, escrevendo o que poderia ser testado, possíveis falhas e os defeitos que geraram as falhas, utilizando a aleatoriedade das cartas e gastando as respectivas unidades de tempo (regras do jogo).

Parte do resultado pode ser observado na Figura 6, com os grupos participantes e a unidade de tempo para cada atividade (Planejamento Geral (PG), Planejamento da Empresa (PE), Execução ou criação do produto de cada empresa (E), Teste Específico (TE), Teste de Junção (TJ), Correção (C), Teste Total (TT)). Teste específico, teste de junção e correção podem se repetir, no caso de falhas. O teste específico pode ocupar uma ou duas unidades de tempo, sendo uma decisão do grupo, pois o teste específico completo é realizado em duas unidades.

Figura 5. Protótipos da aeronave.

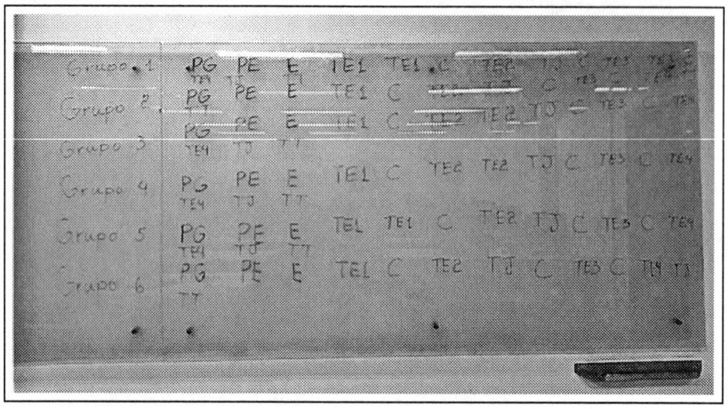

Figura 6. Parte do resultado dos testes.

4.3. Avaliação

Foram aplicados questionários prévios ao professor e aos alunos para conhecer o perfil, conhecimento e experiência com jogos educacionais, mais precisamente com RPG.

Sobre o professor, atua no ensino há oito anos, nunca utilizou jogos educacionais e/ou *framework* para criação de jogos, nunca jogou RPG, mas estava muito motivado em experenciar a criação de um RPG para ser aplicado na disciplina de Teste de Software.

Após a criação e aplicação do jogo em sala de aula, o professor respondeu 11 questões fechadas e duas abertas. O professor respondeu que trabalhou 10% do conteúdo programático da disciplina no jogo e que levou em torno de quatro horas para criar o jogo utilizando o CreativEduc.

Da questão quatro a questão 12 foi utilizada a escala Likert (5 - concordo plenamente, 4 - concordo, 3 - não concordo nem discordo, 2 - discordo e 1 - discordo totalmente). O professor assinalou 4 sobre o CreativEduc ser de fácil compreensão, e assinalou 5 sobre: o CreativEduc oferecer os elementos necessários para a criação de um RPG, que permite moldar o RPG de acordo com a ementa da disciplina, que permite trabalhar a interdisciplinaridade no RPG, que inclui opções para exercitar habilidades sociais e interpessoais no RPG. Acrescentou que ficou satisfeito com o RPG criado a partir das diretrizes propostas no CreativEduc, que os alunos participaram ativamente dos desafios propostos no RPG, mas, sobre uma melhora do desempenho dos alunos, não foi aplicado instrumento avaliativo para verificar o desempenho, no entanto, a motivação dos alunos foi observada.

A partir da análise das respostas, observa-se que a experiência em criar e aplicar um RPG no ensino de testes de software, de acordo com o CreativEduc, foi satisfatória segundo a visão do professor.

O perfil dos alunos indicou que a maioria está no 6º período do curso de Engenharia de Software, que 26% nunca jogaram RPG, mas os demais jogaram pelo menos uma vez, que 74% nunca jogaram RPG educacional, mas 63% jogaram outros tipos de jogos educacionais.

As questões respondidas pelos alunos, após o término do jogo foram: **Q.1** O tema do RPG foi envolvente; **Q.2** Os cenários criados durante a narrativa foram bem explorados de acordo com o tema proposto; **Q.3** O enredo possibilitou a criação de situações problema e conflitos; **Q.4** O número de sessões/aulas foi adequado para a finalização da narrativa; **Q.5** Eu participei em todas as sessões/aulas; **Q.6** Eu pude interagir com outras pessoas durante as sessões/aulas; **Q.7** O RPG promove momentos de cooperação entre os jogadores; **Q.8** Eu me senti bem interagindo com outras pessoas durante as sessões/aulas; **Q.9**O narrador conduziu bem a narrativa; **Q.10** Eu me senti imerso no universo do meu personagem; **Q.11** Os objetivos e metas dados ao meu personagem foram cumpridos; **Q.12** Eu compreendi e exercitei as habilidades do meu personagem; **Q.13** A ficha do meu personagem foi de fácil manuseio e compreensão, se utilizadas fichas; **Q.14** O RPG oferece novos desafios com ritmo adequado; **Q.15** O RPG não se torna monótona nas suas tarefas (repetitiva ou com tarefas chatas); **Q.16** Completar as tarefas do RPG me deu um sentimento de realização; **Q.17** As regras do RPG são claras e compreensíveis; **Q.18** Eu considero RPG fácil de jogar; **Q.19** O uso de cartas cria uma atmosfera de expectativa e aleatoriedade dando mais emoção à narrativa; **Q.20** Eu me diverti com o RPG; **Q.21** Aconteceu alguma situação durante o RPG que me fez sorrir; **Q.22** Houve algo interessante no início do RPG que capturou minha atenção; **Q.23** Eu estava tão envolvido que eu perdi a noção do tempo; **Q.24** Eu esqueci sobre o ambiente ao meu redor enquanto participava do RPG; **Q.25** O conteúdo do RPG é relevante para os meus interesses; **Q.26** É claro para mim como o conteúdo do RPG está relacionado com a disciplina; **Q.27** O RPG é um método de ensino adequado para esta disciplina; **Q.28** Eu prefiro aprender com RPG do que de outra forma (outro método de ensino); **Q.29** O RPG contribuiu para a minha aprendizagem na disciplina; **Q.30** O RPG contribuiu para exercitar habilidades sociais e interpessoais importantes à profissão de ES; **Q.31** O RPG foi eficiente para minha aprendizagem em comparação com outras atividades da disciplina.

Na Tabela 1 são apresentadas as respostas dos alunos, utilizando a escala Likert (5 - concordo plenamente, 4 - concordo, 3 - não concordo nem discordo, 2 - discordo e 1 - discordo totalmente), as repostas estão em percentual de acordo com os 14 alunos participantes. As respostas assinaladas em negrito foram a de maior percentual, sendo que as azuis representam concordo totalmente e concordo, as verdes representam os indecisos, não concordo nem discordo, e as vermelhas alertam para os que discordam.

Observa-se que a maioria das respostas são favoráveis ao RPG aplicado à disciplina de Teste de Software. Sendo que os maiores índices de aceitação estão relacionados à criação de situações problema e conflitos, a qual amplia as possibilidades de praticar a teoria no ensino de ES, além da interação, participação e cooperação que possibilitam o trabalho em equipe mais ativamente.

A diversão, elemento importante em jogos, se mostrou presente ao verificar as respostas da questão 21 e principalmente as respostas das questões 26, 27 e 29, que demonstram que o conteúdo ministrado por meio do RPG foi compreendido, além da importância de trabalhar habilidades interpessoais e sociais refletidas na resposta da questão 30. Exercitaram ética e responsabilidade ao decidirem se fariam um teste completo ou não, pois sem realizar o teste completo, problemas sérios poderiam acontecer com falhas no sistema, a comunicação foi necessária na integração entre os projetos das diferentes empresas, para realização teste de junção/integração), na resolução de conflitos houve alguns conflitos sobre *design* e descrição de falhas, mas foram resolvidos.

No entanto, as questões 10, 16 e 23 alertam para melhorar as características dos personagens e ampliar a imersão dos alunos nos personagens, bem como trazer algum tipo de recompensa ao realizarem as atividades propostas no jogo, pensar em situações, engraçadas ou preocupantes, que possam de fato fazê-los com que percam a noção do tempo.

De acordo com a resposta da questão quatro e relato do próprio professor, a quantidade de sessões pode ser aumentada em pelo menos mais uma sessão para possibilitar a criação da escada semiótica e para finalizarem o jogo com um pouco mais de tempo ou terem mais atividades de correção e testes. Enquanto que a questão 24 sinaliza a necessidade de criar uma atmosfera mais realista para que eles imaginem realmente que estão em outro local, diverso da sala de aula.

Não houve uma avaliação formal para avaliar o aprendizado, mas durante a execução do jogo os alunos compreenderam bem as fases de teste (teste unitário, teste de integração e teste de sistema), que apesar de no jogo estarem com outros nomes, os alunos conseguiram relacionar a quais testes o jogo se referia, relacionando com o conceito aprendido na semana anterior.

Foram identificadas ameaças à validade relacionadas ao tamanho da amostra e ao fato de ter sido possível afirmar se em outra disciplina de ES o resultado seria o mesmo.

O resultado dos questionários pré e pós pesquisa, professores e aluno, estão disponíveis em: https://drive.google.com/drive/folders/1RQrl7LTvEYfqUJzjwOWigKza4Qy30wM5?usp=sharing.

5. Considerações Finais

Este artigo apresentou a criação e aplicação de um RPG na disciplina de Teste de Software de um curso de ES, para testar o uso do CreativEduc, um *framework* que auxilia na criação de RPGs voltados ao ensino de ES. O CreativEduc é fruto de uma pesquisa de doutorado [Haddad 2022] em estágio final, sendo de grande relevância o *feedback* obtido para melhorá-lo e validá-lo.

O RPG, Viagem à Lua, criado a partir do CreativEduc pode ser aprimorado a partir do resultado da avaliação, podendo ser replicado em outras turmas que possuem

Tabela 1. Resultado do questionário pós-jogo alunos.

	5	4	3	2	1		5	4	3	2	1
Q. 1	42,9	**50**	7,1	0	0	Q. 17	7,1	**50**	28,6	14,3	0
Q. 2	**57,1**	35,7	7,1	0	0	Q. 18	**35,7**	21,4	28,6	14,3	0
Q. 3	**78,6**	21,4	0	0	0	Q. 19	**57,1**	28,6	0	7,1	7,1
Q. 4	28,6	**35,7**	7,1	**28,6**	0	Q. 20	**42,9**	35,7	21,4	0	0
Q. 5	**78,6**	14,3	0	7,1	0	Q.21	**50**	42,9	7,1	0	0
Q. 6	**92,9**	7,1	0	0	0	Q. 22	28,6	**35,7**	28,6	7,1	0
Q.7	**71,4**	14,3	7,1	7,1	0	Q. 23	14,3	28,6	42,9	14,3	0
Q. 8	**57,1**	42,9	0	0	0	Q. 24	7,1	35,7	14,3	**42,9**	0
Q. 9	**50**	42,9	7,1	0	0	Q. 25	14,3	**42,9**	35,7	7,1	0
Q. 10	28,6	28,6	35,7	7,1	0	Q. 26	35,7	**64,3**	0	0	0
Q. 11	**42,9**	35,7	21,4	0	0	Q. 27	**42,9**	28,6	14,3	14,3	0
Q. 12	35,7	**57,1**	7,1	0	0	Q. 28	28,6	21,4	35,7	14,3	0
Q. 13	**44,4**	33,3	22,2	0	0	Q. 29	**50**	35,7	14,3	0	0
Q. 14	**42,9**	**42,9**	14,3	0	0	Q. 30	**50**	42,9	7,1	0	0
Q. 15	**42,9**	21,4	21,4	14,3	0	Q. 31	**42,9**	35,7	14,3	7,1	0
Q. 16	28,6	**35,7**	35,7	0	0						

testes de software em seu currículo. Como o jogo trabalha a interdisciplinaridade por utilizar conceitos de requisitos e *design* para prototipação da espaçonave, este pode ainda ser adaptado para aplicação nestas disciplinas também.

Outro fator relevante desta pesquisa é a inserção dos artefatos do DSC que possibilitam uma visão sistêmica do problema, análise de impacto no contexto social da aplicação, trabalho colaborativo e participativo, considera habilidades sociais e interpessoais necessárias para profissionais de tecnologia da informação, ou seja, vai além da técnica por buscar o contexto social de tal forma a tornar as aplicações mais inclusivas e sustentáveis, trazendo um diferencial em relação aos trabalhos relacionados apresentados, pois o CreativEdcu une RPG, ensino de ES aberto a qualquer conteúdo e DSC.

O CreativEduc está sendo aplicado em duas outras disciplinas, Introdução à ES e Gerenciamento de Projeto de Software, e como trabalhos futuros, pretende-se implementar melhorias para disponibilizar o CreativEduc para a comunidade e comparar a GBL com RPG a outros métodos de ensino.

Agradecimento

Esta pesquisa teve apoio da Coordenação de Aperfeiçoamento de Pessoal de Nível Superior - Brasil (CAPES)/Proex, da Universidade Tecnólogica Federal do Paraná e da Universidade Federal do Paraná.

Referências

Association for Computing Machinery (2020). Computing curricula 2020: Paradigms for global computing education. Disponível em: `https://www.acm.org/education/curricula-recommendations`. Acesso em: 29 de janeiro 2024.

Baranauskas, M. C. C. (2014). Social awareness in hci. *Interactions*, 21(4):66–69.

Baranauskas, M. C. C. and Posada, J. E. G. (2017). Tangible and shared storytelling: Searching for the social dimension of constructionism. In *Proceedings of the 2017 Conference on Interaction Design and Children*, IDC '17, page 193–203, New York, NY, USA. Association for Computing Machinery.

Barreto, F., Benitti, F., and Molleri, J. (2008). Utilização de um rpg no ensino de gerenciamento e processo de desenvolvimento de software.

Brenda Alexandre, L. L. (2024). Gamificação no ensino superior. In *Anais do VIII Colóquio Estadual de Pesquisa Multidisciplinar, VI Congresso Nacional de Pesquisa Multidisciplinar e I Congresso de Pós-Graduação da Unifimes*. Disponível em: http://publicacoes.unifimes.edu.br/index.php/coloquio/article/view/3914. Acesso em: 15 de janeiro 2024.

De Almeida Souza, M. R., Furtini Veado, L., Teles Moreira, R., Magno Lages Figueiredo, E., and Costa, H. A. X. (2017). Games for learning: bridging game-related education methods to software engineering knowledge areas. In *2017 IEEE/ACM 39th International Conference on Software Engineering: Software Engineering Education and Training Track (ICSE-SEET)*, pages 170–179.

Ferrari, B., da Silva Junior, D. P., Oliveira, C. M., Ortiz, J. S. B., and Pereira, R. (2020). Socially aware design of games: an early workshop for game designers.

Ferrari, B., Junior, D. S., Oliveira, C., Ortiz, J., and Pereira, R. (2019). Design socialmente consciente de jogos: relato de uma oficina prática para o entendimento do problema e prospecção de ideias. In *Anais do I Workshop sobre Interação e Pesquisa de Usuários no Desenvolvimento de Jogos*, pages 11–20, Porto Alegre, RS, Brasil. SBC.

Ferreira, A., Rolim, T., Barbosa, P. L., Silva, J. A., Félix, R., and Silva, P. C. (2018a). Adversidades e intervenções no ensino da engenharia de software: Uma revisão sistemática na literatura. In *Anais da IV Escola Regional de Informática do Piauí*, pages 178–183, Porto Alegre, RS, Brasil. SBC.

Ferreira, T., Viana, D., Fernandes, J., and Santos, R. (2018b). Identifying emerging topics and difficulties in software engineering education in brazil. In *Proceedings of the XXXII Brazilian Symposium on Software Engineering*, SBES '18, page 230–239, New York, NY, USA. Association for Computing Machinery.

Ferreira, V., Souza, M., and Júnior, P. P. (2024). Caracterização do nível de adequação das matrizes curriculares dos cursos de computação no brasil ao modelo de competências da sbc. In *Anais do XXXII Workshop sobre Educação em Computação*, pages 443–454, Porto Alegre, RS, Brasil. SBC.

Giani Petri, C. v. W. e. A. B. (2019). Meega+: Um modelo para a avaliação de jogos educacionais para o ensino de computação. *Revista Brasileira de Informática na Educação*, 27(03):52–81.

Grando, A. and Tarouco, L. M. R. (2008). O uso de jogos educacionais do tipo rpg na educação. *RENOTE*, 6(1).

Guerra, A. d. S., Oliveira, S., and Furtado, J. (2024). Cones: Um jogo de rpg como instrumento de apoio ao ensino da construção de produto de software. pages 241–246.

Haddad, F. (2022). Framework socialmente consciente para criação de rpgs para contribuir com o processo de ensino e aprendizagem de engenharia de software. In *Anais do XXV Congresso Ibero-Americano em Engenharia de Software*, pages 376–383, Porto Alegre, RS, Brasil. SBC.

Haddad, F., Filho, W. R., Ramos, V., Corrêa, C., and Peres, L. (2024). Mapeamento sistemático da literatura de jogos educacionais destinados ao ensino e aprendizagem de engenharia de software: uma análise do estado da arte. In *Anais do XXIII Simpósio Brasileiro de Jogos e Entretenimento Digital*, pages 1256–1269, Porto Alegre, RS, Brasil. SBC.

Haddad, F. B. B., Miguel Naldi Dias, L., Corrêa, C. G., and Mara Peres, L. (2022). Building a digital educational game supported by socially aware design. In *2022 IEEE Frontiers in Education Conference (FIE)*, pages 1–9.

Hall, E. T. (1959). *The silent language*. Doubleday, Garden City, N. Y.

Ivan, G., Pacheco, C., Méndez, F., and Calvo-Manzano, J. (2020). The effects of game-based learning in the acquisition of "soft skills" on undergraduate software engineering courses: A systematic literature review. *Computer Applications in Engineering Education*, 28:1327–1354.

Lemos, W., Cunha, J., and Saraiva, J. (2019). Ensino de engenharia de software em um curso de sistemas de informação: Uma análise dos problemas e soluções na perspectiva de professores e alunos. In *Anais do XXVII Workshop sobre Educação em Computação*, pages 305–318, Porto Alegre, RS, Brasil. SBC.

Liu, K. (2000). *Semiotics in Information Systems Engineering*. Cambridge University Press.

Marín, B., del Mar Sánchez Vera, M., and Giachetti, G. (2019). An adventure serious game for teaching effort estimation in software engineering. In *IWSM-Mensura*.

Pereira, R., Peres, L., and Silva, F. (2021). Hello world: 17 habilidades para exercitar desde o início da graduação em computação.

Rodríguez, G., González-Caino, P. C., and Resett, S. (2021). Serious games for teaching agile methods: A review of multivocal literature. *Computer Applications in Engineering Education*, 29(6):1931–1949.

Zuppiroli, S., Ciancarini, P., and Gabbrielli, M. (2012). A role-playing game for a software engineering lab: Developing a product line. In *2012 IEEE 25th Conference on Software Engineering Education and Training*, pages 13–22.

A Method for Regression Testing Plan Ordering for Non-Automated Executions in Black Box Testing

Vinicius Hernandes[1], André Carvalho[1], Eulanda Santos[1], Yan Soares[1], Hygo Oliveira[1], Adamor Barros[1], Ronaldo Soares[1], Alexandre Lima[1] Raoni Ferreira[2], Gabriel Martins[2], Lucas Carvalho[2], Nicolas Assumpção[3], José Nascimento[3], Eliane Collins[4], Silvia Ascate[4], Mateus Souza[4]

[1] Universidade Federal do Amazonas (UFAM)

[2]Universidade Federal do Acre (UFAC)

[3]Motorola Mobility LLC

[4]Instituto de Desenvolvimento Tecnológico

{vmh, andre, emsantos, yan.soares}@icomp.ufam.edu.br

{hygo.sousa, adamorb, ronaldo.soares, alexandre.lima}@icomp.ufam.edu.br

{raoni.ferreira, lima.gabriel, lucas.hildelbrano}@sou.ufac.br

{nicolas, josern}@motorola.com

{eliane.collins, silvia.ascate, mateus.souza}@indt.org.br

Abstract. *In this paper, we propose a method for prioritizing regression test cases based on the probability of detecting software execution failures without source code analysis. To achieve this, our method employs the SentenceBERT model to extract embeddings from textual information of development commits and test scripts. These embeddings are then used by machine learning models to predict the probability of detecting a failure. Our experiments show that the proposed method achieves results equal to or better than those of human experts in 92.52% to 94.24% of scenarios when evaluating the APFD (Average Percentage Faults Detected) metric, an overall gain of 10% in APFD mean and a potential gain of up to 6.03% in test plan prioritization counting cases.*

1. Introduction

During the software development process, various testing routines are executed to ensure the quality of the product being developed. Among these routines, regression testing aims to verify whether changes made to components introduce new defects into the product by re-executing existing test cases to verify that previously working functionalities remain unaffected. Regression testing can be divided into the following stages: analysis of modified components, selection of suitable test cases, ordering of test case execution, and generation of documentation for the test results. [Rizwan et al. 2022].

In the first stage, the testing team analyzes information about product changes and scales plans to cover functional modifications executed in the new version of a product, as well as dependencies between these components [Zhang et al. 2022]. After identifying potentially affected components by the product change comes the selection of test cases to be executed. As test cases typically possess some form of tagging and cataloging, information about existing test case scopes is crossed with scope information for affected components during the selection stage. Consequently, test cases are selected based on defined criteria, such as covering affected components and generating a set of test cases capable of identifying the highest number of errors in the product [Pan et al. 2020].

This process affects the effectiveness of the testing plan in finding existing product failures. Usually, this procedure is executed by a group of testers where different levels of expertise among team members complement each other, often ensuring good performance.

Once the test case set has been defined, the subsequent stage involves determining their order of execution. In this stage, despite the numerous possible approaches to define their execution sequence, a common objective exists: to execute tests that are likely to uncover existing failures first. Typically, this ordering is performed based on the experience of the tester or historical information about the execution of test cases [Pan et al. 2020], which in turn affects the efficiency of the plan, given its direct impact on the speed at which failures will be discovered. Finally, after determining the ordering strategy, the tests are executed, and their results are recorded. These results may lead to the implementation of further changes in the software, which will subsequently enter the cycle and repeat until the product is delivered with all necessary corrections to ensure proper functioning.

In this context, test cases serve as units of execution for testing plans and can be categorized based on two characteristics: their level of automation [Tahvili et al. 2018] and functional or structural observation [Mafra et al. 2009]. Considering automation, tests are divided into automated and non-automated tests. Automated tests are executed by a computer in a controlled environment, without human intervention. In contrast, non-automated tests rely on a human tester for their full or partial execution [Tahvili et al. 2018].

In terms of functional characteristics, test cases are categorized as black-box or structural (white-box) based on distinct product features that they observe. While white-box testing is entirely dependent on the implementation of source code and examines the correctness of implementation aspects such as logical decisions, data structures, and loop structures, black-box testing verifies the product's functional capabilities without directly observing the source code [Mafra et al. 2009]. This allows black-box testing to be produced before the functionality is implemented, provided that only the test specification is based on the proposed product features.

In the specific context of automation characteristics, there is a significant interest in automating test case execution due to various reasons. These reasons include attempts to exclude human error during execution and the possibility of increasing the test scale with reduced costs [Rizwan et al. 2022]. However, the automation process can have a very high cost, both in terms of resources [Mafra et al. 2009] and time frames, or may even be impossible to implement. Due to this scenario, many companies still perform manual testing, even though, despite following an execution routine, the tester's interpretation may lead to divergent results [Mafra et al. 2009].

Regression testing cycles are justified by ensuring product quality with respect to execution correctness, which is an indispensable step in various product development scenarios. Due to this necessity, reducing its execution cost, whether financially or temporally, confirms the interest in optimizing resource allocation for the test task [Al-Sabbagh et al. 2021][Mehta et al. 2021][Ramírez et al. 2023]. However, human analysis can be inefficient when seeking the best possible resource utilization, either due to selecting redundant tests (unnecessarily increasing testing effort) or a biased execution order (resulting in potential defect correction delays).

In this perspective, machine learning techniques can be adopted to ensure confidence in the quality of the proposed test order for the execution of regression tests [Palma et al. 2018], [Wu et al. 2019]. This approach reduces the cost of generating testing plans and allows for the rapid analysis of massive data sources [Mehta et al. 2021]. According to [Rizwan et al. 2022], the use of machine learning techniques (ML) has been suitable and successful in automating many testing steps, such as product change identification, test case selection, and ordering. Moreover, advances in natural language processing (NLP) research have shown that these techniques have achieved improved performance in extracting information as well as in categorizing natural language texts, which may be difficult for machines to interpret due to their ambiguity and lack of structure [Tahvili et al. 2018].

Considering this context, this work proposes a framework for ordering regression testing plans, observing non-automated and black-box test cases. The proposed ordering is based on the probability of classification of a test case execution as a failure in a specific product. Therefore, the higher its probability of failure, the higher the priority of executing a test. An important feature of the method is that we use textual information without requiring access to the source code of the tested product. This enables suggesting an ordering of a testing plan according to the probabilities of failure of a specific test case.

The framework obtains the probability of a test execution resulting in a failure by deploying ML techniques, as follows: a classification model is trained to observe the information from a test case and a product change record, associating this tuple with a failure or not. The association is learned from the historical registry of executions, whose data allow us to associate a past execution of a test case with a specific product and its corresponding result. Finally, due to the textual nature of test cases and available product change records, it is necessary to use ML and NLP techniques to obtain codified information useful for the classification model.

The remainder of this work is structured as follows: Section 2 describes some related work relevant to our research problem. Section 3 details the proposed framework. In Section 4, we present the results achieved, along with an explanation of the data employed. Finally, in Section 5, a general summary of the results achieved is presented, as well as future works to be carried out.

2. Related Work

The ordering of test cases is a crucial step in the software testing process, allowing testers to focus on the most important tests based on predefined criteria. Consequently, testing time and resources are utilized more efficiently, increasing the probability of detecting critical failures in the software as quickly as possible. Various techniques for prioritizing test cases have been proposed in the literature, each with its own strengths and weaknesses. This section presents a review on this subject, focusing on approaches most relevant to the work developed here.

In [Mafra et al. 2009], the author proposed a tool that selects a set of ordered test cases according to their relevance. The selection is based on metrics obtained from previous execution results and metrics obtained from analyzing the content of each test case against the product scope. These metrics determine a relevance score for each test case, making it possible to identify the most relevant tests within a testing plan.

The authors in [Zhang et al. 2022] highlight that regression testing selection (RTS) optimizes testing by executing only the subset of tests that can be affected by changes. In this context, they showed that RTS based on ML works well in large code repositories. They developed a combination of RTS based on analysis and RTS based on ML to learn the impact of code changes on test results. Experiments were conducted on a training dataset obtained through mutation analysis. Compared to RTS based on analysis, this study showed that the combination with RTS based on ML selects about 25% fewer test cases, improving the task of prioritizing test cases to be evaluated.

In addition to selecting sets of test cases (TCs), another approach used in the literature is defining the order of execution for TCs to improve test execution time. In this sense, [Palma et al. 2018] developed an evaluative study of TCs from a dataset of open-source projects developed in Java, which compose the defects4j dataset. The authors proposed a logistic regression model for predicting TC priority, with results submitted to traditional quality metrics such as: Traditional Historical Fault Detection Metric (TM), Method Coverage (MC), Changed Method Coverage (CMC), and Size of Tests (ST); and quality metrics based on similarity, such as: Basic Counting (BC), Edit Distance (ED), Hamming Distance (HD), and Improved Basic Counting (IBC). The results indicated that the predictive model suggested by the authors can perform test case prioritization.

The work presented in [Spieker et al. 2017] proposes the RETECS method, focusing on automatically selecting and prioritizing TCs in the context of continuous software integration. The authors emphasize the relevance and difficulty of selecting TCs with higher probability of generating errors due to uncertainty generated by commit information regarding the impact of code changes. RETECS selects and prioritizes TCs using reinforcement learning and neural networks. To evaluate the performance of this method, the authors implemented a normalized APFD metric and identified an agent-based neural network as the best predictor for prioritizing TCs.

In [An and Yoo 2022], the authors also focused on selecting and prioritizing TCs. The Fault Localization (FL) technique was used, which measures the impact of each TC on the test plan suite (TP). In this work, it is reinforced that it is essential that FL performance be directly related to TP-tested test quality. To expand the TCs that comprise each TP, the authors developed the Fault Diagnosability Gain metric, which explores continuous FL results to emphasize parts of the program requiring more information.

Reinforcement learning techniques were also employed in [Omri and Sinz 2022]. In this work, the challenge of prioritizing TCs was approached as an online ranking problem to mitigate the scalability impact in continuous integration environments. The authors validated the proposed method in a case study industrial setting, showing that more than 95% of test failures were reported to software engineers, while only 40% of available TCs were executed.

Finally, in [Shankar and Sridhar 2024] it is highlighted that information loss is the biggest difficulty in prioritizing TCs in continuous integration environments. This loss significantly impacts the regression task performed by tools already produced in the literature. To resolve this problem, the authors developed DeepRP, a Q-learning-based reinforcement learning model that better understands features extracted from source code, version control, and code coverage.

It is worth mentioning that most of the work described in this section refers to the prioritization or selection of TCs related to continuous integration cycles through software versioning. In each cycle, metadata about the tests is generated through logs, test case execution time, instructions that guide the test cases, as well as coding of the version control system. In almost all observed methods, the use of the developed source code is used in the approaches proposed by the other solutions. On the other hand, in this work, the ordering of TCs is defined based on metadata contained in test scripts, commits and historical data related to the tested product, without observing the product's source code itself. In this way, our tool seeks to understand what was modified in the product from the textual artifacts mentioned above. This type of ordering, called black box, demonstrated compatibility and reliability through the APFD metric.

3. Proposed Method

In this work, we propose a framework that aims to optimize the order of execution of test cases to efficiently identify existing failures in product functionality, thereby ensuring a wider time margin for correcting these failures. To achieve this objective, it is necessary to prioritize the execution of test cases within a testing plan related to the changes made in the product. Therefore, there is an implicit interest in executing test cases that will reject the product as early as possible. Consequently, we seek to define an execution order that contains failure situations at the top positions.

To select the execution order, ML models are used to identify the probability of the product failing a test: a characteristic we call *failure probability*. Once the failure probability is calculated, the ordering of test cases is entirely based on this new characteristic. To calculate the failure probability, we provide the ML model with a feature vector composed of information about both the test case and the tested product version. This is done by concatenating two separately extracted feature vectors, one containing features extracted from the test case and another containing features representing the product. To characterize the product, we used commit texts from changes made to that version of the product, while for test case characteristics, we used the test script text. We did so since we believe that NLP ML models can extract characteristics from both to identify possible product failures, since the commits contain information regarding product changes and the test scripts of the tested characteristics.

It is important to note that both product and test case data are natural language texts, making it very challenging to extract computable information efficiently to characterize this textual information. To obtain a feature vector that can represent both sets of textual information, we employ neural networks based on transformer architecture SBERT [Reimers 2019], where the network provides a feature vector expressing the information existing in a text sentence. Therefore, given a product and a testing plan, we are able to establish a sequence of steps (illustrated in Figure 1) capable of ordering test cases based on failure probability. These steps are detailed in the next subsections.

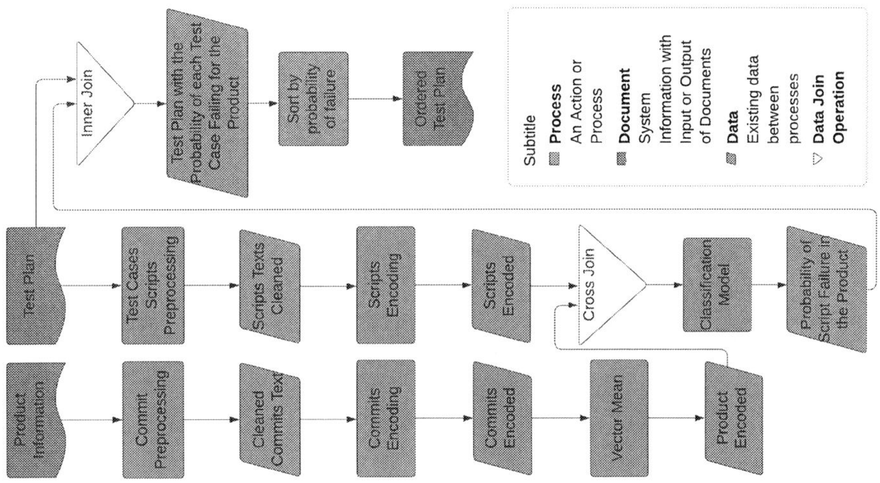

Figura 1. Flowchart of the Ordering Framework

3.1. Product Information and Test Case Preprocessing

The product and testing plan information are abstractions for the entire set of relevant information related to the problem used in our framework. As mentioned earlier, the product information is extracted from commit texts generated during the development of the referred product version. On the other hand, the information in the test plan is the test cases that make it up, each test case has a script of action instructions (test script) to be applied to the product. Both types of information possess textual characteristics close to natural language texts. Therefore, the first step for the proper use of this information involves text preprocessing.

Given the similarity in text type between both data sources, the preprocessing step in both cases consists of filtering out very common or very rare terms and removing known irrelevant texts. For example, during this stage, attention warnings, multiple blank spaces, special characters such as brackets, numbers, HTML tags, among others were removed. In our work, the filters used were essentially based on regular expression searches (REGEX). However, due to the specificities of each textual input (commits and test scripts), it was necessary to develop specific filters for each type of input. Once preprocessing is completed, the next step involves text encoding, in which texts are converted into numerical representation vectors.

3.2. Product Information and Test Case Encoding

The encoding models are responsible for observing textual content and transforming its representation into a numerical vector. The information contained in the vectors generated by the encoding models enables differentiation between texts based on the original textual content, representing it in a numerical form. The encoding model employed in our work was SBERT (Sentence Bidirectional Encoder Representations for Transformers).

3.3. SBERT

The Bidirectional Encoder Representations for Transformers (BERT) encoder is based on a transformer network, where the textual input is encoded into a 768-dimensional vector representation when the standard version of the architecture is used. This representation takes into account not only the content of existing terms in the text but also the arrangement of these terms within the text, as illustrated in Figure 2. SBERT is an extension of BERT, designed specifically for generating sentence representations. The key distinction between them is that SBERT trains BERT on a specific task of sentence encoding—rather than predicting words in a sentence. As a result, SBERT produces full-sentence representations, making them useful for tasks such as text-based information retrieval and text clustering [Reimers 2019].

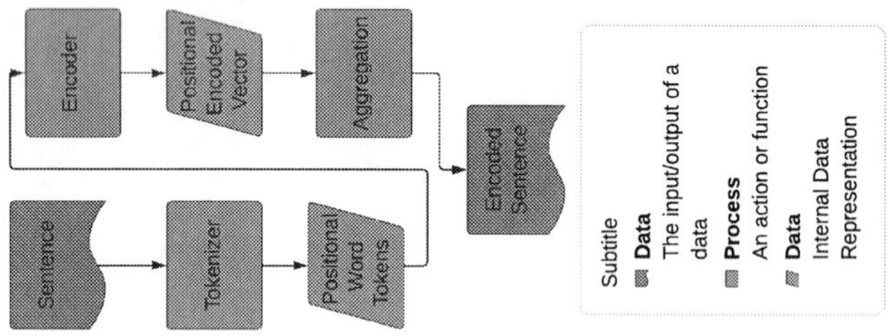

Figura 2. Flowchart of the SBERT Process.

In this work, we employed SBERT to encode the two textual entities: test case scripts and commit messages. The preprocessed texts were then submitted to the pre-trained SBERT model, which transformed the test steps and commits into embeddings. Our goal is that these embeddings condense the semantic content of the texts in a compact yet informative manner. Additionally, the vectorial representation of textual data enables various ML methods to perform tasks with the features extracted by the SBERT network. The next stage of our framework focuses on using some ML methods for the task of test case classification.

3.4. Classification of Test Cases Applied to a Product

As previously mentioned, the ordering of test cases is performed based on the probability of failure for each test case. This probability is calculated at this stage as follows: The encoding step of test case scripts and products generates a 1536-position vector (768 to represent the product and 768 to represent the test case) for each instance of test cases. These vectors are used as input for classification algorithms. Subsequently, the classification algorithm analyzes the received vector and returns the probability that this vector represents an accepted or failed test case, using the class probability output of the model.

Various ML techniques can be employed at this stage, since the objective of the algorithm is to learn to correlate the input vectors with the failure probability of the test case. In this work, the investigated methods were as follows: KNN (K-nearest neighbors) [Batista et al. 2009], Logistic Regressor [Brzezinski and Knafl 1999], MLP (Multi-Layer Perceptron) [Murtagh 1991], Xgboost [Friedman 2001], and random forest [Breiman 2001]. Once the failure probability of test cases is calculated, these can be ordered considering their failure probabilities.

3.5. Test Case Ordering

The failure probability generated by the classification model for each test case is aggregated with the identifiers of the test cases. In the final stage of the proposed framework, the test cases are ordered to prioritize those with higher failure probabilities. Therefore, the framework returns the sequence of execution identifiers for the test cases.

To verify the performance of our framework, an experimental protocol was designed to replicate a scenario of executing test plans. In these experiments, 5 different versions of the framework were tested using 5 classification techniques. The experimental protocol and the obtained results are presented in the next section.

4. Experiments

In this section, we describe the experimental protocol, evaluation metrics, and results obtained in the experiments. First, however, we present details about the dataset used.

4.1. Dataset

The dataset used in our experiments was provided by a large multinational corporation. The content of the dataset meets the requirements of the proposed scenario and allows us to validate the results of the framework and compare them with those obtained by the strategy adopted by this company. The dataset is originally divided into three sets, each serving a purpose of information representation.

The first is the *test case set*, which has 13,890 instances, containing labeled information regarding the functionalities under test by each individual test case and the actual text of the test script. The second set is the *product set*, which contains codification of 943,469 commit messages from 9052 products, distributed across approximately 240 classes corresponding to the type of component altered in the product. Due to the confidential nature of the commit messages, the company provided a sample of over 50,000 commits, which served to explore techniques for filtering and encoding that could be candidates for execution on the dataset by the company itself. With the filters and codification model defined, the company executed the processing of text from commits and provided a dataset containing the encoded vectors of commits. Finally, the third set is the *execution record set*, which contains information about the application of test cases to real products and the results of their executions. This set consists of 142,401 test case execution records.

4.2. Experimental Protocol

The experiments were conducted using the Hold-Out protocol and taking into account a temporal separation, i.e., by considering the time at which the products available in the dataset had their tests initiated. The proportion used was 70% of the products (necessarily the oldest) for training and the remaining 30% for testing (the most recent ones). The dataset was divided in this way since it is the procedure that most resembles the real process in production. In the training partition, 89.6% of the instances (test case executions) are from the non-failure class, while executions labeled as failure correspond to 1.9% of the set. On the other hand, in the testing partition, instances corresponding to the non-failure class represent 87.3%, while failures correspond to 2.2%. In both partitions, the remaining instances belong to classes such as postponed execution, conditional pass, and others that regard specific situations of the testing stage and were not considered in this experiment.

Given the two sets obtained after splitting the dataset, the training set and test set, all classification models were submitted to the same experimental protocol. Using the training partition, we manually set the hyperparameters of the models to optimize our classification metrics. After defining the hyperparameters of the models, we executed the final training and evaluated the models on the testing partition.

4.2.1. Comparison Protocol

In order to better evaluate the models' performance considering the ordering task, we employ three additional approaches as baselines: Real Order, Random Order, and Optimal Order of execution. The first considers the sequence used by the testing team of the partner company. Therefore, this method reflects the behavior of human Q&A analysts at the task of ordering the execution of test cases.

The remaining two methods are automatic methods for ordering the execution of test cases. The Random Order is a method that randomly guesses the order of the execution. It was designed by randomly generating 100 sequences for each test plan and presenting the mean result from these sequences. The sequences disregard any information about the product content or the test cases during their generation. Finally, the Optimal Order is an upper bound of ordering strategies, where it always generates the perfect execution sequence for any test plan, consistently achieving the best possible result under the observed metric.

4.3. Metrics

4.3.1. Classification

The metrics evaluated for the classification models are: accuracy, precision, recall, and F1 score. The values presented in the experiments section are the means of the observed test plan values.

4.3.2. Ordering

To evaluate the ordering, we use the APFD (Average Percentage Faults Detected) metric[Pradeepa and VimalDevi 2013], which is usual for test case priorization tasks. This metric measures the ordering of a test case based on the time at which existing faults are found. Its equation is as follows:

$$APFD = 1 - \frac{TF1 + TF2 + ... + TFm}{nm} + \frac{1}{2n} \tag{1}$$

where TFm indicates how many failures were found by the mth executed test, m represents the total number of failures and n represents the number of test cases used.

Similarly to the classification metrics, APFD will also be reported considering the average of the values achieved by the orderings for test plans.

4.4. Results

Initially, we evaluated the five ML models investigated in terms of classification of test cases into classes failure and non-failure. For this purpose, we considered the classification metrics accuracy, precision, recall, and F1-score. As shown in Figure 3, although four metrics have been used, all indicate the following order of decreasing performance: Xgboost, Knn, Logistic Regression, Random Forest, and MLP. However, it is important to note that Logistic Regression, Random Forest, and MLP exhibit very similar results. Xgboost, on the other hand, achieved inferior results.

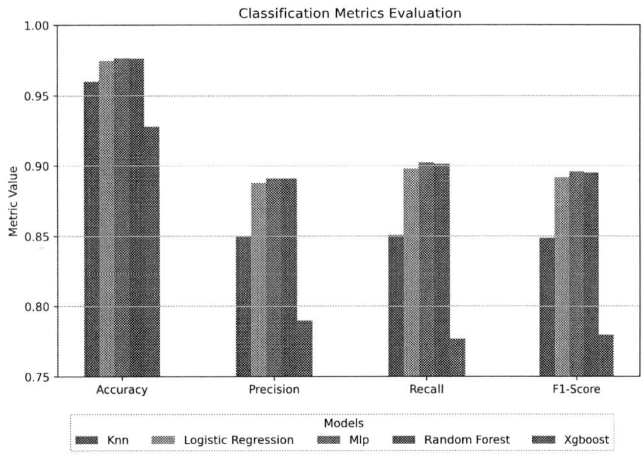

Figura 3. Comparing Machine Learning Algorithms for Classifying Test Cases into Failure and Non-Failure Classes.

As previously mentioned, the objective of our framework is to prioritize the test cases that will result in failures. Therefore, classification is only one necessary step towards ordering. The APFD metric is used to allow us to evaluate the actual ordering results. Here, two APFD values were calculated: one from the real-world data ordering (Real Order) and another from the ordering provided by our framework (Proposed Order). Consequently, for each test plan, we have access to two orderings: Real Order and Proposed Order, whose APFD values were calculated and compared to obtain information on the quality of the orderings for each test plan.

The five classification models were used individually to provide the probability of failure for the ordering step, enabling the testing of five different versions of the framework. Considering these five versions, we observed three possible scenarios for analyzing the ordering quality: (1) Better - scenario where the APFD calculated for the Proposed Order is higher than the APFD calculated for the Real Order; (2) Equal - where both values are similar; and (3) Worse - where the APFD calculated for the Proposed Order is lower than the APFD calculated for the Real Order.

Figure 4 illustrates the behavior of the five framework versions across the three scenarios. For all methods, the test plans are ordered from worse to best APFD results in comparison with its performance in the Real Order. Thus, in the left side are the worst results and on the right side the best results, and the relative improvement (or not) in APFD of the methods can be more easily compared.

Considering the models and scenarios, it is possible to observe the following order of results from worst to best: Knn, Xgboost, Logistic Regression, MLP, with Random Forest obtaining the best results, with 11,79% of the test plans having APFD results above the real order and only 5,76% of them having worse results. It is important to note that, in Figure 4, the width of the areas represents the number of cases where each scenario occurs, while the height of the bars indicates the difference observed in the quality of the ordering.

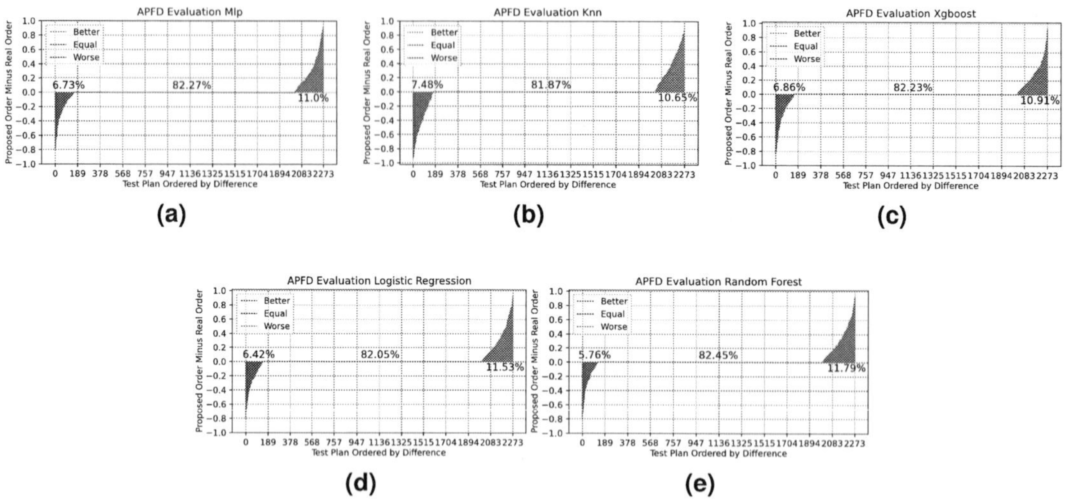

Figura 4. Comparison of the proposed framework using different machine learning algorithms in terms of Actual Percentage of Fault Detection (APFD) against Real APFD. Test plans are ordered from worst to best APFD difference in comparison to to the real order.

To further analyze the impact of our framework in the ordering, Figure 5 presents Violin plots of the APFD differences for test cases with better (a) and worse (b) results when compared to the Real Order, respectively. As can be seen, the worse results of KNN were more frequent and presented larger drops in APFD compared to the other classifiers, which had similar results in that regard. When analyzing the test cases with better APFD, surprisingly KNN had a higher mean APFD difference, but had a smaller number of test cases and highest values compared to all other methods evaluated, which also obtained similar results in comparison with each other, with Random Forest and Logistic Regression having more test cases with higher differences.

4.5. Discussions

Considering the various proposed orderings based on the five versions of the classification models, we can observe that despite the fact that a significant portion of the test plan orderings do not present real gains (Equal), the number of test plans with improved ordering (Better) exceeds the number of worse orderings in all scenarios, as shown in Figure 4.

Therefore, when considering the benefit provided by the framework as the number of plans evaluated as Better minus the number of plans with Worse outcomes, we observe that the framework demonstrates an improvement of 3.17% in its worst-performing classifier version (KNN 10.65% - 7,48%) and 6.03% in its best-performing classifier version

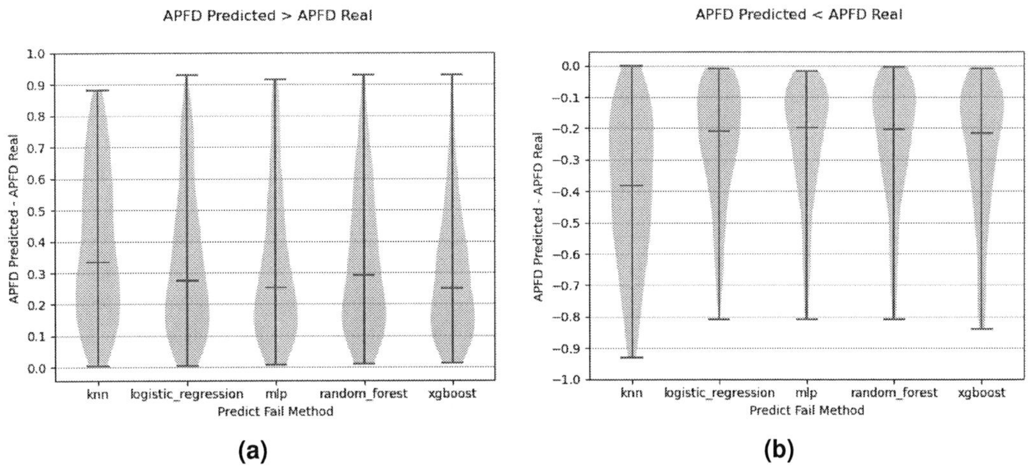

Figura 5. Distribution of differences between predicted and Real APFD for test cases where the framework obtained superior (a) and inferior (b) results in comparison to the Real Order.

(Random Forest 11,79% - 5,76%). Furthermore, our framework attained results superior to or equal to the manual method in between 92.52% and 94.24% of cases, depending on the machine learning algorithm used.

Based on these results, we can affirm that using the test case script and commit logs from a product submitted to this testing succeeded in providing sufficient information to the classification models to achieve a gain of up to 6.03% in the ordering of test plans, using the probability of failure as the ordering criterion.

Furthermore, as can be seen in Figure 4, there is a large number of test plans with APFD value tied between the real order and the order given by our framework. Most of these ties can be explained by the fact that 82.08% of test plans executed in the test set there were no test cases that ended in failure, hence having an APFD value of 1 irregardless of the test case ordering. Due to these cases being the majority, eventual improvements made from our framework may get diluted when analyzing ordering metrics.

Thus, to better visualize the impact of our Framework in the test plans where it *can* make any difference, Figure 6 presents the mean APFD for the different classification methods of our Framework, as well as the Real, Random and Optimal Order APFD results, considering only test plan executions where at least one failure was found. In these cases, the proposed ranking strategy once again demonstrated superior performance, achieving improvements of nearly 10% over the manually performed ordering. However, despite the gains obtained compared to the Real Order and Random Order, there remains a significant gap when contrasted with the Optimal Order. Even in the best scenario (Random Forest), the difference still stands at approximately 30% indicating that there is still room for improvements in the framework.

5. Conclusions

In this work, we propose a framework for ordering regression test plans considering non-automated and black-box testing cases. The ordering is performed based on the probability of classification of a test case execution on a specific product as a failure, which is

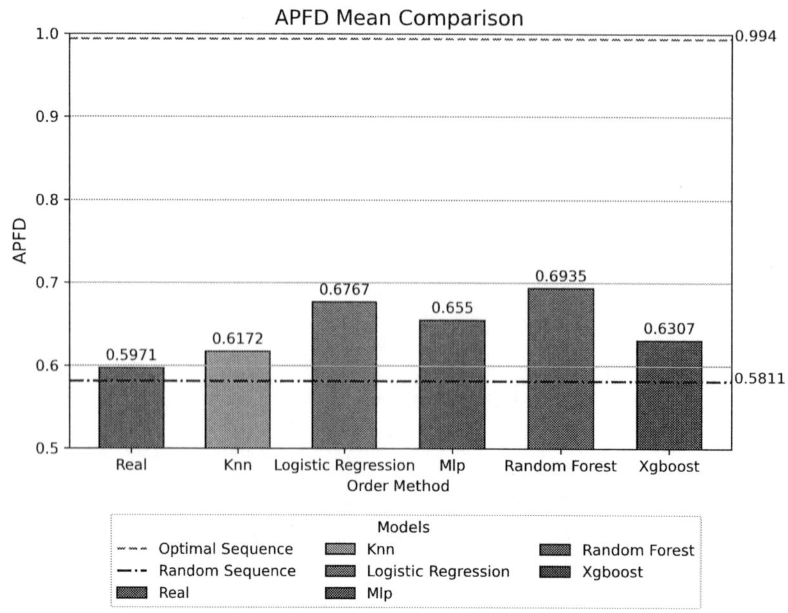

Figura 6. Proposed framework compared to Real, Random and Optimal Order.

calculated by machine learning models. The information used to represent each test case includes textual natural language information from the test case and a product change log to associate this pair with a failure or not.

We evaluated five different versions of the framework by varying the machine learning method used to classify the test cases. The results of the framework were compared to the performance of the sorting made by an expert team from the company owning the data, as well as random and optimal orderings of test case execution. The experiment results showed that the adopted ordering strategy achieved positive gain-loss ratios in all scenarios. Although there was similar performance between automatic and manual ordering in many cases, this scenario only reinforces the good performance of the framework, as our solution was able to equal or outperform the expert team with previously acquired experience in this function.

Another noteworthy point is that the information from commits and test case scripts proved capable of providing indications of a probable failure in the tested product, given that no source code was used.

The threats to the validity of this experiment reside in its use of proprietary data, making it difficult to generalize its performance to other data scenarios. Another point is the impossibility of validating the obtained results by disregarding the intrinsic characteristics of the test set, due to the necessary Hold-Out design feature of the problem.

Finally, new approaches are still needed for the investigated problem, such as expanding the framework's information sources and testing new machine learning model approaches like neural networks with higher learning capacity and techniques like reinforcement learning, where it would also be worthwhile to explore the use of the APFD metric as a reward for the model.

Artifact Availability

Due to our partner industrial compliance, we cannot provide any software developed during this research. Some parts contain sensitive content attached or industrial secrets that can be retrieved into our framework source code. Hence, since this research was conducted on texts extracted from commits and tests scripts from real data, it contains employee information or secrets about products functions. Consequently, even coded, the data and trained models are not allowed to being provided. Moreover, simulated versions of sensitive functions or content would turn the data useless and compromise results, as artificial generated data could not reproduce real-world data. Considering this context, we are unable to elaborate software or data artifacts that can be followed, comprehended, or executed to really reproduce results without compromising the expected confidentially.

Acknowledgments

This research was partially supported by Motorola Mobility Comércio de Produtos Eletrônicos Ltda, under the terms of Federal Law No. 8.387/1991, through agreement No. 02/2021, signed with ICOMP/UFAM. Also, this work was partially supported by the following Brazilian agencies: the Coordenação de Aperfeiçoamento de Pessoal de Nível Superior- Brasil (CAPES-PROEX)- Finance Code 001, the National Council for Scientific and Technological Development (CNPq), and Amazonas State Research Support Foundation- FAPEAM- through the POSGRAD project 2024/2025.

Referências

Al-Sabbagh, K., Staron, M., Hebig, R., and Gomes, F. (2021). A classification of code changes and test types dependencies for improving machine learning based test selection. In *Proceedings of the 17th International Conference on Predictive Models and Data Analytics in Software Engineering*, pages 40–49.

An, G. and Yoo, S. (2022). Fdg: a precise measurement of fault diagnosability gain of test cases. In *Proceedings of the 31st ACM SIGSOFT International Symposium on Software Testing and Analysis*, pages 14–26.

Batista, G., Silva, D. F., et al. (2009). How k-nearest neighbor parameters affect its performance. In *Argentine symposium on artificial intelligence*, pages 1–12. Citeseer.

Breiman, L. (2001). Random forests. *Machine learning*, 45:5–32.

Brzezinski, J. R. and Knafl, G. J. (1999). Logistic regression modeling for context-based classification. In *Proceedings. Tenth International Workshop on Database and Expert Systems Applications. DEXA 99*, pages 755–759. IEEE.

Friedman, J. H. (2001). Greedy function approximation: a gradient boosting machine. *Annals of statistics*, pages 1189–1232.

Mafra, J., Miranda, B., Iyoda, J., and Sampaio, A. (2009). Test case selector: Uma ferramenta para seleção de testes. *Proceedings of SBMF/SAST*.

Mehta, S., Farmahinifarahani, F., Bhagwan, R., Guptha, S., Jafari, S., Kumar, R., Saini, V., and Santhiar, A. (2021). Data-driven test selection at scale. In *Proceedings of the 29th ACM Joint Meeting on European Software Engineering Conference and Symposium on the Foundations of Software Engineering*, pages 1225–1235.

Murtagh, F. (1991). Multilayer perceptrons for classification and regression. *Neurocomputing*, 2(5-6):183–197.

Omri, S. and Sinz, C. (2022). Learning to rank for test case prioritization. In *Proceedings of the 15th Workshop on Search-Based Software Testing*, pages 16–24.

Palma, F., Abdou, T., Bener, A., Maidens, J., and Liu, S. (2018). An improvement to test case failure prediction in the context of test case prioritization. In *Proceedings of the 14th international conference on predictive models and data analytics in software engineering*, pages 80–89.

Pan, C., Yang, Y., Li, Z., and Guo, J. (2020). Dynamic time window based reward for reinforcement learning in continuous integration testing. In *Proceedings of the 12th Asia-Pacific Symposium on Internetware*, pages 189–198.

Pradeepa, R. and VimalDevi, K. (2013). Effectiveness of testcase prioritization using apfd metric: Survey. In *International Conference on Research Trends in Computer Technologies (ICRTCT—2013). Proceedings published in International Journal of Computer Applications®(IJCA)*, pages 0975–8887.

Ramírez, A., Feldt, R., and Romero, J. R. (2023). A taxonomy of information attributes for test case prioritisation: Applicability, machine learning. *ACM Transactions on Software Engineering and Methodology*, 32(1):1–42.

Reimers, N. (2019). Sentence-bert: Sentence embeddings using siamese bert-networks. *arXiv preprint arXiv:1908.10084*.

Rizwan, S., Ali Sobuj, M. S., and Akhond, M. R. (2022). A survey on software test case minimization. In *Proceedings of the 2022 Fourteenth International Conference on Contemporary Computing*, pages 679–684.

Shankar, R. and Sridhar, D. (2024). An improved deep learning based test case prioritization using deep reinforcement learning. *International Journal of Intelligent Engineering & Systems*, 17(1).

Spieker, H., Gotlieb, A., Marijan, D., and Mossige, M. (2017). Reinforcement learning for automatic test case prioritization and selection in continuous integration. In *Proceedings of the 26th ACM SIGSOFT international symposium on software testing and analysis*, pages 12–22.

Tahvili, S., Hatvani, L., Felderer, M., Afzal, W., Saadatmand, M., and Bohlin, M. (2018). Cluster-based test scheduling strategies using semantic relationships between test specifications. In *Proceedings of the 5th International Workshop on Requirements Engineering and Testing*, pages 1–4.

Wu, Z., Yang, Y., Li, Z., and Zhao, R. (2019). A time window based reinforcement learning reward for test case prioritization in continuous integration. In *Proceedings of the 11th Asia-Pacific Symposium on Internetware*, pages 1–6.

Zhang, J., Liu, Y., Gligoric, M., Legunsen, O., and Shi, A. (2022). Comparing and combining analysis-based and learning-based regression test selection. In *Proceedings of the 3rd ACM/IEEE International Conference on Automation of Software Test*, pages 17–28.

A Decade of Turnover Intention Research in IT: Key Insights and Trends

Wagner Vidal Xavier da Silva[1], Suzana Sampaio[2,3]

[1]Graduate Program in Administration and Development – Universidade Federal Rural de Pernambuco (UFRPE), Recife – PE – Brazil

[2]Computer Department – Universidade Federal Rural de Pernambuco (UFRPE) Recife – PE – Brazil

[3]University of Galway, School of Engineering - Galway - Ireland

{wagner.vidal,suzana.sampaio}@ufrpe.br

Abstract. *Employee turnover intention poses challenges for IT organizations, affecting performance and strategic goals. Despite research efforts, the factors driving turnover remain fragmented. This study conducted a systematic literature review of research published between 2015 and 2024, using PRISMA guidelines. A total of 41 studies were analyzed, identifying 29 internal and 25 external factors. Job satisfaction was the most cited internal factor, while organizational commitment was the most frequent external factor. Burnout also emerged as a key driver. These findings support IT organizations in developing targeted HR strategies to improve retention.*

1. Introduction

Information Technology (IT) is one of the fastest-growing industries, standing out as one of the most promising business segments for economic development on a global scale [Farooq *et al.*, 2022]. According to [Sandhya and Sulphey, 2019], more than 30% of significant growth has witnessed $150 billion in the IT and software industry in the last few years. This growth is expected to require around 546,100 new jobs over the next few years [Moquin *et al.,* 2019]. However, the IT sector is facing major challenges, such as rapid technological changes, continual training and retooling of IT professionals, high employee turnover, and economic fluctuations [Gefen *et al.*, 2015; Moquin *et al.,* 2019].

The fast-paced environment of the IT industry, coupled with high expectations of innovation and productivity, creates significant stress and pressure on employees [Ajayi and Udeh, 2024]. Due to that, to maintain professional competence, IT professionals must remain updated on technological advancements and uphold their knowledge base [Pereira *et al.,* 2024]. Moreover, the IT industry has a culture of constant connectivity, high technical expertise, continuous learning, and extended periods of focused work, often under tight deadlines [Ajayi and Udeh, 2024]. In this way, the boundaries between work and personal life can be blurred, further exacerbating stress levels and decreasing overall well-being [Lo, 2015]. This dynamic often leads to burnout among IT professionals [Ajayi and Udeh, 2024].

In such a high-pressure environment, retaining professionals becomes a persistent challenge, particularly for the IT sector [Joseph *et al.*, 2007]. This challenge is further amplified by the phenomenon of turnover intention. Turnover intention refers to the employee's desire to seek new job opportunities or voluntarily switch companies [Pereira *et al.,* 2024]. It is also recognized as a significant predictor of voluntary job resignation [Chouhan, 2022]. Furthermore, this phenomenon directly impacts the organizational well-being and disrupts the supply and demand of the IT labor market [Lo, 2015]. Moreover, previous studies have demonstrated that employees with high turnover intention often display poor performance and high absenteeism rates [Chouhan, 2022].

Turnover intention can negatively impact organizations by leading to the loss of critical skills, knowledge and abilities, ultimately resulting in high replacement costs and a reduced revenue (current and/or future) [Scholtz *et al.,* 2019]. Consequently, mitigating the pretentiousness of this phenomenon has become the focus of attention for the IT industry in recent years [Kumar, 2022]. This concern is legitimate because of the financial repercussions of high turnover rates in an industry that continuously reports poor employee retention [Lo, 2015]. The IT sector is among the top four industries with poor employee retention rates [Rhatigan, 2016] and overall human capital has a significant role in shaping the financial performance of IT organizations [Chouhan, 2022; Gupta and Raman, 2021].

Many variables influence employee turnover intentions [Kanchana and Jayathilaka, 2023]. However, the causes of employee turnover intention are multiple and complex, and still poorly understood globally [Cohen *et al.,* 2016]. To address this salient and persistent issue, the present study systematically reviews the literature on turnover intention among IT professionals from 2015 to 2024. Preliminary results indicate that job satisfaction and organizational commitment are potential constructs in the analyses. Furthermore, the survey method is utilized in most of the studies. Another introductory point is the prevalence of studies in countries with technological prominence, such as the United States and India.

By identifying and analyzing key factors contributing to turnover intention, this study aims to provide actionable insights for IT organizations to develop more effective retention strategies as a potential means to mitigate turnover intention and its associated challenges. Specifically, it examines global trends, antecedents of turnover intention, and methodological approaches, highlighting research gaps and laying the groundwork for future studies. In this context, understanding these elements is crucial in a landscape where the demand for qualified talent exceeds supply [Chouhan, 2022]. Thus, it is essential to mitigate turnover and ensure the retention of a skilled workforce [Pereira *et al.,* 2024].

Thus, to achieve these objectives, the study addresses the primary research question: "What are the main factors influencing turnover intention decisions among IT professionals according to the existing literature?". The following sections of this article are structured as follows. Section 2 introduces the background and related works about the theme. Section 3 documents the research method applied. Section 4 highlights the results, their implications, and discussion, respectively. Finally, section 5 marks the conclusion, limitations, and future research directions.

2. Background

2.1 Turnover Intention

Turnover intention refers to an employee's likelihood of leaving an organization voluntarily. In the IT sector, this issue is particularly prevalent due to job stress, lack of satisfaction, and inadequate compensation [Al-Dalahmeh *et al.,* 2020; Pereira *et al.,* 2024]. Besides that, IT professionals leave the organization due to poor relationships with supervisors, co-workers, and management [Farooq *et al.,* 2022]. Stressors such as job overload [Sarker *et al.,* 2019] also contribute to turnover intention [Tulili *et al.,* 2023].

In the IT sector, a high rate of turnover intention has been noticed due to different challenging issues such as work stress, lack of job satisfaction, and inefficient compensation plans [Al-Dalahmeh *et al.,* 2020; Pereira *et al.,* 2024]. In addition, IT employees face constant changes that accompany rapid technological leaps in the field [Prommegger *et al.,* 2019]. Furthermore, IT professionals suffer from high project error rates that typically occur in IT projects [Standish Group, 2015] and are, therefore, often exposed to feelings of failure [Rampadaruth, 2022]. In this way, mental health is impacted by the constant scenarios of change and tension, increasing the desire to leave work, which is a key factor contributing to burnout among IT professionals [Ajayi and Udeh, 2024].

Burnout is a key factor in turnover intentions, which negatively impacts mental health and job satisfaction [Ajayi and Udeh, 2024). Burnout is often triggered by excessive workload, inadequate recognition, and poor work-life balance, making IT professionals more susceptible to leaving their jobs [Rampadaruth, 2022]. Job satisfaction plays a critical role, as dissatisfied employees are more likely to seek alternative opportunities [Farooq *et al.,* 2022].

Global studies highlight the financial impact of turnover. Due to the shortage of skilled and talented employees, IT organizations have to bear the projected financial loss in revenue, such as the United States $435.7 billion in 2020 [Farooq *et al.,* 2022]. High turnover rates lead to financial losses, knowledge drain, and recruitment challenges [Ajit, 2016; Witt and Burke, 2002]. Understanding the factors driving turnover intention is vital to developing effective retention strategies [Kanchana and Jayathilaka, 2023].

2.2 Employee Retention

Employee retention focuses on organizational efforts to keep skilled workers engaged and committed [Kong, 2022]. In the IT sector, where demand for qualified professionals exceeds supply, companies invest heavily in retention strategies [Kumar, 2022]. Retaining qualified IT professionals to strengthen organizational performance and competitiveness [Zaza *et al.,* 2022]. High-performing employees contribute significantly to organizational success, making retention a priority [Serenko *et al.,* 2022]

Effective retention strategies include competitive salaries, career growth opportunities, and supportive work environments [Al Akasheh *et al.,* 2024]. Organizations also focus on job satisfaction and engagement to reduce turnover [Pereira *et al.,* 2024]. Studies indicate that employees with higher job satisfaction and organizational commitment exhibit lower turnover intentions [Mahindru *et al.,* 2023].

2.3 Related Work

Prior research on turnover intention has identified multiple influencing factors, including job satisfaction, burnout, and organizational commitment [Farooq *et al.,* 2022; Serenko *et al.,* 2022] A study in Japan found that work exhaustion and job satisfaction mediate turnover intention [Serenko *et al.,* 2022]. Another study in Pakistan identified job security, salary, and career management as significant factors [Farooq *et al.,* 2022]. [Alla and Rajaa, 2019] conducted a literature review on employee turnover. The authors concluded that turnover has negative repercussions on the psychological and productivity of employees as well as on the overall organizational performance.

However, it does not directly portray which attributes impact on turnover intention. This study addresses this gap by compiling, through an SLR, the key attributes that influence turnover intention. Moreover, this study extends previous research by analyzing turnover intention globally, covering a broader timeframe (2015–2024). Unlike earlier reviews, it incorporates additional factors such as work integration, burnout, and perceived workload [Farooq *et al.,* 2022]. By consolidating findings, this review offers actionable insights to mitigate turnover and improve retention strategies in the IT sector, and support managers and leaders in effectively mitigating this phenomenon.

3. Research Method

This study follows a systematic literature review (SLR) approach, employing the Preferred Reporting Items for Systematic Reviews and Meta-Analyses (PRISMA) method. The review aims on answering the research question: *What are the main factors influencing turnover intention among IT professionals as identified in the literature?*

To ensure rigor, the methodology aligns with [Kitchenham and Charters, 2007] guidelines, covering research questions, inclusion/exclusion criteria and search strategy Figure 1 illustrates the study selection process, summarizing how studies were filtered and finalized. The study was conducted by two researchers.

3.1. Data Collection

Four electronic repositories were selected: IEEE Xplore, ScienceDirect, ACM Digital, and Google Scholar. The search period spans 2015–2024, reflecting the growing influence of digital transformation and trends around the digital economy, which have been catalyzed by the COVID-19 pandemic, indicate a significant increase in functions and occupations in the IT area [Souza *et al.,* 2023].

The following string was selected also based on the work of [Farooq *et al.,* 2022]: (''turnover intention'' OR ''job change'' OR ''turn away'' OR ''job mobility'' OR ''job movement'' OR ''job flow'' OR ''career change'') AND (''software developer'' OR ''IT professional'' OR ''IT personnel'' OR ''software engineer'' OR ''software coder'' OR "developer" OR "tester") AND (''software industry'' OR ''IT industry'' OR "software engineering") applied to the title, abstract, and keywords. For the Science Direct repository, the research string was adapted due to the limitation of only eight Boolean operators. As a result, the adjusted string was structured as follows: ("turnover intention" AND "software industry") OR ("turnover intention" AND "IT industry") OR ("turnover intention" AND "IT professional").

The inclusion and exclusion criteria were outlined as follows, adapted from the work of [Farooq *et al.,* 2022]. Inclusion criteria involved: studies written in English; peer-reviewed journal or conference papers published between 2015–2024; and research addressing turnover factors in IT/software sectors. Exclusion criteria included: non- English studies; book chapters, white papers, workshop reports; duplicates or inaccessible studies; and studies not relevant to the topic. Figure 1 illustrates the study selection process, summarizing how studies were filtered and finalized.

3.2. Study Selection Process

The selection followed PRISMA's four-step process:

1. Identification – 20,252 studies retrieved from databases
2. Screening – Filtering by title, abstract, keywords, and relevance
3. Eligibility – Exclusion of inaccessible or duplicate papers
4. Inclusion – Final selection of 41 primary studies for analysis

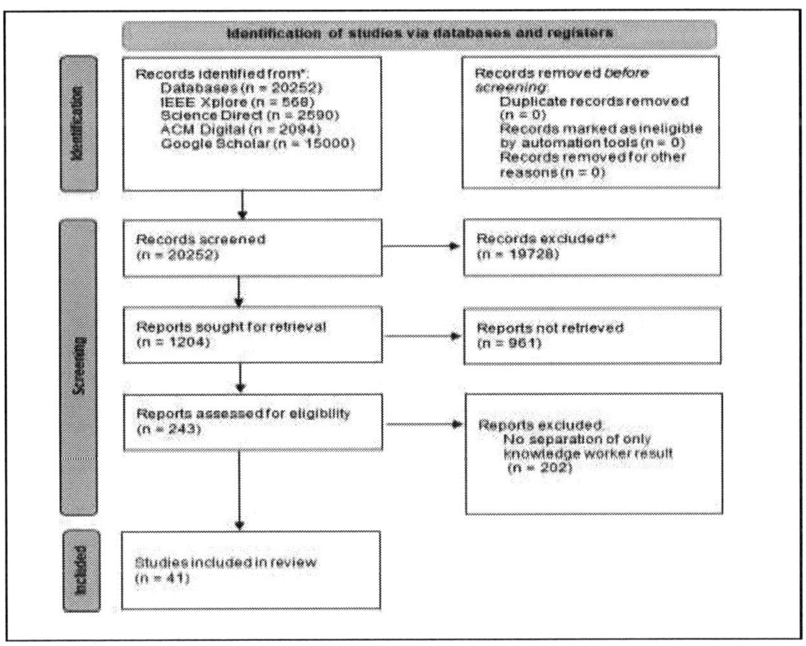

Figure 1. Selection process

3.3. Data Extraction and Synthesis

In this phase, all remaining studies were analyzed, for data extraction and synthesis. The analysis focused on turnover intention factors, classified as:

- internal (job satisfaction, burnout, demographic attributes);
- or external (organizational commitment, compensation, leadership style).

4. Results and Discussion

4.1. Overview of primary studies

This SLR identified 41 relevant studies investigating the factors that impact turnover intention among IT professionals, as described in Table 2. The factors are classified as internal (demographics, job satisfaction, burnout) and external (organizational commitment, leadership style, compensation), as presented in the work of [Pratiwi *et al.,* 2024]. Internal factors include personality traits such as extraversion, openness, emotional resilience, and assertiveness, while external factors encompass aspects related to professional development, organizational skills and knowledge, supportive supervisors, and career anchors [Chouhan, 2022]. Additionally, each study was meticulously analyzed and classified according to its method and country of origin.

Table 1. Primary studies and key findings

Author, Year	Country	Method	Factors affecting turnover intention	
			Internal	External
[Abid *et al.,* 2016]	Pakistan	Quantitative	Demographic (Age; Education; Gender; Organizational Tenure) Perceived Organizational Support	Heedful Relating
[Al Akasheh et *al.,* 2024]	Arab Emirates	Quantitative	Job Satisfaction Job Involvement	Job Environment
[Apostel *et al.,* 2018]	Germany	Quantitative	-	Illegitimate Tasks
[Armstrong *et al.,* 2018]	United States	Quantitative	Work Exhaustion	Organizational Commitment
[Atouba, 2018]	United States	Quantitative	Employee Work Participation Organizational Identification	Internal Communication Adequacy
[Booysen and Malan, 2024]	South Africa	Literature Review	Satisfaction With Benefits	Job Embeddedness Supportive Organizational Climate Transformational Leadership
[Chiu, 2017]	Taiwan	Quantitative	Job Crafting	-
[Cho *et al.,* 2020]	Korea	Quantitative	Job Satisfaction	-
[Chouhan , 2022]	India	Quantitative	Career Adaptability	-
[Dinger *et al.,* 2015]	United States	Quantitative	Perceived Job Alternatives Intrinsic Motivation Job Satisfaction Affective Commitment	-

[Dunukara and Pushpakumari, 2021]	Sri Lanka	Quantitative	-	Advancement Opportunities Pay and Benefits Job Security Supervisor/Management Relations Peer Relations
[Eckhardt *et al.*, 2016]	Germany	Quantitative	Personality Traits Neuroticism Extraversion Conscientiousness	-
[Farooq *et al.*, 2022]	Pakistan	Quantitative	Employee Commitment Recognition Employee Experience Education Level	Recruitment & Section Team & Management Support Performance & Career Management Salary & Compensation Job Security Organizational Demographics (Organization Size and Department Size)
[Gumussoy, 2016]	Turkey	Quantitative	Job Satisfaction Career Commitment Conscientiousness Openness To Experience Career Satisfaction	-
[Haran and Niederman, 2022]	India	Quantitative	Job Satisfaction Organizational Justice	-
[Harden *et al.*, 2018]	United States	Quantitative	Perceived Work Overload Perceived Skill Obsolescence Fairness of Rewards	Organizational Commitment
[Haridas *et al.*, 2022]	India	Quantitative	-	Organizational Career Management
[Idell *et al.*, 2021]	United States	Quantitative	Distrust in organization	-
[Kanchana and Jayathilaka, 2023]	Sri Lanka	Quantitative	Job Satisfaction Demographic (Gender: Male)	-
[Moquin *et al.*, 2019]	United States	Quantitative	Psychological contract breach	-
[Mufitha *et al.*, 2019]	Sri Lanka	Quantitative	Job Satisfaction Professional Commitment	-
[Naqvi and Bashir, 2015]	Pakistan	Quantitative	-	Supervisor Support
[Pereira *et al.*, 2024]	Brazil	Qualitative	Satisfaction With Compensations (Salary)	Remote Work
[Ramalho Luz *et al.*, 2018]	Brazil	Quantitative	Demographic (Age) Affective Commitment Normative Commitment Job Satisfaction Satisfaction With Pay Satisfaction With Promotions	Organizational Commitment

			Satisfaction With The Nature of The Work	
[Ramaprasad *et al.*, 2021]	Indian	Quantitative	Work Engagement	High-Performance Work Systems Organizational Commitment
[Rusbadrol *et al.*, 2017]	Malaysia	Qualitative	Organizational Justice	-
[Santoso *et al.*, 2023]	Indone-sia	Qualitative	Job Satisfaction	Organizational Commitment
[Sasaki *et al.*, 2019]	Japan	Quantitative	Job Satisfaction	-
[Scholtz *et al.*, 2019]	South Africa	Quantitative	Job Satisfaction	Organizational Size Occupational Culture
[Serenko *et al.*, 2022]	Japan	Quantitative	Job Satisfaction	-
[Sethar *et al.*, 2022]	Pakistan	Quantitative	Job Satisfaction	-
[Setiawan *et al.*, 2024]	Jakarta	Quantitative	Employee Engagement	-
[Sharma and Stol, 2020]	Ireland	Quantitative	Job Satisfaction	-
[Singh, 2024]	India	Quantitative	Work-Life Balance	Organizational Commitment
[Sivarethinamohan and Aranganathan, 2015]	India	Quantitative	Role Ambiguity Role conflict Work Exhaustion Promotion Satisfaction Fairness of individual rewards Job security	Supervisor's feedback Leader Member exchange Work Schedule Flexibility Career accommodation
[Souza *et al.*, 2023]	Brazil	Literature Review	Perception Of Material Support	Performance Management Compensation and Development Policies Management Leadership Style Social Support
[Suárez Albanchez *et al.*, 2022]	Spain	Quantitative	Organizational Support Perceived	Organizational Commitment
[Vennila and Vivekanandan, 2017]	India	Quantitative	Work Exhaustion	-
[Vidya, 2023]	India	Quantitative	Emotional Dissonance Burnout Components (Emotional Exhaustion, Depersonalization And Personal Accomplishment)	-
[Zaza *et al.*, 2022]	United States	Quantitative	Burnout	-

[Zentner, 2018]	United States	Quantitative	Job Performance	-

4.2. Key constructs on turnover intention among IT professionals

Job satisfaction was identified in 14 studies, making it the most cited internal factor influencing turnover intention. Employees with higher satisfaction levels are less likely to leave, reinforcing findings from [Pereira *et al.,* 2024] and [Dhakal *et al.,* 2024]. This construct can be understood as the fulfillment of work demands and has a significant impact on employees' well-being in the workplace [Dhamija *et al.,* 2019] [Xavier *et al.,* 2024]. It represents how much an individual experiences pleasures in the organizational context [Ramalho Luz *et al.,* 2018]. In addition, job satisfaction is also known to be a predictor of turnover intention [Grawitch *et al.,* 2007] where the higher the levels of job satisfaction the lower the intention to leave [Xavier *et al.,* 2024].

Organizational commitment appeared in 7 studies as the most frequent external factor. It stands out as the factor that reflects the extent to which an employee aligns with the organization's goals and values and is willing to put in effort to contribute to its success [Singh, 2024]. Additionally, [Mahindru *et al.,* 2023] reinforce that employees with higher organizational commitment exhibit lower turnover intention [Biswas and Varma, 2012; Gupta and Bhatia, 2023; Ramaprasad *et al.,* 2020] as noted by [Suárez-Albanchez *et al.,* 2022].

Burnout was highlighted in some studies as a significant internal factor, leading to decreased productivity and higher attrition rates, aligning with the work of of [Trinkenreich *et al.,* 2024], which states that the few studies investigating its consequences provide evidence that burnout can lead to an increase in staff turnover intention. Moreover, according to [Ajayi and Udeh, 2024], the detrimental effect of burnout on productivity is well-documented, with several studies linking it to decreased work performance, increased absenteeism, and a higher turnover rate.

4.3 Discussion and Implications

The findings confirm that job satisfaction and organizational commitment are critical in understanding turnover intention. In this sense, when these factors are low, employees are more likely to seek opportunities elsewhere, increasing turnover rates. The geographic distribution highlights the growing importance of emerging IT markets in turnover research. Additionally, the dominance of quantitative surveys suggests a need for more diverse methodological approaches, including qualitative and longitudinal studies.

To mitigate turnover intention, IT organizations should focus on enhancing job satisfaction through career development and well-being initiatives; strengthening organizational commitment by fostering engagement and leadership support; and addressing burnout with flexible work policies and mental health support. These insights might contribute to HR strategies aimed at improving talent retention and organizational stability in the IT sector.

5. Conclusion

This in-depth review analyzed 41 studies on knowledge workers' turnover, examining the internal and external factors influencing turnover intention. Searches were conducted in IEEE Xplore, ScienceDirect, ACM Digital, and Google Scholar (2015–2024), identifying 20,252 papers. After applying PRISMA-based inclusion and exclusion criteria, 41 studies were selected and categorized based on key turnover determinants.

Findings revealed that job satisfaction was the most frequently cited internal factor, while organizational commitment was the most prominent external factor. Additionally, burnout emerged as a significant internal driver of turnover intention among IT professionals. Thus, understanding these influences, along with global trends and research methodologies, supports the development of talent retention strategies, mitigating productivity losses, skill gaps, and high rehiring costs.

This study has limitations. Many relevant studies were not freely accessible, and the scope was restricted to four databases, which, while significant, may not cover all pertinent research. Expanding the database scope could enhance future findings. Future research should also investigate the antecedents of job satisfaction, organizational commitment, and burnout, as well as explore qualitative approaches to capture deeper insights into employee motivations and decision-making processes that quantitative methods may overlook.

References

Abid, G., Zahra, I. and Ahmed, A. (2016). Promoting thriving at work and waning turnover intention: A relational perspective. *Future Business Journal*, v. 2, n. 2, p. 127-137.

Ajayi, F. A. and Udeh, C. A. (2024). Combating burnout in the IT Industry: A review of employee well-being initiatives. *International Journal of Applied Research in Social Sciences*, v. 6, n. 4, p. 567-588.

Ajit, P. (2016). Prediction of employee turnover in organizations using machine learning algorithms. *algorithms*, v. 4, n. 5, p. C5.

Al-Dalahmeh, M. L., Héder, M. and Dajnoki, K. (2020). The effect of talent management practices on employee turnover intention in the information and communication technologies (ICTs) sector: Case of Jordan.

Al Akasheh, M., Hujiran, O., Malik, E. F. and Zaki, N. (2024). Enhancing the Prediction of Employee Turnover with Knowledge Graphs and Explainable AI. *IEEE Access.*

Alla, A. A. and Rajaa, O. (2019). A review of the literature on employee turnover. *American International Journal of Social Science*, v. 8, n. 3, p. 22-29.

Apostel, E., Syrek, C. J. and Antoni, C. H. (2018). Turnover intention as a response to illegitimate tasks: The moderating role of appreciative leadership. *International Journal of Stress Management*, v. 25, n. 3, p. 234.

Armstrong, D., Riemenschneider, C., Buche, M. W. and Armstrong, K. R. (2018). Mitigating turnover intentions: are all IT workers warriors?. *AIS Transactions on Replication Research*, v. 4, n. 1, p. 10.

Atouba, Y. C. (2018). Tackling the turnover challenge among IT workers: Examining the role of internal communication adequacy, employee work participation, and organizational identification. *Communication Reports*, v. 31, n. 3, p. 174-187.

Biswas, S. and Varma, A. (2012). Linkages between antecedents of in-role performance and intentions to quit: an investigation in India. *The International Journal of Human Resource Management*, v. 23, n. 5, p. 987-1005.

Booysen, C. and Malan, D. J. (2024). Intention to quit among Generation Y information technology professionals in South Africa. *SA Journal of Industrial Psychology*, v. 50,n. 1, p. 1-13.

Chiu, C. (2017). IT professionals' turnover intention: the role of job crafting and engagement. *PACIS 2017 Proceedings*.

Cho, J.,Yoo, J. and Lim, J. (2020). Analysis of job stress's impact on job performance and turnover of cybersecurity professionals. *ICIC Express Letters*, v.14, p. 409-415.

Chouhan, V. S. (2022). Influence of career adaptability on career satisfaction and turnover intention of IT professionals. *International Journal of Human Capital and Information Technology Professionals (IJHCITP),* v. 13, n. 1, p. 1-15.

Cohen, G. and Blake, R. S. (2016). Goodman, Doug. Does turnover intention matter? Evaluating the usefulness of turnover intention rate as a predictor of actual turnover rate. *Review of Public Personnel Administration*, v. 36, n. 3, p. 240-263.

Dhakal, D. R., Ojha, S. K., Sharma, L. K., Dhungana, B. R. and Chapagain, R. (2024). Employee turnover intention in a service industry: a systematic literature review. *Migration Letters*, v. 21, n. 7, p. 1481-1494.

Dhamija, P., Gupta, S. and Bag, S. (2019). Measuring of job satisfaction: the use of quality of work life factors. *Benchmarking: An International Journal*, v. 26, n. 3, p. 871-892.

Dinger, M., Thatcher, J. B., Treadway, D., Stepina, L. and Breland, J. (2015). Does professionalism matter in the IT workforce? An empirical examination of IT professionals. *Journal of the Association for Information Systems*, v. 16, n. 4, p. 1.

Dunukara, D. M. A. M. and Pushpakumari, M. D. (2021). The Effect of Job-Related Factors and Organisational Factors on Turnover Intention of IT Professionals in the Western Province, Sri Lanka. In: *Proceedings of International Conference on Business Management.*

Eckhardt, A., Laumer, S., Maier, C. and Weitzel, T. (2016). The effect of personality on IT personnel's job-related attitudes: Establishing a dispositional model of turnover intention across IT job types. *Journal of Information Technology*, v. 31, p. 48-66.

Farooq, H., Janjua, U. I., Madni, T. M., Waheed, A., Zareei, M. and Alanazi, F. (2022). Identification and analysis of factors influencing turnover intention of Pakistan IT professionals: An empirical study. *IEEE Access*, v. 10, p. 64234-64256.

Gefen, D., Ragowsky, A., Miller, J., Licker, P. and Stern, M. (2015). The center cannot hold: How leading firms are managing the changing IT boundaries. *Communications of the Association for Information Systems*, v. 36, n. 1, p. 33.

Grawitch, M. J., Trares, S. and Kohler, J. M. (2007). Healthy workplace practices and employee outcomes. *International journal of stress management*, v. 14, n. 3, p. 275, 2007.

Gumussoy, C. A. (2016). The effect of five-factor model of personality traits on turnover intention among information technology IT professionals. AJIT-e: *Academic Journal of Information Technology*, v. 7, n. 22, p. 7-28.

Gupta, K. and Raman, T. V. (2021). Influence of intellectual capital on performance: An analysis of IT and pharmaceutical firms. *International Journal of Human Capital and Information Technology Professionals (IJHCITP)*, v. 12, n. 2, p. 53-71.

Gupta, S. K. and Bhatia, N. (2023). A decade of trend in the employee turnover intention study in India: A systematic review and recommendation. *FIIB Business Review*, p. 23197145231158907.

Haran, V. V. and Niederman, F. (2022). Social context of turnover-mixed methods study of Indian IT professionals. *Journal of Global Information Management (JGIM)*, v. 30, n. 1, p. 1-24.

Harden, G., Boakye, K. G. and Ryan, S. (2018). Turnover intention of technology professionals: A social exchange theory perspective. *Journal of Computer Information Systems*, v. 58, n. 4, p. 291-300.

Haridas, J., Ture, R. S. and Nayanpally, A. K. (2022). Organizational career management and turnover intentions: mediating role of trust in management. *European Journal of Training and Development*, v. 46, n. 1/2, p. 257-275.

Herscovitch, L. and Meyer, J. P. (2002). Commitment to organizational change: extension of a three-component model. *Journal of applied psychology*, v. 87, n. 3, p. 474.

Idell, K., Gefen, D. and Ragowsky, A. (2021). Managing IT professional turnover. *Communications of the ACM*, v. 64, n. 9, p. 72-77.

Joseph, D., Ng, K., Koh, C. and Ang, S. (2007). Turnover of information technology professionals: A narrative review, meta-analytic structural equation modeling, and model development. *MIS quarterly*, p. 547-577.

Kanchana, L. and Jayathilaka, R. (2023). Factors impacting employee turnover intentions among professionals in Sri Lankan startups. *Plos one*, v. 18, n. 2, p. e0281729.

Kitchenham, B. and Charters, S. (2007). Guidelines for performing systematic literature reviews in software engineering. Technical report, Technical report, EBSE Technical Report EBSE-2007-01.

Kong, C. Y. (2022). Assessment of occupational stress towards turnover intention in construction industry.

Kumar, S. (2022). The impact of talent management practices on employee turnover and retention intentions. *Global Business and Organizational Excellence*, v. 41, n. 2, p. 21-34.

Lo, J. (2015). The information technology workforce: A review and assessment of voluntary turnover research. *Information Systems Frontiers*, v. 17, p. 387-411.

Mahindru, R., Kaur, H. and Gupta, R. (2023). Mapping Research on Ageism, Personal and Social Well-Being in IT Professionals: A Literature Review and Bibliometric Analysis. *Acta Universitatis Bohemiae Meridionales*, v. 26, n. 2.

Moquin, R., Riemenschneider, C. K. and Wakefield, R. L. (2019). Psychological contract and turnover intention in the information technology profession. *Information Systems Management*, v. 36, n. 2, p. 111-125.

Mufitha, M. B., Lee, S. T. and Yong, C. C. (2019). Is professional commitment the reason for turnover intentions of IT professionals?. *Advances in business research international journal*, v. 5, n. 1, p. 124-143.

Naqvi, S. M. M. R. and Bashir, S. (2015). IT-expert retention through organizational commitment: A study of public sector information technology professionals in Pakistan. *Applied Computing and Informatics*, v. 11, n. 1, p. 60-75.

Pereira, L. C. O., Albuquerque, N. B. C., Valle, R. S., Gois, S. R. F. S. M. and Goncalves, A. A. (2024). Turnover Intention Among ICT Professionals in Brazilian Public Organizations. *SAGE Open*, v. 14, n. 2, p. 21582440241240313.

Pratiwi, M., Hinduan, Z. R. and Lubis, F. Y. (2024). Unraveling the Factors Contributing to Turnover Intentions Among Knowledge Workers: A Systematic Literature Review. In: *Proceeding of the International Conference on Multidisciplinary Research for Sustainable Innovation*. p. 400-410.

Prommegger, B., Pflügler, C., Wiesche, M. and Krcmar, H. (2019). Understanding IT- Specific Job Embeddedness to Prevent Turnover of IT Professionals. In: Academy of Management Proceedings. Briarcliff Manor, NY 10510: *Academy of Management*, p. 17510.

Ramalho Luz, C. M. D., Luiz De Paula, S. and De Oliveira, L. M. B. (2018). Organizational commitment, job satisfaction and their possible influences on intent to turnover. *Revista de Gestão*, v. 25, n. 1, p. 84-101.

Ramaprasad, B. S., Lakshminarayanan, S. and Pai, Y. P. (2021). Exploring the mediating role of employee attitudes in the relationship between high-performance work systems and turnover intention among IT professionals in India: A serial mediation approach. *Global Business Review*, v. 22, n. 1, p. 197-218.

Ramaprasad, B. S., Rao, S. and Prabhu, K. N. (2020). Commitment profiles and voluntary turnover intentions: An empirical assessment of 'two-faces' conceptualization of normative commitment. Prabandhan: *Indian Journal of Management*, 13(5–7), 7–25.

Rampadaruth, V. (2022). Turnover and Turnaway Intentions of IT Professionals and the Impact of COVID-19 on Their Work. *Human Resource Research*.

Rhatigan, C. (2016). The 4 Industries with the Worst Retention Rates. *TINYpulse*. Viewed on Oct, v. 18, p. 2017.

Rusbadrol, N. and Mahmud, N. (2017). Systematic review on the relationship between organizational justice and turnover intention. *European Proceedings of Social and Behavioural Sciences*, v. 40.

Sandhya, S. and Sulphey, M. M. (2019). An assessment of contribution of employee engagement, psychological contract and psychological empowerment towards turnover intentions of IT employees. *International Journal of Environment, Workplace and Employment*, v. 5, n. 1, p. 22-31.

Santoso, S., Tukiran, M., Aw, P., Pratiwi, I., Elizabeth, R. and Centari, R. E. (2023). The Relationship Between Job Satisfaction, Moonlighting Intentions, Turnover Intention And Organizational Citizenship Behavior: A Literature Review. *International Journal of Economy, Education and Entrepreneurship (IJE3)*, v. 3, n. 2, p. 577-589.

Sarker, F., Vasilescu, B., Blincoe, K. and Filkov, V. (2019). Socio-technical work-rate increase associates with changes in work patterns in online projects. In: 2019 IEEE/ACM 41st Int. Conference on Software Engineering (ICSE). *IEEE*, p. 936-947.

Sasaki, H., Serenko, A., Sato, O. and Prashant, P. (2019). Determinants of Job Satisfaction and Turnover Intention of IT Professionals in Japan. In: *AMCIS*.

Serenko, A., Sasaki, H., Prashant, P. and Sato, O. (2022). Turnover in Japanese it professionals: antecedents and nuances. *Australasian Journal of Information Systems*, v. 26.

Setiawan Wahidin, A. D. D. and Heryjanto, A. (2024). The Effect of Job Stress and Corporate Culture on Turnover Intention Mediated By Employee Engagement (Empirical Study: Workers In The Field of Information Technology In Greater Jakarta). *Journal Research of Social Science, Ecs & Mng*., v. 4, n. 2.

Scholtz, B. M., Van Belle, J., Njenga, K., Serenko, A. and Palvia, P. (2019). The role of job satisfaction in turnover and turn-away intention of IT staff in South Africa. *Interdisciplinary Journal of Information, Knowledge, and Management*, v. 14, n. 1, p. 077-097.

Sethar, W. A., Channar, S. H. and Jatoi, S. (2022). A. Study of turnover intentions of IT professionals: The case study software houses, Hyderabad, Pakistan. *Pakistan Journal of International Affairs*, v. 5, n. 3.

Sharma, G. G. and Stol, K. (2020). Exploring onboarding success, organizational fit, and turnover intention of software professionals. *Journal of Systems and Software*, v. 159, p. 110442.

Singh, A. (2024). A Study on Organizational Commitment, Turnover Intention, and Work-Life Balance among Working Professionals. *International Journal of Interdisciplinary Approaches in Psychology*, v. 2, n. 6, p. 251: 268-251: 268.

Sivarethinamohan, R. and Aranganathan, Mr. P. (2015). A Study on Turnover Intentions of Software Professionals in Chennai City. *International Journal of Management*, v. 6, n. 4, p. 44-51.

Souza, D. S., Kilimnik, Z. M., Sant'Anna, A. S. and Diniz, D. M. (2023).

Organizational Support, Social Support, And Turnover Intention In Brazilians It Professionals. *Revista Economia & Gestão*, v. 22, n. 64.

Standish Group. (2015). The Chaos Report 2015. In T. S. Group (Ed.). https://www.standishgroup.com/. (accessed 25 January 2025).

Suárez-Albanchez, J., Gutierrez-Broncano, S., Jimenez-Estevez, P. and Blazquez-Resino , J. J. (2022). Organizational support and turnover intention in the Spanish IT consultancy sector: Role of organizational commitment. *Cogent Social Sciences*, v. 8,
n. 1, p. 2051790.

Trinkenreich, B., Santos, F. and Stol, K. (2024). Predicting Attrition among Software Professionals: Antecedents and Consequences of Burnout and Engagement. *ACM Transactions on Software Engineering and Methodology*, v. 33, n. 8, p. 1-45.

Tulili, T. R., Capiluppi, A. and Rastogi, A. (2023). Burnout in software engineering: A systematic mapping study. *Information and Software Technology*, v. 155, p. 107116.

Vennila, M. and Vivekanandan, Dr. K. (2017). A study on how emotional dissonance impact work exhaustion, job satisfaction and turnover intention among IT professionals. *International journal of Management*, v. 8, n. 1.

Vidya, K. A. (2023). A Study On Emotional Dissonance And Burnout Influence On Employee Turnover Intention Among Information Technology Professionals.

Witt, L. A. and Burke, L. A. (2002). Selecting high-performing information technology professionals. *Journal of Organizational and End User Computing (JOEUC)*, v. 14, n. 4, p. 37-50.

Xavier, H. B., Sampaio, S. C. B., Sobral, M. F. F. and Cornican, K. (2024). From the table to the sofa: The remote work revolution in a context of crises and its consequences on work attitudes and behaviors. *Education and Information Technologies*, p. 1-40.

Zaza, S., Riemenschneider, C. and Armstrong, D. J. (2022). The drivers and effects of burnout within an information technology work context: a job demands-resources framework. *Information Technology & People*, v. 35, n. 7, p. 2288-2313.

Zentner, A. (2018). Making the jump: Understanding the associativity between perceived job performance and turnover intention of IT professionals in higher education. *Available at SSRN 3145662*.

An Agent-Oriented Model-Driven Development Process for Cyber-Physical Systems

Claudio Navarro[1,2], Lorenzo Devia[3], Jose E. Labra Gayo[2], Carlos Cares[1]

[1]Computer Science and Informatics Department,
University of La Frontera, Temuco, La Araucanía, Chile

[2]Departamento de Informática, Universidad de Oviedo, Oviedo, Spain

[3]Graduate of Civil Engineering in Computer Science,
University of La Frontera, Temuco, La Araucanía, Chile

claudio.navarro@ufrontera.cl, l.devia02@ufromail.cl,
labra@uniovi.es, carlos.cares@ceisufro.cl

Abstract. *Cyber-Physical Systems (CPS) integrate distributed software and hardware, requiring systematic engineering approaches. This paper presents a Model-Driven Development (MDD) process that spans the entire CPS lifecycle, from conceptual modeling (CIM) to functional implementation (Code). By leveraging agent orientation, the approach simplifies system structuring and enables semi-automated transformations through a domain-specific language (DSL). A proof of concept validates the process in a greenhouse automation scenario, demonstrating that the generated software functions as expected on real hardware. The results confirm the feasibility of this end-to-end MDD workflow for CPS development.*

1. Introduction

Cyber-Physical Systems (CPS) integrate computational and physical processes across distributed components, leading to inherent development complexity [Cares et al. 2019, de C Henshaw 2016]. Structured methodologies are required to manage this complexity and align system implementation with high-level objectives [Sjöberg et al. 2023]. Agent orientation has been proposed as a suitable paradigm for structuring CPS, as it allows modeling components as autonomous entities that interact and adapt to their environment [Cares et al. 2019]. However, despite its potential, integrating agent orientation into CPS engineering remains an open challenge. Model-Driven Development (MDD) provides a systematic approach to software and system design through successive transformations from abstract models to concrete implementations [Atkinson and Kühne 2005, Selic 2003, Bézivin 2005]. While previous works have explored the application of MDD in CPS [Staroletov et al. 2019, Cares et al. 2022a, Jiang et al. 2018, Gräßler et al. 2021], a fully integrated process that spans from conceptual modeling to execution in real hardware has not been fully established [Liu et al. 2020]. An extensive systematic literature review on Model-Driven Development for Cyber-Physical Systems, as reported in [Mohamed et al. 2021], identified several underexplored areas, including requirements, socio-technical aspects, and the software of cyber components such as sensors and actuators. The study also noted limited coverage of the full development cycle, particularly model-to-model and model-to-code transformations, as well as the availability of technological solutions. We address these limitations as an integrated set to be covered. This work presents a complete MDD process for CPS, structured in four stages: Computation-Independent Modeling (CIM), Platform-Independent Modeling (PIM), Platform-Specific Modeling (PSM), and Code. The approach leverages agent orientation in the CIM phase using iStar 2.0, which is then systematically transformed through a domain-specific language (DSL) into concrete CPS constructs. To support these transformations, we developed custom tools integrated with diagrams.net, enabling semi-automated model-to-model and model-to-code conversions. The feasibility of the proposed workflow is validated through a proof of concept in greenhouse automation. The generated software is deployed on Arduino-based computing units, verifying sensor-actuator interaction and message exchange via MQTT[1]. Results confirm that the process effectively supports the structured development of CPS while maintaining traceability and reducing manual intervention.

2. Theoretical Background

2.1. Cyber-physical Systems

Cyber-physical systems (CPS) offer solutions to manage intricate physical processes through monitoring and control. These systems utilize both software and hardware components that can detect variables from the physical world and respond accordingly. Owing to the distributed nature of their software and hardware across multiple devices, these systems inherently carry complexity [Cares et al. 2019]. CPS, conceptualized in the early 21st century, has been pivotal to the advent of Industry 4.0 [Lee et al. 2015]. The affordability of electro-mechanical devices has been a key factor in the widespread adoption of Cyber-Physical Systems (CPS). This trend is further driven by their extensive interconnectivity and the economic accessibility of dependable, high-quality sensors and microcontrollers [Norris 2015]. Yet, even with these technological advancements, methodologies and modeling techniques tailored for cyber-physical engineering remain in their nascent stages [Oudina and Derdour 2023, Liu et al. 2017, Cares et al. 2019, Cares et al. 2022b].

2.2. Agent Orientation Overview

Agent orientation is an approach in software engineering that emphasizes the importance of autonomous agents as primary entities in modeling and designing software systems. At its core, this paradigm recognizes agents as autonomous units that interact, perceive, and act based on their set objectives and the environment in which they operate. The foundation for agent-oriented methodologies can be traced back to significant works such as the iStar framework, introduced in 1995. This influential framework has since shaped requirements standards, further agent-oriented methodologies, modeling paradigms, and even the development of security and normative formalisms [Cares et al. 2011]. One of the notable methodologies influenced by the iStar framework is Tropos [Bresciani et al. 2004]. Central to Tropos are concepts like actors, which can further be categorized into agents, roles, and positions, and their objectives captured through goals, *softgoals*, resources, and tasks. Notably, goals can be further detailed or contribute to other goals, while *softgoals* delineate quality goals and non-functional requirements. An integral part of both iStar and Tropos is the representation of agents' interdependencies, viewed through the

[1]Message Queuing Telemetry Transport (MQTT) is a lightweight messaging protocol widely used for communication in IoT and CPS environments.

lens of their objectives and depicted in dependency diagrams. Nevertheless, the landscape of agent-oriented software engineering has also been enriched by other methodologies. GAIA [Wooldridge et al. 2000], O-MASE [Padgham and Winikoff 2005], and PASSI [Burrafato and Cossentino 2002] have each brought significant insights and techniques to the table, contributing to a comprehensive understanding and practice of agent-oriented development.

2.3. Model-Driven Development

In software engineering, models serve as abstract representations that highlight relevant aspects of a system while omitting unnecessary details [Pidd 2003]. They enhance understanding, document system components, and improve team communication, supporting informed design decisions [Selic 2003]. The Model-Driven Development (MDD) paradigm emerged in the early 2000s [Selic 2003, Bézivin 2005], proposing that software can be developed through successive computer-assisted transformations, starting from abstract models and progressing through increasingly detailed representations until executable code is generated. MDD shifts the focus from code-centric to model-based development, where models are the primary artifacts [Staron 2006]. This approach separates system logic from platform-specific implementation, allowing for automated transformations between abstraction levels [Atkinson and Kühne 2005, Bézivin 2005].

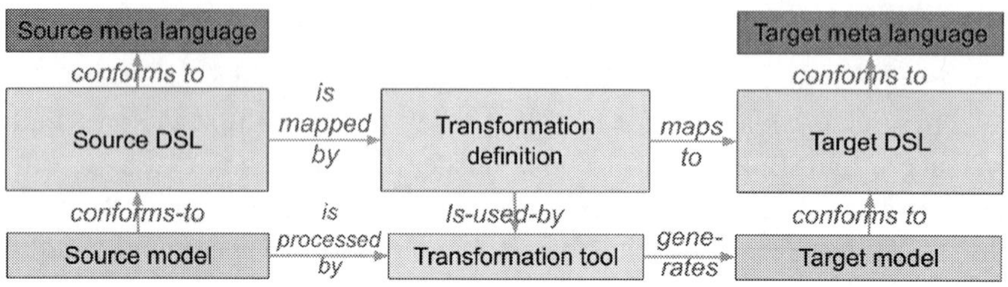

Figure 1. Model-to-model transformation in MDD.

As depicted in Figure 1 (adapted from [Kleppe et al. 2003]), these transformations are crucial for automating model evolution. A transformation definition specifies mappings from source to target models, and transformation tools execute these mappings to generate the target model. This process can be fully automated when the models contain all required information, or semi-automated when additional user input is necessary. Source and target models may use the same or different modeling languages, depending on the metamodels involved. MDD does not impose a fixed number of abstraction levels or specific standards, providing flexibility to adapt modeling approaches to the problem domain. It often leverages domain-specific languages (DSLs) to streamline modeling and transformations at each phase [Kleppe et al. 2003]. MDD approaches underpin modern low-code approaches, not aiming to eliminate manual coding entirely, but rather focusing on automating development tasks to reduce coding effort. Compared to traditional software development, MDD improves precision and efficiency, particularly in complex systems [Pastor et al. 2016].

2.4. Towards an Agent-Oriented MDD approach for CPS development

This work conceptualizes cyber-physical systems (CPS) as a network of cyber-physical components (CPCs) with sensing, actuation, communication, and computational capabilities. Their computational capacity enables local processing, decision-making, and interaction within the system, serving as the execution environment for the software generated through the MDD process. The proposed CPS development process follows a semi-automatic MDD approach based on successive, well-defined stages. Its goal is to systematically capture design definitions, leading to the semi-automatic generation of code. The process considers three key modeling levels: the computation-independent model (CIM), which describes the system domain without technological details; the platform-independent model (PIM), which represents the system design independent of platform constraints; and the platform-specific model (PSM), which details the implementation for a specific platform. Given the conceptual framework reviewed and the nature of CPCs, the CIM level is approached from an agent-oriented perspective using the iStar 2.0 modeling language [Dalpiaz et al. 2016]. The PIM level relies on a domain-specific language (DSL) designed to provide an intermediate description of the CPS functionality, structure, and behavior, independent of specific technologies. Finally, the PSM and Code stages are devoted to code generation, configuration, and customization, as depicted in Figure 2.

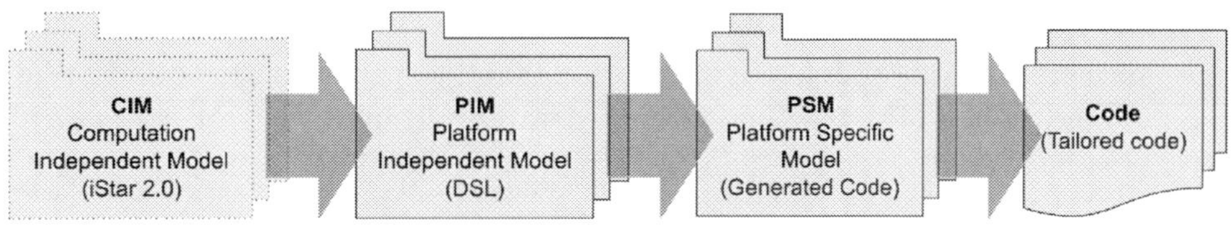

Figure 2. MDD process from Agents to CPS.

3. MDD for CPS: From Agents to Cyber-physical Systems

The following sections describe the CIM, PIM, PSM, and Code phases, detailing the modeling languages, their constructs, the transformations applied, and their role in CPS development.

3.1. Computation-Independent Models (CIM) for CPS

The Computation-Independent Model (CIM) phase defines the CPS at a high level, capturing domain requirements without technological details. This work adopts an agent-oriented approach, conceptualizing CPS as a network of autonomous cyber-physical components (CPCs) that exhibit proactivity, reactivity, and interactivity [Cares et al. 2011]. These CPCs include both physical entities—such as sensors, actuators, and communication modules—and software processes like control algorithms and resource management, bridging the cyber and physical domains. To support modeling in this phase, we use iStar 2.0, leveraging its constructs to define the structural and behavioral aspects of CPS. We developed an iStar 2.0 library for diagrams.net, shown in Figure 3, which facilitates practical modeling. The following sections describe each iStar 2.0 construct, its role in CPS modeling, and its dependency relationships.

Actor, Agent, Role: In iStar, the concept of Actor represents the primary autonomous entities in this paradigm. An actor can be further specified as an Agent, which refers to an autonomous and proactive entity, or as a Role, which abstracts the entity's function within the system without considering its individuality. In the context of CPS, actors are not limited to high-level abstractions of physical hardware components, such as

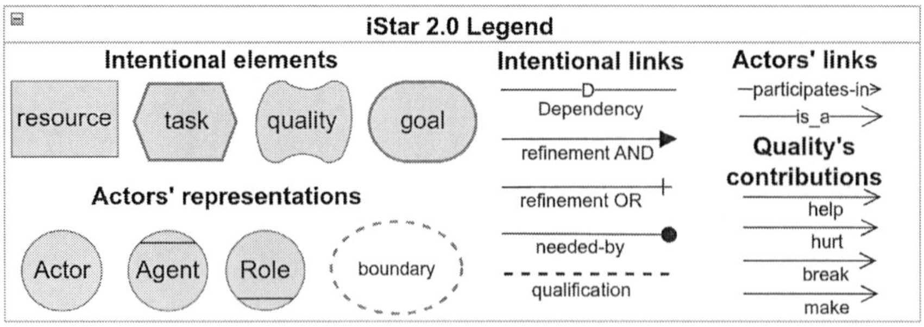

Figure 3. iStar 2.0 legend implemented as a library for diagrams.net.

sensors and actuators, or cyber entities, such as algorithms. They also provide a broader scope for comprehensive requirements modeling, encompassing stakeholders, environmental factors, and even user intentions. This allows for a more holistic representation of the system and its interactions.

Goals: These delineate the objectives an actor seeks to achieve. It is important to note that this element is not prescriptive, meaning that the specific means of achieving the goal are not constrained. For CPS, goals can represent desired states or outcomes, such as maintaining a specific speed or achieving a particular energy consumption level.

Softgoals: Representing non-functional requirements or quality attributes, softgoals in CPS might entail parameters like system resilience, security, or performance.

Resources: They can be tangible or intangible assets used by actors. This could relate to available bandwidth, power sources, computing capacity, or data storage in a CPS environment.

Tasks: Refers to the specific actions actors undertake to achieve their goals. Unlike goals, tasks are prescriptive and must explicitly define how they should be carried out. In the realm of CPS, tasks can encompass activities such as sensing, data acquisition, signal processing, or actuation within the physical environment.

Social dependencies: This construct captures the relations and dependencies between actors, crucial for the interconnected nature of CPS components. Figure 4 illustrates an iStar 2.0 dependency relationship, where the *Depender* agent relies on the *Dependee* agent to obtain the *dependum*. The *dependerElmt* explains *why* the *dependum* is needed, while the *dependeeElmt* specifies *how* it will be provided. In the diagram, both elements are represented as dashed-line boxes to denote that they can correspond to any intentional element in the model. The *dependum* itself can take different forms: a *Goal*, where the *Dependee* is responsible for achieving it with freedom in its execution; a *Quality* (*softgoal*), where the *Dependee* ensures sufficient compliance; a *Task*, which must be executed as prescribed; or a *Resource*, where the *Dependee* provides a specific asset.

Refinement, Needed-by, Contribution, and Qualification links: These links define how intentional elements interact within the model. *Refinement links* specify how goals and tasks are decomposed into more specific elements. *Needed-by links* indicate the resources required for task execution. *Qualification links* associate softgoals with the intentional elements they assess. Finally, *Contribution links* define how intentional elements impact softgoals, either positively (*help, make*) or negatively (*hurt, break*).

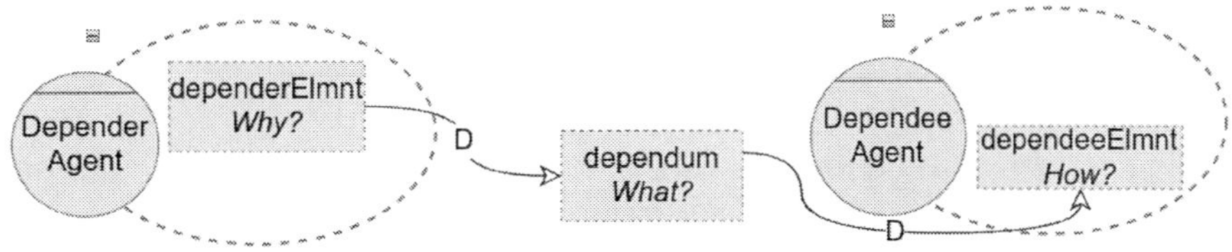

Figure 4. iStar 2.0 dependency relations.

As an example, Figure 5 illustrates a dependency relationship between an actuators and sensors, which can be considered part of a CPS for greenhouse automation. The model shows that both sensors and actuators have the primary *Goals* of measuring and maintaining the appropriate temperature, respectively. Additionally, both components aim to optimize resource usage in terms of energy consumption by analyzing battery usage and adjusting their operation mode accordingly.

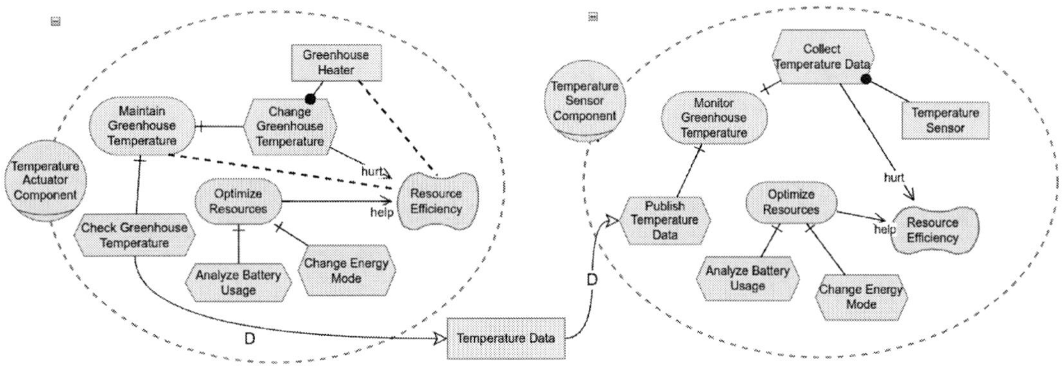

Figure 5. iStar 2.0 dependency relationship between a temperature actuator and a sensor.

It can also be observed that this process *helps* improve *Resource Efficiency*, whereas both collecting temperature data (by the sensor) and changing the temperature (via the heater) *hurt Resource Efficiency*. Furthermore, the model emphasizes *Resource Efficiency* for the actuator through *Qualification links*, ensuring that both the *Greenhouse Heater* and the *Goal* of maintaining the appropriate temperature in the greenhouse are aligned with this concern.

3.2. Platform-Independent Models (PIM) for CPS Modeling

The Platform-Independent Model (PIM) serves as an intermediate stage in the MDD approach, refining the CPS design without committing to specific technologies. To ensure a seamless transition from the agent-oriented CIM phase, we propose a domain-specific language (DSL) tailored for CPS. This DSL is designed to provide a straightforward and structured mapping of high-level agent-oriented constructs into CPS representations, facilitating model transformations and preserving traceability across MDD stages [Atkinson and Kühne 2005, Pastor et al. 2016]. Agent-oriented requirements from

CIM are refined into explicit CPS components at this stage. The transformation process ensures traceability by incorporating semantic annotations into PIM construct attributes, preserving information such as contribution and qualification relations with softgoals (*softgoal_qualification_array* and *softgoal_contribution_array*). These transformations are applied either automatically or with designer input when additional specifications are needed. To support accurate modeling, we developed a diagrams.net library ensuring a consistent representation of PIM constructs, attributes, and their relationships. Figure 6 presents the DSL legend, detailing the constructs and relationships used in this modeling phase.

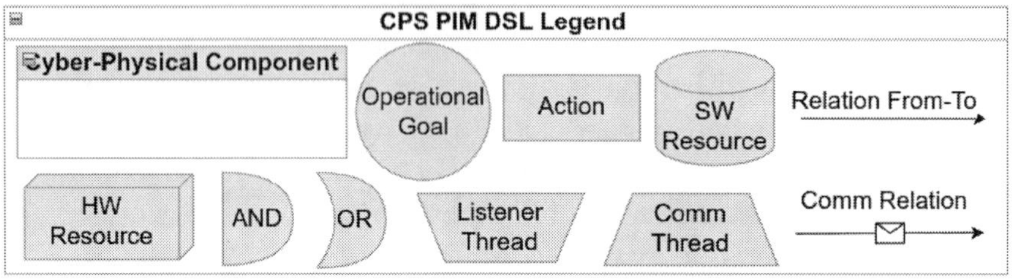

Figure 6. CPS PIM Domain specific language (DSL) legend.

Cyber-physical components (CPC): In PIM modeling, CPS are structured as a network of CPCs, each representing a computational unit that integrates sensing, actuation, and communication while interacting with other components. The focus is on their functional role rather than their specific implementation. CPCs serve as modular containers, encapsulating services such as data storage, computation, and decision-making in a technology-independent manner. This aligns with the component-based approach, where components abstract internal complexity and provide functionality through well-defined interfaces [Crnkovic 2005]. CPCs are derived from *Actors* in the agent-oriented CIM phase. While CIM actors can represent both cyber-physical and non-cyber-physical entities (e.g., stakeholders or external software systems), only explicitly cyber-physical actors are transformed into CPCs, as this work focuses on CPS development rather than general agent-based software. Identifying these actors requires designer interaction during transformation, ensuring correct classification. Once defined, traceability information from the original construct is preserved in the CPC attributes.

Operational Goals: An *Operational Goal* within a *CPC* (which is a computational unit) represents a process or thread aimed at achieving a specific goal from the previous CIM phase, without prescribing how it is fulfilled. It continuously evaluates its achievement based on inputs such as other *Operational Goals* or *Actions* that refine it, as well as internal criteria. This includes the attribute *checkInterval_in_milliseconds*, which defines its evaluation frequency. Additionally, operation modes can be specified through the attributes *operation_modes_enabled* (boolean) and *operation_modes_description* (text), allowing for discrete operational strategies when required [Navarro et al. 2024]. These attributes are defined through user interaction and apply only if discrete operation modes are needed.

Actions: An Action in a CPC represents a prescriptive procedure executed within the component, similar to a function in procedural programming. Unlike an Operational Goal, an Action is not autonomous but is triggered as needed. It returns a boolean value indicating success or failure and may require input parameters and produce output parameters, both defined via user interaction in this phase, without specifying data types. Actions contribute to other Actions or Operational Goals via AND/OR operators, signaling success or failure. Additionally, like Operational Goals, they include the operationModes attribute to specify discrete operation modes when applicable.

SW Resources: An *SW Resource* in PIM represents a non-physical resource, specifically data required for the operation of other elements. It originates from a *Resource* in CIM, where resource types are not yet distinguished. During transformation, user input determines whether a *CIM Resource* should be classified as an *SW Resource* in PIM. If confirmed, the transformation proceeds by assigning a *data_structure* attribute, defined through an interaction with the designer. This definition includes field names and natural language descriptions, ensuring clarity without specifying data types.

HW Resources: A *HW Resource* in PIM represents a physical resource mapped from a *Resource* in CIM, requiring implementation within the corresponding *CPC*. This construct defines the hardware needed for proper system operation. Examples include servomotors, sensors, I/O ports, and battery packs, or complex devices like 3D printers, assumed to have necessary consumables. To determine whether a CIM *Resource* transforms into an *HW Resource* or *SW Resource*, user input is required.

AND, OR Operators: These operators in PIM originate from iStar 2.0 goal and task refinement relations in CIM. They are transformed while preserving their logical structure, now interpreted through the boolean evaluation of *Operational Goals* and *Actions*. In iStar, *Goals* and *Tasks* decompose into more specific elements via **AND** or **OR** refinements, a logic maintained in CPS-PIM: an *AND-refinement-operator* enforces that all related *Operational Goals* and *Actions* must succeed, while an *OR-refinement-operator* allows multiple alternatives, requiring at least one to be achieved. These operators ensure that the hierarchical breakdown of objectives from CIM is preserved in PIM, adapting it to a computational model where goal fulfillment is dynamically evaluated based on process execution.

Relation (from-to): In this PIM modeling language for CPS, each construct combination within a *Cyber-Physical Component* (CPC) has a single, unambiguous relation type. All CIM associations are mapped to this unified relation, where the constructs involved and the relation's direction define its nature.

Listener Thread, Comm Thread, and Comm Relation: Dependencies in CIM are transformed in PIM into structured message-based communication between *Cyber-Physical Components* (CPCs), as shown in Figure 7. The *Comm Thread* in the *Dependee CPC* gathers and transmits the *dependum* as a message via *Comm Relations* to the *Listener Thread* in the *Depender CPC*, which then distributes it internally.

Interactions with the designer allow defining the dependum's data structure (specifying fields but not data types, maintaining a technology-agnostic design). Additionally, designer interaction is required to specify the transmission frequency of the dependum, which is set through a time interval attribute in the *Comm Thread*. Other communication timing preferences—such as unacknowledged send, retransmission on demand, and single confirmation—can also be defined independently of technology at this stage as operation modes. Both the dependum's data structure and communication timing parameters must

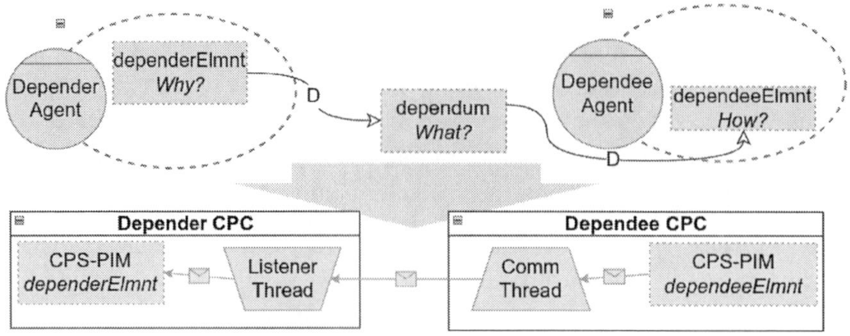

Figure 7. Transformation from CIM dependency relation to PIM communication process.

be adopted by the *Comm Thread* and its corresponding *Listener Thread*. If the *dependeeElmnt* or *dependerElmnt* in CIM is a *softgoal*, it is subsumed in PIM, meaning that no explicit softgoal-equivalent construct appears in the PIM phase, nor does any *Comm Relation* related to it. Instead, softgoal traceability is preserved within the corresponding *Comm Thread* and *Listener Thread* attributes, allowing this information to be leveraged in the PSM phase. This approach standardizes all dependencies in PIM, ensuring a uniform and flexible communication mechanism between CPCs.

Figure 8 illustrates the transformation of the dependency relationship depicted in Figure 5 into a PIM model. This transformation represents both the logical refinement relations between *Operational Goals* and *Actions* and the structured communication process facilitated by *Comm Threads* and *Listener Threads*.

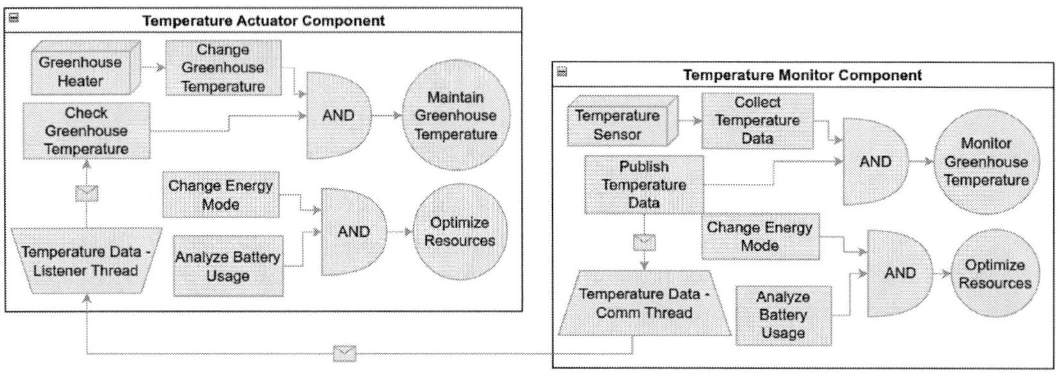

Figure 8. Example CPS PIM DSL: Communication process between a temperature actuator and a sensor.

3.3. Platform-Specific Models (PSM) for CPS Implementation

The Platform-Specific Model (PSM) phase converts PIM representations into functional, executable, or at least compilable code for the selected platform. This process requires interaction with the designer during the PIM-to-code transformation to define data types, such as input and output parameters for *Actions* (attributes *input_parameters* and *output_parameters*) and *dependum* contents to ensure compatibility. Softgoal traceability, contribution, and qualification relations from the CIM phase are included as comments to enhance traceability and improve developer efficiency. Sections for manual modifications are also clearly marked. The following outlines both general and target-specific transformations, with Arduino MKR WiFi 1010 and MQTT as the selected platform.

Cyber-Physical Components (CPC): Mapped to selected platform computing units, i.e., Arduino MKR WiFi 1010.

Operational Goals: Transformed into execution threads using FreeRTOS_SAMD21[2] for multitasking, including timing preferences for goal evaluation. When using operation modes, a switch statement is included to clearly define the behavior of each mode.

Actions: Converted into platform-specific functions, with explicitly defined input/output types determined through interaction with the designer and based on available data types on the target platform. The PIM-to-code transformation also supports function operation modes through switch statements.

SW Resources: Mapped to concrete data structures with defined field types, including traceability indications via block comments in the code.

HW Resources: The PIM-to-code transformation includes block comments with relevant information from previous stages regarding the required hardware in the functions that use them.

Communication Threads and Relations: This transformation maps these PIM constructs to code, inheriting timing synchronization on both sides of the communication, and defining the message data structure (formerly the dependum). It is implemented with MQTT, using PubSubClient.h[3] for constrained environments.

AND/OR Operators: Translated into execution control structures ensuring logical conditions. Functions (when invoked) and threads (periodically) evaluate logical expressions to report their accomplishment status.

This systematic transformation process ensures alignment with the original design while adapting to the constraints of the target platform.

3.4. Code Phase: Final Configuration and Customization

The code generated in the PSM phase is functional—it compiles and runs on the target hardware without programming errors. However, the Code phase focuses on configuring and fine-tuning the generated code for deployment. Typical adjustments include specifying WiFi credentials (SSID and password), selecting hardware connection pins, and adding necessary libraries for specific hardware, such as the DHT11[4] sensor. Additionally, this phase allows programmers to refine operation modes: although structurally defined in the generated code, specific behaviors for each mode often require manual customization. These final adaptations ensure the software aligns with the deployment environment while preserving the MDD structure.

[2] `FreeRTOS_SAMD21` refers to the real-time operating system (FreeRTOS) port adapted for the SAMD21 microcontroller used in Arduino MKR WiFi 1010 boards, enabling multitasking capabilities.

[3] `PubSubClient.h` is an Arduino library that provides MQTT client functionality for embedded devices.

[4] DHT refers to a family of digital humidity and temperature sensors, with DHT11 and DHT22 being common models differing in accuracy and range.

3.5. Demonstrating the MDD Approach: Developing a Cyber-Physical System for Greenhouse Automation

To validate the feasibility of conducting an MDD process for developing a CPS under an agent-oriented approach, we implemented a proof of concept (PoC). This PoC demonstrates the applicability of the approach using a set of integrated tools within diagrams.net, including libraries for CIM and PIM modeling, a containerized XSLT-based web tool for designer interaction, and model-to-model and model-to-code transformations. The PoC is considered successful if the generated software enables cyber-physical components (CPCs) to interact as expected in a greenhouse automation scenario. The system is tested by executing the automatically generated code on Arduino MKR WiFi 1010 units, ensuring that sensors collect data, actuators respond to control commands, and communication between components occurs via MQTT. Success criteria include: Proper execution of the generated Arduino sketches, with manual fine-tuning in the Code stage, Correct sensor data acquisition and transmission, Consistent actuation based on received commands, and Communication logs confirming successful message exchange between CPCs. If any of these criteria are not met, debugging is performed to determine whether the issue stems from the generated code (indicating a limitation in the MDD process) or external hardware/configuration factors.

As part of the CIM modeling stage, various actors were identified and modeled using iStar 2.0. Non-cyber-physical actors, such as the *Administrator* and *Middleware platform* roles, were discarded. The roles corresponding to *Soil Moisture Monitor Component*, *Soil Moisture Actuator Component*, *Temperature Monitor Component*, and *Temperature Actuator Component* were transformed and carried forward through the CPS development stages. Figure 9 illustrates the MDD process from a method engineering perspective, showing its step-by-step workflow alongside diagrams.net modeling tools and the web transformation tool. The final output consists of compiled and configured code for each CPC, fine-tuned during the Code stage and integrated with the hardware, forming the complete CPS.

During the Code stage fine-tuning, minor manual adjustments were necessary to integrate specific hardware components. For example, we manually included the library and reading functions for a DHT22 humidity and temperature sensor. These adjustments were straightforward thanks to the automatically generated traceability comments and the explicit placeholders indicating where manual code additions should be made. Another case involved the MQTT communication for the actuator CPC, where inconsistent readings were observed. This issue was resolved by fine-tuning the memory allocation for the communication thread. After completing the MDD process for the greenhouse automation CPS, we verified that all proof-of-concept (PoC) success criteria were met.

All the assets developed to support this agent-oriented MDD for CPS approach are publicly available, as detailed in the *Artifact Availability* section (see Section 5). These include the diagrams.net libraries for CIM (iStar 2.0) and PIM (DSL) modeling, the corresponding models used in the proof-of-concept, the PSM-generated Arduino sketches refined during the Code stage, and the complete source code of the transformation tool—both frontend and backend, covering transformation definitions, code generation patterns, and model processing logic. Step-by-step usage guidelines and documentation, are also provided.

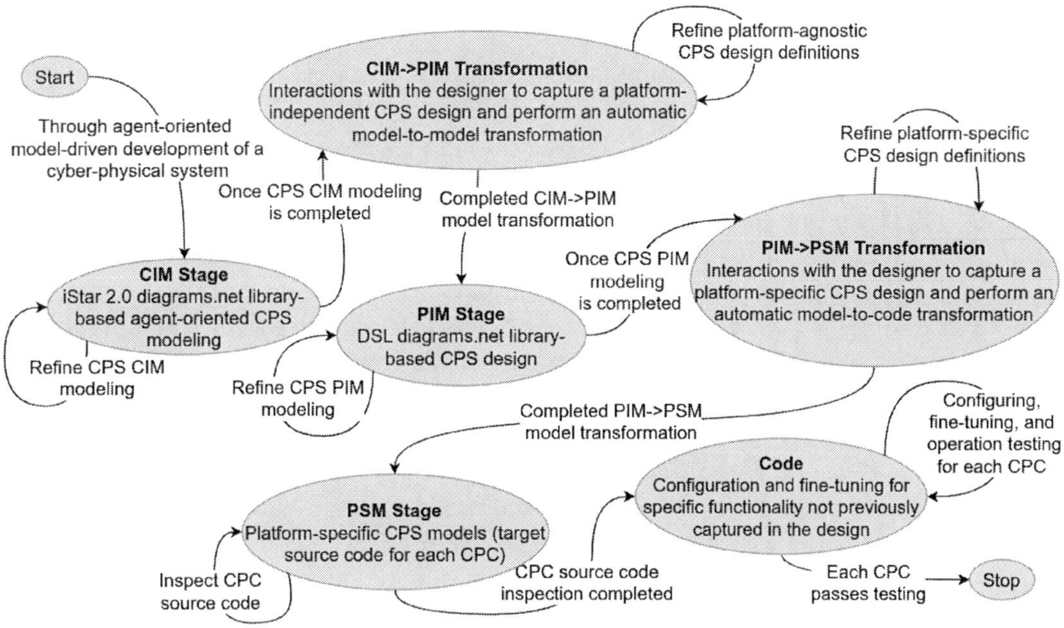

Figure 9. Agent-oriented CPS MDD process.

4. Results and Discussion

The proposed MDD process was successfully applied to CPS development, covering the full cycle from conceptual modeling (CIM) to implementation (Code). The proof of concept demonstrated that CPCs generated through this approach operated as expected, following their defined behaviors and interacting via MQTT according to the initial models. While the validation was conducted in a controlled environment, the results confirm that the process effectively supports CPS design and implementation. Agent orientation played a key role in the initial conceptualization of the CPS during the CIM phase. This paradigm shift enabled high-level abstraction units, simplifying analysis by decomposing the global problem into smaller, more manageable ones. These were then systematically transformed into concrete constructs in later stages, facilitating system implementation. The PoC was instrumental in verifying the process and identifying areas for improvement. As shown in Figure 9, each stage allows refinement through interactions with the web-based transformation tool. Designers provide technology-independent and technology-dependent information via web forms, whose complexity scales with model attributes. However, the current process flow does not allow revisiting previous phases without losing modifications from the current stage, which could be improved to increase design flexibility. A significant advantage was that the CPC software was tested on real hardware, not in a simulated environment. Comparatively, while previous studies have incorporated agent orientation into specific segments of CPS development [Ayala et al. 2019, Daun et al. 2021], this approach spans the entire lifecycle, from conceptualization to implementation. The initial phase leverages iStar 2.0 without specialized CPS extensions, ensuring compatibility with standard iStar 2.0 models. This allows the CIM stage to produce iStar 2.0-compliant models, seamlessly integrable with external iStar 2.0-based processes. Likewise, external iStar 2.0 models can be easily incorporated into this process, maintaining interoperability within the MDD workflow.

5. Conclusion

This work presented an MDD-based approach for CPS development, integrating agent orientation to structure the transition from conceptual modeling (CIM) to implementation (Code). The proposed process was validated through a proof of concept in greenhouse automation, demonstrating that CPCs generated via model transformations operated as expected, interacting through MQTT and adhering to their predefined behaviors. This confirms the feasibility of using MDD to develop CPS from high-level abstractions to functional implementations. Agent orientation played a fundamental role in managing complexity during the CIM phase, allowing high-level abstraction units to facilitate structured decomposition. This contributed to a systematic refinement process across MDD stages, preserving design intent while progressively incorporating CPS implementation details. Unlike previous works that apply MDD partially or focus on isolated phases, this approach covers the entire CPS development cycle, from conceptualization to execution in real hardware. It combines automated model transformations with guided designer interaction, progressively incorporating design details through a semi-automatic process aligned with each development phase, ensuring that technology-independent and technology-specific decisions are captured at appropriate workflow stages. Future improvements include enhancing the navigability of the MDD workflow and refining the usability of transformation tools. Allowing designers to select specific technologies and communication protocols per CPC could provide greater flexibility. The early inclusion of commonly used hardware components constructs could further reduce manual intervention in the Code phase. Additionally, incorporating design patterns from the CIM level may further streamline the initial modeling process by providing reusable templates for frequently occurring component compositions, reducing the need to redefine common structures. Beyond these refinements, a key direction for future work is transitioning from this descriptive implementation towards a formal specification of the languages and transformation rules used in the MDD process. While the current approach effectively supports automation and has been validated in a proof of concept, formalizing the semantics of the proposed DSL and the transformation rules could further enhance the rigor, reproducibility, and interoperability of the process, facilitating its integration with existing MDD frameworks and broader adoption. Furthermore, an in-depth evaluation of this approach's impact on CPS development efficiency is needed. Initial observations suggest a reduction in development time, but a systematic assessment in practical settings is required to compare its effectiveness against traditional methods.

Artifact Availability

The software artifact and documentation supporting this paper are available at Zenodo: `https://doi.org/10.5281/zenodo.15086005`

References

Atkinson, C. and Kühne, T. (2005). A generalized notion of platforms for model-driven development. In *Model-driven software development*, pages 119–136. Springer.

Ayala, I., Amor, M., Horcas, J.-M., and Fuentes, L. (2019). A goal-driven software product line approach for evolving multi-agent systems in the internet of things. *Knowledge-Based Systems*, 184:104883.

Bézivin, J. (2005). On the unification power of models. *Software & Systems Modeling*, 4(2):171–188.

Bresciani, P., Perini, A., Giorgini, P., Giunchiglia, F., and Mylopoulos, J. (2004). Tropos: An agent-oriented software development methodology. *Autonomous Agents and Multi-Agent Systems*, 8:203–236.

Burrafato, P. and Cossentino, M. (2002). Designing a multi-agent solution for a bookstore with the passi methodology. *AOIS@ CAiSE*, 57.

Cares, C., Chebanyuk, O., and Navarro, C. (2022a). A model-driven approach for cyber-physical systems: a method engineering perspective. *Proceedings of the XVII-th International Conference on Software Engineering SoftEngine 2022*, page 14.

Cares, C., Franch, X., Quer, C., and Enric, M. (2011). A reference model for i*. In Yu, E., Giorgini, P., Maiden, N., and Mylopoulos, J., editors, *Social Modeling for Requirements Engineering*, pages 573–606. MIT Press.

Cares, C., Lühr, D., Mora, S., Navarro, C., Olivares, L., Sepúlveda, S., and Vidal, G. (2022b). Architecting autonomous underwater vehicles by adapting software product lines. In *Conference on Integrated Computer Technologies in Mechanical Engineering–Synergetic Engineering*, pages 719–730. Springer.

Cares, C., Sepúlveda, S., and Navarro, C. (2019). Agent-oriented engineering for cyber-physical systems. In *Information Technology and Systems: Proceedings of ICITS 2019*, pages 93–102. Springer.

Crnkovic, I. (2005). Component-based software engineering for embedded systems. In *27th international conference on Software engineering*, pages 712–713.

Dalpiaz, F., Franch, X., and Horkoff, J. (2016). istar 2.0 language guide. *arXiv preprint arXiv:1605.07767*.

Daun, M., Brings, J., Krajinski, L., Stenkova, V., and Bandyszak, T. (2021). A grl-compliant istar extension for collaborative cyber-physical systems. *Requirements Engineering*, 26(3):325–370.

de C Henshaw, M. J. (2016). Systems of systems, cyber-physical systems, the internet-of-things... whatever next? *Insight*, 19(3):51–54.

Gräßler, I., Wiechel, D., Roesmann, D., and Thiele, H. (2021). V-model based development of cyber-physical systems and cyber-physical production systems. *Procedia CIRP*, 100:253–258.

Jiang, Y., Song, H., Yang, Y., Liu, H., Gu, M., Guan, Y., Sun, J., and Sha, L. (2018). Dependable model-driven development of cps: From stateflow simulation to verified implementation. *ACM Transactions on Cyber-Physical Systems*, 3(1):1–31.

Kleppe, A. G., Warmer, J. B., Warmer, J., and Bast, W. (2003). *MDA explained: the model driven architecture: practice and promise*. Addison-Wesley Professional.

Lee, J., Bagheri, B., and Kao, H.-A. (2015). A cyber-physical systems architecture for industry 4.0-based manufacturing systems. *Manufacturing letters*, 3:18–23.

Liu, B., Zhang, Y.-r., Cao, X.-l., Liu, Y., Gu, B., and Wang, T.-x. (2020). A survey of model-driven techniques and tools for cyber-physical systems. *Frontiers of Information Technology & Electronic Engineering*, 21(11):1567–1590.

Liu, Y., Peng, Y., Wang, B., Yao, S., and Liu, Z. (2017). Review on cyber-physical systems. *IEEE/CAA Journal of Automatica Sinica*, 4(1):27–40.

Mohamed, M. A., Kardas, G., and Challenger, M. (2021). Model-driven engineering tools and languages for cyber-physical systems–a systematic literature review. *IEEE Access*, 9:48605–48630.

Navarro, C., Gayo, J. E. L., Jara, F. A. E., and Cares, C. (2024). Componentizing autonomous underwater vehicles by physical-running algorithms. *PeerJ Computer Science*, 10:e2305.

Norris, D. (2015). *The internet of things: Do-it-yourself at home projects for arduino, raspberry pi, and beaglebone black*. McGraw-Hill Education.

Oudina, Z. and Derdour, M. (2023). Toward modeling trust cyber-physical systems: A model-based system engineering method. *International Journal of Advanced Computer Science and Applications*, 14(7):441–452.

Padgham, L. and Winikoff, M. (2005). *Developing intelligent agent systems: A practical guide*. John Wiley & Sons.

Pastor, Ó., España, S., and Panach, J. I. (2016). Learning pros and cons of model-driven development in a practical teaching experience. In *International Conference on Conceptual Modeling*, pages 218–227. Springer.

Pidd, M. (2003). *Tools for Thinking: Modelling in Management Science*. John Wiley and Sons Ltd, 2nd edition.

Selic, B. (2003). The pragmatics of model-driven development. *IEEE software*, 20(5):19–25.

Sjöberg, P., Mendez, D., and Gorschek, T. (2023). Contemporary challenges when developing cyber-physical systems of systems-a case study. In *2023 IEEE/ACM 11th International Workshop on Software Engineering for Systems-of-Systems and Software Ecosystems (SESoS)*, pages 46–53. IEEE.

Staroletov, S., Shilov, N., Konyukhov, I., Zyubin, V., Liakh, T., Rozov, A., Shilov, I., Baar, T., and Schulte, H. (2019). Model-driven methods to design of reliable multiagent cyber-physical systems. In *CEUR workshop proceedings*, volume 2478, pages 74–91.

Staron, M. (2006). Adopting model driven software development in industry–a case study at two companies. In *International Conference on Model Driven Engineering Languages and Systems*, pages 57–72. Springer.

Wooldridge, M., Jennings, N. R., and Kinny, D. (2000). The gaia methodology for agent-oriented analysis and design. *Autonomous Agents and multi-agent systems*, 3:285–312.

Factores Personales que Influyen en la Realización de Tareas bajo *Test-Driven Development*: Meta-Análisis de una Familia de Experimentos

Geovanny Raura [1], **Efraín R. Fonseca C.** [1], **Oscar Dieste** [2]

[1]Departamento de Ciencias de la Computación – Universidad de las Fuerzas Armadas - ESPE
Quito, Ecuador

[2]Departamento de Lenguajes y Sistemas Informáticos e Ingeniería de Software –
Universidad Politécnica de Madrid
Madrid, España

{jgraura, erfonseca}@espe.edu.ec, odieste@fi.upm.es

***Abstract. Background**: Experimentation in Software Engineering often requires experimental subjects to perform some task. **Objective**: To study the extent to which experimental tasks are carried out based on an experiment's instrumental aspects and the subjects' personal characteristics. **Method**: Meta-analysis of a family of experiments in Test-Driven Development. **Results**: Older subjects and those with more professional experience perform less work on the experimental tasks. The nature of the experimental task can influence the level of participation in the experiment. **Conclusions**: The motivations of experimental subjects should be studied, and control mechanisms should be established to ensure proper performance.*

***Resumen. Antecedentes**: La experimentación en Ingeniería del Software requiere frecuentemente que los sujetos experimentales realicen algún tipo de tarea. **Objetivo**: Estudiar el grado en que se realizan las tareas experimentales, en función de los aspectos instrumentales de un experimento y de las características personales de los sujetos. **Método**: Meta-análisis de una familia de experimentos en Test-Driven Development. **Resultados**: Los sujetos de mayor edad y más experiencia profesional realizan menos trabajo en las tareas experimentales. La tarea experimental puede influir en el grado de participación en el experimento. **Conclusiones**: Deben estudiarse las motivaciones de los sujetos experimentales y establecer mecanismos de control que aseguren un correcto desempeño.*

1. Introducción

Las metodologías ágiles han ganado popularidad desde su aparición en la década de los 90, convirtiéndose en un pilar fundamental de las prácticas modernas de desarrollo de software. De entre estas metodologías, el Desarrollo Guiado por Pruebas (TDD, de las siglas del inglés *Test-Driven Development*) [Beck 2003] ha captado significativamente la atención de la academia, la industria y la comunidad científica, debido a su filosofía de mejora, tanto de la calidad del software, como de la productividad de los desarrolladores.

Existen varias revisiones de literatura que sintetizan los hallazgos acerca de TDD ([Rafique and Mišić 2012], [Munir et al. 2014], [Bissi et al. 2016a], entre otras). Un aspecto recurrente en estas investigaciones ha sido la comparación entre TDD y las metodologías tradicionales de programación, utilizando diversas aproximaciones como experimentos controlados [George and Williams 2004], estudios de caso [Nagappan et al. 2008] y encuestas [Bissi et al. 2016b]. Este tipo de estudios ha permitido identificar similitudes y diferencias significativas, enriqueciendo la comprensión sobre las fortalezas y limitaciones de TDD en una variedad de contextos y escenarios.

La literatura también destaca el papel de factores humanos, como la experiencia de los desarrolladores [Fucci et al. 2016], su familiaridad con las herramientas de desarrollo [Madeyski 2010], y el conocimiento de los lenguajes de programación [Pančur and Ciglarič 2011], como elementos influyentes en la aplicación de TDD y en los resultados obtenidos por los programadores. Sin embargo, la relación entre estos factores y los resultados de TDD sigue estando poco explorada, y las conclusiones de los estudios existentes no son concluyentes, lo que resalta la necesidad de investigaciones más profundas y focalizadas [Kollanus 2010].

En esta línea, hemos realizado una familia de experimentos centrados en estudiar factores humanos que influyen en la calidad del código y la productividad de los desarrolladores cuando utilizan TDD. Sin embargo, durante su ejecución, observamos discrepancias entre el comportamiento esperado y real de los sujetos participantes durante la realización de las tareas experimentales. Además de medir ciertas variables respuesta como la calidad y la productividad, revisamos manualmente el código entregado y encontramos que algunos participantes trabajaron considerablemente, mientras que otros apenas realizaron cambios. En casos extremos, los sujetos devolvieron el mismo código proporcionado al inicio.

En un experimento, se espera que los sujetos se comporten profesionalmente, de modo que los efectos observados en las variables respuesta se deriven de los tratamientos ensayados, y no de otros factores. En caso contrario, las conclusiones del experimento sufrirían de una severa amenaza a la validez. Por este motivo, hemos realizado un meta-análisis de nuestra familia de experimentos para averiguar si **el nivel de participación de los sujetos en la realización de las tareas experimentales es aleatorio o puede trazarse a alguna variable**, que en nuestro caso son los aspectos instrumentales de un experimento (tareas, objetos experimentales) y las características personales de los sujetos.

La principal contribución de este trabajo radica en mostrar en qué medida las características personales pueden influir en la ejecución de TDD, lo cual puede tener impacto en la aplicación práctica de esta estrategia de desarrollo, así como implicaciones metodológicas para la investigación empírica en Ingeniería de Software.

El artículo se estructura como sigue. La Sección 2 revisa el estado del arte. En la Sección 3 describimos el diseño experimental, mientras que en la Sección 4 describimos las características principales de las replicaciones experimentales. Los principales resultados del meta-análisis se reportan en la Sección 5. Las Secciones 6 y 7 finalizan el artículo describiendo las amenazas a la validez y las conclusiones, respectivamente.

2. Estado de la Cuestión

En la investigación experimental con humanos, se han realizado diversos estudios que no se centran únicamente en evaluar un determinado tratamiento o factor, sino que también persiguen comprender cómo los sujetos experimentales aplican dicho tratamiento o factor en contextos controlados.

El nivel de participación de los sujetos en las tareas experimentales puede estar influenciado por varios componentes de diseño, como la dificultad de la tarea, los incentivos, la duración del experimento, el diseño de la interfaz y las características del participante. La investigación realizada hasta el momento es limitada, pero algunos resultados son ilustrativos.

La complejidad de una tarea influye significativamente en la probabilidad de que los participantes participen activamente. Cuando una es demasiado compleja, los participantes experimentan sobrecarga cognitiva [Sweller 1988], lo que provoca frustración y abandono. Las tareas que requieren razonamiento abstracto o multitarea pueden abrumar a los participantes [Chandler et al. 2014]. Por el contrario, la baja dificultad puede provocar abandono por aburrimiento.

Los incentivos representan un aspecto muy importante que influye en la realización de las tareas experimentales. Cuando los incentivos son bajos, se produce un mayor abandono. Hauser, David y Schwarz [Hauser and Schwarz 2018] observaron que los participantes pueden abandonar si sienten que la tarea no compensa el tiempo empleado en ella.

La utilización de incentivos monetarios aumenta la retención de los sujetos experimentales. Sin embargo, algunos sujetos pueden realizar la tarea rápido y sin cuidado solo por obtener la recompensa [Oppenheimer et al. 2009]. En general, la motivación intrínseca es la que asegura un grado de compromiso mayor. Cuando los participantes encuentran a la tarea interesante o significativa, participan activamente y la completan con mayor frecuencia [Deci and Ryan 1985].

Los experimentos más largos tienden a presentar tasas de abandono más altas. Los participantes son más propensos a completar tareas de corta duración. En las tareas de duración media (10–30 minutos) la tasa de abandono es moderada. Zhou y Fishbach [Zhou and Fishbach 2016] observaron que, a medida que aumenta la duración de la tarea, la motivación tiende a disminuir, a menos que la tarea se divida en segmentos más cortos y manejables. Los estudios muestran una caída drástica en la retención después de los 30 minutos, especialmente en experimentos en línea [Kittur et al. 2008].

Las diferencias individuales influyen en quién tiene más probabilidades de abandonar la tarea. Las personas con altos niveles de escrupulosidad tienen más probabilidades de completar las tareas que les son asignadas [Diefendorff and Richard 2000]. Las personas con poca paciencia o excesivamente impulsivas abandonan con mayor frecuencia las tareas. En experimentos sobre gratificación diferida, como la famosa *Prueba del Malvavisco* [Mischel et al. 1989], los niños que tenían dificultades con el autocontrol eran más propensos a abandonar las tareas experimentales. De manera similar, los participantes que experimentan estrés o ansiedad tienen un rendimiento inferior, como lo demuestran los estudios sobre ansiedad ante los exámenes y rendimiento cognitivo [Eysenck et al. 2007]. Además, variables demográficas como el nivel educativo y la familiaridad con los procedimientos experimentales afectan la persistencia en la realización de las tareas. Hauser, David y Schwarz [Hauser and Schwarz 2018] encontraron que los participantes con más experiencia en experimentos en línea eran menos propensos a abandonar prematuramente en comparación con los novatos.

El diseño deficiente de la interfaz genera frustración, mientras que las interfaces intuitivas mejoran la retención. Si los participantes tienen dificultades para entender las instrucciones, pueden abandonar prematuramente [Chandler et al. 2014]. Introducir elementos de gamificación (como recompensas o seguimiento del progreso) podrían el abandono [McGonigal 2011].

Los experimentos que generan malestar pueden llevar a un alto abandono. En el bien conocido experimento de obediencia de Milgram [Milgram 1963], algunos participantes se negaron a continuar debido a conflictos morales. En general, los estudios que incluyen dilemas morales reportan altos niveles de abandono [Kogut and Ritov 2005].

En el contexto de los experimentos en Ingeniería de Software, y particularmente en estudios sobre TDD, también se ha comenzado a prestar atención a la influencia que tiene la forma en que los participantes aplican la técnica durante el experimento. Karac et al.[Karac et al. 2025] investigan si esta aplicación práctica impacta los resultados obtenidos en experimentos sobre TDD, mostrando cómo las diferencias individuales pueden afectar los efectos medidos. Por su parte, Santos et al.[Santos et al. 2021] presentan una familia de experimentos centrada en TDD en la que se identifican retos relacionados con la ejecución consistente del tratamiento. Estos trabajos subrayan la importancia de considerar factores personales y contextuales al analizar los resultados de experimentos empíricos en prácticas de desarrollo de software como TDD.

3. Método de Investigación

La investigación en la que se basa este trabajo tenía como objetivo estudiar la influencia de los factores humanos en el desarrollo de software. Para ello, escogimos un experimento base en el área de TDD [Juristo 2016], del cual realizamos siete replicaciones literales nativas tanto internas como externas [Juristo and Gómez 2012] con ciertas diferencias en su contexto o metodología. Cinco replicaciones fueron realizadas en la academia y dos en la industria. A continuación, se presentan los elementos clave del diseño experimental.

3.1. Factores y Niveles

3.1.1. Estrategia de Desarrollo

En este estudio se analizaron dos estrategias de desarrollo: **Desarrollo Guiado por Pruebas** (TDD) y **Desarrollo Iterativo con Pruebas Finales** (*Iterative Test-Last Development*, ITLD por sus siglas en inglés). En uno de los experimentos se introdujo una tercera estrategia denominada **A su manera** (*Your Way, YW por sus siglas en inglés*, pero su utilización no tuvo continuiada. En lo que respecta a TDD, los participantes siguieron el ciclo tradicional:

1. Dividir la tarea principal en sub-tareas pequeñas y manejables.
2. Escribir pruebas mínimas para cada sub-tarea antes de desarrollar el código de producción.

3. Ejecutar las pruebas y validar los resultados para determinar si la implementación es correcta.
4. Refactorizar el código de forma incremental para mejorar su diseño sin alterar su funcionalidad.

En ITLD, aunque se siguen los mismos principios generales, el código de producción se escribe antes que las pruebas, pero en incrementos progresivos. Este enfoque permite una comparación justa con TDD al incorporar pruebas de manera iterativa, evitando problemas asociados con enfoques como *Test Last Development*, donde el código se escribe en su totalidad antes de realizar las pruebas.

3.1.2. Nivel de Descomposición de las Tareas

En varias replicaciones se estudió el **nivel de especificación de las tareas**. Se consideraron dos variantes: **Sliced** (tareas descompuestas) y **No-sliced** (tareas integradas).

En la versión **Sliced**, cada tarea se presenta como una serie de pasos independientes, con especificaciones detalladas del comportamiento esperado y ejemplos de casos de prueba para cada paso. Por ejemplo, si la tarea consiste en implementar una calculadora, los participantes recibirían instrucciones para desarrollar primero la operación de suma con un caso de prueba asociado, luego la resta, y así sucesivamente.

En la versión **No-sliced**, la especificación de la tarea incluyó una descripción general de las funcionalidades requeridas, sin dividirla en pasos. Esto refleja un entorno más cercano a las condiciones reales en las que los requisitos son menos estructurados.

3.2. Tareas Experimentales

Utilizamos dos tareas experimentales:

- **MarsRover API (MR)**. Es un ejercicio de programación que tiene por objetivo el desarrollo de una serie de métodos públicos o API (Aplication Program Interface), que simula el movimiento de un vehículo hacia distintos puntos con diferentes orientaciones (Norte, Sur, Este, Oeste), dentro de un planeta representado por un plano de coordenadas. No se requiere la implementación de una interfaz de usuario.
- **Robert Martin's Bowling Score Keeper (BSK)**. Esta tarea tiene por objetivo calcular el marcador de un único juego de bolos. Igual que MR, esta tarea consiste en la implementación de un algoritmo de programación, sin que tampoco sea necesario el desarrollo de una interface de usuario.

Las tareas experimentales fueron realizadas utilizando el lenguaje de programación Java y JUnit como framework de pruebas. En todos los casos se entregó a los sujetos la estructura básica de código, disponible en [*cita anonimizada*]. Como IDE de desarrollo se utilizó Eclipse.

3.3. Variables de Respuesta y Métricas

El diseño experimental original contemplaba dos variables: la calidad del código y la productividad de los investigadores. El reporte de dichos resultados está en proceso. Sin embargo, al realizar el proceso de medición, pudimos apreciar que independientemente de los valores obtenidos para las variables calidad y productividad, algunos sujetos entregaron código casi sin haber tocado el esqueleto entregado.

Este comportamiento motivó a que se incluyera dentro del reporte de mediciones, una nueva variable respuesta que se denominó: *nivel de participación en la tarea experimental*, con tres valores posibles (nótese que la variable es ordinal): *Nothing*, cuando el código entregado fue *prácticamente* el mismo código que el descargado de *github*; *Insignificant*, cuando los cambios realizados estaban restringidos a unas pocas líneas de código; y *Aceptable* en los casos restantes.

Es importante destacar que el nivel de participación no tiene el mismo significado que otras variables relacionadas, como el grado de adherencia a un procedimiento experimental (*process conformance* [Fucci et al. 2014]). La adherencia estudia en qué grado siguen los sujetos experimentales las instrucciones de los experimentadores. Sin embargo, el nivel de partición representa (a grano grueso) la cantidad de trabajo realizado por los sujetos, independientemente de si ese trabajo es conforme o no a las instrucciones proporcionadas.

Para hacerse una idea de la importancia del nivel de participación, la Tabla 1 muestra el nivel de participación desglosado por replicación experimental. Los niveles de participación *Nothing* e *Insignificant* superan, por mucho, las participaciones *Adequate*.

Tabla 1. Nivel de participación desglosado por replicación experimental

Nivel de participación	**Replicación**						
	1	2	3	4	5	6	7
Nothing	12	2	0	1	11	6	8
Insignificant	58	43	9	23	12	8	32
Adequate	5	23	8	6	18	2	13

3.4. Diseño Experimental

El diseño experimental sigue un enfoque factorial mixto, donde los factores principales (Estrategia de Desarrollo y Nivel de Descomposición de Tareas) son intra-sujetos. También es intra-sujetos el factor Tarea, aunque su interés es principalmente instrumental (son necesarias para la aplicación de los factores principales) y exploratorio. La variable independiente Grupo es entre-sujetos, aunque no tiene interés en la investigación más allá de aplicar las buenas prácticas indicadas en [Vegas et al. 2016]. Los participantes fueron asignados aleatoriamente a los siguientes grupos experimentales indicados en la Tabla 2.

Existen varias consideraciones importantes respecto al diseño experimental base, que sólo podemos enunciar brevemente en este trabajo (los detalles completos están disponibles en [Raura Ruiz 2022]):

- El diseño mostrado en la Tabla 2 sólo fue utilizado en un experimento. En los restantes, se utilizó únicamente la versión **No-Sliced**, ya que la muestra de sujetos era limitada. De esta manera, se mejoró el poder estadístico de los experimentos individuales.
- Al utilizar únicamente la versión **No-Sliced**, el diseño de la Tabla 2 se simplifica a 2-grupos, 2-periodos, 2-tratamientos. En esta configuración es muy difícil identificar efectos de *carry-over*, por lo que conviene minimizarlos por diseño [Vegas et al. 2016].

Tabla 2. Diseño Experimental

Grupos	Sesión Experimental 1 - ITLD	Sesión Experimental 2 - TDD
G1	BSK /Sliced	MR/No Sliced
G2	BSK/ No Sliced	MR/Sliced
G3	MR/Sliced	BSK/No Sliced
G4	MR/No Sliced	BSK/Slicing

- El *carry-over* es el efecto que el primer factor intra-sujetos ejerce sobre el segundo factor [Senn 2003, 10 ss.]. En medicina, el *carry-over* tiene su fundamento en la permanencia de la medicación en el organismo durante un cierto tiempo después de finalizar su administración. En IS, el fundamento es menos evidente y podría obedecer a múltiples causas. En esta investigación, el aspecto que más claramente podría producir *carry-over* es la formación, ya que podría ocurrir que los sujetos utilizasen la estrategia TDD en ITLD. Al contrario es más improbable, ya que ITLD sólo añade la prueba automatizada a los conocimientos en programación que ya poseen los sujetos, y dichas pruebas son un prerequisito para TDD. Por este motivo, se decidió aplicar ITLD siempre antes que TDD, aunque ello implique confundir la Estrategia de Desarrollo y la sesión experimental (esto es, el diseño es entre-sujetos pero no *cross-over*).

3.5. Covariables

Estudiamos los efectos de diferentes covariables, esto es, otras variables independientes que podrían influir en el estudio, tales como la edad de los sujetos, la experiencia en desarrollo y el conocimiento previo de TDD, entre otros aspectos indicados en la Tabla 3.

Habitualmente, las covariables no son de interés para la investigación y se consideran únicamente para reducir la variabilidad en la medición de la variable respuesta. Este no es nuestro caso; de hecho, las covariables son un objeto principal de nuestra investigación. La principal característica de estas covariables (y por esta razón no las consideramos como factores) es que no son controlables por los investigadores: en todos los casos, son características propias de los sujetos experimentales. Los valores de estas covariables fueron obtenidos mediante la aplicación de un cuestionario al inicio de cada experimento. Sin embargo, dependiendo de las condiciones de cada experimento, algunas de ellas fueron descartadas posteriormente.

4. Familia de Experimentos

Tal y como se ha mencionado con anterioridad, este trabajo se basa en siete experimentos replicados en diferentes contextos, los cuales se resumen en la Tabla 4. Todos los experimentos están afectados por el fenómeno de abandono de las tareas.

Cada uno de estos experimentos fue analizado independientemente con el propósito de encontrar relaciones entre el nivel de participación y:

Tabla 3. Covariables

Covariable	Descripción	Métrica
Edad	Indica la edad del sujeto participante	Medida mediante un valor numérico: Tipo entero positivo
Nivel de Educación	Determina el nivel de educación del sujeto, el mismo que puede ser estudiante de pre-grado, estudiante de post-grado u otro.	Medida mediante escala nominal: 1 Bachiller en Ciencias de la Computación 2 Master 3 Otro
Experiencia en programación	Indica la experiencia del sujeto en programación	Medida mediante escala ordinal de likert: 1 Sin experiencia (<2 años) 2 Novato (2 - 5 años) 3 Intermedio (6 - 10 años) 4 Experto (>10 años)
Uso de herramientas de pruebas	Indica si el sujeto ha utilizado o no herramientas automáticas de pruebas	Medida mediante escala nominal: 1 Si 2 No
Experiencia en lenguaje Java	Determina si el sujeto tiene experiencia con el uso del lenguaje Java	Medida mediante escala escala ordinal de likert: 1 Sin experiencia (<2 años) 2 Novato (2-5 años) 3 Intermedio (6-10 años) 4 Experto (>10 años)
Experiencia en JUnit	Indica si el sujeto tiene experiencia previa utilizando el framework JUnit	Medida mediante escala escala ordinal de likert: 1 Sin experiencia (<2 años) 2 Novato (2-5 años) 3 Intermedio (6-10 años) 4 Experto (>10 años)
Uso de la técnica TDD	Permite conocer si el sujeto ha tenido conocimiento previo en la técnica TDD	Medida mediante escala nominal: 1 Si 2 No
Experiencia en TDD	Si el sujeto tiene experiencia en la técnica de TDD, este indicador permite determinar los años de experiencia en su uso	Medida mediante escala escala ordinal de likert: 1 Sin experiencia (<2 años) 2 Novato (2-5 años) 3 Intermedio (6-10 años) 4 Experto (>10 años)
Entrenamiento previo en desarrollo de pruebas unitarias	Determina si el sujeto ha recibido entrenamiento previo en el desarrollo de pruebas unitarias	Medida mediante escala nominal: 1 Si 2 No
Conocimiento del entorno Eclipse	Determina si el sujeto tiene conocimiento previo del IDE de desarrollo Eclipse	Medida mediante escala nominal: 1 Si 2 No
Función actual en la organización	Indica cuál es la función que se encontraba desempeñando el sujeto dentro de la Organización	Medida mediante escala nominal: 1 Manager 2 Developer 3 Analyst 4 Other

- Los componentes instrumentales del experimento: niveles y tareas experimentales.
- Los factores personales indicados en la Tabla 3.

Los análisis estadísticos no mostraron, con pocas excepciones, diferencias estadísticamente significativas. La única excepción fue la **experiencia en programación**, la cual mostró una correlación positiva con el nivel de participación en las tareas en algunos experimentos, indicando que los participantes con mayor experiencia tendieron a finalizar más tareas de manera aceptable. No obstante, este resultado no se confirmó en el meta-análisis posterior, como se indicará en la siguiente sección.

La ausencia de resultados significativos no debería extrañarnos. De existir relación entre los componentes instrumentales o factores personales, y el nivel de participación, dicha relación relación debería estar asociada a un tamaño de efecto muy alto para poder ser detectable con el número de sujetos por replicación disponibles. Por este motivo, decidimos aplicar meta-análisis para analizar todas las replicaciones en conjunto.

Tabla 4. Descripción de los experimentos realizados

Rep.	Contexto	# sujetos	Niveles				
			TDD	ITLD	YOUR WAY	SLICED	NO-SLICED
1	Académico (pregrado)	43	X	X		X	X
2	Académico (pregrado)	35	X	X		X	X
3	Académico (postgrado)	9	X	X		X	X
4	Académico (pregrado)	15	X	X		X	X
5	Industrial	23	X	X	X	X	
6	Industrial	10	X	X		X	X
7	Académico (postgrado)	27	X	X		X	X
Sujetos		162					

5. Síntesis de la Familia de Experimentos

El procedimiento que vamos a utilizar para la síntesis es el meta-análisis de datos agregados[1]. Dado que el nivel de participación es ordinal, lo dicotomizaremos en dos categorías: *NothingOrInsignificant* y *Acceptable*. La primera categoría indica que el trabajo realizado por el sujeto experimental no ha sido satisfactorio, y la segunda lo contrario. Existen otras opciones de meta-análisis que no exigen la dicotomización, como los *proportional odds models* y las tablas de contingencia. Evitamos los primeros por su difícil interpretación, y los segundos porque no nos permiten considerar los experimentos por separado ni determinar la homogeneidad de los mismos.

El procedimiento de meta-análisis aplicado el *odds ratio* (OR) o diferencia media (d) utilizando el método genérico de ponderación por inversa de varianza. Para el cálculo de la heterogeneidad hemos usado el procedimiento de DerSimonian y Laird. Dado que este estudio no es confirmatorio y el tamaño muestral es limitado, usamos el nivel de significación $\alpha = 0{,}1$ para rechazar la hipótesis nula, aunque entendemos que los resultados son mucho más fiables a un nivel de significación $\alpha = 0{,}05$.

A este respecto, el p-valor del "*test for overall effect*" no ha sido incluido en los *forest plots* con el fin de evitar sobrecargar las figuras. Sin embargo, su carácter significativo al nivel $\alpha = 0{,}05$ puede inferirse del valor del intervalo de confianza al 95 %. Sí incluye el p-valor correspondiente al análisis de heterogeneidad, ya que este permite determinar el modelo de efectos (fijos o aleatorios) que debe ser interpretado en cada caso.

El meta análisis ha arrojado tres resultados positivos. En primer lugar, el tipo de tarea experimental influye significativamente en nivel de participación. La influencia de la Tarea puede observarse en la Figura 1. En particular, la tarea **Bowling Score Keeper** propocia que los sujetos realicen una mayor cantidad de trabajo en comparación con **Mars Rover**. El efecto observado es estadísticamente significativo ($p - valor = 0{,}06$) al nivel $\alpha = 0{,}1$, con un tamaño de efecto $OR = 3{,}15$, indicando una influencia moderada en el nivel de participación en la tarea de generar el código.

En segundo lugar, la edad de los participantes también juega un papel en el nivel de participación en las tareas. En este análisis, se consideró la edad como variable dependiente, revelando que los **sujetos de mayor edad tienden a entregar tareas que denotan menor participación**. La influencia de la Edad puede observarse en la Figura 2.

[1]Los datos experimentales están disponibles en `https://doi.org/10.5281/zenodo.15075335`.

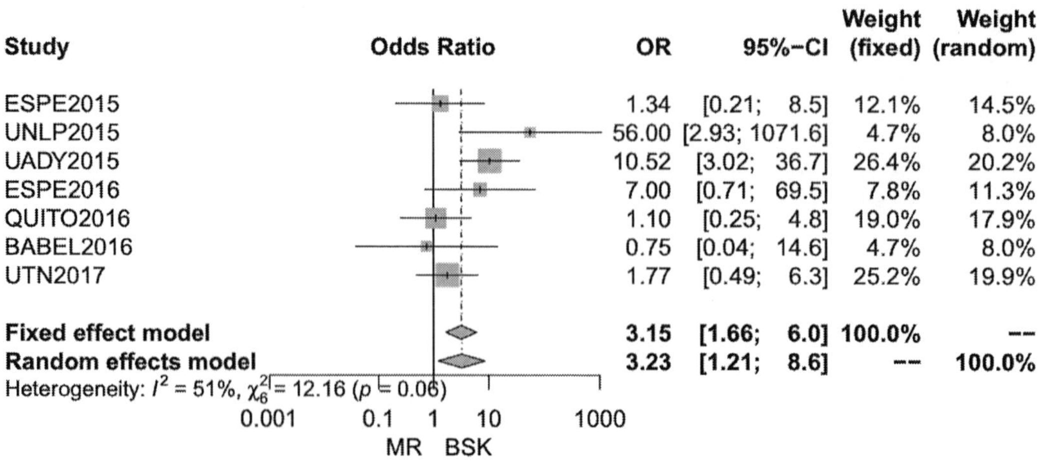

Figura 1. Meta-análisis para el componente instrumental Tarea

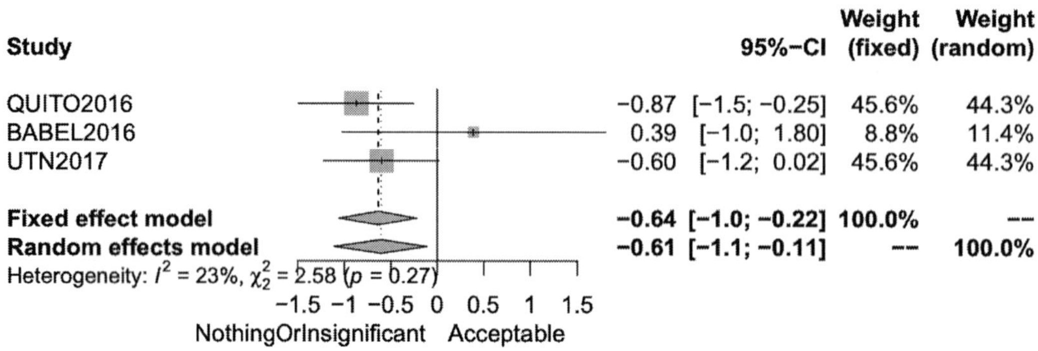

Figura 2. Meta-análisis para el aspecto personal Edad

El tamaño del efecto fue $d = -0{,}64$, lo que representa un efecto medio estadísticamente significativo ($p - value \leq 0{,}0029$). Este hallazgo sugiere que la edad podría estar relacionada con la capacidad o la motivación para completar las tareas asignadas, lo que podría deberse a diferencias en experiencia, hábitos de trabajo o familiaridad con el entorno experimental.

Finalmente, el nivel de educación de los participantes, es una variable ordinal (between-subjects), por lo que hemos realizado un análisis mediante una tabla de contingencia, con un análisis *post-hoc* posterior, en lugar de aplicar un metá-análisis de OR o d. Se obtiene un $p - valor = 0{,}0655$, por debajo del nivel $\alpha = 0{,}1$, lo que lleva a descartar la hipótesis nula, aunque los resultados no son completamente fiables. El análisis *post-hoc* muestra que las diferencias entre grupos no son estadísticamente significativas, pero se observa una tendencia: los participantes con educación de *Master* y *Bachelor* completaron más tareas aceptables (32.5 %), en comparación con el 19.9 % del grupo *Undergraduate*. El grupo *Other* (sin educación universitaria) no completó ninguna tarea de manera aceptable.

El resto de aspectos instrumentales y aspectos personales no han arrojado resultados estadísticamente significativos:

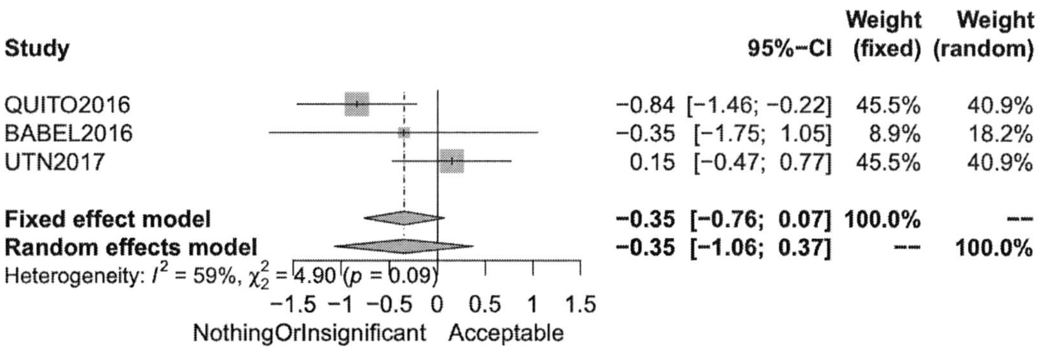

Figura 3. Meta-análisis para la Experiencia Profesional

- Las estrategias TDD e ITLD, esto es, el tipo de estrategia de desarrollo no influencia el nivel de participación.
- El entrenamiento en *Unit Testing*, esto es, el conocimiento previo en pruebas unitarias no afecta al nivel de participación.
- El conocimiento del entorno de desarrollo *Eclipse*.
- La experiencia en programación.
- La experiencia profesional, aunque en este caso el tamaño del efecto $d = -0{,}35$ es pequeño, con un $p - valor \leq 0{,}1055$ no significativo, lo que sugiere que podemos estar ante un error de tipo II. El *forest plot* correspondiente se muestra en la Figura 3.
- El uso de herramientas de prueba.
- La experiencia en *JUnit*.
- La experiencia en el lenguaje de programación Java.

6. Amenazas a la Validez

Existen diversas amenazas a la validez [Shadish et al. 2002] que podrían influir en los resultados obtenidos. Estas amenazas están principalmente relacionadas con el diseño experimental, las condiciones en las que se llevaron a cabo los experimentos y la muestra de participantes utilizada.

La **validez de conclusión** se ve amenaza por dos aspectos principales. En primer lugar, el **tamaño muestral es limitado**, lo que influye en el poder estadístico del análisis. Para paliar esta amenaza, se han realizado varias replicaciones totalizando 162 sujetos, y los resultados de las replicaciones individuales se han combinado mediante meta-análisis. Sin embargo, dado el elevado número de resultados no significativos obtenidos, no podemos descartar la existencia de errores de tipo II, independientemente de que muchos de los efectos implicados serán pequeños, y por lo tanto de difícil detección y no muy interesantes en la práctica.

Otra potencial amenaza a la conclusión es que **sólo se ha considerado el efecto sumativo**, y no interactivo, de las covariables. Podría ocurrir que la edad interaccionase negativamente con TDD pero no con ITLD, y que la experiencia profesional interaccionase inversamente. Sin embargo, estos efectos de segundo orden normalmente son pequeños y difíciles de detectar. Por ello, su estudio debe llevarse a cabo mediante análisis *post-hoc*, que no tienen cabida en esta investigación de tipo experimental.

Una de las principales **amenazas a la validez interna** es el efecto de **práctica**, ya que los participantes pueden mejorar en la tarea a medida que adquieren experiencia con el tiempo. Sin embargo, dado que TDD es una técnica nueva para la mayoría de los sujetos, se espera que la práctica les ayude a comprender mejor sus beneficios en lugar de sesgar los resultados. La **fatiga** es otra amenaza importante, pues las sesiones de entrenamiento y los experimentos se realizaron de manera intensiva, lo que pudo afectar el rendimiento de los participantes, especialmente en tareas repetitivas y de alta concentración.

Otra posible **amenaza a la validez interna** es el **efecto de arrastre** (*carry-over*), ya discutido en la sección 3.4, que ocurre cuando la experiencia adquirida en una condición experimental afecta la siguiente. No podemos descartar que se produzca *carry-over*. Sin embargo, dado que ITLD y TDD comparten estrategias similares, este efecto no se considera problemático e incluso podría haber facilitado la transferencia de conocimientos entre técnicas. Dado que el *carry-over* se confunde con el periodo y grupo experimental [Vegas et al. 2016], además de con la Estrategia de Desarrollo en este diseño concreto, no es posible realizar correcciones durante el análisis que eliminen dicho efecto.

Asimismo, el **orden o periodo de las pruebas** podría ser una fuente de sesgo, pero dado que las sesiones experimentales y de entrenamiento se realizaron secuencialmente, es poco probable que eventos externos hayan influido significativamente en la motivación o habilidades de los participantes.

La medición de la variable respuesta Nivel de Participación se ha realizado de forma subjetiva. Aunque en la medición han participado dos investigadores, es necesario una definición más precisa que evite problemas de **validez de constructo**.

En cuanto a las **amenazas a la validez externa**, la diversidad de los participantes representa una limitación importante. La mayoría de los sujetos experimentales han sido estudiantes, aunque también incorporamos un numero significativo de desarrolladores que trabajan en la industria. Aun así, sería conveniente una muestra más diversa que permitiera generalizar de los resultados.

7. Conclusiones y Trabajos Futuros

La principal contribución de este trabajo es poner de manifiesto que los sujetos experimentales, por diversas razones, pueden realizar de manera inadecuada (lo que denominamos nivel de participación) las tareas experimentales.

Observamos que, conforme los participantes tienen mayor edad, el nivel de participación en las tareas experimentales disminuye. Quizás este efecto podría explicarse por la falta de motivación. En nuestra investigación, los sujetos de mayor edad fueron profesionales que participaban en cursos de entrenamiento y, en ciertos casos, no podían abandonar dichos cursos (ni tampoco los experimentos asociados) dado que debían realizar el entrenamiento dentro de su horario de trabajo.

Otro factor humano que está relacionado con un bajo nivel de participación es la experiencia profesional. Aunque se podría buscar una explicación a dicha relación, lo más probable es que se deba a que está fuertemente correlacionada con la edad (r = 0.66, p-valor <0,001), por lo que exhibe un comportamiento semejante, aunque el meta-análisis, en este caso, no sea estadísticamente significativo al nivel $\alpha = 0{,}05$.

Un factor que se acercó al nivel de significación estadística del 5 % fue el nivel de educación para el caso de los experimentos realizados con estudiantes. El grupo de participantes de *Bachelor* y *Master* fueron quienes entregaron las tareas experimentales más completas. Esto puede parecer lógico en el sentido de que los estudiantes más formados realizan las tareas *mejor* que los menos formados.

Sin embargo, el nivel de participación no mide dicho efecto, sino el grado en el que los estudiantes de *Bachelor* y *Master* han trabajado durante el experimento, independientemente de si han conseguido realizar con éxito las tareas experimentales. Nuestra interpretación es que los sujetos formados en la universidad están más acostumbrados y probablemente aprecian más los cursos de formación del estilo impartido durante la realización del experimento, y por lo tanto se involucran en mayor medida.

Desde nuestra perspectiva, hemos obtenido ciertos hallazgos interesantes que apuntan en dos direcciones: 1) deben estudiarse las motivaciones de los sujetos experimentales y 2) es conveniente establecer mecanismos de control que aseguren un correcto desempeño de los sujetos durante la realización de experimentos.

Finalmente, queremos indicar que el presente estudio es de carácter exploratorio, dado que no hemos pretendido establecer una relación causa-efecto, sino más bien despertar el interés en la realización de un mayor número de estudios empíricos sobre los factores humanos que podrían incidir en los resultados. En particular, el limitado número de sujetos experimentales que participaron en los siete experimentos hace que nuestros resultados deban tomarse con cautela.

Referencias

Beck, K. (2003). *Test Driven Development: By Example*. Addison-Wesley.

Bissi, W., Neto, A. G. S. S., and Emer, M. C. F. P. (2016a). The effects of test driven development on internal quality, external quality and productivity: A systematic review. *Information and Software Technology*, 74:45–54.

Bissi, W., Scanniello, G., Romano, S., and Tortora, G. (2016b). On the perception of test driven development: A replicated study. *Journal of Visual Languages & Computing*, 34:11–24.

Chandler, J., Mueller, P., and Paolacci, G. (2014). Nonnaïveté among amazon mechanical turk workers: Consequences and solutions for behavioral researchers. *Behavior Research Methods*, 46(1):112–130.

Deci, E. L. and Ryan, R. M. (1985). *Intrinsic Motivation and Self-Determination in Human Behavior*. Plenum, New York.

Diefendorff, J. M. and Richard, E. M. (2000). Antecedents and consequences of emotional display rule perceptions. *Journal of Applied Psychology*, 88(2):284–294.

Eysenck, M. W., Derakshan, N., Santos, R., and Calvo, M. G. (2007). Anxiety and cognitive performance: Attentional control theory. *Emotion*, 7(2):336–353.

Fucci, D., Erdogmus, H., Turhan, B., Oivo, M., and Juristo, N. (2016). A dissection of the test-driven development process: does it really matter to test-first or to test-last? *IEEE Transactions on Software Engineering*, 43(7):597–614.

Fucci, D., Turhan, B., and Oivo, M. (2014). Impact of process conformance on the effects of test-driven development. In *Proceedings of the 8th ACM/IEEE International Symposium on Empirical Software Engineering and Measurement*, pages 1–10.

George, B. and Williams, L. (2004). A structured experiment of test-driven development. *Information and Software Technology*, 46(5):337–342.

Hauser, D. J. and Schwarz, N. (2018). Attentive turkers: Mturk participants perform better on online attention checks than do subject pool participants. *Behavior Research Methods*, 48(1):400–407.

Juristo, N. (2016). Experiences conducting experiments in industry: The eseil fidipro project. In *2016 IEEE/ACM 4th International Workshop on Conducting Empirical Studies in Industry (CESI)*, pages 1–3.

Juristo, N. and Gómez, O. S. (2012). *Replication of Software Engineering Experiments*, pages 60–88. Springer Berlin Heidelberg, Berlin, Heidelberg.

Karac, I., Panach, J. I., Turhan, B., and Juristo, N. (2025). Does treatment adherence impact experiment results in tdd? *IEEE Transactions on Software Engineering*, 51(1):135–152.

Kittur, A., Chi, E. H., and Suh, B. (2008). Crowdsourcing user studies with mechanical turk. In *Proceedings of the SIGCHI Conference on Human Factors in Computing Systems*, pages 453–456.

Kogut, T. and Ritov, I. (2005). The "identified victim" effect: An identified group, or just a single individual? *Journal of Behavioral Decision Making*, 18(3):157–167.

Kollanus, S. (2010). Test-driven development: still a promising approach? *Proceedings of the 2010 ACM-IEEE International Symposium on Empirical Software Engineering and Measurement*, pages 1–4.

Madeyski, L. (2010). The impact of test-first programming on branch coverage and mutation score indicator of unit tests: An experiment. *Information and Software Technology*, 52(2):169–184.

McGonigal, J. (2011). *Reality Is Broken: Why Games Make Us Better and How They Can Change the World.* Penguin Press, New York.

Milgram, S. (1963). Behavioral study of obedience. *Journal of Abnormal and Social Psychology*, 67(4):371–378.

Mischel, W., Shoda, Y., and Rodriguez, M. L. (1989). Delay of gratification in children. *Science*, 244(4907):933–938.

Munir, H., Moayyed, M., and Petersen, K. (2014). Considering rigor and relevance when evaluating test driven development: A systematic review. *Information and Software Technology*, 56(4):375–394.

Nagappan, N., Maximilien, E. M., Bhat, T., and Williams, L. (2008). Realizing quality improvement through test driven development: Results and experiences of four industrial teams. *Empirical Software Engineering*, 13(3):289–302.

Oppenheimer, D. M., Meyvis, T., and Davidenko, N. (2009). Instructional manipulation checks: Detecting satisficing to increase statistical power. *Journal of Experimental Social Psychology*, 45(4):867–872.

Pančur, M. and Ciglarič, M. (2011). Impact of test-driven development on productivity, code and tests: A controlled experiment. *Information and Software Technology*, 53(6):557–573.

Rafique, Y. and Mišić, V. B. (2012). Effects of test driven development on external quality and productivity: A systematic review. *Empirical Software Engineering*, 18(5):1094–1117.

Raura Ruiz, J. G. (2022). *Impacto de las características personales de los programadores en la efectividad de Test-Driven Development (TDD)*. PhD thesis, Universidad Nacional de La Plata, La Plata, Argentina. Tesis de doctorado.

Santos, A., Vegas, S., Dieste, O., and Juristo, N. (2021). A family of experiments on test-driven development. *Empirical Software Engineering*, 26(42).

Senn, S. (2003). *Cross-over Trials in Clinical Research*. Statistics in Practice. Wiley.

Shadish, W., Cook, T., and Campbell, D. (2002). *Experimental and Quasi-experimental Designs for Generalized Causal Inference*. Houghton Mifflin.

Sweller, J. (1988). Cognitive load during problem solving: Effects on learning. *Cognitive Science*, 12(2):257–285.

Vegas, S., Apa, C., and Juristo, N. (2016). Crossover designs in software engineering experiments: Benefits and perils. *IEEE Transactions on Software Engineering*, 42(2):120–135.

Zhou, X. and Fishbach, A. (2016). The pitfall of experimenting on the web: How unattended selective attrition leads to surprising (yet false) research conclusions. *Journal of Personality and Social Psychology*, 111(4):493–504.

Challenges and Solutions for Organizational Change in the Software Industry: A Tertiary Study

Rayfran Rocha Lima[1], **Ana Carolina Oran**[2], **César França**[1], **Leonardo Marques**[3]

[1]Cesar School – Recife – PE – Brazil

[2]Federal University of Amazonas – Manaus – AM – Brazil

[3]Sidi – Manaus – AM – Brazil

{ana.oran,lcm}@icomp.ufam.edu.br, {rrl2,franssa}@cesar.school

Abstract. *Organizational Change (OC) in the software industry is essential for maintaining competitiveness in dynamic environments. However, OC initiatives often face inefficiencies due to the lack of structured methodologies and reliance on ad hoc practices. This tertiary study analyzes 17 secondary studies related to the OC theme and its instances affecting key organizational pillars, such as technology, processes, and people. The results reveal limited adoption of OC models in software organizations. In response, it synthesizes 41 OC models, 14 critical success factors, and 6 key characteristics, offering a synthesized overview of structured OC frameworks and their relevance to the software industry context, supporting future adaptation efforts by practitioners.*

1. Introduction

The software industry operates in a fast-paced, innovation-driven environment where organizational agility and continuous adaptation to external and internal demands are essential for maintaining competitiveness [Agazu and Kero 2024]. However, the successful implementation of large-scale changes—such as cultural shifts, digital transformation, software process improvement, and process automation—remains a significant challenge [Lima et al. 2024]. Despite the critical role of these initiatives, they are often not recognized as forms of Organizational Change (OC), a well-established field with decades of consolidated knowledge and best practices [Orieno et al. 2024]. This lack of recognition limits the ability of software organizations to benefit from proven OC models, frameworks, and tools.

The absence of awareness and adoption of OC management theories and tools in the software industry leads to reliance on ad hoc, experience-driven approaches [Beer and Nohria 2000]. These unstructured methods, typically carried out by operational professionals without formal training in OC management, result in recurrent inefficiencies, such as resistance to change, insufficient organizational support, resource constraints, and low stakeholder engagement [Lima et al. 2024]. These challenges compromise the success of change initiatives and hinder their alignment with organizational strategies and goals, reducing the potential for long-term impact.

While some organizations employ external consultants for large specialized transformations—such as implementing CMMI (Capability Maturity Model Integration), adopting Industry 4.0, or integrating agile practices —most OC initiatives implemented in software industry companies are led by internal teams or organizational change teams composed of dedicated volunteers strongly committed to improving current practices, often lack the formal expertise needed to effectively plan, execute, and sustain this type of initiative [Edison et al. 2018].

This paper provides a structured synthesis of existing secondary studies, connecting theoretical and practical perspectives and organizing insights to support organizational change practitioners to navigate the complexities of EOC initiatives in software industry context. Through a systematic review of secondary studies, it presents the foundational OC concepts and key characteristics to be considered throughout the EOCs lifecycle, examining critical factors that can boost or hinder such initiatives.

2. Background

OC is a formal approach to transitioning from the current state to a desired future, focusing the organization's efforts on this change [Lewin 1947]. It refers to planned or unplanned initiatives that may make changes in the elements of an organization, such as structure, culture, processes, and technology aiming to enhance performance, efficiency, effectiveness [Beer and Walton 1987] to respond to internal ou external demands [Agazu and Kero 2024]. Still, the lack of an empirical basis to support theoretical findings [Cummings and Worley 2016] has been a recurring critique, emphasizing the need for more robust evidence to validate OC theories and practices.

Even using other nomenclatures [Lima et al. 2022], in the software and information technology industry, implementing OCs has been a way of life [Miller 2001]. It is a strategic mechanism for companies to establish robust competitive advantages [Davenport and Stoddard 1994], particularly in highly dynamic business environments. These initiatives often implement the steps of the change as three steps (CATS) model: unfreeze, change, refreeze [Lewin 1947].

Despite its significance, various studies [Dikert et al. 2016, Orieno et al. 2024, Beer and Nohria 2000] have shown that the failure or neglect of implementing the knowledge of the management of OC can complicate the implementation of OC in the software industry, making it more susceptible to inefficiency or failure. Consequently, the evolution of many companies relies on individual efforts, leading to unpredictable outcomes. An analysis of 82 cases of OC initiatives implemented in a large software development company, revealed critical challenges, including low familiarity with structured methodologies and minimal adoption of OC management practices due to lack of awareness of this field of knowledge [Lima et al. 2024].

Many studies highlight alternative approaches for managing such initiatives, including PMBoK, Scrum, and CMMI [Zahra et al. 2017, Dikert et al. 2016]. Although PMBoK and Scrum support project management, they do not cover the whole EOC lifecycle, which extends beyond traditional project phases. EOCs require evaluating organizational readiness, aligning with long-term goals, and sustaining outcomes post-implementation. CMMI-SW, focused on process maturity in software organizations, lacks support for broader changes involving technology and people—key pillars in EOC initiatives.

Given the strategic importance of OC initiatives in fostering competitiveness and adaptability, particularly in the dynamic software industry, it is evident that a lack of structured methodologies and the neglect of established OC practices significantly hinder the success of such initiatives. This gap highlights the need for a comprehensive analysis of existing OC models, critical factors, and key characteristics to guide practitioners in overcoming these challenges.

3. Method

This study aims to provide an overview of current research on OC management focusing on available knowledge in the literature applicable to OC initiatives implemented in the software industry context. To consolidate the state-of-the-art from existing literature reviews, a tertiary study [Kitchenham et al. 2010] was conducted to answer three research questions: RQ1. What are the main OC characteristics? RQ2. What existing models could assist in the OC process? RQ3. What are the critical factors for OC initiatives? While RQ1 identifies key aspects that influence management, RQ2 explores models that offer practical support for implementation, and RQ3 reveals critical factors that affect the success and failure of OC initiatives.

The decision to conduct a tertiary study arose from challenges in identifying relevant primary studies [Da Silva et al. 2011] on OC within the software industry context. Initial searches using the term 'Organizational Change' yielded limited results, with only 2% of reviews providing data relevant to this context. Expanding the scope to include terms like "digital transformation", "agile adoption", and "software process improvement" increased the pool from 500 to over 18,000 candidate papers, but the volume and diversity made this approach unfeasible. Consequently, the study focused on identifying and analysing secondary studies that synthesize the state-of-the-art, providing a comprehensive analysis of frameworks, critical factors, and essential elements that corroborate effective organizational changes addressed by these studies.

As the interest was to identify literature reviews on the OC field, a Search String as "Organizational Change" AND "Review" was tested. Although 52 articles were returned, only two addressed interventions implemented in the software industry [Acharya and Colomo-Palacios 2019, Armenakis and Bedeian 1999]. The others addressed the healthcare, construction, public, industrial, and services sectors. To resolve it, it was added synonyms for OC proposed by [Lima et al. 2022] such as transition, transformation, adaptation, redesign, migration, improvement, adoption, restructure.

To refine the Search String, terms related to specific examples of OC initiatives implemented in the software industry that affect three pillars of companies: people, processes, and technology [Taylor 1914] were added. For the people pillar, the term "team" [Dikert et al. 2016, Lima et al. 2022] was added. For the process pillar, the terms "process improvement" and its acronym "SPI" [Bayona et al. 2012] were added. Within the technology pillar, emphasis was placed on two additional terms and their variations: "digital transformation" and "Robotic process automation" their acronyms "DT" and "RPA" [Zaoui and Souissi 2020, Ribeiro et al. 2021]. In addition, the operator OR was used among alternative spellings and synonyms, and the operator AND was applied to obtain the intersection of these results.

After several runs to reduce the noise in the results while ensuring that the reference set, composed of [Lima et al. 2022, Errida and Lotfi 2021, Dikert et al. 2016], was returned, the final Search String was defined as *("Organizational change" OR "transi-*

tion" OR "transformation" OR "adaptation" OR "redesign" OR "migration" OR "improvement" OR "adoption" OR "restructure" OR "SPI" OR "Software process improvement" OR "DT" OR "digital transformation" OR "RPA" OR "robotic process automation") AND "Review". Applied in the Scopus digital library[1] in October 2024, the search returned 190 candidate secondary studies after applying a publication year filter from 2014 to 2024.

The study selection process involved two filtering steps, each applying the inclusion and exclusion criteria. To be included in the selected list, the candidate secondary study must: (i) address OC initiatives, (ii) be a Systematic or Mapping Literature Review, (iii) be published between 2014 and 2024, (iv) be peer-reviewed and published in a journal or conference, and (v) be written in English. In contrast, candidate study must be excluded if it: (i) does not provide any answer to the research questions of this study, (ii) lacks support for their findings with academic studies, or (iii) fails to meet the minimum quality score of 10.

In Filter 1, the result of the analysis of the title and abstract of the retrieved secondary studies generated a set of 25 candidate studies (13% of the total). To ensure consistency in paper selection, statistical tests were applied to evaluate inter-rater agreement. Two independent reviewers screened articles based on predefined criteria, and any discrepancies were resolved through a reconciliation meeting with an additional researcher serving as mediator. Cohen's Kappa coefficient was calculated to quantify agreement, with a threshold of 0.73 indicating substantial consistency [Landis and Koch 1977].

In Filter 2, a full read of each selected study in the previous step was conducted, identifying 8 publications (32%) that must be excluded. Table 1 presents a checklist of nine questions [Ivarsson and Gorschek 2011] used to conduct a quality assessment [Kitchenham et al. 2023], ensuring rigor and reliability of the selected secondary studies while addressing potential biases and validity concerns.

During the Filter 2 step, two researchers independently evaluated each secondary study selected in Filter 1 using a three-point scale: 'Yes' (score of 2, indicating full compliance), 'Partially' (score of 1, indicating partial compliance), and 'No' (score of 0, indicating the criterion is not addressed). The scores were then reviewed in a new reconciliation meeting using a third researcher as mediator. The maximum possible score for a study was 16, reflecting complete adherence to quality criteria, while secondary studies scoring below 11.2 (70% of adherence) were excluded. This process resulted in the final selection of 17 secondary studies, coded from P1 to P18.

Beyond the quality analysis of the secondary studies, data extraction was performed for the following elements: (i) critical factors, (ii) OC Models, (iii) OC characteristics, (iv) Main explored subjects, (v) Field of knowledge, and (vi) Industry where OC was applied. Afterward, data analysis was conducted, involving content analysis [Hsieh and Shannon 2005], synthesis using thematic analysis [Cruzes and Dyba 2011], and critical evaluation of selected secondary studies to derive meaningful insights and results. The thematic synthesis approach involved extracting key data from each secondary study and grouping similar elements into preliminary categories. These categories were iteratively refined by two researchers through discussions and validation against the

[1] `http://www.digitallibrary.edu.pk/scopus.html`

Table 1. Quality Assessment Criteria

Category	Question
Research Design	1. Is the research aim clear and justified?
	2. Is the methodology well-described and aligned with the objectives?
Data Collection	3. Are the data collection methods and sources clearly described?
Data Analysis	4. For qualitative studies: Are the interpretations clear and logical? For quantitative studies: Are statistical analyses well-documented? For quali-quanti studies: use their average score.
	5. Are synthesis methods adequately explained?
Context	6. Is the study context (e.g., industry and scope) sufficiently detailed?
Limitations	7. Are the limitations and threats to validity presented?
Results/Conclusions	8. Are the results supported by empirical data?

study objectives. A third researcher reviewed the final categories to ensure consistency and minimize bias. This process ensured that the synthesized factors were representative and aligned with the research questions.

4. Results

Table 2 presents the distributions of the secondary studies among the following perspectives: Evidence on research questions (RQ1, RQ2, RQ3), Main explored subject, Field of knowledge, Industry where the OC was applied, and Quality Score.

Table 2. Distribution of the selected literature reviews

		Main explored subject				Field of knowledge			Industry			Questions			Primary Studies		
Code	Publication	OC in general	OC in People	OC in Process	OC in Technology	SW Engineering	Management & Bussiness	Social Science &Psychology	Software	Non-Software	Not specified	RQ1. Character.	RQ2. Models	RQ3. Factors	Quantity	Span of Period	Quality Score
P1	Umut & Aslan (2019)	X						X			X			X	18	1999-2018	13
P2	Miake-Lye et al. (2020)	X					X			X			X	X	26	1988-2016	14
P3	Errida & Lotfi (2021)	X					X			X			X	X	29	1958-2020	13
P4	Khaw et al. (2023)	X					X			X		X		X	79	1970-2021	16
P5	Tipu (2022)	X					X				X		X		62	2000-2019	14
P6	Supriharynt et al. (2023)	X					X				X			X	48	2005-2020	13
P7	Orieno et al. (2024)	X					X				X	X			37	1958-2020	13
P8	Dikert et al. (2016)		X			X			X					X	52	1958-2015	16
P9	Acharya & Palacios (2019)		X			X			X					X	23	1951-2019	12
P10	Lima et al. (2022)		X			X			X					X	28	2016-2022	16
P11	Khan & Keung (2016)			X		X			X					X	33	1995-2016	16
P12	Zahra et al. (2017)			X		X			X					X	40	2009-2016	16
P13	Zaoui & Souissi (2020)				X		X		X			X			32	2009-2019	13
P14	Enríquez et al. (2020)				X		X		X			X			54	2012-2020	16
P15	Costa et al. (2022)				X	X			X			X		X	47	2004-2021	12
P16	Moreira et al. (2023)				X	X			X					X	40	2019-2022	14
P17	Plekhanov et al. (2023)				X	X			X			X		X	40	2009-2016	14
	Totals	7	3	2	5	8	8	1	10	3	4	6	3	13	688	72 years	x=14.2
	%	41%	18%	12%	29%	47%	47%	6%	59%	18%	24%	35%	18%	76%			

The main explored subjects in the selected literature reviews were OC in general (41%), OC in people, which are interventions that affect team dynamics and maturity (18%), (iii) OC in the process, which are interventions that generate software process improvement (12%), and OC in technology, which are interventions that involve adoption or creation of new technologies (29%). Since the search was not limited exclusively to studies within the field of Software Engineering, 47% of the reviews pertained to the Software Engineering field, another 47% were related to Management and Business, and 6% of the secondary studies addressed changes in the context of Social Sciences, Psychology, and Human Resource Management. Furthermore, although 24% of the studies did not target a specific industry, 59% were directly associated with the software development sector, while 18% addressed contexts such as healthcare, civil construction, public administration, and various service industries.

Although all selected studies were based on the 'Organizational Change' theme, these studies had different focuses. Several studies were found to address organizational change efforts centered on the implementation of new management models in software development teams (P08, P10), improving software process (P12), analyzing the reactions of change agents and individuals affected by the change (P04), analyzing the readiness of the company and its employees to implement an EOC (P02), analyzing the impact of training and the presence of coaching in the EOC process (P01), analyzing EOC as a tool for promoting environmental, social, and financial sustainability (P05), analyzing aspects such as leadership, organizational culture, and change management (P07). In addition, studies were found that focused on reviewing OC theories in general and proposing future research agendas (P06), identifying the most important factors influencing change management success in the construction field (P03), employees' attitudes toward OC initiatives (P09), applying robotic process automation as a tool to apply OC (P14), and the digital transformation as an instance of OC in companies (P13).

Table 2 shows that most of the selected studies were interested in providing evidence on critical factors that can boost or hinder OC iniciatives (76%), others discussed the characteristics of OCs implemented in each context (35%), and few presented processual and descriptive models (18%). In addition, the quality scores presented in Table 2 indicate that the selected studies adhere well to the established quality criteria. Most studies scored highly across key categories, such as clarity of research aims, well-described methodologies, and robust data collection processes. However, only 40% addressed limitations and threats to validity, while 76% explicitly detailed the synthesis methodologies employed, including meta-analysis, thematic analysis, and narrative review.

4.1. RQ1. What are the main OC characteristics?

Among the selected secondary studies, 39% addressed OC characteristics. The analysis revealed five primary characteristics that must be considered to implement effective OC management. These interrelated characteristics underscore the importance of adopting integrated approaches to OC management.

Characteristic #1: OC initiatives respond to internal and external factors. Organizational change is driven by external pressures, such as market dynamics or regulatory requirements, and internal factors like inefficiencies or cultural shifts. These initiatives can originate from the strategic level (top-down), aligning the organization with long-term goals, or from the tactical and operational levels (bottom-up), addressing practical challenges or opportunities. "Organizations are required to make significant investments for implementing various changes to adapt to the changing context" (P03) "These change initiatives are driven by the need to respond to organizational needs and external environmental pressures, such as consumer trends, regulatory influences, and global competitiveness." (P05)

Characteristic #2: Large-scale or high-impact OC initiatives exhibit the characteristics of episodic organizational change (EOC). Unlike continuous organizational change (COC), which evolves incrementally with lower risks and resource requirements, EOC initiatives are marked by intermittent, intentional transformations that demand greater complexity, authority, and resource allocation [Weick and Quinn 1999]. These large-scale changes can significantly impact one or more fundamental pillars of an organization, including people, processes, and technology [Taylor 1914], necessitating structured planning and governance to ensure successful implementation and long-term sustainability. "EOC are driven by the need to implement planned interventions that address specific organizational challenges, contrasting with incremental adaptation processes" (P03)

Characteristic #3: OC initiatives must be implemented without disrupting daily operations, requiring a balance between continuity and transformation. For example, "to sustain change, it is not sufficient for organizations to be ready for implementing single change initiatives, but they must also have the capacity to maintain daily operations and manage and implement multiple changes" (P03) Another study complement that "Effective change management involves the need to balance operational stability with innovative approaches, ensuring that transitions occur without compromising day-to-day operations" (P07). These perspectives underline that achieving the desired future state requires careful operational continuity management.

Characteristic #4: Many OC initiatives are implemented without sponsoring support or OC management knowledge. However, active sponsorship and reinforcement of changes are vital for sustainability [Lima et al. 2024]. "Visible support from executives ensures alignment and resource allocation, while reinforcement mechanisms solidify the long-term gains of OCs" (P03). "Organizational support and leadership are highlighted as essential elements for successful change, especially in initiatives that require strategic and cultural alignment." (P05). "lack of formal SPI implementation methodology" is an important obstacle" (P11).

Characteristic #5: OC initiatives must be aligned with governance structures. Misalignment between OC initiatives and organizational governance structures can lead to resistance, resource inefficiencies, and dissatisfaction among change agents, particularly in bottom-up initiatives without management approval. Impacting key pillars such as technology, people, and processes, "aligning initiatives with organizational's strategic objectives" (P07) "enhances oversight, fosters coordination, and ensures long-term sustainability" (P05). "It can enhance and constrain value creation" (P17).

Characteristic #6: OC initiative should be integrated with organizational learning. One study observed that "lack of systematic knowledge sharing prevents organizations from learning from past OC initiatives, leading to repeated mistakes" (P15). Another emphasized, "establishing frameworks for capturing lessons learned is essential for fostering continuous improvement and minimizing risks in future initiatives" (P16). These findings highlight the importance of embedding learning mechanisms within the organization to sustain long-term benefits.

The findings underline the interconnected nature of these characteristics. Effective OC management requires an integrated approach, combining strategic planning, leadership, team engagement, and continuous learning. Understanding these elements helps navigate the complexities of OCs and achieve sustainable organizational transformation.

4.2. RQ2. What existing models could assist in OC process?

Among the selected secondary studies, 17% addressed OC models stratified in descriptive and processual models [Errida and Lotfi 2021]. While the descriptive models explain the dynamics and characteristics of OC without prescribing specific actions, focusing on understanding existing conditions and contextual factors influencing change [Powell Jr 2002], the processual models provide structured frameworks outlining specific steps and actions for implementing change, guiding organizations toward a desired future state [Dawson 2019]. Following the analysis and review of the 41 identified models, a categorization was established comprising 17 processual models and 24 descriptive models (see Table 3).

Table 3. Processual and Descriptive Models

Processual Models	
1. Lewin's three-step change model	10. Model of Fernandez and Rainey
2. Kotter's 8-Step Change Model	11. Kickert
3. Lippitt et al.'s change theory	12. Accelerating Implementation Methodology
4. Luecke's seven steps	13. PDCA Model
5. Mento et al.'s change model	14. PDSA Model
6. Jick's 10 steps model	15. Model for improvement
7. Judson's five-phase model	16. Lean Six Sigma
8. ACMP's Standard for Change Management	17. Business Process Management
9. Galpin's wheel of nine wedges	

Descriptive Models		
1. ADKAR	9. Change tracking model	17. Bullock & Batten's change model
2. Kanter et al.	10. Bridges' model of transition	18. Change Management (CM) BoK
3. Armenakis et al.	11. Prosci's CM methodology	19. Cummings and Worley's CM model
4. Greer and Ford	12. CMI (CM maturity)	20. 10 principles of OC management
5. Cawsey et al.	13. GE's change acceleration	21. Beckhard & Harris' Change formula
6. BCG's change delta	14. Burke & Litwin's OC model	22. Processes of change in organizations
7. McKinsey's 7-S	15. Whelan-Berry and Somerville	23. General strategies for changes
8. Carnall's CM model	16. The change leader's roadmap	24. Change first's model

Inspired by the CATS Model [Lewin 1947], the activities mapped by the processual models were compiled, resulting in a total of 15 activities distributed across three stages: Unfreeze, Change, and Refreeze. The Unfreeze Stage focuses on preparing the organization for change. The following activities are proposed: A1. Define the motivation for change; A2. Ensure leadership and stakeholder support for the change; A3. Assemble a dedicated change agent team; A4. Establish a clear vision of the desired future state; A5. Analyze the organization's readiness for change; A6. Implement a risk management strategy; A7. Develop a comprehensive change plan.

The Change Stage involves executing and managing the transition. Continuing the numeration, the recommended activities are: A8. Prepare the organization and its stakeholders for the change; A9. Implement the change plan as designed; A10. Monitor and control the change process to address any emerging issues; A11. Ensure the sustainability of the change through ongoing reinforcement. The Refreeze Stage aims to embed the change into the organization's structure and culture. Key activities include: A12. Institutionalize the change as part of the organization's standard practices; A13. Consolidate the change to ensure it is fully integrated; A14. Evaluate the results and the overall process of the OC initiative; A15. Formalize the completion of the change process.

By structuring the activities across these three stages, organizations can navigate the complexities of change more effectively, ensuring both the smooth implementation and long-term sustainability of organizational change initiatives.

4.3. RQ3. What are the critical success and failure factors for OC initiatives?

Among the selected secondary studies, 94% mentioned critical factors that influence the success or failure of the OC initiatives in the form of opportunities or challenges. These factors were compiled and categorized based on their relevance and frequency in the literature. Table 4 presents a list of 14 critical factors that can boost or hinder the implementation of OC.

Table 4. Critical factors (CF)

CF1. Clear change vision and strategy	CF8. Change readiness and capacity for change
CF2. Change team performance	CF9. Effective communication
CF3. Stakeholder engagement	CF10. Motivation of change agents
CF4. Resistance management	CF11. Training, coaching, and empowerment
CF5. Leadership	CF12. Structured approach for change
CF6. Support and sponsorship	CF13. Learning and knowledge sharing
CF7. Choosing adequate approach	CF14. Evaluation and measurement

A **clear change vision and strategy (CF1)** is crucial for success. This involves aligning the change with the organization's mission, setting clear objectives, and ensuring stakeholders understand the impacts. A lack of clarity was noted as a major barrier. For instance, "defining a clear vision and aligning it with organizational goals ensures a unified direction" (P14), while "without a clearly communicated vision, stakeholders struggle to connect with the change purpose" (P01). Additionally, "ambiguous or misaligned goals create confusion and resistance" (P16).

The performance of the change team (CF2) emerged as another critical factor. High-performing, skilled teams with clear roles and responsibilities are essential for driving OC. However, restrictions on autonomy or insufficient team preparation can undermine their effectiveness. As noted, "high-performing teams with well-defined roles are vital for operationalizing the change strategy" (P13). Similarly, "insufficient autonomy or limited decision-making authority hampers the team's ability to respond dynamically to challenges" (P02). Another study highlighted that "Several studies stated that training improved the chances of succeeding in the transformation" (P08).

Employee motivation (CF10) and stakeholder engagement (CF3) are key to OC success. Recognizing contributions, celebrating small wins, and aligning initiatives with employees' values foster commitment and morale. Engaging supervisors, managers, and external stakeholders ensures aligned support. As noted, "recognizing employees' contributions and celebrating small wins increases morale and commitment" (P15), and "stakeholder engagement, including supervisors and external partners, ensures aligned support across all levels" (P13). Additionally, "aligning change initiatives with employees' values fosters a deeper connection and motivation" (P10). Most models stress that "motivation mobilizes employees to actively participate in change" (P03).

Resistance management (CF4) is frequently discussed, including addressing resistance at individual, team, and organizational levels [Dikert et al. 2016]. "Cultural factors, inadequate transition management, and cynicism were highlighted as barriers that require careful attention and strategic interventions" (P15). "Strategic interventions, such as involving resistant individuals in the planning process, can mitigate opposition" (P13). "People's resistance is considered as the biggest barrier that can make change difficult, if not impossible" (P03).

Leadership (CF5) and structured approaches to change (CF12), such as governance, planning, and risk management, were identified as key enablers. Effective leadership supports alignment and resource allocation, while structured approaches ensure that change is methodically implemented and monitored. For instance, "strong leadership provides direction and ensures alignment of resources with strategic goals" (P12). Another study highlighted that "structured governance frameworks help monitor progress and address risks proactively" (P08). Furthermore, "methodical planning increases the likelihood of success by reducing ambiguity and streamlining the change process" (P16).

Sustaining change and reinforcing new behaviors (CF6) are vital for long-term success. Cultural integration, reinforcement, and lessons learned prevent regression and foster continuous improvement. "Reinforcement strategies (e.g. recognition and formalization) embed changes into the culture" (P15). "Learning from past OCs ensures continuous improvement" (P14). "Integrating new behaviors promotes sustainability" (P05).

Change readiness and capacity (CF8) emphasize urgency, structural and cultural preparation, and adequate resources and skills. Without these, change efforts risk resistance and low engagement. "Readiness assessments are critical to gauge capacity and identify barriers" (P02). "Establishing urgency through targeted communication fosters awareness and reduces inertia" (P12). Moreover, "lack of preparation, especially cultural and structural, leads to disengagement and prolonged resistance" (P15).

Selecting the appropriate methodology (CF7) impacts OC successful. "There is no consensus on the most appropriate change management model, as a single model may not fully address different OC situations. Therefore, combining multiple models may be the best approach to fit an organization's particular needs" (P03). Using an unsuitable methodology "can lead to resource wastage and poor outcomes" (P04).

Effective communication (CF9) affects successful OC, requiring constant updates, transparency about the process, and monitoring communication strategies. Failures can foster distrust and resistance. "Continuous communication ensures stakeholders are informed and engaged, reducing resistance" (P10). Transparency "builds employee trust by conveying the rationale and steps of the change process" (P14). Monitoring channels "helps identify gaps and improve message delivery" (P16). Additionally, "effective and constant communication creates readiness, reduces resistance, and secures buy-in" (P03).

Training, coaching, and empowerment (CF11) are essential to equip employees with the skills and confidence to cope with OC initiatives. Poor training or lack of empowerment hinders adoption of new practices. "Training programs tailored to required skills ensure employees feel prepared and confident" (P12). "Empowering employees with decision-making authority fosters ownership and commitment" (P16). Moreover, "continuous learning and coaching enable effective adaptation to new practices" (P14).

Learning and knowledge sharing (CF13) build institutional knowledge, while **evaluation and measurement (CF14)** monitor and refine change efforts. "Knowledge sharing enhances collective understanding and prevents repeated mistakes" (P03). "Tracking progress with clear metrics and periodic reviews ensures accountability and informed decisions" (P14). Additionally, "knowledge sharing was essential in successful agile transformations" (P08).

The characteristics, activities, and critical factors of OC initiatives are interconnected. While key aspects influence management, existing models provide structured support for implementation and managing factors that determine success or failure. Due to space limitations, a complete mapping of activities and critical factors is available in the supplementary material[2], which includes a compilation of OC models from 1947 to 2018 and a structured mapping of selected secondary studies, highlighting the interconnections among activities, key characteristics, and critical factors discussed in this paper.

5. Discussion

The findings of the study highlight that OC initiatives in the software industry face persistent challenges, with ad hoc, experience-driven practices often prevailing over proven methodologies [Beer and Nohria 2000]. Although practitioners often adopt familiar frameworks such as PMBoK, Scrum framework, and CMMI, these models fail to address critical aspects of EOC initiatives, such as organizational readiness, alignment with organizational governance, and long-term sustainability [Lima et al. 2024]. Furthermore, the low adoption of classical OC models [Kotter 2007, Lewin 1947] further reinforces the need to investigate how existing frameworks can be adapted to better suit the software industry context. To improve effectiveness, software industry companies must increase awareness of OC methodologies and adapt existing models to their specific challenges and characteristics. The synthesized models and factors presented in this study offer a practical foundation for organizations seeking to replace improvised strategies with evidence-based practices.

Integrating descriptive and processual models to address the "why" and "how" of OC offers a promising avenue to improve the efficiency and sustainability of change initiatives in the software industry. Despite expanding [Errida and Lotfi 2021]'s list of OC models from 37 to 41 (17 processual and 24 descriptive), most of the primary studies cited in the selected literature reviews do not reference these models, particularly in software industry contexts [Lima et al. 2024]. While descriptive models help clarify the motivations and contextual factors that drive change, processual models provide step-by-step guidance for execution. This dual perspective enables organizations not only to understand the underlying rationale for change but also to structure their initiatives in a systematic and goal-oriented manner. Practitioners can use this integration as a basis for developing OC roadmaps that align strategic intent with concrete actions, particularly in scenarios such as agile transformations, digital modernization, or process restructuring.

The results of Sections 4.1, 4.2, and 4.3 complement each other, offering a holistic

[2] `http://bit.ly/419HB1J` Supplementary Material

understanding of OC in the software industry. While Section 4.1 explores broader characteristics shaping OC management, Section 4.2 categorizes OC models into processual and descriptive types, providing structured frameworks and theoretical insights. Finally, Section 4.3 identifies critical factors influencing the success or failure of OC initiatives. These findings create a foundation for connecting practical strategies to conceptual principles, supporting practitioners in designing context-aware change strategies that consider both organizational dynamics and technical complexity.

Conducting a literature review of secondary studies enabled us to capitalize on a body of empirical evidence, encompassing nearly 700 primary studies spanning over 70 years (see Table 2). These studies, predominantly case studies, action research, and grounded theory, address a long-standing criticism in the field of OC: the lack of empirical basis to support theoretical findings [Cummings and Worley 2016] and the neglect or lack of knowledge about OC management applied in the software industry [Lima et al. 2024].

These findings advocate for a dual focus on theory and practice. Practitioners must embrace proven OC models, adapting them to the software industry's unique demands, while researchers should aim to fill theoretical gaps. For practitioners, the consolidated set of models, activities, and critical factors can serve as a practical reference to plan, monitor, and adapt OC efforts more effectively.

6. Threats to Validity and Limitations

Despite the adoption of a well-defined protocol and the application of rigorous methodological practices [Kitchenham et al. 2010], some threats to validity remain, along with associated limitations [Zhou et al. 2016].

Internal Validity refers to the reliability of the methods and data used in this study. As the analysis relies on secondary sources, interpretation biases from original authors may persist. To mitigate this, predefined inclusion and exclusion criteria were applied, and independent reviews were conducted by multiple coders. Despite these measures, subjective interpretations during thematic synthesis remain a potential limitation. **External Validity** concerns the generalizability of findings to other contexts. The results are tailored to the software industry, characterized by its rapid technological evolution and volatility. Future studies should investigate cross-industry comparisons to validate the transferability of these findings.

Construct Validity examines whether the study accurately captured its intended constructs. While "critical factors" and "OC models" were derived from established literature [Lewin 1947, Errida and Lotfi 2021, Weick and Quinn 1999], the inclusion of synonyms to address the limited use of "Organizational Change" in software-focused studies may have introduced minor misalignments. Furthermore, synthesizing activities from diverse models, each with distinct contexts and purposes, risks conceptual inconsistency. This mapping provides a starting framework, not a definitive guide. Future research should validate these constructs empirically. **Conclusion Validity** relates to the strength of the evidence supporting the study's conclusions. Synthesizing data from multiple studies added robustness but risked overgeneralization due to variations in study quality and focus. Additionally, excluding non-English secondary studies and those outside the 2014–2024 timeframe might have overlooked relevant insights. Nonetheless, Scopus's comprehensive indexing likely minimized omissions.

Researcher bias remains a concern in qualitative studies. Predefined protocols, peer reviews, and reconciliation meetings minimized subjectivity, with a third researcher ensuring consistency. However, the inclusion of only 17 secondary studies may limit generalizability, and the thematic synthesis process relies on subjective judgment. Expanding the dataset in future research could enhance applicability and impact.

7. Conclusion

This study presented a comprehensive tertiary review of Organizational Change (OC) initiatives implemented in the software industry, focusing on identifying models, critical factors, and key characteristics of OC initiatives. By synthesizing insights from diverse secondary studies, this paper aimed to organize and consolidate knowledge that bridges theory and practice, providing a structured understanding of how OC can be effectively implemented in dynamic and complex environments. To ensure study quality, a self-assessment based on the defined Quality Assessment Criteria (Table 1) confirmed the rigor of the methodology and the findings.

The study revealed critical insights. First, while many well-established OC models exist, their application in the software industry remains limited, often overshadowed by informal, ad hoc approaches. Second, the success of OC initiatives hinges on aligning change efforts with organizational strategy, fostering stakeholder engagement, and investing in clear communication and training. Lastly, the lack of a standardized framework for managing risks and leveraging lessons learned continues to hinder the long-term effectiveness of OC initiatives. These insights underscore the importance of integrating descriptive and processual models to address the software industry's unique challenges.

This paper contributes to academia and industry by advancing the understanding of OC in software companies. For academia, the study highlights gaps in the current research landscape, particularly in the development and contextual adaptation of OC models for technology-driven environments. For industry, the paper offers actionable recommendations to improve the planning, execution, and evaluation of OC initiatives. The findings can guide organizational change teams in adopting structured frameworks and leveraging critical success factors to enhance the effectiveness of their efforts.

Future work could expand this research by applying the snowballing technique [Wohlin 2014] to the selected secondary studies, potentially uncovering additional relevant studies. Empirical research is necessary to validate the applicability of the reviewed models in real-world software industry contexts. Moreover, developing tailored frameworks specifically for the software industry could improve the efficiency of organizational change (OC) initiatives. Finally, adapting processual and descriptive models to the dynamic and high-volatility environments characteristic of the software industry represents another promising direction for future exploration.

References

Acharya, B. and Colomo-Palacios, R. (2019). A systematic literature review on autonomous agile teams. In *2019 19th International Conference on Computational Science and Its Applications (ICCSA)*, pages 146–151. IEEE.

Agazu, B. G. and Kero, C. A. (2024). Innovation strategy and firm competitiveness: a systematic literature review. *Journal of Innovation and Entrepreneurship*, 13(1):24.

Armenakis, A. A. and Bedeian, A. G. (1999). Organizational change: A review of theory and research in the 1990s. *Journal of management*, 25(3):293–315.

Bayona, S., Calvo-Manzano, J. A., and San Feliu, T. (2012). Critical success factors in software process improvement: A systematic review. In *Software Process Improvement and Capability Determination: 12th International Conference, SPICE 2012, Palma, Spain, May 29-31, 2012. Proceedings 12*, pages 1–12. Springer.

Beer, M. and Nohria, N. (2000). Cracking the code of change. *Harvard business review*, 78(3):133–141.

Beer, M. and Walton, A. E. (1987). Organization change and development. *Annual review of psychology*, 38(1):339–367.

Cruzes, D. S. and Dyba, T. (2011). Recommended steps for thematic synthesis in software engineering. In *2011 international symposium on empirical software engineering and measurement*, pages 275–284, NJ, US. ÌEEE.

Cummings, T. G. and Worley, C. G. (2016). *Organization development & change*. South-Western.

Da Silva, F. Q., Santos, A. L., Soares, S., França, A. C. C., Monteiro, C. V., and Maciel, F. F. (2011). Six years of systematic literature reviews in software engineering: An updated tertiary study. *Information and Software Technology*, 53(9):899–913.

Davenport, T. H. and Stoddard, D. B. (1994). Reengineering: business change of mythic proportions? *MIS quarterly*, n/a:121–127.

Dawson, P. (2019). *Reshaping change: A processual perspective*. Routledge.

Dikert, K., Paasivaara, M., and Lassenius, C. (2016). Challenges and success factors for large-scale agile transformations: A systematic literature review. *Journal of Systems and Software*, 119:87–108.

Edison, H., Wang, X., Jabangwe, R., and Abrahamsson, P. (2018). Innovation initiatives in large software companies: a systematic mapping study. In *Proceedings of the 2018 International Conference on Software and System Process*, pages 140–141.

Errida, A. and Lotfi, B. (2021). The determinants of organizational change management success: Literature review and case study. *International Journal of Engineering Business Management*, 13:18479790211016273.

Hsieh, H.-F. and Shannon, S. E. (2005). Three approaches to qualitative content analysis. *Qualitative health research*, 15(9):1277–1288.

Ivarsson, M. and Gorschek, T. (2011). A method for evaluating rigor and industrial relevance of techn. evaluations. *Empirical SW Engineering*, 16:365–395.

Kitchenham, B., Madeyski, L., and Budgen, D. (2023). Segress: Software engineering guidelines for reporting secondary studies. *IEEE Transactions on Software Engineering*, 49(3):1273–1298.

Kitchenham, B., Pretorius, R., Budgen, D., Brereton, O. P., Turner, M., Niazi, M., and Linkman, S. (2010). Systematic literature reviews in software engineering–a tertiary study. *Information and software technology*, 52(8):792–805.

Kotter, J. P. (2007). Leading change: Why transformation efforts fail. In *Museum management and marketing*, pages 20–29. Routledge.

Landis, J. R. and Koch, G. G. (1977). The measurement of observer agreement for categorical data. *Biometrics*, 33(1):159–174.

Lewin, K. (1947). Frontiers in group dynamics: Ii. channels of group life; social planning and action research. *Human relations*, 1(2):143–153.

Lima, R. R., Costa, M. S., Oran, A. C., and França, C. (2022). Factors that boost and hinder the transition from traditional to self-managed teams: A systematic literature review. In *Proceedings of the XXI Brazilian Symposium on Software Quality*, pages 1–11.

Lima, R. R., Oran, A., and França, C. (2024). Beyond continuous improvement: Unraveling the invisible challenges of implementing organizational change in a software company. In *Proceedings of the XXXVIII Brazilian Symposium on Software Engineering*, pages 1–11.

Miller, A. K. (2001). Organizational change. *IEEE Software*.

Orieno, O. H., Udeh, C. A., Oriekhoe, O. I., Odonkor, B., and Ndubuisi, N. L. (2024). Innovative management strategies in contemporary organizations: a review: analyzing the evolution and impact of modern management practices, with an emphasis on leadership, organizational culture, and change management. *International Journal of Management & Entrepreneurship Research*, 6(1):167–190.

Powell Jr, W. R. (2002). Organizational change models. *Futurics*, 26(3/4):20.

Ribeiro, J., Lima, R., Eckhardt, T., and Paiva, S. (2021). Robotic process automation and artificial intelligence in industry 4.0–a literature review. *Procedia Computer Science*, 181:51–58.

Taylor, F. W. (1914). Scientific management: reply from mr. fw taylor. *The Sociological Review*, 7(3):266–269.

Weick, K. E. and Quinn, R. E. (1999). Organizational change and development. *Annual review of psychology*, 50(1):361–386.

Wohlin, C. (2014). Guidelines for snowballing in systematic literature studies and a replication in software engineering. In *Proceedings of the 18th international conference on evaluation and assessment in software engineering*, pages 1–10.

Zahra, K., Azam, F., Ilyas, F., Faisal, H., Ambreen, N., and Gondal, N. (2017). Success factors of organizational change in software process improvement: A systematic literature review. In *Proceedings of the 5th International Conference on Information and Education Technology*, pages 155–160.

Zaoui, F. and Souissi, N. (2020). Roadmap for digital transformation: A literature review. *Procedia Computer Science*, 175:621–628.

Zhou, X., Jin, Y., Zhang, H., Li, S., and Huang, X. (2016). A map of threats to validity of systematic literature reviews in software engineering. In *2016 23rd Asia-Pacific Software Engineering Conference (APSEC)*, pages 153–160. IEEE.

Modelo de referencia de ciberseguridad para prevenir ataques de red a infraestructuras críticas en la era cuántica

Siler Amador Donado

Departamento de sistemas – Universidad del Cauca (Unicauca)
Calle 5 # 4 -70 – Popayán – Colombia

samador@unicauca.edu.co

Resumen. *Este documento presenta un modelo de referencia de ciberseguridad para proteger sistemas ciber-físicos (CPS) en infraestructuras críticas (IC) ante las amenazas de la computación cuántica. La revisión sistemática de la literatura (RSL) revela la urgencia de incorporar criptografía post-cuántica y de abordar retos como la interoperabilidad con sistemas heredados y los altos costos de implementación. MoRCiTO integra controles de acceso, monitorización continua y métodos de detección y mitigación de ciberataques de red, desarrollado mediante investigación-acción en tres ciclos.*

Palabras claves. *Modelo de referencia MoRCiTO, ciberseguridad post-cuántica, infraestructura crítica, sistema ciber-físico, tecnología de la operación.*

Abstract. *This paper presents a cybersecurity reference model for protecting cyber-physical systems (CPS) in critical infrastructures (CI) from quantum computing threats. The systematic literature review (SLR) reveals the urgency of incorporating post-quantum cryptography and addressing challenges such as interoperability with legacy systems and high implementation costs. MoRCiTO integrates access controls, continuous monitoring, and network cyberattack detection and mitigation methods, developed through action research in three cycles.*

Keywords. *MoRCiTO reference model, post-quantum cybersecurity, critical infrastructure, cyber-physical system, operation technology.*

1. Introducción y principales desafíos

Problema: La convergencia entre los CPS y las IC ha incrementado significativamente la dependencia tecnológica en sectores fundamentales como energía, salud, transporte, sistemas financieros y telecomunicaciones. Aunque esta integración proporciona beneficios en eficiencia y control, también expone a estos sistemas a ciberataques potencialmente devastadores, comprometiendo no solo la estabilidad económica, sino también la seguridad pública. Los CPS implementados en IC generalmente son sistemas heredados, difíciles y costosos de reemplazar o actualizar, incrementando aún más su vulnerabilidad. Además, con la llegada de la computación cuántica, se enfrentan a nuevas amenazas, debido a que los algoritmos cuánticos como los propuestos por Shor y Grover podrían romper las soluciones criptográficas actuales (Amador-Donado et al., 2024a, 2024b). Entre los desafíos específicos identificados se destacan la interoperabilidad tecnológica, ausencia de estándares globales, escalabilidad de soluciones, altos costos de implementación, validación práctica limitada, dificultad en detección de amenazas cuánticas, falta de personal capacitado y problemas prácticos en la implementación segura de criptografía post-cuántica (Bernstein & Lange, 2017; Liu et al., 2022; Kalinin & Krundyshev, 2022; Kayan et al., 2022).

Motivación: La relevancia de abordar este problema radica en la necesidad urgente de proteger la integridad operativa y funcional de las IC, dado su impacto directo en la seguridad nacional, estabilidad económica y bienestar social. La llegada de la computación cuántica impone una transición acelerada y planeada hacia soluciones de ciberseguridad robustas, capaces de enfrentar nuevas categorías de ciber-amenazas. Garantizar la continuidad operativa segura en sectores estratégicos constituye una prioridad global, dada la magnitud potencial de las consecuencias asociadas a fallas en estos sistemas críticos.

Contribución: Esta investigación contribuye al cuerpo de conocimiento existente mediante el desarrollo de un modelo de referencia orientado explícitamente hacia la prevención de ataques de red en CPS utilizados en IC, específicamente en el contexto de la era cuántica. Este modelo se destaca por proponer mecanismos de integración efectiva entre tecnologías heredadas y emergentes, fomentar el establecimiento de bases para la estandarización global de soluciones criptográficas post-cuánticas, y proporcionar lineamientos para la escalabilidad y validación práctica de las soluciones implementadas. De esta manera, el estudio pretende reducir la brecha identificada en investigaciones previas y ofrecer un camino viable para enfrentar los retos planteados por el paradigma cuántico en entornos críticos reales.

2. Preguntas y objetivos de la investigación

Objetivo general de la investigación: Proponer un modelo de referencia de ciberseguridad para la tecnología de la operación que apoye la prevención de ataques de red a CPS en IC como advenimiento a la era cuántica. Objetivos específicos de la investigación: **OE1**: Caracterizar los elementos fundamentales a tener en cuenta para la ciberseguridad en la tecnología de la operación por medio del análisis de la literatura existente, que permita clarificar la prevención de los tipos de ataques de red contra CPS en IC como advenimiento a la era cuántica. **OE2**: Proponer un modelo de referencia que clarifique las prácticas a tener en cuenta para prevenir ataques de red a CPS en IC como advenimiento a la era cuántica, con base en los elementos caracterizados en el objetivo anterior. **OE3**: Evaluar el modelo de referencia propuesto a través de un estudio de caso para prevenir ataques de red a CPS en IC.

Para lograr el primer objetivo de la investigación se llevó a cabo una RSL basados en (Kitchenham & Charters, 2007). En https://acortar.link/Y0uU8u se detallan los objetivos de búsqueda y sus correspondientes preguntas de investigación.

3. Resumen del conocimiento actual del dominio del problema

El dominio de la ciberseguridad en CPS ha avanzado significativamente en áreas como detección de amenazas, criptografía y gestión de incidentes. Sin embargo, la llegada de la computación cuántica introduce nuevos riesgos, especialmente por su potencial para vulnerar sistemas criptográficos actuales.

Una RSL preliminar realizada por (Amador Donado et al., 2024a) revela brechas importantes, como la falta de estandarización en protocolos criptográficos post-cuánticos y la necesidad de modelos específicos para CPS. Se identificó que el 65% de los estudios revisados ofrecen soluciones teóricas sin validación empírica, y solo el 20% exploran escenarios concretos en IC. Por ejemplo, la integración de Quantum Key Distribution (QKD) presenta desafíos prácticos relacionados con la complejidad y costos elevados (Diamanti et al., 2016). Aunque la criptografía basada en lattice muestra promesas para la resistencia post-cuántica, aún enfrenta limitaciones de rendimiento. Asimismo, menos del 10% de los estudios abordan la interoperabilidad con sistemas legados. Es crucial superar retos relacionados con interoperabilidad, escalabilidad y adaptación efectiva de estas tecnologías en entornos complejos y distribuidos propios de los CPS (Bernstein & Lange, 2017).

4. Metodología de investigación

Se utilizó la metodología investigación-acción (Mertler, 2020) mediante 3 ciclos, en el primero se realizó la caracterización del modelo mediante la RSL obteniéndose la versión 1.0 de MoRCiTO (Modelo de Referencia de Ciberseguridad para la Tecnología de la Operación), en el segundo ciclo se está realizando la evaluación por expertos para así obtener la versión 2.0 del modelo, y en el tercer ciclo se espera realizar mejoras a partir de los ajustes realizados al modelo y obtener la versión 3 (ver Figura 1(**a**)). Para llevar a cabo la RSL se diseñó el protocolo basados en (Kitchenham & Charters, 2007) (ver Figura 1(**b**)).

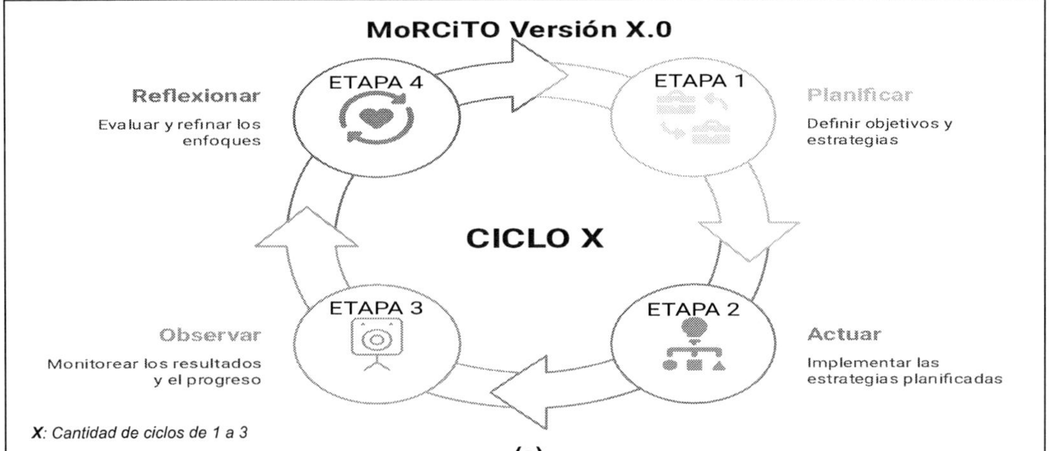

(a)

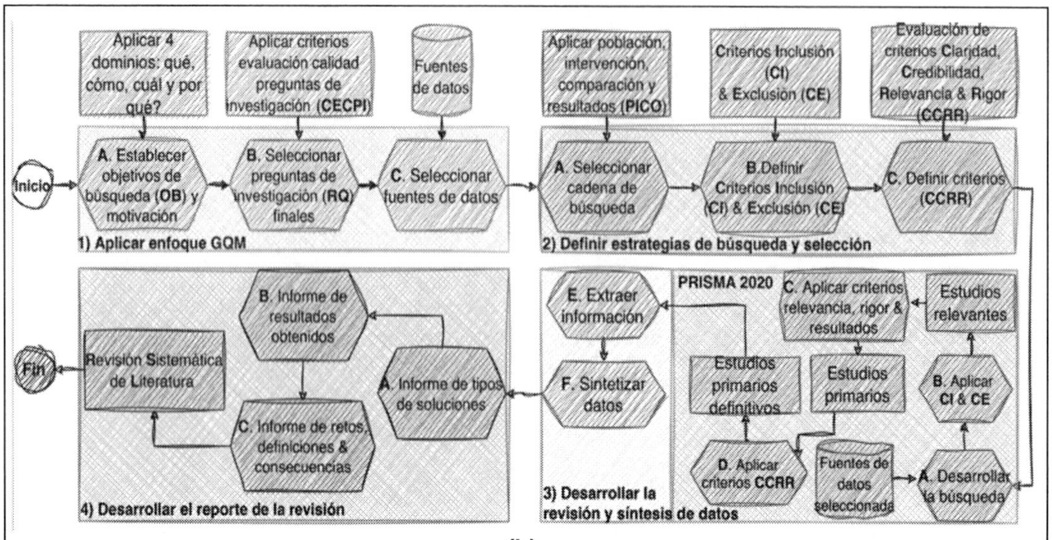

(b)

Figura 1. Metodologías de investigación

A continuación se presenta un resumen de las actividades de investigación realizadas en cada uno de los 3 ciclos:

Ciclo 1-RSL preliminar (MoRCiTO V1.0): Este ciclo tuvo una duración de 19 meses, ya fue desarrollado en su totalidad y se llevaron a cabo las siguientes etapas: **Etapa 1-Planeación:** En esta etapa se identificó y delimitó el tema, se recolectó información pertinente, se revisó la literatura relacionada y se desarrolló un plan de investigación. También se establecieron los objetivos de búsqueda y su motivación, se seleccionaron las preguntas finales de investigación, se seleccionaron las fuentes de datos adecuadas y se aplicaron criterios de evaluación de calidad a dichas preguntas. **Etapa 2-Ejecución:** Se recolectaron y analizaron los datos. Además, se seleccionó la cadena de búsqueda utilizando la técnica PICO (población, intervención, comparación y resultados). También se definieron los criterios de inclusión y exclusión para seleccionar los estudios, así como los criterios de claridad, credibilidad, relevancia y rigor (CCRR). **Etapa 3- Desarrollo**: Se desarrolló un plan de acción, que incluyó la ejecución de la búsqueda bibliográfica, aplicando los criterios previamente definidos de inclusión y exclusión. A partir de esto, se obtuvieron los estudios relevantes, se aplicaron criterios adicionales relacionados con relevancia, rigor y resultados, identificando finalmente los estudios primarios definitivos. Posteriormente, se aplicaron criterios CCRR, se extrajo la información necesaria y se sintetizaron los datos obtenidos. **Etapa 4-Reflexión:** Se compartieron los resultados y se reflexionó profundamente sobre todo el proceso llevado a cabo. Se elaboraron informes sobre los tipos de soluciones encontradas, se presentaron los retos enfrentados y finalmente se preparó el informe detallado con los resultados obtenidos, consolidando la elaboración de la publicación de la RSL preliminar (Amador Donado et al., 2024a) y en proceso de evaluación para su publicación la RSL final en la revista IEEE Access. Otra publicación realizada fue MoRCiTO versión 1.0 (Amador Donado et al., 2024b). También se realizaron 2 presentaciones: 1. En la modalidad de keynote, la charla titulada "Ciberseguridad en IC". 2. En la modalidad de ponencia titulada "Characterization of MoRCiTO: Cybersecurity reference model for operation technology" en el "VI International conference on advances in emerging trends and technologies – ICAETT

2024" celebrado en la Escuela Superior Politécnica del Chimborazo (ESPOCH) en Riobamba, Ecuador, el 17 y 18 de octubre de 2024.

Ciclo 2-Evaluación por juicio de expertos (MoRCiTO V2.0): Para este ciclo se estimó una duración de 13 meses. Este ciclo se encuentra aún en desarrollo y se llevaran a cabo las siguientes etapas: **Etapa 1-Planeación:** Se delimitó el tema de investigación relacionado con la evaluación del modelo versión 1.0. Se recolectó información y se tomó como base de referencia la RSL preliminar realizada en el ciclo 1 para sustentar la investigación. Además, se desarrolló un plan de investigación y se definió con precisión el objetivo de la evaluación por expertos, especificando los criterios que evaluarán: comprensibilidad, aplicabilidad, idoneidad y completitud del modelo versión 1.0, estableciendo el alcance y resultados esperados. **Etapa 2-Ejecución:** Se realizará la recolección y análisis preliminar de datos relacionados con el modelo versión 1.0, determinando su estado actual. Se seleccionarán cuidadosamente los 4 expertos que participarán en la evaluación, considerando criterios como trayectoria académica, experiencia profesional en ciberseguridad, experiencia en CPS e IC. Se elaborará un instrumento para la evaluación del modelo en relación con los criterios definidos (comprensibilidad, aplicabilidad, idoneidad y completitud), utilizando cuestionarios, entrevistas o matrices de valoración mediante la técnica de grupo focal. **Etapa 3-Desarrollo:** Se desarrollará un plan de acción que contemplará la evaluación por expertos del modelo versión 1.0. Se realizará el contacto formal con los expertos, proporcionando los documentos necesarios del modelo junto con el instrumento para la evaluación de comprensibilidad, aplicabilidad, idoneidad y completitud. Posteriormente, se recolectarán las respuestas aportadas por los expertos y se realizará el procesamiento y organización sistemática de los datos obtenidos para facilitar un análisis claro y detallado. **Etapa 4-Reflexión:** Se analizarán los resultados de la evaluación de expertos de la versión 1.0, determinando niveles de concordancia, áreas de mejora y recomendaciones asociadas a la comprensibilidad, aplicabilidad, idoneidad y completitud del modelo. Se formularán ajustes y recomendaciones de mejora, se elaborará un informe de todo el proceso de evaluación, la metodología empleada, los perfiles de los expertos participantes, resultados detallados y las decisiones del análisis realizado. Se espera realizar la publicación de los resultados obtenidos de MoRCiTO versión 2.0.

Ciclo 3-Estudio de caso (MoRCiTO V3.0): Para este ciclo se estimó una duración de 13 meses. Este ciclo de la investigación se encuentra en desarrollo y se llevaran a cabo las siguientes etapas: **Etapa 1-Planeación:** Se identificará el estudio de caso enfocado en el análisis de la versión 2.0. Se delimitará el alcance y se definirán los objetivos específicos de la evaluación. Se recolectará información preliminar y con base en la RSL se elaborará el estudio del caso. Se desarrollará el protocolo del estudio de caso sobre la versión 2.0, especificando las preguntas, los métodos para recolectar datos, los criterios para seleccionar escenarios representativos para su implementación, y los métodos previstos para analizar los datos obtenidos. **Etapa 2-Ejecución:** Se recolectará sistemáticamente los datos específicos mediante la implementación práctica de la versión 2.0 del modelo en contextos seleccionados. Se utilizarán instrumentos definidos en el protocolo, tales como entrevistas a usuarios, observación directa durante la aplicación del modelo y análisis exhaustivo de documentos técnicos. Los datos recopilados serán organizados, registrados y preparados cuidadosamente para garantizar su calidad, precisión y coherencia, facilitando así un análisis riguroso y profundo posterior. **Etapa 3-Desarrollo:** Se desarrollará un análisis de los datos recolectados del estudio de caso sobre la versión 2.0 del modelo. Se aplicarán métodos analíticos cualitativos y cuantitativos que permitan interpretar los datos obtenidos, identificando patrones, fortalezas, debilidades y aspectos relevantes de la implementación práctica del modelo. Posteriormente, se realizará una síntesis sistemática para extraer hallazgos específicos, conclusiones y resultados acerca de la aplicabilidad, efectividad y pertinencia de la versión 2.0. **Etapa 4-Reflexión:** Se publicaran los resultados del estudio de caso realizado sobre la versión 2.0, además, se formularán recomendaciones del análisis detallado del modelo. Finalmente, se elaborará un informe de los resultados obtenidos, conclusiones y las acciones a seguir derivadas del estudio sobre la versión 2.0. Se espera realizar la publicación de MoRCiTO versión 3.0.

5. Solución propuesta y resultados obtenidos

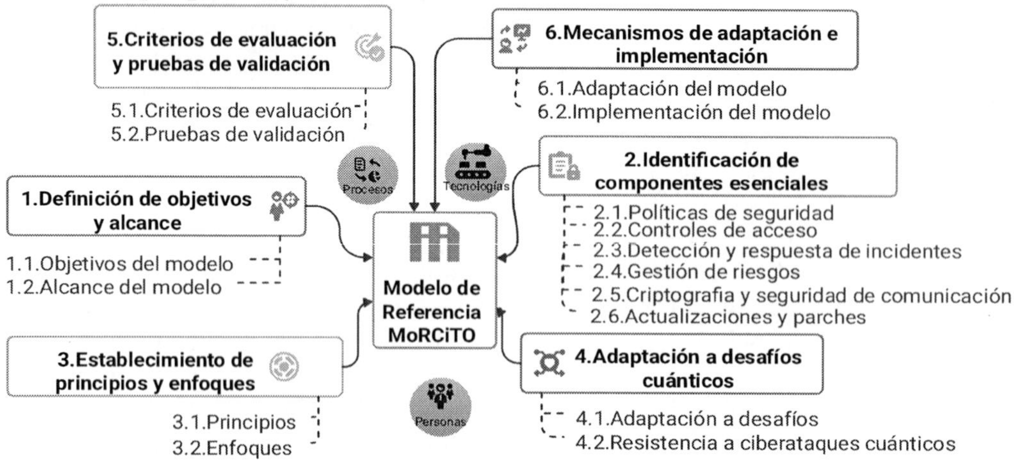

Figura 2. Vista resumida del Modelo de referencia propuesto

MoRCiTO se centra en: 1. Un enfoque modular que integra prevención de ciber-ataques de red y mitigación. 2. Lineamientos para la implementación de criptografía post-cuántica. 3. Un sistema de monitoreo continuo.

Los componentes del modelo funcionan de integradamente estableciendo un enfoque holístico de seguridad en las IC. Las *políticas de seguridad* brindan directrices generales, los *controles de acceso* garantizan protección de los sistemas y los datos, la *detección y respuesta a incidentes* permiten respuestas eficientes a ciberataques, la *gestión de riesgos* identifica y mitiga riesgos potenciales, la *criptografía y la seguridad de la comunicación* protegen la confidencialidad de los datos y las *actualizaciones y parches de seguridad* mantienen los sistemas actualizados y protegidos. MoRCiTO se encuentra en evaluación por expertos y se validará a través de escenarios simulados que repliquen operaciones de IC. Los resultados permitirán la toma de decisiones en la detección de amenazas y la mitigación de riesgos (Amador Donado et al., 2024a, 2024b).

6. Aspectos de la solución sugerida que la hacen diferente o mejor

MoRCiTO se destaca por tres aspectos: su adaptabilidad a entornos operativos, integración de criptografía post-cuántica y un enfoque holístico desde la detección hasta la mitigación de amenazas. Su diseño modular facilita la integración progresiva en IC variadas, siendo eficaz en redes industriales centralizadas y sistemas distribuidos con CPS (Amador Donado et al., 2024b; Bernstein & Lange, 2017).

En una prueba de concepto aplicada a cable-modems Technicolor en Colombia, se evidenció que el 89.1% son vulnerables a ataques por diccionario, permitiendo su control, ataques de phishing e instalación de rootkits. Su evaluación con TRACI confirmó alta exposición de activos, gestión del riesgo y motivación del adversario. Se recomienda cambio de contraseñas, autenticación multifactor y monitoreo continuo (https://acortar.link/27T1Oo). Sin embargo, persisten limitaciones, como dificultad para gestionar escenarios en tiempo real e interoperabilidad con sistemas legados (Amador-Donado et al., 2024a, 2024b). Estas serán abordadas mediante escenarios simulados de ciberataques sin comprometer la IC real (https://acortar.link/8yMNIt).

7. Referencias

Amador Donado, S., Pardo Calvache, C. J., & Raúl Iván, M. P. (2024a). Preliminary Review: Cybersecurity for Operation Technology in Quantum Age Against Network Attacks to Critical Infrastructures. *INGE CUC*, *20*(2), 1-16. https://doi.org/10.17981/ingecuc.20.2.2024.06

Amador-Donado, S., Pardo-Calvache, C.-J., & Mazo-Peña, R. (2024b). *MoRCiTO: Towards a Cybersecurity Reference Model for Operation Technology in Preparation for the Quantum Era to Prevent Network Attacks on Cyber-Physical Systems in Critical Infrastructures*. 22-46. https://revistas.udistrital.edu.co/index.php/revcie/article/view/22581/20496

Bernstein, D. J., & Lange, T. (2017). Post-quantum cryptography. *Nature*, *549*(7671), 188-194. https://doi.org/10.1038/nature23461

Diamanti, E., Lo, H.-K., Qi, B., & Yuan, Z. (2016). Practical challenges in quantum key distribution. *npj Quantum Information*, *2*(1). https://doi.org/10.1038/npjqi.2016.25

Kalinin, M., & Krundyshev, V. (2022). Security intrusion detection using quantum machine learning techniques. *Journal of Computer Virology and Hacking Techniques*, *19*(1), 125-136. https://doi.org/10.1007/s11416-022-00435-0

Kayan, H., Nunes, M., Rana, O., Burnap, P., & Perera, C. (2022). Cybersecurity of Industrial Cyber-Physical Systems: A Review. *ACM Computing Surveys*, *54*(11s), 1-35. https://doi.org/10.1145/3510410

Kitchenham, B., & Charters, S. (2007). *Guidelines for performing systematic literature reviews in software engineering*. UK.

Liu, R., Rozenman, G. G., Kundu, N. K., Chandra, D., & De, D. (2022). Towards the industrialisation of quantum key distribution in communication networks: A short survey. *IET Quantum Communication*, *3*(3), 151-163. https://doi.org/10.1049/qtc2.12044

Mertler, C. A. (2020). *Action Research*. SAGE Publications. https://a.co/d/iS4GfIr

Hacia una arquitectura de referencia para la definición de arquitecturas de software empresariales híbridas, adaptada a las necesidades emergentes de la Ingeniería de Software Cuántica

Carlos Orozco[1]

[1] Facultad de Ingeniería Electrónica – Universidad del Cauca
Calle 5 No. 4-70 – 190003 – Popayán – Cauca – Colombia

carlosorozco@unicauca.edu.co

Resumen. *El auge de la computación cuántica ha abierto un nuevo paradigma en el procesamiento de la información, prometiendo superar los límites de la computación clásica. Sin embargo, el desarrollo de arquitecturas de software que puedan explotar plenamente este potencial es aún un campo de estudio constante, lleno de desafíos sin precedentes. Este artículo presenta el estado actual de la propuesta de doctorado que se centra en el diseño de una arquitectura de referencia que apoye la definición de arquitecturas de sistemas software híbridos, atendiendo a las necesidades y desafíos que propone el avance en el campo de la Ingeniería de Software Cuántico.*

Abstract. *The rise of quantum computing has introduced a new paradigm in information processing, with the potential to surpass the limits of classical computation. However, the development of software architectures capable of fully leveraging this technology remains an active research area, filled with unprecedented challenges. This paper presents the current state of a Ph.D. proposal focused on designing a reference architecture to support the definition of hybrid software systems, addressing the needs and challenges emerging from the progress in Quantum Software Engineering.*

1. Introducción

Las últimas cuatro décadas han marcado un avance notable en la comprensión conceptual y teórica de la computación cuántica. Sin embargo, la implementación de dispositivos cuánticos operativos capaces de solucionar problemas en la industria de software comenzó a suceder en la última década, cuando gigantes como Google (Gibney, 2019a), IBM (Santos, 2016) y Microsoft (Gibney, 2016) decidieron invertir recursos financieros, de infraestructura y de talento humano en el desarrollo de soluciones utilizando dispositivos cuánticos para abordar problemas en sectores como: la inteligencia artificial, la ciencia de datos, el análisis predictivo, la ciberseguridad, la optimización de procesos empresariales, entre otros (Bayerstadler et al., 2021). Como resultado, la integración de la computación cuántica en el desarrollo de nuevas soluciones tecnológicas se ha convertido gradualmente en un punto de enfoque crítico para la industria. Simultáneamente, el sector académico ha buscado clarificar y sistematizar el conocimiento en torno a un campo emergente y relacionado con la computación cuántica, denominado: *Ingeniería de Software Cuántica* (Zhao, 2020).

Este esfuerzo busca adaptar los fundamentos de la *Ingeniería de Software Clásica* —que incluye conceptos, definiciones, prácticas, roles y actividades— al nuevo paradigma que representa la computación cuántica. Para lograrlo, se han desarrollado diferentes soluciones para clarificar y establecer un ciclo de vida del desarrollo de software específico adaptado a las necesidades y retos que define la computación cuántica (Weder et al., 2020; Zhao, 2020), que incluyen documentar las distintas fases de desarrollo de software dentro del ámbito cuántico (Piattini & Murillo, 2022), la creación de marcos de trabajo híbridos clásico/cuántico (Piattini & Murillo, 2022), definir principios y técnicas (Piattini et al., 2021) diseñadas para el desarrollo de algoritmos cuánticos, entre otros. Los esfuerzos académicos complementan los avances industriales, estableciendo un puente entre la teoría y la práctica que promete acelerar la evolución y aplicación de la tecnología cuántica en el software, marcando un hito en la forma en que se enfrentan los retos tecnológicos y se desarrollan soluciones innovadoras En particular, una de las áreas críticas de la *Ingeniería de Software Cuántica* incluye la definición de estrategias que faciliten el diseño de sistemas desde la perspectiva de la *arquitectura de software*, que es el objeto de estudio de interés para el trabajo de investigación presentado en este artículo.

1. Estado del arte

Con el objetivo de analizar la arquitectura de software desde la perspectiva de la computación cuántica, se realizó una Revisión Sistemática de la Literatura (RSL). En general, los resultados destacan: (i) la necesidad de un estado del arte que facilite la síntesis e identificación de líneas de trabajo en el área; (ii) el desarrollo de modelos, metodologías y marcos que impulsen soluciones híbridas y cuánticas, y (iii) la importancia de establecer criterios de calidad para diseñar arquitecturas adaptadas a sistemas software híbridos (clásico-cuántico).

El análisis de la literatura destaca dos tipos de arquitecturas emergentes: (i) *híbridas*, que adaptan prácticas del software clásico a las necesidades de la computación cuántica, y (ii) *puramente cuánticas*, que requieren abordar nuevos desafíos propios del contexto cuántico. Sin embargo, esta área de investigación, aún en etapas preliminares, presenta soluciones limitadas, heterogéneas y sin consenso en definiciones y conceptos clave, lo que dificulta su aplicación industrial. Los resultados de la RSL también evidencian iniciativas metodológicas híbridas que buscan transferir mejores prácticas del software clásico al ámbito de la Ingeniería de Software Cuántica (Conradi & Fuggetta, 2002).

Por otro lado, el análisis de las tendencias presentes en la industria indica que las empresas tienen un creciente interés en adoptar e implementar soluciones que apliquen los beneficios que trae la computación cuántica. Sin embargo, la falta de soluciones generales y estandarizadas obliga a las empresas a invertir esfuerzos y tiempos adicionales en adaptar las soluciones existentes a su propio modelo de negocio (Beck et al., 2001). En este sentido, sólo algunas multinacionales y empresas de la industria de TI como: Google (Gibney, 2019a), IBM (Santos, 2016), Microsoft (Gibney, 2016), IonQ (IonQ, 2024), entre otros, cuentan con la capacidad de desarrollar computadoras cuánticas de alto nivel. Asimismo, algunas empresas de diversos sectores están comenzando a explorar, adquirir y utilizar computadoras cuánticas con capacidades limitadas para resolver necesidades específicas de su negocio, mejorar sus operaciones y desarrollar nuevas soluciones, algunas de ellas son: Alibaba, Tencent, Nokia, Airbus,

Biogen , entre otros (Gibney, 2019b; The Quantum Insider, 2022). De esta manera, se observa una fuerte tendencia hacia el uso de soluciones cuánticas en el sector industrial, sumado a iniciativas en la academia que buscan estandarizar el estado del conocimiento en torno a la definición de arquitecturas de software adaptadas a las necesidades que sugiere la computación cuántica.

Adicionalmente, se identificó una diversidad de enfoques arquitectónicos enfocados en el diseño de soluciones híbridas como cuánticas, esta variedad refleja un panorama heterogéneo de estrategias y patrones arquitectónicos, abarcando desde arquitecturas en capas, pasando por patrones de contención recursiva, que se utilizan para evitar desbordamientos de pila en entornos críticos, hasta llegar a configuraciones de computación cuántica universal (Khan et al., 2022). Por un lado, la variedad puede ser beneficiosa, ya que diferentes arquitecturas pueden adaptarse a necesidades específicas, aprovechar diferentes tecnologías subyacentes o abordar distintos tipos de problemas de manera más eficiente. Asimismo, la experimentación y la diversidad pueden fomentar la innovación de enfoques más efectivos. Por otro lado, una excesiva diversidad sin estandarización puede llevar a complicaciones en términos de: compatibilidad, interoperabilidad, colaboración, complejidad en el desarrollo, inconsistencias en la calidad y desempeño de las aplicaciones, dificultad en la adopción generalizada de tecnologías cuánticas, entre otros. En este sentido, una consolidación hacia estándares comunes puede facilitar la colaboración y la adopción generalizada de tecnologías cuánticas (Khan et al., 2022).

Además, los resultados del análisis de la literatura indican que se han realizado esfuerzos significativos en el estudio de los criterios de calidad o requisitos no funcionales que se deben adoptar, adaptar y definir para cumplir con los desafíos que requiere la industria para el desarrollo de arquitecturas híbridas y cuánticas, y destacan características de calidad conocidas desde el punto de vista de arquitecturas clásicas como: compatibilidad, escalabilidad, eficiencia, seguridad, entre otros, y proponen nuevos elementos directamente relacionados con los desafíos de la computación cuántica, por ejemplo: reducción de errores probabilísticos, calidad de simulaciones, coherencia cuántica y decoherencia cuántica, error cuántico fidelidad de operaciones cuánticas, seguridad cuántica, integración con sistemas clásicos, entre otros (Sodhi, 2018; Sodhi & Kapur, 2021). La superación de estos desafíos es importante para avanzar en el desarrollo de arquitecturas de software cuánticas.

5. Brechas existentes y propuesta de solución

En general, La RSL evidencia la necesidad de estandarizar el desarrollo de arquitecturas de software cuánticas mediante marcos de trabajo comunes que simplifiquen su creación/mantenimiento, promoviendo soluciones híbridas y cuánticas más cohesionadas y eficientes (Khan et al., 2022) que consideren aspectos como: (i) la reducción de costos operativos maximizando el uso de recursos cuánticos, (ii) la compatibilidad con sistemas clásicos al integrar aspectos funcionales y no funcionales de ambos paradigmas, y (iii) la transición eficaz y eficiente de sistemas clásicos a cuánticos mediante enfoques híbridos.

El análisis de la literatura identifica dos áreas clave para el desarrollo de soluciones en computación cuántica: (i) la creación de metodologías puramente cuánticas para mejorar enfoques existentes, y (ii) la exploración de soluciones híbridas que conecten metodologías clásicas con enfoques cuánticos avanzados. En particular, este estudio se centrará en las arquitecturas híbridas porque representan una oportunidad de proponer soluciones que faciliten la transición entre el paradigma de desarrollo de software clásico y cuántico.

En el contexto de la arquitectura de software, esto se podría lograr a través de una arquitectura de referencia (Cervantes et al., 2016); la cual se puede definir como una abstracción de alto nivel que encapsula características comunes y prácticas de diseño que se pueden reutilizar en diferentes contextos, proporcionando una base estandarizada para el desarrollo de software. Como resultado, una arquitectura de referencia sirve como una base atemporal que se puede instanciar y adaptar para cumplir las necesidades propias de un proyecto. En consecuencia, una arquitectura de referencia en el contexto de las arquitecturas de software híbridas podría representar un conjunto estandarizado de componentes, patrones de diseño y prácticas que se aplican a la construcción de software que involucre elementos clásicos y cuánticos.

5. Estado actual de la propuesta de solución

La arquitectura de referencia que surgió como propuesta de solución luego de analizar los resultados reportados en la RSL hace parte de un proyecto de doctorado que se encuentra en etapa de desarrollo. A continuación, se presentan los objetivos definidos para el proyecto y su estado actual.

Objetivo General: Diseñar una arquitectura de referencia adaptada a las necesidades de la *Ingeniería de Software Cuántica* que apoye el diseño de arquitecturas de software empresariales híbridas en la industria de software.

Para dar conformidad al cumplimiento del objetivo general, se definió un total de cuatro objetivos específicos, que son descritos a continuación

OE1. Identificar los estudios, propuestas, alcance, limitaciones y desafíos de la arquitectura de software en el contexto de la computación cuántica, a través de una Revisión Sistemática de la Literatura que permita establecer un estado del cocimiento extendido en torno a las soluciones propuestas por otros autores; **OE2.** Diseñar una arquitectura de referencia para arquitecturas de software empresariales híbridas, que incorpore los principios de la Ingeniería de Software Cuántica y la armonización de los elementos identificados en el OE1; **OE3.** Evaluar la arquitectura de referencia propuesta en el **OE2** a través de la aplicación de la técnica de evaluación de juicio de expertos, para determinar aspectos críticos e insights significativos que permitan mejorar y optimizar la solución y su aplicación en el contexto de aplicaciones empresariales híbridas; **OE4.**Evaluar la arquitectura de referencia propuesta en el **OE2** mediante la validación de escenarios hipotéticos como método mixto de evaluación en un entorno controlado que permita determinar su grado de aplicabilidad.

4.1. Estado actual del proyecto

A partir del análisis realizado por el equipo investigador, se identificó que el marco para guiar el desarrollo de la propuesta se adapta al formalismo propuesto por la *metodología investigación-acción con múltiples ciclos* (Wood-Harper, 1985), donde cada ciclo se divide en cuatro etapas: ***planeación, ejecución, desarrollo y reflexión*** (ver la Figura 1):

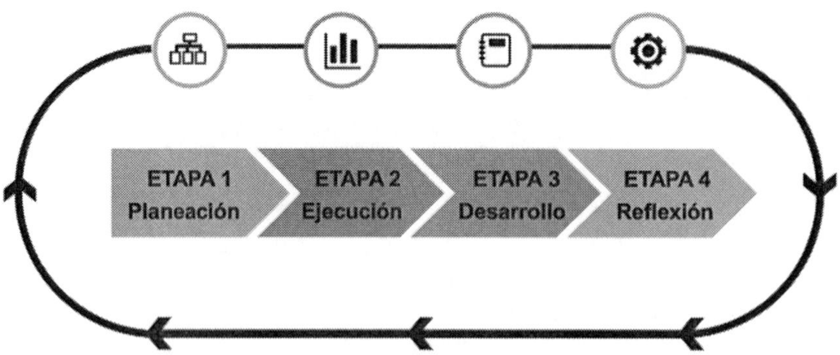

Figure 1. Metodología investigación-acción.

A partir de las actividades propuestas en esta metodología, se identificó que la investigación se debe dividir en cinco ciclos que guíen las actividades, entradas y salidas esperados después realizar el proyecto de investigación. A continuación, se presenta la descripción de cada ciclo planteado en el proyecto:

Ciclo 1: Realizar una Revisión Sistemática de la Literatura que sigue los lineamientos propuestos por (Budgen et al., 2008). El propósito de la revisión de la literatura es identificar el estado del arte actualizado y las brechas existentes en torno a la temática de interés; **Ciclo 2:** Definir una Arquitectura de Referencia para la definición de arquitecturas empresariales híbridas. Para lograrlo, se aplicará un proceso de armonización de las soluciones identificadas en el *Ciclo 1,* siguiendo las actividades que propone (Wood-Harper, 1985); **Ciclo 3:** Evaluar la Arquitectura de Referencia definida en el *Ciclo 2* mediante su validación a través del método de Juicio de Expertos (Almenara & Cejudo, 2013), que describe cada una de las actividades, roles y elementos necesarios para realizar una evaluación teórica que incluya a expertos en Ingeniería de Software y arquitectura de software, quienes determinarán la aplicabilidad de la propuesta e identificarán información que permita mejorar y optimizar la solución propuesta; **Ciclo 4:** Determinar la aplicabilidad de la arquitectura de referencia propuesta en el *Ciclo 2* y refinada durante el *Ciclo 3* en un entorno simulado y controlado. Para ello, se realizará una evaluación adaptando el método para la evaluación de arquitecturas de software a través de escenarios hipotéticos propuesto por (Kazman et al., 1994), conocido como SAAM, en inglés: Software Architecture Analysis Method; **Ciclo 5:** Documentación y socialización del proyecto. Este *Ciclo* es transversal y es realizado durante todo el tiempo que dure el proyecto. En particular, el Ciclo 1 que corresponde a la ejecución de la RSL, se ha completado satisfactoriamente. En la **Tabla 1** se presenta el consolidado de resultados esperados en las siguientes fases del proyecto.

Tabla 1.Resultados esperados durante la ejecución del proyecto.

Resultado	Entrada	Proceso	Salida
1	Reporte estructurado de resultados de la RSL.	Desarrollo de actividades correspondientes al Ciclo 2	Arquitectura de referencia (Versión 1).
2	Arquitectura de referencia (Versión 1).	Desarrollo de actividades correspondientes al Ciclo 3.	Arquitectura de referencia (Versión 2).
3	Arquitectura de referencia (Versión 2).	Desarrollo de actividades correspondientes al Ciclo 4.	Arquitectura de referencia (Versión final).

6. Conclusiones preliminares

Con respecto al trabajo desarrollado hasta el momento se puede concluir que: (i) la RSL permitió conocer el estado del arte en torno a la definición e implementación de soluciones en el área de la arquitectura de software cuántica; (ii) el análisis de las arquitecturas de software cuánticas es un tema emergente que se encuentra en estudio y es susceptible a mejoras relacionadas con el desarrollo de procesos, marcos de trabajo, estándares, entre otros, que faciliten la adopción de soluciones híbridas y cuánticas.

Referencias

Almenara, J. C., & Cejudo, M. del C. L. (2013). La aplicación del juicio de experto como técnica de evaluación de las tecnologías de la información y comunicación (TIC). *Revista Eduweb*, *7*(2), 11–22.

Bayerstadler, A., Becquin, G., Binder, J., Botter, T., Ehm, H., Ehmer, T., Erdmann, M., Gaus, N., Harbach, P., & Hess, M. (2021). Industry quantum computing applications. *EPJ Quantum Technology*, *8*(1), 25.

Beck, K., Beedle, M., Bennekum, A. Van, Cockburn, A., Cunningham, W., Fowler, M., Grenning, J., Highsmith, J., Hunt, A., Jeffries, R., Kern, J., & Marick, B. (2001, February 12). *Manifesto for Agile Software Development.*

Cervantes, H., Velasco-Elizondo, P., & Castro, L. (2016). Arquitectura de software Conceptos y ciclo de desarrollo. *México, México DF.*

Conradi, H., & Fuggetta, A. (2002). Improving software process improvement. *IEEE Software*, *19*(4), 92–99. https://doi.org/10.1109/MS.2002.1020295

Gibney, E. (2016). Inside Microsoft's quest for a topological quantum computer. *Nature*.

Gibney, E. (2019a). Hello quantum world! Google publishes landmark quantum supremacy claim. *Nature*, *574*(7779), 461–463.

IonQ. (2024, February 22). *IonQ*. Https://Ionq.Com.

Kazman, R., Bass, L., Abowd, G., & Webb, M. (1994). SAAM: A method for analyzing the properties of software architectures. *Proceedings of 16th International Conference on Software Engineering*, 81–90.

Khan, A. A., Ahmad, A., Waseem, M., Liang, P., Fahmideh, M., Mikkonen, T., & Abrahamsson, P. (2022). Software Architecture for Quantum Computing Systems-A Systematic Review. *ArXiv Preprint ArXiv:2202.05505.*

Piattini, M., & Murillo, J. M. (2022). Quantum Software Engineering Landscape and Challenges. In *Quantum Software Engineering* (pp. 25–38). Springer.

Piattini, M., & Murillo, J. M. (2022). Quantum Software Engineering Landscape and Challenges. In *Quantum Software Engineering* (pp. 25–38). Springer.

Piattini, M., Peterssen, G., & Pérez-Castillo, R. (2021). Quantum computing: A new software engineering golden age. *ACM SIGSOFT Software Engineering Notes*, *45*(3), 12–14.

Santos, A. C. (2016). The IBM quantum computer and the IBM quantum experience. *ArXiv Preprint ArXiv:1610.06980.*

Sodhi, B. (2018). Quality attributes on quantum computing platforms. *ArXiv Preprint ArXiv:1803.07407.*

Sodhi, B., & Kapur, R. (2021). Quantum computing platforms: assessing the impact on quality attributes and sdlc activities. *2021 IEEE 18th International Conference on Software Architecture (ICSA)*, 80–91.

The Quantum Insider. (2022). *Quantum Technology Investment Update.*

Weder, B., Barzen, J., Leymann, F., Salm, M., & Vietz, D. (2020). The quantum software lifecycle. *Proceedings of the 1st ACM SIGSOFT International Workshop on Architectures and Paradigms for Engineering Quantum Software*, 2–9.

Wood-Harper, T. (1985). Research methods in information systems: using action research. *Research Methods in Information Systems*, *169*, 191.

Ying, M. (2010). Foundations of quantum programming. *Asian Symposium on Programming Languages and Systems*, 16–20.

Zhao, J. (2020). Quantum software engineering: Landscapes and horizons. *ArXiv Preprint ArXiv:2007.07047.*

Detección de Patologías Pulmonares: Un Enfoque Basado en IA con Redes Neuronales Convolucionales

Mgtr. Ing. Pablo Ramirez A[1]

[1]Centro de Altos Estudios de Tecnología Informática – Universidad Abierta Interamericana (UAI), Avenida San Juan 951 - 10° piso
C1147AAU – Capital Federal – Buenos Aires – AR – Argentina

{Pablo.RamirezAmador}@alumnos.uai.edu.ar

Abstract. *Early diagnosis of lung diseases significantly improves survival. This study uses an action research approach with CNNs, ResNet152, and Vision Transformers, optimized with data augmentation. Applying the ISO 25059:2023 standard, the study addresses data interpretability, robustness, and security. Initial results show an accuracy of over 93%, supported by heat maps that highlight key areas in the images, facilitating clinical work. Ethical principles are integrated to protect patient privacy. The project seeks to reduce diagnostic errors and promote the safe use of artificial intelligence in hospitals, with a view to future clinical validation.*

Resumen. *El diagnóstico temprano de enfermedades pulmonares mejora significativamente la supervivencia. Este estudio utiliza un enfoque de investigación-acción con CNNs, ResNet152 y Vision Transformers, optimizados con Data Augmentation. Aplicando la norma ISO 25059:2023, se abordan la interpretabilidad, robustez y seguridad de los datos. Los resultados iniciales muestran una precisión superior al 93%, apoyada por mapas de calor que destacan zonas clave en las imágenes, facilitando la labor médica. Se integran principios éticos para proteger la privacidad del paciente. El proyecto busca reducir errores diagnósticos y promover el uso seguro de inteligencia artificial en hospitales, con miras a validación clínica futura.*

Palabras Clave: Redes Neuronales Convolucionales (CNNs), ResNet152, Vision Transformers, Data Augmentation, Norma ISO 25059:2023, Inteligencia Artificial.

1. Introducción al Campo de la Investigación e Identificación de los Principales Desafíos

El cáncer pulmonar es uno de los principales factores de mortalidad a nivel global, con elevadas tasas de diagnóstico tardío que reducen considerablemente las oportunidades de supervivencia (Tang et al., 2021). Las técnicas convencionales, tales como radiografías torácicas y tomografías computarizadas (CT), tienen restricciones para identificar tumores en sus fases iniciales, lo que ha motivado la búsqueda de tecnologías de vanguardia para optimizar los diagnósticos médicos (Chen et al., 2022).

Las Redes Neuronales Convolucionales (CNN) se distinguen entre estas tecnologías por su habilidad para examinar imágenes e identificar patrones complejos (Tang et al.,

2021). No obstante, su puesta en marcha se topa con retos significativos, tales como la demanda de grandes cantidades de información etiquetada, que resultan complicadas de conseguir en contextos médicos por razones de privacidad y accesibilidad (Qin et al., 2022). Adicionalmente, las CNN plantean desafíos en términos de su interpretación, dado que los expertos en salud necesitan entender cómo el modelo decide para confiar en sus resultados (Cai et al., 2023; Wang et al., 2022). Otra barrera fundamental es la diversidad en la calidad y formato de las imágenes médicas, lo cual puede afectar el desempeño del modelo. Para tratar esta situación, se utilizan métodos de *Data Augmentation*, que producen cambios en los datos de entrenamiento a través de rotaciones, escalados y la adición de ruido, potenciando de esta manera la habilidad del modelo para generalizar en diferentes situaciones (Huang et al., 2021).

La implementación eficaz de estas tecnologías en contextos clínicos exige asegurar la compatibilidad con las infraestructuras ya existentes y la observancia de las regulaciones de seguridad y privacidad de la información (Qin et al., 2022). Igualmente, resulta fundamental la formación de los profesionales de la salud para simplificar la incorporación de estos sistemas en sus rutinas de trabajo cotidianas. El propósito de este estudio es construir un modelo híbrido que fusiona CNN, ResNet152 y Vision Transformers, optimizado a través de la *Data Augmentation* y evaluado bajo los estándares de calidad fijados por la norma ISO 25059:2023, garantizando de esta manera un diagnóstico más precoz, exacto y fiable del cáncer de pulmón (Liu et al., 2023; Martínez et al., 2020).

2. Formulación de las Preguntas y Objetivos de la Investigación, Justificando Por Qué Fueron Elegidos

Es esencial establecer preguntas de investigación precisas y metas claramente establecidas para orientar proyectos científicos que buscan solucionar problemáticas reales a través de un enfoque pragmático. Desde el punto de vista de la investigación-acción, aplicada al diagnóstico médico, este método aspira no solo a la creación de modelos sofisticados de inteligencia artificial (IA), sino también a valorar su influencia en la práctica clínica. Esto asegura que las soluciones sugeridas sean prácticas, seguras y de confianza para los expertos en salud. El estudio se fundamenta en los fundamentos de la norma ISO 25059:2023, la cual define criterios para valorar la calidad de los sistemas de Inteligencia Artificial en cuanto a su interpretación, seguridad y solidez.

Preguntas de Investigación y Objetivos Específicos

1. **Pregunta:** ¿Cómo desarrollar un modelo de inteligencia artificial para la detección de cáncer de pulmón en imágenes médicas que integre una red neuronal convolucional (arquitectura ResNet152) con un modelo Vision Transformer, y que al mismo tiempo cumpla con los criterios de interpretabilidad, solidez y confiabilidad según la norma ISO 25059:2023?
    - **Objetivo Específico:** Desarrollar y entrenar un modelo híbrido de inteligencia artificial que combine una red neuronal convolucional (ResNet152) con un modelo Vision Transformer para la detección de cáncer de pulmón en imágenes médicas, y validar su rendimiento diagnóstico de acuerdo con los criterios de interpretabilidad, solidez y confiabilidad definidos en la norma ISO 25059:2023.

2. **Pregunta:** ¿Qué estrategias de evaluación y validación pueden emplearse para garantizar que el modelo de detección de cáncer de pulmón cumpla con los estándares de interpretabilidad, solidez y confiabilidad establecidos por la norma ISO 25059:2023 en un entorno clínico real?
    - **Objetivo Específico:** Diseñar y aplicar un protocolo de evaluación del modelo en un entorno clínico real, con el fin de medir y verificar su nivel de interpretabilidad, solidez y confiabilidad conforme a los estándares de calidad definidos en la norma ISO 25059:2023.
3. **Pregunta:** ¿Cómo implementar un enfoque de investigación-acción en un entorno hospitalario que permita integrar el modelo de inteligencia artificial en el flujo de trabajo del diagnóstico de cáncer de pulmón y mejorar iterativamente su interpretabilidad, solidez y confiabilidad de acuerdo con la norma ISO 25059:2023?
    - **Objetivo Específico:** Implementar un enfoque de investigación-acción en un entorno hospitalario para la integración del modelo de inteligencia artificial en el flujo de trabajo clínico del diagnóstico de cáncer de pulmón, incorporando la retroalimentación de los especialistas médicos y realizando mejoras iterativas que incrementen la interpretabilidad, solidez y confiabilidad del sistema conforme a los criterios de la norma ISO 25059:2023.
4. **Pregunta:** ¿Cómo validar el modelo propuesto utilizando conjuntos de datos reales para asegurar su aplicabilidad clínica, garantizando que cumpla con los criterios de interpretabilidad, solidez y confiabilidad establecidos por la norma ISO 25059:2023?
    - **Objetivo Específico:** Validar el modelo propuesto mediante experimentación con conjuntos de datos reales, evaluando su precisión, sensibilidad y especificidad, y verificando que cumpla con los requisitos de interpretabilidad, solidez y confiabilidad definidos por la norma ISO 25059:2023, a fin de asegurar su aplicabilidad en contextos clínicos reales.

Estas interrogantes y metas tienen como objetivo enfrentar los retos en la identificación precoz del cáncer pulmonar. La metodología de investigación-acción garantiza que los hallazgos se reflejen en ventajas concretas para los pacientes y los expertos en salud, en concordancia con los estándares internacionales definidos por la norma ISO 25059:2023.

3. Resumen del Conocimiento Actual del Dominio del Problema y Estado de las Soluciones Existentes

El estudio de imágenes médicas juega un rol crucial en la detección precoz del cáncer de pulmón. Los métodos convencionales, como las radiografías torácicas y las tomografías computarizadas (CT), poseen restricciones significativas en términos de precisión y sensibilidad, particularmente en las fases tempranas de la enfermedad, lo que complica la intervención médica en las primeras etapas (Tang et al., 2021; Chen et al., 2022).

Las Redes Neuronales Convolucionales (CNN) han transformado este ámbito al automatizar la identificación de patrones complejos en imágenes médicas, facilitando la detección de rasgos significativos para tumores de diferentes dimensiones y formas. No obstante, estas redes demandan grandes cantidades de información etiquetada, una exigencia difícil de satisfacer en contextos médicos debido a la privacidad de los pacientes y la escasez de datos accesibles (Qin et al., 2022).

Para sortear esta limitación, se emplean estrategias de *Data Augmentation*, las cuales producen cambios en los datos de entrenamiento a través de transformaciones como rotaciones, escalados y adición de luz. Estas metodologías potencian la habilidad del modelo para generalizar en datos nuevos (Huang et al., 2021). Además, arquitecturas de vanguardia como ResNet152 y Vision Transformers han mejorado el desempeño de las CNN, reforzando la identificación de relaciones espaciales complejas (Martínez et al., 2020; Liu et al., 2023).

En contextos clínicos, resulta crucial que los sistemas de Inteligencia Artificial sean entendibles y confiables. De acuerdo con la norma ISO 25059:2023, los expertos en salud deben comprender las determinaciones de los modelos para depositar su confianza en estos. Se emplean métodos como los mapas de calor para facilitar la interpretación de los resultados (Cai et al., 2023; Wang et al., 2022). Además, es esencial asegurar la privacidad y protección de los datos mediante marcos de gobernanza adecuados que garanticen el cumplimiento de las regulaciones (Qin et al., 2022).

Desde una perspectiva de investigación-acción, se sugieren ciclos de mejora iterativos, estudios participativos, validación en equipo y programas de formación continua. Estas metodologías garantizan que los modelos de Inteligencia Artificial sean eficaces, seguros y aceptados en el ámbito clínico.

4. Esbozo de la Metodología de Investigación que se Está Aplicando

La metodología sigue un enfoque de investigación-acción basado en fases iterativas que aseguran la mejora continua del modelo propuesto y su alineación con los criterios de calidad establecidos por la norma ISO 25059:2023. Las fases están integradas en los objetivos específicos de la investigación para garantizar una implementación efectiva en entornos clínicos.

1. **Desarrollar y entrenar un modelo híbrido de inteligencia artificial que combine una red neuronal convolucional (ResNet152) con un modelo Vision Transformer para la detección de cáncer de pulmón en imágenes médicas, y validar su rendimiento diagnóstico de acuerdo con los criterios de interpretabilidad, solidez y confiabilidad definidos en la norma ISO 25059:2023.**
    - Revisión bibliográfica exhaustiva sobre el uso de CNN y arquitecturas avanzadas para detectar cáncer de pulmón (Ramirez A, Pablo., 2023).
    - Selección y recopilación de conjuntos de datos relevantes, priorizando imágenes de tomografía computarizada etiquetadas por expertos.
2. **Diseñar y aplicar un protocolo de evaluación del modelo en un entorno clínico real, con el fin de medir y verificar su nivel de interpretabilidad, solidez y confiabilidad conforme a los estándares de calidad definidos en la norma ISO 25059:2023.**

- Evaluación de infraestructuras tecnológicas disponibles en entornos clínicos.
- Identificación de normativas y protocolos de seguridad y privacidad de datos.

3. **Implementar un enfoque de investigación-acción en un entorno hospitalario para la integración del modelo de inteligencia artificial en el flujo de trabajo clínico del diagnóstico de cáncer de pulmón, incorporando la retroalimentación de los especialistas médicos y realizando mejoras iterativas que incrementen la interpretabilidad, solidez y confiabilidad del sistema conforme a los criterios de la norma ISO 25059:2023.**
   - Diseño y entrenamiento del modelo híbrido utilizando Data Augmentation para mejorar su capacidad de generalización.
   - Implementación de técnicas de explicabilidad, como mapas de calor, para facilitar la interpretación de resultados.
4. **Validar el modelo propuesto mediante experimentación con conjuntos de datos reales, evaluando su precisión, sensibilidad y especificidad, y verificando que cumpla con los requisitos de interpretabilidad, solidez y confiabilidad definidos por la norma ISO 25059:2023, a fin de asegurar su aplicabilidad en contextos clínicos reales.**
   - Evaluación comparativa del modelo frente a otros enfoques existentes.
   - Incorporación de retroalimentación de los usuarios para optimizar el modelo de forma iterativa.

Esta metodología garantiza que el modelo desarrollado sea seguro, eficiente y aplicable en la práctica clínica diaria.

5. Introducción de la Solución Propuesta y de los Resultados Obtenidos hasta la Fecha

La solución propuesta adopta un enfoque de investigación-acción para desarrollar un modelo híbrido que integra Redes Neuronales Convolucionales (CNN), ResNet152 y Vision Transformers, optimizado mediante técnicas de Data Augmentation. El objetivo principal es mejorar la detección temprana de nódulos pulmonares en imágenes de tomografía computarizada (CT), favoreciendo el diagnóstico precoz del cáncer pulmonar.

El modelo combina las fortalezas de las CNN para extraer características visuales esenciales, las conexiones residuales de ResNet152 que permiten entrenar redes más profundas sin degradación, y la capacidad de los Vision Transformers para capturar relaciones espaciales complejas. Hasta ahora, las pruebas realizadas sobre conjuntos de datos reales muestran una precisión superior al 90%, mejorando significativamente la sensibilidad y reduciendo los falsos negativos.

El uso de Data Augmentation genera variaciones de entrenamiento mediante rotaciones, escalado y adición de ruido, incrementando la generalización y evitando sobreajuste. Además, técnicas explicativas como mapas de calor facilitan la interpretación clínica, destacando áreas sospechosas identificadas por el modelo.

La aplicación de la norma ISO 25059:2023 garantiza seguridad, interpretabilidad y robustez, aunque todavía es necesario ampliar los datos con mayor diversidad poblacional y validar continuamente el sistema en entornos clínicos reales.

6. Declaración de los Aspectos de la Solución Sugerida que la Hacen Diferente o Mejor en Comparación con los Enfoques Existentes

La solución propuesta se distingue de los enfoques existentes por integrar un modelo híbrido que combina CNN, ResNet152 y Vision Transformers, optimizado mediante Data Augmentation. Esta combinación permite mejorar la precisión, robustez y capacidad de generalización del modelo, aspectos fundamentales para su aplicabilidad en entornos clínicos. A diferencia de los modelos basados en una sola arquitectura, la solución aprovecha las fortalezas de cada componente: las CNN extraen características relevantes, ResNet152 mejora el aprendizaje profundo mediante conexiones residuales, y Vision Transformers identifican relaciones espaciales complejas.

El uso de Data Augmentation aborda la falta de grandes conjuntos de datos etiquetados, un desafío recurrente en el aprendizaje profundo aplicado a la medicina. Al generar variaciones de los datos de entrenamiento, el modelo mejora su capacidad para generalizar en datos no vistos previamente, reduciendo el riesgo de sobreajuste.

Un aspecto diferencial clave es la implementación de técnicas de explicabilidad, como mapas de calor, que permiten a los profesionales de la salud interpretar las decisiones del modelo y verificar si las áreas resaltadas corresponden a nódulos sospechosos. Esto genera confianza en los resultados y facilita la adopción del sistema en la práctica médica.

Además, la investigación incluye una evaluación comparativa que demuestra mejoras en precisión, sensibilidad y especificidad frente a otros enfoques. Se proponen protocolos de integración clínica que abordan requisitos técnicos, éticos y legales, asegurando que la solución sea segura, efectiva y aplicable en entornos reales. Esta consideración práctica es esencial para cumplir con los estándares de la norma ISO 25059:2023.

7. Declaración de las Cuestiones Pendientes y Descripción de los Próximos Pasos que se Planifican

Aunque el modelo híbrido basado en Redes Neuronales Convolucionales (CNN), ResNet152 y Vision Transformers ha demostrado ser efectivo en la detección temprana de cáncer de pulmón, aún persisten desafíos críticos por abordar. Entre ellos destacan la ampliación del conjunto de datos, aunque no se ha abordado aun, es importante la validación en entornos clínicos reales, la optimización de la interpretabilidad y la consideración de aspectos éticos y legales, todos ellos alineados con la norma ISO 25059:2023.

Ampliar el conjunto de datos, es fundamental para garantizar la capacidad de generalización del modelo. Es necesario recopilar imágenes médicas de diversas fuentes, considerando variaciones entre diferentes edades y sexos, lo que mejorará la robustez del sistema en diferentes escenarios clínicos.

La validación en entornos clínicos reales es esencial para medir el impacto práctico del modelo en el diagnóstico médico. La integración en hospitales permitirá identificar limitaciones y adaptar el sistema a las necesidades específicas del personal de salud.

La optimización de la interpretabilidad del modelo es otro desafío prioritario. Se planea desarrollar herramientas de explicabilidad avanzadas, como mapas de calor detallados y explicaciones en lenguaje natural, que permitan a los médicos comprender y confiar en las decisiones del modelo. Finalmente, es indispensable abordar los aspectos éticos y legales. Se deben establecer protocolos que aseguren la privacidad de los datos de los pacientes y definan claramente el rol de los médicos en la toma de decisiones diagnósticas. Los próximos pasos incluyen colaboraciones con instituciones médicas, implementación en entornos reales, desarrollo de nuevas herramientas de explicabilidad y creación de guías de adopción segura, asegurando que el modelo sea aplicable y confiable en la práctica clínica.

8. Referencias

Cai, W., Wang, X., Zhang, X., & Zhang, Y. (2023). Explainable AI for Medical Imaging: Techniques and Applications. *Journal of Medical Imaging and Health Informatics, 13*(2), 345-358.

Chen, L., Wu, H., Xu, Y., & Zhou, Z. (2022). Deep Learning Approaches for Lung Nodule Detection: Current Trends and Future Directions. *International Journal of Computer-Assisted Radiology and Surgery, 17*(4), 567-580.

Huang, J., Li, F., Zhao, M., & Yang, T. (2021). Data Augmentation Techniques for Medical Image Analysis: A Comprehensive Review. *Computerized Medical Imaging and Graphics, 92*, 101967.

Liu, Y., Lu, H., Zhang, J., & Sun, H. (2023). Advancements in Vision Transformers for Medical Image Analysis: Challenges and Opportunities. *Artificial Intelligence in Medicine, 135*, 102525.

Martínez, R., Sánchez, A., & Paredes, P. (2020). Enhancing Lung Cancer Detection with Hybrid Deep Learning Models: Combining CNNs and Transformers. *Journal of Thoracic Imaging, 35*(3), 210-219.

Tang, S., Zhou, L., & Chen, P. (2021). Automated Lung Cancer Diagnosis Using Deep Learning Techniques: A Review of Recent Advances. *Computational and Structural Biotechnology Journal, 19*, 2453-2467.

Wang, J., Zhao, L., & Li, R. (2022). Improving Model Interpretability in Medical AI: The Role of Explainability Tools. *Frontiers in Medicine, 9*, 858342.

Ramirez Amador, P. (2023). Algoritmos de Inteligencia Artificial para la Detección de Patologías Relacionadas con el Cáncer de Pulmón a través del Análisis de Imágenes utilizando Redes Neuronales Convolucionales y Data Augmentation: un mapeo sistemático de la literatura.

Amador, P. R., Ortega, D. M., & Cesarano, A. (2024). Detection of pulmonary pathologies using convolutional neural networks, Data Augmentation, ResNet50 and Vision Transformers. *arXiv preprint arXiv:2409.14446*.

Identificación Ágil de Microservicios Utilizando DDD y BDD

Nicolás Battaglia[1]

[1]Centro de Altos Estudios en Tecnología Informática (CAETI). Facultad de Tecnología Informática – Universidad Abierta Interamericana – Buenos Aires – Argentina

Nicolas.battaglia@uai.edu.ar

Resumen *La adopción de microservicios mejora la mantenibilidad y escalabilidad frente a arquitecturas monolíticas, aunque su diseño inicial es desafiante. Esta investigación propone un marco ágil que integra Desarrollo Guiado por Comportamiento y Diseño Guiado por el Dominio para identificar microservicios y definir arquitecturas escalables. Un análisis de la literatura y un experimento evidencian que combinar diseño estratégico y prácticas ágiles reduce la deuda técnica y mejora la escalabilidad.*

Abstract *Adopting microservices improves maintainability and scalability compared to monolithic architectures, though initial design remains challenging. This research proposes an agile framework combining Behavior-Driven Development and Domain-Driven Design to identify microservices and define scalable architectures. A literature review and an experiment show that integrating strategic design with agile practices reduces technical debt and enhances scalability.*

1. Introducción

El crecimiento de las arquitecturas basadas en microservicios (MS) se debe a sus ventajas frente a las arquitecturas monolíticas, especialmente al aprovechar la computación en la nube. Los MS facilitan la mantenibilidad y escalabilidad mediante el desarrollo, prueba y despliegue independiente de cada servicio, mejorando la flexibilidad y reduciendo la complejidad. Su modularidad permite que equipos distribuidos trabajen de forma autónoma, acelerando el desarrollo. Además, su tolerancia a fallos asegura que la falla de un servicio no afecte al sistema completo. Integrados con prácticas de DevOps, optimizan recursos y reducen costos, posicionándose como una solución escalable y rentable (De Lauretis, 2019). Sin embargo, el diseño de una arquitectura basada en microservicios no es trivial. Si las "fronteras" entre los microservicios no son las correctas, se pueden generar "malos olores" que con el tiempo generan problemas en la evolución y el mantenimiento (Taibi & Lenarduzzi, 2018). Al tomarse decisiones arquitecturales tempranamente (y con poca información) corremos el riesgo de hacerlo de manera equivocada dado que las decisiones de diseño arquitectónico son (como se afirma en (Fowler, 2012)) aquellas que son más difíciles de modificar durante el ciclo de vida del software. Este problema se agrava cuando se utilizan enfoques ágiles de desarrollo (Kruchten, 2010) dado que los mismos rechazan la utilización de períodos largos de análisis y diseño (por ejemplo, arquitectural) previos al desarrollo. No es de extrañar entonces que muchas compañías hayan decidido dar marcha atrás en sus migraciones a microservicios y volver a centrar sus sistemas críticos en arquitecturas monolíticas (Su et al., 2024).

Por estas razones (entre otras), se discute si en un sistema basado en MS es preferible diseñar los MS tempranamente o debe comenzarse como en un monolito para dividirse (luego, si fuera necesario) en MS (Cardoso, 2021). En (Lewis & Fowler, 2014), como un argumento razonable, se indica que no se debería comenzar con MS sino con un monolito modular y, solo cuando (y sí) se convierte en un problema, descomponerlo en MS (usando técnicas existentes y documentadas). Este problema incluso afecta a desarrolladores más experimentados (Fowler, 2015a). Varios autores han propuesto el uso de Domain-Driven Design (DDD) (Evans, 2004) como una estrategia adecuada para el descubrimiento de MS. Su uso podría reducir los malos olores mencionados anteriormente (Vural & Koyuncu, 2021). DDD propone basar el proceso de construcción de software en una comprensión profunda del modelo de negocios (en colaboración con los expertos del dominio) y de esa manera "descubrir" las abstracciones adecuadas, algunas de las cuales nos pueden ayudar a encontrar las fronteras entre MS. DDD aplicado en el contexto de las arquitecturas ágiles (Waterman, 2014) permitiría reducir el riesgo de tomar decisiones inadecuadas tempranamente. Además, la combinación de DDD con prácticas ágiles consolidadas como Test-Driven Development (Beck, 2022) permitirían asegurar que el diseño emergente (Blair et al., 2010) se mantenga correcto. No obstante, se ha reportado (Zhong et al., 2024) que no existe un soporte pragmático (en términos, por ejemplo, de heurísticas, reglas, etc) para guiar el reconocimiento ágil de microservicios en sistemas complejos. Los equipos de desarrollo enfrentan problemas para mantener consistencia entre modelos de dominio y su implementación. Además, la dificultad que existe para que desarrolladores y técnicos adquieran el conocimiento específico del dominio, valorando a las metodologías ágiles que alientan la participación de stakeholders en el proceso de desarrollo desde las etapas más tempranas. Adicionalmente, la naturaleza técnica de TDD, basada en un nivel de abstracción mucho más bajo (código) que el atacado por DDD, hace que exista un gap entre los conceptos apropiados para razonar sobre MS y los necesarios para aplicar esta técnica. Es en este punto que proponemos, entre otras contribuciones, la utilización sistemática de BDD (North & others, 2006) como un complemento a DDD para descubrir, testear y soportar la evolución de MS.

El objetivo general del trabajo doctoral es proponer un enfoque metodológico que integre Behavior-Driven Development (BDD) y Domain-Driven Design (DDD) para la identificación, diseño e implementación de microservicios. Este enfoque se centrará en evaluar el impacto de nuevos requisitos en la arquitectura, promoviendo la adaptabilidad y evolución del sistema, y previniendo la aparición temprana de malos olores o facilitando su eliminación de manera ágil. Este objetivo general se puede desglosar en objetivos específicos que aborden tanto la identificación de microservicios como la mantenibilidad: 1. Analizar las mejores prácticas actuales de BDD y DDD en el contexto de microservicios, con énfasis en cómo estas metodologías pueden mejorar la mantenibilidad y la capacidad de adaptación a nuevos requisitos. 2. Desarrollar un marco metodológico que combine BDD y DDD para la identificación de microservicios, priorizando la cohesión entre servicios y la facilidad de adaptación a cambios en los requisitos del negocio. 3. Proponer un conjunto de heurísticas de diseño que permitan adaptar las prácticas propuestas por DDD al mundo ágil que ayude al descubrimiento incremental de MS. 4. Evaluar el impacto de nuevos requisitos en la arquitectura de microservicios, midiendo cómo el enfoque propuesto mejora la capacidad de mantener y modificar los servicios sin introducir riesgos, complejidades innecesarias ni malos olores.

5.Comparar los resultados obtenidos con enfoques tradicionales de diseño de microservicios, destacando mejoras en la flexibilidad y la mantenibilidad del sistema a lo largo del tiempo. Este artículo se organiza de la siguiente manera: en la sección 2 abordamos el marco teórico de los temas relevantes en estudio. En la sección 3, describimos aspectos metodológicos del desarrollo de la tesis, los avances obtenidos hasta el momento y los próximos pasos. Por último, introducimos la propuesta sobre la cual se sustentará la tesis.

2. Preguntas de Investigación

A continuación, describimos las preguntas de investigación que motivan nuestro trabajo: 1. ¿Cómo puede el uso de Behavior-Driven Development (BDD) mejorar la identificación temprana de límites contextuales en arquitecturas de microservicios? 2. ¿Qué tan efectivo es combinar DDD con BDD para garantizar la cohesión y granularidad óptimas en el diseño de microservicios? 3.¿En qué medida la integración de DDD y BDD reduce la deuda técnica y mejora la mantenibilidad en sistemas basados en microservicios? 4.¿Qué diferencias significativas se observan en términos de refactorización y escalabilidad entre equipos que utilizan DDD y BDD frente a aquellos que no siguen metodologías específicas?

3. Conocimiento Actual del Problema

Como se dijo previamente, determinar cuáles son los límites de los microservicios es crucial para un buen diseño arquitectónico (Fowler, 2015a; SAID et al., 2024). De esa manera evitamos redundancia y acoplamiento reduciendo el costo de mantenimiento del sistema (Taibi et al., 2017). Como se mencionó en la sección 1, DDD ayuda a identificar y extraer los MS de un dominio mediante la identificación de "*bounded contexts*" que pueden ser interpretados como MS.

La falta de heurísticas o guías para utilizar DDD para la detección temprana de MS en un enfoque ágil hacen que el éxito de este enfoque dependa exclusivamente de la experiencia del arquitecto (Kapferer & Zimmermann, 2020). Existe otro problema, no menor, que tiene que ver con la evolución de los requisitos y su impacto en el diseño de una arquitectura de MS. Si bien hay numerosos estudios que abordan el tema desde la perspectiva ágil, no identificamos en la literatura discusiones sólidas sobre las implicaciones de esta evolución y las consecuencias de tomar las decisiones de diseño en las etapas incorrectas. Nos referimos a entender cuando se viola el principio de "no lo vas a necesitar" (Fowler, 2015b) o sufrir la falacia del gran diseño por adelantado (Zimmermann, 2017). En este contexto, identificamos las arquitecturas ágiles como una conciliación entre la agilidad y la arquitectura (Waterman, 2014) permitiendo reducir el riesgo que genera dedicarle mucho tiempo a planificar y diseñar la arquitectura por adelantado. En los procesos ágiles, la fase inicial de planificación, conocida como "*sprint zero*" (Nord & Tomayko, 2006), define el tiempo necesario entre el inicio del proyecto y el desarrollo, tomando decisiones arquitectónicas clave que son difíciles de cambiar posteriormente. Este enfoque, denominado diseño "*upfront*", busca establecer una base arquitectónica sólida. Sin embargo, tras esta etapa, las decisiones arquitectónicas tienden a ser emergentes (Waterman, 2014), evolucionando con el desarrollo del software. Mientras una planificación prolongada puede retrasar la entrega de valor y reducir la agilidad, una arquitectura 100% emergente exige refactorizaciones continuas para mantener la coherencia, arriesgando que una arquitectura intencionada se vuelva accidental (Booch, 2006). Por ello, el "*sprint zero*" debe equilibrar las decisiones iniciales y las que emerjan durante el desarrollo, aunque los métodos ágiles no definen claramente cuánto de la arquitectura debe decidirse al inicio. Por otro lado, Técnicas como *Test-Driven Development* (TDD) (Hellesoy et al., 2017) simplifican la refactorización del código en procesos ágiles, aunque suelen excluir a interesados como analistas y expertos del dominio. *Behavior-Driven Development* (BDD), en cambio, amplía el alcance al incluir a todos los involucrados en el proceso. Basado en prácticas ágiles como TDD [26] y *Domain-Driven Design* (DDD), BDD utiliza un lenguaje ubicuo propuesto por Evans (Evans, 2004) y adaptado por Dan North (North & others, 2006) para describir requisitos de forma clara y accesible. Este enfoque permite transformar escenarios definidos por analistas en pruebas de aceptación automatizadas, facilitando la comprensión entre técnicos y expertos del dominio (Tuglular et al., 2021). En entornos con requisitos cambiantes, BDD se presenta como una herramienta clave para construir características progresivamente y garantizar que el software cumpla con las expectativas del negocio (Smart & Molak, 2023).

3.1. Trabajos Relacionados

El desarrollo de aplicaciones basadas en microservicios (MS) utilizando Behavior-Driven Development (BDD) es un área poco explorada, a pesar de que BDD está ganando popularidad por su enfoque ágil y centrado en el dominio, facilitando el uso de Domain-Driven Design (DDD). Sin embargo, no existen mecanismos adecuados para identificar MS de manera temprana utilizando los principios ágiles de BDD a partir de escenarios descritos en lenguaje específico de dominio (Ma et al., 2018). Una búsqueda bibliográfica inicial reveló una escasez de estudios relacionados, lo que evidencia un vacío en la literatura y abre la oportunidad para nuevas propuestas.

Entre los trabajos relevantes, (Tuglular et al., 2021) propone un método de BDD para MS que comienza con pruebas a nivel de sistema y microservicio, integrando pruebas negativas tras cubrir las historias de usuario, validado con cinco microservicios. El artículo (Ma et al., 2018) sugiere usar algoritmos de procesamiento del lenguaje natural para recuperar MS en contextos específicos, entrenados con tokens de documentos en sintaxis Gherkin de BDD. En (Rahman & Gao, 2015) se presenta una arquitectura reutilizable para pruebas de aceptación automáticas en MS con BDD, abordando la reusabilidad, el desacoplamiento de pruebas del código fuente y la facilidad de auditoría, aunque identifica desafíos como mantenibilidad y testing de caja negra. Finalmente, (Lima et al., 2021) destaca que BDD permite a usuarios no técnicos escribir casos de prueba, facilitando la detección de fallos de negocio no identificados en pruebas unitarias de los servicios.

4. Estado del proyecto

Este trabajo adopta la metodología Design Science Research (DSR) como enfoque central, dado su enfoque en el desarrollo de artefactos innovadores y su validación rigurosa en entornos prácticos. Hevner et al (Hevner et al., 2004) destacan que la DSR se compone de tres ciclos principales: el ciclo de relevancia, el ciclo de rigor y el ciclo central de diseño. Estos ciclos permiten garantizar que el artefacto no solo sea innovador y técnicamente sólido, sino también ´util y aplicable en contextos reales. Para desarrollar el ciclo de relevancia, el primer punto que se trabajó fue en la realización de un mapeo sistemático sobre el descubrimiento de microservicios utilizando metodologías ágiles

(Battaglia et al., 2024) y, posteriormente, un experimento práctico con estudiantes de posgrado. Para definir el contexto del mapeo, se identificaron 5110 artículos entre 2022 y 2024 y luego se redujo a 194, asegurando su relevancia, calidad y aporte al tema de estudio. Los criterios aplicados son los siguientes: Inclusión: Se incluyen estudios que discutan la identificación de microservicios, que proporcionen enfoques y estrategias. Investigaciones que aborden metodologías ágiles, centrándose en cómo afectan la identificación y diseño de microservicios. Artículos publicados en los últimos dos años y publicaciones en inglés. Exclusión: No se incluyen estudios que no hayan sido revisados por pares, ya que estos no ofrecen la misma garantía de calidad y publicaciones que no aborden el contexto de empresas de tecnología, dado que el enfoque del estudio es específico para este tipo de empresas. Asimismo, se realizó un filtrado sobre el título y resumen para eliminar los que no eran relevantes. A continuación, describimos las preguntas de investigación que motivaron el estudio: Pl: ¿Cuáles son las estrategias más comunes para identificar microservicios en empresas con arquitecturas complejas? P2: ¿Qué técnicas se utilizan para definir los límites de los microservicios en metodologías ágiles? P3: ¿Cuáles son los desafíos y soluciones reportados en la literatura sobre la implementación de microservicios en metodologías ágiles? P4: ¿Cómo se aplica la teoría en la práctica dentro de una empresa? y P5: ¿En qué idiomas y en qué países se produce la investigación sobre descubrimiento de microservicios?.El trabajo realizado revela una diversidad de enfoques y técnicas para identificar y definir los límites de los microservicios, adaptándose a un entorno de desarrollo iterativo e incremental (Ünlü et al., 2024). El principal enfoque se da a partir del uso de DDD y la creación de modelos de dominio que reflejan la lógica del negocio. Otro enfoque es aprovechando la modularidad de arquitecturas SOA, centrándose en unidades funcionales del negocio. Por último, algunos autores proponen la utilización de Event Storming para mapear eventos de negocio y descubrir potenciales MS. Por otro lado, diversos estudios analizan técnicas para descomposición impulsada por dominio, en la que se aprovecha el conocimiento del negocio para identificar límites naturales asi también como técnicas de descomposición basadas en análisis de código para identificar módulos independientes. La aplicabilidad práctica de estas técnicas en entornos empresariales reales sugiere que, aunque la teoría proporciona una base sólida, la implementación exitosa de microservicios requiere una adaptación continua y un enfoque colaborativo para abordar los cambios frecuentes en los requisitos. Otra conclusión relevante es que no existe gran cantidad de estudios versen sobre la creación de arquitecturas basadas en MS desde su concepción ya que, en general, trabajan sobre la descomposición de monolitos previos.

Por otro lado, se realizó un experimento para comparar enfoques en la identificación y diseño de microservicios (MS). Participaron 26 estudiantes divididos en 10 equipos, organizados en dos grupos: el Grupo A, que resolvió el problema sin seguir una metodología específica, y el Grupo B, que utilizó metodologías ágiles y Domain-Driven Design (DDD). El trabajo práctico consistió en identificar los MS necesarios para un escenario de gestión de manufactura, seguido de una segunda etapa en la que se introdujeron nuevos requisitos para analizar el impacto del cambio según el enfoque aplicado inicialmente. En cuanto a la demografía, el 68.5% de los estudiantes no tenían un posgrado finalizado, mientras que el 77% contaban con 4 o más años de experiencia en desarrollo de software. El 65% tenía al menos 3 años de experiencia con metodologías ágiles, y el 57% había trabajado con MS, aunque solo el 35% acumulaba 3 o más años de experiencia en esta área. Respecto a BDD, únicamente el 35% poseía experiencia previa.

Al finalizar el experimento, se encuestó a los alumnos participantes, obteniendo los siguientes resultados: el 97% calificó el enunciado del problema como complejo o muy complejo. Respecto al nuevo requisito, el 57% tuvo que refactorizar su trabajo inicial, y el 87% lo consideró complejo o muy complejo. Entre quienes no usaron metodología, solo el 36% refactorizó, mientras que el 50% de los que usaron DDD y metodologías ágiles rediseñaron su trabajo. El análisis destaca que combinar un diseño inicial ligero con metodologías ágiles es clave para sistemas basados en microservicios (MS). Aunque el diseño inicial no elimina la necesidad de ajustes, facilita la identificación de límites contextuales y dominios clave, optimizando la granularidad y reduciendo riesgos. Los datos sugieren que el enfoque ágil y DDD requiere más refactorización, pero ofrece un marco sólido que equilibra planificación y adaptabilidad, reduciendo la deuda técnica y mejorando escalabilidad y alineación entre objetivos técnicos y de negocio.

4.1. Próximos pasos

Para abordar los ciclos de diseño y evaluación, nos apoyamos en el análisis de la literatura y estudios realizados hasta el momento que nos permiten identificar que BDD puede utilizarse para describir y analizar requisitos, identificando objetivos de negocio y buscando características que ayuden a alcanzarlos asi como colaborar en la identificación y mantenimiento de MS. En base a lo anteriormente expuesto buscaremos, en primera medida, comprender que sucede actualmente en la industria en términos de uso de BDD y TDD para identificar MS y, a partir a los aportes de (Irshad et al., 2021; Smart & Molak, 2023), propondremos un marco inicial de trabajo iterativo para la identificación de MS utilizando DDD y BDD tanto para la incorporación de nuevas características como para el refinamiento de los MS existentes. Esta propuesta se basa en la definición estratégica del dominio con DDD, alcance y propósito, modelado funcional y definición de escenarios utilizando BDD/Gherkin. Por último, se realiza el diseño arquitectónico, modelado de datos y definición de interfaces. En términos concretos, buscamos combinar los beneficios de las arquitecturas ágiles con la naturaleza de DDD y BDD en uso de lenguajes específicos de dominio y la caracterización temprana de microservicios con límites apropiados.

5. Conclusiones

En este trabajo presentamos los aspectos más importantes de la investigación doctoral sobre enfoques ágiles basados en DDD y BDD para especificación de microservicios. La integración de métodos sistemáticos como Domain-Driven Design (DDD) con metodologías ágiles ofrece un enfoque efectivo para abordar la complejidad inherente al diseño de microservicios (MS). Este enfoque iterativo y evolutivo maximiza la capacidad de respuesta ante cambios, asegurando que las soluciones desarrolladas reflejen las necesidades reales del negocio. Además, la combinación de DDD con Behavior-Driven Development (BDD) no solo facilita la identificación y diseño de microservicios desde las primeras etapas del desarrollo, sino que también mejora la mantenibilidad y escalabilidad del sistema. Los resultados de nuestro experimento con estudiantes de posgrado demuestran que el uso de estas metodologías reduce la deuda técnica y mejora la capacidad de adaptación a nuevos requisitos. Sin embargo, persisten desafíos, como la necesidad de heurísticas y guías más pragmáticas para la detección temprana de microservicios en sistemas complejos. También es crucial seguir investigando cómo la evolución de los requisitos impacta en el diseño arquitectónico y cómo mitigar los riesgos asociados a decisiones de diseño tomadas en etapas tempranas.

En resumen, nuestro trabajo propone un marco metodológico que integra DDD y BDD para la identificación, diseño e implementación de microservicios, promoviendo la adaptabilidad y evolución del sistema. Este enfoque no solo aborda los desafíos actuales, sino que también sienta las bases para futuras investigaciones y mejoras en el campo del desarrollo de software basado en microservicios

6. Referencias

Battaglia, N., Garcia, A. N., & Congiusti, A. (2024). Descubrimiento de Microservicios en Metodologías Ágiles: un mapeo sistemático de la literatura. *XXX Congreso Argentino de Ciencias de La Computacion*, 1506–1510.

Beck, K. (2022). *Test driven development: By example*. Addison-Wesley Professional.

Blair, S., Watt, R., & Cull, T. (2010). Responsibility-driven architecture. *IEEE Software*, *27*(2), 26–32.

Booch, G. (2006). The accidental architecture. *IEEE Software*, *23*(3), 9–11.

Cardoso, J. P. S. (2021). *A guide for microservices in greenfield projects*. Instituto Politecnico do Porto (Portugal).

De Lauretis, L. (2019). From monolithic architecture to microservices architecture. *2019 IEEE International Symposium on Software Reliability Engineering Workshops (ISSREW)*, 93–96.

Evans, E. (2004). *Domain-driven design: tackling complexity in the heart of software*. Addison-Wesley Professional.

Fowler, M. (2012). *Patterns of enterprise application architecture*. Addison-Wesley.

Fowler, M. (2015a). *Monolith First*. https://martinfowler.com/bliki/MonolithFirst.html

Fowler, M. (2015b). *YAGNI*. https://martinfowler.com/bliki/Yagni.html

Hellesoy, A., Tooke, S., & Wynne, M. (2017). *The cucumber book: behaviour-driven development for testers and developers*. The Pragmatic Bookshelf.

Hevner, A. R., March, S. T., Park, J., & Ram, S. (2004). Design science in information systems research. *MIS Quarterly*, 75–105.

Irshad, M., Britto, R., & Petersen, K. (2021). Adapting Behavior Driven Development (BDD) for large-scale software systems. *Journal of Systems and Software*, *177*, 110944.

Kapferer, S., & Zimmermann, O. (2020). Domain-specific Language and Tools for Strategic Domain-driven Design, Context Mapping and Bounded Context Modeling. *MODELSWARD*, 299–306.

Kruchten, P. (2010). Software architecture and agile software development: a clash of two cultures? *Proceedings of the 32nd ACM/IEEE International Conference on Software Engineering-Volume 2*, 497–498.

Lewis, J., & Fowler, M. (2014). *Microservices - a definition of this new architectural term*. https://martinfowler.com/articles/microservices.html

Lima, H. R., Souza, K. C., de Paula, L. V., e Martins, L. M. C., Giozza, W. F., & de Sousa, R. T. (2021). Acceptance tests over microservices architecture using behaviour-driven development. *2021 16th Iberian Conference on Information Systems and Technologies (CISTI)*, 1–6.

Ma, S.-P., Chuang, Y., Lan, C.-W., Chen, H.-M., Huang, C.-Y., & Li, C.-Y. (2018). Scenario-based microservice retrieval using Word2Vec. *2018 IEEE 15th International Conference on E-Business Engineering (ICEBE)*, 239–244.

Nord, R. L., & Tomayko, J. E. (2006). Software architecture-centric methods and agile development. *IEEE Software*, *23*(2), 47–53.

North, D., & others. (2006). Introducing BDD. *Better Software*, *12*, 7.

Rahman, M., & Gao, J. (2015). A reusable automated acceptance testing architecture for microservices in behavior-driven development. *2015 IEEE Symposium on Service-Oriented System Engineering*, 321–325.

SAID, M. A. I. T., EZZATI, A., MIHI, S., & BELOUADDANE, L. (2024). Microservices adoption: An industrial inquiry into factors influencing decisions and implementation strategies. *International Journal of Computing and Digital Systems*, *15*(1), 1417–1432.

Smart, J. F., & Molak, J. (2023). *BDD in Action: Behavior-driven development for the whole software lifecycle*. Simon and Schuster.

Su, R., Li, X., & Taibi, D. (2024). From Microservice to Monolith: A Multivocal Literature Review. *Electronics*, *13*(8), 1452.

Taibi, D., & Lenarduzzi, V. (2018). On the definition of microservice bad smells. *IEEE Software*, *35*(3), 56–62.

Taibi, D., Lenarduzzi, V., & Pahl, C. (2017). Processes, motivations, and issues for migrating to microservices architectures: An empirical investigation. *IEEE Cloud Computing*, *4*(5), 22–32.

Tuglular, T., Coşkun, D. E., Gülen, Ö., Okluoğlu, A., & Algan, K. (2021). Behavior-Driven Development of Microservice Applications. *International Journal of Computers*, *15*, 130–137. https://doi.org/10.46300/9108.2021.15.20

Ünlü, H., Kennouche, D. E., Soylu, G. K., & Demirörs, O. (2024). Microservice-based projects in agile world: A structured interview. *Information and Software Technology*, *165*, 107334.

Vural, H., & Koyuncu, M. (2021). Does domain-driven design lead to finding the optimal modularity of a microservice? *IEEE Access*, *9*, 32721–32733.

Waterman, M. G. (2014). *Reconciling agility and architecture: a theory of agile architecture*. Open Access Te Herenga Waka-Victoria University of Wellington.

Zhong, C., Li, S., Huang, H., Liu, X., Chen, Z., Zhang, Y., & Zhang, H. (2024). Domain-driven design for microservices: An evidence-based investigation. *IEEE Transactions on Software Engineering*.

Zimmermann, O. (2017). Microservices tenets: Agile approach to service development and deployment. *Computer Science-Research and Development*, *32*, 301–310.

Explorando el Uso de Inteligencia Artificial en el Descubrimiento y Diseño de Microservicios

Daniel Narváez[1]

[1]CAETI, Facultad de Tecnología Informática – Universidad Abierta Interamericana
Argentina

JoseDaniel.NarvaezF@alumnos.uai.edu.ar

Abstract. *Microservice design is a significant challenge in greenfield software development, especially in ensuring internal cohesion and low coupling. This paper proposes an artificial intelligence-based approach, particularly leveraging natural language processing (NLP) and deep learning, to support the discovery and design of microservices from textual requirements. Employing the Design Science Research (DSR) methodology, the proposed research focuses on prompt engineering techniques and architectural validation to guide and assess the quality of microservice-oriented designs. As part of a doctoral project, this work aims to optimize architectural quality, design time, and costs, addressing challenges and opportunities identified through both a systematic mapping study (MSL) and a systematic literature review (SLR).*

Resumen. *El diseño de microservicios es un desafío significativo en desarrollos desde cero, especialmente para garantizar cohesión interna y bajo acoplamiento. Este trabajo propone un enfoque basado en inteligencia artificial, particularmente en procesamiento de lenguaje natural (PLN) y aprendizaje profundo, para apoyar el descubrimiento y diseño de microservicios a partir de requisitos textuales. Utilizando la metodología de Design Science Research (DSR), la propuesta se centra en técnicas de ingeniería de prompts y validación arquitectónica para guiar y evaluar la calidad de diseños orientados a microservicios. Como parte de un proyecto doctoral, esta investigación busca optimizar la calidad arquitectónica, el tiempo de diseño y los costos, abordando retos y oportunidades identificados mediante un mapeo sistemático de la literatura (MSL) y una revisión sistemática de la literatura (SLR).*

Keywords: Ingeniería de Software, Diseño de Software, Microservicios, Inteligencia Artificial, Aprendizaje Automático, Procesamiento de Lenguaje Natural, Investigación en Ciencia del Diseño.

1. Introducción

El diseño de microservicios ha emergido como una práctica clave en el desarrollo de sistemas modernos debido a su capacidad para promover la modularidad, la escalabilidad y la facilidad de mantenimiento en arquitecturas de software complejas [Taibi et al. 2017]. Este paradigma arquitectónico permite dividir aplicaciones monolíticas en componentes independientes y autónomos, denominados microservicios, que interactúan a través de interfaces bien definidas [Newman 2015]. Sin embargo, el proceso de diseño de microservicios sigue siendo un desafío significativo, especialmente en desarrollos desde cero, donde no existen puntos de referencia arquitectónicos claros [Ait Said et al. 2024].

Esta investigación forma parte de mi proyecto doctoral en el Doctorado en Ciencias Informáticas de la Universidad Abierta Interamericana, el cual aborda el descubrimiento y diseño de microservicios en desarrollos desde cero utilizando requisitos textuales. El objetivo principal de la disertación es proponer una metodología basada en inteligencia artificial (IA), centrada en ingeniería de prompts y validación cuantitativa, para guiar el descubrimiento de microservicios. Este trabajo se alinea con los desafíos y oportunidades explorados en el presente estudio, destacando la importancia de combinar técnicas innovadoras para superar las limitaciones actuales.

Uno de los principales obstáculos es garantizar que los microservicios diseñados cumplan con principios fundamentales, como la cohesión interna y el bajo acoplamiento. Según [Narváez et al. 2024], estos principios son esenciales para maximizar la eficiencia operativa y la flexibilidad del sistema, pero su aplicación práctica depende en gran medida de la experiencia del diseñador y de la calidad de los requisitos disponibles. En entornos donde los requisitos se presentan en forma textual y no estructurada, este desafío se amplifica, lo que aumenta el riesgo de errores de diseño y retrabajo [Taibi et al. 2017].

La integración de IA, particularmente el procesamiento de lenguaje natural (PLN) y el aprendizaje profundo, representa una oportunidad única para abordar estas limitaciones. Estas tecnologías han demostrado su capacidad para extraer información estructurada de textos no estructurados, lo que las hace ideales para analizar documentos de requisitos [Narváez et al. 2024]. Además, estudios recientes destacan la efectividad del clustering y otras técnicas de aprendizaje automático en la identificación de dominios funcionales y módulos coherentes [Ait Said et al. 2024].

Nuestro mapeo sistemático de la literatura (MSL) [Narváez et al. 2024] identificó varias brechas en el uso de IA para el diseño de microservicios. Mientras que algunas investigaciones han explorado el uso de PLN para extraer requisitos, pocas han integrado estas técnicas con herramientas de diseño automatizado que permitan generar microservicios alineados con objetivos arquitectónicos claros. Este vacío teórico y práctico subraya la necesidad de un enfoque más integral que combine la extracción de requisitos textuales con métodos automatizados de diseño y validación.

Además, los desafíos relacionados con la evaluación de la calidad arquitectónica de los microservicios generados, como la medición de cohesión, acoplamiento y alineación con los objetivos del negocio, siguen sin resolverse completamente. Según [Taibi et al. 2017], la falta de herramientas automatizadas para esta evaluación complica la adopción de prácticas de diseño basadas en IA en entornos empresariales.

Por lo tanto, este trabajo propone una metodología experimental que utiliza técnicas de IA para automatizar el descubrimiento y diseño de microservicios desde requisitos textuales. Este enfoque no solo optimiza el tiempo y esfuerzo necesario para el diseño, sino que también mejora la calidad arquitectónica al incorporar métricas objetivas y herramientas de validación automática. La metodología de investigación se basa en Design Science Research (DSR), que ofrece un marco estructurado para la creación y validación de artefactos tecnológicos novedosos [Hevner et al. 2004].

2. Preguntas de investigación

1. ¿Qué técnicas de inteligencia artificial pueden emplearse para identificar y diseñar microservicios a partir de requisitos textuales?
2. ¿Cuáles son los principales desafíos técnicos y metodológicos en la automatización del diseño de microservicios?
3. ¿Cómo se puede evaluar la calidad arquitectónica de los microservicios generados automáticamente?

3. Objetivos

1. Diseñar una metodología basada en ingeniería de prompts para identificar microservicios a partir de requisitos textuales usando IA.
2. Evaluar la calidad arquitectónica mediante métricas como cohesión, acoplamiento, independencia funcional y alineación con los objetivos del negocio.
3. Validar la metodología mediante estudios de caso en entornos controlados y reales.

4. Estado del Arte

El diseño de microservicios ha sido un tema central en la investigación arquitectónica de software en la última década, destacándose como una alternativa escalable y modular frente a las arquitecturas monolíticas y orientadas a servicios (SOA) [Newman 2015, Clements 2002]. A pesar de sus ventajas, la transición a microservicios presenta desafíos significativos, particularmente en entornos de desarrollo desde cero. Entre los problemas más comunes se encuentran la correcta identificación de límites de servicios, la gestión de dependencias, y el aseguramiento de la cohesión interna y bajo acoplamiento entre módulos [Ait Said et al. 2024].

4.1. Enfoques Actuales en el Diseño de Microservicios

Los enfoques tradicionales para el diseño de microservicios se han basado en heurísticas manuales, como la identificación de *bounded contexts* mediante Domain-Driven Design (DDD). Aunque ampliamente aceptadas, estas metodologías dependen de la experiencia del arquitecto y son propensas a errores [Booch et al. 2008]. En organizaciones sin una comprensión clara del dominio, es común diseñar servicios redundantes o con alto acoplamiento, lo que dificulta la escalabilidad y el mantenimiento [Taibi et al. 2017].

Recientemente, se han propuesto técnicas automatizadas para mejorar este proceso. Herramientas como Service Cutter y enfoques de *clustering* han demostrado cierto éxito en la identificación de microservicios a partir de artefactos como bases de datos o código fuente [Ait Said et al. 2024], aunque resultan inadecuadas en escenarios greenfield donde tales artefactos no existen.

Por otro lado, tecnologías emergentes como GreenMicro [Bajaj et al. 2022], SEMGROMI [Vera-Rivera et al. 2023] y GTMicro [Bajaj et al. 2024] han mostrado resultados prometedores en desarrollos desde cero. GreenMicro aplica *clustering* sobre casos de uso y entidades de base de datos, SEMGROMI agrupa historias de usuario mediante PLN para mejorar cohesión y reducir acoplamiento, y GTMicro emplea modelos como BERT para organizar requisitos textuales en microservicios coherentes.

Estas herramientas representan avances significativos para el diseño en escenarios greenfield, aunque enfrentan limitaciones derivadas de la ambigüedad y la calidad de los artefactos de entrada.

4.2. Inteligencia Artificial en el Diseño de Microservicios

La inteligencia artificial ha emergido como una alternativa prometedora frente a las limitaciones de los enfoques tradicionales. En particular, el procesamiento de lenguaje natural (PLN) y el aprendizaje profundo han demostrado eficacia en tareas como la extracción de requisitos y la identificación de patrones en texto no estructurado [Taibi et al. 2017]. Modelos como redes neuronales recurrentes (RNN) y transformers, incluyendo BERT, han sido utilizados con éxito para analizar requisitos textuales, extrayendo entidades y relaciones relevantes para el diseño de software [Narváez et al. 2024].

Herramientas como PF4MD [Li et al. 2023] integran métricas de complejidad y análisis de dependencias para apoyar la descomposición de servicios, mediante visualizaciones que facilitan decisiones arquitectónicas. SEMGROMI y GTMicro aplican PLN y aprendizaje profundo para identificar microservicios, mientras que GreenMicro utiliza clustering para generar estructuras modulares desde etapas tempranas.

Nuestro mapeo sistemático de la literatura [Narváez et al. 2024] identificó que, si bien existen avances en la extracción de requisitos mediante IA, persiste una falta de integración entre estas técnicas y los métodos automatizados de diseño de microservicios. La mayoría de los trabajos se enfocan en etapas aisladas del proceso, como el análisis de dependencias o clustering, sin abordar la transición completa desde requisitos textuales hasta microservicios implementables.

4.3. Brechas y Oportunidades de Investigación

Una de las principales brechas identificadas es la falta de metodologías integradas que combinen técnicas de PLN con aprendizaje profundo y clustering para automatizar el diseño de microservicios en escenarios de desarrollo desde cero. Mientras que estudios previos han explorado la identificación de microservicios en sistemas existentes, pocos trabajos han investigado cómo extraer directamente requisitos textuales y transformarlos en diseños modulares [Ait Said et al. 2024, Taibi et al. 2017].

Además, tecnologías como GreenMicro y SEMGROMI, aunque efectivas, carecen de mecanismos para validar automáticamente la calidad arquitectónica de los microservicios generados. Métricas como cohesión, acoplamiento y alineación con los objetivos del negocio son esenciales para garantizar que los servicios diseñados sean viables tanto técnica como funcionalmente, pero estas métricas rara vez se integran en los enfoques existentes [Bajaj et al. 2022, Vera-Rivera et al. 2023].

Finalmente, la integración de modelos generativos, como los LLMs, representa una oportunidad para automatizar decisiones arquitectónicas y sugerir patrones de diseño basados en conocimiento previo. Sin embargo, su implementación práctica aún requiere mayor investigación y validación empírica para demostrar su efectividad en escenarios reales.

En este contexto, la metodología propuesta busca llenar estas brechas mediante la integración de técnicas avanzadas de IA con herramientas de validación arquitectónica, optimizando tanto la calidad como la eficiencia del proceso de diseño. Este enfoque tiene el potencial de transformar el diseño de microservicios, estableciendo nuevas bases para la investigación y práctica en este campo.

5. Metodología

Este trabajo adopta la metodología Design Science Research (DSR) como enfoque central, dado su enfoque en el desarrollo de artefactos innovadores y su validación rigurosa en entornos prácticos. Hevner et al. [Hevner et al. 2004] destacan que la DSR se compone de tres ciclos principales: el ciclo de relevancia, el ciclo de rigor y el ciclo central de diseño. Estos ciclos permiten garantizar que el artefacto no solo sea innovador y técnicamente sólido, sino también útil y aplicable en contextos reales.

El ciclo de relevancia comenzó con un análisis sistemático de la literatura para identificar las brechas en el diseño de microservicios desde cero. Este análisis incluyó la revisión de enfoques tradicionales, como el Domain-Driven Design (DDD), que aunque efectivos, dependen en gran medida de la experiencia del arquitecto y de artefactos preexistentes [Booch et al. 2008]. Además, se evaluaron enfoques emergentes basados en inteligencia artificial, como el uso de modelos de procesamiento de lenguaje natural (PLN) y técnicas de aprendizaje profundo para extraer información relevante de textos no estructurados [Ait Said et al. 2024, Narváez et al. 2024]. Este análisis permitió identificar la falta de integración entre técnicas de PLN y herramientas automatizadas de diseño de microservicios como una brecha crítica.

En el ciclo de diseño, se conceptualizó una metodología experimental que combina ingeniería de prompts, PLN y métricas cuantitativas de calidad arquitectónica. El artefacto generado no es una implementación completa, sino una especificación arquitectónica preliminar que representa microservicios potenciales. Dicha especificación se genera a partir de requisitos textuales mediante tres fases principales: extracción de entidades y relaciones, agrupamiento en servicios mediante algoritmos de clustering, y evaluación estructural basada en métricas. El proceso es parcialmente automatizado, con posibilidad de intervención manual para ajustes finos, y la selección de técnicas específicas se basó en su eficacia documentada en la literatura [Narváez et al. 2024, Ait Said et al. 2024].

Finalmente, en el ciclo de evaluación, se validará la metodología propuesta a través de experimentos en entornos simulados y casos reales. Las métricas clave incluirán cohesión interna, acoplamiento entre servicios y alineación con los objetivos del negocio, siguiendo las mejores prácticas propuestas en trabajos previos [Taibi et al. 2017, Clements 2002]. Además, se realizarán pruebas de estrés para evaluar la escalabilidad y robustez de los microservicios generados.

6. Solución propuesta

Este trabajo propone una metodología que transforma requisitos textuales en una especificación arquitectónica preliminar de microservicios mediante técnicas de inteligencia artificial. El proceso, sujeto a ajuste manual, se organiza en tres etapas interdependientes. La validación considera métricas como cohesión, acoplamiento e independencia funcional, aplicadas sobre representaciones estructurales.

Extracción de requisitos textuales. Este componente emplea modelos de PLN avanzados, como BERT y transformers, para analizar documentos de requisitos y extraer entidades clave, relaciones y acciones. Por ejemplo, en un dominio de comercio electrónico, puede identificar entidades como "cliente" y "producto", y relaciones como "realiza pedido" o "gestiona inventario". La entrada son textos no estructurados, y la salida es una representación semiestructurada de conceptos funcionales. Esta etapa utiliza técnicas de aprendizaje supervisado o no supervisado, en función de la disponibilidad de datos etiquetados.

Diseño automatizado de microservicios. A partir de los conceptos extraídos, se aplica clustering con algoritmos como k-means o DBSCAN para agrupar funcionalidades relacionadas en módulos coherentes que representen microservicios potenciales. El proceso permite ajustar hiperparámetros según el contexto y contempla retroalimentación humana para refinar resultados. La salida es una propuesta estructurada de microservicios lista para validación arquitectónica.

Validación arquitectónica. Esta etapa aplica métricas como cohesión, acoplamiento y alineación con objetivos del negocio para evaluar la calidad del diseño. Se generan informes con indicadores clave y se prevé el uso de herramientas visuales para inspección manual. El enfoque combina automatización con supervisión humana para garantizar viabilidad técnica y organizacional.

La metodología se valida inicialmente en entornos simulados, utilizando conjuntos de datos sintéticos y reales. Los resultados de estas validaciones servirán como base para futuras implementaciones en entornos empresariales, donde se medirá su impacto en términos de tiempo de diseño, costos y calidad arquitectónica.

7. Resultados iniciales

Como resultado inicial, completamos un mapeo sistemático de la literatura (MSL) que identificó las tendencias actuales y las principales brechas en la aplicación de inteligencia artificial (IA) al diseño de microservicios [Narváez et al. 2024]. Este trabajo exploró técnicas de IA relevantes, como el aprendizaje profundo, modelos de decisión de Markov, y herramientas como Mono2Micro y PF4MD, las cuales han demostrado un impacto significativo en el monitoreo, la detección de anomalías y la adaptación dinámica de sistemas basados en microservicios [Kalia et al. 2020, Li et al. 2023, MAGABLEH and ALMIANI23 2019].

El MSL destacó cómo Mono2Micro facilita la transición de aplicaciones monolíticas a microservicios mediante técnicas de clustering temporoespacial [Kalia et al. 2020]. Por otro lado, PF4MD combina marcos conceptuales de análisis de requisitos, como los Problem Frames, con métricas de complejidad para guiar la descomposición de sistemas en microservicios. Esta herramienta se ha utilizado exitosamente para visualizar dependencias, diseñar reglas de descomposición y mejorar la toma de decisiones arquitectónicas [Li et al. 2023].

A pesar de estos avances, el MSL subrayó la necesidad de soluciones integrales para diseñar microservicios desde cero, una área aún poco explorada. Además, identificó desafíos como la falta de datasets estandarizados para evaluar herramientas de diseño automatizado y la ausencia de métricas ampliamente adoptadas para medir la cohesión interna y el bajo acoplamiento en los servicios generados.

Además, el MSL destacó que la validación en escenarios empresariales reales será crucial para la adopción industrial de estas herramientas. Aunque los experimentos controlados han mostrado resultados prometedores, la implementación práctica enfrenta barreras relacionadas con la interoperabilidad de herramientas y la gestión eficiente de recursos. Estos hallazgos confirman la relevancia del problema abordado y proporcionan una base sólida para el desarrollo de enfoques más avanzados que integren IA en el diseño de microservicios desde la etapa inicial.

Como parte de la evolución de esta línea de investigación, recientemente se publicó un segundo estudio de revisión sistemática en la revista Software (MDPI) [Narváez et al. 2025], que amplía la cobertura del campo incluyendo enfoques emergentes como los modelos generativos (LLMs), el aprendizaje por refuerzo y técnicas de documentación arquitectónica asistida por IA. Este nuevo trabajo analizó 43 estudios entre 2018 y 2024, y reafirmó la utilidad de herramientas como Mono2Micro, SEMGROMI y PF4MD, al tiempo que identificó desafíos persistentes en torno a la consistencia de datos distribuidos, la incorporación de requisitos no funcionales, y la necesidad de validaciones empíricas más robustas. Estos hallazgos refuerzan la necesidad de soluciones integrales como la que se propone en esta investigación doctoral, orientadas a automatizar el diseño de arquitecturas de microservicios desde los requerimientos textuales, garantizando además su validación estructural.

8. Conclusiones y trabajo futuro

Este trabajo propone una metodología basada en inteligencia artificial para el descubrimiento y diseño de microservicios a partir de requisitos textuales, integrando técnicas avanzadas de inteligencia artificial, como procesamiento de lenguaje natural y aprendizaje profundo. La propuesta busca superar las limitaciones de enfoques manuales y heurísticos, enfrentando desafíos clave como la identificación de límites de servicio, la cohesión interna y el bajo acoplamiento.

Los resultados iniciales, sustentados en un mapeo sistemático de literatura y una revisión sistemática más reciente, confirman la pertinencia del problema abordado y evidencian vacíos en la integración entre extracción de requisitos, diseño automatizado y validación estructural. Asimismo, se han identificado métricas fundamentales para evaluar la calidad arquitectónica de los microservicios generados.

La propuesta se orienta a optimizar el esfuerzo de diseño y mejorar la calidad estructural mediante un enfoque híbrido que combina automatización y supervisión humana, ofreciendo una solución escalable para proyectos desarrollados desde cero.

Como trabajo futuro, se plantea la implementación y validación de la metodología en escenarios reales, a través de estudios de caso en distintos dominios. Se evaluará su impacto en términos de eficiencia, calidad arquitectónica y costos. Además, se explorará el uso de herramientas visuales para facilitar la inspección, y se integrarán modelos generativos guiados por prompts junto con mecanismos de validación formal para apoyar decisiones arquitectónicas automatizadas.

Este trabajo pretende contribuir al cuerpo de conocimiento académico y ofrecer soluciones prácticas para la ingeniería de software, consolidando un puente entre los avances en inteligencia artificial y los desafíos actuales del diseño de microservicios.

Referencias

Ait Said, M., Ezzati, A., Mihi, S., and Belouaddane, L. (2024). Microservices adoption: An industrial inquiry into factors influencing decisions and implementation strategies. *International Journal of Computing and Digital Systems*, 15:2210–142.

Bajaj, D., Bharti, U., Gupta, I., Gupta, P., and Yadav, A. (2024). Gtmicro—microservice identification approach based on deep nlp transformer model for greenfield developments. *International Journal of Information Technology*, pages 1–11.

Bajaj, D., Goel, A., and Gupta, S. C. (2022). Greenmicro: identifying microservices from use cases in greenfield development. *IEEE Access*, 10:67008–67018.

Booch, G., Maksimchuk, R. A., Engle, M. W., Young, B. J., Connallen, J., and Houston, K. A. (2008). Object-oriented analysis and design with applications. *ACM SIGSOFT software engineering notes*, 33(5):29–29.

Clements, P. C. (2002). Software architecture in practice. *Diss. Software Engineering Institute*.

Hevner, A. R., March, S. T., Park, J., and Ram, S. (2004). Design science in information systems research. *MIS Quarterly*, 28(1):75–105.

Kalia, A. K., Xiao, J., Lin, C., Sinha, S., Rofrano, J., Vukovic, M., and Banerjee, D. (2020). Mono2micro: an ai-based toolchain for evolving monolithic enterprise applications to a microservice architecture. In *Proceedings of the 28th ACM Joint Meeting on European Software Engineering Conference and Symposium on the Foundations of Software Engineering*, pages 1606–1610.

Li, Y., Li, Z., Bu, Y., Xiao, H., and Deng, Y. (2023). Pf4md: A microservice decomposition tool combining problem frames. In *2023 IEEE 31st International Requirements Engineering Conference (RE)*, pages 359–360. IEEE.

MAGABLEH, B. and ALMIANI23, M. (2019). Deep q learning for self adaptive distributed microservices architecture. *IEEE Acess*.

Narváez, D., Battaglia, N., Fernández, A., and Rossi, G. (2025). Designing microservices using ai: A systematic literature review. *Software*, 4(1):6.

Narváez, D., Rossi, G. H., and Battaglia, N. (2024). Aplicación de inteligencia artificial en el diseño de microservicios. In *XXX Congreso Argentino de Ciencias de la Computación (CACIC)(La Plata, 7 al 11 de octubre de 2024)*.

Newman, S. (2015). *Building Microservices: Designing Fine-Grained Systems*. O'Reilly Media.

Taibi, D., Lenarduzzi, V., and Pahl, C. (2017). Processes, motivations, and issues for migrating to microservices architectures: An empirical investigation. *IEEE Cloud Computing*, 4(5):22–32.

Vera-Rivera, F. H., Cuadros, E. G. P., Perez, B., Astudillo, H., and Gaona, C. (2023). Semgromi—a semantic grouping algorithm to identifying microservices using semantic similarity of user stories. *PeerJ Computer Science*, 9:e1380.

Towards a process for Trustworthy AI systems development

Carlos Mario Braga[1]

[1]Alarcos Research Group – Univ. of Castilla-La Mancha – Ciudad Real – Spain

carlosmario.braga1@alu.uclm.es

Abstract. *This work aims to define a comprehensive Software Development Life Cycle (SDLC) tailored for Trustworthy Artificial Intelligence (AI) systems. These systems are understood as full software solutions that incorporate AI components—such as machine learning models or intelligent agents—whose behavior must align with ethical principles, legal requirements, and technical robustness. The proposed SDLC is grounded on a multidimensional taxonomy of trustworthiness, covering aspects such as lawfulness, non-maleficence, beneficence, autonomy, justice, explicability, and technology. By integrating these principles into all development phases, the SDLC supports the design of AI systems that are not only effective and innovative but also aligned with human values, regulations, and societal expectations. The methodology follows a Design Science Research approach, ensuring the model's relevance, feasibility, and adaptability to evolving technological and regulatory contexts.*

Keywords— Artificial Intelligence, Trustworthy, Process Model

1. Introduction

Norbert Wiener established the foundations of computer ethics in the late 1940s and early 1950s, particularly through his book The Human Use of Human Beings [Wiener 1950], where he analyzed the impact of technologies on human values.

The rise of computational power in the 20th century enabled diverse AI applications, raising ethical concerns—as noted by O'Neil [O'neil 2017]. This led to the publication of numerous ethical guidelines. Algorithm Watch has compiled over 160 such documents.[1] Several works have attempted to synthesize these guidelines into global frameworks for ethical AI [Floridi et al. 2018, Jobin et al. 2019, Thiebes et al. 2021]. However, critiques from legal and technological perspectives persist. Legally, ethics and law are often conflated, which creates a false sense of compliance known as "ethics washing" [Bietti 2020, Steinhoff 2023]. Technologically, ethical principles often lack mechanisms for practical integration into AI development [Whittlestone et al. 2019, Morley et al. 2020, Stix 2021].

To address this gap, a taxonomy that classifies trust-related concerns from ethical, legal, and technical domains is needed. This taxonomy supports the construction of a Software Development Life Cycle (SDLC) for trustworthy AI systems, understood here as complete software systems incorporating AI components whose behavior must align with legal requirements, ethical values, and technical robustness.

As a foundation, this research adopts CRISP-DM, a widely used, non-proprietary model that structures data projects into six phases: business understanding, data understanding, data preparation, modeling, evaluation, and deployment [Shearer 2000]. Despite evolving challenges, CRISP-DM is still considered the de facto standard in data-driven development [Schröer et al. 2021], especially in domains like Data Science [Saltz 2021, Saltz et al. 2022,

[1]https://inventory.algorithmwatch.org/

Abbasi et al. 2016]. However, its usage is declining [Mohan et al. 2011, Piatetsky 2014], and improvements to process models have shown benefits in project outcomes [Mariscal et al. 2010, Saltz et al. 2016].

Despite its widespread adoption, CRISP-DM has shown limitations in addressing modern AI development needs. Its evolution towards data science trajectories and the need for modernization have been discussed in recent works [Martínez-Plumed et al. 2019].

This research proposes a CRISP-DM refinement that integrates trustworthiness dimensions throughout the SDLC. The goal is to support the ethical, lawful, and robust development of AI-enabled systems, particularly relevant now given the increasing impact and autonomy of AI technologies, including Generative AI.

2. Research Questions

This research aims to answer the following questions:

- RQ1: Can we classify and organize the core elements of Trustworthy AI, considering ethical, legal, and technological perspectives in a structured and comprehensive way?
- RQ2: How can these elements be effectively operationalized into a SDLC tailored for the development of full AI-based systems, using an established model as foundation?
- RQ3: What requirements must the proposed SDLC meet to ensure compliance with international standards, long-term applicability, and the ability to address emerging challenges in AI development?

RQ1 aims to define a taxonomy that unifies ethical, legal, and technical perspectives of trustworthiness, RQ2 focuses on translating this taxonomy into actionable tasks within a refined SDLC, and RQ3 evaluates the model's compliance with legal, ethical, and technical standards, and its adaptability to emerging regulations.

3. State of Art

According to [Barletta et al. 2023], the main issues in developing ethical and trustworthy AI systems are the diversity of perspectives, the lack of standardized development practices, and the absence of practical frameworks covering the full SDLC while being usable by all stakeholders.

Recent contributions to Trustworthy AI often focus on assessment and verification tools, such as third-party evaluations or self-assessment checklists [Zhou et al. 2020, Zhang et al. 2021]. Examples include Z-Inspection®, based on the European Commission's framework, and Wasabi [Singh et al. 2023], which supports structured evaluation of trust dimensions. While extensive work exists on audits, verifications, and checklists [Sharma et al. 2023, Xiaomei et al. 2023, Radclyffe et al. 2023], these efforts mostly address what should be done, not how to operationalize trustworthiness in development processes.

Some proposals aim to embed trust principles into the AI lifecycle [Wu et al. 2020, Xue et al. 2022], or improve human-AI interaction across development stages [Wickramasinghe et al. 2020]. However, most of these are partial or focused on specific phases. For example, GreatAI [Schmelczer et al. 2023] targets deployment, TrustOps [Kwak 2022] and AI TRiSM [Habbal et al. 2024] center on risk management, while others address individual dimensions such as fairness or explainability [Zhang et al. 2023, Schmid et al. 2023, Sekiguchi et al. 2020].

In parallel, traditional SDLCs such as Waterfall, Spiral, or Agile are still used in AI projects [Agarwal et al. 2017, Mandal et al. 2013], but they lack explicit mechanisms for integrating legal, ethical, or trust-related aspects [Morley et al. 2020]. Specific models for data science, such as ASUM-DM or Microsoft's Team Data Science Process (TDSP), address technical lifecycle management but do not systematically incorporate trustworthiness dimensions like fairness, accountability, or legal compliance [Saltz et al. 2016, Saltz 2021].

Therefore, despite the variety of existing tools and partial frameworks, there is still a lack of a comprehensive, practical, and evolvable SDLC specifically tailored for Trustworthy AI. As pointed out in prior works [Mandal et al. 2013, Agarwal et al. 2017], adoption of new SDLC strategies remains low due to complexity, compatibility issues, and lack of validation. This research addresses that gap by proposing a refinement of the mature CRISP-DM model, integrating trustworthiness dimensions in a structured and adaptable way, suitable for current and future AI systems under evolving regulatory frameworks.

4. Methodology

This research adopts a Design Science Research (DSR) methodology [Hevner et al. 2010], structured in six iterative phases. This approach ensures that the artifact—the proposed SDLC for Trustworthy AI—is both theoretically grounded and practically validated.

- Problem Identification: The study begins by identifying a critical gap: the absence of comprehensive, practical SDLCs that integrate ethical, legal, and technical dimensions of trust in AI system development.
- Objective Definition: The goal is to design a process model that enables the structured development of full AI-based systems (not only models), ensuring compliance, explicability, and robustness from the outset.
- Design and Creation: The artifact was developed in two steps. First, a taxonomy of trustworthiness was created from a systematic literature review. Second, this taxonomy was operationalized through a refinement of the CRISP-DM model, embedding trust dimensions into each phase and task of the SDLC.
- Evaluation and Validation: The refined SDLC will be assessed via expert reviews, alignment with international standards (e.g., EU AI Act, ISO/IEC, IEEE), and application to a pilot AI project. A comparative analysis (with and without the SDLC) will be conducted to assess practical utility, completeness, and usability.
- Iteration and Improvement: Based on evaluation feedback and real-world testing, the SDLC will be iteratively refined to improve coverage and applicability.
- Practical Use: Finally, the artifact will be deployed in a real development context. A guideline and set of practical resources (techniques, checklists, templates) will be developed to support adoption by AI teams.

5. Proposed Solution and Results

The proposed solution is structured in two key contributions. First, we developed a comprehensive Trustworthy AI Taxonomy that unifies, classifies, and organizes core concepts related to trustworthiness in AI systems. This taxonomy was constructed after conducting a systematic literature review (SLR), in which 67 selected papers were analyzed to extract the ethical, legal, and technological foundations of Trustworthy AI. The taxonomy includes seven top-level principles—*Lawfulness*, *Beneficence*, *Non-Maleficence*, *Autonomy*, *Justice*, *Explicability*, and *Technology*, as shown in Fig. 1 —each decomposed into second-level concepts to ensure consistent interpretation across disciplines. It is conceived as a sociotechnical system, supporting the integrated management of trust-related aspects throughout the AI lifecycle.

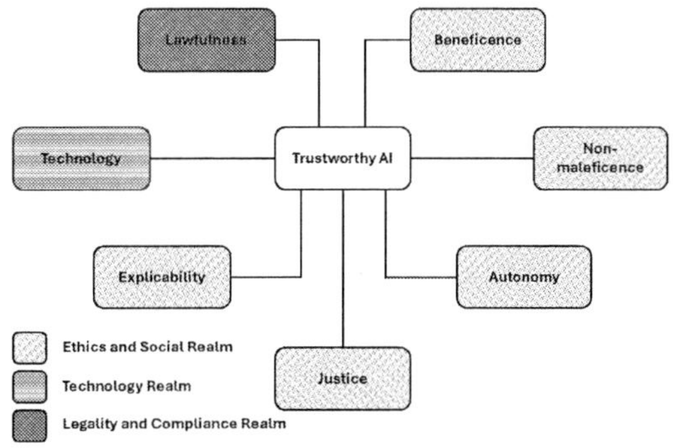

Figure 1. First Level of Trustworthy AI Taxonomy.

The taxonomy includes seven key dimensions: *Lawfulness*, concerning compliance with laws and regulations; *Beneficence*, focused on promoting human and environmental well-being; *Non-maleficence*, ensuring safety, privacy, and harm prevention; *Autonomy*, supporting human oversight and self-determination; *Justice*, targeting fairness and bias mitigation; *Explicability*, ensuring transparency and interpretability; and *Technology*, addressing infrastructure, algorithms, and security to operationalize trust principles.

Each of these dimensions has been further decomposed into a second level of concepts, derived from literature and aligned with the principles of a sociotechnical system. These subcomponents provide additional granularity and semantic clarity, ensuring consistent interpretation and application across different domains and contexts. The complete structure of this second level is illustrated in Figure 2, which presents the detailed Trustworthy AI taxonomy and the classification of its elements into ethical, legal, and technological realms.

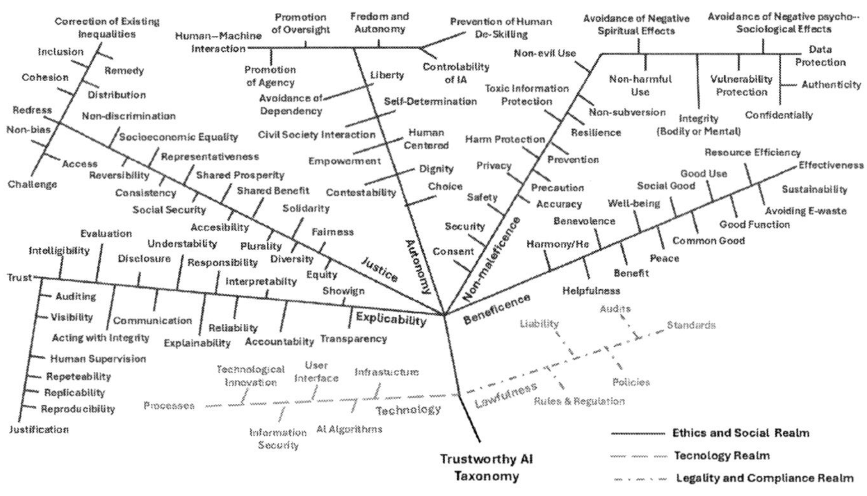

Figure 2. Detailed Trustworthy AI Taxonomy.

The second contribution is the development of CRISP-TAI, a modernized and specialized refinement of CRISP-DM tailored for the development of trustworthy AI systems. To construct this model, a second SLR was conducted to analyze 35 existing CRISP-DM refinements, applying a comparison framework based on eight evaluation metrics (including alignment with trust principles, risk management, and tool compatibility). From this process, 18 high-quality refinements were selected, leading to the extraction of 130 design considerations, which were consolidated into 100 structured changes to the original CRISP-DM model.

These changes include structural modifications, new tasks and deliverables, and the introduction of a new phase (Continuous Deployment and Monitoring) that addresses post-deployment responsibilities such as fairness evaluation, explainability for end users, continuous risk mitigation, and regulatory compliance.

The structure of CRISP-TAI including its phases and tasks is summarized in Figure 3. This figure provides a high-level visual overview of how trustworthiness principles are embedded across the entire process lifecycle, highlighting the integration of a new iterative phase for continuous deployment and monitoring.

The result is a complete and operational process model named CRISP-TAI, which embeds trustworthiness into all phases of the SDLC while preserving the structure and usability of CRISP-DM. The model is supported by a full definition of phases, tasks, activities, deliverables, and traceability logs. The two main scientific contributions—(i) the Trustworthy AI taxonomy and (ii) the CRISP-TAI process model—have been submitted to peer-reviewed JCR journals and are currently under review. The venue names have been intentionally omitted to preserve the anonymity required by double-blind review processes.

These contributions lay the foundation for a practical and actionable methodology to build trustworthy AI systems, operationalizing abstract ethical, legal, and technical principles into concrete development tasks.

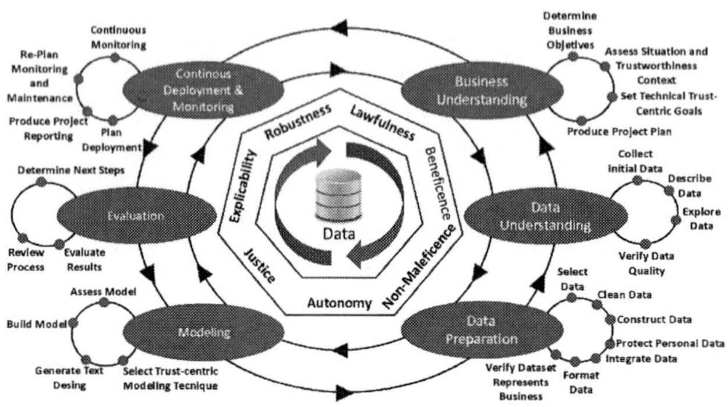

Figure 3. Phases and task of the CRISP-DM refinement for Trustworthy AI.

6. Key Distictive Aspects of Our Proposal

The key differentiating factors of our proposal compared to existing approaches are the following:

- It is based on an exhaustive analysis of the core concerns around AI trustworthiness, integrating ethical, legal, and technological dimensions into a unified sociotechnical system.
- Rather than focusing only on evaluation or audit phases, it provides practical guidance from the earliest stages of system development, embedding trust requirements into all lifecycle phases.
- It specializes and modernizes the most widely used SDLC for data projects, CRISP-DM, ensuring compatibility with industry practices while enhancing it to support Trustworthy AI.
- It introduces a new, iterative phase for continuous deployment and monitoring, supporting long-term compliance, retraining, fairness evaluation, and stakeholder engagement.
- Finally, the model was built following a structured design methodology and is supported by a detailed taxonomy, systematic refinements, and traceability of changes, allowing both transparency and future adaptability.

7. Next Steps

With CRISP-TAI fully defined, upcoming work focuses on validation, refinement, and dissemination. First, we will assess its alignment with international standards such as the EU AI Act [European Parliament and the Council 2024], IEEE P7000 series, and ISO/IEC 24027. Recent studies have translated these frameworks into actionable developer-oriented requirements, reinforcing the importance of integrating trust principles throughout the lifecycle [Baldassarre et al. 2024].

We will test CRISP-TAI in real-world AI projects to evaluate its practical applicability, completeness, and ease of use compared to conventional practices. These pilots will also help identify barriers and inform future improvements.

To foster adoption, a practical guide will be developed with checklists, templates, and traceability aids, ensuring accessibility for diverse teams and maturity levels.

Long-term sustainability will be addressed through mechanisms for updating the model as regulations, risks, and technologies evolve, ensuring its continued relevance.

Lastly, we will explore dissemination via publications and open-source formats.

8. Acknowledgments

This research would not have been possible without the support of the following projects: Di4SPDS (PCI2023145980-2), funded by MCIN/AEI/10.13039/501100011033 and by the European Union (Chist-Era Program), AETHER-UCLM (PID2020-112540RB-C42) funded by MCIN/AEI/10.13039/501100011033, ALBA (TED2021-130355B-C31), funded by MICIU/AEI /10.13039/501100011033 and the European Union NextGeneration EU/ PRTR, and MESIAS (2022-GRIN-34202) funded by FEDER.

References

Abbasi, A. et al. (2016). Big data research in information systems: Toward an inclusive research agenda. *Journal of the association for information systems*, 17(2):3.

Agarwal, P. et al. (2017). SDLC model selection tool and risk incorporation. *Int. J. Comput. Appl*, 172(10):6–10.

Baldassarre, M. T., Gigante, D., Kalinowski, M., and Ragone, A. (2024). Polaris: A framework to guide the development of trustworthy ai systems. In *Proceedings of the IEEE/ACM 3rd International Conference on AI Engineering-Software Engineering for AI*, pages 200–210.

Barletta, V. S. et al. (2023). A rapid review of responsible AI frameworks: How to guide the development of ethical AI. In *Proceedings of the 27th International Conference on Evaluation and Assessment in Software Engineering*, pages 358–367.

Bietti, E. (2020). From ethics washing to ethics bashing: a view on tech ethics from within moral philosophy. In *Proceedings of the 2020 conference on fairness, accountability, and transparency*, pages 210–219.

European Parliament and the Council (2024). Artificial intelligence act. `https://www.europarl.europa.eu/doceo/document/TA-9-2024-0138_EN.html`. Final text approved on 13 March 2024.

Floridi, L. et al. (2018). AI4People—an ethical framework for a good AI society: opportunities, risks, principles, and recommendations. *Minds and machines*, 28:689–707.

Habbal, A. et al. (2024). Artificial intelligence trust, risk and security management (AI TRiSM): Frameworks, applications, challenges and future research directions. *Expert Systems with Applications*, 240:122442.

Hevner, A. et al. (2010). Design science research in information systems. *Design research in information systems: theory and practice*, pages 9–22.

Jobin, A. et al. (2019). The global landscape of AI ethics guidelines. *Nature machine intelligence*, 1(9):389–399.

Kwak, J. H. (2022). Trustops: A risk-based AI engineering process. In *2022 13th International Conference on Information and Communication Technology Convergence (ICTC)*, pages 2252–2254. IEEE.

Mandal, A. et al. (2013). Investigating and analysing the desired characteristics of software development lifecycle (SDLC) models. *International Journal of Software Engineering Research & Practices*, pages 9–15.

Mariscal, G. et al. (2010). A survey of data mining and knowledge discovery process models and methodologies. *The Knowledge Engineering Review*, 25(2):137–166.

Martínez-Plumed et al. (2019). CRISP-DM twenty years later: From data mining processes to data science trajectories. *IEEE transactions on knowledge and data engineering*, 33(8):3048–3061.

Mohan, K. et al. (2011). What methodology attributes are critical for potential users? understanding the effect of human needs. In *Advanced Information Systems Engineering: 23rd International Conference, CAiSE 2011, London, UK, June 20-24, 2011. Proceedings 23*, pages 314–328. Springer.

Morley, J. et al. (2020). From what to how: an initial review of publicly available AI ethics tools, methods and research to translate principles into practices. *Science and engineering ethics*, 26(4):2141–2168.

O'neil, C. (2017). *Weapons of math destruction: How big data increases inequality and threatens democracy*. Crown, New York City, U.S.

Piatetsky, G. (2014). CRISP-DM, still the top methodology for analytics, data mining, or data science projects. *KDD News*.

Radclyffe, C. et al. (2023). The assessment list for trustworthy artificial intelligence: A review and recommendations. *Frontiers in artificial intelligence*, 6:1020592.

Saltz, J. S. (2021). CRISP-DM for data science: strengths, weaknesses and potential next steps. In *2021 IEEE International Conference on Big Data (Big Data)*, pages 2337–2344. IEEE.

Saltz, J. S. et al. (2016). Big data team process methodologies: A literature review and the identification of key factors for a project's success. In *2016 IEEE International Conference on Big Data (Big Data)*, pages 2872–2879. IEEE.

Saltz, J. S. et al. (2022). Current approaches for executing big data science projects—a systematic literature review. *PeerJ Computer Science*, 8:e862.

Schmelczer, A. et al. (2023). Trustworthy and robust AI deployment by design: A framework to inject best practice support into AI deployment pipelines. In *2023 IEEE/ACM 2nd International Conference on AI Engineering–Software Engineering for AI (CAIN)*, pages 127–138. IEEE.

Schmid, A. et al. (2023). The importance of an ethical framework for trust calibration in AI. *IEEE Intelligent Systems*.

Schröer, C. et al. (2021). A systematic literature review on applying CRISP-DM process model. *Procedia Computer Science*, 181:526–534.

Sekiguchi, K. et al. (2020). Organic and dynamic tool for use with knowledge base of AI ethics for promoting engineers' practice of ethical AI design. *AI & Society*, 35(1):51–71.

Sharma, V. et al. (2023). Framework for evaluating ethics in AI. In *2023 International Conference on Innovative Data Communication Technologies and Application (ICIDCA)*, pages 307–312. IEEE.

Shearer, C. (2000). The CRISP-DM model: the new blueprint for data mining. *Journal of data warehousing*, 5(4):13–22.

Singh, A. M. et al. (2023). Wasabi: A conceptual model for trustworthy artificial intelligence. *Computer*, 56(2):20–28.

Steinhoff, J. (2023). AI ethics as subordinated innovation network. *AI & Society*, pages 1–13.

Stix, C. (2021). Actionable principles for artificial intelligence policy: three pathways. *Science and Engineering Ethics*, 27(1):15.

Thiebes, S. et al. (2021). Trustworthy artificial intelligence. *Electronic Markets*, 31:447–464.

Whittlestone, J. et al. (2019). The role and limits of principles in AI ethics: Towards a focus on tensions. In *Proceedings of the 2019 AAAI/ACM Conference on AI, Ethics, and Society*, pages 195–200.

Wickramasinghe, C. S. et al. (2020). Trustworthy AI development guidelines for human system interaction. In *2020 13th International Conference on Human System Interaction (HSI)*, pages 130–136. IEEE.

Wiener, N. (1950). *The human use of human beings: Cybernetics and society*. The riverside press, Cambridge, Massachusetts.

Wu, W. et al. (2020). Ethical principles and governance technology development of AI in china. *Engineering*, 6(3):302–309.

Xiaomei, S. et al. (2023). Research on trustworthiness analysis technology of artificial intelligence software. In *2023 IEEE International Conference on Control, Electronics and Computer Technology (ICCECT)*, pages 802–806. IEEE.

Xue, L. et al. (2022). Ethical governance of artificial intelligence: An integrated analytical framework. *Journal of Digital Economy*, 1(1):44–52.

Zhang, J. et al. (2023). Fairness in design: A framework for facilitating ethical artificial intelligence designs. *International Journal of Crowd Science*, 7(1):32–39.

Zhang, T. et al. (2021). Trusted artificial intelligence: technique requirements and best practices. In *2021 International Conference on Cyberworlds (CW)*, pages 303–306. IEEE.

Zhou, J. et al. (2020). A survey on ethical principles of AI and implementations. In *2020 IEEE Symposium Series on Computational Intelligence (SSCI)*, pages 3010–3017. IEEE.

Hacia el desarrollo de un modelo adaptativo para gestionar la deuda social en entornos de desarrollo de software ágil distribuido

Eydy del C. Suarez Brieva[1]

[1]Universidad Popular del Cesar
80, Valledupar – Cesar- Colombia

eydysuarez@unicesar.edu.co

Abstract. *The misalignment of socio-technical congruence in software development teams—understood as the disconnect between social and technical factors—can lead to suboptimal decisions and unforeseen costs, giving rise to the concept of social debt. Through a systematic literature review, various solutions for detecting social debt have been identified; however, these approaches operate in isolation. Therefore, this study proposes the development of an adaptive model to manage social debt in distributed agile teams, integrating its causes, effects, and mitigation strategies. The model is grounded in an Action Research approach structured into four iterative cycles.*

Resumen. *La desalineación de la congruencia sociotécnica en equipos de desarrollo de software, entendida como la desarticulación entre factores sociales y técnicos, puede generar decisiones subóptimas que conllevan a costos imprevistos dando origen al concepto de deuda social. Mediante una revisión sistemática de la literatura, se identificaron soluciones para detectar la deuda social; sin embargo, estas propuestas operan de forma independiente. Por ello, se propone el desarrollo de un modelo adaptativo para gestionarla en equipos ágiles distribuidos, integrando causas, efectos y estrategias. El modelo se sustenta en un enfoque de Investigación-Acción estructurado en cuatro ciclos.*

1. Introducción

La Ingeniería de Software es una disciplina centrada en actividades realizadas mayormente por personas [Pantaleo and Rinaudo, 2015]. Sin embargo, la IA generativa ha cobrado importancia al automatizar tareas como la escritura de código, la simulación de escenarios complejos y la detección y corrección de errores, lo que mejora la productividad y reduce los tiempos de respuesta [Terragni *et al.*, 2025]. Tradicionalmente, estas tareas eran ejecutadas por grupos organizados de trabajo especializado y a pesar del surgimiento de la IA generativa y de sus beneficios, el factor humano en el desarrollo de software sigue siendo esencial en la planificación, asignación de recursos y consideraciones *éticas y sociales* en los proyectos de software. El desarrollo de software requiere profesionales con habilidades sociales y técnicas, capaces de compartir conocimiento, implementar buenas prácticas, definir roles y responsabilidades, y fomentar la transparencia en su trabajo. Aunque la IA generativa mejora la eficiencia de los equipos, no reemplazará por completo el talento humano, ya que ciertas actividades requieren pensamiento lógico complejo, creatividad en el diseño de software, interacción con clientes para comprender sus necesidades, resolución de problemas imprevistos y consideraciones éticas y regulatorias [de Campos *et al*., 2024]. Además, la supervisión humana sigue siendo clave para mitigar sesgos en el desarrollo de software.

Cabe destacar que el Reporte del Estado de la Agilidad 2023 [State of Agile, 2023] destaca el crecimiento del trabajo remoto, impulsado por el Desarrollo Global de Software (DGS), este modelo plantea desafíos en la comunicación y colaboración entre equipos distribuidos. Factores como la diferencia horaria, el idioma y las costumbres pueden dificultar la coordinación en comparación con equipos co-localizados [García *et al*., 2022]. Para enfrentar estos retos, las empresas deben garantizar una comunicación efectiva entre sus miembros. En consecuencia, una comunicación, coordinación o cooperación deficiente y la desalineación de los factores sociales y técnicos entre los miembros del equipo, puede generar "costos adicionales en el estado del proyecto, originado por decisiones sociotécnicas subóptimas", lo cual da lugar a la deuda social en adelante DS [Tamburri *et al.* 2013]. La DS debe ser supervisada y mitigada oportunamente, ya que su prolongación puede afectar significativamente la eficiencia y productividad del equipo. Ignorar su importancia puede desencadenar en conflictos personales e interpersonales, barreras lingüísticas, culturales, desconfianza, irritabilidad, así como dificultades en la toma de decisiones, lo que impacta directamente en el bienestar emocional y social de los miembros del equipo [Lambiase, 2024]. Es de anotar, que la DS también se manifiesta en problemas técnicos visibles en artefactos de software, como documentación incomprensible y componentes de software incompletos [Caballero-Espinosa *et al*., 2023]. Además, la automatización impulsada por la IA generativa podría reducir la interacción y el rol de los desarrolladores, afectando su motivación y aumentando la incertidumbre laboral.

Considerando lo expuesto anteriormente, se realizó una Revisión Sistemática de la Literatura (RSL) para analizar las causas, efectos y estrategias de prevención de la DS en equipos ágiles distribuidos. A partir del análisis de los 47 artículos primarios, se identificaron herramientas, modelos y métricas; sin embargo, ninguna de las propuestas ofrece una solución integral que combine la identificación de la DS con estrategias específicas para su mitigación. Teniendo en cuenta esta brecha, se propone el desarrollo de un modelo adaptativo para gestionar la DS en equipos de desarrollo de software ágil distribuido. Para ello, se incorpora una ontología que representa formalmente el conocimiento asociado a la DS, esta permite estructurar, conceptualizar y relacionar de manera explícita los elementos como causas, efectos, riesgos, métricas y estrategias de mitigación. Al proporcionar una representación semántica, la ontología se convierte en un componente esencial del modelo adaptativo, ya que facilita la integración y análisis de datos mediante técnicas de analítica de datos. De este modo, la ontología no solo mejora la capacidad de detección y comprensión de la DS, sino que también permite la adaptación de estrategias de intervención personalizadas ajustadas al contexto especifico de cada equipo ágil.

Además de la introducción presentada, esta propuesta se divide en 8 secciones. La Sección 2 expone los objetivos de investigación. La Sección 3 presenta un resumen del conocimiento actual del dominio del problema. En la Sección 4 se presenta la metodología de investigación. La Sección 5 solución propuesta y resultados. La Sección 6 aborda la descripción de las actividades pendientes. La Sección 7 ilustra implicaciones y en la Sección 8 las referencias bibliográficas.

2. Objetivos del proyecto de investigación

A continuación, se presenta el objetivo general y los objetivos específicos definidos para la investigación.

2.1. Objetivo General

Construir un modelo adaptativo como apoyo a la gestión de la deuda social en equipos de desarrollo de software ágil distribuido.

2.2. Objetivos específicos

OE1. Caracterizar los elementos fundamentales que contribuyen a la deuda social en equipos de desarrollo de software ágil mediante el análisis de la literatura existente, con el fin de clarificar los conceptos, factores, métodos y relaciones que inciden en su manifestación y gestión.

OE2. Desarrollar una ontología de dominio específico con el propósito de organizar y utilizar el conocimiento relacionado con la gestión de la deuda social en equipos de desarrollo de software ágil distribuido, haciendo uso de los términos y relaciones identificadas en el OE1.

OE3. Construir un modelo adaptativo para identificar las causas y efectos que genera la DS en equipos de desarrollo de software ágil distribuido y, con base en los efectos detectados, establecer estrategias de mitigación para su gestión. Este modelo analizará en tiempo real la acumulación de deuda social, ajustando dinámicamente sus estrategias según el contexto organizacional. Se fundamentará en el análisis de literatura (OE1) y la creación de una ontología (OE2).

OE4. Evaluar el modelo adaptativo de gestión propuesto en el OE3 mediante la validación de juicio de expertos, que permita identificar áreas de mejora y proponer acciones correctivas en el modelo propuesto.

3. Resumen del conocimiento actual del dominio del problema

La DS se define como un "costo adicional en el estado del proyecto, derivado de decisiones sociotécnicas subóptimas, que resultan de la ruptura de la congruencia sociotécnica (STC)" [Tamburri *et al*., 2015]. La falta de identificación, evaluación y adopción de medidas para controlar o minimizar los costos generados por la DS, puede afectar negativamente el bienestar mental y emocional de los trabajadores [Saeeda *et al*., 2024], dando origen a lo que en el entorno laboral se conoce como: factores de riesgo psicosocial. Según la [Organización Internacional del Trabajo, 2013], estos riesgos surgen de "las interacciones entre el trabajo, su entorno, la satisfacción laboral y las condiciones organizativas", además de factores como las "capacidades del trabajador, necesidades, cultura y situación personal, que pueden influir en su salud, rendimiento y satisfacción laboral".

Desde esta perspectiva, la DS se refiere a la ausencia de acciones y servicios que afectan el bienestar de los equipos, sea co-localizados o distribuidos. A partir de la RSL, se identificó herramientas para prevenir y gestionar la DS, se destacó la importancia del seguimiento periódico a las interacciones humanas y al desarrollo de habilidades blandas y técnicas de los individuos. Se definieron 2 ejes de estudio: (i) tipos de solución, que incluyen: (a) (14) modelos conceptuales y estadísticos [Yilmaz, O'Connor, and Clarke 2016], [Anwar *et al*., 2019], (b) (3) marco de trabajo [Catolino *et al*., 2021], (c) (3) herramientas automatizadas, (d) (4) modelos predictivos [Almarimi *et al*., 2022) y (e) (2) otros modelos [Khan *et al.*, 2019], y (ii) las categorías de análisis abarcan: (a) (11) métricas para determinar la DS, (b) (9) causas de la DS, (c) (2) efectos de la DS y (d) (6) gestión de la DS. Se puede señalar que predomina el uso de modelos conceptuales y estadísticos, evidenciando un enfoque basado en métricas para detectar la DS en equipos de desarrollo de software ágil distribuido.

4. Esbozo de la metodología de investigación

Para esta propuesta, se adopta la metodología Investigación-Acción, debido a su enfoque práctico y participativo, lo que permite ajustar y refinar el *modelo adaptativo* en función de la problemática planteada. Esta metodología consta de cuatro ciclos, con una duración total de *54 meses*, cada uno guiado por las etapas de *planeación, ejecución, desarrollo y reflexión*, como se ilustra en la Figura 1. Cada ciclo, contempla actividades específicas, seguidas de una evaluación para identificar áreas de mejora y optimizar el modelo. Estas actividades se desarrollarán de la siguiente manera: (i) primer ciclo (20 meses), Se realizará la RSL y, posteriormente, se llevará a cabo la caracterización de la información a partir de los estudios primarios, (ii) segundo ciclo (12 meses), se elaborará una *ontología de dominio específico*, denominada OntoSocialDebt, para gestionar el conocimiento sobre la deuda social, (iii) tercer ciclo (14 meses), se construirá el *modelo adaptativo V 1.0* y (iv) cuarto ciclo (8 meses), se realizará una validación por juicio de expertos. A continuación, se presenta un resumen de las actividades de investigación realizadas.

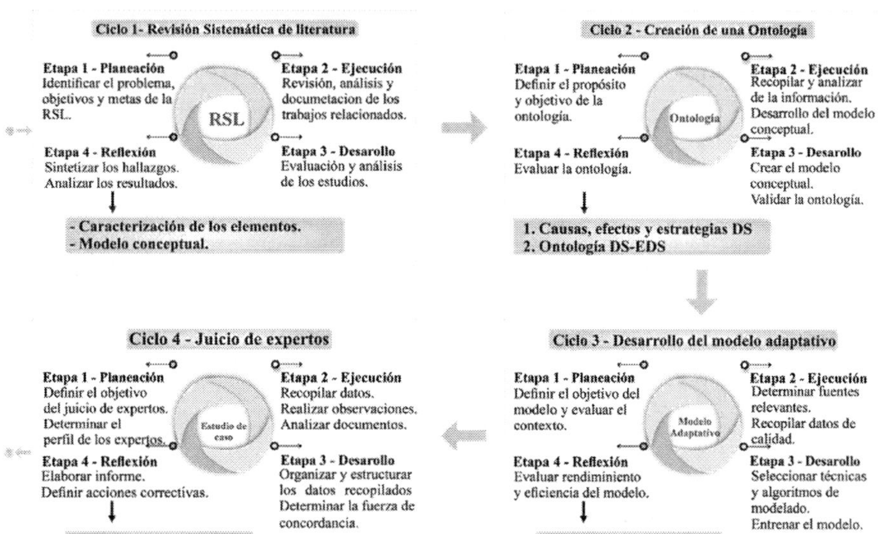

Figura 1. Proceso metodología Investigación – Acción

En el primer ciclo, se desarrolló la caracterización de los elementos mediante una RSL, identificando 47 artículos publicados entre 2013 y 2024. Estos abordan las causas que generan la deuda social y su relación con deficiencias en factores como la comunicación, coordinación y colaboración. Asimismo, se analizaron factores que contribuyen a la acumulación de la DS y estrategias para mitigar sus efectos. Además, se profundizó en categorías clave relacionadas con el fenómeno de la deuda social, abordando aspectos como causas, métricas para su identificación, efectos generados, estrategias de mitigación y enfoques para su gestión. Por otro lado, se identificaron iniciativas de solución, que centraron en determinar la presencia de cuatro olores comunitarios: silo organizacional, nube negra, cuello de botella y lobo solitario. A continuación, se presentan los objetivos de búsqueda y preguntas de investigación definidas para la realización de la RSL.

Objetivos de búsqueda:

OB1. Categorizar los estudios e investigaciones teniendo en cuenta criterios demográficos, con el propósito de evaluar el interés científico de la comunidad académica con relación al tema de DS, causas, efectos y procedimientos empleados para mitigar y controlar su presencia en el contexto de desarrollo ágil de software.

OB2. Analizar la diversidad de estudios identificados y relacionados con el tema DS, basándose en el esquema de clasificación propuesto por [Wieringa *et al*., 2006] mediante la definición de criterios de calidad, seleccionar los artículos primarios teniendo en cuenta factores como claridad, suficiencia, relevancia y contribución investigativa.

OB3. Recopilar información actualizada, relevante y validada sobre el tema en estudio. Este proceso permitirá identificar las tendencias actuales, así como anticipar retos y desafíos futuros relacionados con la DS en el contexto de desarrollo ágil de software.

Preguntas de investigación:

RQ1. ¿Cuáles son los tipos de investigación identificados y las contribuciones reportadas sobre la DS en el contexto de desarrollo de software ágil distribuido?

RQ2. ¿Cuáles son los dominios en los que se puede generar e impactar la DS en el contexto de desarrollo de software ágil distribuido?

RQ3. ¿Existe algún tipo o propuesta de solución definida para prevenir, identificar y gestionar la DS en equipos de desarrollo de software ágil distribuido?

RQ4. ¿Cuáles son las características de las empresas en las cuales se han realizado estudios para determinar la DS en equipos de desarrollo de software ágil distribuido?

RQ5. ¿Qué patrones permiten identificar y gestionar la DS en equipos de desarrollo de software ágil distribuido?

RQ6. ¿Cuáles son los desafíos y/o trabajos futuros identificados que contribuyen a determinar la deuda social en equipos de desarrollo de software ágil distribuido?

En el segundo ciclo, se definió el propósito y alcance de la ontología para identificar y gestionar la DS en equipos de desarrollo de software. Se clasificaron sus causas según factores sociales, culturales, organizacionales, individuales y de equipo, permitiendo analizar su origen, efectos negativos y su impacto en la productividad, calidad técnica, gestión de proyectos y cultura organizacional. Además, se avanzó en el diseño preliminar de la ontología, formulando preguntas de competencia. La evaluación de la ontología, realizada en cada fase, busca identificar errores, garantizar la calidad del diseño y documentar el progreso. Es de anotar que, para los ciclos 3 y 4, aún no se ha avanzado en el desarrollo de las actividades. Por lo tanto, estas serán relacionadas en la Sección 6. Declaración de las actividades pendientes.

5. Introducción de la solución propuesta y resultados obtenidos

El análisis realizado evidencia la existencia de herramientas para detectar la DS mediante la identificación de causas, tales como: *silo organizacional*, *lobo solitario*, *cuello de botella* y *nube negra* [Caballero-Espinosa *et al*., 2023]. Sin embargo, aún es necesario explorar nuevas causas que puedan impactar el bienestar social de los miembros del equipo y la empresa, y que aún no estén incluidos en estas herramientas. Si bien existen múltiples métricas para evaluar la comunicación, colaboración y coordinación en equipos de desarrollo de software, la literatura revisada sugiere la necesidad de definir y profundizar en nuevas métricas que permitan determinar con mayor precisión la presencia de DS en equipos de desarrollo de software ágil distribuidos geográficamente [Ahmad 2023], [Dreesen *et al.*, 2021]. Además, se destaca la importancia de implementar estrategias efectivas de mitigación, considerando intervenciones culturales, organizacionales y técnicas para reducir su impacto. Es importante destacar que todas estas soluciones operan de manera independiente, y hasta el desarrollo de esta propuesta, no se evidencia en la literatura un modelo adaptativo que integre de manera sistemática la identificación y gestión de la DS [Palomba *et al.*, 2021], [Tamburri *et al.*, 2019] . Por ello, se plantea el desarrollo de un modelo adaptativo o herramienta automatizada que apoye a las empresas en la gestión la DS, recopilando datos sobre sus causas subyacentes y permitiendo la identificación de áreas críticas que requieren intervención. Con base en los datos recopilados, el modelo facilitará la implementación de acciones y estrategias personalizadas para abordar los problemas de la DS en equipos de desarrollo de software, mejorando la productividad de los miembros del equipo, la eficiencia y calidad del software. Dado que la dinámica de los equipos es cambiante, el modelo debe ser un proceso continuo y adaptable a las necesidades emergentes del entorno.

6. Declaración de las actividades pendientes

Para el desarrollo final de esta propuesta está pendiente el desarrollo de las siguientes actividades.

Ciclo 2 – Construcción de la ontología: Se desarrollará siguiendo la metodología REFSENO , estructurada en 6 etapas de las cuales están pendientes: (i) reutilización de ontologías y metadatos, se aprovechará la información disponible en la web para extraer conocimientos relevantes; (ii) elaboración del modelo conceptual, creación de un glosario de términos, identificación y jerarquización de clases y definición de atributos y relaciones; (iii) implementación: selección de la herramienta para el desarrollo de la ontología, (iv) evaluación: validación con la metodología FOCA para identificar errores y documentar el progreso en cada fase y (v) con base en los resultados de la evaluación, se realizan los ajustes pertinentes a la ontología, con el fin de mejorar su precisión, coherencia y capacidad de representación del dominio.

Ciclo 3- Construcción del Modelo adaptativo: las actividades pendientes incluyen: (i) definición del modelo, detallará los métodos y estrategias para la identificación y gestión de la DS, (ii) diseño del modelo, establecerá los métodos para la recolección y limpieza de los datos, (iii) desarrollo del modelo, se seleccionarán los algoritmos, técnicas de modelado y datos más adecuados para su entrenamiento y (iv) evaluación del modelo, abordará su aplicación en un contexto real para determinar su eficacia en la resolución del problema.

Ciclo 4- Validación juicio de expertos: se definirán objetivos, se seleccionarán expertos según su experiencia, y se precisará el problema a abordar. Se prepararán materiales, se diseñará un instrumento de evaluación considerando eficiencia, eficacia, rendimiento y usabilidad, y se definirán unidades de análisis de la DS. Posteriormente, se socializará el cuestionario, se recopilarán datos y se aplicarán las mejoras sugeridas

7. Implicaciones esperadas

- La RSL evidencia un creciente interés en la investigación sobre la DS, pero persisten vacíos en su comprensión y gestión. Se requiere profundizar en la identificación de decisiones subóptimas, sus criterios de evaluación, actores involucrados y métricas de impacto. Además, es crucial desarrollar mecanismos de seguimiento y mitigación para evitar su acumulación.

- El modelo adaptativo mejorará la gestión de la DS en equipos de desarrollo de software ágil distribuido, ayudando a reducir su impacto negativo en la productividad, motivación y colaboración. Asimismo, proporcionará acciones adaptables al contexto organizacional, facilitará la identificación temprana de los factores que generan la DS y permitirá mitigar sus efectos antes que afecten el desempeño y la calidad del software. Además, fomentará un entorno colaborativo y saludable, y mediante métricas e indicadores evaluar su estado y evolución a lo largo del tiempo.
- Fortalecimiento de la cultura organizacional enfocándose en el bienestar físico, social y emocional de los miembros del equipo de desarrollo de software ágil.

8. Referencias

Almarimi, Nuri, Ali Ouni, Moataz Chouchen, and Mohamed Wiem Mkaouer. 2022. 'Improving the Detection of Community Smells through Socio-technical and Sentiment Analysis'. *Journal of Software: Evolution and Process* 35. doi: 10.1002/smr.2505.

Anwar, Rayhab, Mobashar Rehman, Khor Siak Wang, Manzoor Ahmed Hashmani, and Amjad Shamim. 2019. 'Investigation of Knowledge Sharing Behavior in Global Software Development Organizations Using Social Cognitive Theory'. *IEEE Access* 7:71286–98. doi: 10.1109/ACCESS.2019.2912657.

Caballero-Espinosa, Eduardo, Jeffrey C. Carver, and Kimberly Stowers. 2023. 'Community Smells—The Sources of Social Debt: A Systematic Literature Review'. *Information and Software Technology* 153. doi: 10.1016/J.INFSOF.2022.107078.

de Campos, Aline, Jorge Melegati, Nicolas Nascimento, Rafael Chanin, Afonso Sales, and Igor Wiese. 2024. 'Some Things Never Change: How Far Generative AI Can Really Change Software Engineering Practice'.

Catolino, Gemma, Fabio Palomba, Damian A. Tamburri, and Alexander Serebrenik. 2021. 'Understanding Community Smells Variability: A Statistical Approach'. *Proceedings - International Conference on Software Engineering* 2021-May:77–86. doi: 10.1109/ICSE-SEIS52602.2021.00017.

Dreesen, Tim, Phil Hennel, Christoph Rosenkranz, and Thomas Kude. 2021. 'The Second Vice Is Lying, the First Is Running into Debt. Antecedents and Mitigating Practices of Social Debt: An Exploratory Study in Distributed Software Development Teams'. *Proceedings of the Annual Hawaii International Conference on System Sciences* 2020-Janua:6826–35. doi: 10.24251/hicss.2021.818.

García, German David, Cesar Jesus Pardo Calvache, and Francisco Javier Alvárez Rodríguez. 2022. 'Society 5.0 and Soft Skills in Agile Global Software Development'. *Revista Iberoamericana de Tecnologías Del Aprendizaje* 17(2):197–207. doi: 10.1109/RITA.2022.3166966.

Khan, Rafiq Ahmad, Mohd Yazid Idris, Siffat Ullah Khan, Muhammad Ilyas, Sikandar Ali, Aziz Ud Din, Ghulam Murtaza, Abdul Wahid Khan, and Saeed Ullah Jan. 2019. 'An Evaluation Framework for Communication and Coordination Processes in Offshore Software Development Outsourcing Relationship: Using Fuzzy Methods'. *IEEE Access* 7:112879–906. doi: 10.1109/ACCESS.2019.2924404.

Lambiase, Stefano. 2024. 'Cultural and Socio-Technical Aspects in Software Development'. Pp. 482–87 in *ACM International Conference Proceeding Series*. Association for Computing Machinery.

Lambiase, Stefano, Gemma Catolino, Damian A. Tamburri, Alexander Serebrenik, Fabio Palomba, and Filomena Ferrucci. 2022. 'Good Fences Make Good Neighbours?' Pp. 67–78 in. Association for Computing Machinery (ACM).

Organización Internacional del Trabajo. 2013. *La Organización Del Trabajo y Los Riesgos Psicosociales: Una Mirada de Género*. San José.

Palomba, Fabio, Damian Andrew Tamburri, Francesca Arcelli Fontana, Rocco Oliveto, Andy Zaidman, and Alexander Serebrenik. 2021. 'Beyond Technical Aspects: How Do Community Smells Influence the Intensity of Code Smells?' *IEEE Transactions on Software Engineering* 47(1):108–29. doi: 10.1109/TSE.2018.2883603.

Pantaleo, Guillermo., and Ludmila Rinaudo. 2015. *Ingeniería de Software*. 1st ed. edited by Alfaomega. Ciudad Autónoma de Buenos Aires: Alfaomega Grupo Editor Argentino.

Saeeda, Hina, Muhammad Ovais Ahamd, and Tomas Gustavsson. 2024. 'A Multivocal Literature Review on Non-Technical Debt in Software Development: An Insight into Process, Social, People, Organizational, and Culture Debt'. *E-Informatica Software Engineering Journal* 18(1):240101. doi: 10.37190/e-inf240101.

State of Agile. 2023. *The 17th State of Agile Report 17th State of Agile*. Raleigh, NC.

Tamburri, Damian A., Philippe Kruchten, Patricia Lago, and Hans Van Vliet. 2013. 'What Is Social Debt in Software Engineering?' Pp. 93–96 in *2013 6th International Workshop on Cooperative and Human Aspects of Software Engineering, CHASE 2013 - Proceedings*.

Tamburri, Damian A., Philippe Kruchten, Patricia Lago, and Hans van Vliet. 2015. 'Social Debt in Software Engineering: Insights from Industry'. *Journal of Internet Services and Applications* 6(1). doi: 10.1186/s13174-015-0024-6.

Tamburri, Damian A., Fabio Palomba, Alexander Serebrenik, and Andy Zaidman. 2019. 'Discovering Community Patterns in Open-Source: A Systematic Approach and Its Evaluation'. *Empirical Software Engineering* 24(3):1369–1417. doi: 10.1007/s10664-018-9659-9.

Terragni, Valerio, Annie Vella, Partha Roop, and Kelly Blincoe. 2025. 'The Future of AI-Driven Software Engineering'. *ACM Transactions on Software Engineering and Methodology*. doi: 10.1145/3715003.

Wieringa, Roel, Neil Maiden, Nancy Mead, and Colette Rolland. 2006. 'Requirements Engineering Paper Classification and Evaluation Criteria: A Proposal and a Discussion'. *Requirements Engineering* 11(1):102–7. doi: 10.1007/s00766-005-0021-6.

Yilmaz, Murat, Rory V. O'Connor, and Paul Clarke. 2016. 'Effective Social Productivity Measurements during Software Development - An Empirical Study'. *International Journal of Software Engineering and Knowledge Engineering* 26(3):457–90. doi: 10.1142/S0218194016500194.

IoT Security Evaluation: A Set of Combined Strategies of Inspection, Testing, and Experimentation

Bruno Pedraça de Souza

PESC/COPPE – Universidade Federal do Rio de Janeiro (UFRJ)

bpsouza@cos.ufrj.br

Abstract. *IoT software systems research has significantly expanded recently, particularly with AI technologies' emergence and widespread adoption. Given their critical nature of continuous connectivity, such systems demand robust security measures. Therefore, it is fundamental to apply technologies that support their quality assurance (QA), specifically security. This thesis proposes strategies combining quality assurance technologies (software inspection, testing, and continuous experimentation) to enhance the final quality of these systems.*

1. Research Context and Problem

Over the past decade, IoT-based systems have grown in popularity, especially with the advancement of Artificial Intelligence (AI) technologies, cost reduction of devices and sensors, and sustainability. IoT generally integrates with other software systems, devices, sensors, middleware, and actuators to perceive, receive, and send environmental data (Motta et al., 2018). As with any paradigm shift, the emergence of IoT software systems brings challenges in their development, deployment, and ongoing evaluation, such as ensuring and addressing security concerns (Motta et al., 2019a).

Security[1] is one of the most important quality requirements. Issues related to security have often been a challenge for the software engineering community, for instance, cyber-attacks, and system code vulnerabilities. In IoT software systems, security challenges are even more critical and difficult as new attack surfaces emerge, such as device vulnerabilities, IoT Botnets, social engineering, etc (Pessoa and Travassos., 2024). To deal with these issues, quality assurance (QA) techniques, such as software inspection, testing, and continuous experimentation (CE), play an essential role and can be used to mitigate them.

Software inspection, testing techniques, and CE are typically applied sequentially throughout the development lifecycle. Inspections focus on identifying defects within software artifacts, like requirements and code, without needing an executable system. Conversely, testing involves executing the software to reveal failures in its behavior. Both software inspection and testing evaluate requirements. CE is a method for conducting experiments in many iterations to evaluate and evolve conjectural requirements of the software systems according to the final user's feedback (Auer and Felderer, 2018). A conjectural requirement is a 'possible requirement' with some level of uncertainty and must be experienced through an experimental study. Once

---

[1] We follow ISO definition regarding security: "*the degree to which a product or system protects information and data so that persons or other products or systems have the degree of data access appropriate to their types and levels of authorization*."

evaluated, the conjectural requirement is implemented as a real system (or feature) requirement or discarded.

To better illustrate some IoT security issues that QA techniques and CE can assess, I will use a real example in a research project case. The problem is secure communication channels[2] that must be implemented in an IoT software system. It was necessary to ensure the communication channel was secure when exchanging data between things (devices) and software systems. To achieve this, a viable solution would be to implement an encryption solution. It is worth highlighting that the software in the system had low-cost devices, so choosing the 'best' encryption algorithm would not be feasible. A brief example is described below.

> *The security requirement specified for the project context was: The software system must use DES[3] algorithms. Such a requirement demonstrates that it was not clear enough for the development team to implement, thus requiring a requirements inspection step. Thus, the security requirement specified was verified by software inspection and corrected. The corrected requirement is that the software system must use a cryptography component to process data received/sent from/to systems and devices (De Paiva et al., 2023). Once this requirement was corrected and implemented, it was possible to describe the test cases for the testing. However, our development team has encountered another issue, which DES algorithm to use? So, after identifying some algorithms, the development team chose SPECK. SPECK was chosen because it was proposed to be used in low-power computing devices, such as sensor networks, including IoT devices (De Paiva et al., 2023).*
>
> *Thus, our team did not know the impact of incorporating SPECK into the software system. This issue was difficult to evaluate since the development team must consider the software and hardware characteristics. One possible solution was CE since the development team could have different software versions using different encryption algorithm solutions. So, De Souza et al. (2023b) applied CE to evaluate the solution of the secure communication channel and choose the best way to implement the cryptography algorithm and how it would impact the software system's performance. As their results, the authors infer that CE can be useful to evaluate some security issues.*

It is well-known that software inspection, testing techniques, and CE are useful when used correctly, although they have limitations. In this Doctoral Symposium paper, I discuss how using software inspection, testing, and CE combined can be more effective in enhancing the quality of IoT software systems.

This thesis proposes a set of strategies to evaluate the security of software systems. Figure 1 shows an extract of two combinations. The current version of the strategies is composed of seven strategies. Each strategy must be applied individually. Furthermore, each of these processes is used in a specific development context. Section 4 introduces an excerpt of the proposal.

---

[2] A secure communication channel is defined as transmitting data between two or more parties that protect the confidentiality, integrity, and authenticity of the information exchanged.

[3] DES means Data encryption standard.

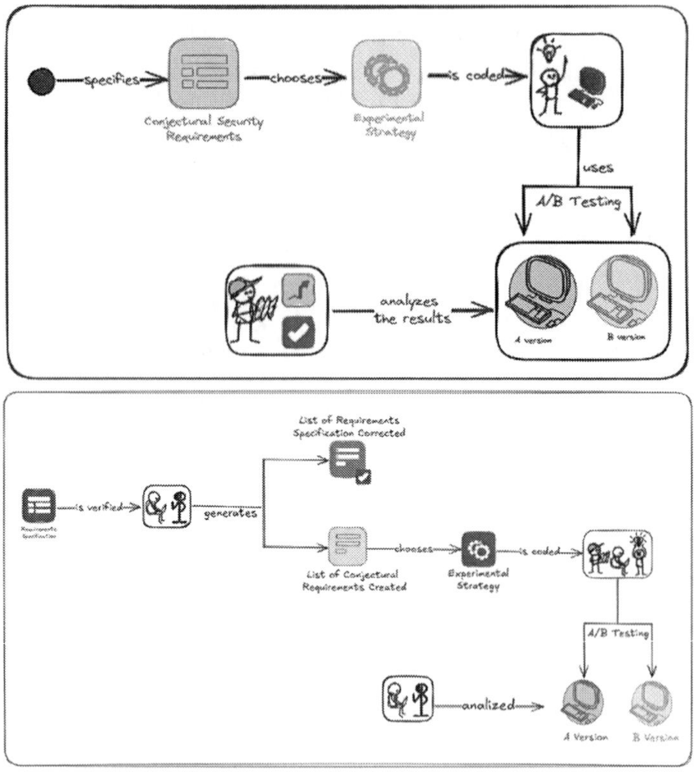

Figure 1. Set of the Combination of QA techniques and CE to evaluate security.

2. Research Goals and Questions

For this thesis proposal, I present the main research question (RQ) guiding this proposal: "*Does the combination of software inspection, testing techniques, and continuous experimentation increase confidence in the systems' quality regarding evaluating security requirements in IoT software systems?*" This research question was split into the following secondary questions:

RQ1: *What are the available security requirements issues in the technical literature concerning IoT software systems?* This research aims to identify and categorize the security problems prevalent in IoT software, as reported in the state of the art.

RQ2: *What can verification, validation, and continuous experimentation technologies be used separately to tackle security requirements issues in IoT software systems?* This research question aims to identify the main V&V for assessing the security requirements found in RQ1 in the technical literature. Furthermore, we strive to identify the strategies and processes used by CE.

RQ3: *How can verification, validation, and CE technologies be combined to address security requirements in IoT software projects?* The goal of this RQ3 is to figure out how verification, validation, and CE can be merged or used to ensure that security requirements are met according to the users' goals.

RQ4: *Would a computational infrastructure support the development team choose the most appropriate strategy to solve such security issues?* This research question aims to verify whether a computational tool helps the development team choose the proper set of verification, validation, and CE technologies to assess security requirements in IoT software systems.

RQ5: *Do the proposed strategies and their computational support tool present adequate results in the development team's respective uses?* This research question aims to evaluate their combination and computational support tools through experimental studies to acquire evidence of their usefulness, efficiency, and effectiveness[4].

Each RQ is associated with at least one sub-objective. Thus, this research aims to provide QA strategies that combine software inspection, software testing, and experimentation technologies to have (conjectural) security requirements implemented with high quality in IoT software systems. To do so, we split the general goal and better detail, it consists in conducting a series of experimental studies the following sub-objectives:

1. Identify and investigate the IoT security requirements available in technical literature through secondary studies.
2. Identify quality assurance technologies, such as software inspection, software testing, and CE, to evaluate IoT software systems' security.
3. Propose strategies to combine software inspection, testing, and experimentation to address the security requirements of IoT software systems.
4. Build and evaluate the feasibility of a computational infrastructure for supporting software practitioners to operationalize the combination of adequate software inspections, software testing, and experimentation technologies for IoT software systems.

Up to now, I have reached sub-objective 3, in which we proposed a set of strategies.

3. Research Methodology

A well-defined research method is necessary in any scientific work since its steps must be clearly defined and described. Thus, in this ongoing thesis proposal, we are conducting an evidence-based methodology (Mafra et al., 2006). It consists of conducting a series of experimental studies (primary and secondary) to mature the approach to be designed, engineered, and adopted by practitioners. Besides, this methodology has traditionally been used in research carried out by the Experimental Software Engineering (ESE) group at COPPE/UFRJ, and it is an extension of the method proposed by Shull et al. (2001), as presented in Figure 2.

[4] *Effectiveness*: number of security issues resolved by total number of issues identified.

Figure 2. Research methodology.

- *Literature Studies*: we have conducted two studies (Erthal et al., 2023; De Souza et al., 2023a) to observe the State of the Art of Continuous Experimentation in IoT Software Systems and Software Engineering.

- *Thesis Proposal*: this step aims to define initial strategies for evaluating security requirements and vulnerabilities using software inspection, testing, and CE in software development (Figure 1).

- *Set of Experimental Studies*: to validate the thesis proposal, it is intended to plan and execute primary studies regarding the proposed approach. The study follows Mafra's methodology (2006). So, four primary studies, from a feasibility study to a case study, are planned to evaluate and evolve the proposed strategies and software technology before transferring it to the industrial environment. Figure 3 shows the methodology applied in this step (to be carried out).

    - The feasibility study evaluates whether the proposed software technology achieves its goal of assessing security/vulnerability requirements using the selected approach.

    - The observational study aims to improve the proposed software technology to understand its application better. In general, it can allow its evolution to a second version (in progress).

    - Case studies 1 and 2 aim to verify whether the proposed strategy fits or can be used in industrial scenarios/development contexts.

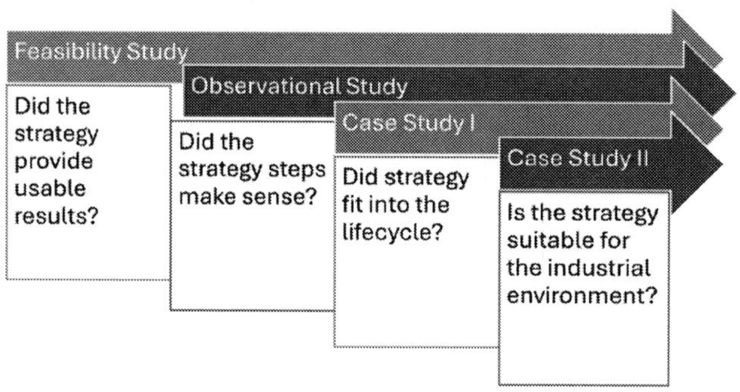

Figure 3. Steps to be executed in Experimental Studies.

4. IoT Security Evaluation: Towards Combined Strategies

This section presents an initial proposal to use and combine software inspection, software testing, and CE to support the quality of security requirements in the IoT context. These combinations can potentially strengthen IoT software security and guide the implementation and evaluation of security aspects throughout the development process.

Seven strategies were proposed for the evaluation of security aspects. Some of them are already known as inspection, testing, and CE. However, I proposed specific artifacts to support the security assessment of each technique. The strategies are:

The strategies can be used individually, as happens in traditional software development, i.e., they can only be used for inspection, tests, and experimentation. The choice of the most appropriate strategy will rely on the characteristics of the IoT software systems and their artifacts. Each strategy focuses on the security aspects of the IoT software system and comprises planning and execution. Next, I will present one strategy and its characteristics.

4.1 Evaluating Security Requirements and Conjectural Requirements Using Software Inspections and Experimentation

Experimentation and inspection together form one of the seven strategies. This strategy is initiated in the first phase of the development process, requirements specification, and is applied as the requirements documents are being defined. Initially, a checklist is used to verify the requirements artifacts, identifying defects and inconsistencies. Once these documents have been inspected, any detected defects must be corrected. These defects can be identified by applying a specific checklist (Figure 4a). CE is closely linked to inspection, requiring a thorough understanding of the system requirements. This knowledge is essential for distinguishing between system requirements and conjectural ones. As requirements inspection relies on the proposed checklist, experimentation utilizes a template to generate conjectural security requirements (Figure 4b).

Questions	
16	Are security requirements necessary?
17	Are highly complex passwords required, for example using a combination of numbers, characters and symbols (letters and special characters)?
18	Are passwords required to be updated every x days?
19	Are there ways described to protect delivered and received data from unauthorized people?
20	Are encrypted communication channels required?
21	Have authentication mechanisms been identified? Is it explained in the requirement document? For instance, two-factor authentication (2FA), or digital certificates.
22	Are requirements specified with sufficient information about security policies?
23	Is there a need to have backup policies?
24	Is communication among subsystems clearly defined?
25	Is it specified that only devices registered in the system send and receive data?
26	Are there requirements to finish the session if the maximum inactivity time is exceeded?
27	Have audit and continuous monitoring policies been described?
28	Are Virtual Private Networks (VPNs) necessary?

A

Conjectural Requirements (CRs)		
ID: CR [2]	CR: [Proposed]	Priority: [High]
Description of CRs	**The software system is expected to have** a secure communication channel. **So** encrypted communication. **However, we do not know:** 1. the impact of using encrypted communication channels on system performance. **The hypotheses are:** H0: There is no difference between SAFE IoT level of protection and performance when using or not using an encryption algorithm. H1: The SAFE IoT level of protection improves, and performance decreases when using an encryption algorithm. H2: The SAFE IoT level of protection improves, and performance does not decrease when using an encryption algorithm. H3: The SAFE IoT level of protection does not improve, and performance decreases when using an encryption algorithm.	
Metric Defined	The metrics used were the level of protection and time (in seconds) of sending messages to a broker.	
Experimental Method	We used A/B testing to evaluate this conjectural security requirement.	

B

Figure 4.A The checklist for evaluating security requirements. Figure 4.B The template for specifying and configuring CE.

The step of checking the requirement artifact is vital because it defines and divides the requirements into system and conjectural requirements. Then, the software engineer can differentiate what is a requirement and what is a conjectural requirement. A system will implement the conjectural requirements to determine whether they are required or not. Even if the system has not been implemented, planning an experimental study on the conjectural requirement is still possible. Figure 5 shows the flow of the strategy to be followed.

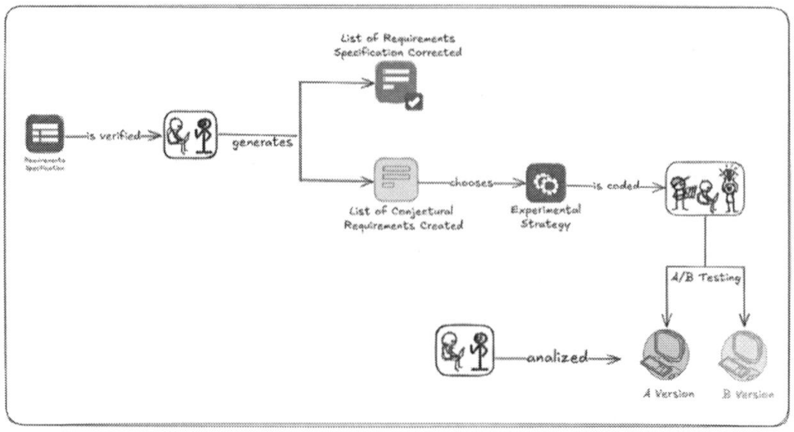

Figure 5. Strategy to assess security requirements using software inspection and conjectural security requirements using experimentation software.

The strategy's application scenario would be to apply the checklist to all requirements artifacts created. Then, we can list all requirements, specifically security, for which the development team is unsure about their implementation and verify their feasibility through CE. Finally, the development team corrects the system requirement artifacts and plans the conjectural requirements evaluations.

4. Preliminary Results and Ongoing Studies

Several results were obtained following the methodology steps (Section 3). Regarding the literature studies, organizing the body of knowledge on continuous experimentation in Software Engineering was possible. The first literature study aimed to characterize CE by examining its definitions, processes, and experimental strategies (Erthal et al., 2023). The second literature study explored works that applied CE to contemporary software systems (CSSs), highlighting the main challenges and opportunities of using CE in CSSs (Souza et al., 2023). These literature studies provided a foundation for this thesis. In alignment with these studies, IoT software projects were crucial in establishing combined strategies. I have successfully achieved sub-objective 3.

As for the next steps, I am evaluating the checklist proposed to verify if it is effective and efficient in detecting defects within the specified requirements for security. I am also planning experimental studies to evaluate each proposed strategy using cases. All artifacts, like the security checklist and the conjectural requirement template, must be evaluated. The strategy must be validated before implementing computational support. It is worth highlighting this research began in mid-2020 and is expected to be completed in the middle of 2026.

5. The Road Ahead

This research originated from an initial problem encountered in an IoT software project and was further shaped by two literature studies. The motivation behind this thesis proposal is the potential to combine software inspection, software testing, and continuous experimentation to assess the security aspects of IoT software systems while maintaining a high level of quality.

Security, a major concern for any software system, requires special attention and has been extensively studied over the last few years. However, final solutions are far from being provided. Therefore, creating means to facilitate the evaluation of this requirement is advantageous. Once the strategies are evaluated and validated, the aim is to transfer them to the industrial environment so that development teams can take a more evidence-based approach.

References

Auer, F., and Felderer, M. (2018) "Current state of research on continuous experimentation: a systematic mapping study." 44th Euromicro Conference on Software Engineering and Advanced Applications (SEAA), 2018, p. 335-344.

De Paiva, B.D., De Souza, B.P., and Travassos, G. H. (2023) "CryptoComponent: um Componente de Criptografia para Sistemas de Software IoT de Baixo Custo." In Anais Estendidos do XIV Congresso Brasileiro de Software: Teoria e Prática (pp. 90-99).

De Souza, B.P., de Paiva, B.D., and Travassos, G. H. (2023a) "Using Experimentation to Evaluate Security Requirements in IoT Software Systems." In 2023 Symposium on Internet of Things (SIoT) (pp. 1-5).

De Souza B.P., Santos P.S., and Travassos G.H. (2023b) "On Challenges and Opportunities of Using Continuous Experimentation in the Engineering of Contemporary Software Systems." In Proceedings of the XIX Brazilian Symposium on Information Systems 2023 May 29 (pp. 372-379).

Erthal, V.M., De Souza, B.P., dos Santos, P.S.M., and Travassos, G.H. (2023). "Characterization of continuous experimentation in software engineering: Expressions, models, and strategies." Science of Computer Programming, 229, 102961.

ISO/IEC 27000, 2018. Information technology — Security techniques — Information security management systems — Overview and vocabulary. https://standards.iso.org/ittf/PubliclyAvailableStandards/index.html.

Mafra, S.N., Barcelos, R.F., and Travassos, G. H. (2006) "Aplicando uma metodologia baseada em evidência na definição de novas tecnologias de software." In Anais do XX Simpósio Brasileiro de Engenharia de Software, 2006, p. 239-254. SBC.

Motta, R. C., DE Oliveira, K. M., Travassos, G. H. (2018) "On challenges in engineering IoT software systems," Proceedings of the XXXII Brazilian Symposium on Software Engineering, New York, NY, USA, ACM, 2018, p. 42–51. DOI: 10.1145/3266237.3266263.

Motta, R. C., Silva, V., Travassos, G. H. (2019) "Towards a more in-depth understanding of the IoT Paradigm and its challenges." JOURNAL OF SOFTWARE ENGINEERING RESEARCH AND DEVELOPMENT, v. 7, p. 1, 2019.

Las estrategias de retención de talento en la transformación digital y su impacto en la rotación de personal de tecnología

Eduardo Augusto Ferreira[1,2]

[1]Centro Federal de Educação Tecnológica Celso Suckow da Fonseca (CEFET/RJ)
Rio de Janeiro – RJ – Brasil

[2]Universidad de Ciencias Empresariales y Sociales (UCES)
Ciudad Autónoma de Buenos Aires – Argentina

eduardo.ferreira@cefet-rj.br

Abstract. *The turnover of personnel in the Information Technology (IT) sector is a key challenge in digital transformation. This doctoral work investigates the relationship between retention strategies and turnover reasons in IT companies in Brazil. The hypothesis suggests a significant relationship between these strategies and the professionals' decision to stay or leave. The methodology combines qualitative interviews and thematic analysis, along with a multi-agent system (MAS) simulation in GAMA to assess key factors in turnover. Preliminary findings show that, despite applied strategies, turnover remains a challenge, especially given high competitiveness and technological evolution. This study contributes to the development of more effective human resource management policies.*

Resumo. *La rotación de personal en el sector de Tecnología de la Información (TI) es un desafío clave en la transformación digital. Este trabajo doctoral investiga la relación entre estrategias de retención y motivos de rotación en empresas de TI en Brasil. La hipótesis plantea una relación significativa entre dichas estrategias y la permanencia o salida de los profesionales. La metodología combina entrevistas cualitativas y análisis temático, junto a una simulación de sistemas multiagente (SMA) en GAMA para evaluar factores clave en la rotación. Los hallazgos preliminares reflejan que, pese a las estrategias aplicadas, la rotación sigue siendo un reto, especialmente ante la alta competitividad y la evolución tecnológica. Este estudio contribuye al desarrollo de políticas de recursos humanos más eficaces.*

1. Introducción

La rotación de personal en el sector de tecnología de la información (TI) constituye un desafío estructural de alto impacto para las empresas brasileñas, especialmente en el contexto de la transformación digital. Esta investigación aborda dicho fenómeno entre 2017 y 2022 desde una perspectiva analítica y crítica, examinando sus causas, repercusiones y las estrategias de mitigación aplicadas. El estudio se inscribe en las dinámicas complejas del mercado laboral, marcadas por la expansión del trabajo remoto, la globalización de la oferta laboral y la creciente escasez de talento especializado, fenómenos acentuados por la crisis pandémica de COVID-19. En este contexto, el reporte [Brasscom 2023] informa que el sector brasileño de TI, con 2,02 millones de trabajadores (4 %) del empleo nacional), generó 117 mil nuevos puestos en 2022 y consolidó su liderazgo en América Latina con una participación del 36,4 %.

Esta investigación se articula en torno a tres interrogantes fundamentales: (C1) *¿Qué estrategias de retención implementan las empresas brasileñas para reducir la rotación de profesionales de TI?* (C2) *¿Cuáles son los principales factores que motivan la rotación en el sector de TI durante la transformación digital?* (C3) *¿Qué relación existe entre dichas estrategias y los motivos de rotación en el contexto de la transformación digital?*

La hipótesis formulada (H1) sostiene que *las estrategias de retención de talento adoptadas están determinadas por los factores que impulsan la rotación de personal en el sector de TI.*

Para abordar estos interrogantes, se adopta un diseño metodológico descriptivo y cualitativo. El proceso de recolección de datos contempla entrevistas semiestructuradas con profesionales de TI, seguidas de un análisis temático orientado a identificar patrones recurrentes y relaciones significativas en las narrativas obtenidas. Complementariamente, se desarrolla una simulación basada en sistemas multiagentes (SMA) mediante la plataforma GAMA [Drogoul et al. 2013], que modela las interacciones entre empleados y su entorno laboral, considerando factores como la satisfacción, el compromiso organizacional y las políticas de recursos humanos. Esta simulación permite evaluar el impacto dinámico de diversas estrategias de retención bajo múltiples escenarios, enriqueciendo así el análisis cualitativo con una perspectiva experimental y predictiva.

Por fin, este trabajo ofrece una aproximación integral al problema de la rotación en el sector de TI, contribuyendo al conocimiento científico sobre las estrategias de retención y su efectividad en un contexto marcado por la transformación digital.

2. Estado del Arte y Contexto Teórico

En este capítulo se exploran de forma ampliada los conceptos fundamentales y las teorías clave que respaldan esta investigación, proporcionando un marco teórico más detallado que contextualiza la rotación de personal en el sector de tecnología de la información (TI) y las estrategias de retención de talento. Esta revisión incorpora un análisis más profundo de las fuentes académicas y sus aportes al campo de estudio, destacando la evolución histórica de las teorías y su aplicación en el contexto contemporáneo.

2.1. Rotación de Personal: Conceptos y Causas

La rotación de personal, definida como el proceso de salida e incorporación de empleados, es un fenómeno complejo que impacta significativamente la gestión organizacional y la continuidad operativa [Chiavenato 2020]. Esta dinámica resulta de la interacción entre factores internos, como políticas salariales, clima laboral y estilos de liderazgo, y factores externos, como la coyuntura económica y la oferta laboral competitiva [Aranibar Gutiérrez et al. 2017]. En el ámbito de TI, la rotación es especialmente intensa debido a la constante demanda de habilidades actualizadas y a un mercado que valora la innovación y la adaptabilidad.

2.2. Teorías Clave sobre la Rotación de Personal

La literatura especializada ofrece un corpus teórico amplio para abordar la rotación. La Teoría del Equilibrio Organizacional [Porter et al. 1974]enfatiza la importancia del equilibrio entre el esfuerzo del trabajador y las recompensas recibidas. Otros autores [Aranibar Gutiérrez et al. 2017] sostienen que la rotación es un proceso multicausal influenciado por insatisfacciones acumulativas, expectativas no cumplidas y la percepción de oportunidades externas más atractivas. Esta visión es complementada por modelos como la Teoría del Desglose Laboral, que destaca las fases de evaluación interna antes de una decisión de salida.

2.3. Rotación en el Sector TI y Transformación Digital

En el sector TI, hay estudios [Frufrek and Pansanato 2017, Steil et al. 2022] que subrayan que la transformación digital ha reconfigurado las demandas laborales, intensificando la búsqueda de perfiles especializados y elevando la competencia por talento. En [et. al. 2019] comparan esta realidad con otras industrias en América Latina, concluyendo que el mercado brasileño enfrenta desafíos únicos debido a la escasez de profesionales calificados, lo que incrementa la volatilidad laboral.

2.4. Enfoque en Sistemas Multiagentes (SMA)

El enfoque basado en Sistemas Multiagentes (SMA) se ha convertido en una herramienta metodológica relevante para simular interacciones complejas, como la rotación laboral [Wooldridge 2009]. Esta investigación emplea la plataforma GAMA [Drogoul et al. 2013] para modelar agentes que representan profesionales de TI, integrando variables como satisfacción, compromiso y políticas de retención. Esta simulación no solo complementa el análisis cualitativo mediante escenarios prospectivos, sino que también permite experimentar con diferentes estrategias para evaluar su impacto en la rotación.

El uso de SMA se justifica por su capacidad de representar dinámicas emergentes. A diferencia de modelos estadísticos o de aprendizaje automático, los SMA permiten simular comportamientos heterogéneos en entornos organizacionales. Con esta ampliación del marco teórico, se profundiza el análisis de la rotación de personal en TI, integrando perspectivas teóricas clásicas, estudios sectoriales específicos y enfoques computacionales avanzados para abordar sus causas y posibles estrategias de mitigación.

3. Metodología de Investigación

Esta sección expone directamente el enfoque metodológico y las técnicas aplicadas para analizar la rotación de personal y las estrategias de retención en el sector de TI en Brasil. El diseño metodológico integra investigación cualitativa y simulación computacional para abordar el fenómeno desde una perspectiva analítica y práctica.

3.1. Enfoque y Tipo de Investigación

El enfoque metodológico es cualitativo, centrado en un diseño descriptivo y evaluativo. Según la metodología elegida [Cohen 2019] por los autores, la investigación descriptiva detalla las características del fenómeno, mientras que la evaluativa examina el impacto de las estrategias de retención. Esta aproximación permite explorar de manera integral las percepciones de los profesionales de TI y su relación con las políticas empresariales de retención de talentos.

3.2. Técnicas de Recolección de Datos

La recolección de datos incluyó entrevistas semiestructuradas y análisis documental. Se entrevistó a 20 profesionales de TI de empresas brasileñas. Las entrevistas, de 30 minutos, exploraron temas como satisfacción laboral y políticas de retención. La muestra, aunque limitada, incluyó desarrolladores, analistas y gerentes con 2 a 30 años de experiencia en empresas de distintos tamaños del sector TI brasileño. Se utilizó muestreo intencional acorde con el enfoque cualitativo, recomendándose estudios futuros con muestras mayores.

También se revisaron documentos internos de recursos humanos, a los que tuvimos acceso como parte de los contactos empresariales, para analizar las prácticas formales de gestión del talento.

3.3. Simulación con Sistemas Multiagentes (SMA)

Como complemento al análisis cualitativo, se desarrolló una simulación basada en Sistemas Multiagentes (SMA) usando la plataforma GAMA [Drogoul et al. 2013]. Este modelo, seguido en el trabajo [Ferreira 2024], representó dinámicas laborales simulando interacciones entre empleados y empresas. El modelo no distingue tipos de empresas ni proyectos, lo que limita el análisis de retención por tipo organizacional. Se propone incorporar perfiles organizacionales en futuras versiones. Como en el Cuadro 1, se incluyeron factores como satisfacción laboral y oportunidades externas para observar patrones emergentes y evaluar el impacto de diversas políticas de retención bajo escenarios múltiples.

Cuadro 1. Descripción de las variables en el modelo de rotación de personal

Variable	Descripción	En el análisis temática?	En la literatura?
s_i	Satisfacción laboral del empleado i	Sí	Sí
e_i	Nível de compromiso del empleado i con la empresa	No	Sí
a_i	Afinidad del empleado i con el equipo o la empresa	No	Sí
p_i	Percepción de las estrategias de retención por parte del empleado i	Sí	Sí
w_i	Salario del empleado i	Sí	Sí
b_i	Calidad de la relación del empleado i con su jefe directo.	Sí	Sí

El estudio incluye una variedad de variables relacionadas con la retención de talento y la rotación de profesionales en el contexto organizacional. Para el análisis temático, se incluyó la satisfacción laboral del empleado, respaldada por la literatura antes mencionada. Otra variable, la percepción de las estrategias de retención desde el punto de vista de los empleados, también se abordó en el análisis temático y contó con apoyo literario. El salario también se presentó como un factor crítico; la literatura muestra su impacto en el tiempo de permanencia de los profesionales. Finalmente, la variable de la calidad de la relación entre el empleado y su supervisor también se consideró relevante para el análisis temático y se sustentó en la literatura. Sin embargo, algunos factores, a pesar de ser reconocidos en la literatura, no se incluyeron en el análisis temático. Entre estos se encuentran el compromiso del empleado con la empresa y su gusto por el equipo de trabajo, que también influyen en la dinámica organizacional. Aunque las variables ya fueron estudiadas, su integración en un modelo SMA permite analizarlas de forma dinámica y contextual.

A diferencia de enfoques tradicionales, el SMA representa decisiones individuales con mayor detalle.

La probabilidad de que un empleado deje la empresa se modela mediante la función logística:

$$P(leave_i) = \frac{1}{1 + e^{-(\beta_0+\beta_1 s_i+\beta_2 e_i+\beta_3 a_i+\beta_4 p_i+\beta_5 w_i+\beta_6 b_i)}}$$

donde $\beta_0, \beta_1, ..., \beta_6$ son los coeficientes del modelo que reflejan el impacto de cada variable en la decisión del empleado de abandonar la empresa. Así, la tasa de rotación global (r) de la empresa se calcula como el promedio de las probabilidades de salida ajustadas por el tiempo medio de permanencia (t):

$$r = \frac{1}{N} \sum_{i=1}^{N} \frac{P(leave_i)}{t}$$

donde N es el número total de empleados en la empresa.

Cabe señalar que, si bien el modelo SMA ofrece una visión sistémica útil, simplifica las dinámicas organizacionales reales, pero parcial. Aun así, proporciona una base estructurada para analizar y prever la rotación, apoyando la gestión de recursos humanos y la definición de estrategias de retención.

3.4. Análisis de Datos

El análisis de los datos se realizó mediante un análisis temático [Braun 2006]. Este proceso incluyó la codificación de respuestas, identificación de temas clave y elaboración de categorías que reflejan las percepciones de los participantes. La integración de los hallazgos de las entrevistas con los resultados de la simulación permitió obtener una perspectiva más profunda del fenómeno, destacando la relación entre estrategias de retención y patrones de rotación.

En conjunto, esta metodología, al integrar métodos cualitativos y simulaciones computacionales, proporciona un enfoque robusto y multidimensional para el análisis de la rotación de personal y las estrategias de retención en el sector de TI en Brasil.

4. Resultados Preliminares y Análisis

Esta sección presenta los resultados iniciales derivados de la investigación, incluyendo hallazgos cualitativos de las entrevistas y análisis computacionales obtenidos mediante simulaciones basadas en SMA.

Las entrevistas semiestructuradas con 20 profesionales de TI permitieron identificar factores clave de rotación. La falta de reconocimiento, el estancamiento profesional y la desconexión entre expectativas y políticas organizacionales emergieron como motivos recurrentes de salida. Por el contrario, la flexibilidad laboral y las oportunidades de desarrollo fueron destacadas como estrategias efectivas de retención. En la revisón de la literaura, se identificaron tres temas principales: satisfacción laboral, calidad del liderazgo y percepción de políticas de retención. Las respuestas mostraron que políticas centradas en el bienestar, el reconocimiento y la capacitación impactan positivamente en la intención de permanencia.

La simulación, ejecutada en la plataforma GAMA, modeló tres escenarios durante doce (12) ciclos (meses), como en las Figuras 1 y 2: políticas de retención fuertes, moderadas y débiles. Las políticas fuertes incluyen aumentos salariales regulares, bonos de desempeño y promociones; las moderadas contemplan solo aumentos anuales sin promociones; y las débiles no poseen incentivos claros. La simulación confirmó que políticas sólidas, combinando incentivos financieros y promociones internas, redujeron la rotación, manteniéndola en un rango entre 5,8 % y 12,9 % durante los 12 meses. En contraste, las estrategias moderadas mostraron tasas superiores, fluctuando entre 10,5 % y 18,5 %, mientras que las políticas débiles resultaron en la mayor rotación, alcanzando valores entre 18,7 % y 35,4 %, evidenciando un aumento progresivo a lo largo del ciclo de simulación. Estos resultados refuerzan la eficacia de las políticas sólidas para mitigar la rotación y subrayan el impacto negativo de estrategias débiles.

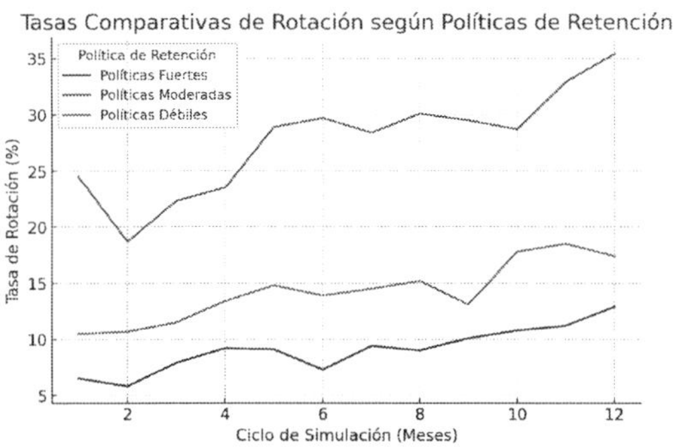

Figura 1. Evolución de la Tasa de Rotación en los 12 ciclos de Simulación

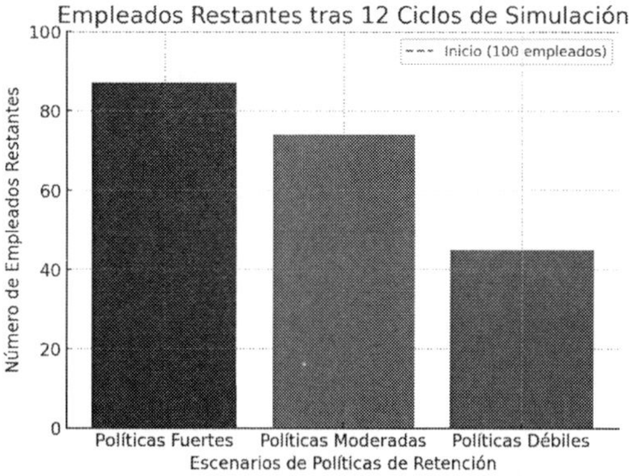

Figura 2. Empleados Restantes tras 12 Ciclos de Simulación

En la Figura 2 muestra el número de empleados restantes al finalizar los 12 ciclos de simulación, partiendo de 100 empleados en cada escenario. Las políticas fuertes (barra azul) resultaron en la mayor retención, con 87 empleados al final del período, destacando la eficacia de incentivos y planes de carrera. Las políticas moderadas (barra roja) retuvieron 74 empleados, evidenciando un impacto intermedio. En contraste, las políticas débiles (barra verde) resultaron en una significativa pérdida, con solo 45 empleados restantes, subrayando el efecto negativo de la falta de estrategias de retención. Este resultado preliminar reafirma la relación entre políticas sólidas y la reducción de la rotación laboral.

4.1. Revisión Crítica y Validación del Análisis

El análisis temático y el modelo fueron presentados al grupo de investigación[1], compuesto por doctorandos e investigadores de la universidad latinoamericana UCES, donde se discutieron críticamente los hallazgos y su coherencia.

Se recomienda integrar enfoques cuantitativos en futuras investigaciones para validar hallazgos y enriquecer el análisis. Además, se reconoce como limitación la ausencia de un análisis sobre diversidad (género, edad, etnicidad), relevante en un sector aún marcado por sesgos.

[1]Enlace IPS - Instituto de Pesquisa Socioeconomica: `https://ipsocioeconomica.org/`

5. Discusión

Esta sección interpreta las evidencias recolectadas en las entrevistas y los resultados de la simulación multiagente (SMA) realizada en GAMA, abordando las preguntas clave de la investigación (C1, C2, C3) y sus implicaciones prácticas y teóricas.

Las entrevistas revelaron que las estrategias de retención varían según el tamaño y madurez tecnológica de las empresas. Mientras las grandes empresas ofrecen beneficios completos, como salud y bienestar, los entrevistados destacaron que las oportunidades de desarrollo profesional y la flexibilidad laboral son más determinantes para su permanencia. Las entrevistas están centradas principalmente a C1 y C2, mientras que la simulación contribuye al análisis de C3, al evaluar la relación entre estrategias y rotación.

En cuanto a los motivos de rotación, las entrevistas identificaron la falta de reconocimiento, oportunidades de crecimiento y equilibrio vida-trabajo como causas principales. La simulación evidenció que ambientes laborales favorables redujeron la rotación al 20 %, mientras que condiciones adversas la aumentaron al 70 %. Ambas metodologías subrayan la importancia de políticas de retención integrales.

6. Conclusiones y Próximos Pasos

Esta investigación ha demostrado que las estrategias de retención de talento en empresas de TI están estrechamente vinculadas a los factores que impulsan la rotación de personal. A través de una metodología que combinó revisión de la literatura, entrevistas semiestructuradas y simulaciones multiagente (SMA), se confirmó la hipótesis planteada: las políticas de retención más eficaces son aquellas que abordan de forma integral aspectos como incentivos financieros, oportunidades de desarrollo profesional y un ambiente laboral saludable. Así, a diferencia de estudios previos que abordan la rotación de forma aislada, esta tesis integra análisis cualitativo y simulación computacional en el contexto brasileño, aportando una mirada integral.

Las entrevistas evidenciaron que la falta de reconocimiento, el estancamiento profesional y el desequilibrio vida-trabajo son las principales causas de rotación. Por otro lado, políticas centradas en bienestar, desarrollo y reconocimiento fueron identificadas como determinantes para la permanencia. Estos hallazgos fueron validados mediante la simulación, que mostró que las estrategias de retención fuertes reducen significativamente la rotación, mientras que la ausencia de incentivos aumenta su incidencia.

Aunque se han obtenido hallazgos relevantes, este doctorado sigue en curso, con finalización prevista para diciembre de 2025. Las próximas fases incluyen la validación cruzada y la ampliación del análisis del modelo. El estudio presenta limitaciones por su enfoque en Brasil, muestra reducida y simplificación del modelo, lo que restringe la generalización. Factores macroeconómicos, aunque no centrales, son abordados en la tesis completa con comparaciones internacionales.

Sin embargo, la integración metodológica entre análisis cualitativo y la simulación representa un aporte valioso, ofreciendo una base sólida para futuras investigaciones y estrategias de retención. Los trabajos futuros podrían explorar escenarios más complejos, ampliar el tamaño muestral , desarrollar modelos más realistas. Además, se espera que las investigaciones venideras profundicen en nuevas estrategias de retención adaptadas a la evolución tecnológica y a las necesidades emergentes del sector de TI.

7. Disponibilidad de Artefactos

En línea con la política de ciencia abierta, esta investigación pone a disposición los principales artefactos utilizados para garantizar transparencia y replicabilidad. Las entrevistas semiestructuradas a 20 profesionales de TI fueron transcritas y anonimizadas, y están disponibles en Zenodo: `https://zenodo.org/records/14888729`, junto con el análisis temático realizado en Taguette. El proyecto está documentado según las categorías emergentes. El código fuente del modelo SMA en GAMA y su respectiva descripción se encuentran en: `https://anonymous.4open.science/r/staff_turnover-F611/`

Referencias

Aranibar Gutiérrez, M. F. y Melendres Carlos, V. D., Ramírez Barón, M. C., and García Rivera, B. R. (2017). Los factores de la rotación de personal en las maquiladoras de exportación de ensenada, bc. *Revista Global de Negocios*, 6(2):25–40.

Brasscom (2023). *Relatório setorial 2022: Macrossetor de TIC.*

Braun, Virginia y Clarke, V. (2006). Using thematic analysis in psychology. *Qualitative Research in Psychology*, 3(2):77–101.

Chiavenato, I. (2020). *Gestão de pessoas: O novo papel da gestão do talento humano.* Atlas, 5 edition.

Cohen, N. y Rojas, G. G. (2019). *Metodología de la investigación, ¿para qué?: La producción de los datos y los diseños.* Teseo.

Drogoul, A., Huynh, N. Q., and Truong, Q. C. (2013). Coupling environmental data and models with simulations of complex systems: The gama platform. *Environmental Modelling & Software*, 39:44–55.

et. al., D. A. (2019). *The Adoption of Digital Technologies in Developing Countries.* Centro de Estudios de Estado y Sociedad (CEDES).

Ferreira, E. y Rete, O. (2024). Simulação de rotatividade de pessoal de ti através de um sistema de multiagentes: Desenvolvimento e aplicações. In *Anais do XVIII Workshop-Escola de Sistemas de Agentes, seus Ambientes e Aplicações (WESAAC 2024)*, pages 73–84.

Frufrek, G. L. and Pansanato, L. T. E. (2017). Rotatividade de pessoal: Pesquisa com profissionais de empresas brasileiras de desenvolvimento de software. *iSys: Revista Brasileira de Sistemas de Informação*, 10(2):5–29.

Porter, L. W. y Steers, R. M., Mowday, R. T., and Boulian, P. V. (1974). Organizational commitment, job satisfaction, and turnover among psychiatric technicians. *Journal of Applied Psychology*, 59(5):603–609.

Steil, A. V., Bello, J. d. S. A., Freitas, A. F. d., Kronbauer, J., and Cuffa, D. d. (2022). Reasons for professionals to stay or leave information technology organizations. *Revista de Administração Mackenzie*, 23(1):1–28.

Wooldridge, M. (2009). *An introduction to multiagent systems.* Wiley, 2 edition.

Insights into API Management Quality Characterization, Measurement and Evaluation

Eder dos Santos[1,2]

[1]Instituto de Tecnología Aplicada – Universidad Nacional de la Patagonia Austral (UNPA)

[2]Consejo Nacional de Investigaciones Científicas y Técnicas (CONICET)
Río Gallegos – Santa Cruz – Argentina

esantos@uarg.unpa.edu.ar

Abstract. *APIs have become a cornerstone in software ecosystems: organizations have been increasingly connecting software applications to share complex digital assets. However, managing APIs is non-trivial, and companies have been struggling with different quality-related issues in managing their APIs. The main goal of this work is to create a framework that allows characterizing, assessing, and improving API Management and API governance, particularly focusing on API Gateways as the core elements of API Management ecosystems.*

1. Introdcution

In recent years, information systems have increasingly adopted Everything-as-a-Service (XaaS) models [Duan et al. 2015], which are primarily built on microservice architectures. These architectures provide organizations with the flexibility to break down their systems into highly scalable services for more efficient management [Gamez-Diaz et al. 2017]. Within this framework, Application Programming Interfaces (APIs) [De 2023] have become key elements in the development of modern software products [Iyer and Subramaniam 2015]. APIs have extended to enterprise information systems [Yamamoto et al. 2018] and form the foundation of today's digital business, where industries share their commercial assets through new business models. This shift has given rise to what is known as the API Economy, where APIs serve as essential enablers for monetization, collaboration, and integration across diverse platforms and industries [Tan et al. 2016].

In general terms, an API is defined as a software-to-software interface through which applications communicate with each other over a network, without user interaction. Software developers access APIs as interfaces to code libraries, frameworks, or data sources, enabling them to avoid low-level programming tasks and/or accelerate development [De 2023]. Currently, several authors [De 2023] [Preibisch 2018] suggest that the term API refers to Web APIs built using REST principles, and the expressions API, Web API, REST API, and RESTful API are considered synonymous. Therefore, the term API will be used throughout this document.

APIs are managed through API management platforms, whose central component is the API Gateway. An API management platform provides the essential capabilities for creating, analyzing, and managing APIs in a secure and scalable environment. The services and functions of the API Gateway enable the inspection of all incoming and outgoing traffic and provide different levels of support for fulfilling a wide range of functional and non-functional requirements related to APIs, such as access control, network-level security, encryption, validation, transformation and routing of messages, resource availability, logging, caching, threat protection, monetization, documentation, developer registration, and tracking of products consuming the API, lifecycle management, auditing, and operational and performance analysis [De 2023] [Preibisch 2018] [Gamez-Diaz et al. 2017]. As a result, the API Gateway facilitates the operation of API, contributes to the separation of concerns and decoupling, facilitates service integration and scaling, and accelerates development.

The growing adoption of APIs has led to the proliferation of various API Gateway products. The global API Management market grew by 13.7% and reached 3.3 billion USD in 2023[1]. Additionally, current industry "state of the market" reports[2,3,4] indicate that there are 65+ API Gateway offerings available nowadays. In such a competitive landscape, it is essential to understand how software quality can be defined, and what these products provide to satisfy the stakeholders' requirements. Nonetheless, several authors agree that, in general, the quality of API is largely overlooked, and it is simply assumed that they are sufficiently "good", "secure", and/or "stable" for adoption [Bermbach 2017], and there is scarce evidence of research in the API Management field.

The remainder of this work is structured as follows: section 2 describes related work; section 3 presents the research questions and objectives that the work aims to achieve; section 4 outlines the research methodology used; section 6 details the proposed solution under development; and finally, section 6 concludes with the final considerations and limitations.

2. Related Work

2.1. Software Product Quality

There is a wide range of standards applicable to various areas of knowledge in Software Engineering, with a common objective related to quality. In general, software quality can be viewed from two perspectives: the first is based on the ISO 9001 standard, which focuses on quality policy across the entire organization. The terminology of this standard may be unfamiliar to software professionals, and quality management auditors may not be well-versed in software engineering vocabulary. The second perspective seeks to decompose software quality into a set of desired characteristics of a software product and select measures and evaluation methods to determine if the desired level of those characteristics has been achieved. Over time, various quality models have been developed from this standpoint, including FURPS, Boehm, Dromey, and McCall, among others [Nistala et al. 2019].

The terminology for quality attributes of software products differs from one model to another; each model has a different number of hierarchical levels and a distinct set of characteristics [Nistala et al. 2019]. A milestone in the definition of quality standards was the publication of the ISO/IEC 9126:1991 standard, which was later replaced by

[1]https://www.gartner.com/en/documents/5594559
[2]https://www.gartner.com/en/documents/4829031
[3]https://www.postman.com/state-of-api/
[4]https://apilandscape.apiscene.io/

the ISO/IEC 9126:2001 and ISO/IEC 14598:1999 standards. Currently, the international ISO/IEC 25000:2014 standards series, known as SQuaRE (Software Product Quality Requirements and Evaluation), unifies and replaces the ISO/IEC 9126 and ISO/IEC 14598 series. SQuaRE is considered the current de facto standard for software product quality and consists of a series of 27 standards that address aspects related to quality management, requirements, software and data quality models, as well as measurement and evaluation processes for quality.

2.2. API management quality

With the growing proliferation of APIs and the subsequent recognition of their importance, several technical challenges have been identified [Espinha et al. 2015]. In line with this, [Yamamoto et al. 2018] argues that the quality of APIs has become a highly relevant issue, asserting that research in Software Engineering focused on Web APIs is urgent. In this regard, various studies indicate that formal evaluation methods are rarely used in practice for the evaluation and selection of API products, leading to the need for empirical research on the evaluation and selection practices adopted in the industry for both open-source products [Ayala et al. 2013] [Sarrab and Rehman 2014] and commercial "off-the-shelf" products [Ayala et al. 2011], while also addressing international standards related to software product quality.

Nevertheless, studies addressing the quality of API Gateways are scarce. [Ofoeda et al. 2019] highlights the limited research on the topic: out of a total of 104 papers analyzed, 20 main research areas were identified, and none of these areas were explicitly related to the terms "software quality" or "API Gateway". Finally, only four papers were related to the research area of "API Management".

3. Research Questions and Goals

The main goal of this doctoral research is to develop an comprehensive, platform-neutral API Gateway quality framework that can be used to create open tools for the characterization, measurement, evaluation, and improvement API Management software quality.

In the search for effective strategies for both providers and consumers of API Management solutions, the following research questions (RQ) have been proposed for exploration:

RQ1: *What quality characteristics can be identified and how can they be specified in a formal basis?* This question aims to explore what dimensions and properties are essential to evaluate API Gateway software quality and how they can be articulated in a precise, formalized manner. This might involve defining these characteristics using a systematic framework, a set of metrics, or through formal models to ensure clarity and avoid ambiguity in quality assessment.

RQ2: *What relevance do these characteristics have from the perspective of the different stakeholders?* This question seeks to assess the degree of importance of each quality characteristic from various perspectives. By examining the priorities of different stakeholders, businesses or organizations can make more informed decisions about which aspects of quality to emphasize, ensuring that they strike a balance between customer satisfaction, technical feasibility, cost-efficiency, and compliance with regulations.

RQ3: *How can these characteristics be measured and assessed?* The goal of this RQ is to establish reliable, repeatable, and valid ways of assessing quality that allow for consistent evaluations over time, across different versions, or across different API Gateway products. This ensures that quality can be tracked, improved, and communicated effectively across all stages of development and use.

RQ4: *How are these quality characteristics related to API Management practices and capabilities?* This RQ aims to explore the relationship between software quality and API management practices and capabilities, providing insights for developers and organizations to align their practices with desired quality outcomes, particularly in the context of increasingly complex and distributed architectures.

Based on this, the following specific objectives are outlined: a. To study and analyze quality models, as well as measurement and evaluation methods for quality applied to API Management in general and API Gateways in particular. b. To propose a theoretical and conceptual metamodel for the standardized specification, measurement, and evaluation of quality characteristics in line with the capabilities of API Gateways. c. To identify the quality characteristics applicable to API Gateways and specify them based on the proposed metamodel. d. To determine the relevance of the identified quality characteristics from the perspective of different stakeholders. e. To design and/or implement tools and frameworks that support the proposed approach.

To provide a consistent and integrated solution, the ISO/IEC 25000 international standards series will be adopted as a reference, and the Goal / Question / Metric (GQM) approach [Basili et al. 1994] will be applied as the evaluation framework.

4. Research Methods and Activities

This research combines different empirical and non-empirical research strategies: solution-seeking strategies [Stol and Fitzgerald 2018] will be adopted for the generation of artifacts and for the adoption of models and tools, while knowledge-seeking strategies [Stol and Fitzgerald 2018] will be used for the analysis, validation, and quality evaluation of the results. As a general framework, the Design Science Research (DSR) framework [Peffers et al. 2007] will be applied. The activities and methods to be applied in each case are outlined below.

1. A review of the literature and other sources of information related to metamodels, models, and quality methods applied to API in general and to API Gateways in particular. To achieve this, a systematic mapping study (SMS) following the guidelines proposed by [Petersen et al. 2015] [Shaw 2003] has been planned.
2. Identification of the quality characteristics applicable to API Gateways and their specification based on the proposed metamodel. To achieve this objective, the GQM paradigm, which is conceptually compatible with SQuaRE and specific to the software development domain, will be adopted.
3. Evaluation of the relevance of the identified quality characteristics from the perspective of different stakeholders. For the preliminary definition, sampling studies such as questionnaires and interviews [Stol and Fitzgerald 2018] will be conducted.
4. Development of a metamodel for the standardized specification, measurement, and evaluation of quality characteristics. To achieve this, the theoretical formu-

lation method proposed by [Ralph 2018] will be applied, and the design will be supported by the principles of the Model Driven Architecture (MDA) approach. This framework allows the establishment of analysis and evaluation models for API Gateway products; as a result, a set of relevant quality attributes and associated metrics will be obtained.

5. Design of a quality model as a set of instances of the specified metamodel.

The validation of the described activities will be carried out using different methods, namely: a. Expert judgment studies, as described in [Stol and Fitzgerald 2018]. b. Development of artifacts to support the proposed approach, following the DSR principles. c. Design of case studies to evaluate a set of at least 10 real API Gateways and statistically analyze the results, as proposed in [Kitchenham et al. 1995] [Pfleeger 1995]. d. Communication of the obtained results through scientific publications and the doctoral thesis.

5. Results

Our research has made significant strides in advancing the understanding of quality traits in API Management, supported by empirical studies and key publications. Four of these publications notably highlight these contributions.

Initially, an SMS was conducted [dos Santos and Casas 2024] following the rigorous framework presented in [Petersen et al. 2015]. The primary objective of this work was to examine the definitions, measurement methods, and evaluation criteria used to assess API Management software quality, with a particular emphasis on methodological perspectives [Shaw 2003], API Management capabilities, and software quality attributes. From an initial set of 1205 papers, 21 identified studies conducted between 2000 and 2023 were identified, highlighting the novelty of the research topic.

The findings indicated that current research landscape is heterogeneous and primarily focuses on technical analysis and specific solution development. Key quality characteristics included performance efficiency, reliability, functional suitability, and security, which align with various API Management capabilities and current industry trends. The results also suggested that research is predominantly informal or lacking in theory, highlighting the need of defining a tailored quality metamodel to define, measure, and assess API Management software quality. Finally, threats to validity were addressed, and research gaps to encompass future research were identified.

As the second main contribution of this research, [dos Santos and Casas 2023] presented a methodical exploration of how practitioners perceive the quality traits associated with API management requirements in alignment with the quality characteristics outlined in ISO/IEC 25010. A comprehensive survey targeted professionals in various roles in Rio Gallegos City, Argentina, including developers, system administrators, and functional analysts. The outcomes of this study revealed that Functional Suitability, Performance Efficiency, and Security emerged as the most prominent quality characteristics for API management, corroborating the findings obtained in [dos Santos and Casas 2024]. These insights are critical for future research and practical applications in API management platforms, guiding developers to enhance functionality and security in their platforms. The study also provided a data-driven approach to assist platform providers in refining their offerings based on user needs, ultimately aiming to create more efficient and reliable API Management solutions.

The third advancement of this research introduced API-MQM, a tailored quality metamodel that builds on the ISO/IEC 25010 standard and integrates the GQM framework [dos Santos and Casas 2025], following the principles of Model-Driven Architecture (MDA). The proposed metamodel encompasses API Management capabilities and practices as key quality requirements, along with software quality characteristics, measurement and assessment, and tools that support the evaluation framework. The proposal was validated through both theoretical and empirical methods [Cachero et al. 2007] [Shaw 2003].

The last contribution of the current research is under peer review. The primary artifact is a catalog of 59 metrics, compiled from 68 industry-leading API Gateway products. These metrics were categorized into distinct groups based on clear definitions found in recent literature [De 2023] [Beyer et al. 2016] [Gregg 2013]. The DSR approach was adopted to design the catalog, and a quantitative analysis method was proposed and systematically performed. This study revealed that most metrics focus on specific API Management capabilities, namely latency and response time, API performance, error capturing, and traffic monitoring. Other features such as caching, saturation, resource utilization, and system health were scarcely addressed by the examined products, which highlights potential gaps in the current research landscape. The proposed artifacts in this study provide an objective foundation for a deeper understanding of API Management software quality and lay the groundwork for future investigation.

6. Concluding Remarks and Future Work

With the widespread adoption of APIs in modern software ecosystems, the need for robust API management practices has become increasingly relevant. Therefore, a comprehensive understanding of software product quality is essential for addressing API Management activities, capabilities, threats, and challenges, ultimately enhancing the success and trustworthiness of API-based systems and services.

Although software quality has become paramount in API Management, the field remains under-explored in scientific research. The primary objective of this paper was to present the ongoing work of the doctoral thesis, which aims to define a framework for characterizing, measuring, evaluating, and improving the software product quality of API Gateways. This framework is based on three key pillars: the ISO/IEC 25000 standards as a formal reference model, the GQM approach as a guiding framework, and API Management capabilities as quality requirements.

This paper also outlined the research objectives, methodology, and planned activities of the research. Notable activities include published work such as the systematic mapping of the literature, the identification and weighting of quality characteristics from the perspective of industry professionals, the definition of a metamodel as a flexible and conceptually coherent framework, and work under review, specifically the development of a preliminary catalog of metrics derived from a comprehensive analysis of API Gateway products offered in the industry.

Finally, it is anticipated that by the end of this research, a set of artifacts will be available to support the processes of characterizing, measuring, evaluating, and improving the quality of API gateways. These artifacts will include a quality model based on the API-MQM metamodel, evaluation methods, tools, and case studies focused on both experimental environments and real-world applications.

Referências

Ayala, C., Franch, X., Conradi, R., Li, J., and Cruzes, D. (2013). Developing software with open source software components. *Finding Source Code on the Web for Remix and Reuse*, pages 167–186.

Ayala, C., Hauge, Ø., Conradi, R., Franch, X., and Li, J. (2011). Selection of third party software in off-the-shelf-based software development—an interview study with industrial practitioners. *Journal of Systems and Software*, 84(4):620–637.

Basili, V. R., Caldiera, G., and Rombach, H. D. (1994). The goal question metric approach. In *Encyclopedia of software engineering*.

Bermbach, D. (2017). Quality of cloud services: Expect the unexpected. *IEEE Internet Computing*, 21(1):68–72.

Beyer, B., Jones, C., Petoff, J., and Murphy, N. (2016). *Site Reliability Engineering: How Google Runs Production Systems*. O'Reilly, Sebastopol, CA.

Cachero, C., Calero, C., and Poels, G. (2007). Metamodeling the quality of the web development process' intermediate artifacts. In *Web Engineering: 7th International Conference, ICWE 2007 Como, Italy, July 16-20, 2007 Proceedings 7*, pages 74–89. Springer.

De, B. (2023). *API Management: An Architect's Guide to Developing and Managing APIs for Your Organization*. Apress Berkeley, CA.

dos Santos, E. and Casas, S. (2023). API management and SQuaRE: A comprehensive overview from the practitioners' standpoint. In *Argentine Congress of Computer Science*, pages 137–150. Springer.

dos Santos, E. and Casas, S. (2024). Unveiling quality in API management: A systematic mapping study. In *2024 L Latin American Computer Conference (CLEI)*, pages 1–10, Buenos Aires, Argentina. IEEE.

dos Santos, E. and Casas, S. (2025). AN API MANAGEMENT SOFTWARE QUALITY METAMODEL BASED ON SQUARE AND GQM. In *Engenharias e soluções: Ciência e tecnologia para o desenvolvimento humano*, pages 249–266. Atena Editora, 1 edition.

Duan, Y., Fu, G., Zhou, N., Sun, X., Narendra, N. C., and Hu, B. (2015). Everything as a service (XaaS) on the cloud: Origins, current and future trends. In *2015 IEEE 8th International Conference on Cloud Computing*, pages 621–628, New York City, NY, USA. IEEE.

Espinha, T., Zaidman, A., and Gross, H.-G. (2015). Web API growing pains: Loosely coupled yet strongly tied. *Journal of Systems and Software*, 100:27–43.

Gamez-Diaz, A., Fernandez, P., and Ruiz-Cortes, A. (2017). An analysis of RESTful APIs offerings in the industry. In Maximilien, M., Vallecillo, A., Wang, J., and Oriol,

M., editors, *Service-Oriented Computing*, volume 10601, pages 589–604. Springer International Publishing. Series Title: Lecture Notes in Computer Science.

Gregg, B. (2013). Thinking methodically about performance. *Commun. ACM*, 56(2):45–51.

Iyer, B. and Subramaniam, M. (2015). The strategic value of APIs. *Harvard Business Review*, 1(7):2015.

Kitchenham, B., Pickard, L., and Pfleeger, S. L. (1995). Case studies for method and tool evaluation. *IEEE software*, 12(4):52–62.

Nistala, P., Nori, K. V., and Reddy, R. (2019). Software quality models: A systematic mapping study. In *2019 IEEE/ACM International Conference on Software and System Processes (ICSSP)*, pages 125–134. IEEE.

Ofoeda, J., Boateng, R., and Effah, J. (2019). Application Programming Interface (API) Research: A Review of the Past to Inform the Future. *International Journal of Enterprise Information Systems*, 15(3):76–95.

Peffers, K., Tuunanen, T., Rothenberger, M. A., and Chatterjee, S. (2007). A design science research methodology for information systems research. *Journal of management information systems*, 24(3):45–77.

Petersen, K., Vakkalanka, S., and Kuzniarz, L. (2015). Guidelines for conducting systematic mapping studies in software engineering: An update. *Information and Software Technology*, 64:1–18.

Pfleeger, S. L. (1995). Experimental design and analysis in software engineering. *Annals of Software Engineering*, 1(1):219–253.

Preibisch, S. (2018). *API development: a practical guide for business implementation success*. Springer Science+Business Media, New York, NY.

Ralph, P. (2018). Toward methodological guidelines for process theories and taxonomies in software engineering. *IEEE Transactions on Software Engineering*, 45(7):712–735.

Sarrab, M. and Rehman, O. M. H. (2014). Empirical study of open source software selection for adoption, based on software quality characteristics. *Advances in Engineering Software*, 69:1–11.

Shaw, M. (2003). Writing good software engineering research papers. In *25th International Conference on Software Engineering, 2003. Proceedings.*, pages 726–736, Portland, OR, USA. IEEE.

Stol, K.-J. and Fitzgerald, B. (2018). The abc of software engineering research. *ACM Transactions on Software Engineering and Methodology (TOSEM)*, 27(3):1–51.

Tan, W., Fan, Y., Ghoneim, A., Hossain, M. A., and Dustdar, S. (2016). From the service-oriented architecture to the web API economy. *IEEE Internet Computing*, 20(4):64–68.

Yamamoto, R., Ohashi, K., Fukuyori, M., Kimura, K., Sekiguchi, A., Umekawa, R., Uehara, T., and Aoyama, M. (2018). A quality model and its quantitative evaluation method for web APIs. In *2018 25th Asia-Pacific Software Engineering Conference (APSEC)*, pages 598–607.

Impulsando el pensamiento crítico de los jefes de proyecto IT en el proceso de adopción de la GenAI

Miguel Ballesteros Cáliz[1]

[1]Programa de Doctorado en Ingeniería Informática – ETS Ingeniería Informática
Universidad de Sevilla – España

mbcaliz@us.es

Abstract. *This research focuses on IT project managers, analyzing their critical thinking skills and behavior in complex decision-making. The main objective is to provide tools to strengthen this competency, which could become a key differentiating value for these professionals in the process of Generative AI (GenAI) adoption.*

Resumen. *La investigación se centra en los jefes de proyecto IT, analizando su habilidad de pensamiento crítico y su comportamiento en la toma de decisiones complejas. El objetivo principal es proporcionar herramientas para fortalecer esta competencia, que podría convertirse en un valor diferencial clave para estos profesionales en el proceso de adopción de la IA Generativa (GenAI).*

1. Introducción

Los proyectos impulsan el cambio y posibilitan la generación de valor en las organizaciones. A pesar de su creciente complejidad y dinamismo, cada vez más organizaciones optan por ejecutar su estrategia a través de proyectos [PMIGruposProcesos 2023]. En este contexto, los enfoques híbridos de gestión de proyectos se han consolidado, mostrando diversas maneras de combinar prácticas, herramientas y técnicas de enfoques predictivos y ágiles [PMIPulseProfession 2024].

Un elemento común a todos los proyectos son las personas. El principio fundamental del Manifiesto Ágil otorga prioridad a los individuos y sus interacciones por encima de procesos y herramientas [ManifiestoAgil 2001]. Incluso en los enfoques predictivos, comienza a reconocerse que el conocimiento tácito de las personas puede aportar más valor al resultado final que las tecnologías y procesos empleados [ScrumManager 2024]. Entre todas las personas involucradas, el rol del jefe de proyecto (project manager) es el más relevante y crucial para asegurar el cumplimiento de los objetivos y la entrega de los resultados esperados [PMBOK 2021].

Tradicionalmente, las habilidades más valoradas en los jefes de proyecto han sido las relacionadas con la gestión, como la planificación, coordinación, medición y supervisión del trabajo. Sin embargo, las habilidades de liderazgo, centradas en las personas [DeMarco and Lister 2013], han ganado protagonismo. Estas habilidades pueden ser desarrolladas y representan un activo tanto para los profesionales como para los proyectos y sus interesados [PMBOK 2021]. En su última actualización, el Project Management Institute (PMI) destacó en el Triángulo del Talento tres dimensiones clave para los jefes de proyecto: dominar el mayor número posible de formas de trabajar, desarrollar habilidades de poder o *power skills*, y tener una robusta visión de negocio [PMITalentTriangle 2024].

Las *power skills* deben complementarse con sólidas habilidades técnicas (*technical skills*), y algunos estudios incluso las consideran más relevantes [Jonesa et al. 2018]. Además, son habilidades críticas en la ingeniería del software [Watson and Blincoe 2017] y permiten a los jefes de proyecto trabajar de manera más inteligente. Este enfoque también se refleja en las certificaciones profesionales de mayor reconocimiento, como el examen *Project Management Professional* (PMP), en el cual el 42 % de las preguntas se centran en el dominio "Personas" [PMP 2021]. Existe una correlación directa entre las *power skills* y el éxito de los proyectos, siendo estas una ventaja competitiva para las organizaciones que las priorizan, las cuales muestran mayores niveles de madurez en la gestión de proyectos y agilidad organizacional [PMIPulseProfession 2023]. Entre las *power skills* esenciales, el pensamiento crítico (*critical thinking*) se destaca como una habilidad clave de liderazgo [Jonesa et al. 2018] que permite abordar los desafíos y la complejidad inherentes a los proyectos [PMINavigatingComplexity 2014]. Los jefes de proyecto emplean el pensamiento crítico para recopilar información imparcial, observar eventos que identifican patrones y relaciones, resolver problemas, analizar datos y evidencias, aplicar razonamientos diversos y enfrentar temas complejos como la ambigüedad y la incertidumbre [PMBOK 2021]. Dotar a los jefes de proyecto de esta capacidad resulta esencial para la toma de decisiones acertadas [Ping 2012].

La introducción de la *GenAI*, con el lanzamiento de ChatGPT de OpenAI en noviembre de 2022, democratizó el acceso a esta tecnología y aceleró su impacto en la profesión [PMIreportAI 2023]. Sin embargo, solo uno de cada cinco profesionales de proyectos ha utilizado la *GenAI* en más del 50 % de sus proyectos recientes. A este grupo de alta adopción se les denomina *Trailblazers*, mientras que los *Explorers*, con una adopción máxima del 15 %, representan el otro extremo. Los *Trailblazers* coinciden en los beneficios y la eficacia de la *GenAI* en la gestión de proyectos; sin embargo, la mayoría de las tareas realizadas con esta tecnología se centran en automatización y asistencia básica. A medida que las tareas se vuelven más complejas, como las de nivel *Augmenting*—que apoyan la toma de decisiones con múltiples interdependencias y variables—se evidencia una brecha significativa entre los *Trailblazers* y los *Explorers* [PMIreportGenAI 2024].

El pensamiento crítico es un rasgo humano que, en cierta medida, puede ser potenciado por la IA. Por ejemplo, las herramientas de IA pueden acelerar y optimizar la resolución de problemas [PMIreportAI 2023]. Los expertos predicen que, a medida que la *GenAI* se integre más en los flujos de trabajo, el pensamiento crítico se convertirá en una habilidad indispensable [PMIreportGenAI 2024]. Cuanto más complejas sean las tareas gestionadas con IA, mayor será la necesidad de interacción humana. Así, la experiencia y el conocimiento contextual de los profesionales sobre el entorno, la organización y la gestión del proyecto influirán significativamente en la calidad de los resultados finales obtenidos con IA [PMIreportAI 2023].

En este marco, la investigación enfrenta el desafío de analizar la habilidad de pensamiento crítico en los jefes de proyecto IT, diseñar artefactos para su mejora y examinar cómo esta capacidad humana coexiste con la *GenAI*, especialmente ante la aceleración de su adopción.

2. Conocimiento actual del dominio del problema

Numerosos estudios han destacado la importancia de las *power skills* en los profesionales del sector IT, subrayando especialmente el pensamiento crítico como una de las competencias clave. Otros estudios [Garousi et al. 2019] se centran en identificar las diferencias entre las habilidades desarrolladas durante la educación y las necesidades reales de la industria, entre las que se encuentran las *power skills* como el trabajo en equipo y la comunicación, el liderazgo y el pensamiento crítico. Se han desarrollado modelos específicos para evaluar la competencia en pensamiento crítico en la gestión de proyectos [Dubrie and Pun 2013], así como guías generales para el desarrollo de habilidades, como el *Project Manager Competency Development Framework* [PMCDF 2017]. Además, en el ámbito educativo, se han diseñado modelos basados en el uso de juegos para mejorar la capacidad de pensamiento crítico [Barnabè et al. 2023] y también se ha comenzado a explorar la convivencia entre ChatGPT y el pensamiento crítico como mecanismos para la resolución de problemas [Sharma 2024].

A pesar de su relevancia, el informe de 2023 del PMI señala que las organizaciones siguen sin priorizar el desarrollo del pensamiento crítico, debido principalmente a la falta de valor percibido y al coste asociado. En promedio, solo destinan un 25 % de su presupuesto de formación a este tipo de habilidades interpersonales, y casi la mitad (47 %) de los profesionales de proyectos afirman que su organización no las consideró al momento de su contratación o ascenso. Esto evidencia que el pensamiento crítico no está suficientemente integrado en las descripciones de puestos de trabajo ni en los planes de desarrollo profesional [PMIPulseProfession 2023].

3. Objetivos de la investigación

El objetivo principal de la investigación es **el estudio de la habilidad de pensamiento crítico de los jefes de proyecto IT para la toma de decisiones complejas en el proceso de adopción de la GenAI.**

El universo objeto de estudio o *target* se define como:

- Sector: Tecnología de la Información (IT), dado que este sector tiene una alta probabilidad de priorizar el pensamiento crítico [PMIPulseProfession 2023] y lidera claramente la adopción de la *GenAI* [PMIreportGenAI 2024].
- Región: Europa, donde se observa con mayor frecuencia la falta de percepción sobre el valor del desarrollo del pensamiento crítico [PMIPulseProfession 2023].

Para alcanzar el objetivo principal se plantean los siguientes objetivos específicos, organizados en torno a tres preguntas de investigación:

Pregunta 1 (P1): **¿Cuál es el comportamiento de los jefes de proyecto IT, basado en la habilidad de pensamiento crítico, para la toma de decisiones complejas?**

1. Analizar si los jefes de proyecto IT son observadores: ¿Son capaces de detectar y predecir problemas y oportunidades que surgen en el proyecto?
2. Examinar si los jefes de proyecto IT son analíticos: ¿Recopilan, comprenden e interpretan datos, así como otro tipo de información, incluida la interacción con personas?
3. Investigar cómo los jefes de proyecto IT obtienen sus conclusiones: ¿Se basan en la información analizada, en su experiencia previa o en su propio conocimiento?

4. Identificar los métodos, técnicas y herramientas utilizados por los jefes de proyecto IT en la aplicación de esta habilidad.

Pregunta 2 (P2): **¿Cómo se puede desarrollar y mejorar la competencia de pensamiento crítico de los jefes de proyecto IT para la toma de decisiones complejas?**

1. Determinar los factores que influyen en el desarrollo de esta competencia.
2. Establecer si es posible identificar diferentes niveles de desarrollo para esta competencia.
3. Proponer métodos, técnicas y herramientas que puedan utilizarse para fortalecer esta competencia.
4. Desarrollar recomendaciones dirigidas a las organizaciones para que prioricen el desarrollo del pensamiento crítico en los jefes de proyecto IT.

Pregunta 3 (P3): **¿Cómo influye la adopción de la *GenAI* en el desarrollo y la aplicación de la competencia de pensamiento crítico de los jefes de proyecto IT para la toma de decisiones complejas?**

1. Analizar cómo influye la adopción de la *GenAI*: ¿El aumento de la productividad generado por la *GenAI* libera tiempo para fomentar la interacción humana y potenciar el pensamiento crítico?
2. Proponer mecanismos de soporte a la toma de decisiones complejas basados en la convivencia de la *GenAI* y el pensamiento crítico.

4. Metodología y actividades

La investigación se aborda como un proyecto utilizando el marco de referencia *Design Science Research* (DSR) [vom Brocke et al. 2020], para garantizar una mayor adaptabilidad a los continuos cambios del sector IT y de la tecnología *GenAI*.

Las fases y actividades, así como las preguntas de investigación a las que están asociadas, son las siguientes:

1. **Fase I: Identificación del problema y motivación**
   Se realizará un trabajo inicial para conocer el estado actual del tema objeto de estudio. Las actividades principales incluyen:
   - Exploración preliminar de artículos de investigación, mediante la herramienta Consensus, para profundizar en el conocimiento del dominio del problema.
   - Revisión de informes recientes publicados por las organizaciones más relevantes del sector.
   - Estudio de guías y métodos de referencia: Se analizarán documentos clave como la Guía del PMBOK [PMBOK 2021] y Scrum [Schwaber and Sutherland 2020], los cuales se han consolidado como estándares entre los millones de profesionales que aplican habilidades de gestión de proyectos.
2. **Fase II: Definición de objetivos de la solución**
   - Definición de manera precisa de la motivación, los objetivos, el universo objeto de estudio y las preguntas de la investigación.

- Revisión sistemática de literatura: Se utilizará la metodología PRISMA [Page 2021] para identificar y sintetizar las investigaciones previas más relevantes relacionadas con el tema de estudio. *(P1, P2.1, P3.1)*
- Investigación cualitativa: Se llevarán a cabo entrevistas exploratorias a jefes de proyecto IT con el objetivo de evaluar el estado actual de la habilidad de pensamiento crítico e identificar cómo esta habilidad se aplica en la toma de decisiones complejas. *(P1, P2.1, P3.1)*
- Investigación cuantitativa: Se distribuirán cuestionarios a jefes de proyecto IT para abordar las preguntas de investigación que no hayan sido respondidas durante las fases previas. *(P1, P2.1, P3.1)*
  Se realizará una explotación detallada de la información obtenida, utilizando técnicas estadísticas y analíticas para extraer información clave.

3. **Fase III: Diseño y desarrollo**
   Se desarrollarán herramientas y recursos para mejorar la competencia de pensamiento crítico en jefes de proyecto IT, incluyendo aquellos basados en *GenAI*. Este enfoque permitirá diseñar artefactos prácticos que apoyen tanto a los profesionales como a las organizaciones en el desarrollo de esta habilidad. *(P2.2, P2.3, P2.4, P3.2)*
4. **Fase IV: Evaluación**
   En esta fase final se llevarán a cabo casos de uso que implementen las soluciones desarrolladas y se podrán identificar mejoras como retroalimentación de la fase de diseño y desarrollo. Se trata por tanto de un proceso iterativo que permitirá reducir el grado de incertidumbre de la solución. *(P2.2, P2.3, P2.4, P3.2)*
   Por último, se sintetizarán los hallazgos obtenidos a lo largo de la investigación, generando las conclusiones relevantes sobre el comportamiento de los jefes de proyecto IT en relación con el pensamiento crítico, así como las recomendaciones prácticas para organizaciones y profesionales del sector.

5. Planificación

La planificación de las actividades a llevar a cabo se representa en la Figura 1, en la que se estima un periodo de tiempo de tres años para acometer el trabajo: año 1 (Fase I), año 2 (Fase II) y año 3 (Fases III y IV).

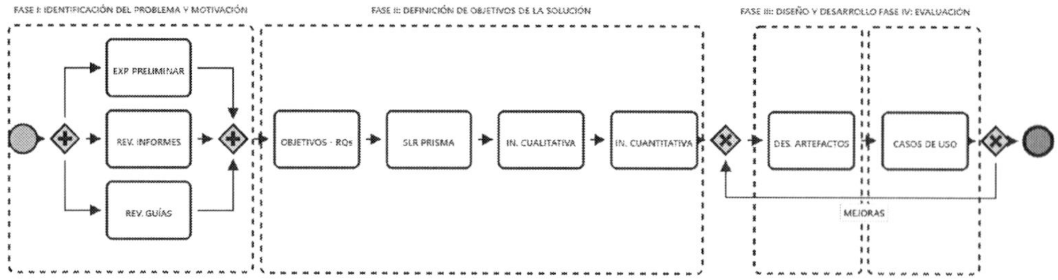

Figura 1. Proceso con notación BPMN de Fases de la investigación

La investigación se encuentra actualmente en la actividad de revisión sistemática de literatura PRISMA, habiéndose completado la **fase de identificación del problema y motivación**, así como la definición de manera precisa de la motivación, los objetivos, el universo objeto de estudio y las preguntas de la investigación.

Revisión sistemática de literatura (PRISMA)

La revisión sistemática de literatura se está llevando a cabo con base en la metodología PRISMA, utilizando la base de datos Scopus como principal fuente de búsqueda. A continuación, se detallan las acciones realizadas:

1. **Opciones de búsqueda:** Se han definido dos enfoques para las búsquedas, la primera (248 resultados), centrada exclusivamente en jefes de proyecto IT y una segunda (212 resultados), más amplia, abarca todos los sectores para analizar cuál ofrece resultados más relevantes. La segunda opción incluye una condición adicional en la consulta, dado el elevado número de resultados inicial.
2. **Criterios de inclusión y exclusión:** Las investigaciones deben estudiar el comportamiento de los jefes de proyecto en relación con el pensamiento crítico, preferentemente mediante encuestas, entrevistas o dinámicas de grupo. Quedan fuera del análisis los estudios que no aporten información sobre el comportamiento humano o que no guarden relación directa con la toma de decisiones complejas.
3. **Resultados preliminares:** Se ha realizado la fase de screening, en la que se seleccionaron una serie de artículos relevantes para el tema objeto de estudio (31 resultados).
   Un hallazgo preliminar es que gran parte de los artículos seleccionados se centran en el desarrollo de algoritmos, herramientas o tecnologías que apoyan a los jefes de proyecto en la toma de decisiones para resolver problemas específicos. Sin embargo, estos estudios suelen centrarse más en los aspectos técnicos que en el análisis del comportamiento humano o las habilidades cognitivas, como el pensamiento crítico
4. **Próximos pasos:** Se procederá al análisis detallado de los artículos seleccionados. A estos se sumarán los artículos citados en dichas investigaciones que resulten de interés (snowballing) para garantizar un enfoque más completo. Por último, se sistematizarán los hallazgos para vincularlos a las preguntas y objetivos de la investigación.

6. Propuesta de solución

A pesar de que las principales guías, métodos y certificaciones de referencia para la gestión de proyectos han comenzado a dar mayor relevancia al pensamiento crítico, la revisión realizada hasta el momento revela que no existe una investigación focalizada específicamente en el análisis del comportamiento de los jefes de proyecto IT en relación con esta habilidad. En particular, se carece de estudios que exploren cómo estos profesionales emplean el pensamiento crítico para tomar decisiones complejas en proyectos con altos niveles de incertidumbre y cambio.

El objetivo principal de esta investigación es cerrar esta brecha de conocimiento, proporcionando un enfoque práctico y basado en evidencia que ayude tanto a las organizaciones como a los jefes de proyecto IT a mejorar su pensamiento crítico. Esto se logra alineando esta competencia clave con las necesidades del negocio, especialmente en un contexto donde la adopción acelerada de tecnologías como la *GenAI* pone aún más de relieve la importancia del pensamiento crítico como un valor diferencial.

Esta investigación aporta un enfoque novedoso al:

1. **Explorar en profundidad el comportamiento humano en contextos complejos**: Mientras otros estudios se centran principalmente en herramientas, algoritmos y tecnologías de soporte a los jefes de proyecto IT, esta investigación se orienta a analizar el comportamiento de estas personas.
2. **Proponer un marco de desarrollo específico para la competencia de pensamiento crítico**: Con base en los hallazgos obtenidos, la investigación desarrollará un marco práctico y adaptable que incluirá los siguientes elementos:
   - Definición de niveles de desarrollo de la competencia: Una clasificación estructurada que permita identificar los diferentes grados de madurez en el uso del pensamiento crítico.
   - Herramientas de evaluación: Instrumentos que faciliten medir el nivel de competencia de pensamiento crítico, identificar brechas y proporcionar un diagnóstico claro.
   - Planes de desarrollo personalizados: Propuestas concretas de actividades, como mentorías, capacitaciones y simulaciones prácticas, diseñadas para fortalecer esta habilidad.
   - Recomendaciones organizacionales: Estrategias para que las organizaciones puedan integrar y aprovechar el pensamiento crítico en su cultura y proyectos, generando puntos de contacto para percibir y valorar mejor la formación y el desarrollo de esta habilidad [PMIPulseProfession 2023].
   - Casos de uso prácticos: Ejemplos reales que ilustren cómo implementar las soluciones propuestas y permitan evaluar los beneficios esperados que estas generan en el entorno IT.
3. **Contextualizar el impacto de la GenAI**: Esta investigación examina cómo las herramientas de *GenIA* pueden complementar o desafiar esta competencia, y cómo su adopción puede influir en las prácticas profesionales de los jefes de proyecto IT.

En resumen, esta propuesta no solo pone el énfasis en el factor humano y en las habilidades interpersonales dentro de un sector altamente tecnológico, sino que también ofrece soluciones prácticas, alineadas con las demandas emergentes del sector IT. Este enfoque integral tiene el potencial de redefinir las estrategias de formación y desarrollo profesional en gestión de proyectos, aportando valor tanto a los individuos como a las organizaciones.

Referencias

Barnabè, F., Armenia, S., Nazir, S., and Pompei, A. (2023). Critical thinking skills enhancement through system dynamics-based games: Insights from the project management board game project. *Systems*.

DeMarco, T. and Lister, T. (2013). *Peopleware: productive projects and teams*. Addison-Wesley.

Dubrie, V. R. and Pun, K. F. (2013). Assessing critical thinking capabilities of project management practitioners: A progressive model. *The West Indian Journal of Engineering*, 36(1):19–24.

Garousi, V., Giray, G., Tüzün, E., Catal, C., and Felderer, M. (2019). Aligning software engineering education with industrial needs: A meta-analysis. *Elsevier*.

Jonesa, K., Leonardb, L. N. K., and Lang, G. (2018). Desired skills for entry level is positions: Identification and assessment. *Journal of Computer Information Systems*.

ManifiestoAgil (2001). Manifiesto por el desarrollo Ágil de software. Technical report, agilemanifesto.org.

Page, M. J. (2021). The prisma 2020 statement: an updated guideline for reporting systematic reviews. *BMJ*.

Ping, F. H. (2012). Influence of overconfidence, critical thinking and creative thinking on project manager's decision making skills–a conceptual paper. *SSM*.

PMBOK (2021). *El estándar para la dirección de proyectos y Guía de los fundamentos para la dirección de proyectos*. Project Management Institute, 7th edition.

PMCDF (2017). *Project Manager Competency Development Framework*. Project Management Institute, 3th edition.

PMIGruposProcesos (2023). *Grupos de Procesos: Guía Práctica*. Project Management Institute.

PMINavigatingComplexity (2014). *Navigating Complexity: A Practice Guide*. Project Management Institute.

PMIPulseProfession (2023). Pulse of the profession 2023 report: Power skills, redefining project success, 14th edition. Technical report, Project Management Institute.

PMIPulseProfession (2024). Pulse of the profession 2024 report: The future of project work, 15th edition. Technical report, Project Management Institute.

PMIreportAI (2023). Shaping the future of project management with ai. Technical report, Project Management Institute.

PMIreportGenAI (2024). Genai adoption report: First movers' advantage, the immediate benefits of adopting generative ai for project management. Technical report, Project Management Institute.

PMITalentTriangle (2024). Pmi talent triangle. Technical report, Project Management Institute.

PMP (2021). Project management professional (pmp) examination content outline. Technical report, Project Management Institute.

Schwaber, K. and Sutherland, J. (2020). *La Guía Scrum*. Ken Schwaber and Jeff Sutherland, 2th edition.

ScrumManager (2024). *Scrum Master*. Scrum Manager, 4th edition.

Sharma, D. (2024). Critical thinking and problem-solving in the age of chatgpt: Experiential-bibliotherapy-blogging project. *Business and Professional Communication Quarterly*, 87(4).

vom Brocke, J., Hevner, A., and Maedche, A. (2020). Introduction to design science research. *Springer Nature Switzerland*.

Watson, C. and Blincoe, K. (2017). Attitudes towards software engineering education in the new zealand industry. *28th Annual Conference of the Australasian Association for Engineering Education (AAEE 2017)*.

Model-Driven Software Engineering to Foster the Adoption of Digital Twins

Arturo Barriga[1]

[1]Quercus Software Engineering Group (https://quercusseg.unex.es), Departamento de Ingeniería Sistemas Informáticos y Telemáticos, Universidad de Extremadura, Avenida de la Universidad s/n, Cáceres, 10003, Spain

arturobc@unex.es

Abstract. *Digital twins are virtual replicas of physical systems that offer significant benefits in terms of productivity and sustainability. However, most digital twin solutions are tailored to specific use cases, and there is a lack of domain-independent development frameworks. As a result, developers must build each system from scratch, which increases project timelines and costs and hinders the scalability of solutions. This ongoing doctoral project proposes a Model-Driven Software Engineering (MDSE) approach to simplify the development of digital twins. Ultimately, the presented approach aims to promote the widespread adoption of digital twins across sectors, making their development more accessible, scalable, and cost-effective.*

1. Introduction

A digital twin is a virtual representation of a physical system that is continuously updated and synchronized with its real counterpart via real-time data streams [Minerva et al. 2020, Sharma et al. 2022]. By integrating technologies such as the Internet of Things (IoT) and machine learning, digital twins create a dynamic, data-driven environment that allows users to simulate scenarios, optimize performance, and proactively identify potential failures or undesirable outcomes before they occur [Rathore et al. 2021, Segovia and Garcia-Alfaro 2022, Minerva et al. 2020]. Moreover, digital twin applications span numerous industries, including manufacturing [Friederich et al. 2022], smart cities [Wang et al. 2023], and energy [Stadtmann et al. 2023]. In this regard, digital twin systems offer substantial benefits, such as improving efficiency and sustainability, and supporting informed decision-making.

However, a major challenge in digital twin development is the lack of domain-independent frameworks [Macías et al. 2023, Mihai et al. 2022, Fuller et al. 2020], which forces developers to build custom solutions for each specific use case. This lack of standardization means that each digital twin must be developed from scratch, which leads to a significant increase in both time and cost and limits the scalability of systems [Lehner et al. 2021, Vale et al. 2023]. This not only raises the barriers to entry for organizations but also hinders the widespread adoption of digital twin technology.

To address these issues, this ongoing doctoral project proposes a Model-Driven Software Engineering (MDSE) approach that includes an abstract syntax, a concrete graphical syntax, and Model-to-Text (M2T) transformations to facilitate the development of digital twins. In this sense, MDSE is a software development methodology that focuses on the use of models as central artifacts throughout the development process [Brambilla et al. 2017]. By using high-level models to represent system structure and behavior, along with M2T transformations, MDSE enables the automatic generation of executable code and other necessary artifacts directly from the models [Hailpern and Tarr 2006, Stahl et al. 2006]. This approach reduces the need for manual coding, minimizes human errors resulting from laborious tasks, and speeds up the development process [Brambilla et al. 2017, Hailpern and Tarr 2006, Stahl et al. 2006]. As a result, developers can focus on refining the logic and functionality of the system instead of dealing with repetitive manual tasks, which speeds implementation and improves consistency throughout the system.

In this context, the proposed MDSE approach involves defining the conceptual model of digital twins from a domain-independent perspective, identifying the essential properties, components, and functionalities of various digital twins documented in the literature. This conceptual model will then be formalized through a metamodel, specifying the rules and semantics governing the structure and behavior of valid digital twin systems. To facilitate intuitive model creation, a graphical editor will be implemented, allowing users to design digital twin systems without requiring extensive programming knowledge. Finally, M2T transformations will be developed to automate the generation of executable code from the models, thereby significantly reducing manual coding efforts [Hailpern and Tarr 2006, Stahl et al. 2006].

Therefore, this project aims to encourage the widespread adoption of digital twins by making their development process more consistent, accessible, scalable, and cost-effective. By simplifying the design, validation, generation, and deployment phases, this approach not only promises to reduce development time and costs but also to promote wider use of digital twin technology across diverse industries, ultimately driving innovation and improving operational efficiency.

It should be mentioned that, although the proposed MDSE approach is domain-independent and could be applied to a variety of industries, this doctoral project pays special attention to the agricultural sector due to its important role in Extremadura, the author's region. In this regard, to validate the applicability of the proposed solution, this doctoral project also aims to implement agricultural digital twins in Extremadura, thus validating the proposed approach in real-world use cases.

The remainder of this manuscript is organized as follows. Section 2 presents an explicit formulation of the research questions and objectives of the doctoral project. Section 3 provides a summary of the current state of knowledge in the problem domain. Section 4 outlines the research methodology employed throughout the project. Section 5 presents the proposed solution and discusses the results obtained so far. Finally, Section 6 presents some of the challenges faced and outlines the next steps planned for the project.

2. Research Questions and Objectives

Given the context and background that justifies the development of this proposal, the main Research Questions (RQs) guiding the doctoral project are:

- **RQ1:** How can a conceptual model of digital twins be defined to effectively capture their essential components, features, and functionalities in a domain-independent manner?
- **RQ2:** How can MDSE be applied to the definition, validation, generation, and deployment of digital twins across industries?

- **RQ3:** What are the challenges of applying MDSE to digital twin development, and how can they be addressed?
- **RQ4:** How can the proposed MDSE approach be validated to assess its applicability and effectiveness in real-world digital twin implementations?

These research questions have been carefully selected. RQ1 is formulated to establish a foundational understanding of digital twins, ensuring that the proposed approach is applicable across multiple domains. RQ2 focuses on how MDSE methodologies can be applied to digital twin development, addressing the limitations of current ad-hoc implementations. RQ3 examines the challenges encountered when applying MDSE to digital twin development, identifying potential obstacles and proposing solutions to ensure the effectiveness of the methodology. Finally, RQ4 ensures that the proposed methodology is validated in practical use cases.

To address these research questions, the doctoral project aims to achieve the following objectives:

- **Ojective 1:** Define a domain-independent conceptual model that identifies the key characteristics, components, relationships, and functionalities of digital twins.
- **Ojective 2:** Propose and implement an MDSE approach to streamline the definition, validation, implementation, and deployment of digital twins across diverse industries.
- **Ojective 3:** Validate the applicability of the proposed model-driven approach in real-world case studies, with special attention to the agricultural sector.
- **Ojective 4:** Disseminate the findings and results of this research through presentations at relevant conferences and publications in high-impact journals.

The following section describes existing MDSE approaches to digital twin development, identifying their limitations and areas for improvement.

3. Current Knowledge and State of Existing Solutions

Traditionally, MDSE has been successfully applied to fields closely related to digital twins, such as the Internet of Things (IoT) and Cyber-Physical Systems (CPS) [Ciccozzi and Spalazzese 2016, Moin et al. 2020, Barriga et al. 2021, Barriga et al. 2023, Ihirwe et al. 2020]. Then, with the rise of digital twin technology, researchers have begun investigating the application of MDSE in this domain [Bibow et al. 2020, Dalibor et al. 2020, Vale et al. 2023], aiming to streamline the development process, reduce its complexity, and enhance automation.

In this regard, [Bibow et al. 2020] proposes an MDSE approach for creating reactive digital twins by defining event-driven rules. This work was later extended by [Dalibor et al. 2020] to include a graphical control interface (cockpit) for monitoring and interacting with physical entities. However, these solutions primarily focus on predefined rule-based behavior and lack support for complex data-driven intelligence, such as machine learning models.

Similarly, [Vale et al. 2023] introduces an MDSE framework for industrial digital twins, validating their approach through an iron ore sintering plant case study. While beneficial for industrial settings, this approach is domain-specific and does not generalize to other applications, such as agricultural or healthcare digital twins. Additionally, it is not specified whether the system supports automatic code generation capabilities.

Therefore, although significant progress has been made in relation to MDSE and digital twins, there are still a number of challenges to be addressed:

- **Lack of domain-independent digital twin frameworks:** Most existing MDSE-based digital twin proposals are designed for specific industries, limiting their adaptability and reusability across different domains.
- **Limited support for intelligent digital twin models:** Many approaches rely on predefined rule-based logic rather than incorporating machine learning and advanced simulation models. However, this integration is essential, as it enables digital twins to continuously learn from data, adapt to changing conditions, and perform intelligent tasks, thus enhancing their capabilities [Rathore et al. 2021].
- **Absence of comprehensive automation:** While some approaches enable code generation, few provide full automation, including the deployment infrastructure.
- **Fragmented digital twin service modeling:** Many frameworks do not fully define the range of services digital twins can offer, such as predictive analytics or testing of hypothetical scenarios.

Therefore, there is a clear need for comprehensive, domain-independent digital twin development frameworks. This doctoral project aims to fill this gap.

4. Research Methodology

The research methodology for this doctoral project follows a structured approach based on the principles of Design Science Research (DSR) [Hevner et al. 2010] and is organized into different phases:

- **Identify problem and motivation:** A thorough review of existing research is conducted to identify gaps and limitations in current modeling techniques for digital twins. The findings from this review provide a foundation for defining the research problem. Thus, this phase establishes the motivation for the research.
- **Define the objectives for a solution:** Based on the definition of the problem, the objectives to be met by an effective MDSE solution are established.
- **Design and development:** An MDSE approach is implemented to streamline digital twin definition, validation, generation, and deployment. For more details on the steps involved in this phase, see Section 5 where the solution is presented.
- **Demonstration:** The proposed MDSE approach is applied to selected digital twin use cases to showcase its feasibility. The purpose of this step is to illustrate how the approach can be applied in real-world situations.
- **Evaluation and refinement:** The effectiveness of the MDSE approach is systematically assessed based on predefined criteria. Insights gained from this phase can guide iterative refinements to enhance the solution.
- **Communication:** The research findings are disseminated through academic publications, presentations, and discussions within the research community. This phase ensures that the contributions of the research reach a broader audience and contribute to advancing knowledge in the field of digital twins and MDSE.

5. Proposed Solution and Preliminary Results

This section begins with an introduction to metamodeling layers. Next, the proposed solution is defined, as well as its novelty and advantages compared to existing approaches. Finally, the results and progress achieved to date are presented.

5.1. Layers of Metamodeling

In MDSE, metamodeling is structured into four hierarchical layers: M0, M1, M2, and M3 [Brambilla et al. 2017], each serving a different function (see Figure 1). The M0 layer represents actual instances of the system, such as code. The M1 layer contains models that describe the structure and behavior of M0 instances, offering an abstract representation of real-world entities. The M2 layer, or metamodel level, defines the language and rules for creating M1 models, ensuring consistency in their structure and semantics. Finally, the M3 layer establishes the fundamental rules for defining metamodels (M2).

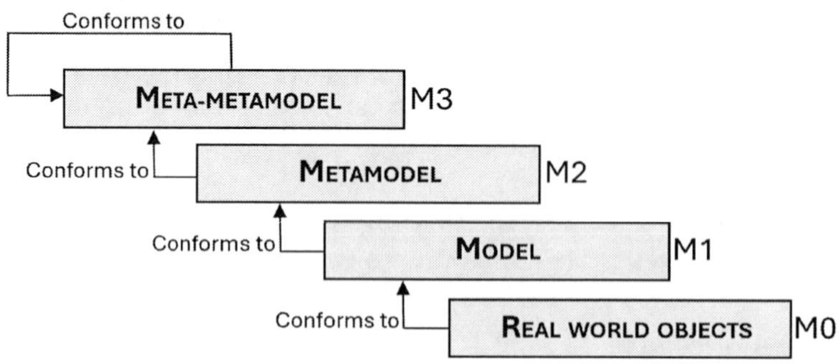

Figure 1. Layers of metamodeling. Adapted from [Brambilla et al. 2017].

5.2. Proposed Solution

Thus, to implement an MDSE approach for digital twin development, it is crucial to focus on these layers. This involves addressing the following steps:

- **Identification of the conceptual model of digital twins:** This step consists of defining in a domain-agnostic manner the fundamental characteristics and relationships of the various digital twin systems documented in the literature.
- **Metamodel (M2) formulation:** The next step involves formalizing the structure and semantics of the conceptual model of digital twins through the creation of a metamodel (M2). This metamodel provides a standardized framework that ensures consistency in the definition of digital twin models (M1). To achieve this, the Eclipse Modeling Tools [Eclipse Foundation b] are utilized.
- **Implementation of a graphical syntax for model representation:** A graphical syntax is a visual language. In this MDSE approach, this syntax allows users to design digital twin models (M1) adhering to the metamodel (M2) specifications without the need for deep technical knowledge. The Sirius [Eclipse Foundation c] and Eugenia [Kolovos et al. 2017] tools are used for this purpose.
- **M2T transformations:** Finally, M2T transformations are implemented to enable the automatic generation of all system code and deployment infrastructure (M0) from the defined digital twin models (M1). The Acceleo tool [Eclipse Foundation a] is used for this purpose.

5.3. Novelty and Advantages of the Proposed Approach

The proposed approach overcomes the limitations of related studies (see Section 3). First, it provides a domain-independent development framework for digital twins, making it applicable to a wide range of industries. Furthermore, by integrating machine learning, the proposed approach enables the creation of intelligent digital twins that go beyond predefined rule-based logic. In addition, its code generation capabilities enable the creation of all system code and deployment infrastructure, providing an end-to-end solution.

5.4. Progress and Achievements to Date

The author is in the second year of the doctoral program and has made significant progress, focusing on familiarizing with the necessary technologies and tools. A comprehensive literature review on MDSE and digital twins has also been conducted.

As part of this ongoing research, the author has published a paper in a high-impact journal [Barriga et al. 2024], where an MDSE approach to streamline the development of distributed intelligent systems is introduced. The applicability of the proposal is illustrated with an agricultural digital twin integrating various intelligent capabilities.

Moreover, in 2024, the author participated in the *Sociedad de Ingeniería de Software y Tecnologías de Desarrollo de Software* (SISTEDES) congress, where he presented in the Software Engineering for Digital Twins (ISGD) track. This experience provided valuable feedback from experts in the field.

6. Major Challenges and Future Work

One of the main challenges facing this doctoral project is the lack of universal agreement on what constitutes a digital twin, as different authors conceptualize them differently, although some elements consistently appear. This complicates the formulation of a domain-independent approach. In addition, the complexity of the technologies involved, such as IoT, cloud computing, and machine learning, presents a significant challenge.

Future work will focus on extending the capabilities of digital twins supported by the MDSE solution, including advanced prescriptive and autonomous capabilities. In this sense, prescriptive capabilities enable digital twins to recommend specific actions, while autonomous capabilities allow digital twins to execute them without human intervention. Given its complexity, the initial version overlooks these two functions.

Acknowledgements. This work was funded by project TED2021-129194B-I00 funded by MCIN/ AEI/ 10.13039/501100011033 and for European Union NextGenerationEU/ PRTR; the 0100_TID4AGRO_4_E project, co-financed by the European Regional Development Fund (ERDF) through the European Commission's INTERREG VI-A Spain-Portugal Program (POCTEP) 2021-2027; the Government of Extremadura, Council for Economy, Science and Digital Agenda under the grant GR21133; Arturo Barriga was supported by a pre-doctoral fellowship (59391100602202300000186) (PD23034) awarded by the Government of Extremadura and co-financed by the European Social Fund Plus (ESF+).

References

Barriga, A., Barriga, J. A., Pérez-Toledano, M. A., and Clemente, P. J. (2024). Model-driven development towards distributed intelligent systems. *ACM Transactions on Internet Technology*.

Barriga, J. A., Chaves-González, J. M., Barriga, A., Alonso, P., and Clemente, P. J. (2023). Simulate iot towards the cloud-to-thing continuum paradigm for task scheduling assessments. *J. Object Technol.*, 22(1):1–31.

Barriga, J. A., Clemente, P. J., Sosa-Sánchez, E., and Prieto, Á. E. (2021). Simulateiot: Domain specific language to design, code generation and execute iot simulation environments. *IEEE Access*, 9:92531–92552.

Bibow, P., Dalibor, M., Hopmann, C., Mainz, B., Rumpe, B., Schmalzing, D., Schmitz, M., and Wortmann, A. (2020). Model-driven development of a digital twin for injection molding. In *International Conference on Advanced Information Systems Engineering*, pages 85–100. Springer.

Brambilla, M., Cabot, J., and Wimmer, M. (2017). *Model-driven software engineering in practice*. Morgan & Claypool Publishers.

Ciccozzi, F. and Spalazzese, R. (2016). Mde4iot: supporting the internet of things with model-driven engineering. In *International Symposium on Intelligent and Distributed Computing*, pages 67–76. Springer.

Dalibor, M., Michael, J., Rumpe, B., Varga, S., and Wortmann, A. (2020). Towards a model-driven architecture for interactive digital twin cockpits. In *International Conference on Conceptual Modeling*, pages 377–387. Springer.

Eclipse Foundation. Acceleo - generate anything from any emf model. `https://eclipse.dev/acceleo/`. Accessed: 2025-02-18.

Eclipse Foundation. Eclipse modeling tools. `https://www.eclipse.org/downloads/packages/release/2021-03/r/eclipse-modeling-tools`. Accessed: 2025-02-18.

Eclipse Foundation. Sirius - the easiest way to get your own modeling tool. `https://eclipse.dev/sirius/`. Accessed: 2025-02-18.

Friederich, J., Francis, D. P., Lazarova-Molnar, S., and Mohamed, N. (2022). A framework for data-driven digital twins of smart manufacturing systems. *Computers in Industry*, 136:103586.

Fuller, A., Fan, Z., Day, C., and Barlow, C. (2020). Digital twin: Enabling technologies, challenges and open research. *IEEE access*, 8:108952–108971.

Hailpern, B. and Tarr, P. (2006). Model-driven development: The good, the bad, and the ugly. *IBM systems journal*, 45(3):451–461.

Hevner, A., Chatterjee, S., Hevner, A., and Chatterjee, S. (2010). Design science research in information systems. *Design research in information systems: theory and practice*, pages 9–22.

Ihirwe, F., Di Ruscio, D., Mazzini, S., Pierini, P., and Pierantonio, A. (2020). Low-code engineering for internet of things: a state of research. In *Proceedings of the*

23rd ACM/IEEE international conference on model driven engineering languages and systems: companion proceedings, pages 1–8.

Kolovos, D. S., García-Domínguez, A., Rose, L. M., and Paige, R. F. (2017). Eugenia: towards disciplined and automated development of gmf-based graphical model editors. *Software & Systems Modeling*, 16:229–255.

Lehner, D., Pfeiffer, J., Tinsel, E.-F., Strljic, M. M., Sint, S., Vierhauser, M., Wortmann, A., and Wimmer, M. (2021). Digital twin platforms: requirements, capabilities, and future prospects. *IEEE Software*, 39(2):53–61.

Macías, A., Navarro, E., Cuesta, C. E., and Zdun, U. (2023). Architecting digital twins using a domain-driven design-based approach. In *2023 IEEE 20th International Conference on Software Architecture (ICSA)*, pages 153–163. IEEE.

Mihai, S., Yaqoob, M., Hung, D. V., Davis, W., Towakel, P., Raza, M., Karamanoglu, M., Barn, B., Shetve, D., Prasad, R. V., et al. (2022). Digital twins: A survey on enabling technologies, challenges, trends and future prospects. *IEEE Communications Surveys & Tutorials*, 24(4):2255–2291.

Minerva, R., Lee, G. M., and Crespi, N. (2020). Digital twin in the iot context: A survey on technical features, scenarios, and architectural models. *Proceedings of the IEEE*, 108(10):1785–1824.

Moin, A., Rössler, S., and Günnemann, S. (2020). Thingml+ augmenting model-driven software engineering for the internet of things with machine learning. *arXiv preprint arXiv:2009.10633*.

Rathore, M. M., Shah, S. A., Shukla, D., Bentafat, E., and Bakiras, S. (2021). The role of ai, machine learning, and big data in digital twinning: A systematic literature review, challenges, and opportunities. *IEEE Access*, 9:32030–32052.

Segovia, M. and Garcia-Alfaro, J. (2022). Design, modeling and implementation of digital twins. *Sensors*, 22(14):5396.

Sharma, A., Kosasih, E., Zhang, J., Brintrup, A., and Calinescu, A. (2022). Digital twins: State of the art theory and practice, challenges, and open research questions. *Journal of Industrial Information Integration*, 30:100383.

Stadtmann, F., Rasheed, A., Kvamsdal, T., Johannessen, K. A., San, O., Kölle, K., Tande, J. O., Barstad, I., Benhamou, A., Brathaug, T., et al. (2023). Digital twins in wind energy: Emerging technologies and industry-informed future directions. *IEEE Access*.

Stahl, T., Völter, M., and Czarnecki, K. (2006). *Model-driven software development: technology, engineering, management*. John Wiley & Sons, Inc.

Vale, S., Reddy, S., Subramanian, S., Chaudhuri, S. R., Nistala, S. H., Deodhar, A., and Runkana, V. (2023). A model-driven approach for knowledge-based engineering of industrial digital twins. In *2023 ACM/IEEE 26th International Conference on Model Driven Engineering Languages and Systems (MODELS)*, pages 13–23. IEEE.

Wang, H., Chen, X., Jia, F., and Cheng, X. (2023). Digital twin-supported smart city: Status, challenges and future research directions. *Expert Systems with Applications*, 217:119531.

Desarrollo y Evaluación de un Tutor Inteligente para el aprendizaje de programación basado en los Modelos de Lenguaje Extenso

M.C. Oleksiy Levchuk

Departamento de Ciencias de la Computación – Centro de Investigación Científica y de Educación Superior de Ensenada (CICESE) – Ensenada, Baja California – México

levchuk@cicese.edu.mx

Abstract. *The emergent behavior of automatic programming following the popularization of Generative Artificial Intelligence has raised uncertainty about the future of programming and its teaching. This doctoral work proposes the design and evaluation of an architecture for the development of Intelligent Tutoring Systems for programming learning, integrating Large Language Models to provide a personalized user experience. The architecture is developed using a design-based research methodology, assessing its effect on cognitive engagement and learning through formative prototype evaluations and a summative evaluation conducted via an intervention study.*

Resumen. *El comportamiento emergente de la programación automática tras la popularización de la Inteligencia Artificial Generativa ha generado incertidumbre sobre el futuro de la programación y su enseñanza. Este trabajo doctoral propone diseñar y evaluar una arquitectura para el desarrollo de Sistemas de Tutoría Inteligente para el aprendizaje de programación que integran Modelos de Lenguaje Extenso para ofrecer una experiencia de usuario personalizada. La arquitectura se desarrolla con una metodología de investigación basada en diseño, evaluándose su efecto en el compromiso cognitivo y el aprendizaje mediante pruebas formativas del prototipo y una evaluación sumativa a través de un estudio de intervención.*

1. Introducción

Los recientes avances en Aprendizaje Profundo, impulsados por el uso de GPUs para realizar cálculos intensivos de manera altamente paralela (Goodfellow et al., 2016) y la introducción de la arquitectura de red neuronal Transformador (Vaswani et al., 2017) han permitido el desarrollo de Modelos de Lenguaje Extenso (**LLMs**) con la capacidad de procesar y generar información de manera coherente y contextualmente relevante. El acceso a grandes volúmenes de datos provenientes de diversas fuentes textuales facilitó el preentrenamiento (fase en la que un LLM aprende estructuras del lenguaje antes de su ajuste para tareas específicas) de estos modelos para capturar patrones lingüísticos complejos, haciendo posible el desarrollo de la Inteligencia Artificial Generativa (**IAG**), IA diseñada para crear contenido nuevo en diferentes formatos (Radford et al., 2019).

Los LLMs pueden utilizarse para desarrollar agentes conversacionales capaces de generar respuestas coherentes y contextuales (Brown et al., 2020), útiles en tareas como traducción, creación de contenido, diseño de prototipos y asistencia educativa (Rahman & Watanobe, 2023). En el ámbito de la programación, estos modelos pueden actuar como asistentes inteligentes que sugieren fragmentos de código, explican conceptos y ofrecen soluciones a errores comunes. Por ejemplo, GitHub Copilot y Llama-Code son capaces de generar código de manera eficiente, facilitando la escritura y depuración de programas. Sin embargo, aunque los LLMs están transformando la práctica del desarrollo de software, la evidencia sugiere que no reemplazan a programadores humanos, sino que elevan los requisitos de su labor y preparación profesional (Vaithilingam et al., 2022).

Los Sistemas de Tutoría Inteligente (**ITS**) son aplicaciones de software diseñadas para proporcionar instrucción y retroalimentación personalizada, adaptándose a las necesidades específicas de cada usuario. Esta área, con varias décadas de desarrollo, ha demostrado en ciertos contextos igualar o superar la efectividad de un tutor humano (Zhai & Wiebe, 2023). Sin embargo, su arquitectura tradicional carece de conciencia contextual (limitando su cobertura temática) y está asociada con altos costos y tiempos de desarrollo (Liu et al., 2023). El reciente éxito de los LLMs en tareas de programación abre oportunidades para fortalecer la arquitectura y aumentar la efectividad de los ITS.

Un estudio reciente que analiza más de 4 millones de conversaciones entre humanos y el asistente conversacional Claude (Tamkin et al., 2025) señala que el uso de la IAG se concentra en el desarrollo de software y las tareas de escritura, con un mayor impacto en ocupaciones relacionadas con la informática y las matemáticas. Dado que los procesos de desarrollo ya están siendo transformados por la IAG, es crucial que los futuros ingenieros de software tengan acceso a herramientas educativas de vanguardia. No obstante, la integración de LLMs en ITS presenta desafíos clave en la depuración y evaluación de su comportamiento debido a la naturaleza probabilística de los LLMs (Bommasani et al., 2021), además de la dificultad de combinarlos eficazmente con los módulos y las subrutinas de un ITS, aspectos que se abordarán en este trabajo doctoral.

2. Planteamiento del problema

Esta investigación busca responder las siguientes preguntas de investigación y alcanzar los objetivos establecidos para abordar la cuestión de integración de LLMs en ITS.

1. ¿En qué áreas de un ITS para programación los LLMs pueden contribuir a la personalización del contenido y en cuáles presentan limitaciones?
2. ¿Qué características de diseño de un ITS para programación basado en LLMs promueven el compromiso cognitivo de los estudiantes?
3. ¿Cómo se pueden ajustar los LLMs en el contexto de un ITS para programación para potenciar el aprendizaje en comparación con otros enfoques de enseñanza?

2.1. Objetivo General

Diseñar y evaluar una arquitectura para el desarrollo de un ITS para programación que integre LLMs con el objetivo de personalizar el contenido educativo, fomentar el compromiso cognitivo y mejorar el aprendizaje, proporcionando asistencia a los estudiantes en la resolución de problemas computacionales.

2.2. Objetivos Específicos

- Diseñar estrategias para integrar LLMs en ITS, identificando componentes clave para personalizar el contenido según distintos perfiles de estudiantes.
- Explorar y comparar estrategias de ajuste fino de LLMs para fomentar el compromiso cognitivo de los estudiantes durante el aprendizaje de programación.
- Implementar evaluaciones formativas e iterativas de la arquitectura desarrollada, integrando principios de diseño instruccional y experiencia de usuario.
- Realizar una evaluación sumativa del prototipo desarrollado en contextos educativos reales para medir su impacto en el aprendizaje de programación.

3. Trabajo relacionado

El compromiso cognitivo (grado de esfuerzo mental y atención que se invierte en el proceso de aprendizaje o resolución de problemas) de los estudiantes se debe tomar en cuenta para comprender los desafíos en la enseñanza y el aprendizaje de programación, donde las altas tasas de fracaso reflejan la necesidad de enfoques que no solo enseñen a producir código, sino que también fomenten una mayor atención en la comprensión de los conceptos subyacentes (Halverson & Graham, 2019). Un metaanálisis de más de 5000 artículos sobre la enseñanza y el aprendizaje de programación (Scherer et al., 2020) identificó que los enfoques constructivistas que combinan autonomía con orientación docente en entornos colaborativos con retroalimentación inmediata y el uso de herramientas tecnológicas son más efectivos que los métodos educativos tradicionales.

En el contexto de los ITS basados en LLMs existen varios prototipos que intentan alinearse con los enfoques educativos constructivistas, como Ruffle&Riley, que genera guiones de tutoría a partir de textos de lecciones y fomenta un modelo de aprendizaje basado en la enseñanza a otros: su evaluación mostró altos niveles de compromiso y comprensión por parte de los estudiantes (Schmucker et al., 2023). Sin embargo, la investigación se ha centrado principalmente en evaluar las capacidades de los LLMs de manera independiente, fuera del contexto de un ITS, observando su efecto positivo en estudiantes de programación (Qureshi, 2023; Denny et al., 2023), así como su inevitable integración en la educación, señalando la necesidad de establecer límites y promover un uso responsable de los LLMs (Rahman & Watanobe, 2023).

La integración de un LLM dentro de la arquitectura de un ITS depende del ajuste fino, un proceso que adapta el modelo a tareas específicas mediante su entrenamiento con datos especializados. Sonkar y colaboradores (2024) emplearon un conjunto de datos pedagógicos sintéticos para ajustar varios LLMs a la tarea de proporcionar ayuda personalizada, logrando mejoras significativas en la calidad de las explicaciones y la capacidad de guiar a los estudiantes. Gao y colaboradores (2024) ajustaron un LLM al contexto de la enseñanza de Inteligencia Artificial, mejorando su capacidad para asistir en el aprendizaje autorregulado dentro de un sistema de visualización interactiva.

Una revisión bibliográfica realizada en el marco de esta investigación identificó que las primeras referencias a ITS que integran LLMs en alguno de sus módulos o subrutinas datan de 2023, lo que evidencia la reciente emergencia de este campo de estudio. Además, la literatura existente no ofrece un consenso sobre la metodología óptima para el diseño y desarrollo de estos sistemas, ya que los estudios disponibles presentan limitaciones o insuficiencias en la evaluación de su diseño arquitectónico.

4. Metodología de investigación

La estrategia de investigación adoptada se fundamenta en el enfoque metodológico *Design Science Research* (Johannesson & Perjons, 2021), el cual se utiliza para crear artefactos innovadores que resuelven problemas prácticos, mientras se genera conocimiento teórico sobre su funcionamiento y posibles mejoras. En este contexto, los pasos fundamentales incluyen: identificación del problema, diseño y desarrollo, demostración, evaluación y, finalmente, comunicación (Figura 1).

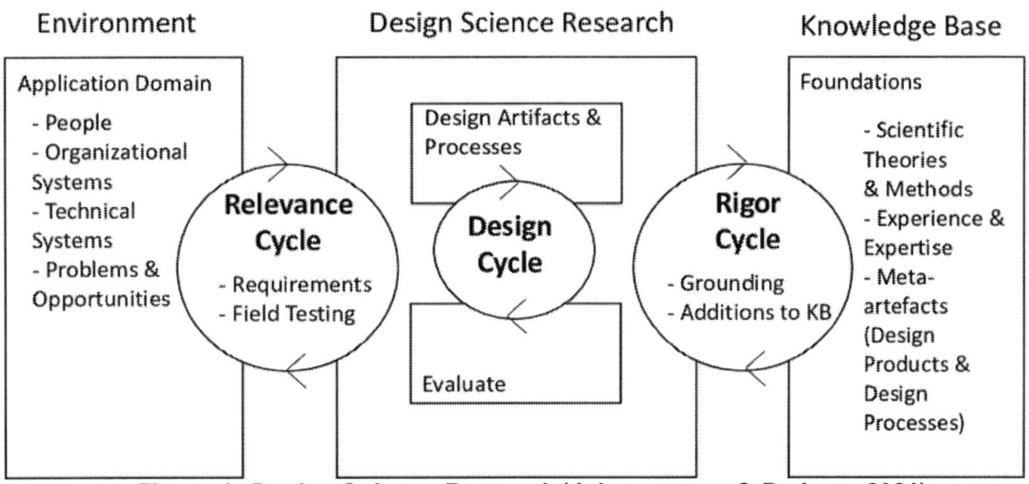

Figura 1: *Design Science Research* (Johannesson & Perjons, 2021)

Algunas de las fases de desarrollo previamente mencionadas se abordaron de manera parcial durante mi estancia de maestría, por ejemplo:

1. Se realizaron entrevistas a 10 profesores-investigadores y se aplicaron encuestas a 150 estudiantes de programación de diversos niveles educativos para explorar su percepción y uso de agentes conversacionales en la enseñanza y el aprendizaje de programación. Los resultados revelaron un marcado uso de estas herramientas entre los estudiantes, así como una actitud receptiva por parte de los profesores. Esta tendencia generalmente positiva hacia su adopción en el entorno educativo destaca la necesidad de avanzar hacia soluciones más estructuradas y personalizadas, como los ITS basados en LLMs (Levchuk, 2024).
2. Se llevó a cabo una revisión de la literatura sobre las capacidades de distintos LLMs para realizar tareas relacionadas con la programación en entornos escolares, identificando el ajuste de instrucciones como una técnica factible para trabajar con LLMs de forma remota sin modificar directamente los parámetros del modelo base. Además, bajo las métricas propuestas, el modelo GPT-4 fue seleccionado como el más pertinente para proporcionar retroalimentación personalizada a los estudiantes usando la técnica previamente mencionada.
3. Se exploro la técnica de ajuste de instrucciones para crear el prototipo de un ITS para programación que combina la funcionalidad de un agente conversacional con un cuaderno computacional. Emplea una API privada de GPT-4 para comunicarse directamente con el LLM seleccionado y una serie de instrucciones prediseñadas para controlar el contenido textual generado y su interacción con el usuario para prevenir plagio académico (Levchuk et al., 2024).

5. Solución propuesta y trabajo a futuro

Para abordar una cuestión tan multimodal como el diseño de una arquitectura que permita la incorporación de LLMs dentro de los ITS, se propone dividir el proyecto en varios pasos alineados directamente con las tres preguntas de investigación:

1. **Revisión bibliográfica:** Para identificar y mapear la literatura disponible mediante una revisión de alcance, se analizarán artículos que evidencien el uso de LLMs para potenciar la funcionalidad de los ITS. Los resultados se presentarán en una investigación registrada en la plataforma *Open Science Framework* y contribuirán al desarrollo de una arquitectura basada en el estado del arte.
2. **Métricas de personalización:** Con base en la primera pregunta de investigación y en la evidencia bibliográfica que respalda el uso de LLMs para la generación de material didáctico (Denny et al., 2023), el apoyo en la resolución de ejercicios (Qureshi, 2023) y la automatización del proceso de tutoría (Schmucker et al., 2023), se pretende establecer directrices de diseño que garanticen no solo la eficiencia técnica en la incorporación de un LLM dentro de cierto módulo o subrutina del ITS, sino también la maximización de su capacidad de personalización de contenido educativo para estudiantes de programación.
3. **Diseño de la arquitectura:** Con base en la segunda pregunta de investigación y en la evidencia bibliográfica de que niveles altos de personalización se asocian con una disminución de la carga cognitiva intrínseca (Lange, 2021), así como en estudios que indican que la personalización del aprendizaje mejora el rendimiento (59 %) y el compromiso cognitivo (36 %) de los estudiantes (du Plooy et al., 2024), se diseñarán prototipos que aprovechen esta capacidad para fomentar el compromiso cognitivo. Dado que la programación demanda habilidades cognitivas avanzadas, es crucial analizar la carga cognitiva (cantidad de esfuerzo mental requerido para procesar información en la memoria de trabajo) que enfrentan los estudiantes y su capacidad para gestionarla.
4. **Ajuste de los LLMs:** Se abordarán y evaluarán diversas técnicas de ajuste de LLMs, como el ajuste fino, la recuperación y generación, la ingeniería de instrucciones y el aprendizaje por refuerzo, entre otras. Se emplearán librerías como Hugging Face Transformers y PyTorch, con su posterior evaluación mediante herramientas como PandaLM. Este proceso implicará la interacción con modelos de código abierto (Llama, DeepSeek, etc.) y de código cerrado (GPT-4, Bard, etc.), con el objetivo de identificar combinaciones que permitan una mayor personalización y, por consiguiente, un mayor compromiso cognitivo.
5. **Enfoque en la cognición:** Con base en la tercera pregunta de investigación y en la evidencia de que promover procesos cognitivos entre estudiantes mejora la adquisición de conocimientos en programación (Singh & Rajendran, 2024), así como en estudios que reportan una fuerte correlación positiva entre el compromiso cognitivo y el éxito/productividad académica (Khan et al., 2023), se diseñará una interfaz de usuario que facilite interacciones intuitivas pero desafiantes. Esta interfaz ofrecerá apoyo sin revelar directa ni indirectamente la solución al problema planteado, mediante la implementación de elementos visuales dinámicos, retroalimentación inmediata y personalizada, así como mecanismos para el monitoreo y la intervención del profesor.

6. **Evaluaciones formativas:** Se realizarán evaluaciones formativas de los módulos y componentes del prototipo de ITS basado en la arquitectura propuesta, integrando tanto retroalimentación cualitativa obtenida a través de entrevistas y encuestas dirigidas a estudiantes y profesores, como datos cuantitativos relacionados con el rendimiento funcional del sistema (pruebas A/B).
7. **Evaluación sumativa:** Se llevará a cabo un estudio de intervención con evaluación sumativa para medir el impacto del ITS en el compromiso cognitivo y el aprendizaje de programación en los estudiantes. El estudio incluirá un grupo de control y un grupo de tratamiento, con una duración de ocho semanas dentro del currículo de clases de programación. Se aplicarán pruebas de rendimiento antes y después de la intervención, así como una prueba de retención un mes después. Se analizarán métricas clave como el progreso en habilidades, el tiempo de resolución, la precisión y la complejidad de las tareas.

6. Ventajas de la solución propuesta

A diferencia de investigaciones centradas en evaluar la capacidad de los LLMs para generar contenido específico, desempeñar tareas concretas o simular roles particulares, este trabajo doctoral propone el diseño y la evaluación de una arquitectura para el desarrollo de ITS basados en LLMs para el aprendizaje de programación. En contraste con la aplicación de estos modelos para suplir funcionalidades específicas dentro de módulos individuales (Fernández et al., 2024), se busca integrar la IAG de manera holística, con el objetivo de optimizar múltiples subrutinas y módulos del sistema, siempre que se identifiquen beneficios significativos en esta sinergia, representando una aplicación más amplia y unificada de los LLMs en la educación de programación, superando las limitaciones de enfoques tradicionales.

La arquitectura propuesta se centra en fomentar la autonomía de los estudiantes, permitiéndoles resolver problemas por sí mismos mientras adquieren un entendimiento más profundo a través de retroalimentación personalizada. Simultáneamente, el sistema proporciona herramientas para monitorear y gestionar las interacciones entre estudiantes y LLMs, asegurando un control efectivo del proceso educativo y facilitando intervenciones pedagógicas en momentos críticos. Este enfoque integral y centrado en la cognición tiene el potencial de transformar la forma en que los ITS basados en LLMs se diseñan y utilizan en el aprendizaje de programación y otros dominios educativos.

7. Conclusiones

Esta investigación propone generar conocimiento sobre el diseño, implementación y evaluación de una arquitectura para el desarrollo de ITS para programación que integren LLMs para personalizar el contenido educativo, fomentar el compromiso cognitivo y mejorar el aprendizaje. Se busca identificar la configuración óptima de los componentes que permiten la personalización del contenido, determinar características de diseño que fomenten el compromiso cognitivo y explorar distintas estrategias de ajuste fino para maximizar el aprendizaje adquirido. Los resultados esperados contribuirán al avance de la Ingeniería de Software, proporcionando lineamientos para la integración efectiva de LLMs en ITS y su aplicación en la enseñanza de programación.

Dado que se trata de un campo emergente, esta investigación no busca crear una herramienta definitiva, sino generar conocimiento y responder la pregunta controversial: ¿Como podemos asegurarnos de que la integración de LLMs en los ITS fomente un aprendizaje activo en lugar de generar dependencia? Explorar algo trascendental en lugar de centrarse en un LLM en particular ayudaría a preservar la relevancia de este trabajo, además de que se hará público el prototipo desarrollado en base a la arquitectura diseñada a través de la plataforma de GitHub y se compartirá con la comunidad científica a través de publicaciones en revistas de impacto.

8. Referencias

Bommasani, R., Hudson, D. A., Adeli, E., Altman, R., Arora, S., von Arx, S., ... & Liang, P. (2021). "On the opportunities and risks of foundation models". arXiv preprint. https://doi.org/10.48550/arXiv.2108.07258

Brown, T., Mann, B., Ryder, N., Subbiah, M., Kaplan, J. D., Dhariwal, P., ... & Amodei, D. (2020). "Language models are few-shot learners". Advances in neural information processing systems, 33, 1877-1901. https://doi.org/10.48550/arXiv.2005.14165

Denny, P., Prather, J., Becker, B. A., Finnie-Ansley, J., Hellas, A., Leinonen, J., ... & Sarsa, S. (2024). "Computing education in the era of generative AI". Communications of the ACM, 67(2), 56-67. https://doi.org/10.1145/3624720

Du Plooy, E., Casteleijn, D., & Franzsen, D. (2024). "Personalized adaptive learning in higher education: a scoping review of key characteristics and impact on academic performance and engagement". Heliyon, 10(21), e39630. https://doi.org/10.1016/j.heliyon.2024.e39630

Fernández, L. R., Mena, A. L. F., Magaña, M. P. T., Magaña, M. A. R., & Fernández, M. A. R. (2024). "Inteligencia artificial en la educación: Modelo de lenguaje de gran tamaño (LLM) como recurso educativo". Revista IPSUMTEC, 7(2), 157-164. https://doi.org/10.61117/ipsumtec.v7i2.321

Gao, L., Lu, J., Shao, Z., Lin, Z., Yue, S., Ieong, C., ... & Chen, S. (2024). "Fine-tuned large language model for visualization system: A study on self-regulated learning in education". IEEE Transactions on Visualization and Computer Graphics. http://dx.doi.org/10.1109/TVCG.2024.3456145

Goodfellow, I., Bengio, Y., & Courville, A. (2016). "Deep learning". MIT Press.

Halverson, L. R., & Graham, C. R. (2019). "Learner Engagement in Blended Learning Environments: A Conceptual Framework". Online Learning, 23, 145-178. https://doi.org/10.24059/olj.v23i2.1481

Johannesson, P., & Perjons, E. (2021). "An Introduction to Design Science". In Springer eBooks. https://doi.org/10.1007/978-3-030-78132-3

Khan, H., Gul, R., & Zeb, M. (2023). "The Effect of Students' Cognitive and Emotional Engagement on Students' Academic Success and Academic Productivity". Journal Of Social Sciences Review, 3(1), 322-334. https://doi.org/10.54183/jssr.v3i1.141

Lange, C. (2021). "The relationship between e-learning personalization and cognitive load". Open Learning the Journal of Open Distance And e-Learning, 38(3), 228-242. https://doi.org/10.1080/02680513.2021.2019577

Levchuk, O. (2024). Diseño y evaluación de un tutor inteligente basado en Inteligencia Artificial Generativa para la adquisición de habilidades de programación. Tesis de Maestría en Ciencias. CICESE, Baja California, México. 92 pp.

Levchuk, O., Sánchez, C., Pacheco, N., López, I., & Favela, J. (2024). "Interaction Design (IxD) of an Intelligent Tutor for Programming Learning Based on LLM". Avances en Interacción Humano-Computadora, 9(1), 1–10. https://doi.org/10.47756/aihc.y9i1.137

Liu, Z., He, X., Liu, L., Liu, T., & Zhai, X. (2023). "Context matters: A strategy to pre-train language model for science education". In International Conference on Artificial Intelligence in Education, 666-674. Cham: Springer Nature Switzerland. https://doi.org/10.1007/978-3-031-36336-8_103

Qureshi, B. (2023). "Exploring the use of chatgpt as a tool for learning and assessment in undergraduate computer science curriculum: Opportunities and challenges". ArXiv preprint. https://doi.org/10.48550/arXiv.2304.11214

Radford, A., Wu, J., Child, R., Luan, D., Amodei, D. & Sutskever, I. (2019). "Language Models are Unsupervised Multitask Learners". OpenAI.

Rahman, M. M., & Watanobe, Y. (2023). "ChatGPT for Education and Research: Opportunities, Threats, and Strategies". Applied Sciences, 13(9), 5783. https://doi.org/10.3390/app13095783

Scherer, R., Siddiq, F., & Viveros, B. S. (2020). "A meta-analysis of teaching and learning computer programming: Effective instructional approaches and conditions". Computers In Human Behavior, 109, 106349. https://doi.org/10.1016/j.chb.2020.106349

Schmucker, R., Xia, M., Azaria, A., & Mitchell, T. (2023). "Ruffle&riley: Towards the automated induction of conversational tutoring systems". ArXiv preprint. https://doi.org/10.48550/arXiv.2310.01420

Singh, D., & Rajendran, R. (2024). "Cognitive engagement as a predictor of learning gain in Python programming". Smart Learning Environments, 11(1). https://doi.org/10.1186/s40561-024-00330-9

Sonkar, S., Ni, K., Chaudhary, S., & Baraniuk, R. G. (2024). "Pedagogical alignment of large language models". arXiv preprint. https://doi.org/10.48550/arXiv.2402.05000

Tamkin, A., Liu, K., Valle, R., & Clark, J. (2025). "Which Economic Tasks are Performed with AI? Evidence from Millions of Claude Conversations". Anthropic. assets.anthropic.com/m/2e23255f1e84ca97/original/Economic_Tasks_AI_Paper.pdf

Vaithilingam, P., Zhang, T., & Glassman, E. L. (2022). "Expectation vs. experience: Evaluating the usability of code generation tools powered by large language models". CHI EA '22: CHI Conference on Human Factors in Computing Systems Extended Abstracts, Article 332, 1–7. https://doi.org/10.1145/3491101.3519665

Vaswani, A., Shazeer, N., Parmar, N., Uszkoreit, J., Jones, L., Gomez, A. N., Kaiser, Ł., & Polosukhin, I. (2017). "Attention is all you need". Advances in Neural Information Processing Systems, 30, 5998–6008. https://doi.org/10.48550/arXiv.1706.03762

Zhai, X., & Wiebe, E. (2023). "Technology-based innovative assessment". In Classroom-Based STEM Assessment: Contemporary Issues and Perspectives, 99–125.

Mitigation of Cognitive Biases in Innovative Software Engineering Projects: A Proposal

Alberto Guerral[1]

[1]CESAR, Recife Center for Advanced Studies and Systems
Apolo Street, Recife – Brazil

ahcg@cesar.school

Abstract.

Cognitive biases are critical in software engineering (SE) affecting replanning, failures and even cancellations. This work aims to identify and mitigate cognitive biases in the management of innovative projects in SE, in a large multinational company. Using the Design Science Research (DSR) method, a (1) Systematic Literature Review (SLR) will be carried out, (2) complementary research, (3) study of technological alternatives and (4) application of an artifact in the company's project portfolio to identify the behavior of the five most impactful biases in SE, proposing a framework with practical recommendations to eliminate them, contributing to future research in the industry.
Keywords: *cognitive bias, project, software, innovation, psychology*

1. Introduction

The pervasive influence of cognitive biases on projects, particularly in the context of replanning and failure or cancellation, has emerged as a significant concern in the field of software engineering. Evidence points to a relationship between cognitive biases and their substantial impacts on software engineering projects [Mohanani et al. 2020]. However, despite this recognition, there is a notable dearth of comprehensive studies and research that explicitly focus on the direct implications of cognitive biases on projects, as well as effective solutions to alleviate the challenges they pose.

Although preliminary studies have identified the presence of cognitive biases in system development and software engineering, there remains a significant gap in exploring strategies to deal with these biases [Borowa et al. 2021], [Chattopadhyay et al. 2020], and [Mohanani et al. 2020]. Some of these biases include anchoring, fixation, confirmation, overconfidence, and optimism, each with distinct characteristics that profoundly influence the dynamics of software projects. Despite being recognized as critical factors, these biases remain relatively unexplored in the academic domain. Furthermore, strategic models designed to eliminate or mitigate these biases are conspicuously scarce in the existing literature.

The recognition of cognitive biases as powerful contributors to challenges in software engineering projects highlights the need for further investigation into their manifestation, impact, and potential countermeasures. This research work aims, in addition to contributing to the existing gap in the literature, investigating aspects of cognitive biases in the context of innovation software projects, as well as pragmatically helping companies that invest in these projects to substantially reduce the negative impact of these biases. Building on existing studies, especially those by [Borowa et al. 2021], [Chattopadhyay et al. 2020], and [Mohanani et al. 2020], this research work seeks to provide a more comprehensive understanding of the key specific biases that significantly affect the outcomes of innovative software engineering projects, by identifying them, understanding how they impact these projects, and exploring mitigation mechanisms for them. In doing so, it aspires to contribute to the advancement of knowledge and the development of practical solutions to increase the success and resilience of software projects in the face of cognitive biases.

2. Research Problem

Cognitive biases are natural characteristic of the human mind, first observed by Kahneman and Tversky et al apud [Borowa et al. 2021]. They have their roots in the dual nature of human reasoning, with two distinct mental systems: System 1, responsible for quick judgments based on limited data, and System 2, which involves rational and logical thinking based on a larger set of data. If we do not deliberately analyze our choices, System 1 will make hasty judgments.

Cognitive biases arise from various sources and depend on each individual's thought process, including software engineers. Some biases result from development style, such as hyperbolic discounting, while others are caused by limited cognitive capacity [Chattopadhyay et al. 2020]. For example, the availability bias can lead programmers to choose solutions based on examples readily available in memory.

The concept of cognitive biases was first introduced in 1974 by Tversky and Kahneman apud [Chattopadhyay et al. 2020]. Since 1990, software engineering researchers have been examining these biases, reported in publications, especially those by [Mohanani et al. 2020]. Of the more than 200 cognitive biases found in management, psychology, and sociology studies, 37 different types have been examined in software engineering. These studies have shown that biases can distort code features, increase defect rates, and result in insufficient effort during requirements analysis.

Fleischmann et al apud [Zhou 2020] grouped cognitive biases into eight categories: perception, pattern recognition, memory, decision-making, action orientation, stability, social, and interest. The Cognitive Biases Codex, described by John Manoogian, 2016, categorizes more than 200 biases into four categories: too much information, not enough meaning, need to act fast, and what to remember.

Systematic deviations from the best choices and judgments are called cognitive biases and can compromise the success of a project [Wyrich et al. 2022]. [Mohanani et al. 2020] demonstrate that cognitive biases can occur in software engineering in several ways. The anchoring effect is the most frequently examined in the software engineering literature. Common problems in software engineering tasks can be explained by cognitive biases, helping to develop better practices and methods [Mohanani et al. 2022]. Studying biases is challenging because they can have different names depending on the field or context [Mohanani et al. 2020].

The most frequent biases in software engineering, according to [Mohanani et al. 2020], include:

A. Anchoring Bias: People rely too heavily on the first information received when making decisions, disproportionately influencing subsequent thinking.

B. Fixation Bias: Inability to adequately adjust the evaluation of a situation, even with new information.

C. Confirmation Bias: Tendency to seek, interpret, and remember information that confirms existing beliefs [Rafiq et al. 2021].

D. Overconfidence Bias: Overestimation of one's abilities and aptitudes, leading to an illusion of control and neglect of useful information.

E. Optimism Bias: Tendency to produce overly optimistic estimates and predictions, influenced by the initial phase of projects and the ability to assess risks [Mohanani et al. 2020].

3. Related Work

The review of related studies in this work focuses on the analysis of cognitive biases in the context of project management for innovation in software engineering and related areas, such as computer science and information systems. In order to delineate the current research frontier, studies published from 2020 onwards were considered in this period, in which a significant gap in specific analyses in this area is observed.

The search for relevant literature, was conducted in renowned databases, including ACM Digital Library, IEEE Explore, and ScienceDirect - Elsevier. Initially, 149 papers were identified, which were subsequently filtered based on rigorous criteria, explained in Systematic Literature Review, resulting in a selection of 12 studies directly pertinent to the theme of cognitive biases in software and innovation projects.

Among these studies, various perspectives were explored. The study by [Kavitha et al. 2022], for example, investigated the role of cognitive biases in the responsible development of AI systems, while [Mohanani et al. 2021] examined the effects of these biases on the definition and framing of desiderata in software engineering projects. Some studies, such as [Catto and Maccari 2021], addressed broader themes related to innovation and project management without a specific focus on cognitive biases, while others, such as [Zhou 2020], explored less studied aspects, such as biases in technical communication. The study [Mohanani et al. 2020] was very comprehensive in terms of exploring cognitive biases in software engineering and can be applied to the study of innovation project management, since it is one of the most complete among those found. 37 cognitive biases were studied, grouped into 8 categories, and mitigation techniques were addressed for only 6 of them. Additionally, it was mentioned that proving a bias in a laboratory is not the same as proving that it has a significant impact on real projects.

In the study [Chattopadhyay et al. 2020], a field study involving ten developers was conducted to examine the prevalence of cognitive biases in the workplace and analyze their effects on development. The findings showed, through the studies of the Systematic Literature Review, that cognitive biases are common and negatively impact developers' problem-solving skills, such as exploration, sense-making, and contextualization. The fixation bias occurred most frequently in this category; it was linked to 477 developmental actions, of which 428 were reversed, although the study did not use mitigation techniques but only questioned developers if they had used actions to combat them.

Table 1 shows the degree of relationship between the studies and the research questions, obtained from reading and verifying whether each of them answered these questions. The variations were Weak (0), when it did not directly answer any question, Moderate (1-2), when it answered between one or two and Strong (3), when it answered the three research questions: RQ1: What are the main cognitive biases related to software innovation project management? RQ2: What are the impacts of cognitive biases on software innovation project management? RQ3: What strategies can be adopted to mitigate the effects of cognitive biases on software innovation project management?

Tabela 1. Degree of relationship between the studies and the research questions

STUDY	RQ1	RQ2	RQ3	DEGREE
[Kavitha et al. 2022]	X			MODERATE
[Borowa et al. 2021]		X		MODERATE
[Nicodeme 2021]				WEAK
[Mohanani et al. 2021]	X	X		MODERATE
[Mohanani et al. 2022]	X	X	X	STRONG
[Catto and Maccari 2021]				WEAK
[Geyer et al. 2022]				WEAK
[Buffardi 2023]		X		MODERATE
[Zhou 2020]				WEAK
[Wyrich et al. 2022]				WEAK
[Chattopadhyay et al. 2020]	X	X	X	STRONG
[Mohanani et al. 2020]	X	X	X	STRONG

Although the selected studies provided valuable insights into cognitive biases in the context of software engineering and innovation project management, few of them addressed specific strategies to mitigate them, and in a superficial way, leaving room for future study and research. This related work section highlighted the importance of additional research that effectively identifies and evaluates such strategies, aiming to promote more efficient and innovative project management in this domain.

4. Research Objectives

The main objective of the research is to identify the behavior, in innovation project management, of the five most common cognitive biases in software engineering in general and to develop a strategy to mitigate them.

To achieve the general objective, the research is divided into specific objectives, which include investigating and mapping the five most common cognitive biases in software engineering projects, analyzing how these biases affect the decision-making process in the management of innovation projects and the quality of the results, building an artifact using AI to identify these biases in a portfolio of projects of a large multinational company, and proposing a framework to mitigate these biases, based on consolidated organizational models.

The expected contributions of this research include promoting greater awareness of cognitive biases in the management of innovation projects in software engineering and offering practical guidelines to mitigate them. The strategies developed are expected to improve the quality and effectiveness of projects, resulting in more impartial and effective solutions, contributing to the advancement of software engineering.

5. Proposed Methodology

The proposed research work plan involves using the DSR (Design Science Research) method.

According to [Vaishanvi and Library. 2009] and [Wieringa 2014], design science is defined as an approach that seeks to create things that serve human purposes. It involves the development of validated artifacts that meet identified needs, as well as the generation of justified theories about these artifacts to contribute to the knowledge base shared by design scientists.

The interaction between design and research activities is highlighted, with an emphasis on solving practical problems through design and validation of proposed solutions.

The philosophical line used by DSR is pragmatism, whose philosophical approach emphasizes the importance of practice, experience, and practical consequences in evaluating theories and beliefs. Pragmatists believe that the value of an idea or concept lies in its usefulness and effectiveness in solving real-world problems.

The thesis development method will consist of four stages:

1. **Use of Systematic Literature Review (SLR)** [Guerra 2024], to identify studies and solutions that aim to solve problems of cognitive biases in the management of innovative software projects.
2. **Deepening of the problem**, through the investigation of the greatest impacts of cognitive biases, how they can affect the management of innovation projects and definition of the biases to be the object of the work research.
3. **Evaluation of technological alternatives** for the construction of an artifact, using Artificial Intelligence (AI) LLM (Large Language Model), trained to identify cognitive biases in the data collected from the research. A research questionnaire will be formulated, in an objective way, to guide the interviews, where the main focus will be on the project planning phase, analyzing the responses of stakeholders, testimonies, facts and context. At this stage, research participants will be clearly informed about how AI will be used to process data, about open and closed questions, about the confidentiality of the data obtained and free from any type of constraint. By following these guidelines, the research will be conducted in an ethical and legally sound manner for the participants.
4. **Evaluation of results**, based on the application of the artifact, in approximately 50 innovative software engineering projects in a large multinational company. Once the presence of cognitive biases is detected, a framework containing recommendations for each project will be used. This framework will be developed based on organizational strategic concepts or models, with well-founded guidelines to mitigate each bias found.

6. Proposed Timeline

The author is a PhD student who began in the second half of 2023.

The first stage of the research, SRL, was completed in 2024 and focused on identifying the state of the art regarding the presence of cognitive biases in innovative software projects and possible existing mitigation techniques.

Based on the SLR, a scientific article was prepared, which was submitted and accepted for publication as a "Short Paper", at ICEIS 2024 – 26th International Conference on Business Information Systems, with issue number 183, entitled "Impact of Cognitive Biases on Innovative Software Engineering Projects". The event was held in the city of Angers, France, between April 28 and 30, 2024.

The proposed schedule also considers: 2024, Preparation of the Thesis Plan; 2025, Qualification of the Thesis Plan; 2025-2026, Evolution of the Thesis; 2027, Thesis Defense.

7. Final Considerations

Through the SRL, it was possible to identify studies and solutions that propose solutions to problems related to cognitive biases in software innovation projects. When reviewing the studies, it was observed that biases directly impact project management, influencing everything from the definition of objectives to the testing phase. Notably, study [Mohanani et al. 2020], offered a holistic approach, identifying 37 biases in software. However, the analysis also highlighted existing gaps, indicating that, despite the extensive research on cognitive biases in the human sciences, specific exploration in software engineering, especially in innovation project management, continues to be a field to be widely investigated. The complexity of these interactions requires continued attention and deeper analyses to develop effective strategies to mitigate biases and promote success in software innovation projects.

The works found related to software engineering are still few and very recent, and they are not applied to innovation projects. The main focus of this research work is to evaluate the presence of main cognitive biases in the management of innovation projects, using an artifact built with the help of AI, to understand their impacts and to apply a framework with mitigation recommendations for each bias found. Therefore, it is expected to contribute, in a pragmatic way, to the evolution of management, efficiency and quality of delivery of innovation software projects.

Referências

Borowa, K., Zalewski, A., and Kijas, S. (2021). The influence of cognitive biases on architectural technical debt. In *Proceedings - IEEE 18th International Conference on Software Architecture, ICSA 2021*, pages 115–125. Institute of Electrical and Electronics Engineers Inc.

Buffardi, K. (2023). Cognitive reflection in software verification and testing. pages 1–10. Institute of Electrical and Electronics Engineers (IEEE).

Catto, S. L. and Maccari, E. A. (2021). Innovation projects management: a systematic literature review. *Revista de Administração da UFSM*, 14:848–863.

Chattopadhyay, S., Nelson, N., Au, A., Morales, N., Sanchez, C., Pandita, R., and Sarmal, A. (2020). A tale from the trenches: Cognitive biases and software development. In

Proceedings - International Conference on Software Engineering, pages 75–86. IEEE Computer Society.

Geyer, F., Szakal, V. A., Kara, P. A., and Simon, A. (2022). Cognitive-bias-induced differences in the perceived video quality of rugged and conventional smartphones. In *Proceedings - 16th International Conference on Signal-Image Technology and Internet-Based Systems, SITIS 2022*, pages 592–599. Institute of Electrical and Electronics Engineers Inc.

Guerra, A. (2024). Impact of cognitive biases on innovative software engineering projects - "https://bit.ly/4hrh4yk". Acessado em: 31 de março de 2025.

Kavitha, J., Kiran, J. S., Prasad, S. D., Soma, K., Babu, G. C., and Sivakumar, S. (2022). Prediction and its impact on its attributes while biasing machinelearning training data. In *Proceedings of the 3rd International Conference on Smart Technologies in Computing, Electrical and Electronics, ICSTCEE 2022*. Institute of Electrical and Electronics Engineers Inc.

Mohanani, R., Ralph, P., Turhan, B., and Mandic, V. (2022). How templated requirements specifications inhibit creativity in software engineering. *IEEE Transactions on Software Engineering*, 48:4074–4086.

Mohanani, R., Salman, I., Turhan, B., Iguez, P. R., and Ralph, P. (2020). Cognitive biases in software engineering: A systematic mapping study.

Mohanani, R., Turhan, B., and Ralph, P. (2021). Requirements framing affects design creativity. *IEEE Transactions on Software Engineering*, 47:936–947.

Nicodeme, C. (2021). Tackle cognitive biases in videosurveillance. In *IEEE International Symposium on Industrial Electronics*, volume 2021-June. Institute of Electrical and Electronics Engineers Inc.

Rafiq, U., Melegati, J., Khanna, D., Guerra, E., and Wang, X. (2021). Analytics mistakes that derail software startups. In *ACM International Conference Proceeding Series*, pages 60–69. Association for Computing Machinery.

Vaishanvi, V. and Library., A. D. (2009). *Proceedings of the 4th International Conference on Design Science Research in Information Systems and Technology.* ACM.

Wieringa, R. (2014). *Design science methodology for information systems and software engineering*. Springer.

Wyrich, M., Merz, L., and Graziotin, D. (2022). Anchoring code understandability evaluations through task descriptions. In *IEEE International Conference on Program Comprehension*, volume 2022-March, pages 133–140. IEEE Computer Society.

Zhou, Q. (2020). Cognitive biases in technical communication. In *IEEE International Professional Communication Conference*, volume 2020-July, pages 39–46. Institute of Electrical and Electronics Engineers Inc.

Model-Driven Engineering for Implementation and Testing of Large Language Model Architectures

Jesús Carreño-Bolufer[1]

[1]Valencian Research Institute for Artificial Intelligence (VRAIN),
Universitat Politècnica de València
Camino de Vera s/n, Valencia, Spain

jecarbo@vrain.upv.es

Abstract. *Large Language Model (LLM) architectures such as DeepSeek-V3 demonstrate reductions in computational costs through the design of efficient architectures, but their development reveals technical debt in the software engineering principles associated with LLM development, partly caused by the multidisciplinary nature of the field. Consequently, it leads to increased development costs and challenges in software quality. To address these issues, this thesis proposes the integration of Model-Driven Engineering into the LLM development life cycle. A conceptual metamodel formalises LLM architectural constructs (RQ1), enabling automated code generation via model transformations (RQ2) and facilitating Model-Based testing (RQ3).*

1. Motivation

The adoption of artificial intelligence (AI)-based applications is growing rapidly in almost all domains. In particular, generative artificial intelligence (GenAI) [Banh and Strobel 2023] has captured much of the attention due to technologies such as Large Language Models (LLMs), including ChatGPT or Google Gemini [Baldassarre et al. 2023, Gozalo-Brizuela and Garrido-Merchan 2023].

LLMs are able to perform advanced tasks such as grammar correction, cross-domain reasoning, arithmetic computations and code execution [Bommasani et al. 2022]. There are multiple benchmarks to evaluate their performance in different areas [Zhao et al. 2024]. However, achieving results that exceed the state of the art requires a significant amount of computational resources. The training of GPT-4 is estimated to have cost around $78 million, while that of Gemini Ultra amounted to $191 million [Perrault and Clark 2024].

In the face of these high costs, approaches have emerged to develop more efficient models [Wan et al. 2024]. A remarkable example is DeepSeek-V3 [DeepSeek-AI 2024], an open-source LLM whose capabilities are comparable to those of models such as LLaMa-3 [Grattafiori et al. 2024] and GPT-4 [OpenAI 2023], but with a cost and training time up to ten times lower [towards data science 2025]. This has been possible thanks to optimisations in its architecture, which has improved efficiency during the training stage [DeepSeek-AI 2024].

In this way, we find synergies with software engineering, leading to an emerging line of research called SE4AI [Martínez-Fernández et al. 2022]. This line proposes the adoption and/or creation of software engineering processes that optimise the construction of intelligent systems.

In the context of software engineering, Model-Driven Engineering (MDE) [Pastor and Molina 2007] has been noted for reducing the complexity of software development through higher levels of abstraction and automation of manual tasks. In this thesis, we explore the adoption of model-based technologies to reduce cost and effort in AI development (MDE4AI) [Rädler et al. 2024]. In particular, we focus on building LLMs from design and quality assurance, considering the architecture design, implementation and testing stages.

2. Problem statement and Existing Solutions

In the field of artificial intelligence, there are several subcategories. This thesis is framed within the subdomain of Deep Learning (DL) which is part of the set of intelligent applications based on Machine Learning (ML) [Banh and Strobel 2023]. As illustrated in Figure 1, within Deep Learning is Generative Artificial Intelligence, from which LLMs emerge.

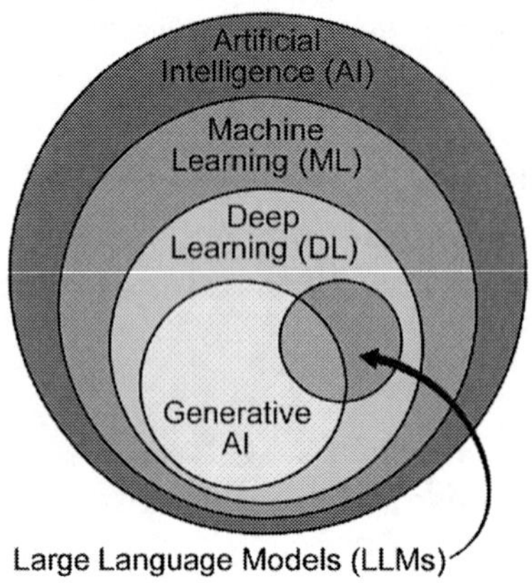

Figure 1. Classification of LLMs within artificial intelligence [Shahab et al. 2024].

The development life cycle of an LLM model can be decomposed into several phases and stages [Amershi et al. 2019, Google-Cloud 2025, Zhang et al. 2019]. This process encompasses five major phases: Analysis (1), Data (2), Software (3), Model (4) and Deployment (5) (see Figure 2).

To reduce the costs associated with LLMs, optimisation focuses mainly on the training stage (4.1), specifically on decreasing the computational costs [Hoffmann et al. 2022]. It has been shown that improving the architectural design of the AI model allows for more computationally efficient training[DeepSeek-AI 2024], achieving adequate results with lower demand on resources [Wan et al. 2024]. Examples of design decisions are the selection of parameters such as the size of the model, the number of layers, the number of heads in the multi-head attention mechanism, or the use of Mixture of Experts (MoE) in the neural network, where a router determines which components of the network are activated, thus optimising the use of computational resources.

However, to reach this goal there is a technical debt in applying software engineering [Liu et al. 2020, Sculley et al. 2015, Foidl et al. 2019, Alahdab and Çalıklı 2019] in the earlier stages of architecture design, implementation and testing (see Figure 2, Phase 3). This lack of SE principles increases development cost and decreases software quality in aspects such as maintainability, reusability and testability [ISO/IEC 25010:2023 2023].

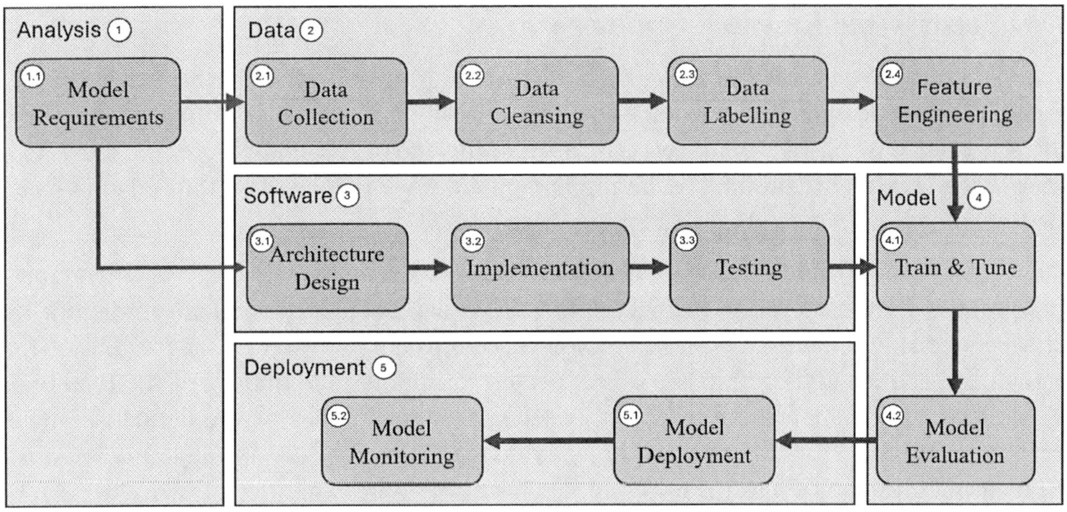

Figure 2. LLM development life cycle. The arrows guide the workflow, but it may loop back to any previous stage.

One of the main factors behind this technical debt is the multidisciplinary nature of the field. AI model development projects involve diverse profiles, such as data scientists, software engineers, domain specialists, cloud infrastructure experts, among others [Foidl et al. 2019].This requires developers to possess knowledge in software engineering and ML to build correct AI models. Furthermore, compared to other types of software, modules in these systems tend to be coupled, which hinders their modularity and evolution.

To address these challenges, proposals have emerged that are framed within the Software Engineering for Artificial Intelligence or SE4AI research domain. [Martínez-Fernández et al. 2022]. More specifically, the MDE4AI [Rädler et al. 2024] line applies the concepts of Model-Driven engineering to encapsulate the complexity associated with the design and automate the implementation of AI models. This is possible by means of model transformation rules that automate the generation of software artefacts. In this domain, the systematic review by Naveed [Naveed et al. 2024] explores the intersection of MDE and Machine Learning. In this review, effort reduction is highlighted, followed by quality improvement. In addition, we find solutions for the automatic generation of neural network code. [Díaz et al. 2015, Al-Azzoni 2020], and modelling for complexity reduction of cyber-physical systems based on deep reinforcement learning [Gatto et al. 2019]. On the other hand, Hartmann's proposal [Hartmann et al. 2019] aims to build ML algorithms into independent and reusable units with MDE techniques.

Considering the reviews and papers previously analysed, no MDE proposals have been identified that address the architecture of the AI model of an LLM in a comprehensive way. The proposals that apply MDE techniques focus on specific components, such as neural networks, or on general aspects of Machine Learning. This justifies and supports the main objective of the thesis, which is to comprehensively address the design and implementation of the architecture for LLMs using an MDE approach.

3. Objectives and Research Questions

The main objective of this thesis is the application of Model-Driven engineering to guide the architecture design, implementation and testing stages in the development of AI models associated with LLMs. In this way, by abstracting and encapsulating specific technical knowledge, as well as automating the implementation, we reduce the effort, cost, and errors inherent to manual coding [Pastor and Molina 2007].

As specific objectives, the proposal is expected to reduce costs and development times. Furthermore, it is expected to reduce the technical complexity inherent to LLM systems, facilitating the reuse of knowledge through the use of conceptual models [Pastor and Molina 2007]. Finally, it is expected to improve the quality of the resulting LLMs through the application of model-based testing techniques on the defined models [ref model based]. To address these objectives, the thesis focuses on the application of MDE in the Software Phase (see Figure 2, Phase 3), addressing the following research questions:

- **RQ1** Is it possible to characterise the conceptual constructors needed to define the software architecture of an LLM in a complete way?
- **RQ1** Is it possible to automatically implement the architecture of an LLM using model transformation rules?
- **RQ3** Is it possible to automatically generate test suites for testing an LLM from its conceptual model?

4. Research approach

For the development of this thesis, research approach based on Design Science Research (DSR) [Wieringa 2014] is defined. Thus, the research process is structured in the following phases:

- **Awareness of the Problem:** Inefficiency in the specification of Large Language Models (LLMs) and quality problems in the products developed due to the lack of software engineering practices in their architecture design, implementation and testing.
- **Suggestion:** A solution based on MDE is proposed to improve both development efficiency and software quality in LLMs.
- **Development:** The central artifact of the thesis is the conceptual model that describes the constructs associated with the architectural design of an LLM.
- **Evaluation:** The evaluation will be carried out considering the efficiency of the development, evaluating aspects such as reduction of implementation time, reduction of complexity and ease of integration of components in the process of building LLMs. Additionally, quality improvement will be analysed considering aspects such as reusability, maintainability and testability [ISO/IEC 25010:2023 2023]. The proposal will be applied in two case studies framed in European projects i) Music360[1]: Analysis of the impact of music in different contexts [Giachetti et al. 2023], and ii) Better [2]: Precision medicine based on genomic analysis.

[1]Music360. https://music-360.eu/

[2]Better. https://www.better-health-project.eu/

Our proposal consider three iterations that also applies the Design Science principles, these iterations are aligned with the research questions proposed, as follows.

1. **Iteration 1 (Year 1)**. Definition and generation of a conceptual model for LLMs architecture specification. Aligned with RQ1. This proposed conceptual model will be supported by a MOF metamodel that formalises its abstract syntax [Object Management Group 2019]. In addition, specific model editors will be implemented to provide notational support to the conceptual model, as well as model transformation tools to automate the generation of software artifacts.
2. **Iteration 2 (Year 2)**. Definition and implementation of Model-to-Text (M2T) transformation rules to generate the LLMs architecture software and configuration of components according the to LLM conceptual model instantiation [Pastor and Molina 2007]. Aligned with RQ2. The transformations will be supported by existing open-source technologies to facilitate its communication to the community and application by practitioners.
3. **Iteration 3 (Year 3)**. Definition and implementation of the suite for the generation of test cases from the LLMs models. Aligned with RQ3. The implementation of this test cases generation will be based on the principles of model-based testing considering approaches such as Marin's [Marín et al. 2017] in our research team.

5. Current status

As a starting point for the development of the thesis, the activities in the life cycle of an LLM were identified (Figure 2). Considering this life cycle, the thesis applies MDE principles framed within the software phase (see Figure 3, Phase 3). Thus, the main definitions for addressing the Research Questions and planning proposed are given below.

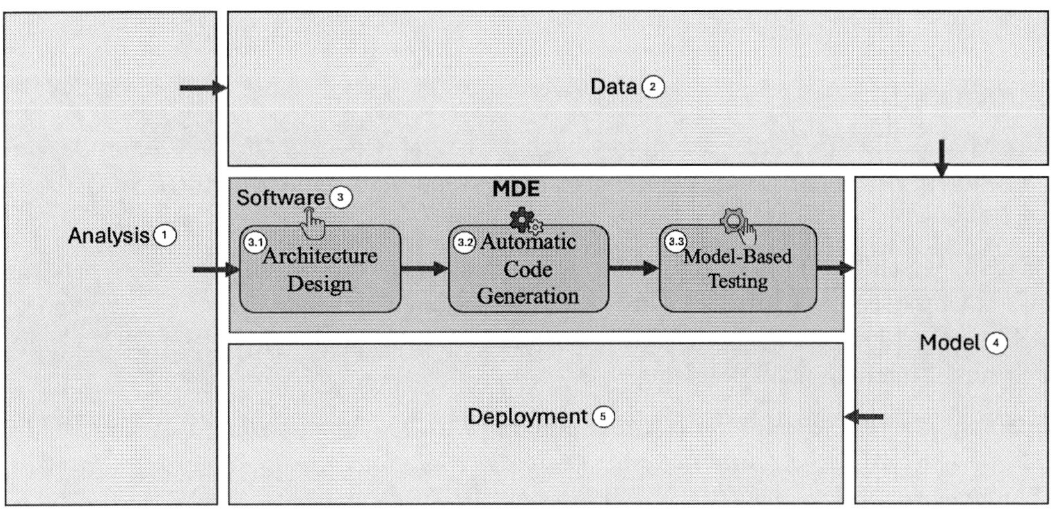

Figure 3. LLM Development life cycle highlighting the Software Phase where the MDE solution is applied.

- **Architecture Design (Stage 3.1)**: Associated with RQ1-Year 1. This stage is supported by metamodel and a modelling tool that will allow the metamodel to be instantiated in accordance with the requirements established in the analysis phase (Phase 1).

- **Automatic Code Generation (3.2)**: Associated to RQ2-Year 2. The implementation stage will be automated by means of model transformation rules for code generation in frameworks such as PyTorch[3]. This process will be automatic and transparent to the designer, adopting a Model is the Code approach [Pastor and Molina 2007]. In this way, modifications to the architecture during the life cycle can be made at the design level, avoiding direct programming on the code.
- **Model-Based Testing (3.3)**: Associated with RQ3-Year 3. The testing of the LLM model, before and after training (Phase 4), can be supported on the conceptual model designed, especially in those techniques that require configuration or parametrisation of the architecture. An example of this is the Mutation Testing technique [Çetiner et al. 2024], which can be applied for assessing the robustness of Deep Neural Networks (DDNs) and Transformer-based [Vaswani et al. 2023] models.

At the time of writing this paper, the thesis has been in progress for three months, including the definition of the methodology and a proposed solution. Currently, RQ1 is being addressed, whose objective is the conceptualisation of the architecture of an LLM, specifically the Transformer architecture [Vaswani et al. 2023], used as a reference in different LLMs such as GPT-4 [OpenAI 2023] and DeepSeek [DeepSeek-AI 2024]. In order to properly establish the conceptual constructs associated with the configuration of the LLM architecture, a systematic literature review is being carried out to identify the design decisions made by experts in the field.

Ackowledgments

Work partially funded by Horizon Europe RIA programme Music360 grant No 101094872.

References

Al-Azzoni, I. (2020). Model driven approach for neural networks. In *2020 International Conference on Intelligent Data Science Technologies and Applications (IDSTA)*, pages 87–94.

Alahdab, M. and Çalıklı, G. (2019). Empirical analysis of hidden technical debt patterns in machine learning software. In Franch, X., Männistö, T., and Martínez-Fernández, S., editors, *Product-Focused Software Process Improvement*, pages 195–202, Cham. Springer International Publishing.

Amershi, S. et al. (2019). Software engineering for machine learning: A case study. *2019 IEEE/ACM 41st International Conference on Software Engineering: Software Engineering in Practice (ICSE-SEIP)*, pages 291–300.

Baldassarre, M. T., Caivano, D., Fernandez Nieto, B., Gigante, D., and Ragone, A. (2023). The social impact of generative ai: An analysis on chatgpt. In *Proceedings of the 2023 ACM Conference on Information Technology for Social Good*, pages 363–373.

Banh, L. and Strobel, G. (2023). Generative artificial intelligence. *Electronic Markets*, 33(1):63.

[3]PyTorch. https://pytorch.org/

Bommasani, R. et al. (2022). On the opportunities and risks of foundation models.

DeepSeek-AI (2024). Deepseek-V3 Technical report.

Díaz, V. G., Espada, J. P., García-Bustelo, B. C. P., and Lovelle, J. M. C. (2015). Towards a standard-based domain-specific platform to solve machine learning-based problems. *Int. J. Interact. Multim. Artif. Intell.*, 3:6–12.

Foidl, H., Felderer, M., and Biffl, S. (2019). Technical debt in data-intensive software systems.

Gatto, N., Kusmenko, E., and Rumpe, B. (2019). Modeling deep reinforcement learning based architectures for cyber-physical systems. In *2019 ACM/IEEE 22nd International Conference on Model Driven Engineering Languages and Systems Companion (MODELS-C)*, pages 196–202.

Giachetti, G., Catalá, D., de Miguel, B., Carrascosa, C., de Miguel, M., and Pastor, O. (2023). Music360: Modeling the value of music. In *CAiSE Research Projects Exhibition*, pages 105–110.

Google-Cloud (2025). Ai platform: Machine learning solutions overview. Available: `https://cloud.google.com/ai-platform/docs/ml-solutions-overview` [Accessed: 20-02-2025].

Gozalo-Brizuela, R. and Garrido-Merchan, E. C. (2023). Chatgpt is not all you need. a state of the art review of large generative ai models. *arXiv preprint arXiv:2301.04655*.

Grattafiori, A. et al. (2024). The llama 3 herd of models.

Hartmann, T., Moawad, A., Fouquet, F., and Le Traon, Y. (2019). The next evolution of mde: a seamless integration of machine learning into domain modeling. *Software & Systems Modeling*, 18:1285–1304.

Hoffmann, J., Borgeaud, S., Mensch, A., Buchatskaya, E., Cai, T., Rutherford, E., Casas, D. d. L., Hendricks, L. A., Welbl, J., Clark, A., et al. (2022). Training compute-optimal large language models. *arXiv preprint arXiv:2203.15556*.

ISO/IEC 25010:2023 (2023). Systems and software engineering — Systems and software Quality Requirements and Evaluation (SQuaRE) — Product quality model . Technical report, International Organization for Standardization.

Liu, J., Huang, Q., Xia, X., Shihab, E., Lo, D., and Li, S. (2020). Is using deep learning frameworks free? characterizing technical debt in deep learning frameworks. In *2020 IEEE/ACM 42nd International Conference on Software Engineering: Software Engineering in Society (ICSE-SEIS)*, pages 1–10.

Marín, B., Gallardo, C., Quiroga, D., Giachetti, G., and Serral, E. (2017). Testing of model-driven development applications. *Software Quality Journal*, 25:407–435.

Martínez-Fernández, S., Bogner, J., Franch, X., Oriol, M., Siebert, J., Trendowicz, A., Vollmer, A. M., and Wagner, S. (2022). Software engineering for ai-based systems: A survey. *ACM Trans. Softw. Eng. Methodol.*, 31(2).

Naveed, H., Arora, C., Khalajzadeh, H., Grundy, J., and Haggag, O. (2024). Model driven engineering for machine learning components: A systematic literature review. *Information and Software Technology*, 169:107423.

Object Management Group (2019). Meta Object Facility (MOF) Core Specification, Version 2.5.1. Technical Report formal/2019-10-01, Object Management Group (OMG). Available: `https://www.omg.org/spec/MOF/2.5.1/PDF` [Accessed 20-02-2025].

OpenAI (2023). GPT-4 Technical Report.

Pastor, O. and Molina, J. C. (2007). *Model-driven architecture in practice: a software production environment based on conceptual modeling*, volume 1. Springer.

Perrault, R. and Clark, J. (2024). Artificial intelligence index report 2024.

Rädler, S., Berardinelli, L., Winter, K., Rahimi, A., and Rinderle-Ma, S. (2024). Bridging mde and ai: a systematic review of domain-specific languages and model-driven practices in ai software systems engineering. *Software and Systems Modeling*, pages 1–25.

Rädler, S., Berardinelli, L., Winter, K., Rahimi, A., and Rinderle-Ma, S. (2024). Bridging mde and ai: a systematic review of domain-specific languages and model-driven practices in ai software systems engineering. *Software and Systems Modeling*.

Sculley, D., Holt, G., Golovin, D., Davydov, E., Phillips, T., Ebner, D., Chaudhary, V., Young, M., Crespo, J.-F., and Dennison, D. (2015). Hidden technical debt in machine learning systems. In Cortes, C., Lawrence, N., Lee, D., Sugiyama, M., and Garnett, R., editors, *Advances in Neural Information Processing Systems*, volume 28. Curran Associates, Inc.

Shahab, O., El Kurdi, B., Shaukat, A., Nadkarni, G., and Soroush, A. (2024). Large language models: a primer and gastroenterology applications. *Therapeutic Advances in Gastroenterology*, 17.

towards data science (2025). DeepSeek V3: A New Contender in AI-Powered Data Science. Available: `https://towardsdatascience.com` [Accessed 14-02-2025].

Vaswani, A., Shazeer, N., Parmar, N., Uszkoreit, J., Jones, L., Gomez, A. N., Kaiser, L., and Polosukhin, I. (2023). Attention is all you need.

Wan, Z., Wang, X., Liu, C., Alam, S., Zheng, Y., Liu, J., Qu, Z., Yan, S., Zhu, Y., Zhang, Q., Chowdhury, M., and Zhang, M. (2024). Efficient large language models: A survey.

Wieringa, R. J. (2014). *Design science methodology for information systems and software engineering*. Springer.

Zhang, J. M., Harman, M., Ma, L., and Liu, Y. (2019). Machine learning testing: Survey, landscapes and horizons.

Zhao, W. X., Zhou, K., Li, J., Tang, T., Wang, X., Hou, Y., Min, Y., Zhang, B., Zhang, J., Dong, Z., Du, Y., Yang, C., Chen, Y., Chen, Z., Jiang, J., Ren, R., Li, Y., Tang, X., Liu, Z., Liu, P., Nie, J.-Y., and Wen, J.-R. (2024). A survey of large language models.

Çetiner, G., Yayan, U., and Yazici, A. (2024). Mutation-based white box testing of deep neural networks. *IEEE Access*, 12:160156–160174.

Engenharia de Requisitos de Explicabilidade em Sistemas Baseados em Aprendizado de Máquina

Lívia Mancine[1,2]

[1]Instituto de Informática – Universidade Federal de Goiás (INF/UFG)
Goiânia – GO – Brazil

[2]Instituto Federal Goiano (IF Goiano)
Goiânia – GO – Brazil

livia.mancine@ifgoiano.edu.br

Abstract. *Explainability is the ability to make the predictions of a Machine Learning (ML) model clear and understandable to people. The adoption of ML models in critical decision-making requires explainability to be incorporated as a fundamental requirement in the decision-making process. As a recent topic, explainability in ML-based systems still lacks systematized processes, which opens space for further research. This PhD work aims to develop and contribute with a Requirements Engineering approach for the analysis and specification of explainability requirements in ML-based systems. The Design Science methodology will serve as the model to guide this research.*

Resumo. *A explicabilidade é a habilidade de tornar as previsões de um modelo de Aprendizado de Máquina (AM) claras e compreensíveis para as pessoas. A adoção de modelos de AM em decisões críticas exige que a explicabilidade seja incorporada como um requisito fundamental no processo de tomada de decisão. Por ser um tema recente, a explicabilidade em sistemas baseados em AM ainda carece de processos sistematizados, o que abre espaço para novas pesquisas. Este trabalho de doutorado visa desenvolver e contribuir com uma abordagem de Engenharia de Requisitos para análise e especificação de requisitos de explicabilidade em sistemas baseados em AM. A metodologia Design Science servirá de modelo para conduzir esta pesquisa.*

1. Introdução

O uso emergente de componentes de Inteligência Artificial (IA) em diversos segmentos de software levanta preocupações sobre a confiabilidade dos resultados gerados pela IA. Além disso, surgem dúvidas sobre a responsabilidade em casos de resultados indesejados, bem como a necessidade de compreender os motivos que levaram a resultados bem-sucedidos. O uso intensivo de componentes de IA, em especial de Aprendizado de Máquina (AM), integrados a software tradicional é impulsionada por fatores, como a grande quantidade de dados gerados e o crescente poder computacional [Giray 2021]. Exemplos desses sistemas podem ser observados em domínios como saúde [Jiang et al. 2017] e finanças [Goodell et al. 2021]. Tais domínios, considerados críticos na tomada de decisão, necessitam de explicações dos sistemas baseados em IA nos quais estão envolvidos, pois esses sistemas são classificados como de alto risco devido aos impactos adversos sobre pessoas ou grupos afetados [Senado Federal do Brasil 2023].

Especialmente na área de saúde, os sistemas de AM enfrentam desafios, como viés em dados clínicos e a opacidade dos modelos [Khattak et al. 2024, Lin et al. 2024]. A confiança, essencial em sistemas críticos [Khattak et al. 2024], é impactada por esses fatores, dificultando a construção de relações seguras entre *stakeholders* e limitando sua adoção prática [Vayena et al. 2018]. Nesse contexto, a transparência torna-se fundamental para fornecer explicações claras e acessíveis sobre as decisões dos algoritmos, fortalecendo a confiança e viabilizando sua adoção [Vayena et al. 2018, Habibullah et al. 2024].

O requisito de explicabilidade tem se tornado uma preocupação emergente em sistemas baseados em AM [Mancine et al. 2024], sendo considerado um requisito não funcional (RNF), que impacta substancialmente a qualidade desses sistemas [Chazette et al. 2022, Umm-E-Habiba 2023]. Assim, aspectos como confiança e transparência devem ser abordados desde as etapas iniciais do ciclo de vida de sistemas de IA/AM [Baldassarre et al. 2024].

Embora a explicabilidade em sistemas baseados em AM tenha despertado interesse crescente na comunidade de ER, *esse recente tema ainda carece de processos sistematizados*. Investigar a sistematização de atividades de processos de ER para abordar explicabilidade torna-se relevante para diferentes *stakeholders*, como especialistas de domínio, usuários finais, desenvolvedores de sistemas e entidades legais, trazendo-lhes explicações adaptadas sobre os resultados dos modelos de AM e, assim, promovendo mais confiança e transparência [Habibullah et al. 2024]. Considere como exemplo um sistema de suporte à decisão clínica baseado em AM, como no diagnóstico de uma doença. Médicos precisam entender as recomendações para avaliar diagnósticos; pacientes necessitam de informações claras para tomar decisões sobre tratamentos; desenvolvedores requerem detalhes técnicos para aprimorar modelos; e entidades regulatórias demandam transparência para garantir conformidade legal. O direito à explicação, previsto no PL 2338/2023 [Senado Federal do Brasil 2023], reforça a importância de explicações acessíveis, especialmente em áreas críticas como saúde, finanças e direito.

Com base nos desafios identificados, o problema de pesquisa a ser investigado nesta proposta de doutorado é *a carência de abordagens de ER que tratem explicabilidade como RNF fundamental, desde a etapa de concepção do sistemas baseados em AM*. Nesse cenário, a atividade de ER mais investigada tem sido a elicitação, *com poucos estudos sobre análise, especificação, validação e gerenciamento* [Mancine et al. 2024]. Para esta proposta de doutorado, será elaborada *uma abordagem de ER para as atividades de análise e especificação de explicabilidade para sistemas baseados em AM*.

Este artigo está assim organizado: a Seção 2 apresenta os objetivos e a questão de pesquisa. A Seção 3 descreve os trabalhos relacionados. A Seção 4 relata o método de pesquisa. A Seção 5 apresenta os resultados preliminares. Por fim, a Seção 6 conclui o artigo e descreve as próximas etapas da pesquisa.

2. Questão de Pesquisa e Objetivos

Apesar das pesquisas sobre ER para AM terem crescido recentemente, a especificação de requisitos de AM de forma compreensível para *stakeholders* é pouco explorada, embora seja considerada a mais desafiadora do desenvolvimento de sistemas baseados em AM [Villamizar et al. 2024]. Um estudo sobre ER e explicabilidade em AM [Mancine et al. 2024] apontou que a ER precisa ser mais investigada em todas as suas atividades. Os autores destacaram que a fase de elicitação foi a mais abordada, seguida da análise, ressaltando a necessidade de aprofundar a especificação. Além disso, a maioria dos estudos se concentra em abordagens teóricas, sem validação em ambientes reais.

Dado o contexto do problema apresentado, este trabalho visa responder a seguinte questão de pesquisa: "*O quanto uma abordagem de ER auxilia na análise e especificação do RNF de explicabilidade em sistemas baseados em AM?*" Assim, o objetivo geral desta pesquisa de doutorado é *desenvolver uma abordagem de ER que contemple as atividades de análise e especificação do RNF de explicabilidade em sistemas baseados em AM*.

Para alcançar esse objetivo geral, definem-se como objetivos específicos:

1. mapear o estado da arte sobre explicabilidade, ER e sistemas baseados em AM [Mancine et al. 2024];
2. coletar pontos de vista de desenvolvedores de sistemas baseados em AM sobre tratamento de explicabilidade;
3. definir técnica de análise de requisitos de explicabilidade;
4. definir técnica de especificação de requisitos de explicabilidade;
5. experimentar a abordagem de análise e especificação elaborada em projetos de sistemas baseados em AM que demandam explicabilidade.

3. Trabalhos Relacionados

Na pesquisa de [Li and Han 2023], é proposta uma estrutura para análise de requisitos de explicabilidade em sistemas de AM, usando *iStar* para modelar um *framework* de explicabilidade. A abordagem baseada em objetivos visa recomendar métodos XAI a desenvolvedores de forma sistemática e automática. A usabilidade do *framework* foi avaliada entre desenvolvedores com diferentes níveis de conhecimento de explicabilidade. O trabalho de [Barrera et al. 2024] utiliza *iStar* como metamodelo para sistemas de AM, permitindo identificar RNF, entre eles, explicabilidade, selecionar algoritmos adequados e analisar fontes de dados alinhadas aos objetivos do projeto. Os autores realizaram um estudo de caso na indústria. Entretanto, os estudos de [Li and Han 2023] e [Barrera et al. 2024] focaram apenas em métodos XAI que fornecem explicações técnicas, sem considerar outros aspectos de explicabilidade para diferentes *stakeholders*.

Com uma abordagem diferente [Guizzardi et al. 2022], a Engenharia de Requisitos Baseada em Ontologia (ObRE) foi proposta para elicitação e análise de requisitos éticos, com foco em explicabilidade e autonomia. A ontologia foi validada quanto à conformidade com os objetivos da União Europeia para sistemas éticos, mas não houve validação por estudos de caso reais, nem avaliação com especialistas.

A proposta deste artigo visa explorar as lacunas de pesquisa existentes quanto ao requisito de explicabilidade. Há uma oportunidade de desenvolver abordagens que contemple a análise e a especificação da explicabilidade para sistemas baseados em AM desde a concepção do sistema, considerando as necessidades dos diferentes *stakeholders* e validando a proposta por meio de estudos de caso.

4. Metodologia de Pesquisa

A metodologia a ser seguida nesta pesquisa é a do paradigma de *Design Science*, utilizado para conduzir e comunicar pesquisas aplicadas, como na Engenharia de Software

[Engström et al. 2020]. O objetivo das pesquisas baseadas em *Design Science* é gerar conhecimento prescritivo para profissionais, além de compartilhar *insights* empíricos obtidos em investigações aplicadas a contextos específicos [Engström et al. 2020]. Na Figura 1 é descrito o método de pesquisa deste trabalho de doutorado. A estrutura utilizada foi baseada na proposta de [Storey et al. 2017], e apresenta elementos como: teoria proposta, contribuição empírica do estudo em termos da instância de solução de problema e os ciclos de design e validação correspondentes, suporte para a avaliação do valor do conhecimento produzido em termos de relevância, rigor e novidade.

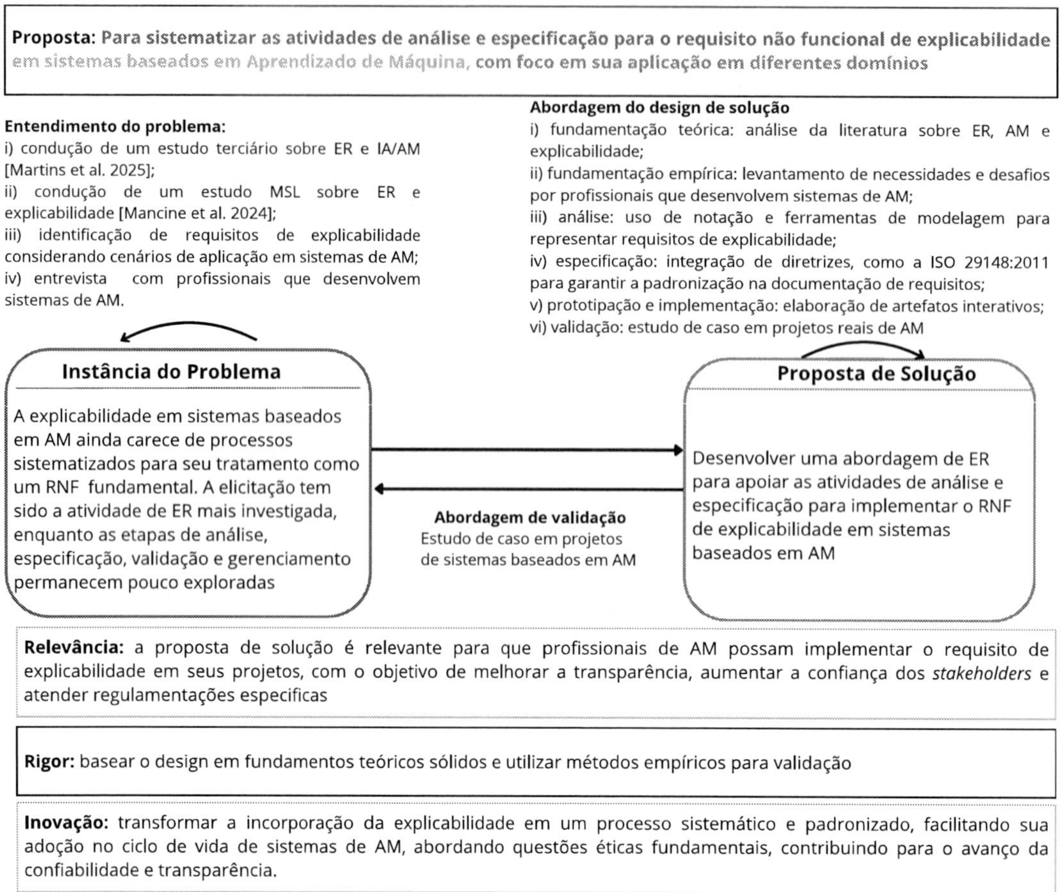

Figura 1. Método de Pesquisa deste doutorado baseado em Design Science.

Considerando a Figura 1, o entendimento do problema envolve a compreensão detalhada do seu contexto, causas e consequências, fornecendo uma base para a proposição de soluções. Nesta proposta, esse entendimento está sendo construído por meio de estudos sistemáticos da literatura sobre o tema [Martins et al. 2025] e [Mancine et al. 2024]; identificação de requisitos de explicabilidade com base em regulamentações e diretrizes internacionais e nacionais, e pela condução de uma entrevista semiestruturada com profissionais da área. Essa entrevista visa oferecer *insights* sobre o estado da prática ao tema investigado. A proposta parte desse conhecimento sobre o problema e seu contexto, alinhando-se ao objetivo geral da pesquisa descrito na Seção 2. Com base nisso, a abordagem de design de solução permite definir uma solução para o problema apresentado e planejar sua validação. A validação será conduzida por meio de estudos de caso em sistemas baseados em AM.

Espera-se como solução uma abordagem de ER para apoiar a análise e especificação de explicabilidade em projetos de AM, viabilizada por artefatos interativos que promovam a colaboração entre os *stakeholders*. Esses artefatos têm o potencial de facilitar a comunicação, a colaboração e o engajamento dos *stakeholders*, além disso, ao integrar IA na criação desses artefatos, é possível elevar a qualidade e a eficiência das soluções propostas [Bogucka et al. 2024]. Por fim, a metodologia adotada ressalta o rigor, a relevância e a inovação da proposta apresentada.

Como contribuição, este trabalho busca avançar a ER para sistemas baseados em AM, fornecendo um processo sistemático para análise e especificação de requisitos de explicabilidade. Para isso, há atividades essenciais para a condução desta pesquisa, como as descritas a seguir.

i) Fundamentação teórica:
- Foi conduzido um estudo terciário que sintetizou a relação entre a ER para AM [Martins et al. 2025], no qual foram discutidas lacunas e apresentada uma agenda de pesquisa. O estudo foi submetido para avaliação em um periódico especializado e, após uma análise inicial pelos revisores, respondemos às suas dúvidas e aguardamos um retorno;
- Realizou-se um estudo secundário, um Mapeamento Sistemático da Literatura (MSL), focado na ER e no requisito de explicabilidade no contexto de AM, publicado em [Mancine et al. 2024]. Com base nesse estudo, foram identificadas lacunas específicas relacionados à ER para a explicabilidade;
- Revisão de diretrizes e regulamentações para IA.

ii) Fundamentação empírica:
- Com o objetivo de alinhar os estudos sistemáticos ao estado da prática, está em andamento uma entrevista semiestruturada com pesquisadores e profissionais da área de AM, incluindo aqueles que atuam no Centro de Excelência em Inteligência Artificial[1] (CEIA) da UFG, além de possíveis parcerias com outros centros de IA no Brasil. A entrevista vai investigar a percepção da explicabilidade no contexto da ER em sistemas baseados em AM. Este estudo foi aprovado pelo Comitê de Ética em Pesquisa da UFG sob o parecer de número 7.416.401, vinculado ao Certificado de Apresentação para Apreciação Ética (CAAE) 85638924.3.0000.5083.

iii) Abordagem de análise:
- Uso de notações e linguagens de modelagem da ER para modelar o requisito de explicabilidade;
- Emprego de técnicas da ER, como cenários e casos de uso para compreender a influência da explicabilidade na interação dos *stakeholders*, permitindo a classificação de diferentes aspectos, como nível de detalhe e público-alvo.

iv) Abordagem de especificação:
- Definição de um modelo estruturado para especificar o requisito de explicabilidade baseados em diretrizes e normas, como a ISO/IEC/IEEE 29148:2011, para descrever requisitos de explicabilidade de forma consistente e compreensível;
- Especificação de diferentes níveis de explicabilidade conforme o público-alvo, detalhando o que deve ser explicado e para quem.

[1]https://ceia.ufg.br/

- Artefatos interativos implementados em uma ferramenta de software de apoio às atividades de análise e especificação de explicabilidade

v) Validação:

- Estudo de caso para implementação do processo sistematizado para análise e especificação do requisito de explicabilidade em sistema baseado em AM.

Dessa forma, a metodologia adotada busca garantir que a abordagem proposta seja efetiva na análise e especificação da explicabilidade em sistemas baseados em AM. A combinação de artefatos interativos e estudos de caso permitirá validar a abordagem em cenários reais, alinhando os requisitos às necessidades dos diferentes *stakeholders*. A partir das etapas descritas, espera-se que os resultados contribuam para a ER de sistemas baseados em AM, oferecendo um processo sistemático e aplicável na prática.

5. Resultados Preliminares

Esta pesquisa iniciou-se em junho de 2023 com a realização de uma revisão sistemática sobre ER e sistemas baseado em AM [Martins et al. 2025]. Embora abrangente, a revisão destacou a explicabilidade como uma lacuna para pesquisas futuras. Caracterizado como um estudo terciário, o trabalho evidenciou a necessidade de abordar a explicabilidade sob a perspectiva da ER, considerando que os *stakeholders* possuem diferentes níveis de compreensão e exigem explicações em distintos níveis de detalhamento. Assim, a documentação de requisitos deve especificar o que deve ser explicado e para quem, garantido que as informações sejam adequadas ao público-alvo.

O resultado dessa revisão, impulsionou a condução de um MSL para identificar características específicas da ER em relação a explicabilidade em sistemas baseados em AM. Nesse MSL, utilizamos pesquisas automáticas em seis bases de dados. Dos 200 artigos retornados, após aplicar os critérios de seleção, analisamos e relatamos os resultados de 27 artigos. Os estudos da literatura mostram que a explicabilidade é um requisito de qualidade emergente em sistemas baseados em AM, desafiando os paradigmas clássicos da ER, especialmente nas fases de análise e especificação. Embora a elicitação e a análise sejam as atividades mais exploradas, há uma carência de estudos empíricos. Como RNF, a explicabilidade pode contribuir para requisitos como conformidade legal, justiça e ética. Portanto, sua abordagem na ER deve ser ampliada para todas as atividades, incluindo a adaptação de técnicas clássicas ao contexto de AM.

Para identificar aspectos de explicabilidade, está sendo desenvolvido um documento de especificação de requisitos de explicabilidade (ERS), seguindo as diretrizes da ISO/IEC/IEEE 29148:2011. A saúde, como um sistema crítico de AM, é utilizada como exemplo, com base em regulamentações e diretrizes nacionais e internacionais, incluindo recomendações da Organização Mundial da Saúde (OMS), o Projeto de Lei n. 2338/2023 [Senado Federal do Brasil 2023], que regulamenta a IA no Brasil, e o estudo sobre IA na saúde do Núcleo de Informação e Coordenação do Ponto BR[2] (NIC.br).

6. Considerações Finais

Este artigo apresentou uma pesquisa de doutorado em andamento que tem como objetivo desenvolver uma abordagem de ER que contemple as atividade de análise e especificação

[2]https://www.nic.br/noticia/na-midia/inteligencia-artificial-pode-aprimorar-a-saude-no-brasil-aponta-estudo-inedito/

do RNF de explicabilicabilidade em sistemas baseados em AM. A proposta de criar um artefato interativo dessa abordagem visa permitir que diferentes *stakeholders* utilizem esse requisito em projetos de AM.

Foram realizados estudos sistemáticos, atualmente, está sendo conduzida uma entrevista com desenvolvedores de AM para verificar sua percepção sobre o requisito de explicabilidade. As próximas atividades, como a definição de técnicas de análise e especificação serão conduzidas por meio de estudo teóricos e práticos, incluindo a aplicação da abordagem em projetos reais de AM. Essa aplicação ocorrerá no CEIA. Paralelamente, está prevista a produção de artigos científicos com os resultados obtidos, visando à publicação em eventos e periódicos das áreas de Engenharia de Software, ER, AM e nos domínios de aplicação, como a saúde, destacando o caráter multidisciplinar da pesquisa. A qualificação deste doutorado ocorrerá em agosto de 2025 e sua defesa está programada para março de 2027.

A implementação da abordagem proposta pode enfrentar desafios como a adaptação da explicabilidade para diferentes *stakeholders*, a validação em cenários reais e a aceitação pelos desenvolvedores. Para mitigar esses riscos, serão desenvolvidos artefatos interativos ajustáveis, validados por estudos de caso no CEIA e refinados com *feedback* de especialistas. Além disso, a abordagem será construída de forma colaborativa para garantir alinhamento com as necessidades práticas dos *stakeholders*.

Referências

Baldassarre, M. T., Gigante, D., Kalinowski, M., Ragone, A., and Tibidò, S. (2024). Trustworthy ai in practice: an analysis of practitioners' needs and challenges. In *Proceedings of the 28th International Conference on Evaluation and Assessment in Software Engineering*, pages 293–302.

Barrera, J. M., Reina-Reina, A., Lavalle, A., Maté, A., and Trujillo, J. (2024). An extension of istar for machine learning requirements by following the prise methodology. *Computer Standards & Interfaces*, 88:103806.

Bogucka, E., Constantinides, M., Scepanovic, S., and Quercia, D. (2024). Ai design: A responsible ai framework for pre-filling impact assessment reports. *IEEE Computer Society*.

Chazette, L., Brunotte, W., and Speith, T. (2022). Explainable software systems: from requirements analysis to system evaluation. *Requirements Engineering*, 27(4):457–487.

Engström, E., Storey, M.-A., Runeson, P., Höst, M., and Baldassarre, M. T. (2020). How software engineering research aligns with design science: a review. *Empirical Software Engineering*, 25:2630–2660.

Giray, G. (2021). A software engineering perspective on engineering machine learning systems: State of the art and challenges. *Journal of Systems and Software*, 180:111031.

Goodell, J. W. et al. (2021). Artificial intelligence and machine learning in finance: Identifying foundations, themes, and research clusters from bibliometric analysis. *Journal of Behavioral and Experimental Finance*, 32:100577.

Guizzardi, R., Amaral, G., Guizzardi, G., and Mylopoulos, J. (2022). Eliciting ethicality requirements using the ontology-based requirements engineering method. In *International Conference on Business Process Modeling, Development and Support*, pages 221–236. Springer.

Habibullah, K. M. et al. (2024). Explainable ai: A diverse stakeholder perspective. In *2024 IEEE 32nd International Requirements Engineering Conference (RE)*, pages 494–495. IEEE.

Jiang, F. et al. (2017). Artificial intelligence in healthcare: past, present and future. *Stroke and vascular neurology*, 2(4).

Khattak, F. K., Subasri, V., Krishnan, A., Pou-Prom, C., Akinli-Kocak, S., Dolatabadi, E., Pandya, D., Seyyed-Kalantari, L., and Rudzicz, F. (2024). Mlhops: Machine learning health operations. *IEEE Access*.

Li, T. and Han, L. (2023). Dealing with explainability requirements for machine learning systems. In *2023 IEEE 47th Annual Computers, Software, and Applications Conference (COMPSAC)*, pages 1203–1208. IEEE.

Lin, H., Han, J., Wu, P., Wang, J., Tu, J., Tang, H., and Zhu, L. (2024). Machine learning and human-machine trust in healthcare: A systematic survey. *CAAI Transactions on Intelligence Technology*, 9(2):286–302.

Mancine, L., Soares, J. L., Kudo, T., and Bulcão-Neto, R. (2024). Estado da arte sobre engenharia de requisitos e explicabilidade em sistemas baseados em aprendizado de máquina. In *Anais Estendidos do XXX Simpósio Brasileiro de Sistemas Multimídia e Web*, pages 143–158, Porto Alegre, RS, Brasil. SBC.

Martins, M. C., Campos, L. M. C., Soares, J. L. R., Kudo, T. N., and Bulcão-Neto, R. F. (2025). Requirements engineering for machine learning-based ai systems: A tertiary study. *Journal of Software Engineering Research and Development (JSERD)*. Submitted and under review.

Senado Federal do Brasil (2023). Projeto de Lei Nº 2338, de 2023. Disponível em: `https://www25.senado.leg.br/web/atividade/materias/-/materia/157233`. Acesso em: 28 jan. 2025.

Storey, M.-A., Engstrom, E., Höst, M., Runeson, P., and Bjarnason, E. (2017). Using a visual abstract as a lens for communicating and promoting design science research in software engineering. In *2017 ACM/IEEE International Symposium on Empirical Software Engineering and Measurement (ESEM)*, pages 181–186. IEEE.

Umm-E-Habiba (2023). Requirements engineering for explainable ai. In *2023 IEEE 31st International Requirements Engineering Conference (RE)*, pages 376–380.

Vayena, E., Blasimme, A., and Cohen, I. G. (2018). Machine learning in medicine: addressing ethical challenges. *PLoS medicine*, 15(11):e1002689.

Villamizar, H., Kalinowski, M., Lopes, H., and Mendez, D. (2024). Identifying concerns when specifying machine learning-enabled systems: a perspective-based approach. *Journal of Systems and Software*, 213:112053.

A Model for Non-Intrusive Capture of Metrics for Early Project Estimation in Agile Environments

José Gamaliel Rivera Ibarra[1]

[1]Instituto Tecnológico de Sonora
Ciudad Obregón, Sonora, México

Abstract. *Early estimation in agile projects is essential for determining feasibility, costs, and planning. However, lacking detailed initial requirements introduces uncertainty and leads to inconsistent results. Although the literature proposes predictive models based on historical data to improve accuracy, the lack of databases tailored to each company's context prevents practitioners from applying these models effectively. This work presents a non-intrusive model for capturing key metrics (such as software size) in agile environments to facilitate the creation of historical databases. The model will be calibrated and validated through empirical studies to support the gradual adoption of a hybrid estimation approach that combines data-driven techniques with expert judgment. Preliminary results indicate that the scarcity of historical data in practice reduces estimation accuracy, highlighting the need for automated metric capture. This approach aims to enhance the reliability of early estimations in agile projects and provide objective support for decision-making in software project management.*

1. Introduction

Early estimation in agile development projects is fundamental for assessing feasibility, defining budgets, planning, and establishing a strategic foundation for decision-making during project execution. During the initiation and planning phases, such estimation provides stakeholders (investors, technical teams, and clients) with a clear view of feasibility, enabling them to anticipate risks, allocate resources efficiently, and align expectations from the outset [McConnell 2006].

Nonetheless, projects in early stages often yield imprecise estimates. The Cone of Uncertainty [Barry et al. 1981] stated that estimating based on vague and ambiguous requirements (characteristic of early stages and agile projects) can result in errors ranging between 60% and 160% of the actual final value [Cohn 2005], which may lead teams to fall short of their objectives [Prakash and Viswanathan 2017].

Researchers and practitioners have worked for decades to develop methods that yield more accurate estimates [Jadhav et al. 2022]. These methods primarily aim to determine the effort required for software development – that is, the amount of work necessary to complete a task satisfactorily [Sudarmaningtyas and Mohamed 2021]. Estimation approaches are broadly classified into three groups: expert judgment–based methods, which rely on the opinions of experienced professionals; data-driven (or quantitative) methods, which build predictive models from historical data to forecast effort; and hybrid methods, which combine data objectivity with professional expertise to enhance accuracy in early-stage estimation [Vera et al. 2018].

Agile development teams have predominantly relied on expert judgment for initial estimations. Although this approach allows for agility and flexibility, it generally produces inconsistent results due to the subjectivity and variability in interpreting requirement complexity [Zarour and Zein 2019]. In this context, using historical data provides an objective basis for enhancing estimation accuracy [Alsaadi and Saeedi 2022].

Researchers in agile project estimation advocate data-driven methods [Rivera et al. 2024]. They primarily employ regression analysis and machine learning techniques [Hameed et al. 2023, Rosa and Jardine 2023] to build predictive models that use software size as the primary independent variable or effort predictor [Ünlü et al. 2022]. However, these models require a large amount of historical data [Sudarmaningtyas and Mohamed 2021], forcing reliance on public sources that present various limitations:

- *Obsolete Records*: Many databases, such as ISBSG, NASA93, COCOMO81, or MAXWELL, contain old project records (from 1970 to 1999) [Beata et al. 2015], hindering their application in today's technological context.
- *Lack of Organizational Context*: These databases aggregate projects from various companies without including information about specific processes, tools, technologies, and methodologies, which limits model comparability and adaptability [Usman et al. 2014].
- *Non-Standardized Metrics*: Using subjective metrics, such as Story Points, prevents objective comparisons between projects [Hacaloğlu and Demirörs 2018].

Function Points (FP) provide a standardized metric for objectively measuring the functional size of software in completed projects [Hussain et al. 2013]. This measurement allows for calculating other relevant metrics, such as team velocity and defect density, and is fundamental for constructing historical databases that serve as input for predictive models [Hussain et al. 2013, Commeyne et al. 2016]. However, functional size measurement (FSM) techniques require considerable analytical effort [Sahab and Trudel 2020], which is often impractical in agile environments [Soubra et al. 2020], where teams prioritize activities that directly add value to the customer. Although some authors [Sahab and Trudel 2020, Özgesu Özen et al. 2020, Tenekeci et al. 2024] have proposed tools to perform FSM from source code, these have not yet achieved widespread adoption.

The lack of automated and nonintrusive mechanisms to capture metrics from ongoing and past (postmortem) projects poses an obstacle to creating the databases that would allow agile teams to adopt a hybrid estimation approach— that combines quantitative methods with expert judgment to improve early-stage estimation accuracy [Yogi and Chinthala 2013].

This work employs a Design Science Research framework to design and validate a non-intrusive model for capturing key metrics, such as functional size and team productivity, through an automated tool that facilitates the creation of historical databases from recent projects within the same company. Our approach implements an iterative process that involves artifact design, demonstration, and evaluation, which enables us to rigorously develop the model and seamlessly integrate it into existing agile workflows. Although our long-term vision is for this data to serve as input for a hybrid estimation approach, the scope of this work is limited to the design, development, and validation of the non-intrusive capture model.

The remainder of this article is organized as follows: Section 2 presents the research questions and objectives, clarifying the focus and expected contributions of our work. Section 3 details the research methodology, including the phases and activities undertaken to design, develop, and validate the proposed model. Section 4 outlines the preliminary results obtained so far, highlighting both the insights from the literature and the initial diagnostic of professional practice. In Section 5, we compare our approach with existing solutions, discussing key differences and potential advantages. Finally, Section 6 addresses the challenges that remain and outlines the next steps required to refine and fully implement our proposal.

2. Research Questions and Objectives

This research seeks to answer the following key questions:

- How can agile teams non-intrusively capture key project metrics using existing tools (Git, Jira, CI/CD) to build contextualized historical databases?
- What technical and methodological criteria enable the integration of non-intrusive metric capture with existing agile tools (e.g., Git, Jira, CI/CD)?
- How effective and applicable is the proposed non-intrusive model for automatically capturing metrics in agile environments, as evaluated through empirical studies in real-world settings?

The general objective is to develop and validate a non-intrusive model for capturing key agile project metrics that integrates with existing tools, enabling the creation of contextualized historical databases to support future estimation practices. The specific objectives include:

- Identify key metrics for early agile estimation and define standardized capture methods aligned with the Goal-Question-Metric (GQM) framework [Misra et al. 2005].
- Design a conceptual model for non-intrusive metric capture, including technical specifications for tool integration (APIs, automation scripts).
- Implement a functional prototype that automates metric extraction from agile tools (e.g., Jira, Git) and stores data with contextual metadata.
- Evaluate the model's accuracy and applicability in real-world agile environments.

3. Research Methodology

This research adopts a Design Science Research (DSR) framework [Alan et al. 2020], combined with a mixed-methods approach (qualitative and quantitative), and is structured into three main phases as illustrated in Figure 1.

Phase 1: Problem Identification and Solution Objectives

In this phase, we identify the core problem – the lack of reliable, context-specific historical databases in agile environments – and define the objectives of our solution. A systematic mapping study (SMS) is conducted following Kitchenham's methodology [Kitchenham and Charters 2007] to review current estimation techniques and their limitations. Concurrently, we diagnose professional practice through surveys and semi-structured interviews with agile practitioners to determine the key challenges in early estimation and data capture.

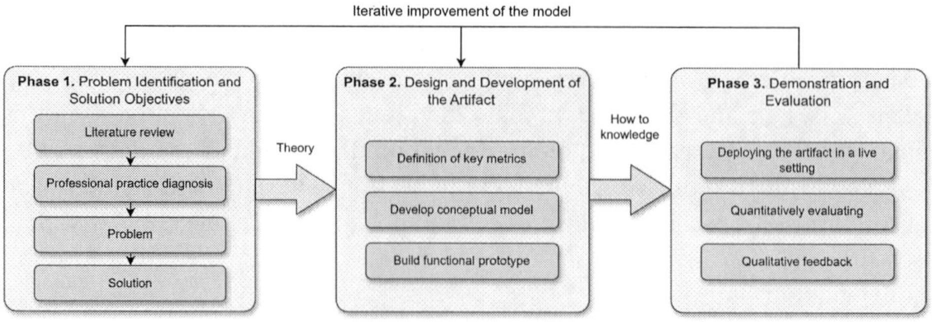

Figure 1. Research methodology based on the DSR framework [Alan et al. 2020]

Phase 2: Design and Development of the Artifact

Based on the findings from Phase 1, we design the conceptual model for non-intrusively capturing key metrics (e.g., functional size, team productivity). This phase involves:

- Defining key metrics using the GQM framework to align with estimation objectives.
- Developing the theoretical framework and data flow processes for constructing context-specific historical databases.
- Building a functional prototype that integrates with agile tools (Jira, Git, CI/CD, SonarQube) via APIs and automation scripts to capture metrics non-intrusively. For example: (a) Extracting task progress from Jira (e.g., Sprint Burndown), (b) deriving code activity from Git commits, (c) logging build/deployment metrics from CI/CD pipelines; and (d) parsing code quality data from SonarQube. This ensures that metric capture leverages existing workflows without manual intervention or disruption.

Phase 3: Demonstration and Evaluation

We validate the proposed model through empirical experiments in a real-world agile development environment in this phase. Key activities include:

- Deploying the artifact in a live setting to capture metrics from current and post-mortem projects.
- Quantitatively evaluate the accuracy of the captured metrics against manual measurements using performance indicators (e.g., MAE).
- Collecting qualitative feedback from agile teams regarding the model's non-intrusive integration and practical utility.
- Incorporating a feedback loop for iterative improvement of the model.

This DSR-based methodology ensures that the proposed model is rigorously designed, developed, and validated, addressing the key challenges of early estimation in agile environments.

4. Preliminary Results

Preliminary findings from the SMS [Rivera et al. 2024] and the professional practice diagnosis have revealed the following:

- Most early estimation methods proposed in the literature use data-driven approaches, primarily based on regression analysis and machine learning techniques [Hameed et al. 2023, Rosa and Jardine 2023].
- There is a marked dependence on expert judgment in agile practice, which results in inconsistent estimations.
- The lack of historical databases limits the adoption of quantitative methods, as automated mechanisms for non-intrusively capturing metrics are absent.

In response to these limitations, this work proposes the development of an automated tool that:

- Non-intrusively captures key metrics, integrating with agile environments' software development and project management tools.
- Enables the construction of a contextualized historical database that is standardized (e.g., using Function Points) [Commeyne et al. 2016].
- Facilitates, in future stages, the integration of hybrid estimation models that combine objective data with expert judgment, allowing for continuous feedback and improvement of the estimation process.

With this proposal, our vision is to build a hybrid early estimation model for agile projects based on the following pillars (however, this work focuses on a non-intrusive metric capture model):

1. *Hybrid Approach*: Since no single estimation technique has proven superior in all contexts, combining expert judgment with data-driven methods offers greater accuracy and adaptability [Usman et al. 2014]. This approach allows professionals to select, combine, and prioritize different estimation methods according to the project's context and needs.
2. *Nonintrusive Tools*: Metric capture should not interrupt the workflow of agile teams. Therefore, we propose automated tools that extract key metrics (e.g., functional size) from current and past projects. These tools integrate with CI/CD, Git, SonarQube, and Jira, minimizing manual intervention.
3. *Database*: Results from previous projects support estimations. Thus, the model aggregates data from dispersed sources (Jira, Git, CI/CD) into a unified repository, creating a historical database that includes recent projects from the company, with standardized metrics (e.g., Function Points for size, velocity for productivity) and contextual metadata (team configuration, technologies, agile practices). This structure enables objective comparison while preserving project-specific context.
4. *Feedback*: The estimation model must be continuously adjusted and improved based on metrics obtained during project execution. Nonintrusive metric capture provides real data that allows for updating and refining predictive models, while experts can identify new predictors from the feedback, generating a framework for continuous improvement.

5. Differences with Previous Approaches

Various studies have developed tools to measure the functional size of software from source code [Sahab and Trudel 2020, Özgesu Özen et al. 2020, Tenekeci et al. 2024]; however, these solutions have not addressed two critical aspects:

- *Nonintrusive Integration*: Existing tools have not investigated how to capture metrics without disrupting the workflow of agile teams.
- *Construction of Historical Databases*: These tools' primary focus has been on calculating functional size without structuring and storing the data in a way that can be used to model future estimations.

Our proposal differs by prioritizing the automated and nonintrusive capture of key metrics, enabling the construction of a historical database that serves as input for the progressive application of hybrid estimation models. These models combine data-driven methods—especially those based on machine learning—with expert judgment. The following table compares approaches based on expert judgment, data-driven methods, and the hybrid approach (the basis of our proposal).

Table 1. Comparison between estimation approaches for early stages of agile projects

Feature	Expert-based	Data-driven	Hybrid (proposal)
Source of data and information	Subjective experience of experts	Databases of previous projects	Combine both sources
Precision	Variable, depends on the experience of the experts	Variable, high when there is enough historical data	It is constantly improving with data from new projects
Applicability in agile environments	High, but prone to bias and human error	Low, lack of historical data is an obstacle	High, non-intrusive tool builds database
Adaptability	Depends on experts to adjust to new projects	Depends on updating the models with new data	Dynamic, data is automatically captured and fed back to the models

6. Challenges and Next Steps

Although the proposal presents a promising approach, we have identified several challenges:

- *Integration of Estimation Approaches*: An important challenge is to establish a set of criteria that enables the coherent combination of different estimation methods, thereby implementing a hybrid approach adaptable to various scenarios.
- *Incorporation of advanced methods*: To apply machine learning-based techniques, collaboration with experts and the availability of specialized tools are required, which might not be present in current teams and environments.

The following steps in this research are:

- *Model Design*: Determine the key metrics for early-stage estimation, specify the processes and data flow required to build historical databases, and detail criteria for non-intrusive integration.
- *Model Extension*: Investigate the possibility of expanding the model to integrate additional sources of information, such as physiological or interaction metrics (e.g., messaging and email applications), which could enhance future predictive estimation models.

- *Implementation and Calibration*: Develop a functional prototype and use post-mortem projects to verify its ability to automatically extract metrics, comparing these results with manual measurements performed by experts.
- *Experimental Evaluation*: Design and execute an experiment in an agile development environment to assess the model's effectiveness in obtaining metrics and collect team feedback on its utility and applicability.

References

Alan, vom Brocke Jan, M. A., and Hevner (2020). *Introduction to Design Science Research*, pages 1–13. Springer International Publishing.

Alsaadi, B. and Saeedi, K. (2022). Data-driven effort estimation techniques of agile user stories: a systematic literature review. *Artificial Intelligence Review*, 55:5485–5516.

Barry, B. et al. (1981). Software engineering economics. *New York*, 197:40.

Beata, Przemysław, K. A. P., and Czarnacka-Chrobot (2015). Application of function points and data mining techniques for software estimation - a combined approach. In Beata, Świerczek Jaroslaw Kobyliński Andrzej, and Czarnacka-Chrobot, editors, *Software Measurement*, pages 96–113. Springer International Publishing.

Cohn, M. (2005). *Agile Estimating and Planning*. Prentice Hall, Upper Saddle River, NJ, USA.

Commeyne, C., Abran, A., and Djouab, R. (2016). Effort estimation with story points and cosmic function points - an industry case study. In *Software Measurement News*.

Hacaloğlu, T. and Demirörs, O. (2018). Challenges of using software size in agile software development: A systematic literature review. *Academic Papers at IWSM Mensura 2018*.

Hameed, S., Elsheikh, Y., and Azzeh, M. (2023). An optimized case-based software project effort estimation using genetic algorithm. *Information and Software Technology*, 153:107088.

Hussain, I., Kosseim, L., and Ormandjieva, O. (2013). Approximation of cosmic functional size to support early effort estimation in agile. *Data & Knowledge Engineering*, 85:2–14. Natural Language for Information Systems: Communicating with Anything, Anywhere in Natural Language.

Jadhav, A., Kaur, M., and Akter, F. (2022). Evolution of software development effort and cost estimation techniques: Five decades study using automated text mining approach. *Mathematical Problems in Engineering*, 2022:5782587.

Kitchenham, B. and Charters, S. (2007). Guidelines for performing systematic literature reviews in software engineering. Technical report, Technical report, EBSE Technical Report EBSE-2007-01.

McConnell, S. (2006). *Software Estimation: Demystifying the Black Art*. Microsoft Press, USA.

Misra, S., Kumar, V., and Kumar, U. (2005). Goal-driven measurement framework for software innovation processes. volume 2, pages 710–716.

Prakash, B. and Viswanathan, V. (2017). A survey on software estimation techniques in traditional and agile development models. *Indonesian Journal of Electrical Engineering and Computer Science*, 7:867–876.

Rivera, J. G., Borrego, G., and Palacio, R. R. (2024). Early estimation in agile software development projects: A systematic mapping study. *Informatics*, 11.

Rosa, W. and Jardine, S. (2023). Data-driven agile software cost estimation models for dhs and dod. *Journal of Systems and Software*, 203:111739.

Sahab, A. and Trudel, S. (2020). Cosmic functional size automation of java web applications using the spring mvc framework. In *IWSM-Mensura*.

Soubra, H., Abufrikha, Y., Abran, A., et al. (2020). Towards universal cosmic size measurement automation. In *Joint Proceedings of the 30th International Workshop on Software Measurementand the 15th International Conference on Software Process and ProductMeasurement (IWSM Mensura 2020), Mexico City, Mexico, October 29-30,2020.*

Sudarmaningtyas, P. and Mohamed, R. B. (2021). A review article on software effort estimation in agile methodology. *Pertanika Journal of Science & Technology*, 29.

Tenekeci, S., Ünlü, H., Dikenelli, E., Selçuk, U., Soylu, G. K., and Demirörs, O. (2024). Predicting software size and effort from code using natural language processing. In Trudel, S., Demirörs, O., Moulla, D. K., and Hacaloglu, T., editors, *Joint Proceedings of the 33rd International Workshop on Software Measurement and the 18th International Conference on Software Process and Product Measurement (IWSM-MENSURA 2024), Montréal, Canada, September 30 - October 4, 2024*, volume 3852. CEUR-WS.org.

Usman, M., Mendes, E., Weidt, F., and Britto, R. (2014). Effort estimation in agile software development: A systematic literature review. In *Proceedings of the 10th International Conference on Predictive Models in Software Engineering*, pages 82–91. Association for Computing Machinery.

Vera, T., Ochoa, S., and Perovich, D. (2018). Survey of software development effort estimation taxonomies.

Yogi, M. K. and Chinthala, V. (2013). A hybrid approach to sizing problem in software project estimation. *International Journal for Scientific Research and Development*, 1(1):29–34.

Zarour, A. and Zein, S. (2019). Software development estimation techniques in industrial contexts: An exploratory multiple case-study. *International Journal of Technology in Education and Science*, 3:72–84.

Özgesu Özen, Özsoy, B., Aktılav, B., Güleç, E. C., and Demirörs, O. (2020). Automated estimation of functional size from code. In *2020 Turkish National Software Engineering Symposium (UYMS)*, pages 1–7.

Ünlü, H., Hacaloglu, T., Büber, F., Berrak, K., Leblebici, O., and Demirörs, O. (2022). Utilization of three software size measures for effort estimation in agile world: A case study. In *2022 48th Euromicro Conference on Software Engineering and Advanced Applications (SEAA)*, pages 239–246.

Minería de procesos e inteligencia artificial para el diseño, sostenibilidad y mejora de procesos colaborativos.

Martín Rubio

[1]Instituto de Computación, Facultad de Ingeniería,
Universidad de la República, Uruguay

mrubio@fing.edu.uy

Abstract. *In recent decades, process mining has played a key role in improving organizational processes. Today's growing complexity, with collaborative processes involving multiple actors, demands new perspectives for design and improvement. At the same time, sustainability and artificial intelligence (AI) have gained relevance. This doctoral work aims to expand the scope of process mining and AI by integrating techniques, practices, and tools for the design, sustainibility and improvement of collaborative processes.*

Resumen. *En las últimas décadas, la minería de procesos ha sido clave para mejorar procesos en las organizaciones. Hoy, la complejidad creciente, con procesos colaborativos que involucran múltiples actores, exige nuevas perspectivas de diseño y mejora. Al mismo tiempo, la sostenibilidad y la inteligencia artificial (IA) han cobrado protagonismo. Este trabajo doctoral busca ampliar el alcance de la minería de procesos y la IA, integrando técnicas, prácticas y herramientas para el diseño, sostenibilidad y mejora de procesos colaborativos.*

1. Introducción

La minería de procesos es una disciplina que emerge de la necesidad de analizar datos desde una perspectiva de procesos [van der Aalst 2016]. Para esto, se integran enfoques que provienen de la ciencia de datos y ciencia de procesos con el objetivo de analizar los datos generados a partir de la ejecución de procesos de negocio. Un proceso de negocio es un conjunto de actividades o tareas que son llevadas a cabo por las organizaciones en un entorno organizacional y técnico, para cumplir con sus objetivos [Weske 2019]. Por ejemplo, un proceso bancario en un banco o un proceso de salud en un hospital.

El principal insumo para la minería de procesos son los logs de eventos (event log) que se generan a partir de la ejecución de los distintos procesos. El enfoque tradicional abarca una perspectiva intra-organizacional, en donde existe una única organización o actor principal asociado a todo el proceso en estudio. Las realidades cada vez más complejas donde se deben integrar ecosistemas y tecnologías diversos, definen procesos colaborativos [van der Aalst 2011], con dependencias e interacciones entre distintos participantes en un único proceso general. Esta naturaleza distribuida, inmersa en diferentes contextos técnicos, compliejiza la recolección y preparación de datos de los procesos.

Adicionalmente, surge el interés en disminuir el impacto de las actividades humanas en el medioambiente, donde los procesos están naturalmente involucrados. Para dimensionar y mejorar la sostenibilidad de procesos es clave poder medir su ejecución con elementos de sostenibilidad, por lo que interesa definir para la minería de procesos una nueva dimensión de sostenibilidad a la hora de analizar los procesos. La sostenibilidad puede definirse como la habilidad de emplear cualquier recurso en el presente sin comprometer el uso de ese recurso para satisfacer las necesidades propias de las generaciones futuras, además asegurando el balance entre el crecimiento económico, bienestar social y medioambiental [Brundtland 1987].

En los últimos años la inteligencia artificial (IA) ha irrumpido en todas las áreas, incluyendo la minería de procesos, propiciando la integración de nuevos enfoques de diseño, automatización y análisis de datos, como aprendizaje automático (AA) para predicción de eventos futuros en los procesos con base en eventos existentes, o creación de nuevo contenido con modelos de lenguaje de gran tamaño (LLMs) como ChatGPT entrenados con una gran cantidad de datos, para asistir en diversas tareas, por ejemplo, el modelado de procesos o el análisis de trazas de ejecución de procesos.

En este contexto, es que esta tesis doctoral busca extender el alcance actual de la minería de procesos con inteligencia artificial, integrando nuevos artefactos como técnicas, prácticas, metodologías y herramientas para el diseño, la sostenibilidad y mejora de procesos colaborativos. El resto del artículo se organiza de la siguiente forma: en la sección 2 se plantean las preguntas y objetivos de investigación, en la sección 3 se presenta el estado del arte, luego en la sección 4 se muestra la metodología de investigación, la propuesta de solución y el avance actual se presenta en la sección 5 y finalmente en la sección 6 el trabajo pendiente.

2. Preguntas y objetivos de la investigación

El objetivo general es definir nuevas técnicas, prácticas, metodologías y herramientas de aplicación de minería de procesos e inteligencia artificial para el diseño, sostenibilidad y mejora de procesos colaborativos, a los efectos de reducir el esfuerzo de modelado, mejorar la ejecución y sostenibilidad de procesos colaborativos y reducir el gap existente entre modelos y su ejecución real. Las preguntas específicas son:

- **RQ1.** ¿Qué técnicas, prácticas, metodologías y herramientas basadas en minería de procesos son requeridas para el diseño, sostenibilidad y mejora de procesos colaborativos?
- **RQ2.** ¿Cuál es el alcance actual de las propuestas existentes y que limitaciones presentan?
- **RQ3.** ¿Cómo puede integrarse la inteligencia artificial para mejorar la aplicación de minería de procesos para el diseño, sostenibilidad y mejora de procesos colaborativos?

3. Estado del arte

La aplicación de minería de procesos (descubrimiento, conformidad, extensión, predicción) sobre los datos de ejecución de procesos de negocio [van der Aalst 2011] se han enfocado principalmente en procesos de tipo orquestación que se realizan en una única organización (intra-organizacionales), y más recientemente, a procesos colaborativos (inter-organizacionales) [Hernandez et al. 2021, Liu et al. 2023, Peña et al. 2024, Liu et al. 2024], principalmente descubrimiento de procesos. Se ha definido una nueva propuesta de log de eventos orientado a objetos, Object Oriented Event Data (OCED)

[Fahland et al. 2024] como el sucesor al estándar tradicional XES (IEEE 1849-2016) [Group et al. 2016] para la representación de los logs de procesos, particularmente con una visión orientada a objetos. El log orientado a objetos permite ampliar las posibilidades de análisis de los procesos, en particular de procesos colaborativos.

Por otro lado, ha cobrado importancia de la orientación hacia procesos más sostenibles y la relevancia de enfoques como Green BPM. En [Couckuyt and Looy 2020] la revisión muestra que el foco principal ha sido medir y controlar las emisiones o la energía en los procesos de negocio, en la dimensión medioambiental. La evaluación de las TICs en [Hernández González et al. 2019] para gestionar recursos energéticos de forma eficiente controlando el impacto de las actividades que se realizan, y [Calero et al. 2021] la influencia del software de soporte en el consumo de energía, ej. plataformas BPMS, algoritmos de inteligencia artificial [Schwartz et al. 2020] y descubrimiento de procesos [Delgado et al. 2023]. La noción de "Ciencia de Datos Verde" (GDS) se introduce en [Van Der Aalst 2016] por la posible "contaminación" que puede causar la ciencia de datos.

Los avances en la inteligencia artificial han propiciado la integración de nuevos enfoques de automatización y análisis de datos, como aprendizaje automático (AA) para predicción de eventos futuros [Di Francescomarino and Ghidini 2022, Ceravolo et al. 2024], o creación de nuevo contenido con modelos de lenguaje de gran tamaño (LLMs) como ChatGPT para asistir en diversas tareas. En particular, se han utilizado LLMs para generación de descripciones textuales desde datos de procesos y logs de eventos, modelado de procesos desde su descripción textual, o uso de descripciones textuales de modelos y logs de eventos para minería de procesos [Grohs et al. 2024, Kourani et al. 2024, Berti et al. 2024b], así como evaluación de requisitos para uso de LLMs [Berti et al. 2024a] y herramientas asociadas.

El foco de este trabajo de tesis es en procesos colaborativos, en el cual se podrán utilizar de base propuestas y herramientas existentes para procesos tradicionales adaptándolas y/o extendiéndolas al contexto más complejo de ese tipo de procesos.

4. Metodología de investigación

Para guiar la investigación se siguen los lineamientos de Design Science para Sistemas de Información e Ingeniería de Software [Wieringa 2014, Hevner et al. 2004, Venable 2006]. En Design-Science para trabajos de investigación se atacan problemas no resueltos aún, utilizando enfoques únicos e innovadores, o problemas resueltos pero con enfoques más efectivos o eficientes, contribuyendo en ambos casos, al conocimiento en fundamentos (teorías, frameworks, construcciones, modelos, métodos, instanciaciones) y metodologías (técnicas de análisis de datos, formalismos, medidas, criterios de validación). Se trabajará principalmente con el primer enfoque, en la creación de artefactos como framework general y metodología de trabajo, modelos (procesos, AA, LLMs e ingeniería del prompt), algoritmos de: minería de procesos, registro y manejo de datos, medidas de sostenibilidad, entre otros. A continuación se describen las principales etapas:

1. En primer lugar se define el problema identificando hipótesis y preguntas de investigación que guiarán el trabajo a realizar, que se presentaron en la Sección 2.
2. Realizar el estado del arte al inicio de la investigación sobre las temáticas seleccionadas siguiendo los lineamientos de revisiones sistemáticas de la literatura y map-

ping studies planteados en [Kitchenham 2004, Kitchenham and Charters 2007].

3. Con base en el estado del arte realizado, se identifican propuestas que pueden servir de base para su aplicación en sostenibilidad de procesos colaborativos, de minería de procesos, aprendizaje automático e inteligencia artificial generativa.
4. Para la validación de resultados se realizarán estudios de caso y/o experimentos controlados [Yin 2014, Wohlin et al. 2012]. Por ejemplo, experimentos controlados para validar la adecuación de las propuestas generadas con usuarios expertos (ej. medidas y análisis de sostenibilidad), estudios de caso en el contexto de procesos colaborativos de e-Government (AGESIC)[1].
5. Comunicación de resultados. Serán validados en la comunidad científica con publicaciones en congresos y revistas de primer nivel regional e internacional.

5. Solución propuesta y avances

La solución propuesta busca materializar una visión integral para la mejora de procesos colaborativos, considerando la perspectiva de sostenibilidad mediante la minería de procesos y la inteligencia artificial como se muestra en la figura 1.

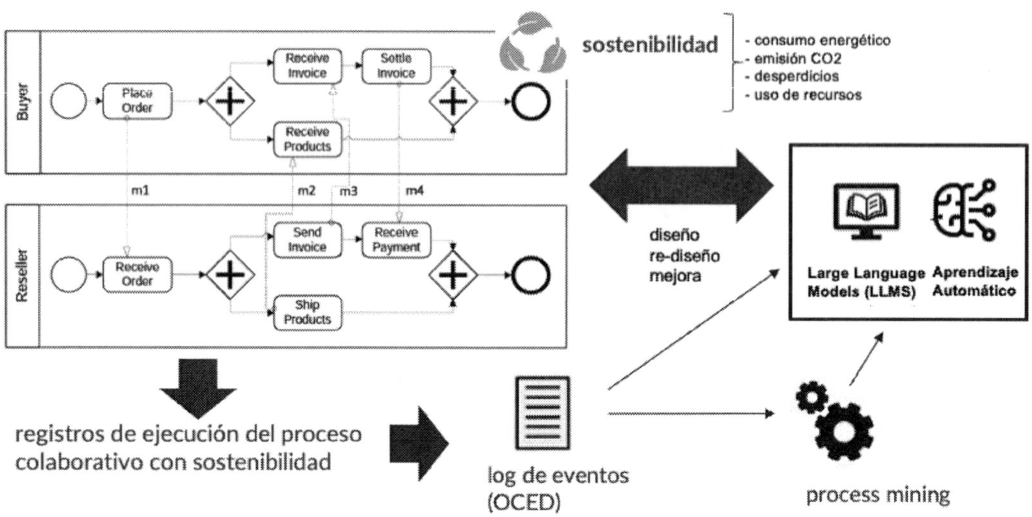

Figura 1. Visión general de la solución propuesta

La propuesta incorpora elementos de sostenibilidad en el registro de los logs de procesos, con base en los descritos en [Hernández González et al. 2019, Mancebo et al. 2017] y métricas asociadas, utilizando logs de eventos OCED. Tanto los logs de eventos como los modelos de procesos colaborativos, serán insumo para minería de procesos potenciada con inteligencia artificial (LLMs, aprendizaje automático) para apoyar el diseño, re-diseño y análisis de trazas de ejecución y modelos de procesos, para su sostenibilidad y mejora asociada. Por ejemplo, en la integración con LLMs se considerarán elementos como prompt engineering específicos [Grohs et al. 2024, Kourani et al. 2024, Berti et al. 2024a], generación aumentada por recuperación (RAG en inglés) para contexto específico, para procesos colaborativos. De esta manera, se espera mejorar los resultados obtenidos con minería de procesos tradicional.

[1]https://www.gub.uy/agencia-gobierno-electronico-sociedad-informacion-conocimiento/

La propuesta incluirá la definición de técnicas, prácticas, metodologías y herramientas de soporte que guíen y promuevan el uso del enfoque definido como parte de las tareas de análisis y mejora de procesos en las organizaciones.

5.1. Revisión sistemática de la literatura

Actualmente se encuentra en curso una revisión sistematica para recolectar la información existente acerca de la minería de procesos aplicada con un enfoque de sostenibilidad. Para llevar a cabo esta revisión se siguen los lineamientos propuestos por Kitchenham [Kitchenham 2004][Kitchenham and Charters 2007]. Para la elaboración de la revisión se está utilizando en la plataforma Parsifal [Parsifal 2025] que brinda soporte a los lineamientos antes mencionados, lo cual ayuda a la ejecución, documentación y análisis de los resultados obtenidos en la revisión.

Partiendo de las preguntas de investigación definidas se genera la cadena de búsqueda que luego fue utilizada en cada una de las fuentes. Las fuentes se seleccionaron con base en el cubrimiento de publicaciones internacionales tanto de conferencias como revistas de primer nivel en el área, incluyendo Springer, IEEE Xplore, Scopus, Science Direct. Además, de los resultados obtenidos en las fuentes antes mencionadas también se consideró importante incluir artículos de conferencias específicas del área [Genero Bocco et al. 2023], particularmente los artículos presentados en el workshop Process Mining 4 Sustainability en 2024. [István Koren 2024]

A modo de resumen de los resultados preliminares se obtuvo un total de 434 artículos, de los que solamente 11 fueron considerados artículos relevantes. También se realizará snowballing [Wohlin 2014] partiendo de los estudios primarios para extender los resultados. Actualmente, se están procesando los 11 artículos relevantes que fueron clasificados con el objetivo de obtener los estudios primarios y de esta manera continuar con la realización de la revisión sistemática. Los estudios primarios serán analizados desde seis perspectivas, donde para cada una se cuenta con una pregunta que será calificada con base en la escala de Likert. Las perspectivas definidas son: técnicas de minería de procesos aplicada para sostenibilidad, medidas de sostenibildiad, tipo de log de eventos utilizado (XES/OCED), técnicas de inteligencia artificial utilizadas (si alguna, aprendizaje automático, IA generativa), datos de sostenibilidad definidos, tipo de procesos utilizados (orquestación, colaborativos).

5.2. Generación de logs OCED

Obtener logs de procesos, suele tener una complejidad considerable. Contar con el conjunto de datos de procesos de calidad es un problema recurrente tanto para el análisis de procesos como para tareas de investigación. Generar logs en forma sintética es una forma de atacar este inconveniente y de obtener datos nuevos y confiables para la experimentación utilizando la propuesta de integración de elementos de sostenibilidad.

Dentro de las técnicas de inteligencia artificial para entrenar redes profundas se encuentran las Redes Generativas Antagónicas (GANS) que han demostrado muy buenos resultados a la hora de generar datos sintéticos [Goodfellow et al. 2014]. Particularmente, las Conditional Tabular GANs (CTGANs)[Xu et al. 2019] son redes que se especializan en generar datos sintéticos a partir de datos tabulares. En ese sentido, se está trabajando en el entrenamiento de distintos modelos generativos utilizando CTGANs para la generación de logs de eventos de procesos sintéticos basados en OCED. Los primeros resultados muestran que es posible generar log sintéticos de buena calidad utilizando estas tecnologías, lo cual será un insumo relevante para la experimentación con distintos datasets.

6. Trabajo pendiente

Un elemento clave es la identificación de elementos de sostenibilidad y la definición de prácticas basadas en integración de datos a los procesos. Particularmente, en mi tesis de maestría [Rubio et al. 2021] [Rubio et al. 2023] trabajé en la integración de datos organizacionales a los logs de procesos, que se trasladará a la nueva propuesta con OCED, utlizando el metamodelo y la implementación de [Calegari and Delgado 2023].

En este año, se trabajará en el análisis de las herramientas que brinda la inteligencia artificial, particularmente el aprendizaje automático y la inteligencia artificial generativa, para el diseño y modelado de procesos considerando su sostenibilidad, mejora de modelos existentes, análisis de sostenibilidad con base en trazas de ejecución reales, entre varias otras posibilidades. La integración de estos elementos a la minería de procesos es parte clave de la propuesta que se generará en este trabajo doctoral.

Se integrarán y definirán técnicas, prácticas, metodologías y herramientas de soporte adecuadas, incluyendo prompt engineering específicos, uso de generación aumentada por recuperación para contexto específico, diseño y re-diseño de procesos sostenibles, considerando y extendiendo/adaptando propuestas existentes, y definiendo nuevas para alcanzar los objetivos planteados.

A partir de los trabajos en curso y las definiciones propuestas, se prevé realizar experimentos y validar la propuesta con casos reales de procesos colaborativos del Estado uruguayo, utilizando datos de AGESIC.

Referencias

Berti, A., Kourani, H., Häfke, H., Li, C.-Y., and Schuster, D. (2024a). Evaluating large language models in process mining: Capabilities, benchmarks, and evaluation strategies. In *Enterprise, Business-Process and Inf.Sys. Modeling*, pages 13–21. Springer.

Berti, A., Schuster, D., and van der Aalst, W. M. P. (2024b). Abstractions, scenarios, and prompt definitions for process mining with llms: A case study. In *Business Process Management Workshops*, pages 427–439. Springer.

Brundtland, G. (1987). Report of the world commision on enviroment and development: our common future. In *United Nations*.

Calegari, D. and Delgado, A. (2023). A model-driven engineering perspective for the object-centric event data (oced) metamodel. In *Int. Conf. on Business Process Management*, pages 508–520. Springer.

Calero, C., Moraga, M. Á., and Piattini, M. (2021). *Software Sustainability*, pages 1–15. Springer.

Ceravolo, P., Comuzzi, M., De Weerdt, J., Di Francescomarino, C., and Maggi, F. M. (2024). Predictive process monitoring: concepts, challenges, and future research directions. *Process Science*, 1(1):2.

Couckuyt, D. and Looy, A. V. (2020). A systematic review of green business process management. *Business Process Management Journal*, 26(2):421–446.

Delgado, A., García, F., Moraga, M. Á., Calegari, D., Gordillo, A., and Peña, L. (2023). Adding the sustainability dimension in process mining discovery algorithms evaluation. In *Business Process Management Forum*, pages 163–177. Springer.

Di Francescomarino, C. and Ghidini, C. (2022). *Predictive Process Monitoring*, volume 448 of *Lecture Notes in Business Information Processing*, pages 320–346. Springer.

Fahland, D., Montali, M., Lebherz, J., van der Aalst, W. M. P., van Asseldonk, M., Blank, P., Bosmans, L., Brenscheidt, M., Ciccio, C. D., Delgado, A., Calegari, D., Peeperkorn, J., Verbeek, E., Vugs, L., and Wynn, M. T. (2024). Towards a simple and extensible standard for object-centric event data (OCED) - core model, design space, and lessons learned. *CoRR*, abs/2410.14495.

Genero Bocco, M., Piattini Velthuis, M. G., Cruz Lemus, J. A., and Díaz García, (2023). *Métodos de investigación en informática*. Ra-Ma.

Goodfellow, I., Pouget-Abadie, J., Mirza, M., Xu, B., Warde-Farley, D., Ozair, S., Courville, A., and Bengio, Y. (2014). Generative adversarial nets. *Advances in neural information processing systems*, 27.

Grohs, M., Abb, L., Elsayed, N., and Rehse, J.-R. (2024). Large language models can accomplish business process management tasks. In *Business Process Management Workshops*, pages 453–465. Springer.

Group, X. W. et al. (2016). Ieee standard for extensible event stream (xes) for achieving interoperability in event logs and event streams. *IEEE Std*, 1849:1–50.

Hernandez, J. D., Tello, E., Marin, H. M., Ramirez, U. M., and Mata, J. A. (2021). Merging event logs for inter-organizational process mining. In *New Perspectives on Enterprise Decision-Making Applying AI Techniques*, pages 3–26. Springer.

Hernández González, A., Calero, C., Pérez Parra, D., and Mancebo, J. (2019). Approaching green BPM characterisation. *Journal of Software: Evolution and Process*, 31(2).

Hevner, A. R., March, S. T., Park, J., and Ram, S. (2004). Design science in information systems research. *MIS Q.*, 28(1):75–105.

István Koren, Janina Bauer, N. G. B. P. (2024). 1st international workshop on process mining for sustainability (pm4s). In *Process Mining Workshops: ICPM 2024 International Workshops, Denmark, Revised Selected Papers*.

Kitchenham, B. (2004). Procedures for performing systematic reviews. Technical Report TR/SE-0401, Keele University and Empirical Soft. Eng. Joint Report, Keele, UK.

Kitchenham, B. A. and Charters, S. (2007). Guidelines for performing systematic literature reviews in software engineering. Technical Report EBSE 2007-001, Keele University and Durham University Joint Report, Keele, UK.

Kourani, H., Berti, A., Hennrich, J., Kratsch, W., Weidlich, R., Li, C.-Y., Arslan, A., Schuster, D., and van der Aalst, W. M. P. (2024). Leveraging large language models for enhanced process model comprehension. *CoRR*, abs/2408.08892.

Liu, C., Li, H., Zeng, Q., Lu, T., and Li, C. (2024). A technique for discovering bpmn collaboration diagrams. *Software and Systems Modeling*, 23:1323–1343.

Liu, C., Li, H., Zhang, S., Cheng, L., and Zeng, Q. (2023). Cross-department collaborative healthcare process model discovery from event logs. *IEEE Transactions on Automation Science and Engineering*, 20(3):2115–2125.

Mancebo, J., García, F., Pedreira, O., and Moraga, M. Á. (2017). Bpms-game: Tool for business process gamification. Business Process Management Forum, pages 127–140. Springer.

Parsifal (2025). Parsifal systematic review tool. Accessed: 2025-03-29.

Peña, L., Andrade, D., Delgado, A., and Calegari, D. (2024). An approach for discovering inter-organizational collaborative business processes in BPMN 2.0. In *Process Mining Workshops*, pages 487–498. Springer Nature Switzerland.

Rubio, M., Delgado, A., and Tansini, L. (2021). Process mining and data mining integration frameworks for evidence-based business intelligence: a systematic review. In *24th Iberoamerican Conf. on Software Engineering (CIbSE)*, pages 28–41. Curran Assoc.

Rubio, M., Delgado, A., and Tansini, L. (2023). An integrated approach to process and organizational data mining. In *Latin American Computer Conf.*, pages 1–10. IEEE.

Schwartz, R., Dodge, J., Smith, N. A., and Etzioni, O. (2020). Green ai. *Commun. ACM*, 63(12):54–63.

Van Der Aalst, W. (2016). Green data science - using big data in an "environmentally friendly" manner. In *Proceedings of the 18th International Conference on Enterprise Information Systems - Volume 1: ICEIS*, pages 9–21. SciTePress.

van der Aalst, W. (2016). *Process Mining: Data Science in Action, 2nd.ed.* Springer.

van der Aalst, W. M. P. (2011). Intra- and inter-organizational process mining: Discovering processes within and between organizations. In *The Practice of Enterprise Modeling*, pages 1–11, Cham. Springer.

Venable, J. (2006). A framework for design science research activities. In *Emerging Trends and Challenges in Information Technology Management*, pages 184–187. Idea group publishing.

Weske, M. (2019). *Business Process Management - Concepts, Languages, Architectures, 3rd Ed.* Springer.

Wieringa, R. J. (2014). *Design Science Methodology for Inf. Systems and Software Engineering*. Springer.

Wohlin, C. (2014). Guidelines for snowballing in systematic literature studies and a replication in software engineering. In *Proceedings of the 18th international conference on evaluation and assessment in software engineering*, pages 1–10.

Wohlin, C., Runeson, P., Höst, M., Ohlsson, M. C., and Regnell, B. (2012). *Experimentation in Software Engineering*. Springer.

Xu, L., Skoularidou, M., Cuesta-Infante, A., and Veeramachaneni, K. (2019). Modeling tabular data using conditional gan. *Advances in neural information processing systems*, 32.

Yin, R. K. (2014). *Case Study Research: Design and Methods, 5th Ed.* SAGE Publications, Inc.

Plataforma para la Gestión de Datos Espaciales y su Aplicación en Gestión en el área Salud

Raquel Sosa

[1]Instituto de Computación – Facultad de Ingeniería – Universidad de la República
Julio Herrera y Reissig 565 – Montevideo – Uruguay

raquels@fing.edu.uy

Abstract. *Different organisms generate spatial data. Health organizations have their own data that could be spacialized. Using these data together allows for spatial analysis to support health service management and planning. However, joint analysis of such data presents several challenges. This paper proposes mechanisms that facilitate joint data management to support access assessment and health service planning. Specifically, it proposes a platform, built using the Design Science Research approach, to generate the design and implementation iteratively. It will be evaluated through exchanges with health experts and technicians.*

Resumo. *Los datos espaciales son generados por diferentes organismos. Las organizaciones de salud tienen datos propios que pueden ser espacializados. Usar estos datos en conjunto permite realizar análisis espaciales para apoyar en la gestión y planificación de los servicios de salud. Sin embargo, el análisis conjunto de dichos datos presenta diferentes desafíos. Este trabajo busca proponer mecanismos que faciliten la gestión conjunta de datos, para brindar soporte a la evaluación de acceso y planificación de los servicios de salud. En particular, se propone una plataforma, construida siguiendo el enfoque Design Science Research, en forma iterativa para generar el diseño e implementación. Se evaluará mediante instancias de intercambio con expertos en salud y técnicos.*

1. Introducción

Los datos espaciales son generados usualmente por organismos y empresas que tienen competencia en esta tarea. En niveles oficiales de gobierno hay organismos que incluso tienen la obligación y competencia de generar y mantener dichos datos. Para la gestión de los datos espaciales a nivel de gobierno se crearon las Infraestructuras de Datos Espaciales (IDEs) [Bernabé Poveda and López Vázquez 2012][Shekhar et al. 2017], las cuales siguen lineamientos y estándares vinculados al área. Esto posibilita que organizaciones que no son productoras de datos espaciales puedan utilizarlos para optimizar sus operaciones de negocio a nivel territorial.

Muchas organizaciones, especialmente las de salud, tienen información relativa a personas (p. ej. usuarios, funcionarios, pacientes, clientes) que puede ser geolocalizada. En sus bases de datos se tiene generalmente la dirección de las personas, la cual puede ubicarse en un mapa. De esta forma, si bien esta información no es información espacial, decimos que es espacializable (i.e. puede ser transformada en información espacial).

Las organizaciones de salud ubican sus servicios en el territorio en el que trabajan de acuerdo a cierta lógica: hospitales de diferentes grados de complejidad en los servicios que brindan, hospitales especializados (por ejemplo en pediatría, traumatología) y servicios de primer nivel de atención como policlínicas (que pueden ubicarse en diferentes lugares para cubrir mejor el territorio en el que están los usuarios).

Como escenario motivador consideramos el Sistema Nacional Integrado de Salud (SNIS) de Uruguay. En este contexto, el Ministerio de Salud Pública (MSP)[1] establece las regulaciones, el programa Salud Digital[2] apoya al MSP en el uso de las TICs en el área salud y los Prestadores de Servicios de Salud son las instituciones que atienden directamente a la población. Salud Digital también lidera la iniciativa de la Historia Clínica Electrónica Nacional (HCEN)[3]. Los prestadores de servicios de salud en general se ubican en un área a la que brindan atención (la mayoría trabaja en un solo Departamento). Dentro de los prestadores se destaca ASSE (Administración de Servicios de Salud del Estado)[4] que es el único que tiene cobertura en todo el país. ASSE es un servicio público y es el que tiene la mayor cantidad de usuarios[5]. Como dato de referencia, a fines de 2019 (último dato publicado) contaba con 1.361.467 usuarios. Adicionalmente la Universidad de la República cuenta con el Hospital Universitario[6] que, si bien no está integrado al SNIS como un prestador, a través de un convenio con ASSE atiende a sus usuarios.

En este escenario, resulta de interés realizar análisis espaciales, por ejemplo, para saber y visualizar cuántos usuarios están dentro de un radio dado de las policlínicas o cuántos usuarios están a menos de media hora de una puerta de emergencia. Sin embargo, para poder realizar estos análisis se necesita poder convertir la información de las organizaciones en información espacial, para luego poder realizar su análisis en conjunto con datos espaciales de propósito general. Dicha conversión requiere que los datos de las organizaciones sean gestionados de forma de contribuir a su calidad con el fin de lograr análisis lo más confiables posible. Asimismo, dado que las instituciones de salud no son generadoras de datos espaciales de propósito general, se necesita seleccionar y gestionar datos espaciales externos.

Sin embargo, el análisis conjunto de dichos datos presenta desafíos en términos del procesamiento de datos espacializables, la gestión de la calidad de ambos tipos de datos y su análisis espacial conjunto. El problema de investigación consiste entonces en definir mecanismos que aborden estos desafíos en un ambiente homogéneo e integrado, apuntando a facilitar las tareas de análisis espacial para la evaluación y planificación de servicios de salud.

Este trabajo propone la plataforma denominada DAMRESP (DAta Management for HealthcaRE Spatial Planning) que apoya en la gestión conjunta de datos espaciales provistos por terceros y datos propios de las organizaciones, con el fin de posibilitar su utilización en análisis espaciales de interés para las organizaciones. La propuesta se centra en el área de la salud y, en particular, en la evaluación del acceso a los servicios de

[1] http://https://www.gub.uy/ministerio-salud-publica/

[2] https://www.gub.uy/agencia-gobierno-electronico-sociedad-informacion-conocimiento/saluduy

[3] https://www.gub.uy/agencia-gobierno-electronico-sociedad-informacion-conocimiento/node/312

[4] https://www.asse.com.uy/

[5] Cant. Usuarios ASSE hasta 2019 - https://www.asse.com.uy/contenido/Datos-Usuarios-ASSE-6604

[6] Hospital de Clínicas - https://www.hc.edu.uy/

salud por parte de los usuarios y en la planificación de dichos servicios. Para la construcción de la plataforma se está utilizando una metodología basada en Design Research Science, siguiendo un proceso iterativo para el desarrollo sucesivo de los componentes de la plataforma.

DAMRESP incluye componentes que abordan los principales desafíos de esta gestión conjunta de información: procesar datos espacializables, gestionar la calidad de ambos tipos de datos y realizar análisis espaciales. Los resultados esperados del trabajo son el diseño e implementación de la plataforma DAMRESP, guías de uso de sus componentes, y un caso de estudio en el área de salud, que constituye un escenario de referencia mostrando cómo utilizar la plataforma.

La evaluación de la plataforma se realizará mediante distintos tipos de instancias intercambio con organizaciones de salud de Uruguay. En particular, se planea realizar entrevistas con referentes de las organizaciones de salud, así como grupos focales y talleres con usuarios analistas.

El resto del trabajo se organiza de la siguiente manera. En la Sección 2 se detallan las preguntas y objetivos de investigación. En la Sección 3 se analiza conocimiento existente en el área. En la Sección 4 se presenta un esbozo de la metodología que se está siguiendo. En la Sección 5 se expone la solución propuesta y en la Sección 6 se presentan las conclusiones del trabajo y los próximos pasos.

2. Preguntas y Objetivos de Investigación

Se plantea como pregunta principal de investigación la siguiente:

¿Cómo facilitar la gestión de datos empresariales espacializables y datos espaciales en una organización de salud, para que de forma conjunta posibiliten evaluar y planificar el acceso a los servicios que brinda?

En base a esta pregunta principal se definen las siguientes preguntas de investigación específicas, que buscan abordar los siguientes desafíos: espacializar datos de las organizaciones (i.e. empresariales), gestionar datos de las organizaciones y datos espaciales de forma conjunta, permitir el diseño de análisis espaciales, y diseñar análisis que permitan la evaluación y planificación del acceso a los servicios de salud.

- RQ1 - ¿Cómo espacializar datos empresariales?
- RQ2 - ¿Cómo gestionar datos espaciales externos y datos de la organización en forma conjunta?
- RQ3 - ¿Cómo posibilitar el diseño de análisis espaciales de datos empresariales espacializables y datos espaciales?
- RQ4 - ¿Qué iniciativas existen vinculadas a las preguntas de investigación anteriores?
- RQ5 - ¿Cuáles son los análisis de uso más relevante para la evaluación y planificación de servicios de Salud?
- RQ6 - ¿Qué componentes pueden facilitar estas tareas para trabajar con los datos?

En línea con estas preguntas de investigación, el objetivo de este trabajo es definir una plataforma que guíe a una organización del área de salud en la utilización de sus datos y datos espaciales externos, con el fin de evaluar el acceso de los usuarios a los servicios de salud y planificar la gestión futura de dichos servicios. En particular, se busca que la plataforma provea las guías como procesos a seguir y que brinde también herramientas para asistir dichos procesos.

3. Conocimiento Actual

Se han estudiado diferentes aplicaciones de tecnologías GIS (Sistemas de Información Geográfica) en el área de salud. En general se distinguen las aplicaciones de tiempo real (p. ej. ruteo de ambulancias, seguimiento epidemiológico) y las aplicaciones de análisis que permiten evaluar el acceso y planificar la evolución de los servicios de salud [Jijón et al. 2022] [Ebube Jones 2023] [Latorre et al. 2024]. En este segundo grupo es interesante poder responder preguntas tales como: "¿todos los usuarios tienen acceso a los servicios de salud?, ¿cuántos niños viven en un determinado radio de una policlínica que brinda consultas pediátricas?, ¿existen usuarios que quedan fuera del área de cobertura de determinados servicios?"

En los trabajos analizados, aunque hay un gran desarrollo de métodos analíticos, un gran desafío son los problemas de la calidad de los datos [Khashoggi and Murad 2020] para poder aplicar esos métodos. Por ejemplo, los datos de los usuarios en general se basan en direcciones, pero los procesos de geocodificación tienen un bajo índice de efectividad, con lo que se podrían terminar realizando los análisis con menos de la mitad de los usuarios reales (incluso podría haber un sesgo porque la población con menos recursos en general no tiene direcciones formales).

En el área de gestión de datos espaciales hay muchos trabajos orientados a las IDEs que apuntan a organismos de gobierno de diferentes niveles, que son los generadores de dichos datos. También hay normas específicas de calidad de datos espaciales que tienen un énfasis en el componente geométrico [Breunig et al. 2020]. Por otro lado hay estándares y propuestas de gestión de datos empresariales y calidad de datos que están orientados a datos alfanuméricos tradicionales de las organizaciones (p. ej. DAMA[7], ISO[8], normas AENOR[9]).

En Uruguay, la AGESIC propone un Modelo de Referencia de Calidad de Datos [AGESIC 2020] que incluye dimensiones y factores tanto para datos alfanuméricos como datos espaciales. Aunque es un trabajo que considera ambos tipos de datos no apunta al análisis espacial de los datos.

En resumen, a nuestro leal saber y entender no hay propuestas para facilitar la gestión conjunta de datos espaciales y espacializables de las organizaciones, con el fin de que organizaciones de salud puedan realizar análisis espaciales de su interés. Este trabajo propone brindar un marco integrado considerando las normas de ambos tipos de datos y proveyendo herramientas concretas que ayuden en dicha gestión para lograr atender las consultas mencionadas al comienzo de esta sección. Por ejemplo, para atacar el problema de las direcciones informales se desarrolló la herramienta GISO que prevee asistir en la georreferenciación manual cuando no se encuentra la dirección en forma automática (además de tener la capacidad de usar varios servicios de georeferenciación).

[7]http://www.dama.org

[8]https://www.iso.org/obp/ui/#iso:std:iso:8000:-1:ed-1:v1:en

[9]https://tienda.aenor.com/norma-une-especificacion-une-0080-2023-n0071383

4. Metodología de Investigación

Este trabajo sigue una metodología de investigación basada en el paradigma de Design Science Research [Hevner et al. 2004][Schoormann et al. 2023]. Se busca resolver un problema de la realidad basándose en el desarrollo de artefactos que ayuden a proveer una solución y su evaluación. Estos artefactos pueden ser tanto especificaciones de procesos como piezas de software. A su vez el trabajo se desarrolla considerando un escenario motivador como guía de la realidad sobre la que se aplicará la solución para evaluarla. Se plantea un trabajo iterativo para ir abordado sucesivamente las preguntas de investigación y con la evaluación de los artefactos ir retroalimentando el diseño general.

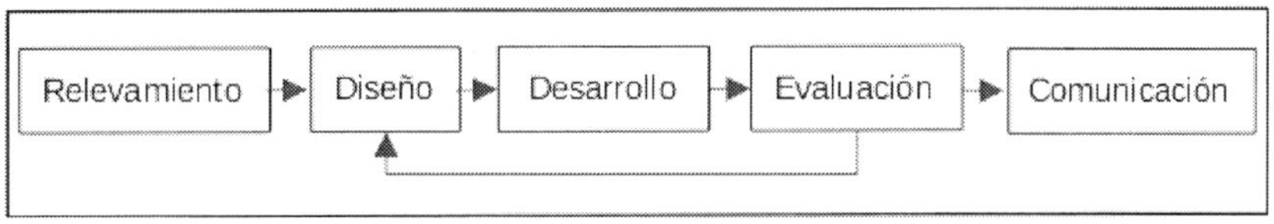

Figura 1. Proceso de Investigación basado en DSR

En la Figura 1 se muestra el proceso seguido en cada iteración, dónde las flechas indican la secuencia de las actividades a realizar (y la iteración). El relevamiento consiste en el análisis de conocimiento existente (utilizando diferentes técnicas de análisis bibliográfico como rapid reviews y mapping study [Budgen et al. 2008] [Kitchenham and Charters 2007][Cartaxo et al. 2020] y en el análisis de las necesidades del escenario planteado. Luego de esta etapa se diseñan artefactos que aborden estas necesidades, para luego desarrollarlos y finalmente evaluarlos. De acuerdo al tipo de artefacto se aplican tanto técnicas de validación de software como técnicas más cualitativas para su evaluación. En el caso de los artefactos que involucran la definición de procesos se espera trabajar tanto con expertos del área salud como con técnicos del área informática que apliquen dichos procesos a sus propios datos. También se prevee la Comunicación de este trabajo a través de publicaciones en ámbitos tanto académicos como de la industria y gobierno.

5. Solución Propuesta

La solución propuesta se guía por un Escenario Motivador que define algunas de las situaciones a las que se busca dar respuesta. Este escenario se inspira en el sistema de salud de Uruguay, considerando tanto a ASSE por ser el mayor prestador de servicios de salud como a otros prestadores con menor cantidad de usuarios o localizados en algunas zonas más acotadas. Es de destacar que ASSE al ser un servicio público atiende a la población económicamente más vulnerable y atiende a población tanto urbana como de zonas periféricas y rurales. Dicha solución se propone como un Plataforma que comprende varios componentes que se presentan en las siguientes subsecciones.

5.1. Plataforma Propuesta

Teniendo en cuenta el escenario motivador presentado en la Sección 1 (i.e. sistema de salud de Uruguay), se considera la posición y capacidades de una organización prestadora de servicios de salud. Dichas organizaciones poseen sus propios sistemas HIS (Health Information Systems) y se integran a HCEN para tener completo acceso a los datos clínicos de sus usuarios. Sin embargo, estas organizaciones no son generadoras de datos espaciales.

Por esto, se propone una plataforma que guíe a estas organizaciones en la gestión propia de datos espaciales externos para usarlos en conjunto con sus datos espacializables, con el fin de que puedan realizar análisis espaciales orientados a la evaluación del acceso a los servicios de salud y la planificación. Un esquema general de la Plataforma se muestra en la Figura 2.

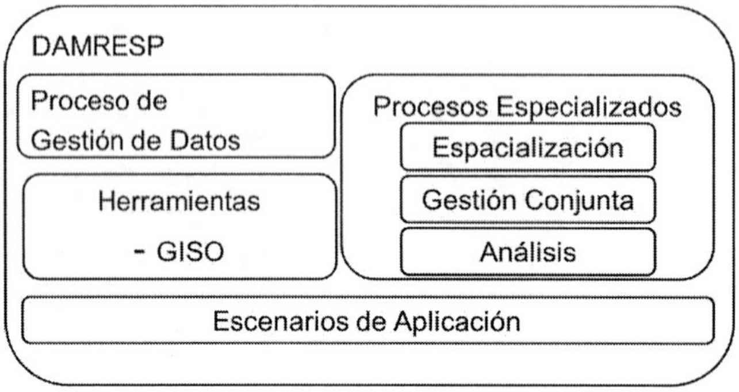

Figura 2. Esquema General de la Plataforma DAMRESP

La Plataforma se compone de un Proceso de Gestión de Datos que contempla el ciclo de vida de ambos tipos de datos dentro de la organización. A su vez se consideran algunos procesos especializados:

- Espacialización - es el proceso que guía la transformación de los datos de la organización en datos espaciales a través de la geocodificación.
- Gestión Conjunta - es el proceso que permite gestionar conjuntamente aspectos de ambos tipos de datos, por ejemplo, la calidad.
- Análisis - es el proceso que guía el análisis espacial de ambos tipos de datos en conjunto.

El desarrollo y refinamiento de los diferentes procesos de la Plataforma genera el desarrollo de herramientas que brindan soporte a dichos procesos. Actualmente ya se cuenta con una herramienta llamada GISO que apoya en la espacialización de datos alfanuméricos y algunos ejemplos básicos de análisis espacial.

Los Escenarios de Aplicación (incluyendo el escenario motivador) apuntan a brindar escenarios de referencia que muestren la forma en la que se puede utilizar la plataforma y faciliten su adopción.

5.2. Herramienta GISO

Esta herramienta, pensada para un usuario no especialista GIS, provee cuatro funcionalidades principales que se muestran en la Figura 3. Dichas funciones se deberían usar siguiendo las flechas como pasos, pero se puede iterar en el uso de dichas funcionalidades.

- Carga de datos de la organización en formato CSV - dichos datos pueden ser de usuarios, policlínicas o cualquier elemento que posea una dirección y puede incluir otros datos alfanuméricos como datos personales (género, edad) o datos clínicos (enfermedades crónicas, condiciones especiales).

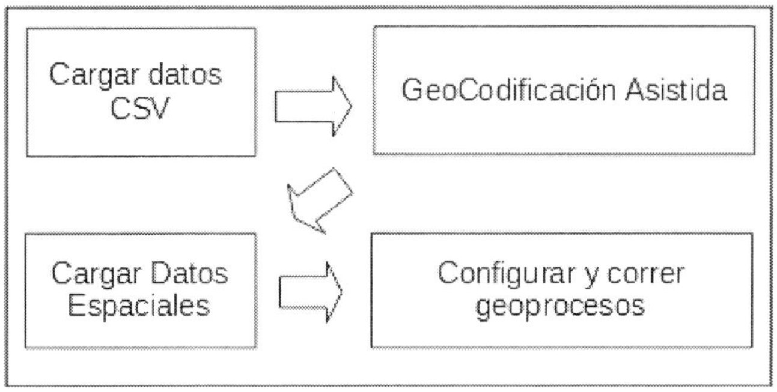

Figura 3. Funciones Herramienta GISO

- Geocodificación de los datos CSV - se usan servicios externos para la geocodificación y para los casos en que no se puede identificar una ubicación se le provee al usuario una interfaz gráfica para la geocodificación manual.
- Carga de Datos Espaciales - datos externos que se usan para contextualizar el análisis espacial (por ejemplo calles, ciudades, barrios, límites administrativos)
- Configuración y ejecución de Geoprocesos - se brinda una interfaz gráfica de mapas en la que se puede definir operaciones espaciales (distancia, intersecciones, áreas) y también se pueden realizar filtros por atributos alfanuméricos (por ejemplo: género de los usuarios, rangos de edades, embarazadas)

Esta herramienta fue usada con datos reales de direcciones y con datos simulados del dominio de salud para su validación. Usando dos servicios externos de georeferenciación se logró un 60% de éxito para direcciones de la forma "calle esq. calle"o "ruta km". Dado que la herramienta cuenta con un asistente visual, el usuario puede realizar la georreferenciación manual para las direcciones restantes. Tanto el diseño de la herramienta, su implementación como su validación técnica fueron presentados en un trabajo previo [Sosa et al. 2024]. En los siguientes pasos se prevee una validación a través de talleres con usuarios para evaluar la facilidad de uso y realizarlo con un mayor volumen de datos reales.

6. Conclusiones y Próximos pasos

Esta propuesta busca que se pueda trabajar integradamente con datos de las organizaciones y datos espaciales, desde el punto de vista de una organización de salud que no es generadora de datos espaciales, pero que puede hacer uso de los mismos para evaluar y planificar sus servicios. La solución propuesta integra metodología con herramientas prácticas que apuntan a simplificar tanto la gestión de los datos como de su calidad.

El trabajo de doctorado cuenta con una publicación en una conferencia regional que abarca un estudio inicial del proceso de espacialización, parte del Escenario Motivador y la herramienta GISO, incluyendo algunos Procesos de Análisis [Sosa et al. 2024]. Se ha trabajado en relevamientos iniciales en los temas de gestión de datos y calidad de datos. Los próximos pasos apuntan a trabajar en el refinamiento de los componentes de la Plataforma DAMRESP.

7. Disponibilidad de Artefactos

El código fuente y la documentación de la herramienta GISO están disponibles en: https://gitlab.fing.edu.uy/open-lins/giso

Referências

AGESIC (2020). Marco de trabajo para la gestión de calidad de datos en gobierno digital. Technical report, Agencia de Gobierno Electrónico y Sociedad de la Información y del Conocimiento.

Bernabé Poveda, M. A. and López Vázquez, C. M. (2012). *Fundamentos de las Infraestructuras de Datos Espaciales*. UPM Press.

Breunig, M., Bradley, P. E., Jahn, M., Kuper, P., Mazroob, N., Rösch, N., Al-Doori, M., Stefanakis, E., and Jadidi, M. (2020). Geospatial data management research: Progress and future directions. *International Journal of Geo-Information 9(2):95*.

Budgen, D., Turner, M., Brereton, P., and Kitchenham, B. A. (2008). Using mapping studies in software engineering. In *PPIG*, volume 8, pages 195–204.

Cartaxo, B., Pinto, G., and Soares, S. (2020). *Rapid Reviews in Software Engineering*, pages 357–384. Springer International Publishing.

Ebube Jones, S. (2023). The applications of geographic information systems (gis) in public health. *Journal of Applied Geographical Studies*, Vol. 3, Issue No.1:1–14. https://doi.org/10.47941/jags.1620.

Hevner, A. R., March, S. T., Park, J., and Ram, S. (2004). Design science in information systems research. *MIS Q.*, 28(1):75–105.

Jijón, A. F., Costa, R., Nicova, K., and Furnari, G. (2022). Review of the use of gis in public health and food safety. Technical report, European Food Safety Authority (EFSA). DOI:10.2903/sp.efsa.2022.EN-7639.

Khashoggi, B. F. and Murad, A. (2020). Issues of healthcare planning and gis: a review. *International Journal of Geo-Information 9(6), 352*. https://doi.org/10.3390/ijgi9060352.

Kitchenham, B. and Charters, S. (2007). Guidelines for performing systematic literature reviews in software engineering. Technical report, Keele University, University of Durham.

Latorre, L., Rego, E., and Leo, L. D. (2024). Reporte técnico: Gis. Technical report, Banco Interamericano de Desarrollo. DOI: http://dx.doi.org/10.18235/0013017.

Schoormann, T., Möller, F., Di Maria, M., and Große, N. (2023). Guiding design principle projects: A canvas for young design science researchers. *Journal of Information Systems Education, 34(3)*, pages 307–325.

Shekhar, S., Xiong, H., and Zhou, X. (2017). *Encyclopedia of GIS*. Springer Cham.

Sosa, R., Rienzi, B., González, L., Cortés, J., Sediey, V., and Segura, V. (2024). Towards a platform for assisted geocoding and geoanalysis: the case of health information. In *IEEE URUCON 2024 Proceedings*. inPress.

Integrating ISO/IEC 29110 into Agile Workflows: A Practical Intervention Strategy for Very Small Entities

Luis T. Portela-Peñúñuri

Department of Computing and Design - Sonora Institute of Technology
Ciudad Obregón, Sonora, México.

tadeo.portela@potros.itson.edu.mx

Abstract. *Very Small Entities (VSEs), crucial to the software industry, often struggle to balance agile practices with the need for standardized processes to ensure quality. This research addresses the challenge of adopting ISO/IEC 29110 in agile VSEs, where resource constraints and a preference for informality hinder standardization. We propose a multi-faceted intervention strategy focusing on gradual, low-intrusion adoption of ISO/IEC 29110, leveraging existing tools and aligning with agile principles. The methodology mapping, case studies, and professional surveys to develop and validate this strategy. The expected outcome is an implementation strategy, supported by tools and instruments, to enhance both process and product quality in VSEs.*

Keywords: ISO/IEC 29110, Agile Methods, Very Small Entities.

1. Introduction

Around the world, micro, small, and medium-sized enterprises (MSMEs) play a crucial role in the global economy, contributing approximately 40% of the Gross Domestic Product in both developing and developed countries [Madgavkar et al., 2024][Sabando-Vera et al., 2022, p. 10]. In the software industry, a subgroup of MSMEs known as Very Small Entities (VSEs) plays a similar role by contributing to the growing demand for software [Muñoz et al., 2021]. These entities with no more than 25 employees represent a substantial share of the global software market. Estimates suggest that between 93.5% and 99% of all software companies worldwide fall into this category, depending on the country [ISO/IEC, 2024][Stojanov, 2022].

VSEs are characterized by flat organizational structures, fewer hierarchical levels, and limited human and financial resources. Due to their small team sizes, their management processes tend to be informal and less well-documented, reflecting a preference for working software over comprehensive documentation [Laporte & O'Connor, 2016]. In software development, VSEs often encounter challenges in managing small-scale projects, adapting to evolving requirements, and responding to changes rather than strictly following a plan [Beck et al., 2001]. Consequently, there is a need for lightweight management processes that encourage client interaction and provide the flexibility to accommodate changes, emphasizing customer collaboration over contract negotiation [Muñoz et al., 2018]. Furthermore, all available human and financial resources of VSEs are typically dedicated to essential tasks necessary for the enterprise's survival [Muñoz et al., 2021]. As a result, VSEs tend to adopt agile methodologies to implement and take advantage of less regulated approaches.

However, the adoption of agile methodologies also entail certain risks and drawbacks, such as insufficient documentation, scope creep, technical debt and knowledge vaporization, [Santos et al., 2023][Nolan et al., 2021]. These risks and challenges can lead to maintenance difficulties, limited reusability, insufficient reliability, and performance degradation, thereby putting long-term software quality at risk [Pinna et al., 2023]. It is important to mention that developing high-quality products or services is fundamental to their survival and growth [Muñoz et al., 2021][Laporte et al., 2023]. Another issue to consider is that the 17th State of Agile Report (2023) shows that most participants in their study do not implement projects in a purely agile or purely traditional manner. Only a small proportion of the respondents, 15%, claim to implement all aspects of their projects consistently, either agile, traditional, or balanced. 42% reported using a hybrid of agile or other. This means that some companies may completely lack a structured engineering method or practice, which can lead to inconsistency, lack of direction, and difficulty in measuring business value [CertiProf, 2022].

To meet the demand for high-quality products, the International Organization for Standardization (ISO) highlights the importance of establishing systematic processes to ensure quality products and services (ISO, 2024). There are several options for VSEs to encourage adopting software engineering practices through process standardization and software process improvement (SPI) models. Some examples of these models are the following: MoProSoft, Competisoft and MPS.BR, along with international standards such as ISO/IEC 29110 offers guidelines designed explicitly for VSEs for implementing standardized best practices in software engineering [Suárez & León, 2019].

The ISO/IEC 29110 standard was released in 2011 and is mainly based on MoProSoft and ISO/IEC/IEEE 12207. It is not intended for any particular life cycle, whether waterfall, iterative, incremental, evolutionary, or agile [Muñoz et al., 2019]. According to [Minero et al. 2020], adopting the standard could significantly reduce long-term costs by minimizing errors, rework, and maintenance issues; it could also provide a set of good practices that can aid agile methodologies in enhancing the quality of their products and processes, and offers support in areas such as project planning, cost and effort estimation, progress tracking, quality control, and managing changes and work products; the standard also contributes to clarity in roles, agile risk management, and rework reduction within agile projects [Negrete et al., 2021]. It helps formalize essential artifacts within the software development process, improving the overall process without disrupting the agile methods [Muñoz et al., 2021]. By enhancing the quality of the final product, the standard also boosts the operational efficiency of VSEs, shortens the time-to-market for new products, and increases customer satisfaction [Sommerville, 2020][INCOSE, 2023].

Despite the benefits highlighted in this section, the lack of formal agile practices and barriers to adopting standardized processes in VSEs are still being reported in the literature [Laporte et al., 2023]. This persistence suggests that the strategies for adopting standardized processes are still insufficient or outdated, particularly in the face of technological advancements and changes in the VSE context, which introduce not only new features to the existing challenges but also new opportunities to address them.

2. Research questions and objectives

Addressing the challenges of adopting standardized processes requires considering the needs and context of agile VSEs. To understand how this could be achieved, first, it is necessary to answer the following questions:

1. What intervention strategy would facilitate a gradual and seamless adoption of standardized processes within the context of agile VSEs while overcoming the current challenges identified in the state of the art and the state of practice? The following sub-questions also need to be addressed:

1.1 What are the most significant challenges and specific needs faced by software development VSEs, particularly those employing agile methods, when attempting to adopt standardized processes based on ISO/IEC 29110?

1.2 What is the gap between the characteristics of VSEs using agile methods and the basic profile defined by the ISO/IEC 29110 standard?

1.3 What support tools and instruments could facilitate the gradual and seamless adoption of the management and implementation processes established by the standard?

The primary objective of this project is to develop an intervention strategy that facilitates the gradual and seamless adoption of standardized processes in the context of agile VSEs while overcoming the challenges currently identified in both the state-of-the-art and the state of practice. The goal is to enhance both process and product quality. In addition to this objective, this research also focuses on the following specific goals:

1. Identify the factors that influence the effective adoption of the ISO/IEC 29110 standard disciplines in VSEs that utilize agile methods through an analysis of the state of the art and the state of practice.

2. Determine the factors that have the most significant impact on software process and product quality during the adoption of ISO/IEC 29110 disciplines in VSEs that utilize agile methods.

3. Analyze available tools and instruments, assessing and comparing their capabilities to address the specific gaps between agile VSE practices and ISO/IEC 29110 requirements, prioritizing solutions that offer seamless integration with existing agile workflows.

4. Integrate tools and instruments to support the implementation of ISO/IEC 29110 disciplines in agile VSEs, considering the identified factors, challenges, needs, and industry best practices.

5. Evaluate the impact of applying these tools and instruments in an agile VSE within a controlled environment, analyzing their effectiveness in improving software process and product quality.

3. Current knowledge of the problem domain.

The complexities surrounding the adoption of Software Process Improvement (SPI) strategies within VSEs have garnered considerable attention. Software engineering literature research explores these challenges [Ragkhitwetsagul et al., 2024]. It is widely acknowledged that the implementation of SPI strategies can substantially enhance software quality, augment productivity, and fortify the competitive standing of such enterprises [Küpper et al., 2019]. Nonetheless, Small and Medium-sized Enterprises (SMEs) frequently encounter significant impediments when embarking on SPI initiatives. These obstacles predominantly arise from constrained financial and human capital, an incomplete foundational knowledge of SPI methodologies, and the inherent complexity often associated with conventional SPI models [Oktaba et al., 2005]. To mitigate these issues, a range of tailored solutions has been conceived to facilitate the assimilation of SPI within SMEs. Prominent among these are specialized software process models, including MoProSoft, COMPETISOFT, and ISO/IEC 29110. Each model is designed to streamline and adapt best practices, aligning them with the specific exigencies of smaller software development firms [Oktaba et al. 2005]. Key features of these instruments are delineated below:

MoProSoft [Oktaba et al. 2005] offers a suite of functionalities specifically designed to assist VSEs in the adoption and implementation of SPI strategies. This model furnishes adjustment guidelines that empower organizations to customize the SPI framework to their unique operational and strategic imperatives. Processes are described with varying degrees of granularity, enabling VSEs to adopt procedures that are optimally suited to their business context and maturity level.

COMPETISOFT [Suárez and León 2019] has been deployed across numerous Ibero-American nations, including Spain, Argentina, and Colombia. It emphasizes the commitment of senior management, the organizational ethos, corporate culture, and the receptiveness of personnel involved in implementation as crucial factors for favorable outcomes. This model provides tools for process assessment and continuous improvement, such as PMCompetiSoft and EvalSoft. PMCompetiSoft, an agile process improvement model, facilitates incremental enhancements and cultivates a culture of ongoing refinement.

ISO/IEC 29110 [Suárez & León, 2019] is centered on simplifying the selection and deployment of SPI practices for VSEs. It offers profiles and implementation guides specifically tailored to diverse VSEs. The central aim of ISO/IEC 29110 is to enhance accessibility to, and the application of software engineering standards within VSEs. This, in turn, promotes adherence to internationally recognized best practices in software development, ultimately enhancing software quality and organizational competitiveness.

4. Research Methodology

This research will employ design cience research methodology [Peffers et al., 2007], focusing on the creation and evaluation of an intervention strategy to facilitate the adoption of standardized practices proposed by the ISO/IEC 29110 standard in agile VSEs. The methodology will incorporate elements of qualitative and quantitative research to provide a comprehensive understanding of the problem and the effectiveness of the proposed solution. The research will be structured in the following phases:

Phase 1 - Problem Identification and Motivation: To define the specific challenges VSEs face in adopting ISO/IEC 29110 standardized practices within agile workflows, and to justify the need for an intervention strategy. Methods: Systematic Mapping Review (SMR) to analyze the barriers and enablers to ISO/IEC 29110 adoption in VSEs, particularly within agile contexts. This includes: examining resource constraints, agile principles that may conflict with standardization, and the need for process improvement; analysis of the gap between current VSE agile practices and the standardized practices outlined in ISO/IEC 29110; identify the specific factors that influence VSEs to effectively adopt standarized practices; identify the factors that have the most significant impact on software process and product quality during the adoption of ISO/IEC 29110 practices in VSEs that utilize agile methods.

Phase 2 - Objectives of a Solution: To define clear and measurable objectives for the intervention strategy, focusing on improved adoption of ISO/IEC 29110 practices and enhanced process and product quality. Methods: Define objectives that specify how the intervention strategy will lead to VSEs adopting ISO/IEC 29110 practices. Objectives should include measurable outcomes related to process improvement and product quality. Determine what support tools and instruments could facilitate the gradual and seamless adoption of the management and implementation processes established by the standard.

Phase 3 - Design and Development: To design and develop the intervention strategy and its supporting tools and instruments, tailored to the specific needs and context of VSEs using agile. Methods: Design a multi-faceted intervention strategy that addresses the identified challenges and facilitates the adoption of ISO/IEC 29110 practices. Develop or adapt supporting tools and instruments that VSEs can use to implement ISO/IEC 29110 disciplines in agile VSEs. The design should consider gradual adoption, low intrusiveness, compatibility with agile, and usability for VSEs.

Phase 4 - Demonstration: To demonstrate the application of the intervention strategy in VSEs. Methods: Demonstrate how the intervention strategy can be implemented in VSEs using agile methodologies. This may involve pilot implementations or case studies to show the strategy in practice.

Phase 5 - Evaluation: To rigorously evaluate the impact and effectiveness of the intervention strategy on VSEs' adoption of ISO/IEC 29110 practices and the resulting improvements in process and product quality, and to use the evaluation results to iteratively refine the intervention strategy. Methods: Evaluate the impact of applying the intervention strategy and its supporting tools in VSEs. This may involve a controlled environment, pilot studies, or real-world implementations. Quantitative: Measure process metrics and product quality metrics before, during, and after the intervention. Qualitative: Gather feedback from VSEs on the usability, feasibility, and effectiveness of the intervention strategy, the perceived benefits and challenges of adopting ISO/IEC 29110, and suggestions for improvement. This can be done through interviews, surveys, and focus groups.

Iteration: Analyze the evaluation data to identify areas where the intervention strategy is effective and areas that need improvement. Based on the evaluation findings, iterate back to Phase 3 (Design and Development) to refine the intervention strategy, supporting tools, and implementation guidance. This iterative process (between Phase 3 and Phase 5) may be repeated multiple times until the intervention strategy demonstrates a satisfactory level of effectiveness and usability. Once the intervention strategy has been refined through iterations, a final evaluation should be conducted to assess its overall impact and effectiveness.

Phase - 6 Communication: To communicate the research findings and the validated intervention strategy to relevant stakeholders, including VSEs, agile practitioners, and the research community. Develop practical guidelines and resources to support VSEs in adopting ISO/IEC 29110 based on the research findings.

5. Introduction of the proposed solution

This research proposes a multi-faceted intervention strategy designed to facilitate the gradual and seamless adoption of ISO/IEC 29110-based software development practices in agile VSEs. The intervention strategy directly addresses the challenges identified in the literature and practice, emphasizing low intrusiveness, leveraging existing VSE tools and practices, and providing measurable improvements in both process and product quality. The intervention strategy is based on the idea that VSEs are more likely to adopt standardized processes if they are easy to follow and they don't have to change their way of working, only complement it. Currently, the research project is in the SMR stage. So far, we have identified 339 articles using a search string across five databases. Initially, 42 articles were selected for analysis, revealing four key factors, for the time being:

- A lack of resources and a reliance on informal project management, which often do not align with the structured requirements of the standard [Muñoz et al., 2021].

- The need to produce numerous high-quality artifacts, which conflicts with agile methodologies that prioritize working software over comprehensive documentation [Muñoz et al., 2018].

- The limited availability of tools to support the procedures mandated by ISO/IEC 29110 and a need for more supporting materials and guidance [Muñoz & Peralta, 2020].

- Additionally, cultural barriers within organizations have been identified, related to the perceived utility of the standard and resistance to changing current work methods [Muñoz et al., 2021].

This intervention strategy differs from existing approaches as it promotes a gradual adoption that allows VSEs to adopt standardized processes gradually, starting with the most critical elements and generating maturity over time. Low Intrusiveness will be a priority in the intervention strategy with the purpose of minimizing disruption in the workflow of VSEs and making use of existing tools and processes whenever possible. The intervention strategy is explicitly designed to be compatible with agile principles and practices and seeks to integrate ISO/IEC 29110 practices in a way that complements, rather than conflicts with, agility.

Usability: The implementation strategy focuses on providing practical, easy-to-understand guidance and tools that are directly relevant to the needs of VSE developers and managers and leverage the tools the VSE is already familiar with to integrate them into an environment that promotes the adoption of standardization.

The implementation strategy includes mechanisms to measure the impact of adopting the standardized processes of ISO/IEC 29110 both on the products and on the processes themselves, allowing VSEs to track their progress and demonstrate the value of standardization.

Following the completion of the SMR, the research will proceed to confirm and contrast the factors identified in the state-of-the-art with those observed in the state-of-practice. Therefore, the subsequent steps include the completion of Phase 1.

This phase is crucial because it will enable the identification of gaps between VSE practices and the standard's processes. This, in turn, will contribute to the identification of the intervention strategy's most specific characteristics and potential tools and instruments that could assist in implementing standardized processes.

6. References

Beck, K., Beedle, M., Bennekum, A. van, Cockburn, A., Cunningham, W., Fowler, M., & Thomas, D. (2001). Manifesto for Agile Software Development. Recuperado de https://agilemanifesto.org/

CertiProf. (2022). *Agile Adoption Report 2022.* p. 18. Retrieved from https://cdn.shopify.com/s/files/1/0299/9215/7283/files/CertiProf_Agile_Adoption_Report_2022_SP.pdf?v=1733935623

Digital.ai. (2023). *The 17th State of Agile Report.* consulted at https://digital.ai/resource-center/analyst-reports/state-of-agile-report/

INCOSE (Ed.). (2023). INCOSE systems engineering handbook (5a ed.). John Wiley & Sons.

ISO/IEC (2024). Systems and software engineering - Lifecycle profiles for Very Small Entities (VSEs) (ISO/IEC 29110-1-1:2024(en) https://www.iso.org/obp/ui/en/#iso:std:iso-iec:tr:29110:-1:ed-2:v1:en

Küpper, S., Pfahl, D., Jürisoo, K., Diebold, P., Münch, J., & Kuhrmann, M. (2019). How has SPI changed in times of agile development? Results from a multi-method study. Journal of Software: Evolution and Process, e2182. https://doi.org/10.1002/smr.2182

Laporte, C. Y., & O'Connor, R. V. (2016). Implementing Process Improvement in Very Small Enterprises with ISO/IEC 29110: A Multiple Case Study Analysis. 2016 10th International Conference on the Quality of Information and Communications Technology (QUATIC), 125–130. https://doi.org/10.1109/QUATIC.2016.033

Laporte, C. Y., Verret, G., & Muñoz, M. (2023). A Software Project That Partially Failed: A Small Organization That Ignored the Management and Technical Practices of Software Standards. Computer, 56(5), 138–144. https://doi.org/10.1109/MC.2023.3253979

Madgavkar, A., Piccitto, M., White, O., Ramirez, M. J., Mischke, J., & Chockalingam, K. (2024). A microscope on small businesses: Spotting opportunities to boost productivity. McKinsey Global Institute. https://www.mckinsey.com/mgi/our-research/a-microscope-on-small-businesses-spotting-opportunities-to-boost-productivity#/

Minero, García.,, J. J. & Lara, E. (2023). Automatización de los procesos del estándar ISO/IEC 29110 a través de la Adopción de DevOps. RISTI - Revista Ibérica de Sistemas e Tecnologias de Informação, 49, 37-51. https://doi.org/10.17013/risti.49.37-51

Muñoz, M., Mejia, J., & Lagunas, A. (2018). Implementation of the ISO/IEC 29110 standard in agile environments: A systematic literature review. 2018 13th Iberian Conference on Information Systems and Technologies (CISTI), 1–6. https://doi.org/10.23919/CISTI.2018.8399332

Muñoz, M., Mejia, J., Peña, A., Lara, G., & Laporte, C. Y. (2019). Transitioning international software engineering standards to academia: Analyzing the results of the adoption of ISO/IEC 29110 in four Mexican universities. Computer Standards & Interfaces, 66, 103340. https://doi.org/10.1016/j.csi.2019.03.008

Muñoz, M., Mejia, J., Peña, A., Laporte, C., Gasca-Hurtado, G. P., & Gómez-Álvarez, M. C. (2021). An Exploratory Analysis of the Perception of the Utility of Proven Practices of the Software Basic Profile of ISO/IEC 29110 by a Set of VSEs in Mexico. Communications in Computer and Information Science, 439–456.

https://doi.org/10.1007/978-3-030-85521-5_29

Muñoz, M., Mejia, J., Peña, A., Laporte, C., & Gasca-Hurtado, G. P. (2020). What Motivates VSEs to Adopt an International Standard Such as ISO/IEC 29110? An Exploratory Analysis. En Systems, Software and Services Process Improvement (pp. 730–741). Springer International Publishing. https://doi.org/10.1007/978-3-030-56441-4_55

Negrete, M., Infante, U., & Muñoz, M. (2021). A case study of improving a Very Small Entity with an Agile Software Development Based on the Basic Profile of the ISO/IEC 29110. In *Advances in Intelligent Systems and Computing*.

Nolan, Aaron, Ben, Strickland., Adam, Quinn., Kyle, Gallagher., Murat, Yilmaz., Paul, M., Clarke. (2021). Exploring Aspects of Agile Software Development Risk - Results from a MLR. 486-502. doi: 10.1007/978-3-031-15559-8_35

Oktaba, H., Alquicira, C., Ramos, A. S., Martínez, A. M., Osorio, G. Q., López, M. R., Lira, F. L., López, M. E. R., Orozco, M. J., Ordóñez, Y. F., & Lemus, M. Á. F. (2005). Modelo de procesos para la industria de software MoProSoft (Versión 1.3). Secretaría de Economía.

Peffers, K., Tuunanen, T., Rothenberger, M. A., & Chatterjee, S. (2007). A design science research methodology for information systems research. Journal of Management Information Systems, 24(3), 45-77. https://doi.org/10.2753/mis0742-1222240302

Pinna, A., Lunesu, M. I., Orrù, S., & Tonelli, R. (2023). Investigation on Self-Admitted Technical Debt in Open-Source Blockchain Projects. Future Internet, 15(7), 232. https://doi.org/10.3390/fi15070232

Ragkhitwetsagul, C., Krinke, J., Choetkiertikul, M., Sunetnanta, T., & Sarro, F. (2024). Adoption of automated software engineering tools and techniques in Thailand. Empirical Software Engineering, 29(3), 90. https://doi.org/10.1007/s10664-024-10472-6

Sabando-Vera, D., Yonfa-Medranda, M., Montalván-Burbano, N., Albors-Garrigos, J., & Parrales-Guerrero, K. (2022). Worldwide research on open innovation in SMEs. Journal of Open Innovation: Technology, Market, and Complexity, 8(1), 20. https://doi.org/10.3390/joitmc8010020

Santos, R. B. M. D., Figueiredo, P. S., & Marques, F. T. (2023). Challenges to agile software project management practices in the context of the COVID-19 pandemic. Gestão & Produção, 30, e9722. https://doi.org/10.1590/1806-9649-2022v29e9722

Sommerville, I. (2020). Software engineering (10th ed.). Pearson Education.

Stojanov, Z. (2022, June). Software Maintenance Management in Micro Software Companies. Southeast European Review of Business and Economics, 3(1), 75–92. https://doi.org/10.20544/SERBE.05.01.22.P05

Suárez, D. R., & León, G. (2019). Las PyME de desarrollo de software. Modelos de mejora de sus procesos en Latinoamérica. Revista Espacios, 40(28), 9.

Multi-View Spectral Clustering for Monolith-to-Microservices Migration

Gonzalo Rivera-Lazo[1], **Fernando Montoya**[1,2,3], **Hernán Astudillo**[4]

[1]AISA Research Group – Corriente Sur
Valparaíso, Chile

[2]Universidad Técnica Federico Santa María
Santiago, Chile

[3]Fundación Instituto Profesional Duoc UC
Santiago, Chile

[4]ITiSB - Universidad Andrés Bello
Viña del Mar, Chile

gonzalo@corrientesur.com, fernando.montoya@usm.cl, hernan.astudillo@unab.cl

Abstract. *The migration from monolithic architectures to microservices poses significant challenges, particularly in achieving modularity, decoupling and functional coherence. This paper explores a multi-view spectral clustering approach to systematically decompose monoliths by integrating structural dependencies, domain semantics and dynamic behavior into a unified weighted affinity model. The method uncovers optimal service boundaries that balance cohesion, coupling and complexity, generating multiple architectural options tailored to weighted quality attributes. Validation on a real-world application demonstrates how the framework enables flexible, quality-driven decompositions, supporting more informed and adaptive architectural decisions.*

1. Introduction

The migration from monolithic architectures to microservices is a key strategy in modern software engineering, offering benefits like scalability, maintainability and resilience [Richardson 2018]. However, determining optimal service boundaries remains a significant challenge, as it requires balancing multiple quality attributes—such as coupling, cohesion, performance and development costs—based on business priorities. While state-of-the-art techniques like static analysis, graph clustering and machine learning assist in automating microservice decomposition [Gysel et al. 2016, Mazlami et al. 2017, Taibi and Systä 2019], they often rely on single-metric optimization. This narrow focus limits their ability to address the multidimensional and dynamic nature of real-world architectural decision-making.

Microservice migration is not merely a technical refactoring but a strategic transformation that involves balancing multiple trade-offs, as illustrated in Figure 1. Architects must evaluate how different service boundaries impact performance, development complexity and adaptability. For instance, some services may prioritize latency optimization, while others focus on modularity. Existing approaches lack systematic guidance for assessing these trade-offs, leaving architects without structured methods to explore multiple viable decompositions. Quality attributes play a fundamental role in shaping architectural decisions. Software quality standards define models and attributes that influence decomposition strategies [Lago and van Vliet 2005]. For example, scalability and availability are crucial in microservices due to their impact on system resilience, while adaptability is essential in dynamic environments [Papazoglou and van den Heuvel 2007]. Current methods fail to provide a parametrizable approach over multiples views, forcing architects to manually adjust service boundaries when automated partitions do not align with business goals.

To address this gap, we introduce multi-view spectral clustering as a principled approach for microservice decomposition. Multi-view clustering refers to the process of integrating multiple heterogeneous views—such as structural dependencies, domain semantics and runtime performance—into a unified model that reveals latent grouping structures [Chao et al. 2021, Zhou et al. 2024]. In our approach, these views are encoded into a weighted affinity matrix, allowing architects to prioritize quality attributes dynamically via a tunable weighting system. Spectral clustering is then applied to this multi-view matrix to identify candidate decompositions that are both technically coherent and aligned with business goals. To determine the optimal number of services, we employ an iterative selection process driven by a composite quality function that balances cohesion, coupling and complexity—enabling dynamic control over microservice granularity.

The remainder of this paper is structured as follows: Section 2 reviews existing approaches to microservice decomposition. Section 3 details our multi-view spectral clustering approach. Section 4 presents experimental results and evaluates our method. Finally, Section 5 summarizes our findings and outlines future research directions.

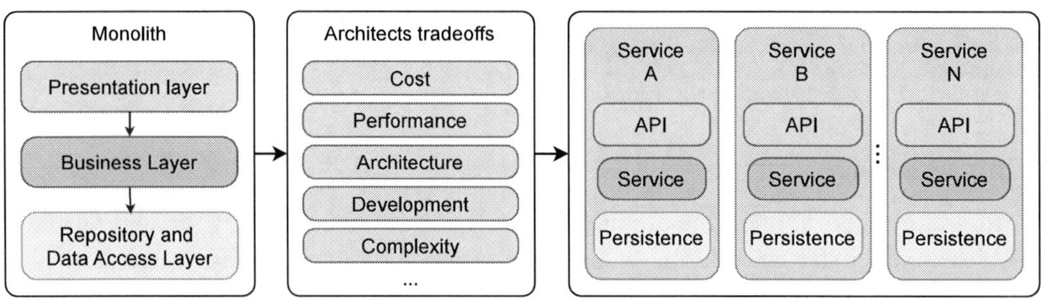

Figure 1. Architectural tradeoffs in the iterative migration of a monolithic application to a microservices-based architecture.

2. Related Work

The migration of monolithic systems to microservices is a well-studied problem with various proposed approaches. This shift was initially driven by industry demands to decouple large, tightly integrated systems into modular architectures, aiming to improve primarily maintainability, enhance scalability and reduce infrastructure costs.

The most related work is a study from [Asseldonk 2021] that evaluates the impact of incorporating multiple viewpoints (static, semantic and dynamic dependencies) on microservices decomposition quality. Results show that combining static and dynamic data improves modularity, but adding semantic information decreases decomposition quality due to an overemphasis on semantic dependencies.

[Andrade et al. 2023] conducts a comparative analysis of static and dynamic techniques, concluding that neither approach consistently outperforms the other. However, the dynamic data collection process requires significantly more effort.

Other approaches, such as execution trace analysis, infer service partitions based on dynamic behavior [Mazlami et al. 2017]. While this improves accuracy in runtime dependency detection, it overlooks domain-driven constraints that influence maintainability and business alignment. Business process mining techniques [Taibi and Systä 2019] enhance microservice identification by emphasizing functional cohesion, yet they remain limited in incorporating performance metrics and technical dependencies.

Machine learning-based techniques, such as repository mining and historical code evolution analysis, have also been explored [Fritzsch et al. 2019]. [Andrade et al. 2022] compared static and dynamic analysis techniques for identifying candidate microservices. Their study demonstrated that neither approach consistently outperforms the other, though dynamic data collection introduces higher overhead. They utilized a complexity metric to assess the effectiveness of each decomposition strategy.

Given the current state-of-the-art in single-perspective methods, we identified an opportunity to apply a multi-view spectral clustering approach that integrates multiple architectural perspectives: structural, semantic and performance driven into a unified model that outputs a solution related to a combination of quality attributes.

3. Proposal

We propose a Multi-view spectral clustering approach to segment monolithic applications into microservices as shown in Figure 2. By integrating multiple views, our method generates multiple architecture options, enabling architects to dynamically prioritize quality attributes based on business and technical needs.

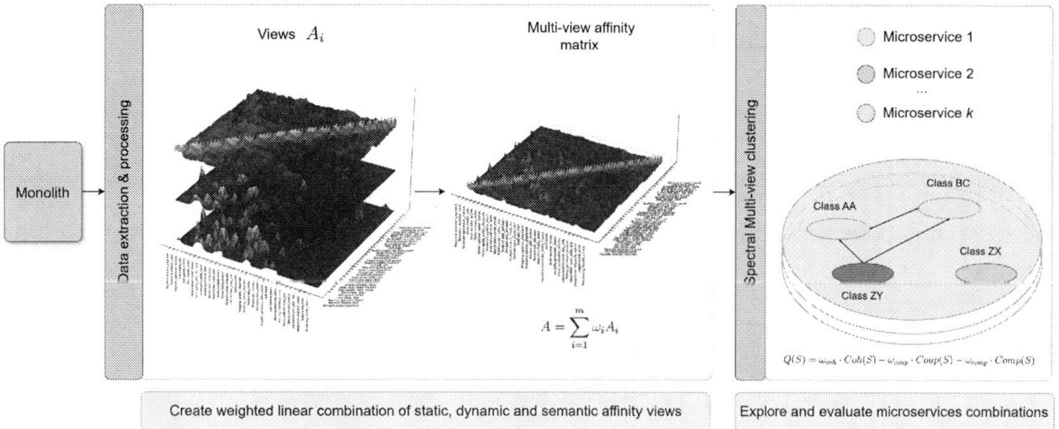

Figure 2. Multi-view spectral clustering pipeline, integrating dependency graphs, dynamic call graphs and semantic data to derive microservices architectures.

3.1. Problem Formulation

Given a monolithic system M composed of n components $C = \{C_1, C_2, ..., C_n\}$, our objective is to partition M into k microservices $S = \{S_1, S_2, ..., S_k\}$ while optimizing multiple quality attributes, such as cohesion, coupling, maintainability and scalability. These attributes are weighted according to a predefined prioritization scheme, allowing the exploration of multiple architectural alternatives.

To achieve this, we first create multiple affinity matrices $A_c, A_d, A_p, \ldots, A_m$, each representing a distinct architectural perspective such as structural dependencies, semantic relationships and performance metrics. Then, the number of clusters k^* is determined by a weighted evaluation of quality attributes that the resulting microservice architecture must satisfy. This ensures that the decomposition aligns with the prioritized architectural goals. Formally, we aim to solve:

$$\arg\max_{S} \sum_{i=1}^{k^*} \left(Q(S_i) - \lambda \sum_{j \neq i} C(S_i, S_j) \right) \tag{1}$$

where $Q(S_i)$ represents the quality metrics of microservice S_i, $C(S_i, S_j)$ denotes the coupling between services S_i and S_j, λ is a tunable weight and k^* is determined based on the weighted prioritization of quality attributes.

3.2. Multi-View Spectral Clustering Approach

To capture different architectural properties, we define multiple embedding functions, each corresponding to a distinct view:

- **Static analysis** (G_c): Models the static coupling between architectural components by analyzing function calls, inter-module dependencies and invocation patterns. This perspective enables the identification of cohesive modules and tightly coupled elements that influence decomposition decisions.
- **Component semantics** (G_d): Captures domain-driven relationships between architectural elements by employing Natural Language Processing (NLP) techniques (e.g., identifier tokenization, documentation analysis). This view facilitates the grouping of components based on conceptual similarity and domain alignment within the architecture.
- **Dynamic analysis** (G_p): Encodes the execution characteristics as the dynamic behavior of the monolith. This view provides insights user-driven architectural decisions.

Each graph G_i represents a different perspective of the monolith, but it is not necessarily limited to these perspectives. The framework allows the aggregation of other types of inputs, provided they can be vectorized, such as historical development commits, pull request information and team ownership structures. This flexibility ensures a comprehensive and adaptable partitioning strategy.

We define a weighted multi-view affinity matrix A as:

$$A = \sum_{i=1}^{m} \omega_i A_i \tag{2}$$

where A_i represents the affinity matrix corresponding to the ith view and ω_i is a tunable weight that adjusts the importance of each perspective [Chao et al. 2021].

This matrix captures inter-component relations specific to the perspective of view V_i. To ensure consistency for spectral processing, each affinity matrix A_i is symmetrized to guarantee $A_i = A_i^\top$ and subsequently used to compute the corresponding normalized Laplacian matrix $\mathcal{L}_i = I - D_i^{-1/2} A_i D_i^{-1/2}$, where D_i is the degree matrix of A_i.

Spectral clustering is then applied on A, using its eigenvectors to project the components into a lower-dimensional space where clustering is performed. The partitioning S is obtained by applying K-Means to the eigenvector representation of A.

Algorithm 1 Multi-View Spectral Clustering for Microservices Decomposition

Require: Graph views $G_c, G_d, G_p, \ldots, G_m$, weight parameters $\omega_c, \omega_d, \omega_p, \ldots, \omega_m$
Ensure: Partitioning $S = S_1, S_2, ..., S_k$

1: Compute affinity matrices $A_c, A_d, A_p, \ldots, A_m$ from $G_c, G_d, G_p, \ldots, G_m$ respectively.
2: Construct the weighted multi-view affinity matrix $A = \sum_{i=1}^{m} \omega_i A_i$.
3: Determine the optimal number of clusters $k*$ by maximizing $Q(S)$.
4: Compute the eigenvectors of A and project the components into the eigen-space.
5: Apply K-Means clustering on the eigenvector representation with $k*$ clusters.
6: Return optimal partitioning S.

3.3. Optimal Cluster Selection

To determine the optimal number of clusters k, we adopt a quality-driven selection method based on a weighted combination of key architectural quality attributes. For a given clustering solution S, the overall quality score is defined as:

$$Q(S) = \omega_{\text{coh}} \cdot \text{Coh}(S) - \omega_{\text{coup}} \cdot \text{Coup}(S) - \omega_{\text{comp}} \cdot \text{Comp}(S), \tag{3}$$

where:

- $\text{Coh}(S)$ denotes the average intra-cluster cohesion. Measures the internal semantic similarity among components within the same cluster. Higher values indicate better modular grouping.
- $\text{Coup}(S)$ represents the inter-cluster coupling. Captures the semantic or structural similarity between components across different clusters. Lower values are preferred.
- $\text{Comp}(S)$ quantifies the overall complexity of the decomposition (e.g., measured in lines of code). Represents the aggregated implementation cost (e.g., sum of lines of code per cluster). Lower values imply simpler, more manageable services.

The weights $\omega_{\text{coh}}, \omega_{\text{coup}}, \omega_{\text{comp}} \in [0, 1]$ satisfy the constraint $\omega_{\text{coh}} + \omega_{\text{coup}} + \omega_{\text{comp}} = 1$, enabling dynamic prioritization of architectural quality attributes based on design goals. The proposed framework is flexible and can be extended to support alternative evaluation strategies, such as Pareto-based optimization or the inclusion of additional quality attributes.

The optimal number of clusters k^* is obtained by maximizing the quality function $Q(S)$ across a candidate range $[k_{\text{min}}, k_{\text{max}}]$:

Algorithm 2 Optimal Cluster Selection via Quality Maximization

Require: Candidate cluster range $[k_{min}, k_{max}]$, quality metric function $Q(S_k)$
Ensure: Optimal number of clusters k^*

Initialize $best_k \leftarrow k_{min}$, $best_score \leftarrow -\infty$
for $k \leftarrow k_{min}$ to k_{max} **do**
    Compute partitioning S_k using Spectral Clustering with k clusters
    Compute quality score $Q(S_k)$
    if $Q(S_k) > best_score$ **then**
        $best_score \leftarrow Q(S_k)$
        $best_k \leftarrow k$
    end if
end for
Return $best_k$

$$k^* = \arg \max_{k \in [k_{\min}, k_{\max}]} Q(S_k), \tag{4}$$

where S_k denotes the clustering solution obtained with k clusters. The selection process iteratively evaluates each candidate k by computing its corresponding quality score using Equation 3.

4. Evaluation and Results

To assess the effectiveness of the proposed multi-view spectral clustering approach for monolith-to-microservices decomposition, we conducted a preliminary evaluation using a representative set of software components extracted from a real-world e-commerce codebase, consisting of 18 parent classes, each containing approximately 4 to 5 methods.

To simulate the decision-making process of a software architect, we iteratively evaluate the clustering results over a grid of weight combinations $(w_{\text{coh}}, w_{\text{coup}}, w_{\text{comp}})$, reflecting different trade-offs among quality attributes. For each combination, we compute evaluation metrics and select clustering configurations accordingly, as illustrated in Figure 3. The optimal number of clusters is dynamically determined by maximizing a weighted quality score that combines cohesion, coupling and complexity.

The results indicate that, for this repository and the input views considered, increasing the number of services does not lead to a substantial reduction in coupling, although it may yield marginal improvements in cohesion. Notably, there appears to be a trade-off point where high cohesion is attained with relatively low complexity, suggesting that moderate values of k may provide a balanced and effective decomposition. In contrast, excessive fragmentation—reflected in high complexity—can adversely affect modularity and maintainability. Moreover, the observed coupling remains largely unaffected by the granularity of the decomposition. This behavior may result from persistent shared dependencies or tightly coupled responsibilities that span across service boundaries. Additionally, the optimal number of clusters $k* = 18$, obtained under uniform weighting of the input views and quality attributes, appears to be strongly influenced by the structure of the original monolith rather than by the intended post-decomposition objectives. Consequently, more sophisticated decomposition strategies—such as those guided by domain-driven design principles—may be necessary to achieve meaningful decoupling.

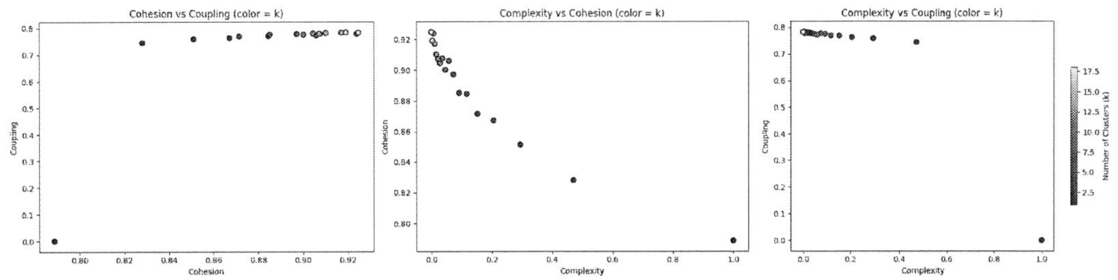

Figure 3. The three scatter plots illustrate the interplay between architectural quality attributes — cohesion, coupling and complexity — under varying numbers of clusters k (potential microservices). The color of each point indicates the value of k, which serves as a proxy for microservice granularity.

5. Discussion & Conclusion

The experimental results demonstrate the potential of multi-view spectral clustering to support monolith decomposition by integrating structural, semantic and runtime-based views. This multi-perspective approach offers software architects a more informed basis for identifying service boundaries.

However, several limitations remain. The effectiveness of the clustering depends heavily on the appropriate weighting of affinity matrices, which requires domain expertise. Additionally, the incorporation of dynamic behavioral data—such as execution traces and request flow patterns—could further improve boundary accuracy. Scalability also requires further evaluation, particularly for large-scale enterprise systems with thousands of components.

Future work should explore adaptive weight tuning, dynamic component reconfiguration during migration and guidance based on technical goals such as scalability—highlighted as critical in recent systematic studies [Martínez Saucedo et al. 2025]. It is also essential to investigate various granularity levels and benchmark the approach against state-of-the-art methods and datasets.

These improvements will contribute to a more automated, scalable and parametrizable methodology for transitioning monolithic systems into microservices architectures.

References

Andrade, B., Santos, S., and Silva, A. R. (2022). From monolith to microservices: Static and dynamic analysis comparison. arXiv:2204.11844.

Andrade, B., Santos, S., and Silva, A. R. (2023). A comparison of static and dynamic analysis to identify microservices in monolith systems. In Tekinerdogan, B., Trubiani, C., Tibermacine, C., Scandurra, P., and Cuesta, C. E., editors, *Software Architecture*, pages 354–361, Cham. Springer Nature Switzerland.

Asseldonk, L. v. (2021). From a monolith to microservices: the effect of multi-view clustering. Master's thesis, Utrecht University.

Chao, G., Sun, S., and Bi, J. (2021). A survey on multiview clustering. *IEEE Transactions on Artificial Intelligence*, 2(2):146–168.

Fritzsch, J., Bogner, J., Wagner, S., and Zimmermann, A. (2019). Microservices migration patterns: A survey. In *Proceedings of the International Conference on Software Maintenance and Evolution (ICSME)*.

Gysel, M., Kölbener, L., Giersche, W., and Zimmermann, O. (2016). Service cutter: A systematic approach to service decomposition. *IEEE Software*.

Lago, P. and van Vliet, H. (2005). Explicit assumptions enrich architectural models. In *Proceedings. 27th International Conference on Software Engineering, 2005. ICSE 2005.*, pages 206–214.

Martínez Saucedo, A., Rodríguez, G., Gomes Rocha, F., and dos Santos, R. P. (2025). Migration of monolithic systems to microservices: A systematic mapping study. *Information and Software Technology*, 177:107590.

Mazlami, G., Cito, J., and Leitner, P. (2017). Extraction of microservices from monolithic software architectures. In *Proceedings of the 24th International Conference on Software Analysis, Evolution and Reengineering (SANER)*.

Papazoglou, M. P. and van den Heuvel, W.-J. (2007). Service oriented architectures: approaches, technologies and research issues. *The VLDB Journal*, 16(3):389–415.

Richardson, C. (2018). *Microservices Patterns: With Examples in Java*. Manning Publications.

Taibi, D. and Systä, K. (2019). From monolithic systems to microservices: A decomposition framework based on process mining. In *International Conference on Cloud Computing and Services Science*.

Zhou, L., Du, G., Lü, K., Wang, L., and Du, J. (2024). A survey and an empirical evaluation of multi-view clustering approaches. *ACM Comput. Surv.*, 56(7).

Arquitectura de un videojuego serio de RV para obtener estrategias de educación personalizadas para el desarrollo de habilidades cognitivas específicas

Abdiel Labrado-Flores, Ulises Juárez-Martínez, Lisbeth Rodríguez-Mazahua, Ignacio López-Martínez, Mónica Ruiz-Martínez

Tecnológico Nacional de México/I.T.Orizaba, Orizaba, 94320, México

m23011387@orizaba.tecnm.mx, ulises.jm@orizaba.tecnm.mx, lisbeth.rm@orizaba.tecnm.mx, igancio.lm@orizaba.tecnm.mx, monica.rm@orizaba.tecnm.mx

Abstract. *Mathematical learning is crucial, and cognitive skills are key to enhancing it. In Mexico, deficiencies in mathematics from early education pose an educational challenge. This article presents a scalable and modular architecture for a serious virtual reality game, based on MVC, designed to foster mathematical learning and personalized cognitive development. Applying a hybrid methodology (Design Thinking, ADDIE, and the Game Development Process), the proposal is an educational solution that leverages personalization algorithms, along with the user's lifestyle and cognitive performance, to tailor a strategy plan that enhances their cognitive skills and mathematical learning.*

Resumen. *El aprendizaje matemático es crucial, y las habilidades cognitivas son clave para impulsarlo. En México, las deficiencias en matemáticas desde educación básica representan un reto educativo. Este artículo presenta una arquitectura escalable y modular de un videojuego serio de realidad virtual, basada en MVC, para fomentar el aprendizaje matemático y el desarrollo cognitivo personalizado. Aplicando una metodología híbrida (Design Thinking, ADDIE y el Proceso de Desarrollo de Videojuegos), la propuesta es una solución educativa que usa algoritmos de personalización, además del estilo de vida y desempeño cognitivo del usuario, para adaptar un plan de estrategias que potencie sus habilidades cognitivas y aprendizaje matemático.*

1. Introducción

Desde temprana edad, las habilidades cognitivas son esenciales para el aprendizaje, la resolución de problemas, la toma de decisiones y la adaptación al entorno. Su desarrollo, ligado al procesamiento de información, puede fortalecerse a través del aprendizaje de las matemáticas, un lenguaje universal de la ciencia y la tecnología, debido a la intensa actividad mental que implican. Sin embargo, en México, el desempeño en matemáticas presenta serias deficiencias. Según el informe PISA 2022, el alumnado mexicano obtuvo un promedio de 395 puntos, frente a la media internacional de 500 [OCED, 2023]. Además, en PLANEA 2018, el 59% de los estudiantes mostró un dominio insuficiente en matemáticas [INEE 2018], y la Evaluación Diagnóstica 2022-2023 reportó un promedio de aciertos del 57%, con niveles bajos en secundaria y quinto de primaria [Mejoredu 2023].

Patrama et al. (2023) y Márquez Sembrano (2023) destacan la importancia de recursos tecnológicos, como los videojuegos educativos, para abordar este problema. Videojuegos como los de Pratama et al. (2023), Rebollo et al. (2022) y Merino-Campos et al (2023) demostraron ser efectivos para aumentar el interés en el aprendizaje y fomentar el desarrollo de habilidades cognitivas. No obstante, según Quintanar Stephano (2020), la calidad del aprendizaje está influenciada por factores del estilo de vida. Sin embargo, pocas herramientas digitales consideran el Perfil de Estilo de Vida (PEV) o la Bitácora de Rutina Diaria (BRD), a pesar de su impacto directo en habilidades cognitivas específicas, como el razonamiento visoespacial y la memoria de trabajo, las cuales pueden evaluarse mediante pruebas psicométricas del cociente intelectual total (CIT). Integrar estos factores en videojuegos serios podría optimizar el aprendizaje y fortalecer las herramientas educativas.

Para abordar estas deficiencias educativas mediante un videojuego serio, se diseñó una arquitectura fundamentada en el patrón Modelo-Vista-Controlador (MVC), que separa presentación, lógica y manejo de datos. Este diseño surge dentro de una metodología híbrida que integra *Design Thinking*, el Proceso de Desarrollo de Videojuegos (GDP) y el modelo instruccional ADDIE, asegurando un enfoque flexible y centrado en los objetivos educativos. En el contexto de un videojuego de realidad virtual, la arquitectura permite gestionar eficientemente las interacciones del usuario, el procesamiento de datos y la transferencia de información. La Vista distingue la visualización de interfaces 2D y los escenarios 3D para capturar las señales del jugador; el Controlador separa los módulos próximos al usuario de aquellos dedicados a la gestión de datos y eventos, mejorando el control de errores; y el Modelo organiza tanto los datos ingresados por el usuario como los generados por el videojuego, facilitando su uso en el modelo de clasificación.

A continuación, la organización del artículo es la siguiente: la sección 2 presenta el estado del arte con una revisión de trabajos relacionados; la sección 3 describe la metodología utilizada; en la sección 4 se detalla la arquitectura propuesta; finalmente, la sección 5 expone las conclusiones y la sección 6 aborda los trabajos futuros.

2. Estado del Arte

Las matemáticas cubren diversas áreas que emplean habilidades cognitivas asociadas al razonamiento fluido, como el cálculo, geometría, secuencias y estadística. Estas disciplinas incluyen aspectos no verbales, abstractos y visuales, donde el razonamiento visoespacial es crucial para entender el entorno y crear ideas. En este contexto, diversos estudios exploraron videojuegos diseñados para potenciar estas habilidades.

Thomsen y Timcenko (2023) desarrollaron un videojuego serio con realidad virtual inmersiva y contenidos matemáticos contextualizados en situaciones cotidianas para reforzar conocimientos. González-Campos et al. (2021) diseñaron *GTCards*, centrado en transformaciones geométricas mediante elementos tridimensionales para reforzar el razonamiento visoespacial. Rebollo et al. (2022) crearon *GameMultiplyAR* para el aprendizaje lúdico de las tablas de multiplicar con realidad aumentada, mientras que Rossano et al. (2021) desarrollaron *Math is Magic*, destacando el impacto de una narrativa sólida en la motivación para aprender matemáticas.

Urakami et al. (2021) analizaron el interés sostenido en videojuegos cognitivos mediante *BrainTagger Suite*, identificando factores como retroalimentación, incentivos y diversidad de mecánicas. Yu-Sheng et al. (2022) concluyeron que la realidad virtual inmersiva mejora la confianza y percepción del aprendizaje en geometría. Casaú Civit (2022) demostró la viabilidad de adaptar actividades simples a entornos de realidad virtual en aritmética, y Van der Stappen et al. (2019) evidenciaron que las recompensas colaborativas en *MathBuilder* incrementan la motivación en resolución de problemas.

Pusey et al. (2021) diseñaron una herramienta para analizar desafíos cognitivos en videojuegos de rompecabezas, evaluando claridad, soluciones múltiples y uso de pistas en títulos como *The Witness*, *Untitled Goose Game* y *Baba Is You*. Finalmente, Chatain et al. (2022) exploraron el impacto de la interacción con la realidad virtual en la motivación al aprender derivadas, aunque sin profundizar en la calidad del aprendizaje.

En síntesis, los estudios revisados reflejan buenos avances en videojuegos serios para el aprendizaje matemático y cognitivo, pero sin abordar el diseño arquitectónico de sus herramientas, clave para garantizar funcionalidad y experiencia de usuario. Aunque algunos aluden al proceso metodológico, el diseño contextual suele opacar el análisis estructural, dejando en segundo plano aspectos como la lógica y la gestión de datos.

Este trabajo cubre esa brecha con una propuesta arquitectónica basada en una metodología que equilibra objetivos educativos, experiencia de usuario y desarrollo técnico. Su diseño asegura una separación clara entre módulos y optimiza la comunicación entre el usuario y el videojuego.

3. Metodología

Para el desarrollo del proyecto se adoptó una metodología híbrida que integra el Proceso de Desarrollo de Videojuegos (GDP), el modelo de diseño instruccional ADDIE y el marco de trabajo *Design Thinking*. La combinación de estas metodologías permite garantizar que el videojuego cumpla con los objetivos educativos, los requerimientos tecnológicos y la experiencia del usuario (UX) de manera equilibrada.

El *Design Thinking* [Dinngo 2024] se empleó como marco general debido a su enfoque iterativo y centrado en el usuario, lo que permite definir necesidades reales y ajustar la solución de manera progresiva. ADDIE [Ghirardini et al 2014] proporciona una estructura pedagógica para asegurar que las estrategias implementadas cumplan con los principios del aprendizaje, mientras que el GDP [Piskunov 2024] establece el flujo de producción técnica para transformar la propuesta en un videojuego funcional.

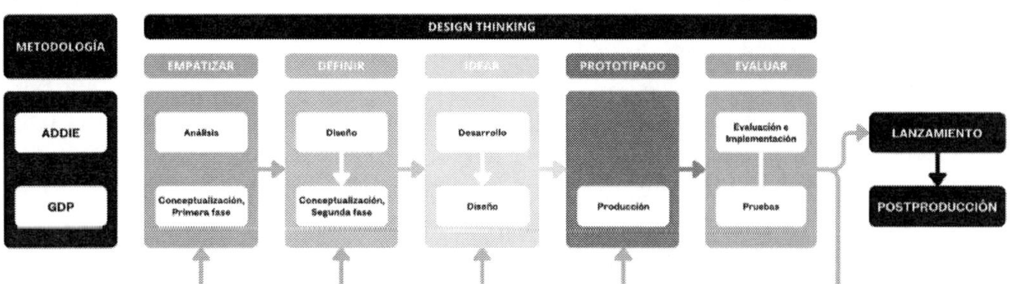

Figura 1. Metodología híbrida para el desarrollo del videojuego serio.

Como se muestra en la Figura 1, la integración de estas metodologías se distribuyó en cinco etapas, alineadas con sus principios, y hasta la fase de ideación se logró lo siguiente:

(1) Empatizar (*Design Thinking*): se realizó una investigación sobre fundamentos educativos y pruebas psicométricas (ADDIE - Análisis). Se revisaron videojuegos serios y no serios con desafíos cognitivos, identificando elementos clave para el diseño (GDP – Conceptualización I).

(2) Definir (*Design Thinking*): se establecieron objetivos educativos, métricas y variables para evaluar el impacto, así como se diseñó la BRD. (ADDIE - Diseño). Se definió el concepto del videojuego, es decir, temática, historia y otros elementos. (GDP – Conceptualización II).

(3) Idear (*Design Thinking*): se diseñaron los desafíos y mecánicas principales según los objetivos educativos (ADDIE - Desarrollo). Se desarrolló la arquitectura del sistema a partir de las funcionalidades definidas, además del diseño preliminar de la Vista, es decir, pantallas e interfaces; y de la estructura de datos para los módulos del Modelo (GDP - Diseño).

(4) Prototipar (*Design Thinking*): desarrollo del prototipo funcional implementando la arquitectura modular y las funcionalidades definidas. La arquitectura cobra relevancia al guiar la programación de la lógica y comunicación a través de la capa Controlador (GDP - Producción).

(5) Evaluar (*Design Thinking*): diseño de un plan de pruebas para aplicar y validar la solución (ADDIE – Evaluación e Implementación), así como para obtener retroalimentación y ajustar el prototipo hasta alcanzar una versión satisfactoria (GDP - Pruebas).

Aunque esto es opcional, en cada etapa la metodología permite volver entre fases si la solución no se acerca al objetivo, logrando ajustar la idea. Una vez que sea funcional según lo esperado, lo siguiente es el lanzamiento o despliegue, así como el mantenimiento periódico, si la herramienta lo requiere.

Este enfoque integra el diseño centrado en el usuario (*Design Thinking*), la planificación educativa (ADDIE) y la producción técnica (GDP) en un marco estructurado y adaptable. Así, se garantiza que el videojuego no solo sea atractivo y funcional, sino que también cumpla con objetivos pedagógicos medibles y ajustables mediante iteraciones estratégicas.

4. Arquitectura del Videojuego

En la Figura 2 se presenta la arquitectura del videojuego serio, diseñada para su uso en *Google Cardboard*, siendo así accesible a los estudiantes al requerir sólo un smartphone y un dispositivo de realidad virtual económico. La implementación se basa en el patrón arquitectónico MVC (Modelo-Vista-Controlador), el cual, según Taylor et al (2009), busca separar la gestión de datos de su representación e interacción con el usuario, permitiendo un desarrollo independiente. Esta separación permite aislar responsabilidades, facilitar la escalabilidad al integrar nuevas funciones sin afectar los módulos existentes y reutilizar componentes ya desarrollados, manteniendo la comunicación eficiente entre las capas.

La Vista constituye el punto de interacción directa entre el usuario y el sistema. Incluye la interfaz del juego, pantallas informativas y la configuración, permitiendo al usuario interactuar con escenarios virtuales, recibir mensajes contextuales sobre su desempeño, navegar entre pantallas y personalizar aspectos técnicos o estéticos del juego. La experiencia de juego está optimizada exclusivamente para la realidad virtual, dejando fuera las pantallas informativas y parcialmente la configuración, que sirven como soporte complementario.

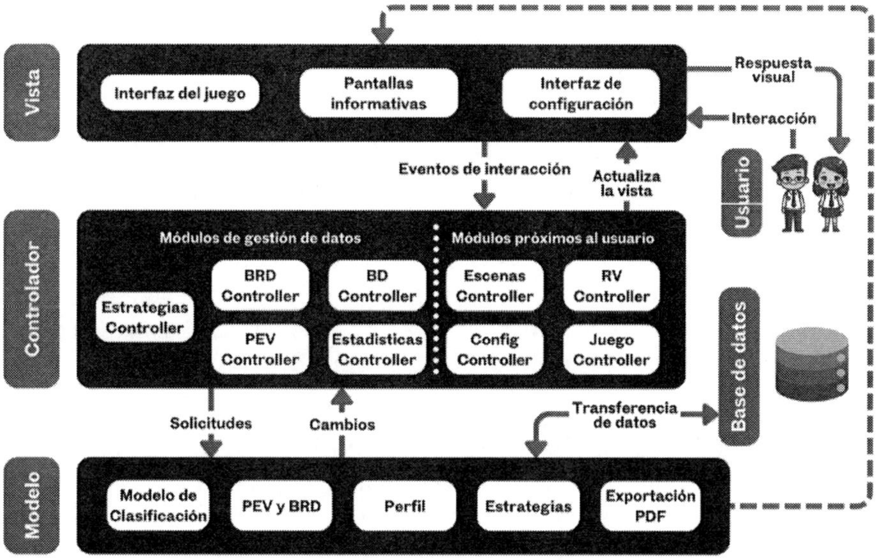

Figura 2. Arquitectura del videojuego serio.

El Controlador gestiona la comunicación entre la Vista y el Modelo, dividiendo su funcionalidad en dos grupos principales. Los controladores cercanos al usuario procesan señales generadas por sus acciones y filtran los datos para garantizar su integridad. Incluyen el controlador de escenas, que coordina las transiciones; el de RV, que gestiona las interacciones tridimensionales; el del juego, que administra desafíos, eventos y animaciones; y el de configuración, que permite ajustes personalizados. Los controladores orientados a la gestión del videojuego procesan la lógica del sistema, alejando al usuario de interacciones directas con el Modelo. Estos incluyen el controlador de estrategias, encargado de generar recomendaciones personalizadas; los controladores de la BRD y el PEV, que recopilan datos del estilo de vida del jugador; el de estadísticas, que evalúa el progreso cognitivo; y el de la base de datos, que asegura la persistencia y accesibilidad de la información

El Modelo organiza y transfiere los datos esenciales del sistema. Contiene un modelo de clasificación que identifica estrategias personalizadas, un perfil del jugador que almacena información general y desempeño en desafíos, y los datos recopilados del PEV y la BRD que estructuran el estilo de vida del jugador. Además, gestiona un repositorio de estrategias diseñadas para diferentes contextos de usuario y permite la exportación de estas en formato PDF para consulta externa.

Esta arquitectura facilita la colaboración interdisciplinaria, permitiendo que diseño gráfico y programación trabajen sin interferencias. La separación de responsabilidades optimiza el mantenimiento y la detección de errores, mientras que su compatibilidad con distintos lenguajes y motores garantiza escalabilidad y reutilización de código.

Además de seguir el patrón MVC, incorpora principios de desarrollo como SOLID y *Clean Code* para mejorar su modularidad. Su rendimiento será evaluado mediante pruebas de carga, estrés y métricas de eficiencia en dispositivos móviles, mientras que la calidad del software se asegurará con un enfoque *Test-Driven Development* (TDD), incluyendo pruebas unitarias en módulos clave y pruebas de usabilidad para optimizar la experiencia del usuario.

5. Conclusiones

Aunque los videojuegos serios se siguen consolidando como herramientas clave para la gamificación y la educación, muchas propuestas no logran un equilibrio efectivo entre educación, entretenimiento y estimulación cognitiva. Esto subraya la importancia de emplear metodologías híbridas como la combinación de *Design Thinking*, GDP y ADDIE, que permiten abordar estos aspectos de manera coherente, proporcionando un análisis contextual de la situación y necesidades del usuario final, métricas para la evaluación de los objetivos educativos y una arquitectura adecuada que integre las funcionalidades y requerimientos necesarios para lograr la solución.

La arquitectura del videojuego no debe considerarse un componente secundario, sino una parte central del diseño. Basada en el patrón MVC, esta arquitectura simplifica la interacción entre módulos, aislando responsabilidades de manera efectiva entre la presentación, la lógica y la gestión de datos. Esta distribución facilita la modularidad y reutilización de código, así como el mantenimiento, además de permitir el trabajo colaborativo eficiente entre disciplinas al asegurar que las capas no interfieran entre sí.

Para validar la efectividad de la arquitectura, métricas como la precisión en la personalización de estrategias, la mejora en habilidades cognitivas específicas y la adecuación de las recomendaciones al desempeño del usuario, aseguran que esta soporte los objetivos educativos propuestos. No obstante, su aplicación está sujeta a ciertas condiciones: (1) el videojuego serio es de realidad virtual e (2) incluye pantallas que no utilizan este formato; (3) se necesita una distinción clara entre módulos de interacción y de gestión de datos; (4) el objetivo es generar estrategias basadas en el estilo de vida del usuario mediante (5) un modelo de clasificación; y (6) se quiere lograr una organización estructurada del código, asegurando la correcta separación de funcionalidades.

6. Trabajo a Futuro

Siguiendo con el proceso metodológico, el siguiente paso consiste en diseñar las interfaces, definir los desafíos y construir los escenarios alineados con la arquitectura propuesta. Este proceso seguirá tres fases principales: (1) conceptualización y prototipado de interacciones entre capas, asegurando la correcta comunicación entre módulos; (2) iteración basada en pruebas preliminares de usabilidad, ajustando mecánicas y flujo de interacción según la experiencia del usuario; y (3) consolidación del diseño final para su implementación en el prototipo funcional. Una vez desarrollado, el prototipo será sometido a pruebas de validación técnica y educativa, midiendo su rendimiento, la experiencia de usuario y el impacto en el aprendizaje. Se diseñará un plan de pruebas estructurado que evaluará variables clave como la interacción con la interfaz, la respuesta a los desafíos y la efectividad del contenido en el desarrollo de habilidades cognitivas.

Para su implementación en escenarios reales, la arquitectura se integrará en entornos educativos mediante un enfoque progresivo. La planificación contempla tres etapas: (1) recolección de datos iniciales sobre las habilidades cognitivas de los usuarios, permitiendo establecer una línea base; (2) ejecución de un caso de estudio con sesiones estructuradas de uso del videojuego, asegurando condiciones controladas para evaluar su impacto; y (3) análisis de la progresión cognitiva a través de métricas cuantitativas y cualitativas, validando la efectividad de la solución. La compatibilidad con hardware accesible como *Google Cardboard* y la optimización para smartphones facilitarán su adopción en aulas y entornos domésticos, promoviendo el aprendizaje adaptativo y midiendo el avance del usuario en matemáticas.

Agradecimientos. Los autores agradecen el patrocinio del Consejo Nacional de Humanidades, Ciencia y Tecnología (CONAHCyT) y al Tecnológico Nacional de México (TecNM) por apoyar este trabajo de investigación.

Referencias

Casaú Civit, P. (2022) "Design of a virtual reality game to enhance the learning of mathematics," Ph.D. thesis, UPC, Centre de la Imatge i la Tecnologia Multimèdia. Disponible en: http://hdl.handle.net/2117/394004.

Chatain, J., Ramp, V., Gashaj, V., Fayolle, V., Kapur, M., Sumner, R. W., and Magnenat, S. (2022) "Grasping Derivatives: Teaching Mathematics through Embodied Interactions using Tablets and Virtual Reality," In: Proceedings of the 21st Annual ACM Interaction Design and Children Conference (IDC '22), ACM, New York, NY, USA, pp. 98–108. https://doi.org/10.1145/3501712.3529748.

Dinngo (2024) Design Thinking en español, Disponible en: https://designthinking.es. Consultado: Abril 19, 2024.

Ghirardini, B., Landriscina, F., and Shapiro, B. (2014) Metodologías de E-learning. Una guía para el diseño y desarrollo de cursos de aprendizaje empleando tecnologías de la información y las comunicaciones, FAO, Roma, Italia, pág. 140. ISBN: 978-92-5-307097-8.

González-Campos, J. S., Arnedo-Moreno, J., and Sánchez-Navarro, J. S. (2021) "GTCards: A Video Game for Learning Geometric Transformations," In: TEEM'21, Barcelona, Spain, pp. 205–209. https://doi.org/10.1145/3486011.3486445.

INEE (2018) "PLANEA. Resultados nacionales 2018," INEE, Ciudad de México. Disponible en: https://www.inee.edu.mx/evaluaciones/planea/resultados-planea/.

Márquez Sambrano, J. D. (2023) "Recursos tecnológicos interactivos en el desempeño académico de la asignatura de matemáticas," Universidad de Guayaquil. Disponible en: http://repositorio.ug.edu.ec/handle/redug/68465.

Mejoredu (2023) "Evaluación diagnóstica del aprendizaje de las y los alumnos de educación básica 2022-2023. Informe de resultados," Mejoredu. Disponible en: https://www.mejoredu.gob.mx/images/Informe_diagnostica.pdf.

Merino-Campos, C., Del-Castillo, H., and Pascual-Gómez, I. (2023) "Enhancing adolescent reasoning skills through a video game program," Education and Information Technologies, vol. 28, pp. 12737–12756. https://doi.org/10.1007/s10639-023-11691-y.

OECD (2023) "PISA 2022 Results (Volume II): Learning During – and From – Disruption," OECD Publishing, Paris. Disponible en: https://doi.org/10.1787/a97db61c-en.

Piskunov, E. (2024) Stages of Game Development | Your Guide On Game Development Process, Disponible en: https://ilogos.biz/stages-of-game-development-your-guide-on-game-development-process/. Consultado: Abril 19, 2024.

Pratama, M., Yanfi, Y., and Nusantara, P. D. (2023) "WizardOfMath: A top-down puzzle game with RPG elements to hone the player's arithmetic skills," Procedia Computer Science, vol. 216, pp. 338–345. https://doi.org/10.1016/j.procs.2022.12.144.

Pusey, M., Wong, K. W., and Rappa, N. A. (2021) "The Puzzle Challenge Analysis Tool: A Tool for Analysing the Cognitive Challenge Level of Puzzles in Video Games," Proc. ACM Hum.-Comput. Interact., vol. 5, no. CHI PLAY, p. 276. https://doi.org/10.1145/3474703.

Quintanar Stephano, J. L. (2020) "Bases biológicas de la memoria en el aprendizaje," Investigación y Práctica en Psicología del Desarrollo, vol. 6, pp. 93–103. https://doi.org/10.33064/ippd62849.

Rebollo, C., Remolar, I., Rossano, V., and Lanzilotti, R. (2022) "Multimedia augmented reality game for learning math," Multimedia Tools and Applications, vol. 81, no. 11, pp. 14851–14868. https://doi.org/10.1007/s11042-021-10821-3.

Rossano, V., Mangialardo, F., and Roselli, T. (2021) "Math is magic: an adaptive serious game to reinforce math competences," In: TEEM'21, Barcelona, Spain, pp. 162–166. https://doi.org/10.1145/3486011.3486439.

Taylor, R. N., Medvidovic, N., and Dashofy, E. (2009) Software Architecture: Foundations, Theory, and Practice, Wiley, Hoboken, NJ, USA.

Thomsen, L. A. and Timcenko, O. (2023) "Real mathematics in virtual worlds," In: IRSPBL23: TEE 23, pp. 124-128. Disponible en: https://vbn.aau.dk/ws/portalfiles/portal/538997960/Transforming_Engineering_Education_2023.pdf.

Urakami, J., Hu, Y. Z., and Chignell, M. (2021) "Monitoring Cognitive Performance with a Serious Game," In: CHI EA '21, Yokohama, Japan, artículo 48, pp. 1-7. https://doi.org/10.1145/3411763.3443431.

van der Stappen, A., Liu, Y., Xu, J., Yu, X., Li, J., and van der Spek, E. D. (2019) "MathBuilder: A Collaborative AR Math Game for Elementary School Students," In: Extended Abstracts of the Annual Symposium on Computer-Human Interaction in Play Companion Extended Abstracts (CHI PLAY '19 Extended Abstracts), ACM, New York, NY, USA, pp. 731-738. https://doi.org/10.1145/3341215.3356295.

Yu-Sheng, S., Cheng, H. W., and Lai, C. F. (2022) "Study of Virtual Reality Immersive Technology Enhanced Mathematics Geometry Learning," Frontiers in Psychology, vol. 13, p. 760418. https://doi.org/10.3389/fpsyg.2022.760418.

Alianza Europea de Innovación para la Educación del Tesing Proyecto ENACTEST

Niels Doorn[1], **Fernando Pastor Ricós**[2], **Beatriz Marín**[2], **Tanja Vos**[1,2]

[1]Open Universiteit (OU), The Netherlands

[2]Universitat Politècnica de València (UPV), Spain

niels.doorn@ou.nl, fpastor@pros.upv.es, bmarin@dsic.upv.es, tvos@dsic.upv.es

Abstract. *La importancia de las pruebas de software es indiscutible, pero su falta de implementación adecuada puede provocar aplicaciones con errores y problemas. Esta situación se debe a un desajuste entre las habilidades demandadas por la industria, las necesidades de aprendizaje de los estudiantes y los métodos actuales que se utilizan para la enseñanza de las pruebas en instituciones educativas. El proyecto ENACTEST busca cubrir este desajuste mediante el desarrollo de cápsulas de enseñanza para las pruebas del software (testing) adaptadas a las demandas de la industria y a los procesos cognitivos de los estudiantes. El consorcio incluye universidades, centros de formación profesional y pequeñas empresas, que representa un entorno socioeconómico amplio.*

1. Introducción

Hoy en día, los sistemas de software se utilizan ampliamente en diversos campos, lo que amplifica las consecuencias de sus fallos, pudiendo causar daños significativos a la sociedad. Las pruebas de software son fundamentales para garantizar la calidad y minimizar los riesgos asociados con los fallos. Sin embargo, en muchas organizaciones falta una cultura de pruebas del software, ya que estas suelen ocupar un lugar secundario en el proceso de desarrollo debido a la presión por entregar actualizaciones rápidas y a la creciente complejidad de los sistemas modernos. Las pruebas del software en la industria enfrentan numerosos desafíos, como el conocimiento insuficiente de metodologías de pruebas, sesgos en los supuestos utilizados para diseñar casos de prueba y la desacertada selección de herramientas para optimizar el proceso, entre otros [Afzal et al. 2020] [Juhnke et al. 2021] [Garousi et al. 2020a].

Para preparar mejor a los profesionales de la industria, es fundamental intervenir la raíz del problema: la educación de las pruebas de software. Aunque se han realizado varios esfuerzos académicos para mejorar este ámbito, como se refleja en revisiones sistemáticas de la literatura [Scatalon et al. 2019] y [Garousi et al. 2020b], numerosos problemas aún persisten. Entre ellos, la desconexión entre la teoría y la práctica reduce el interés de los estudiantes; los ejemplos en clase están alejados de los proyectos reales; los estudiantes carecen de confianza en sus habilidades para probar el software, y la falta de experiencia práctica limita la capacidad de los profesionales novatos para llevar a cabo el proceso completo de pruebas en entornos industriales.

El proyecto ENACTEST enfrenta estos desafíos mediante el desarrollo de materiales didácticos, llamados *cápsulas*, cuya principal característica es que son breves y fáciles de integrar en los cursos existentes sin imponer una carga de trabajo adicional a los profesores. Las cápsulas presentan técnicas de enseñanza novedodas, adaptadas a las necesidades de aprendizaje de los estudiantes y alineadas con las demandas de la industria para mejorar sus habilidades en el proceso de pruebas del software. Las cápsulas corresponden a materiales didácticos de diversa naturaleza (por ej. ejercicios, casos de estudio, juegos, herramientas, etc.), que han sido diseñados para fomentar el aprendizaje de tópicos de pruebas específicos, por ej. pruebas de mutación, pruebas de regresión, etc.

2. Objetivos del proyecto

El proyecto ENACTEST (2022-2025) tiene como objetivo crear materiales didácticos coherentes y oportunos para la enseñanza de las pruebas del software, considerando tanto las necesidades de la industria como los modelos cognitivos de los estudiantes. Para ello, en el proyecto ENACTEST se ha analizado la viabilidad de incorporar nuevas técnicas de enseñanza/aprendizaje en la educación superior, con el fin de mejorar las competencias de los estudiantes y, por ende, las habilidades de los futuros profesionales de la informática. Este propósito se puede resumir en la reducción de las brechas en la educación sobre pruebas desde tres perspectivas interconectadas en la educación de la informática: los estudiantes, la industria y el ámbito académico, como se ilustra en la Figura 1.

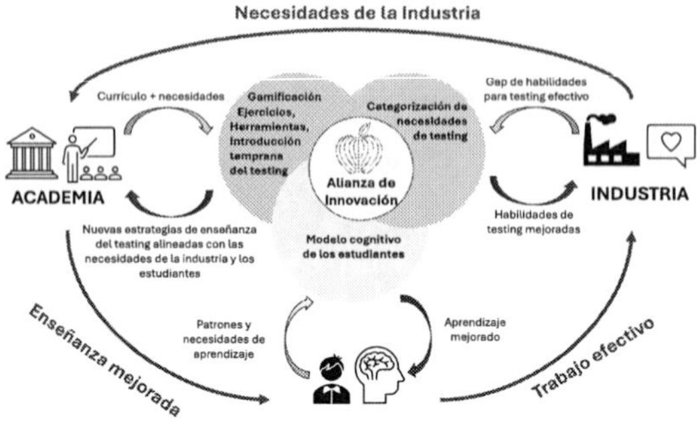

Figure 1. Proyecto ENACTEST (https://enactest-project.eu).

Para alcanzar el objetivo general de ENACTEST, se han definido los siguientes objetivos específicos:

- Identificar los modelos cognitivos que utilizan los estudiantes y los expertos cuando tienen que lidiar con pruebas, especialmente al diseñar casos de prueba.
- Categorizar las necesidades y habilidades que requiere la industria para las pruebas del software y las habilidades fundamentales que se deberían incluir en los planes de estudio.
- Diseñar y desarrollar materiales para la enseñanza de las pruebas del software (cápsulas) para incorporarlos a la educación de manera fácil. Estos materiales tendrán en cuenta los modelos cognitivos de los estudiantes y las necesidades de la industria.
- Proporcionar evidencia de mejora en los resultados de aprendizaje para los estudiantes y una mejor transferencia de conocimientos a la industria.

3. Beneficiarios

El consorcio del proyecto está compuesto por un grupo diverso de beneficiarios para garantizar que los resultados beneficien a la totalidad del panorama socioeconómico. El consorcio incluye universidades (4), centros de formación profesional (1) y pequeñas empresas (4). Los beneficiarios del proyecto ENACTEST son: Universitat Politècnica de València (UPV), España; Katholieke Universiteit Leuven (KULeuven), Bélgica; Universidade do Porto (UP), Portugal; Università degli Studi di Napoli Federico II (UNINA), Italia; Research Institutes of Sweden (RISE), Suecia; Centro Superior de Formacion Europa-Sur (CESUR), España; NEXO QA, España; INOVA+, Portugal; CTG, Bélgica.

4. Resultados

Para alcanzar los objetivos del proyecto ENACTEST, se ha realizado la especificación de requisitos, modelos e implementación de un caso para realizar las pruebas, y se ha diseñado un experimento que ha sido realizado en diferentes centros de educación superior y centros de formación profesional para descifrar el proceso cognitivo de los estudiantes cuando diseñan casos de pruebas utilizando distintas estrategias [Doorn et al. 2023]. Además, se han realizado tres grupos focales con profesionales para entender las necesidades de la industria en el proceso de pruebas y las carencias existentes en la transferencia de conocimiento en los equipos de pruebas. También, se ha llevado a cabo un mapeo de cursos donde se enseñan las pruebas del software en los países de la alianza de innovación, y se ha entrevistado a profesores para comprender los problemas y necesidades relacionados con la enseñanza de las pruebas en la práctica [Tramontana et al. 2024].

Teniendo en cuenta los resultados sobre el proceso cognitivo de los estudiantes, las necesidades de la industria y las necesidades académicas, se han diseñado las siguientes cápsulas:

1. GIPPPY: Juego en línea para la introducción temprana del testing y del pensamiento computacional [Lapeña et al. 2022] - UPV.
2. INCITE: Entrevistas semiestructuradas para enseñar testing y promover el momento A-HA en estudiantes - UPV.
3. GADGETS: Colección de juegos análogos para practicar estrategias de testing siendo consicentes de los supuestos que pueden sesgar el proceso - UPV.
4. FRAFOL: Framework para el aprendizaje de testing de mutación - UP.
5. GAMFLEW: Juego para aprender pruebas de caja blanca - UP.
6. TES Game: Juego para la detección de test smells y refactorización - UNINA.
7. Testing Robot Challenge: Herramienta para competir mediante el testing manual con testing automático en diversos desafíos - UNINA.
8. TESCAV: Herramineta para visualizar de cobertura en modeos - KU Leuven.
9. ModelDefenders: Juego para aprender testing de modelos basado en mutaciones - KU Leuven
10. Herramienta para aprender testing basado en estados - RISE.
11. BDD: Artefactos y ejercicios para aprender testing de acepación usando BDD - NexoQA.
12. Cyber: Artefactos y ejercicios para las pruebas de ciberseguridad - NexoQA.
13. TDD: Artefactos y ejercicios para el desarrollo dirigido por pruebas - CESUR.
14. AGILE: Artefactos y guías para aplicar testing en procesos ágiles - CESUR.
15. WCAG: Artefactos y ejemplos para enseñar testing de accessibilidad y WCAG - CTG.
16. TDTech: Base de conocimiento y ejercicios de técnicas de diseño de casos de prueba - CTG.

17. DELTA: Herramienta para la detección de cambios a través de la interfaz gráfica d elos sistemas para aprender testing de regresión y validar cambios no intencionales que afectan la experiencia de usuario [Pastor Ricós et al. 2025].

Las cápsulas están en un proceso continuo de refinamiento y validación. Los metadatos de las cápsulas han sido definidos según los estandares IEEE LOM y ARIANDE, donde se describe el tipo de recurso educativo (juego, entorno, ejercicio), el nivel de interacción, los prerrequisitos, los objetivos de aprendizaje, su nivel de cumplimiento según la taxonomía de Bloom, el nivel de los estudiantes (grado, master, doctorado), el tema específico dentro de la disciplina del software testing, el enfoque educativo, y el acceso a la cápsula junto a los materiales (videos, poster, etc.) que la soportan. Las cápsulas junto a los materiales y recursos desarrollados serán publicados en el sitio web del proyecto ENACTEST durante el 2025. Esto permitirá que la comunidad en general pueda acceder a ellas y utilizarlas para sus fines educativos y profesionales. Finalmente, para potenciar una cultura de pruebas y reforzar la importancia de ellas a toda la sociedad, se publican noticias quincenales en el sitio del proyecto [1].

Agradecimientos Este proyecto ha sido financiado en la convocatoria ERASMUS-EDU-2021-PI-ALL-INNO con el número 101055874, 2022-2025

References

Afzal, A., Le Goues, C., Hilton, M., and Timperley, C. (2020). A study on challenges of testing robotic systems. In *13th ICST*, pages 96–107. IEEE.

Doorn, N., Vos, T., and Marín, B. (2023). Towards understanding students' sensemaking of test case design. *Data & Knowledge Engineering*, page 102199.

Garousi, V., Felderer, M., Kuhrmann, M., Herkiloğlu, K., and Eldh, S. (2020a). Exploring the industry's challenges in software testing: An empirical study. *Journal of Software: Evolution and Process*, 32(8):e2251.

Garousi, V., Rainer, A., Lauvås Jr, P., and Arcuri, A. (2020b). Software-testing education: A systematic literature mapping. *Journal of Systems and Software*, 165:110570.

Juhnke, K., Tichy, M., and Houdek, F. (2021). Challenges concerning test case specifications in automotive software testing: assessment of frequency and criticality. *Software Quality Journal*, 29:39–100.

Lapeña, A., Marin, B., and Vos, T. (2022). Gipppy: Game for introductory programming practice in python. In *INTED2022 Proceedings*, pages 5598–5606. IATED.

Pastor Ricós, F., Marín, B., Vos, T., Neeft, R., and Aho, P. (2025). Delta gui change detection using inferred models. *Computer Standards & Interfaces*, 92:103925.

Scatalon, L., Carver, J., Garcia, R., and Barbosa, E. (2019). Software testing in introductory programming courses: A systematic mapping study. In *50th SIGCSE*, pages 421–427. ACM.

Tramontana, P., Marin, B., Paiva, A., Mendes, A., Vos, T., Amalfitano, D., Cammaerts, F., Snoeck, M., and Fasolino, A. (2024). State of the Practice in Software Testing Teaching in Four European Countries. In *17th ICST*, pages 59–69. IEEE.

[1] https://enactest-project.eu/news/

Building a Smart City that Stimulates Innovation Using Open Source and Decentralised Technologies

Sandro Sawicki[1], Rafael Z. Frantz[1], Gerson Battisti[1], Fabricia Roos-Frantz[1] Luiz Antonio Rasia[1], Odaylson Eder[2], Carlos Molina–Jimenez[3], Jon Crowcroft[3]

[1]Unijuí University – Ijuí/RS – Brazil

{sawicki, rzfrantz, battisti, rasia, frfrantz}@unijui.edu.br

[2]Municipal Secretariat of Economic Development, Tourism and Technology of Santa Rosa

odaylson.eder@santarosa.rs.gov.br

[3]University of Cambridge – Cambridge –UK

{carlos.molina, jon.crowcroft}@cl.cam.ac.uk

Abstract. *We are developing Santa Rosa municipality as a smart and sustainable region that stimulates innovation. A place that will take advantage of the data–driven economy and data–centric applications with Equality, Diversity and Inclusion (EDI) as a priority. To this end, have built a pilot smart city lab for testing technologies in real-life conditions; we are currently exploring decentralised technologies and technologies with low environmental cost. Also, we are following competency frameworks for smart cities rather than deploying technologies indiscriminately. 12 years of work have produced tangible results and practical experience that we share in this paper.*

1. Introduction

The city of Santa Rosa was founded in 1931; with a current population of 73,575 inhabitants and a municipality that expands over 488.42 km^2 is becoming an important industrial and commercial hub in the south of Brazil. Its geographical location a few kilometres of Argentina's and Paraguay's borders give the city and the region a potential that the city council is determined to capitalise. Their overall objective is to develop Santa Rosa as a smart city and to launch the region as the innovation hub of the South of Brazil that will take advantage of the data-centric economy to boost the economy of the region at least for the next 20 years. They aim at a socio–technical system, therefore, have taken a multi–dimensional vision that combines technical, economic and social dimensions. Therefore, sustainability and Equality, Diversity and Inclusion (EDI) are priorities – they want Santa Rosa to be sustainable and EDI compliant by design. Further, they have an integral view where the surrounding rural area is regarded as an extension of the city as it contributes to its economy. They regard smart cities as complex systems, therefore, in the development of Santa Rosa they are following a competency framework that includes planning, testing and embedding. From a technological perspective, firstly we setup a project to build an innovation ecosystem and a hardware infrastructure based on open technologies for sensing the urban and rural areas of the municipality. We are currently developing applications on this ecosystem to provide citizens with digital services that use the sensing data. We also make the data open to academy, companies and to the general public. Here in after we will use "we" to refer to the authors of this document.

2. Collaborations, projects and objectives

To progress towards the fulfilment of their overall objective, in 2021 the city council signed up a formal collaboration with the Applied Computing Research Group[1] (GCA) of Unijuí University to submit a joint project proposal to a call of the Secretary of Innovation, Science and Technology of the state of Rio Grande do Sul. Fortunately, we succeeded and the project was awarded 1.3 million Reais for the creation of the SmartLive Lab within Unijuí's premises. The lab is equipped with hardware, software for testing smart city technologies and facilities (e.g, meeting rooms) for collaborating with other institutions; for example, they have been collaborating with the University of Cambridge since 2019. We have been granted three complementary projects that cover three topics included in our multidimensional approach, use the SmartLive Lab and target specific objectives: **i) Economic sustainability** is covered by a 36 month project that investigates open source decentralised technologies for integrating digital services. **ii) Environmental sustainability** is covered by a 36 month project that is manufacturing and testing biodegradable sensors in the SmartLive Lab. **iii) Connected places** is covered by 24 month project that is deploying a hardware–software infrastructure in the rural farming area to integrate it with the smart and sustainable infrastructure of the city.

3. Development under a competency framework

We are collaborating with members of the Digital Cities for Change (DC2) [2] team in validating their DC2–FC (Digital Cities for change) competency framework for developing smart cities. In Santa Rosa, we are following the DC2–FC rather than deploying technologies indiscriminately. As required by DC2–FC, we test technologies in our SmartLive Lab and generated knowledge before full scale deployment.

The DC2–FC framework. DC2–FC was designed at the University of Cambridge [Bastidas et al. 2023] to help smart city planners to identify tasks, roles and competencies needed to deliver projects successfully. The creation of public value through responsible use of technology is central to DC2–FC and in line with our views over smart cities. Three members of Santa Rosa's development team have been interviewed to asses compliance with DC2–FC and help us identified gaps.

The SmartLive Lab. We use this lab as a pilot for testing technologies in real–life conditions (actual deployment in the city at small scale) before full scale deployment (called embedding in DC2–FC). The lab is a knowledge generator too: it is an experimental lab for undergrad, MsC and PhD students including some international ones.

4. Technologies

Currently, the SmartLive Lab has 26 LoRa outdoor 8 dBi Omni 915/923 MHz antennas; 260 sensors compatible with LoRa including 40 temperature and humidity sensors (RAK1901 WisBlock), 40 ultrasonic ambient light sensors (RAK 12010), 40 noise sensors (RAK 18000), 10 water level sensors (RAK12014), 20 ultrasonic MQ3 gas (RAK 12004), 40 sensors for assessing the water pH, and several modules for prototyping and 3D printing. We have a DELL computer with 256GB, 2TB and Linux that hosts the open source ChirpStack Network Server.

The lab is a generator of technologies needed to meet our overall objective. A priority is to retain control of Santa Rosa's data (our main asset) to be able to share it,

[1] www.gca.unijui.edu.br

[2] https://www-smartinfrastructure.eng.cam.ac.uk/projects-and-case-studies/dc2-digital-cities-change

say, under data contract agreements and not necessarily for free. Therefore, we welcome experimental open source decentralised technologies [Crowcroft et al. 2024] that enable data–sharing to stimulate innovation, fair competition (e.g. among SMEs) and redistribution of data and value [Blancato 2024]. Data is an asset and to help innovation, it should flow (like money) rather than remaining static in possession of a few. To ease its flow, we need a data sharing infrastructure —similar to the road infrastructure. We have reservations about purchasing technologies from the cloud monopolies because they make money from abusing their business power, rather than from innovation. In response, we are currently assessing emerging decentralised technologies that follow the P2P interaction model rather than the traditional client–server model prevalent in the current cloud; for example, we are comparing BlueSky *vs* X, Matrix *vs* Whatsapp, and other messaging services. Further, we believe in open governance and think that the city council should be a regulator, not a controller; therefore, we are building technologies that are secure, protect privacy and individual freedom; precisely, we are developing applications on top of decentralised ID systems like Trustchain[3] and Privacy Enhancing Technologies (PETs) like AWS Nitro and compartments created on Morello Boards[4].

5. Results

We have deployed 12 LoRa antennas that cover both the rural and urban areas: 9 in the urban space and 3 in rural area. They receive sensor measurements. Incidentally, we have installed two LoRa–based meteorological stations in town to collect metrics about air quality, wind, luminosity, temperature, humidity, noise and UV radiation. We have also deployed a LoRa antenna in the rural area and associated sensors that collect soil (temperature, humidity and luminosity) and air (temperature and humidity) properties. Each antenna potentially covers a 10 km radius. As of the writing of this paper, we have other 10 LoRa–based meteorological stations and 14 LoRa antennas being deployed to achieve 100% coverage of the city. We have been collecting sensor data since Aug 2023 and stored 410275 entries as historical series. We regard the records as open data and share them with academy, companies, and soya–bean producers. The former use them in research and innovation projects tackling real-world problems in the city, such as in traffic and health. The latter used them for understanding the relationship between rainfall and current soil humidity and temperature. We have also built plots that we share with the general public on dashboards [5].

In the SmartLive Lab, we rely on software engineering techniques. For example, we use Search-Based Software Engineering (SBSE) to solve optimisation problems like antenna deployment. We also need software engineering techniques (e.g. run–time control–loop and reflection) for building self–adaptive applications; the need emerges from our interest in decentralised applications that are underpinned by peer–to–peer networks that are inherently self–organised, self–adaptable and, in general, self*.

6. Social and economic impact

Our LoRaWan network and servers are open and available to local companies. Some of them have deployed sensors in their warehouses that send data to our server through our antennas. Similarly, in rural areas, fish farmers are also using our antennas; they have deployed sensors to monitor fish tanks. We have also developed a system that notifies

[3]https://github.com/alan-turing-institute/trustchain

[4]https://www.arm.com/architecture/cpu/morello

[5]https://livelab.unijui.edu.br/

farmers about the likelihood of the Asian Rust affecting soya–bean–growing areas. Being the regional hub, we are happy to share our facilities with neighbour cities. EDI comes naturally to us; our regions is home to more than 20 ethnics that came from different regions of the world. We treasure and retain their traditions. EDI is already visible in our research team that is composed of people from different ages, genders, races and nationalities. We have seven females and eight males, PhD students; some of them are from ethnic minorities, others from neglected regions of Brazil. We admit that in Santa Rosa there are still some inequalities that we are already solving. We can mention that the health service is deploying home and body sensors for remote monitoring of the elderly.

7. Pending tasks

At the head of our to–do list is to build a web page to bring the SmartLive Lab online with information about its facilities and opportunities for the general public. Likewise, we will endow our data repository with APIs available to the general public to retrieve (e.g. sensor data) and upload data (e.g. historical photos). We also need to release under open source licences, several pieces of code that we have implemented, including Python scrips for record management and several independent data dashboards for web applications. We are also working on a decentralised digital identity system to grant the general public, access to our repository and pieces of code.

On the technical side, we have plans to deploy 10 additional meteorological stations by 2025 to collect real–time weather data at a granularity that enables to build a map of the region's microclimates. A pressing problem is the implementation of legal and technical mechanisms for sharing data that is currently in several siloed repositories. In the list are two data silos owned by Santa Rosa's medical service. Data sharing will motivate the use and development of data–centric applications such a AI. To cite an specific example, it has come to the city council's attention that, in comparison with other regions of Brazil, Santa Rosa has a high incidence of cancer. The medical sector and researchers from Unijuí would like to have access to the medical and other repositories to correlate data to investigate the cause which might be associated to genetic, eating habits or other factors. We also have plans to make all the sensor data available to the general public.

Acknowledgements

Research partially funded by the Co-ordination for the Brazilian Improvement of Higher Education Personnel (CAPES) and the Brazilian National Council for Scientific and Technological Development (CNPq) under grants 311011/2022-5, 309425/2023-9, 402915/2023-2. EPSRC/EP/X015785/1(G115169) grant funded Carlos and Jon. Thanks to Arturo Dina and Aristeo Hernández for proof–reading this document.

References

Bastidas, V., Oti-Sarpong, K., Nochta, T., Wan, L., Tang, J., and Schooling, J. (2023). Leadership of urban digital innovation for public value: A competency framework. *IET (The Institution of Engineering and Technology) Smart Cities*, 6(3). https://doi.org/10.1049/smc2.12063.

Blancato, F. G. (2024). Innovation is overrated: a provocation. *Communications of the ACM*, 67(3). https://dl.acm.org/doi/10.1145/3624727.

Crowcroft, J., Molina-Jimenez, C., Toliver, D., and Nakib, H. D. (2024). The Centre for ReDecentralisation (CRDC). www.cl.cam.ac.uk/research/srg/projects/crdc/. Visited on 10 May 2024.

Development of San Marcos as a Smart and Sustainable City with the Support of Search-based Software Engineering

Arturo Dina Valente[1], Luciana M. Cardoso[1], Mateus D. Kuhn[1], Misael Lorenzo[2], Higinio Torres Lucena[2], Sandro Sawicki[1], Fabricia Roos-Frantz[1], Rafael Z. Frantz[1], Carlos Molina-Jiménez[3]

[1]Unijuí University – Ijuí/RS – Brazil

{arturo.valente, luciana.c, mateus.kuhn}@sou.unijui.edu.br

{sawicki, frfrantz, rzfrantz}@unijui.edu.br

[2]Gobierno Municipal – San Marcos – México

sanmarcospresidencia@gmail.com

[3]University of Cambridge – Cambridge – United Kingdom

carlos.molina@cl.cam.ac.uk

Abstract. *The authorities of San Marcos' municipality (Mexico) have funded a project to develop it as a smart and sustainable place. This requires funding, technology, and expertise that they scarcely have, since they are afflicted by digital exclusion. To face the challenge, they have teamed up with Unijuí University and Santa Rosa city (Brazil) under Memoranda of Understanding (MOU) and with University of Cambridge under academic collaboration. In this paper, we (the team) discuss the main technical problems, technology used, results achieved and pending. Our strategy is to use low-cost technologies with optimised deployments to minimise maintenance and environmental costs.*

1. Introduction

In this paper we discuss a project funded by the authorities of the municipality of San Marcos (henceforth referred to as San Marcos) in 2022 to develop it as a smart, innovative, and sustainable place. San Marcos is located in State of Guerrero, Mexico and has 40 km of virgin coastline. It is home to 50,000 inhabitants, 12,000 of which live in San Marcos city— the municipal seat. The project includes the development of San Marcos city as a smart city and the 40 km of coastline as smart tourism destination. We have a team to meet the challenge: Santa Rosa contributes its 10 years of experience gained from its own development; Unijuí contributes technical know–how and shares its SmartLive Lab used for technology evaluation; Cambridge brings research expertise. We conceive smart and sustainable cities as places that offer conditions for integral human development. In our view, they are complex socio-technical systems, therefore, their development demands a multidisciplinary effort grounded in the intensive use of digital technologies. A smart city depends on communication networks, monitoring sensors, data-sharing repositories, methodologies, and algorithms (e.g. artificial intelligence) for urban analytics and end-user data-centric applications. It is common knowledge that the development of smart places is challenging and significantly harder in places like San Marcos municipality that are afflicted by digital exclusion [Alshamaila et al. 2024]. San Marcos suffers from a lack of public-private initiatives and economic, social, and technological constraints. The hurdles can prove to be too high to overcome unless innovative approaches are taken. The remainder of this paper explains the objectives of the project and the novel approach that we are taking to fulfill them in spite of the limitations mentioned above. In brief, we prefer open source (as opposed to cloud) technologies and open science. We welcome data-sharing and aim at reducing environmental costs through optimisation and biodegradable sensors. We have already achieved some results.

2. Objectives and strategies

Our goal is to redirect San Marcos' development from traditional and short-sighted to smart and sustainable. Specific short-term goal to fulfil by 2026 are to deploy antennas and sensors for testing and training. The strategy is to take advantage of open science and data-sharing to provide San Marcos with open source environmentally friendly technologies and to transfer technical skills to San Marcos to make it technically sustainable.

3. Technologies selected for reducing financial and environmental costs

We have selected LoRa (Long Range) antennas to leverage the experience gained from previous work in Santa Rosa. Additionally, LoRa is affordable; antennas cost from 350 to 500 dollars. Technical factors in favour include that it is a low-power alternative for Internet of Things (IoT) devices operating in unlicensed bands, such as the 902-928 MHz band in Mexico and Brazil. The use of Chirp Spread Spectrum (CSS) provides high resistance to interference and great range. A LoRa network includes antennas that capture radio signals from sensors and spreads radio signals to actuators. It also includes gateways that convert radio signals into digital data, forward them to central servers and transmit data in the opposite direction.

Communication coverage is more costly to achieve in regions afflicted by geographical (e.g. mountains) and urban (e.g. buildings) obstacles that block signal propagation. In places that suffer from digital divide, the lack of electrical grids and Internet aggravates the problem. In those places, antenna deployment is harder since they need to be placed at carefully selected locations; this effort demands proper software engineering techniques aimed at optimisation. San Marcos falls within this category. The optimisation of antennas is an (NP-hard) problem, i.e. a computationally complex problem with no polynomial-time solution for large inputs. The problem can be addressed with techniques that aim at near–optimal solutions like those used in Search-Based Software Engineering (SBSE) [Harman et al. 2008]. In San Marcos, we will use SBSE to solve other complex problems of design, testing and maintenance; examples are traffic management, deployment of video-cameras and waste collection. SBSE bridges the gap between theoretical research and practical engineering applications. To optimise antenna deployment, we have implemented *SmartSignal*, which is composed of a set of algorithms that use Simulated Annealing technique. This optimisation technique is derived from the simulation of a physical cooling process used to crystallise metals. *SmartSignal* can find the minimum number of antennas and their locations to cover a given area. We have coded it in GNU Octave (open source version of MatLab), it consists of 257 LOC and calls a Simulated Annealing library (*optim library*) to solve the NP-hard optimisation problem. *SmartSignal* is open source and available, with directions to run to replicate and validate, at GitHub[1] for the benefit of other cities interested in reducing the amount of hardware, energy consumed by their networks, and environmental costs. We favour low-cost open source experimental technologies rather than purchasing ready-to-use expensive technologies from dominant cloud providers. Thus, we store sensor data in an

[1] https://github.com/gca-research-group/lora-metaheuristic-model

open source ChirpStack Network Server deployed on Linux. We are manufacturing and testing biodegradable piezoresistive sensors in our laboratory; we can use them to monitor mechanical parameters such as pressure, tension, humidity, wearability, and temperature.

4. Benefits

The project will benefit biodiversity and reduce hazards. We will use sensors to monitor water levels (e.g. RAK12014), temperature, pollution, and other parameters of the 22 km^2 Tecomate Pesquería lagoon. It is home to several bird and fish species and, in our view, a candidate to join the list of Ramsar sites. Knowledge of water level variations can be used to anticipate its natural flooding cycle and evacuate affected villages [2]. Similarly, monitoring air particles can alert the authorities to wildfires that frequently affect the municipality during the dry season. Also, we can use sensors to monitor the rich biodiversity and weather conditions of the 40 km long coastline to produce maps (e.g. of native species) and attract eco-tourists. In San Marcos city, monitors can help with traffic management; noise sensors (RAK 18000) can be used to detect problems caused by about 7,500 motorbikes that roar through the streets. The project contributes to EDI (Equity, Diversity, and Inclusion) in several ways. For example, people from neglected villages without access to mobile coverage, mobile phones, or electrical grids can resort to LoRa to send messages. They can use devices such as the LoRa-based TTGO LoRa32 to request emergency assistance. We can use sensors (e.g. NEO-6M GPS Module) to monitor elderly and for incorporating people with disabilities into the labour market; there are about 550 of them that we regard as people with coolabilities (special talents), e.g. the enhanced imagination and creativity of individuals with ADHD.

5. Proposed solution and results

We suggest the use of LoRa/LoRaWAN antennas deployed at strategic locations determined by *SmartSignal*. We report here *SmartSignal's* approach and results. Firstly, the region under study is georeferenced using Google MyMaps. Secondly, we export, in Keyhole Markup Language (KML) format, the coordinates of the polygon that defines the geographical limits of the area to be signal-covered and the coordinates of the vertices of the geometric figures that delimit the obstacles and restrictions. The results are three files: city, obstacles, and restrictions. Thirdly, we use a text editor to convert the KML files into Comma Separated Values (CSV) format. Finally, we load these files into *SmartSignal* as input data in the main interface and run it. In *SmartSignal's* runs, we use the graphical interface (provided by Octave) that allows the user to import CSV files with coordinates, define antenna parameters, and observe the generated coverage. The use of *SmartSignal* is iterative and stochastic, differing from other techniques by avoiding converging on local minima. *SmartSignal* starts with an arbitrary initial solution, initially placing N antennas and a high initial temperature, then perturbation is applied. Interactions are used to lower the temperature and explore the best solutions [Harman et al. 2008]. A result is accepted when the new antenna arrangement improves coverage or cost reduction. Upon completion, *SmartSignal* generates a CSV file with the results. We then import this file into the Google Earth tool to visualise the coverage and antenna positions in a real geospatial environment. The result is a meaningful representation for non-technical people, such as municipal authorities. One of our results is shown in Figure 1.a The left side shows, in blue lines, the overlap of the coverage of the antennas. The right side shows the locations of the antennas and two obstacles: a mountain and the Tecomate Lagoon.

[2]We will build a digital twin of the Tecomate Pesquería lagoon.

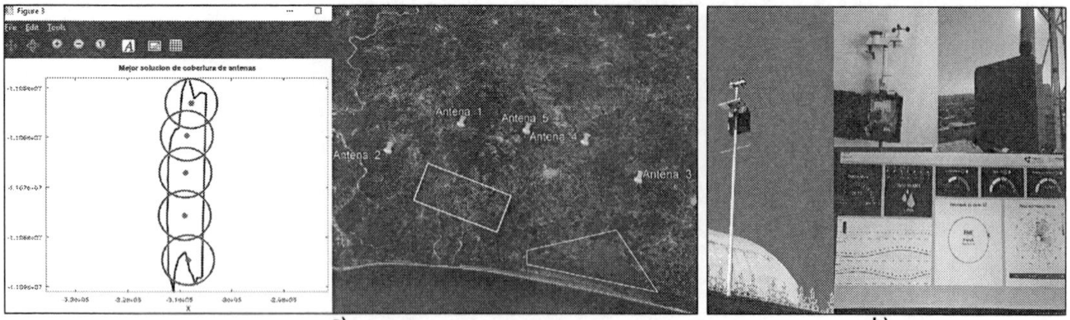

a) b)

Figure 1. a) Antenna coverage. b) Weather station, gateway, and dashboard.

With the simulations (using five antennas of 5 km radius), we managed to cover 75% San Marcos' area and revealed that the antenna that we have deployed in San Marcos city is 5.8 km away from the nearest optimal location; we will relocate it. To master the technology, we have deployed a weather station with seven sensors that measure temperature, humidity, rainfall, luminosity, UV index, wind speed, and direction. To reduce expenses through resource sharing, we transmitted the data to a network server located in Santa Rosa instead of purchasing a brand new server for San Marcos. Figure 1.b shows the LoRa infrastructure that we have installed in San Marcos city. The dashboard shows plots of the data collected by the station.

6. Pending tasks

Pending is the deployment of a ChirpStack Network Server locally to store San Marcos' data and share it with our current and other collaborators. Testing of properties of the biodegradable sensors (e.g. lifespan and robustness to accidental exposure to the elements) is on our agenda. Our to-do list also includes the gradual deployment of additional antennas and sensors at locations suggested by our optimisation results (see Section 5). Additionally, we need to train more experts in data sharing and smart city technologies.

Acknowledgements

Research funded by the Co-ordination for the Brazilian Improvement of Higher Education Personnel (CAPES) and Brazilian National Council for Scientific and Technological Development (CNPq) under grants 311011/2022-5, 309425/2023-9, 402915/2023-2. EPSRC/EP/X015785/1(G115169) grant funded Carlos Molina. Arturo thanks Jesús Gallardo, Carlos Gallegos, Hermenegildo Cisneros, Gilberto Ramírez and Daniel Martínez for helping in the deployment of the antenna; he also thanks Karen Dimayuga for her support and Aristeo Hernández for proof–reading the document.

References

Alshamaila, Y., Papagiannidis, S., and Alsawalqah, H. (2024). Smart cities in Jordan: Challenges and barriers. *Cities*, 154:105327.

Harman, M., McMinn, P., De Souza, J. T., and Yoo, S. (2008). Search based software engineering: Techniques, taxonomy, tutorial. In *LASER Summer School on Software Engineering*, pages 1–59. Springer.

Automated Unobtrusive Techniques for Linking requirements and testing in agile software development AUTOLINK PROJECT

Fernando Pastor Ricós[1], Ashley van Can[2], Beatriz Marín[1], Fabiano Dalpiaz[2], Tanja Vos[1,3]

[1]Universitat Politècnica de València (UPV), Spain

[2]Utrecht University (UU), The Netherlands

[3]Open Universiteit (OU), The Netherlands

Abstract. *Software professionals often face challenges in defining requirements and conducting thorough testing, particularly within agile development environments. The rapid and frequent iterations of agile methods encourage developers to take shortcuts to meet tight release deadlines, which may lead to low-quality software. To enhance software quality, the AUTOLINK project explores the synergies between requirements engineering and software testing, aiming to seamlessly integrate them into agile environments. AUTOLINK seeks to develop techniques that enable practitioners to improve software quality by testing it against its requirements in a way that is unobtrusive, cost-effective, and requires minimal effort.*

1. Introduction

Many of the recent disasters that occurred due to software faults are rooted in the human aspects of software engineering: "developers don't understand the problem they're trying to solve" [Somers 2017]. As a consequence, "the serious problems that have happened with software have to do with requirements, not coding errors [Somers 2017]. Hence, representing requirements and testing the developed software against them is crucial.

Over the past decades, the release of the agile manifesto [Beck et al. 2001] led to unprecedented changes in the methods that software development teams employ to build software. Traditional approaches borrowed from systems engineering (e.g., waterfall, the V-model) have been gradually replaced with methods that focus on the quick release of working software (e.g., Scrum, Kanban, XP). The World Quality Report [SOGETI 2019] has been arguing for years that this has led to blurred boundaries between development and quality assurance techniques like requirements engineering and testing. Consequently, serious attention needs to be given to the study of intelligent automation of end-to-end testing based on requirements, to truly provide business assurance, as organizations scale to enterprise agility [SOGETI 2019].

Software engineering research has studied agile development in many ways [Dingsøyr et al. 2012], especially in terms of human collaboration [Conboy et al. 2010] and its relationships with innovation theories [Nerur and Balijepally 2007]. Despite the acknowledged impact of agile development on requirements engineering and testing [Paetsch et al. 2003], there is a substantial lack of studies that describe how requirements are specified, managed, and tested in agile development [Inayat et al. 2015]

[Schön et al. 2017]. This is a serious issue for robust approaches that focus on the problem to solve and on validating its solution, like the V-model, were replaced by alternatives that aim at development and release speed [Bosch 2015], at the cost of decreasing software reliability [da Costa et al. 2016].

Concretely, user stories are the primary tool for managing requirements in agile development, with adoption rates reaching 90% [Cohn 2004, Kassab 2015, Lucassen et al. 2016]. However, they are often created hastily without adhering to quality standards. Although poorly written user stories may spark team discussions [Lucassen et al. 2017], they are difficult to trace back to test cases and code. Regarding testing, most testing frameworks, like Gherkin and Cucumber, rely on scripts to automate manual steps. These tools support BDD by generating test scripts from user stories and automating acceptance criteria checks. However, their lack of flexibility to adapt to changes results in high maintenance efforts [Vos and Aho 2017, Binamungu et al. 2018].

The AUTOLINK project aims to tackle these challenges by developing innovative tools, powered by natural language processing and machine learning, that integrate requirements engineering with software testing in agile practices. By leveraging unobtrusive software tools, this approach seeks to encourage companies to adopt these techniques more rigorously, ultimately resulting in higher-quality software.

2. Goals of the AUTOLINK Project

The main goals of the AUTOLINK Project are:

- *O1. Enhancing traceability of requirements*: To support practitioners in validating their system functionalities, we develop techniques to automatically extract testing-relevant behavioral information from requirements, which can serve as a starting point for testing activities (including manual, automated, and scriptless testing). In addition, achieving ubiquitous traceability involves ensuring that trace links between software artifacts (e.g., from requirements to code) are consistently available without requiring extra effort. By promoting the disciplined creation of user stories, we will apply artificial intelligence techniques to extract trace links between requirements and the software.
- *O2. Automating requirements validation through scriptless testing*: Trace links support requirements validation by connecting user stories to software artifacts. To provide value while avoiding the maintenance challenges of test scripts, we will explore how user stories, enriched with acceptance criteria, can be automatically validated using scriptless testing. A key challenge lies in guiding intelligent agents to select the appropriate actions and determine the next tests to perform.
- *O3. Designing seamless tools to enhance agile development*: We will develop a tool-supported approach that incorporates the results of O1 and O2, designed for integration into software companies. Our goal is to ensure the method is seamless and unobtrusive, allowing it to blend into existing development practices without necessitating significant changes to developers' workflows.
- *O4. Collecting evidence of value for software companies through empirical studies*: The tools and methods developed in O3 will allow us to assess the practical impact of the automated techniques from O1 and O2. By conducting case studies with partnering software companies we aim to gather empirical evidence demonstrating the benefits our approach offers to software developers.

3. Beneficiaries

The AUTOLINK project is a collaborative research project emerges from research groups that focus on different, yet complementary sub-fields of software engineering: automated scriptless testing and requirements engineering. These groups are: Open Universiteit (OU), The Netherlands; Utrecht University (UU), The Netherlands, and Universitat Politècnica de València (UPV), Spain. Also, six industry partners: ING Bank, Mendix Technology, TestCompass, Newspark, AXINI, and B00, are actively involved. Collaboration with these industry partners is essential for testing solutions and addressing challenges in real-world environments, ensuring the project's practical impact and relevance.

4. Results

The results of the project so far are:

- In collaboration with Mendix, we analyzed real-world backlog items, aiming to determine how requirements are documented in agile teams, and where additional information relevant to the project is stored.
- A collection of open-source issue tracking systems (ITSs) of real projects, in addition to the studied ITSs of Mendix, was analyzed to determine how requirements are represented in practice. In this study, we found that ITSs lack an organized and standardized representation of requirements. The identified challenges led to the experimentation with LLMs on the automated identification and classification of requirements [van Can and Dalpiaz 2025].
- A study to compare AI-based techniques as well as their performance against humans to derive domain models from collections of user stories was performed.
- A state model is inferred while testing at the GUI level with the scriptless testing tool TESTAR. To do that, an action selection mechanism has been designed and implemented to derive all possible actions from the available widgets.
- A listener mode is implemented such that TESTAR state models can also be inferred when the software is being tested by other means than TESTAR (i.e., manual testing, scripted automation, etc.).
- A preliminary prototype for improved action selection incorporating the use of LLMs into the TESTAR loop that has been tried out on open-source web applications, including prompts containing user requirements. This prototype is available at `https://github.com/TESTARtool/TESTAR_dev/tree/autolink` with an open-source 3-Clause BSD License.
- An industrial case study was performed using the LLM-empowered TESTAR at ING on real websites including chatbot functionality for requirements.

Results of AUTOLINK show that the project is aligned with the latest developments in GenAI and Large Language Model (LLM) technologies, which strongly support the research goals of the project. While our initial efforts concentrated on improving action selection mechanisms through reinforcement learning, the incorporation of state-of-the-art LLMs has broadened our scope. This integration holds significant promise for achieving our ambitious initial objectives: creating advanced tools capable of intelligently and autonomously extracting, connecting, and validating user requirements.

Acknowledgement This research is partially funded by the Dutch Research Council (NWO) through the Open Technology Programme 2021-II TTW, project AUTOLINK (19521), 2023-2027.

References

Beck, K., Beedle, M., Van Bennekum, A., Cockburn, A., Cunningham, W., Fowler, M., Grenning, J., Highsmith, J., Hunt, A., Jeffries, R., et al. (2001). The agile manifesto.

Binamungu, L. P., Embury, S. M., and Konstantinou, N. (2018). Maintaining behaviour driven development specifications: Challenges and opportunities. In *25th SANER*, pages 175–184. IEEE.

Bosch, J. (2015). Speed, data, and ecosystems: the future of software engineering. *IEEE Software*, 33(1):82–88.

Cohn, M. (2004). *User stories applied: For agile software development.* Addison-Wesley Professional.

Conboy, K., Coyle, S., and Wang, X. (2010). People over process: Key challenges in agile development,(99), 48–57.

da Costa, D., McIntosh, S., Kulesza, U., and Hassan, A. (2016). The impact of switching to a rapid release cycle on the integration delay of addressed issues: an empirical study of the mozilla firefox project. In *13th MRS*, pages 374–385.

Dingsøyr, T., Nerur, S., Balijepally, V., and Moe, N. B. (2012). A decade of agile methodologies: Towards explaining agile software development.

Inayat, I., Salim, S. S., Marczak, S., Daneva, M., and Shamshirband, S. (2015). A systematic literature review on agile requirements engineering practices and challenges. *Computers in human behavior*, 51:915–929.

Kassab, M. (2015). The changing landscape of requirements engineering practices over the past decade. In *5th EmpiRE Workshop*, pages 1–8. IEEE.

Lucassen, G., Dalpiaz, F., van der Werf, J., and Brinkkemper, S. (2016). The use and effectiveness of user stories in practice. In *22nd REFSQ*, pages 205–222. Springer.

Lucassen, G., Dalpiaz, F., van der Werf, J., and Brinkkemper, S. (2017). Improving user story practice with the grimm method: A multiple case study in the software industry. In *23rd REFSQ*, pages 235–252. Springer.

Nerur, S. and Balijepally, V. (2007). Theoretical reflections on agile development methodologies. *Communications of the ACM*, 50(3):79–83.

Paetsch, F., Eberlein, A., and Maurer, F. (2003). Requirements engineering and agile software development. In *12th WET ICE*, pages 308–313. IEEE.

Schön, E.-M., Thomaschewski, J., and Escalona, M. J. (2017). Agile requirements engineering: A systematic literature review. *Computer standards & interfaces*, 49:79–91.

SOGETI (2019). The world quality report 2019-2020.

Somers, J. (2017). The coming software apocalypse. *The Atlantic*, 26:1.

van Can, A. T. and Dalpiaz, F. (2025). Locating requirements in backlog items: Content analysis and experiments with large language models. *Information and Software Technology*, 179:107644.

Vos, T. and Aho, P. (2017). Searching for the best test. In *IEEE/ACM 10th International Workshop on Search-Based Software Testing (SBST)*, pages 3–4. IEEE.

Comparing LLMs in business rule-following

Nikson Bernardes Fernandes Ferreira[1], William Freitas[1], Hallyson Melo[1], Andre Carvalho[2], Thiago Borges[1], Rodrigo Marques[1]

[1] Institute de Desenvolvimento Tecnológico (INDT)
[2] Universidade Federal do Amazonas (UFAM)

{nikson.ferreira,william.freitas,hallyson.melo}@indt.org.br
{thiago.borges, rodrigo.marques}@indt.org.br
andre@icomp.ufam.edu.br

Abstract. *Large Language Models (LLMs) have shown great capabilities in language understanding and instruction following. However, to the author's knowledge, no prior work has evaluated their performance in real industry internal rule-following scenarios compared to humans. The present R&D project aims to analyze the applicability of LLMs in improving efficiency in task analysis and scheduling through automatic team assignment, following a set of internal business rules. The study was funded by SUFRAMA and is a collaboration between INDT and Motorola Mobility. The experiment results show that lightweight open LLMs, on average, have worse accuracy than mean worker (57.5% x 86.25%) with a higher divergence rate (90% x 45%).*

1. Introduction

Large Language Models (LLMs) can accomplish numerous Natural Language Processing (NLP) tasks thanks to their instruction-following ability. However, in real-world applications, people often expect LLMs to generate outputs that conform to user-provided rules [Sun et al. 2024]. In this work we are interested in Inferential Rule-following that differs from following instruction in the objectivity of the task. Instructions describe the objective or the steps to perform it, inferential rule following gives abstract predicate entailments, namely rules, and the model is responsible for applying the rules in a given context finding a correspondence (if it exists) with the input [Sun et al. 2024]. Companies usually expect their employees to strive for rules to perform internal processes. In this sense, evaluthe evaluation of the LLMs' capabilities to help workers to perform their usual job is attreled to its inferential rule-following abilities.

To try to decide if this technology can help in a work environment, previous works have been made to try to create benchmarks or ways for checking and evaluating the rule-following capabilities of a large language model, such as RuleBench [Sun et al. 2024] and the LLM Comparator [Kahng et al. 2024]. However, LLMs often come with a warning to use them carefully, as they tend to generate false data. So evaluating their contribution to a real work environment is quite challenging. On the other hand, this could help to decide if LLMs can help or get in the way of users when they need to follow a set of rules and do their activities on a larger scale.

This research projetct aims to compare lightweight local running LLMs to find out how well they can help the users perform their tasks. Local models are used instead of external services, e.g. ChatGPT or Gemini, due to the common confidentiality of internal organization rules. In this way, four human evaluators were selected to evaluate a set of instructions and check if they could categorize tasks to specific teams. Meanwhile, the rules they used were stored so they could also be followed by the LLMs later on and metrics could then be extracted.

2. Project Objectives

The Instituto de Desenvolvimento Tecnológico (INDT) is a technology-focused organization commited to advancing progress through innovation. Its activities broad several research and development areas including Advanced Manufacturing, Industry 4.0, Hardware and Firmware, Communication and Networks, Autonomous Vehicles, Robotic, Materials and Chemical, and Biotech serving and colaborating with various large companies of these sectors.

One of the colaborations are in the field of software testing. It was identified that the partner Motorola had thousands of tasks written in free natural language to analyze and execute. In 2023, It was proposed a research and project aiming to improve efficience in the process automaticaly standadizing input descriptions avoiding missunderdanding and enhance readability. In 2024, the project was extended to also reduce task redundance and automatic execution team assignment. The present work cover automatic team assignment which should consider a set of internal rules that limit team roles.

The objective of the present case study is to evaluate the applicability and the impact of open Large Language Models (LLMs) on performing inferential rule-following on team assignment company's processes, i.e., to discern business rules to define which one should me responsable for execution of the input task.

3. Proposed Method and Technologies

As described in [Sun et al. 2024], a rule can be understood in logical terms as entailment $\sigma \models \phi$, which means *"if σ holds, then ϕ also hold"*, where σ and ϕ are first order logic formulas. For instance, consider the predicates $isFalling(X)$ and $sell(X)$ which reads *"X is falling"* and *"sell X"*, respectively for a free variable X. One possible rule can be $isFalling(X) \models sell(X)$. In inferential rule-following, the objective is to find a substitution for one or more rules and apply implication given an input context, e.g., in the sentence *"NVIDIA stocks is falling"*, the model should find the substitution *[X/"NVIDIA stocks"]* and, then, the consequence *"Sell NVIDIA stocks"*.

In our case study, the rules defines which team should perform a determined task given teams limitations and explore the tradeoff between them. An Exemple of potential rules is $requires(X, y) \vee isExecuted(X, N) \models executes(a, X)$ where upper case terms are free variables which should be instantiated and lower ones, constants; the rule is read as *"if X requires y or it is executed N times, the team 'a' executes X"*.

A set of state-of-art lightweight open source LLM models were evaluated for confidentiality reasons. All models are inputed with the same prompt following the template shown in the Figure 1 instructing the model about the company context, the objective and the business-rules in natural language as if-then-else expressions. Exploring the causality of the model and following works such as [Wei et al. 2023], the model first provides a reasoning about the input, then provides a response. All time experiments were performed using llama.cpp framework with greedy sampling in a user grade computer aiming realistic time that even small companies could obtain: 16GB 12th Gen Intel® Core™ i712700H x 20 and a RTX 30606 GB.

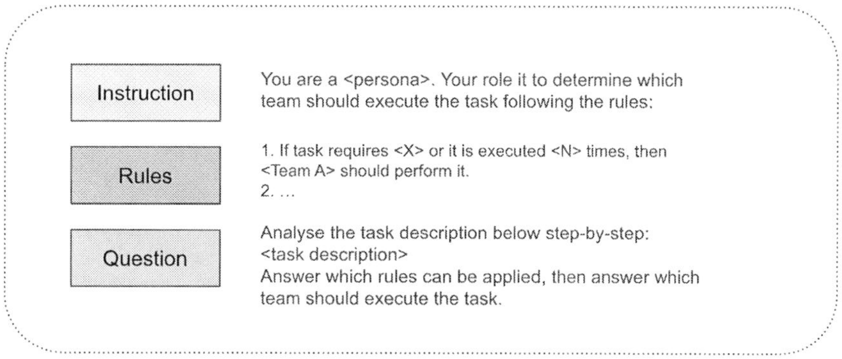

Figure 1. Inferential rule following prompt template used.

Model	MMLU	Accuracy (%)	avg time (s)	std time (s)
Llama3.2-3B	58	50	4.92	2.09
Phi-4-mini-4B	67.3	45	7.40	5.22
Gemma34B	59.6	75	5.11	1.42
DeepSeekR1-distil-Llama-8B	-	60	14.15	1.99
Humans	-	86	70.1	60.54

Table 1. Comparing open LLM MMLU benchmark, performance in business-rule following task and time perform a task in a user grade computer. All models are quantized in 4 bits.

A group of four human evaluators (selected by their experience level) performed this categorization of twenty tasks manually without communicating with each other. We recorded the time required for each assimilation, including time to consult resources. The majority vote was considered as the correct output, then the accuracy for each user was calculated and set as baseline for the approach. The discordance rate between workers also was evaluated. If there is one worker that disagrees with others, it is counted as discordance. The discordance rate is calculated by the number of cases where a discordance occurs over the total of cases.

4. Results

In 45% of cases where workers are assigned to independently perform the evaluation in the study, at least one of them gave a different response from others (divergence rate). It means that all workers agreed on only 55% of 20 tasks. Considering the majority vote as the correct categorization, the users hit on average 86,25% with a standard deviation of 8,54%. The results indicate that even humans can struggle to perform a relatively simple task making some mistakes, such as directing the task to a team. The low concordance and high accuracy indicate that workers tended to make different errors. These divergences can be related to previous experience or some arbitrary subjectivity of the user. On average, humans take 70.1 seconds to analyse the problem and provide a response in the case study. It varies considerably depending on problem complexity, it is possible to see on standard deviation that is 60,56 seconds, minimum of 10 seconds and maximum of 390 s.

For comparison, Table 1 also presents a common benchmark with results publicly available: the Massive Multitask Language Understanding (MMLU) benchmark evaluates LLMs pre-training in language understanding, knowledge and problem solving using questions from several fields with diverse range of difficulties. It is presented here to illustrate that there is no apparent relation between the global performance indicated by the classical benchmark and the result obtained in a specific business-rule following the experiment. The models' performance varies significantly from model to model. The Gemma-3-4B model performed better than the Phi-4-Mini that presented 112.9% gemma performance on the MMLU benchmark while it presented the worst performance on study.

In addition, Gemma-3 and DeepSeek-R1 distiled performed nearest to human level performance, however, it is still a long difference to it. The first performs the objective 36.1% of time in a sequential usage in a user grade computer. This time can be reduced even more with batched generation. LLMs disagreed in 90% of cases.

The present case-study evaluated the capacity and performance of low-scale LLM models to follow and apply internal business rules. Based on the average performance of humans, it indicates that it is possible to use low scale open LLM models to help company following internal business-rules at a slight performance drop compared with human. However, there are still opportunities for improvements. The project next steps are to analyse rules to turn them more concise and suitable for models' understanding and to try to apply the project idea for other activities besides team assignment, such as automatic labeling task's requisites. Additionally, the authors aim to implement a agentic approach that proposes and checks rules instantiation.

Acknowledgements

The present research is resulting of a Instituto de Desenvolvimento Tecnológico (INDT)'s R&D project benefiting from SUFRAMA tax incentives from Informatics Law No. 8387/1991. It is result from a cooperation between INDT - Instituto de Desenvolvimento Tecnologico and Motorola Mobility Comercio de Produtos Eletrônicos Ltda.

References

Kahng, M., Tenney, I., Pushkarna, M., Liu, M. X., Wexler, J., Reif, E., Kallarackal, K., Chang, M., Terry, M., and Dixon, L. (2024). Llm comparator: Visual analytics for side-by-side evaluation of large language models.

Sun, W., Zhang, C., Zhang, X., Yu, X., Huang, Z., Chen, P., Xu, H., He, S., Zhao, J., and Liu, K. (2024). Beyond instruction following: Evaluating inferential rule following of large language models.

Wei, J., Wang, X., Schuurmans, D., Bosma, M., Ichter, B., Xia, F., Chi, E., Le, Q., and Zhou, D. (2023). Chain-of-thought prompting elicits reasoning in large language models.

Test Case Creation Approach using LLM for Android System

Bruno Cerdeira[1], Hermann Hernani[1], Luan Marques[1], Luiz Souza[1], Silvia Ascate[1]
Eliane Collins[1], André Carvalho[2]

[1]Instituto de Desenvolvimento Tecnológico – (INDT)
Av. José Moacir Teberga de Toledo, 1520 - Planalto, Manaus - AM, 69044-235

[2]ICOMP – Instituto de Computação
Universidade Federal do Amazonas (UFAM), Manaus – AM, Brazil.

bruno.cerdeira@indt.org.br, hermann.oliveira@indt.org.br
luan.marques@indt.org.br, luiz.souza@indt.org.br, silvia@indt.org.br
eliane.collins@indt.org.br, andre@icomp.ufam.edu.br

Abstract. *This research project presents a method to generate functional test cases for new Android features using the Large Language Model (LLM) LLama. The objective is to reduce manual effort and avoid process bottlenecks, benefiting software testing teams and developers. The approach uses LLM-generated prompts based on Android feature specifications for automated test case generation. A feasibility study evaluated 57 test cases, revealing that 19.3% were well-written, 63.2% had acceptable quality, and 26.3% had medium complexity. The research was conducted under contract with the Institute of Technological Development (INDT) and its funded by the R&D program of EMBRAPII for Motorola LTDA/Flextronic Ltda.*

1. Context

As the mobile system market is very competitive, there is a constant need for effective strategies to ensure the delivery of high-quality applications. Software testing is fundamental in the development process that aims to evaluate and improve the quality of products. Mobile systems have some characteristics and limitations such as the battery life, amount of input data, and different inputs. This context increases the complexity of test case maintenance. Furthermore, generating test scripts requires constant monitoring and updates for new devices, OS versions, resolution variations, and Google adopts a rapid Android release cycle with frequent updates and new features.

New techniques have been used to solve these gaps, such as Artificial Intelligence, which has contributed significantly to the generation of tests. LLMs provide language understanding abilities and adaptability across various fields, including software testing. It can be used to create functional test cases for specific contexts Lima Jr et al. (2024).

LLMs have been successfully implemented in various testing tasks. Liu et al. (2023) propose GPTDroid, a system that uses LLMs to generate testing scripts to provide Graphical user interface (GUI) page information to the LLM for mobile apps and execute them. In Lima Jr et al. (2024), a case study investigates the integration of LLMs in creating test cases. The authors generate test cases using a real software application and evaluate their effectiveness based on quality factors like Clarity, Correctness, Completeness, and Consistency.

2. Study Objectives

The aim of this research project is to evaluate the feasibility of incorporating the LLM Llama 2.0[1] (Llama2) model into the test case creation process in the mobile systems industry, without the need for additional training, based on the analysis of the quality and complexity of the generated tests. Quality was analyzed following criteria such as clarity, completeness, objectivity, and maintainability Lima Jr et al. (2024), while complexity was evaluated considering the test case configuration, test steps, number of components, and test case abstraction level Tran et al. (2021).

These are the contributions of this study: A process to create test cases from Llama 2.0 helping test professionals and students; evaluation of the test cases created using the quality and complexity metrics; and benefits professionals in the Android software testing market and companies in this business.

3. Methods and Technologies

INDT - Instituto de Desenvolvimento Tecnológico, provides solutions in the areas of Software, Hardware & Firmware, Communication and Networks, Advanced Manufacturing, Autonomous Vehicles and Robotics, Materials and Chemistry, and BioTech. The projects are carried out in collaboration with companies in these sectors, in which problems are identified and ways to solve them are developed through research and development.

In this context, in March 2024 the partner company had to re-think how it would handle with the advance of LLMs in the context of creating test cases for software engineering. Consequently, this research project initially aimed to prove the feasibility of using LLMs to create test cases in large-scale systems that met the criteria already mentioned in the previous section (quality and complexity). The feasibility study has the following process flow represented in Figure 1, with four stages, from describing the features to refining the final result after generating the test case using the Llama2.0 script.

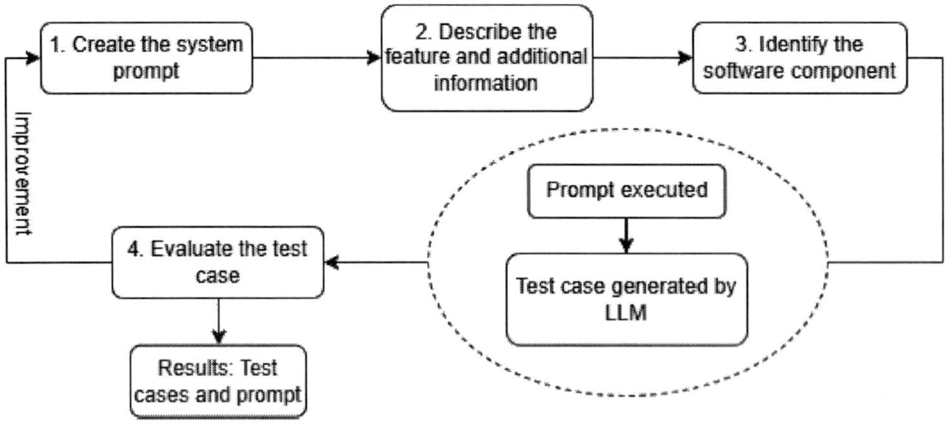

Figure 1. The proposed solution

The system prompt was initially created using the Zero-shot prompting technique, providing a natural language description of the task without prior examples Jaremko et al. (2025). Guidelines for impersonation, response formatting, and evaluation criteria were

[1]Meta. 2024. Llama 2. https://llama.meta.com/

included to enhance the model's output. A detailed feature description (2) was then provided to help understand its functionality and objectives, facilitating the generation of test cases. Identifying the software components that interact with these features clarifies dependencies, enabling the LLM to create targeted test cases focused on specific interactions (3). The evaluation process (4) involved testers manually reviewing and executing the generated test cases to ensure they met quality and complexity standards.

DEFAULT_SYSTEM_PROMPT = """
You are a helpful, respectful and honest assistant. Always answer as helpfully as possible, while being safe. Your answers should not include any harmful, unethical, racist, sexist, toxic, dangerous, or illegal content. Please ensure that your responses are socially unbiased and positive in nature.
If a question does not make any sense or is not factually coherent, explain why instead of answering something not correct. If you don't know the answer to a question, please don't share false information.
Imagine that you're an experient QA tester, and you have to write a new Test Case base on the feature described.
You know that your team Test Case pattern has 3 columns; the first one is the initial setup column, where all the pre-setup required to run the test case is described. The second one is the steps columns, which can be more than one and specify all the steps to execute the test case.
The third one shows the Expected results for each Test step column.
Generate a score ranging from 1 (low) to 5 (high) that represents the importance level of the test case for the final user."""

3.1. Feasibility Study

Writing quality was evaluated using the following factors: clarity, objectivity, completeness, and maintainability, each rated on a scale from 1 to 3 in which 1 represents poor, 2 is acceptable, and 3 is good. Clarity assessed the precision and comprehensibility of the test case descriptions. Objectivity focuses on the conciseness and relevance of the information provided. Completeness ensured that the test case included all necessary setup details and expected outcomes. Maintainability examined the ease with which the test case could be adapted to future changes.

Test case complexity was rated from 1 to 3, considering setup, steps, components involved, and abstraction level. The Llama2.0 model was implemented in a Google Colab Python script using Android features. Four test analysts created the test cases, and two professionals evaluated their quality based on writing and complexity.

4. Results

Using the developed prompt, 57 test cases were generated based on the requirements outlined in Figure 2. Some test cases lacked expected results for each step, affecting completeness, while missing or inadequate initial setup data impacted complexity. A limitation of the method is the need for test analysts to map interacting features manually, and the limited number of evaluated Android features lacks statistical relevance.

The results show that 82.5% of the generated test cases had acceptable quality, with 63.2% partially acceptable due to issues with completeness and complexity, and 19.3% fully acceptable without modifications. The approach worked well for high-level descriptions, such as the "Select to Speak" feature, enabling the creation of comprehensible and effective test cases. Minimal modifications were needed, facilitating integration into the platform's overall test suite.

The LLM's non-persistent nature affected test consistency, making it challenging to generate accurate test cases and apply few-shot strategies effectively. Additionally, varying the number of steps in a test case proved difficult.

Feature	Android Version	Generated TCs	Feature	Android Version	Generated TCs
Flash Notification	14	3	Vibration & Haptics	13	10
Regional Preferences	14	6	Screen Reader	13	5
Select to Speak	14	1	Live Transcribe	13	7
Live Caption	14	5	Apps Language Preferences	13	1
Quick Tiles Settings	13	4	Talkback	13	1
Dark Mode at Bedtime	13	5	Safety - SOS	13	9

Figure 2. Google Android Features used in the feasibility study

Despite the good quality of test creation, there are opportunities for improvements to achieve completeness and complexity, especially when it comes to understanding how different features interact with each other. These improvements aim to benefit test professionals, students, and software testing teams and developers seeking to optimize Android feature validation by providing more comprehensive and effective test cases. In future works, the LLM prompts will be updated with information about the initial setup and the Android platform description for the model to infer the components interact with a specific feature.

Acknowledgment

This research was done during the year 2024 and was funded as provided for in arts. 21 and 22 of decree no. 10,521/2020, under the terms of Federal Law no. 8,387/1991, through agreement no. 003/2021, signed between INDT - Instituto de Desenvolvimento Tecnologico, Flextronics da Amazonia Ltda and Motorola Mobility Comercio de Produtos Eletrônicos Ltda.

References

Julia Jaremko, Dagmar Gromann, and Michael Wiegand. Revisiting implicitly abusive language detection: Evaluating llms in zero-shot and few-shot settings. In *Proceedings of the 31st International Conference on Computational Linguistics*, pages 3879–3898, 2025.

Roberto F Lima Jr, Luiz Fernando PB Presta, Lucca S Borborema, Vanderson N Silva, Marcio LM Dahia, and Anderson Santos. A case study on test case construction with large language models: Unveiling practical insights and challenges. In *Congresso Ibero-Americano em Engenharia de Software (CIbSE)*, pages 388–395. SBC, 2024.

Zhe Liu, Chunyang Chen, Junjie Wang, Mengzhuo Chen, Boyu Wu, Xing Che, Dandan Wang, and Qing Wang. Chatting with gpt-3 for zero-shot human-like mobile automated gui testing. *arXiv preprint arXiv:2305.09434*, 2023.

Huynh Khanh Vi Tran, Michael Unterkalmsteiner, Jürgen Börstler, and Nauman bin Ali. Assessing test artifact quality - a tertiary study. *Information and Software Technology*, 139:106620, 2021.

Music360: Software Engineering for Assessing the True Value of Music

Jesús Carreño [1], Giovanni Giachetti[1,2], Daniel Catalá [1], Blanca de Miguel [1], Conrado Carrascosa [1], María de Miguel [1]

[1]Universitat Politècnica de València
Camino de Vera s/n, Valencia, Spain

[2] Universidad Andres Bello, Chile

Abstract. *While it is well known that music influences our emotions, health and work, there is a lack of standardised information to measure and share the true impact of music and how this relates to the distribution of royalties. The Music360 project, led by a European consortium, aims to assess the value of music and connect stakeholders across the music value chain to build a common data analytics platform that goes beyond traditional metrics to explore the impact of music. The Music360 platform is based on a novel model-driven approach that will be applied to empirical case studies in the form of living labs in healthcare, media, retail, etc. to evaluate how music enhances well-being, patient recovery, brand identity and revenue potential.*

1. Introduction

Various studies demonstrate that music can influence our emotions, decisions, and even our health [Zhou et al. 2022, Martin-Saavedra et al. 2018]. As a result, many venues, such as bars, shopping malls, supermarkets, and hospitals, use background music to enhance the experience for their customers [Choo et al. 2021], users [Fu et al. 2020], and employees [Mao 2022]. These establishments are required to pay licensing fees for the use of music, which are typically managed by Collective Management Organizations (CMOs). CMOs distribute royalties to the various rights holders associated with the musical works played, including singers, musicians, songwriters, and composers.

However, the payment of music royalties does not take into account the real impact that music has on people in different places and contexts [Eidsvold-Tøien 2023]. For example, a store or bar might pay a licensing fee based on its square footage, when a more accurate measure would be the actual number of listeners or the contribution of music to the customer's purchase decision. On the other hand, to determine the distribution of music royalties between the different rights holders, the CMOs apply what the lawsuit calls "fair compensation" [Commission et al. 2020], using reference data such as the top 20 radio stations in a country. However, this distribution model does not consider to local artists, while the superstar artists receive the most royalties.

To overcome these challenges, the Music360 project[1] aims to create a fair and sustainable European music ecosystem by developing a platform that collects and shares detailed music usage data with different stakeholders, while maintaining data confidentiality. To achieve this goal, the Music360 platform considers the use of model-driven

[1]Music360. https://music-360.eu/

engineering approaches [Gaševic et al. 2009, Schumacher et al. 2014] to ensure consistent terminology and facilitate information interoperability among different stakeholders of the music value chain [Giachetti et al. 2023].

Music360 focuses on background music, such as live music, music broadcast on the radio, music streamed, or music distributed by other means such as tape or disk, as it accounts for 28% of the royalty collection for songwriters and composers, more than streaming, which accounts for 21% [Commission et al. 2020]. It is an interdisciplinary research effort involving experts in the social sciences, economics, and technology. Specifically, to measure the actual value of music in three specific areas: Therapeutic, Social and Cultural. To this end, Music360 requires conducting empirical studies, called living labs, to understand the real-world impact of music and how the technology developed can provide an appropriate platform for assessing the true value of music.

2. Music360 Objectives

The Music360 project aims to develop a new perspective on the value of music and to enable the collection of more reliable data [Guilhot et al. 2024]. The project started in March 2023 and will run for three years (see Figure 1). The main objective of the project is to provide mechanisms for information interoperability and facilities for research scenarios aimed at developing new technologies and studies around the music value ecosystem. The specific objectives are the following:

1. Conceptualize and measure the monetary and non-monetary value of music, including economic, societal, cultural, and therapeutic perspectives. This will be based on a thorough and broad literature review [de Miguel-Molina et al. 2024].
2. Define a standardized, trusted, and unified collection and representation of music data (such as recordings, plays, claims, etc.) to ensure that all stakeholders have a clear understanding of the information presented .
3. Develop a distributed information network between different music stakeholders to analyze the value of music and to make information widely and transparently available to address challenges related to the fair distribution of neighbouring and author rights while respecting confidentiality requirements.
4. Conduct living labs to test and validate the platform solutions for capturing music value data (such as music fingerprinting devices) and defining appropriate measures for the monetary and non-monetary value of music in different contexts.

3. Music360 Current Status

The Music 360 project is in its second year of development (from March 2024 to February 2026). The main milestones achieved so far are described below.

- Implementation of the Music360 platform V1.0, which adapts the conceptual models and evaluates them using data collected from the living labs. Novel data analysis mechanisms were implemented to generate a set of reports on music usage, which were positively validated by CMOs and policy makers. For the transparent and secure exchange of information between the different stakeholders involved in the music ecosystem, a specific distributed architecture was defined (obtained in May 2024) [McLaren et al. 2024].

- The Music360 conceptual model V2.0, based on a literature review and previous studies, together with the first preliminary results from living labs conducted, was obtained in March 2025. The Music360 metamodel can be found in Zenodo [2].
- Live demonstrations of the platform for stakeholders (November 2024 and January 2025), including data from four countries: Ireland, the Netherlands, Finland and Portugal. The feedback from these demonstrations was positive and generated interest among stakeholders such as artists and CMOs.

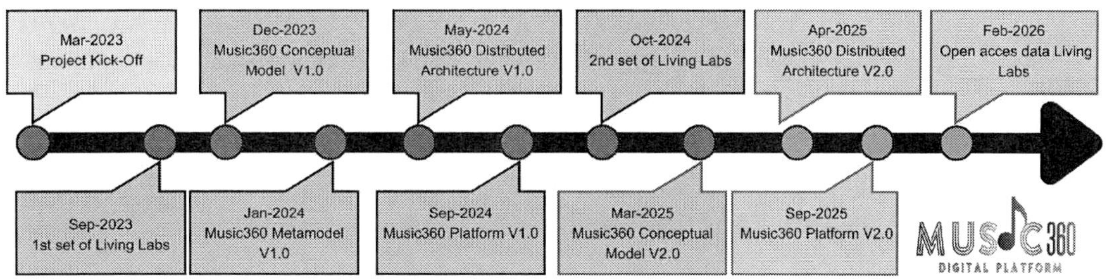

Figure 1. Music360 Project Sumarized Roadmap till Feb 2026

4. Relevance for the CIBSE Community

1. Provide new technology for measuring and analyzing the value of music that can be used by practitioners and researchers to develop specific studies.
2. Provide a novel distributed architecture that facilitates the comparison and communication of results from different studies with relevant partie.
3. Conducting empirical studies that combine social, economic, and computer sciences to define appropriate measures of the value of music in various domains.
4. Create novel solutions based on model-driven software engineering (Music360 conceptual model), data science, IoT, and artificial intelligence to support the project objectives [Giachetti et al. 2024].

5. Conclusions

Music360 aims to provide robust methods and tools to assess the value of music in a more standardised and contextual way. By integrating model-driven software engineering principles with data science and AI, it is possible to create a fairer and more transparent system for valuing and distributing music royalties. This will address the challenges faced by CMOs and the music industry as a whole to ensure a fairer distribution of royalties, and help researchers to understand the multi-faceted value of music for the benefit of all stakeholders involved in the creation, distribution and consumption of music.

6. Acknowledgement

This work is part of the Music360 project funded by the European Union's Horizon Europe research and innovation programme, Grant Agreement No. 101094872.

[2]Music360 Ontology V2. https://doi.org/10.5281/zenodo.15063314

References

Choo et al. (2021). The sound of music on the pocket: A study of background music in retail. *Psychology of Music*, 49(5):1381–1400.

Commission, E., Directorate-General for Education, Youth, S., Culture, et al. (2020). *Feasibility study for the establishment of a European Music Observatory – Final report*. Publications Office of the European Union.

de Miguel-Molina, M., de Miguel-Molina, B., Catala-Perez, D., Carrascosa-Lopez, C., Pastor-López, Ó., and Giachetti Herrera, G. (2024). The economic value of music: a literature review.

Eidsvold-Tøien, I. (2023). Remunerating authors and performers: Are statutory fair compensation provisions sufficient? In *The Exploitation of Intellectual Property Rights*, pages 187–215. Edward Elgar Publishing.

Fu, V. X., Oomens, P., Klimek, M., Verhofstad, M. H., and Jeekel, J. (2020). The effect of perioperative music on medication requirement and hospital length of stay: a meta-analysis.

Gaševic, D., Djuric, D., and Devedžic, V. (2009). *Model driven engineering and ontology development*. Springer Science & Business Media.

Giachetti, G., Catalá, D., de Miguel, B., Carrascosa, C., de Miguel, M., Carreño, J., and Pastor, O. (2024). Smart model-driven engineering to improve the music valuation.

Giachetti, G., Catalá, D., de Miguel, B., Carrascosa, C., de Miguel, M., and Pastor, O. (2023). Music360: Modeling the value of music. In *CAiSE Research Projects Exhibition*, pages 105–110.

Guilhot, D., Calvo, G., Gordijn, J., Bon, A., Wieringa, R., Teekens, S., Lucassen, F., Giachetti, G., Catalá, D., de Miguel, B., et al. (2024). Music360: Assessing the true value of music. In *OpenLivingLab Days Conference 2024*, page 281.

Mao, N. (2022). The role of music therapy in the emotional regulation and psychological stress relief of employees in the workplace. *Journal of healthcare engineering*, 2022(1):4260904.

Martin-Saavedra et al. (2018). Standardizing music characteristics for the management of pain: A systematic review and meta-analysis of clinical trials. *Complementary therapies in medicine*, 41:81–89.

McLaren, A., Wang, Y., van de Velde, C., Green, E., Wieringa, R., and Gordijn, J. (2024). Value-based security requirements in a highly decentralized digital ecosystem: the music360 case. In *17th IFIP WG 8.1 Working Conference on the Practice of Enterprise Modeling Forum*, pages 1–15. CEUR-WS.

Schumacher, F., Gey, R., and Klingner, S. (2014). Semantics for the music industry: the development of the music business ontology (mbo). In *Proceedings of the 10th International Conference on Semantic Systems*, pages 77–83.

Zhou, L., Yang, Y., and Li, S. (2022). Music-induced emotions influence intertemporal decision making. *Cognition and Emotion*, 36(2):211–229.

Quality concerns when integrating quantum and classical computing: a systematic mapping study

Cristian Marquez[1], **Johana Ojeda**[1] **and Kelly Garcés** [1]

[1]Department of Systems and Computing Engineering – Universidad de los Andes
Bogotá – Colombia
(e-mail: c.marquezb, j.ojedaa, kj.garces971@uniandes.edu.co)

Abstract. *This article presents a systematic mapping review to categorize software quality research for hybrid computing systems; meaning the combination of classical software and quantum technologies to solve a problem. This work attempts to categorize primary studies with respect to quality attributes and metrics in hybrid systems reported in state of the art literature. Moreover, it identifies potential research areas and surveys the challenges of the practical integration of quantum software into classical infrastructures.*

1. Introduction

Hybrid computing systems present several challenges, including heterogeneity of quantum hardware due to multiple quantum phenomena [Elsharkawy et al. 2023, Sodhi and Kapur 2021], multiple ways to represent data in Qubits [Moguel et al. 2022], lack of software standardization [Elsharkawy et al. 2023, Cerezo et al. 2022, Sodhi and Kapur 2021], limited monitoring tools [Moguel et al. 2022, Alvarado-Valiente et al. 2023], error-prone algorithm development [Sodhi and Kapur 2021], shortage of quantum experts [Sodhi and Kapur 2021], and limited visibility between quantum and classical computing boundaries [Vietz et al. 2021]. While current literature focuses on specific topics such as quantum verification [Gheorghiu et al. 2019], compilation [Heyfron and Campbell 2018], simulation [Dong et al. 2022], and development [Cruz-Lemus et al. 2021], these studies typically adopt a theoretical perspective without addressing practical strategies for software quality attributes. These challenges and advancements motivate our systematic mapping study to examine progress in software quality for hybrid quantum-classical systems.

2. Systematic mapping review process

We conducted a systematic mapping review using *Web of Science* and *Scopus* databases. The search focused on studies addressing quality attributes and metrics in hybrid quantum-classical systems. A total of 559 papers were identified; out of which, 484 articles matched the search criteria from *Web of Science*, while *Scopus* yielded 75 results. Following a two-phase screening process, we selected 16 articles for detailed analysis. Our analysis revealed that while 87% of studies focus on quality metrics and attributes, only 43% address integration challenges, highlighting a significant research gap in hybrid systems.

The study primarily addresses two main research questions: (1) *What are the challenges of integrating quantum computing systems with an existing classical computing infrastructure?* and (2) *What attributes and/or metrics of classical software qual-*

ity are relevant to the quantum realm, and which are unique in the context of quantum computing?. Additional analyses are available in our supplementary material at `https://zenodo.org/records/15072607`.

3. Mapping Results

3.1. Integration Challenges

Hybrid quantum/classical systems present challenges in four main areas. First, scalability and performance issues arise from supporting diverse quantum technologies [Elsharkawy et al. 2023], managing high latency, and addressing lack of standardization [Cerezo et al. 2022]. Second, data and encoding challenges include difficulty in defining boundaries between quantum and classical systems [Vietz et al. 2021], and scarcity of standardized datasets [Cerezo et al. 2022]. Third, algorithmic development faces the need for unique algorithms per problem, limited component reuse [Moguel et al. 2022], and lack of standardization [Alvarado-Valiente et al. 2023]. Finally, developer expertise requirements encompass both quantum and traditional computing knowledge, including software integration and cloud computing [Vietz et al. 2021, Sodhi and Kapur 2021].

3.2. Quality Attributes and Metrics

Our review identified that hybrid systems currently use classical software quality attributes [Silva et al. 2023] found in the literature. The only software-related metrics reported include quantum volume (now known as layer fidelity), and total quantum factor [Verduro et al. 2021]. While other metrics such as T1 (Energy relaxation) and T2 (Dephasing) are relevant for quantum systems [Youssef 2020].

4. Conclusions

The systematic mapping review reveals that quantum computing technologies remain in their early developmental stages, evidenced by the limited literature addressing quality assurance in quantum computing. Current studies focus on establishing theoretical quality attributes derived from classical software standards, with minimal exploration of quantum or hybrid specific metrics. Moreover, documented quality attributes require validation in operational environments to assess their practical utility.

The analysis of hybrid systems shows that cloud services represent the most viable solution for accessing quantum hardware, given the challenges of maintaining stable qubits and meeting specialized requirements. However, this approach inherits traditional cloud computing challenges while confronting quantum-specific issues such as system availability and exponential error propagation.

Finally, we found that the field requires quantum-specific standards and empirical validation of quality metrics. The development of observability tools and testing frameworks for hybrid quantum-classical systems represents a clear research opportunity. Future work should focus on establishing robust quality assurance practices that can be validated in operational environments.

5. References

Due to space limitations, all references cited in this paper can be consulted in our supplementary material available at `https://zenodo.org/records/15072607`.

Towards a Software Toolkit for Specifying and Monitoring Smart Contracts in the Application Integration Domain*

Mailson Teles-Borges[1], Eldair F. Dornelles[1], Fabricia Roos-Frantz[1], Antonia M. Reina-Quintero[2], Sandro Sawicki[1], José Bocanegra[3], Rafael Z. Frantz[1]

[1]Unijuí University – Ijuí/RS – Brazil

mailson.borges@sou.unijui.edu.br

{eldair.dornelles, frfrantz, sawicki, rzfrantz}@unijui.edu.br

[2]University of Seville – Seville – Spain

reinaqu@us.es

[3]Universidad Distrital Francisco José de Caldas – Bogotá – Colombia

jjbocanegrag@udistrital.edu.co

1. Introduction

This paper contributes a toolkit that we have developed to ease the implementation of smart contracts. It is an ongoing project, yet, we have already implemented four of its core components: Jabuti DSL, Jabuti CE, the Transformation Engine, and the Monitoring System. Jabuti DSL is a domain-specific language for writing smart contracts for Enterprise Application Integrations [Dornelles et al. 2022]. It includes constructs for encoding operations frequently found in smart contracts for the application integrations. Our toolkit is aimed at developers of Jabuti DSL smart contracts. It provides a comprehensive programming environment that should encourage the adoption of the language. In the following sections, we will discuss only the last three components.

2. Software Toolkit

Jabuti CE[1] is an editor for writing contracts in Jabuti DSL. It includes a VSCode Plug-in and a Language Server. The VSCode Plug-in connects to the VSCode Editor and integrates with both the Language Server and the Transformation Engine. The Language Server provides editor features such as code formatting, syntax and semantic validation, auto-completion, colour highlighting, and code transformation.

The Transformation Engine transforms contracts written in Jabuti DSL into executable smart contracts. It consists of five components: Grammar Parser, Validators, Canonical Parser, Code Generator, and Code Formatter. The Jabuti DSL grammar is based on ANTLR, so the Grammar Parser also uses ANTLR to generate the Abstract

*Research funded by the Co-ordination for the Brazilian Improvement of Higher Education Personnel (CAPES) and the Brazilian National Council for Scientific and Technological Development (CNPq) under grants 311011/2022-5, 309425/2023-9, 402915/2023-2. Antonia M. Reina has been funded by projects PID2020-112540RB-C44 and TED2021-130355B-C32. Thanks to Carlos Molina-Jimenez from Cambridge University for his valuable feedback in early versions of this work.

[1]The source code of Jabuti DSL, Jabuti CE, the Transformation Engine, and the Monitoring System is available on GitHub: https://github.com/gca-research-group/smart-contract-execution-monitoring-system?tab=readme-ov-file#project-repositories

Syntax Tree (AST) of the smart contract. The AST is a structured data format that links each token value in a hierarchical sequence of relationships. Validators, also implemented using ANTLR, perform syntactic and semantic checks. The Canonical Parser converts the generated AST into the format required by the Code Generator. The Code Generator uses a *template rendering library*, currently *ejs*[2], to transform the Jabuti DSL smart contract into the format of target platform. Finally, the Code Formatter corrects formatting errors.

The Monitoring System mediates between integrated applications and blockchain platforms. It manages blockchain connections and smart contract execution. It captures execution events and detects clause violations. The system forwards contractual events to integrated applications. Monitoring System is event driven and is activated on demand. It consists of three main components: Event Handler, Contract Invoker, and Event Updater. The Event Handler polls and prepares events awaiting processing. The Contract Invoker connects to the target blockchain, executes the smart contract, and captures execution events. Lastly, the Event Updater evaluates the Contract Invoker's response and makes the results available to the integrated application.

3. Usage of the toolkit in a case study

Imagine a contract with a single rule between a shop-owner and a supplier that dictates that *delivery trucks are expected only from 6:00 pm to 11:59 pm.* Next, imagine that Alice (a developer) proceeds to implement it using our toolkit. (1) Alice uses Jabuti CE to encode the rule in Jabuti DSL. The result is a Jabuti DSL smart contract stored in a .jabuti file. (2) In this example, she wishes to deploy the smart contract in Hyperledger Fabric, thus she uses the Transformation Engine to transform it into Golang (Solidity would be another alternative). (3) She deploys the Golang smart contract into the Monitoring System to finish her task. (4) When a delivery is completed, the shop-owner generates an event reporting the truck's arrival and departure times and sends it to the Monitoring System. (5) The Monitoring System launches the smart contract into execution. (6) If the smart contract detects a rule breach, it sends a violation event to the shop-owner and the supplier to enable compensatory actions.

The main advantages of this approach are: firstly, Jabuti DSL can encode rules directly and intuitively, Jabuti CE automates code specification and transformation; secondly, the Monitoring System simplifies the connection and management of the interaction between the integration and the blockchain; it lowers the adoption barrier; finally, the blockchain serves as an immutable storage of transaction records.

4. Future Work

The adoption of AI to automate the transformation process that runs into the Transformation Engine is in our plans. Managing and deploying a Hyperledger Fabric network can be cumbersome, even for testing purposes. Therefore, we would like to implement a tool to automate the deployment of local Hyperledger Fabric networks. We plan to evaluate the performance of the Monitoring System under stressful conditions.

References

Dornelles, E. F., Parahyba, F., Frantz, R. Z., Roos-Frantz, F., Reina-Quintero, A. M., Molina-Jiménez, C., Bocanegra, J., and Sawicki, S. (2022). Advances in a DSL to specify smart contracts for application integration processes. In *Ibero-American Conference on Software Engineering (CIbSE)*, pages 46–60.

[2]https://ejs.co/

An API for Developing Secure Integration Processes *

Regis Schuch[1], Rafael Z. Frantz[1], Antonia M. Reina Quintero[2], José Bocanegra[3]
Sandro Sawicki[1], Fabricia Roos-Frantz[1], Carlos Molina-Jiménez[4]

[1]Unijuí University – Ijuí/RS – Brazil

{regis.schuch, rzfrantz, sawicki, frfrantz}@unijui.edu.br

[2]University of Seville – Seville – Spain

reinaqu@us.es

[3]Universidad Distrital Francisco José de Caldas – Bogotá – Colombia

jjbocanegrag@udistrital.edu.co

[4]University of Cambridge – Cambridge – United Kingdom

carlos.molina@cl.cam.ac.uk

1. Introduction

Integration processes are applications that retrieve data from several remote and independent services, process it locally to implement new services, and potentially transmit data to other integrated services. They are prevalent in smart cities and other domains. Current integration processes protect data in transit but lack mechanisms to prevent data exfiltration during execution. A viable solution is to execute the integration process within a Trusted Execution Environment (TEE), implemented in hardware such as Intel SGX, Amazon Nitro, and Morello Board Compartments[1] [Intel 2025, ARM 2025]. These and similar technologies provide APIs that are (i) technology-specific and (ii) general-purpose. Consequently, TEEs are challenging to employ in integration processes. In this paper, we briefly introduce *iDevS*, our API that aims to address this issue by simplifying and encapsulating the common actions involved in integration processes. Integration processes interact with digital services through *receive* and *send* actions to securely retrieve and transmit data. Implementing these actions within TEEs is challenging due to technological variations in execution models, attestation mechanisms, and security policies. The iDevS API abstracts these complexities, standardising secure integration within TEEs. It provides classes that encapsulate these actions, ensuring secure and attested execution. By transparently handling cryptographic and attestation processes, it enables integration processes to execute seamlessly in TEEs such as Intel SGX, AWS Nitro Enclaves, and Morello Board, offering 29 operations across 9 classes. Due to space constraints, this paper focuses on the *send* action; however, the iDevS API also supports the implementation of other relevant actions, such as deployment, compilation, and compartment creation. To validate iDevS, we developed a complete study of a case with the support of our API, which is available on GitHub[2].

*Research funded by the Co-ordination for the Brazilian Improvement of Higher Education Personnel (CAPES) and the Brazilian National Council for Scientific and Technological Development (CNPq) under grants 311011/2022-5, 309425/2023-9, 402915/2023-2. AETHER-US PID2020-112540RB-C44, ALBA-US TED2021-130355B-C32MICIU/AEI/10.13039/501100011033, "EU NextGenerationEU/PRTR" grants funded Antonia. EPSRC/EP/X015785/1(G115169) grant funded Carlos Molina.

[1]We exclude software-based solutions such as homomorphic encryption, as they remain immature.

[2]https://github.com/gca-research-group/tee-compartimentalisation-study-case

2. Implementing the Send Action

The implementation of the *send* action demands operations from the `Process`, `Service`, and `Launcher` classes of the iDevS API. The `Process` class abstracts operations typically performed by integration processes, such as `getServicePublicKey()` for retrieving a service's public key and `encrypt()` for securing data prior to transmission. The `Service` class encapsulates operations commonly executed by digital services, including `verifyCertificate()` to authenticate the sender and `decrypt()` to restore the original dataset. The `Launcher` class abstracts operations required to mediate secure communication between the integration process and the digital service, such as `lockupService()` to locate the destination service and `getCertificate()` to retrieve the integration process's attestation certificate. Listing 1 presents a pseudocode that shows the use of the iDevS API to encrypt, attest, and validate data during the implementation of a *send* action.

```
Process::
void write (UUID srvId, Dataset data) {
  Key puK_ = getServicePublicKey(srvId);
  EncDataset dataEnc = encrypt(puK_, data);
  new Launcher().write(srvId, this.progId, dataEnc);
}

Launcher::
void write (UUID srvId, UUID progId, EncData data) {
  Service srv = lockupService(srvId);
  SignedCertificate signedCert = getCertificate(progId);
  new Service().post(signedCert, data);
}
```

```
Service::
void post(SignedCertificate signedCert, EncData data) {
  boolean verified = verifyCertificate(signedCert);
  if (verified) {
    Dataset data = decrypt(this.prK_, data);
    storeLocalData(data);
  }
}
```

Listing 1. API operations (in bold) to implement the *send* action.

The *send* action begins with the execution of the `write()` operation in the `Process` class, taking as parameters the ID of the target service and the dataset to be sent to the service. This operation starts by retrieving the service's public key, the it encrypts the dataset, and creates a `Launcher` object to invoke the `write()` operation on it by passing as parameters the ID of the service, the ID of the process, and the encrypted dataset. The `write()` operation in the `Launcher` class starts by locating the target service and retrieving the integration process's attestation certificate. It then creates a `Service` object to invoke the `post()` operation, forwarding to the service the signed certificate and the encrypted dataset. The `post()` operation begins by validating the attestation certificate, then it decrypts the dataset, and so securely stores the data locally.

3. Conclusion and Future Work

We present *iDevS*, a domain-specific, technology-agnostic API to secure integration processes in TEEs, mitigating data exfiltration during execution. The iDevS API abstracts integration actions, such as *receive* and *send*, from the TEE execution and attestation mechanisms, enabling deployment across different TEEs without requiring modifications to the integration logic. We validate its effectiveness through a study of a case implemented with Morello Board compartments. Future work will assess the generalisability of the API in TEEs such as Intel SGX, AWS Nitro Enclaves, and ARM TrustZone.

References

ARM (2025). ARM Morello Program. `https://www.arm.com/architecture/cpu/morello`. [online: access in 21-jan-2025].

Intel (2025). Intel® Software Guard Extensions (Intel® SGX). `https://www.intel.com/content/www/us/en/products/docs/accelerator-engines/software-guard-extensions.html`. [online: access in 21-jan-2025].

¿Cómo perciben los ingenieros de software su productividad trabajando de forma remota?

Aurora Vizcaíno[1], Gabriela Aranda[2], Elvira Rolón[3], Kelly Garces[4], Juan Pablo Soto[5]
[1]Universidad de Castilla-La Mancha – Ciudad Real, España
[2]Universidad Nacional de Comahue – Neuquén, Argentina
[3]Universidad Autónoma de Tamaulipas – Tampico, México
[4]Universidad de los Andes – Bogotá, Colombia
[5]Universidad de Sonora – Hermosillo, México

aurora.vizcaino@uclm.es, gabriela.aranda@fi.uncoma-edu.ar, erolon@docentes.uat.edu.mx, kj.garces971@uniandes.edu.co, juanpablo.soto@unison.mx

Resumen. *El trabajo remoto se afianzó tras la pandemia de COVID-19. Mientras grandes empresas buscan el retorno a oficinas, este estudio analiza la percepción de ingenieros de software en México, España, Colombia y Argentina sobre el teletrabajo.*

1. Introducción

El desarrollo distribuido y global ha sido una tendencia en el software durante décadas [Manjavacas et al., 2020]. La pandemia de COVID-19 impulsó la adopción del teletrabajo, una modalidad que sigue vigente y enfrenta desafíos globales como la comunicación, la coordinación, el control y la gestión del conocimiento [Ozkaya, 2021; Šmite et al., 2023a, 2023b]. Los distintos tipos de formas de trabajar han sido caracterizados por [Šmite et al., 2023a] como: *presencialidad* (siempre en la oficina); *office-first* (más tiempo en la oficina que en casa), *office-remote mix* (enfoque que permite total flexibilidad), *remote-first* (que implica trabajar más tiempo fuera de la oficina que en ésta) y modo *remoto* (teletrabajo todos los días). Aunque el teletrabajo aporta flexibilidad, puede afectar la productividad y generar aislamiento, reduciendo la cohesión del equipo. Empresas como Amazon y Google promueven el retorno a oficinas, argumentando beneficios en el rendimiento [Ebert et al., 2024]. Este artículo analiza si los empleados concuerdan con esa visión en España, México, Colombia y Argentina.

2. Metodología de trabajo

Para llevar a cabo este estudio, se realizó una encuesta (https://github.com/GrupoAlarcos/Encuesta-de-productividad/blob/main/EncuestaProductividad.pdf). Se recibieron 287 respuestas, de las cuales 250 fueron válidas tras eliminar encuestas incompletas o de personas sin experiencia presencial. La muestra final incluyó 25 respuestas de Argentina, 65 de Colombia, 59 de España y 101 de México.

3. Resultados obtenidos

La mayoría de los encuestados tenían entre 25 y 45 años de edad, predominando hombres (67%). En Argentina hay más encuestadas mujeres (33%) y en Colombia el menor porcentaje (12%). En cuanto a experiencia, la mayoría en España, Colombia y

Argentina cuenta con una experiencia de 5 a 30 años, mientras que en México predominan los menos experimentados.

Más del 48% trabaja en grandes empresas y la mayoría en España, Colombia y México lo hace para multinacionales. En cuanto a modalidad laboral, la mayoría trabaja 4-5 días a la semana desde casa, predominando el modelo '*remote-first*'.

En términos de productividad, más del 60% considera que su rendimiento teletrabajando es igual o mayor al de la oficina. En Argentina y Colombia, destacan un aumento en la concentración al teletrabajar. Sobre cuestiones técnicas, la mayoría tiene conexión a Internet igual o mejor en casa y las herramientas de comunicación no afectan negativamente su rendimiento.

En cuanto a trabajo en equipo, la percepción general es que la productividad del equipo se mantiene o mejora. Sin embargo, la compartición de conocimiento, la confianza y la colaboración pueden verse afectadas, especialmente en Colombia y México. La falta de cohesión y relaciones personales preocupa en algunos casos, aunque la mayoría no percibe un impacto negativo en su productividad.

4. Conclusiones

Los resultados sugieren que los empresarios deben desarrollar estrategias para mejorar la colaboración y confianza en equipos remotos. Si optan por el regreso a oficinas, deberían ofrecer incentivos como horarios flexibles y facilidades para mejorar el balance laboral.

Agradecimientos

Nos gustaría agradecer a Manuel Casas su colaboración generando la encuesta y gráficos.

Referencias

Ebert, C. (2024). Industry Trends 2024: Innovation needs competence. In Computer, vol. 57(4), pp. 93-98. https://doi.org/10.1109/mc.2024.3364288

Manjavacas, A., Vizcaíno, A., Ruíz, F. & Piattini, M. (2020). Global software development governance: Challenges and solutions. In Journal of Software: Evolution and Process, vol. 32(10). https://doi.org/10.1002/smr.2266

Ozkaya, I. (2021). The Future of Software Engineering Work. IEEE Software, 38(05), pp. 3-6. https://doi.org/10.1109/ms.2021.3089729

Šmite D., Christensen, E., Tell, P. & Russo, D. (2023a). The Future Workplace: Characterizing the Spectrum of Hybrid Work Arrangements for Software Teams. IEEE Software, vol. 40(02), pp. 34-41. https://doi.org/10.1109/ms.2022.3230289

Šmite, D., Moe, N., Klotins, E. & Gonzalez-Huerta, J. (2023b). From forced Working-From-Home to voluntary working-from-anywhere: Two revolutions in telework. Journal of Systems and Software, Vol. 195, 111509. https://doi.org/10.1016/j.jss.2022.111509

Unraveling Software Antipatterns and Smells Definitions

Richard Rivera[1], Pamela Flores[1], Carlos E. Anchundia[1], Marcela Mosquera[1], Alejandro Jiménez[1], Xavier Carpio[1]

[1]Departamento de Informática y Ciencias de la Computación.
Escuela Politécnica Nacional. Quito, Ecuador

{richard.rivera01, pamela.flores, carlos.anchundia evelyn.mosquerae, alejandro.jimenez, xavier.carpio}@epn.edu.ec

Abstract. *Software technical debt may persist if the root cause is misidentified. We argue that this stems from misconceptions about antipatterns and smells. This article reviews the literature to clarify their similarities and differences. Findings suggest that both terms are used interchangeably, with "smell" being more common, though this ambiguity may affect optimal solutions in software projects.*

1. Introduction and Methodology

Antipatterns and smells concepts have become essential for identifying and mitigating design and implementation flaws. "Antipattern" was introduced by [Brown et al. 1998] to define recurring poor solutions to common software problems. On the other hand, "smells" serve as heuristics to identify potential issues in source code [Fowler et al. 2018]. Although the terms could confuse academic and industry contexts when reviewing publications, forums, and books. This research examines the current use of these terms and their practical implications through the questions: **RQ1:** Are antipatterns and smells the same? **RQ2:** What are the implications of confusing these terms?

An exploratory review of the literature was carried out, taking Fowler and Brown as references, given their proposal of concepts and classifications. In addition, the exploration included articles related to classification proposals and taxonomies of antipatterns and smells, among which Neil, Laplante, Wakem Jerzyks, and Madeysky stand out. We gather information such as definitions, classification, structure, and impact on projects.

2. Key Results

Similarities. In software project management, the terms are used as synonyms to denote technical debt issues. Also, researchers and practitioners prioritize problem-solving over conceptual distinctions [Tahir et al. 2018]. Additionally, there are antipatterns, such as "Spaghetti Code," which can be addressed based on their impact on the project. Structurally, researchers organize antipatterns and smells into catalogs, which exhibit striking similarities, potentially confusing for an inexperienced observer (Fig. 1).

Differences. We have grouped different classification schemes into "collections". At first glance, it can be seen that antipatterns focus on high-level context, while smells focus on low-level aspects of implementation (Fig. 1). It is a finding that smells such as "Blob" or "Functional Decomposition" were first classified as antipatterns by [Brown et al. 1998]. Conversely, the presence of antipatterns can be revealed through the manifestation of smells, necessitating a potential restructuring. However, a smell can be identified through various technological tools associated with basic refactoring, such as clean code principles [Sabir et al. 2019].

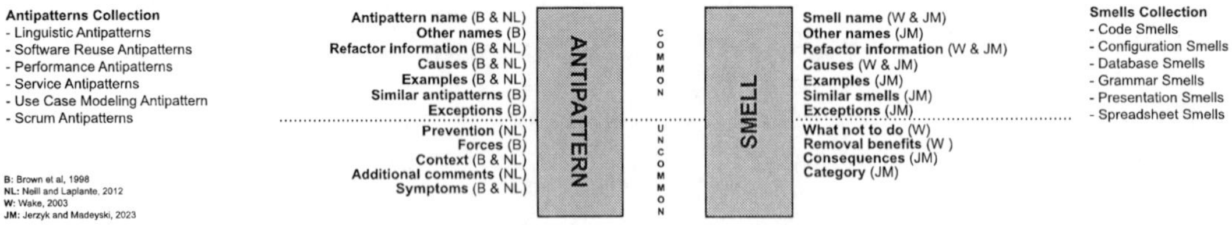

Figure 1. Antipattern and Smell relationship and analogy

3. Discussion

RQ1, antipatterns and smells are different, though both negatively impact software maintainability. Their definitions should not be overlapped, obscuring their true significance. Antipatterns and smells are related to different levels of software project issues.
RQ2, smells are like visible moisture on a wall, signaling underlying issues, whereas antipatterns resemble hidden plumbing leaks that require deeper investigation. While smells can be quickly addressed, antipatterns demand extensive structural changes and a thorough understanding of the development environment (Fig. 2).

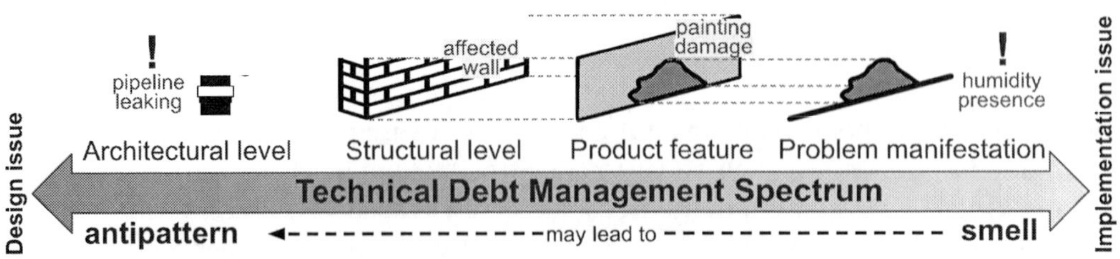

Figure 2. Antipattern and Smell relationship and analogy

4. Conclusions and Future Work

It has been examined how the terms antipattern and smell are often interpreted as similar. However, this can be a mistake when dealing with technical debt due to possible implications for treating causes within a software project. With this knowledge, future work will explore the traceability between antipatterns and smells to distinguish these concepts better.

References

Brown, W. H., Malveau, R. C., McCormick, H. W. S., and Mowbray, T. J. (1998). *AntiPatterns: refactoring software, architectures, and projects in crisis.*

Fowler, M., Beck, K., Brant, J., and Opdyke, W. (2018). *Refactoring: improving the design of existing code.* Addison-Wesley.

Sabir, F., Palma, F., Rasool, G., Guéhéneuc, Y.-G., and Moha, N. (2019). A systematic literature review on the detection of smells and their evolution in object-oriented and service-oriented systems. *Software: Practice and Experience*, 49(1):3–39.

Tahir, A., Yamashita, A., Licorish, S., Dietrich, J., and Counsell, S. (2018). Can you tell me if it smells? a study on how developers discuss code smells and anti-patterns in stack overflow. In *Proceedings of the 22nd International Conference on Evaluation and Assessment in Software Engineering 2018*, EASE '18, page 68–78. ACM.

Gestión de autorización de acceso a microservicios en sistemas de gestión pública: una propuesta de automatización

Rafael Palau H.[1,2], Magalí Gonzalez T. [2], Luca Cernuzzi [2]

[1] Ministerio de Economía y Finanzas (Paraguay)

[2] Departamento de Electrónica e Informática, Universidad Católica "Nuestra Señora de la Asunción" (UC) – Asunción – Paraguay

rafael_palau@mef.gov..py,{mgonzalez,lcernuzz}@uc.edu.py

Abstract. *This study presents SIARE-Artefactos, to automate the registration of access authorization to resources. It is designed with microservices, Java Spring Boot Starter, and OAuth 2.0 integrated into CI/CD processes. The results demonstrate a 60% reduction in configuration time and enhanced system reliability.*

1. Antecedentes y Motivación

La modernización de los sistemas de software de la administración pública adopta cada vez más arquitecturas de microservicios [Fowler & Lewis, 2014]. Los enfoques tradicionales para la gestión de recursos y la autorización a menudo se basan en procesos manuales poco eficientes, propensos a errores y difíciles de escalar. OAuth 2.0[1] ha surgido como un estándar de la industria para la autorización abierta en aplicaciones web, proporcionando flujos específicos de autorización para servicios web.

El Sistema Integrado de Administración de Recursos del Estado Paraguayo (SIARE) gestiona más de 780 endpoints REST, 2.198 acciones HTTP y 62 perfiles de usuario; un desafío considerable, especialmente en lo que respecta al registro y autorización de acceso. Cada nueva implementación o adición de perfil requiere un esfuerzo manual de configuración de 125 minutos por perfil y entre 17 y 75 minutos por back-end. La solución SIARE-Artefactos, diseñada para automatizar el registro de la autorización de acceso dentro del SIARE basado en el sistema SIARE-Autodiscovery[2], que gestiona automáticamente el registro y despliegue de API [Guayuan et al., 2023].

2. SIARE-Artefactos y resultados experimentales

El proceso (Figura 1) comienza con la identificación de anotaciones La aplicación escanea los Controllers al momento del inicio de la aplicación en tiempo de despliegue. Estas anotaciones, como @GetMapping, identifican endpoints, métodos y acciones que deben registrarse automáticamente. Luego de validar las configuraciones de entorno, el sistema registra en back-usuarios (sistema de autorización) todos los recursos identificados, asegurando que todos los endpoints, métodos HTTP y acciones asociadas estén correctamente identificados, documentados y autorizados.

---

[1] https://oauth.net/2/

[2] https://gitlab.com/dgic.mh.py/SIARE

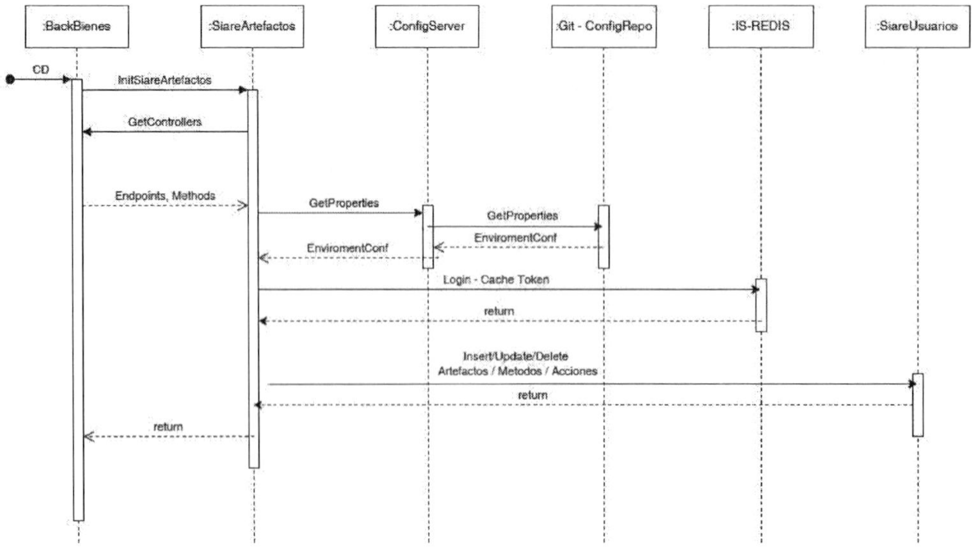

Figura 1. Secuencia de SIARE-Artefactos

La arquitectura y los objetos del sistema se dividieron en cuatro capas principales, cada una con un propósito específico para mejorar la mantenibilidad y la eficiencia operativa. La **Capa Cliente**, es responsable de gestionar la comunicación con los sistemas de back-end. El **Módulo de Inicio**, inicializa el proceso de registro automatizado de recursos escaneando las anotaciones en los controladores de Spring Boot. La capa, **Capa Proveedora**, gestiona las interacciones con las API. Finalmente, la **Capa de Configuración** gestiona la configuración centralizada de todo el sistema.

Tabla 1. Tiempo (horas) mensual dedicado.

Proyecto	2024-7	2024-8	2024-9	2024-10	2024-11	2024-12
SIGEBYS	30,5	48	41	7	10	14
Total	119,25	85,75	46,5	48,75	20	65,5
Promedio trimestral	42,50	35,17	39,83	32,00	**19,33**	10,33
Porcentaje de variación	103,66%	82,75%	113,27%	80,33%	**60,42%**	53,45%

SIARE-Autodiscovery logró reducir el tiempo promedio de registro de recursos de un rango de 17 a 75 minutos a un impresionante intervalo de 3 a 5 segundos. La validación reveló una notable reducción del 68% en errores de configuración y resultó en una reducción del 60% en el esfuerzo manual del equipo (tabla 1), evidenciando el potencial para transformar los sistemas de administración pública a gran escala.

Referencias

Fowler, M., & Lewis, J. (2014). Microservices: A definition of this new architectural term. Retrieved from: martinfowler.com.

Guayuan, M. B., Mello-Román, J. C., Heikel, R. F. P., Cremona, M. L., Aquino, M. A., Yegros, I. G., & Wenninger, C. M. (2023, June). Automatic Deployment of Microservices in API Manager. *CISTI 2023 Proceedings*.

Preliminary Results of a Systematic Mapping Study of AIOps Practices and Trends

Juan Ignacio Irabedra[1] **, Martín Solari** [1]

[1] Universidad ORT Uruguay

juanignacioirabedra@gmail.com,

martin.solari@ort.edu.uy

Abstract. *This work aims at identifying the main AIOps techniques reported in peer-reviewed literature in the last six years (1) and classify the techniques according to what software quality attribute to they contribute to. It presents the preliminary results of a systematic mapping study considering peer-reviewed literature. 72 peer-reviewed studies were analyzed in order to extract strategies and practices. Anomaly detection and fault prediction were the strategies most often applied on AIOps. Classical machine learning techniques, as well as deep learning techniques were the most frequently found groups of techniques in literature. Availability and maintainability are the most frequently software quality attributes improved by applying AIOps techniques.*

1. Introduction

Organizations have reacted to an emerging culture of acceleration, and in particular in the collection of feedback. This enables IT organizations to produce large volumes of real-time operational data.

At the same time the adoption of AI in the software industry also grew larger [Durrani et al. 2024]. The availability of large operational records as well as the know-how of machine learning (ML) models and artificial intelligence (AI) in general settles the ground for an emerging trend: using AI to enhance software development and operation, which would be named AIOps.

AIOps is a set of organizational practices and AI tools that use vast amounts of data created by disparate systems to assist IT organizations operations that lead to more effective and faster decisions to resolve operational incidents even before clients report them [Zhang et al. 2024] [Potts and Carver 2024].

The research questions that guide this study are:

- RQ1. What software engineering problems do AIOps practices solve?
- RQ2. What AI strategies and tools are used for solving software engineering problems?
- RQ3. Which software quality attributes are impacted when applying AIOps?

2. Results

This section presents the findings after analyzing 72 peer-reviewed primary studies published between 2020 and 2025.

The most commonly addressed problems in the AIOps practice are anomaly detection, defect prediction, ops data management and root cause analysis. The number of occurrences of each problem in the primary studies is presented in table 1.

Table 1. Software engineering problems results

Software engineering problem	Occurrences
Anomaly detection	28
Defect prediction	11
Ops data management	8
Root cause analysis	8
Resource allocation	5
Metric prediction	5
ML lifecycle support	2
Support development	2
Correlation analysis	2
Change point detection	1

Table 2 presents the frequency in which software quality attributes were the main quality attributes impacted on the studies considered by the systematic mapping of literature when solving software engineering problems.

Table 2. Software quality attributes are impacted when applying AIOps

Software quality attributes are impacted when applying AIOps	
Software quality attribute	Occurrences
Availability	44
Maintainability	18
Security	5
Performance	5
Functionality	2

3. Artifact Availability

Following open science transparency and reproducibility principles, all research artifacts involved have been published and made available on Zenodo and can be accessed here.

References

Durrani, U. K., Akpinar, M., Fatih Adak, M., Talha Kabakus, A., Maruf Ozturk, M., and Saleh, M. (2024). A decade of progress: A systematic literature review on the integration of ai in software engineering phases and activities (2013-2023). *IEEE Access*, 12.

Potts, W. C. and Carver, C. (2024). Best practices implementing aiops in large organizations. In *2024 International Conference on Smart Applications, Communications and Networking (SmartNets)*.

Zhang, C., Chen, W., and Xie, Y. (2024). Research on aiops-based intelligent monitoring technology for meteorological business. In *2024 IEEE 7th Advanced Information Technology, Electronic and Automation Control Conference (IAEAC)*.

Personality, Security, and User Satisfaction in Context-Aware Applications

Nelly Condori-Fernandez[1], Denisse Muñante[2], Franci Suni-Lopez[3], Maya Daneva[4]

[1] Centro Singular de Investigación en Tecnoloxías Intelixentes (CiTIUS), Universidade de Santiago de Compostela – Santiago de Compostela – Spain

[2]ensIIE & SAMOVAR – Évry – France

[3]Laboratorio de Inteligencia Artificial – Universidad de Lima – Perú

[4]University of Twente – The Netherlands

n.condori.fernandez@usc.es, denisse.munantearzapalo@ensiie.fr

fsuni@ulima.edu.pe, m.daneva@utwente.nl

Abstract. *This study explores how personality traits influence the perception of security and satisfaction of context-aware applications. Through a web-based survey using animated videos, we find that openness and agreeableness influence security perceptions, while satisfaction is more context-dependent. A positive correlation was also found between perceived security and satisfaction.*

1. Introduction

Context-aware applications play a critical role across various domains, requiring a careful balance between security and user satisfaction. These applications, which adapt to users' context (e.g., location, behavior, preferences), introduce unique challenges in terms of how security and satisfaction are perceived. Although previous studies have recognized the importance of both attributes, there is a lack of empirical evidence on how personality traits influence user perceptions on these applications. This study extends previous work [Condori-Fernández et al. 2020] by addressing three research questions: how users perceive satisfaction in terms of trust and usefulness (RQ1), the relationship between perceived security and satisfaction (RQ2), and how personality traits influence perceptions of security and satisfaction in context-aware applications (RQ3). The artifacts of this study are available in[1].

2. Study Design, Data analysis and Key findings

Study design: Participants were divided into two groups (engineering and non-engineering) and assessed security, satisfaction, and personality traits after watching two animated videos (see Note [1]): one presenting the core functionality of the app, and another highlighting potential security vulnerabilities.

Data analysis: Descriptive statistics summarized participant demographics and initial responses. Pearson and Spearman correlation tests examined the relationships between perceived security and satisfaction. Regression analysis and non-parametric tests explored the influence of personality traits on these perceptions.

[1]https://osf.io/c8mnr/?view_only=381f8fb6916f4783886a548e6f00d480

Key findings: For RQ1, participants with engineering background consistently rated trust and usefulness as highly important, while non-engineering participants tended to perceived their importance with a low intensity and showed more variability influenced by context. Regarding RQ2, strong positive correlations were found between perceived security and satisfaction. In general, it does not depend on the participants' background, however for non-engineering participants this correlation was more evident. For RQ3, openness was associated with higher perceived importance of confidentiality and integrity, while agreeableness showed mixed associations with authentication and accountability. No significant link was found between personality traits and satisfaction. These relationships are visually summarized in Figure 1, which highlights the correlations for RQ2 (green links) and the associations for RQ3 (red links), distinguishing significant and non-significant links.

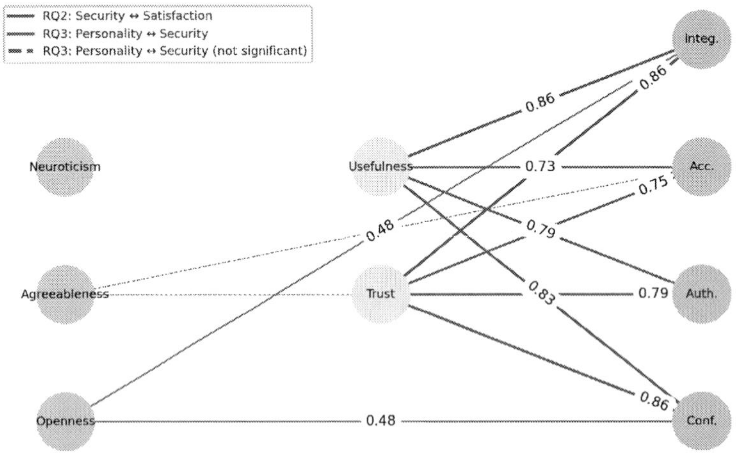

Figura 1. Relationships among personality traits, perceived security, and user satisfaction (not grouped by participant background). Conf. = Confidentiality, Auth. = Authenticity, Acc. = Accountability, Integ. = Integrity.

3. Conclusions

Our findings suggest that user perceptions of security and satisfaction are interdependent, with personality traits influencing security perceptions. This highlights the need for user-centered security design. Threats to validity include the post-hoc formulation of research questions and the use of a partial Big Five Inventory, which may limit the personality analysis. In addition, the representativeness of the sample and interpretation variability between backgrounds may affect generalizability. Further studies should use more diverse samples and explore how contextual and cultural factors shape the role of personality in perceptions of security and satisfaction.

Referências

Condori-Fernández, N., Suni-Lopez, F., Muñante, D., and Daneva, M. (2020). How can personality influence perception on security of context-aware applications? In *Proceedings in 10th International Workshop on Socio-Technical Aspects in Security*, Guildford, United Kingdom. LNCS.

Using Gamification to Teach Security Analysis in Higher Education

Clara Ayora[1], Jose Luis de la Vara[1]
[1]Universidad de Castilla-La Mancha
Avda. España s/n, 02071 – Albacete – Spain
{clara.ayora, joseluis.delavara}@uclm.es

Abstract. *Teaching security analysis at university allows future professionals to acquire with the necessary skills to protect and maintain the integrity of digital infrastructures. This work presents a board game and its practical use for teaching security analysis in 1st-year bachelor students. The game has been employed in the past four years and our perception of use is positive. Being a game with a simple and most-likely known mechanics, it could be adapted and used by other educators to teach software engineering topics.*

1. Introduction

Security analysis is an integral aspect of requirements engineering to ensure systems are robust and resilient against potential threats [McGraw 2004]. As future professionals, university computer science students will design and maintain essential systems, e.g., e-banking. Understanding security analysis is vital to protect data, ensure privacy, and safeguard against cyber threats [Stallings 2015]. Early learning enables students to identify vulnerabilities, implement security measures, and respond to incidents.

Simultaneously, gamification has gained attention in higher education [Chung 2019, Schreuders 2016]. Defined as applying game-design elements in non-game contexts [Chung 2019], gamification enhances student engagement, motivation, and learning outcomes. By leveraging motivational factors like rewards and progress tracking, gamification creates a dynamic and interactive educational experience.

Following [Schreuders 2016], we present a game for teaching security analysis in higher education. It is called '*Cyberpatrol*' and is a board game with a mechanics like the '*game of the goose*'. Upon landing on the squares, players must answer whether a statement about security analysis is true or false. The statements are about *Security Fundamental Concepts*, *Encryption Types*, *Protection Measures,* and *Security History*.

2. Game description and discussion

The board of the game can be found in [Ayora 2025]. The mechanics is as follows: **1.** Students are grouped in teams of four students each. **2.** Teams start with 0 points. **3.** A playing order is established for the teams. **4.** Using turns, each team rolls a die to determine how many squares they move on the board. **5.** Depending on the type of square a team lands on (Figure 1), they must answer a question about *security concepts* (square with a light bulb), *encryption* (padlock), *protection* (shield), or *history* (clock and scroll), *suffer an attack* (hacker), *challenge another team* (swords), or *roll the die again* (pipe). **6.** Teams will earn 3 points if they answer correctly or lose 1 point if they answer incorrectly. **7.** When suffering an attack, a team will lose 5 points. **8.** When landing on a challenge square, the corresponding team can challenge another by selecting two questions that both teams need to answer. If one team wins (i.e., one team has more correct answers than the other), it will earn 5 points, and the losing team will lose 3 points. In case of a tie, the team that issued the challenge will lose 1 point and the challenged team will gain 1 point. **9.** During the game, why a statement is true or false is explained if needed. **10.** A game ends when a team reaches the final square or when the teaching session finishes **11.** The team with the highest number points is the winner.

Figure 1. Types of squares

The game has been used the past four years in a 1st-year course on "*Information Systems*" of a Bilingual (in Spanish and English) Bachelor's Degree in Computer Science and Engineering at the *University of Castilla-La Mancha* in *Albacete, Spain.* This course introduces what information systems are, their role, and how they are managed and used (including security aspects). Around 50 students, including exchange ones, attend the course each year. Being a 1st-year course, students have no (or very little) knowledge about security analysis. To encourage students' participation, winning students are rewarded with 0.25 additional points to their grade for the exam on security analysis. Security analysis is the last unit of the course. The board game is currently implemented in Excel. We have used it as part of a content review session.

During these four years, our perception and experience using the game has been positive and we plan to continue using it. First, the game has remained unchanged since its initial use, beyond adding questions, showing a suitable design for teaching security analysis. Second, students appear to enjoy playing, especially the challenges, showing interest in security analysis and eagerness to win the game. Third, we consider that the game contributes to students' learning on security analysis. These perceptions could be further analyzed via empirical studies, e.g., surveys and experiments.

Given its simple mechanics and design, the game can be easily adapted to other topics, e.g., by defining different question categories and symbols. Educators could use the game to teach (or reinforce) software engineering topics such as software modelling or processes. As potential improvements, multiple-choice questions could be used instead of true/false ones. This would increase the game difficulty. Besides, the board game could be implemented in a mobile app so that students can play (alone or in groups) even after the teaching session. This could help students with the course exam.

Acknowledgement. This work has received funding from the REBECCA project (HORIZON-KDT 101097224; MCIN/AEI PCI2022-135043-2; NextGen.EU/PRTR).

References

Ayora, C., et al. (2025). Cyberpatrol-game board. *CIbSE 2025*. Zenodo. https://doi.org/10.5281/zenodo.15088573

McGraw, G. (2004). Software security. *IEEE Security & Privacy*, *2*(2), 80-83.

Stallings, W., et al (2015). *Computer security: principles and practice*. Pearson.

Chung, C. et al. (2019). Students' acceptance of gamification in higher education. *(IJGBL)*, *9*(2), 1-19.

Schreuders, Z. C. et al. (2016). Gamification for teaching and learning computer security in higher education. In ASE 16.

A Non-Intrusive Model for Capturing Metrics for Early Project Estimation in Agile Environments

José Gamaliel Rivera Ibarra[1], Gilberto Borrego[1], Ramón René Palacio Cinco[2]

[1]Instituto Tecnológico de Sonora
Ciudad Obregón, Sonora, México

[2]Unidad Navojoa, Instituto Tecnológico de Sonora, México
Navojoa, Sonora, México

{joseg.rivera,gborrego,ramon.palacio88271}@potros.itson.edu.mx

Abstract. *Early estimation is crucial in agile projects, but a lack of detailed initial requirements often makes it inaccurate. While data-driven models improve accuracy, the absence of company-specific databases hinders the reliance on historical data. This work presents a non-intrusive model for capturing key metrics (e.g., software size) in agile settings to facilitate building these databases. The model aims to support a hybrid estimation approach that combines data-driven techniques with expert judgment. Preliminary results highlight the need for automated metric capture to enhance the reliability of early agile estimations.*

1. Introduction

Early estimation is fundamental in agile projects to ensure their feasibility, plan activities, and allocate resources efficiently. Nevertheless, initial estimates are often imprecise, as illustrated by the well-known Cone of Uncertainty [Barry et al. 1981]. This difficulty is accentuated in agile environments due to the changing nature of requirements and the priority given to the early delivery of customer value. While data-driven estimation methods promise objectivity and greater accuracy [Alsaadi and Saeedi 2022], their application in agile organizations is limited by the frequent absence of relevant historical data. Additionally, existing predictive models are often based on outdated information, lack specific organizational context, and employ non-standardized metrics [Rivera et al. 2024]. The agile philosophy, focused on maximizing customer-delivered value (as defined in the Agile Manifesto [Beck et al. 2001]), can generate resistance in teams to adopt complementary activities, such as project metric collection, if their immediate value is not evident. In this context, our research addresses the lack of non-intrusive mechanisms for metric capture, a factor that significantly hinders the adoption of hybrid estimation approaches that integrate both data and expert judgment. Therefore, the general objective of this research is to develop an inherently non-intrusive model for capturing key software metrics (size and quality) and development process metrics (effort and productivity) in agile projects, and to facilitate the creation of historical databases for hybrid estimation models to improve their accuracy and reliability. To achieve this objective, we seek to answer the following research questions:

- How can agile teams non-intrusively capture key software size and quality metrics, as well as team effort and productivity metrics, to create historical databases?

- What impact does the availability of historical data have on the accuracy of estimations in agile projects?
- How can a hybrid estimation approach that combines historical data-based methods with expert judgment be integrated into agile environments?

2. Methodology

We will conduct this research in three phases: (1) **Understanding** through a literature review and diagnosing professional practice. (2) **Designing and Calibrating** the non-intrusive capture model and its prototype. (3) **Validating and Evaluating** through a case study in a real agile environment.

3. Preliminary Results and Proposal

Preliminary findings reveal a strong dependence on expert judgment, resulting in inconsistent estimations and a scarcity of historical data for data-driven methods. To address this, we propose an automated tool that captures key metrics (size, quality, effort, productivity) nonintrusively by integrating with agile tools. This tool will enable the construction of standardized historical databases, facilitating the integration of hybrid estimation models that combine data and expert judgment to improve accuracy and reliability, utilizing automated tools and a continuous feedback mechanism.

4. Next Steps

- *Model Design*: Define key metrics, data flow, and non-intrusive integration criteria.
- *Model Extension*: Investigate the incorporation of additional data sources.
- *Implementation and Calibration*: Develop a prototype and calibrate it using postmortem projects.
- *Experimental Evaluation*: Evaluate the model's effectiveness in an agile environment and collect team feedback.

5. Conclusions

This research proposes a non-intrusive model for capturing key metrics in agile projects. It seeks to overcome the lack of historical data and facilitate the adoption of hybrid estimation approaches. We expect this model to improve the accuracy and reliability of estimations in agile environments, optimizing planning and resource allocation.

References

Alsaadi, B. and Saeedi, K. (2022). Data-driven effort estimation techniques of agile user stories: a systematic literature review. *Artificial Intelligence Review*, 55:5485–5516.

Barry, B. et al. (1981). Software engineering economics. *New York*, 197:40.

Beck, K., Beedle, M., van Bennekum, A., Cockburn, A., Cunningham, W., Fowler, M., Grenning, J., Highsmith, J., Hunt, A., Jeffries, R., Kern, J., Marick, B., Martin, R. C., Mellor, S., Schwaber, K., Sutherland, J., and Thomas, D. (2001). Manifesto for agile software development.

Rivera, J. G., Borrego, G., and Palacio, R. R. (2024). Early estimation in agile software development projects: A systematic mapping study. *Informatics*, 11.

Challenges in adopting ISO/IEC 29110 standardized processes in agile VSEs

Luis T. Portela-Peñúñuri[1], Gilberto Borrego[1], Ramón R. Palacio[2]

[1]Department of Computing and Design - Sonora Institute of Technology. Ciudad Obregón, Sonora, México.

[2]Sonora Institute of Technology - Unidad Navojoa, Sonora, México.

tadeo.portela@potros.itson.edu.mx,
{gborrego,ramon.palacio}@itson.edu.mx

Abstract. *Very small software entities (VSEs) face challenges when attempting to incorporate structured quality practices into their agile environment. The ISO/IEC 29110 standard aims to address these challenges; however, its adoption still faces some issues. This study identifies adoption barriers through an ongoing systematic mapping aiming to prioritize those with the highest impact on standard adoption. Preliminary results highlight organizational barriers, technical challenges, and psychosocial factors. These findings lay the groundwork for future research to compare factors with case studies, aiming to develop an adaptive framework that closes the gap between agility and standardization, enabling VSEs to adopt critical disciplines of the standard.*

Keywords: ISO/IEC 29110, Agile Methods, VSEs, Systematic Mapping

1. Introduction

Very small entities (VSEs) are vital to the global economy, particularly in the software industry. There's a growing need for these organizations to adopt engineering practices that ensure reliable, efficient, and secure software that meets user requirements [Muñoz et al., 2021][Stojanov, 2022]. However, VSEs often struggle to implement standardized processes, such as those in the ISO/IEC 29110 standard [ISO, 2015][Muñoz et al., 2021], due to perceived rigidity and misalignment with agile principles [Muñoz et al., 2018]. While VSEs prioritize agility to adapt quickly to changes in software development [Beck et al., 2001], the challenge remains: How can they adopt standardized processes without losing their agility? The objective of this study is to identify and analyze the key factors that hinder the adoption of standardized practices within VSEs. Additionally, the study aims to explore these barriers in practice through interviews and focus groups with experts seeking a deeper understanding of the challenges VSEs encounter when implementing standards.

2. Methods

The study uses a systematic mapping review (SMR) following Kitchenham and Charters (2007) guidelines, focusing on VSEs and their challenges in adopting the ISO/IEC 29110 standard. The search string utilized boolean operations AND(&), OR(|) and produced: ("iso/iec 29110"|"iso 29110" | "29110 standard" | iso/iec29110) & (implementation | adoption | deployment) & (challenges | obstacles | issues) in ACM, IEEExplore, Wiley, SpringerLink, and ScienceDirect databases.

The inclusion criteria focus on studies published in English from 2011 to 2024 that explicitly mention the standard and present empirical data—such as case studies, surveys, or interviews—related to its implementation. Acceptable sources include academic journals, international conferences, and book chapters. Exclusion criteria include duplicate publications, abstracts, opinion articles, editorials, and PowerPoint presentations. We identified 339 studies, narrowing it down to 280 after removing duplicates. From these, 51 articles were selected for preliminary analysis based on title, abstract, or introduction criteria. A quality assessment is pending, along with qualitative research involving expert interviews and focus groups. The insights from this research will be analyzed to compare them with the findings from the SMR.

3. Preliminary results and conclusions

51 articles were analyzed and the data was extracted[i] to report preliminary results:

Fig. 1 results for each source by year and % of mentions for each factor

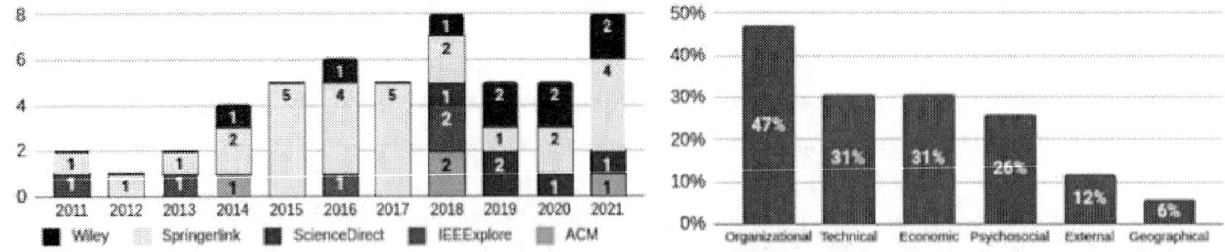

Preliminary results show that VSEs face significant challenges in implementing standards, such as resource constraints, knowledge gaps and resistance to change. Technical issues, skill shortages and financial limitations also hinder adoption. Additionally, motivation and perceived value are key psychosocial factors. Understanding all factors is essential for bridging the gap between agility and standards.

References

Beck, K., Beedle, M., Bennekum, A. van, Cockburn, A., Cunningham, W., Fowler, M., ... & Thomas, D. (2001). Manifesto for Agile Software Development. retrieved from https://agilemanifesto.org/

ISO (2015). ISO/IEC 29110-2-1:2015 - Software engineering - Lifecycle profiles for VSEs: Framework and taxonomy. ISO https://www.iso.org/standard/62712.html

Kitchenham, B. and Charters, S. (2007) Guidelines for Performing Systematic Literature Reviews in Software Engineering, Technical Report EBSE 2007-001, Keele University and Durham University Joint Report.

Muñoz, M., Mejía, J., Peña, A., Laporte, C. Y., & Gasca-Hurtado, G. P. (2021). Beyond factors that motivate the adoption of the ISO/IEC 29110 in Mexico: An exploratory study of the implementation pace of this standard and the benefits observed. IET Software, 15(6), 412–427. https://doi.org/10.1049/sfw2.12041

Stojanov, Z. (2022, June). Software maintenance management in micro-software companies. Southeast European Review of Business and Economics, 3(1), 75–92. https://doi.org/10.20544/serbe.05.01.22.p05

[i] The artifacts associated with this submission are publicly available on Zenodo under DOI: https://doi.org/10.5281/zenodo.15062258

AUTHOR INDEX